The
CHICKAMAUGA
Campaign

A Mad Irregular Battle: From the Crossing of the Tennessee
River through the Second Day, August 22 - September 19, 1863

David A. Powell

SB

Savas Beatie

California

Library of Congress Control Number: 2014950391

ISBN 13: 978-1-61121-174-0

05 04 03 02 01   5 4 3 2 1
First edition, first printing

SB

Published by
Savas Beatie LLC
989 Governor Drive, Suite 102
El Dorado Hills, CA 95762

Phone: 916-941-6896
(E-mail) sales@savasbeatie.com

Savas Beatie titles are available at special discounts for bulk purchases in the United States by corporations, institutions, and other organizations. For more details, please contact Special Sales, P.O. Box 4527, El Dorado Hills, CA 95762, or you may e-mail us at sales@savasbeatie.com, or visit our website at www.savasbeatie.com for additional information.

Proudly published, printed, and warehoused in the United States of America.

For my mother, N. Geraldine Powell,
who first encouraged my love of reading.

Table of Contents

Table of Contents (continued)

Table of Contents, continued

Preface

". . . for the purpose of preserving and suitably marking for historical and professional military study the fields of some of the most remarkable maneuvers and most brilliant fighting in the war of the rebellion."

— *enabling legislation, Chickamauga and Chattanooga
National Military Park, August 19, 1890*

The battle of Chickamauga was the second bloodiest engagement of the American Civil War, behind only Gettysburg in the quantity of blood spilled. As an historical subject, Chickamauga lags much further behind in the amount of ink spilled in writing about the engagement. Indeed, the quantity of Chickamauga literature lags not just behind Gettysburg, but behind most of the war's major engagements. Given the size, scope, complexity, fascinating cast of characters, and desperate nature of the fighting at Chickamauga, this is all the more surprising.

Only two modern monographs have attempted to explore the battle in detail. The Centennial of the Civil War kicked off in 1961 with Glenn Tucker's *Chickamauga: Bloody Battle in the West*, followed three decades later in 1991 with *This Terrible Sound: The Battle of Chickamauga*, by Peter Cozzens. Both volumes had and still have considerable merits, but much remains to be said about a wide variety of aspects of the battle. Other works devoted to the battle have been confined to guidebooks, introductory monographs, or overviews. More technical works, such as my own (with David Friedrichs, cartography) *The Maps of Chickamauga: An Atlas of the Chickamauga Campaign, Including the Tullahoma Operations, June 22-September 23, 1863* (2009) and *Failure in the Saddle: Nathan Bedford Forrest, Joseph Wheeler, and the Confederate Cavalry in the Chickamauga Campaign* (2010) explore aspects of the battle, but are more limited in scope.

This dearth of attention is unfortunate, and a bit mystifying. Chickamauga became our nation's first national military park in part because so many veterans from so many different corners of the country fought here in September 1863 at either Chickamauga or the Union riposte, Chattanooga. It certainly does not lack primary sources, as I have discovered over the years. Indeed, hundreds of veterans left their stories in official reports, journals, letters, diaries, reminiscences, regimental histories, and newspapers.

Several reasons account for this historical void. First, Chickamauga was the most confusing large scale battle of the war. The fighting, especially on September 19, was conducted largely in wooded terrain where, time and again flanks were turned and battle lines collapsed into retreat, with enemy troops appearing as if from nowhere to enter the hellish combat. Everyone who has studied this battle, casual student and professional historian alike, has found Chickamauga an exceedingly difficult battle to grasp, let alone write about. Second, Chickamauga remains the only clear-cut victory achieved by the Confederate Army of Tennessee. (Other tactical successes such as Perryville and Murfreesboro were overshadowed by subsequent strategic retreats.) The fruits of that hard-bought Rebel victory, however, began to quickly evaporate and disappeared altogether two months later on the hills surrounding Chattanooga. Third, Chickamauga does not have the benefit of "brand" recognition: neither army was led by a general named Ulysses S. Grant or William T. Sherman or Robert E. Lee or Stonewall Jackson. Finally, the campaign was fought in the war's Western Theater. Historians have spent over a century dissecting actions large and small waged in Virginia, Maryland, and Pennsylvania, and are only now turning their gaze and their pens westward in a significant way. That attention is long overdue. Had Chickamauga been waged in northern Virginia between Lee and Grant, McClellan, or Hooker, it is reasonable to conclude it would today be the recipient of extensive attention. For all of these reasons, the more I walked the fields and the more I read the accounts of the participants, the more I felt the desire to, in my own small way, remedy this oversight.

Those of you who have read my earlier works learned my interest in Chickamauga began as a board game project. Research to determine battle strengths and tactical positions morphed into a search for any and all accounts of the battle I could find. That interest, in turn, fed my desire to write on the battle.

The book you are now holding is the first of three projected volumes exploring all aspects of the campaign. *A Mad Irregular Battle* (a descriptor coined by John B. Turchin, a Union brigade commander and veteran who wrote his own history of the bloody affair) covers events from the Tullahoma campaign, which set the stage for Chickamauga, up to and including much of the fateful night of September 19, 1863. The story line ends with the conclusion of the fighting as darkness fell on September 19. The second volume, *Glory or the Grave: The Breakthrough, Union Collapse, and the Retreat to Chattanooga, September 20, 1863*, begins with the fateful consultations both army commanders held with their subordinates that same evening, meetings which set the stage for all that happened on Sunday, September 20. As you will see, William Rosecrans and Braxton Bragg handled those meetings quite differently. *Glory or the Grave* carries the action through the climactic fighting of that day and the chaotic Union retreat to Rossville that night. This second installment is already written and should follow shortly on the heels of the first. A third volume concludes the narration, discussing Rosecrans's retreat into Chattanooga and Bragg's pursuit, ending on September 23. The costs of the battle, the command fallout, various appendices and underlying data, including my research into numbers engaged, losses, and a full bibliography, will also be included. Together, these three volumes will provide my version of a comprehensive, detailed narrative exploring the second largest battle of the American Civil War.

The reason for writing a multi-volume work is simple: the vast amount of material available simply begged to be used. My personal files contain thousands of primary sources, both published and unpublished, over and above the material found in the *Official Records*. These accounts breathe life into the barebones framework of the battle, and I humbly acknowledge the debt I owe (indeed, all of us owe) to those veterans of long ago who took the time to tell their stories in letters home, in diary and journal entries, in newspaper articles and editorials, personal memoirs, regimental histories, and elsewhere.

I would also like to acknowledge that the foundation of this massive collection stems not merely from my own work, but from the tireless efforts of Dr. William G. Robertson, who began mining this material in the 1980s. When Dr. Robertson generously opened his files to me on a trip to Fort Leavenworth, I was both humbled and appreciative. I have tried to model my own approach to research on that generosity, and repay that kindness wherever possible.

In the mid-2000s I penned a pair of monographs on various aspects of Chickamauga. One (as noted above) was a Confederate cavalry study eventually published in 2010 as *Failure in the Saddle*. The second was an unpublished study of the fighting on Horseshoe Ridge. It was during the writing phase of *The Maps of Chickamauga* that I realized how little of the material I had available was actually being used. After serious thought, I decided to take the plunge and tackle the whole grand affair, incorporating my unpublished Horseshoe Ridge work into the larger project. I organized the massive array of sources I had at my disposal and began to write, finding the time between other writing obligations.

At that time I still envisioned a one-volume project. It did not take me long to realize the manuscript that was largely writing itself was quickly becoming too long for a single book. I suspected finding a publisher willing to undertake the costs and risks of producing a multi-volume history would be daunting, and perhaps impossible.

I was pondering this dilemma when Theodore Savas stepped in and made me the offer I couldn't refuse. Ted was aware I was working on something of this sort and called me one day in late 2011 to suggest dividing up my manuscript into its current format: a pair of large narrative volumes and one of valuable ancillary material. That invigorating conversation galvanized me into two years of hard work, the first fruits of which you now hold in your hands.

First, a few housekeeping matters. Other than an order of battle with strengths and losses, the bulk of the appendices will appear in the third installment. All of the sources used to create this first installment are listed in full in the footnotes, and the complete bibliography (including the works most directly consulted or cited in the text) will appear at the end of the second installment. Everything else, including appendices concerning things like civilians on the battlefield and discussions of the more salient controversies, a complete list of sources, even if they were not used in the text, and my complete order of battle research, with notes, will appear in the third ancillary installment.

The issue of spelling is an important one. Today, the town of LaFayette, Georgia (pronounced la FAY-ett) is written without a space between "La" and "Fayette." There are, of course, variations. In the 1860s, the most common usage was La Fayette (with the space), which is also the spelling adopted in the *Official Records* and how it appears in most military correspondence at the time. I have adopted the same convention. Similarly, some of the civilians living on the battlefield had unusual names. Two of these bear mention. The Vittetoe name is variously spelled Viditoe, Vittitoe, or Vittatoe. The Viniard name has similar variations, such as Vineyard or Vinyard. For consistency in all cases, I have used the spelling found in James Alfred Sartain, *History of Walker County Georgia*, 2 vols. (Thomasson Printing and Office Eqpt. Co., Inc., 1972).

Acknowledgments

The *Chickamauga Campaign* is the result of 15 years of research, study, and writing. While the vast bulk of that work has been mine, I would still be floundering, lost in the woods of north Georgia, were it not for the help of a great many other people. Two men, James Ogden, Park Historian at Chickamauga-Chattanooga National Military Park, and Dr. William Glenn Robertson, former head of the Combat Studies Institute, U.S. Army Command

and General Staff College, Fort Leavenworth, Kansas, have been indispensable and hugely influential in bringing this project to fruition. No one knows more about this campaign than they do. They have been unstinting with their help and generous with their own research and in offering up opinions concerning the often vexing hows and whys of Chickamauga. I could not have finished this study without their help, and I thank them both.

I must also thank my partner in cartography, David Friedrichs. Dave was my co-author and graphics expert through our first mutual effort, *The Maps of Chickamauga*. His maps also graced *Failure in the Saddle* and are used extensively in these new volumes. Given the crude nature of the hand-drawn scrawling I pass over to David, I am always amazed at how well the final maps turn out. It is my sincere hope that we complete many more projects together.

My wife Anne has been an immense help as she always is. In addition to all else she puts up with, Anne lets me run around the country on research trips while she tends to home fires alone. She has been a continual supporter of my work, letting me steal hours away from my home life to research and write. I know, it is time to walk the dogs again.

I must also thank Theodore P. Savas, managing director of Savas Beatie, for embracing this project and for all his excitement and help along the way. Ted, who has a deep personal interest in this campaign, personally performed the developmental editing for this series (and for all the books I have published with his company). Marketing director Sarah Keeney has also offered wonderful help, as have copy editor Mary Gutzke and production manager Lee Merideth, whose work shaped this book into its final form.

A host of others bear mention. Frank Crawford, Lee White, Dr. Keith Bohannon, Scott Day, Sam Elliott, Rick Manion, John Reed, Zack Waltz; and many more helped in ways large and small. For all of you just mentioned, and for those too numerous to thank individually (you know who you are), know I am grateful for your help and friendship along the way. If you tramped with Jim Ogden and me on one of the Chickamauga Study Group Tours, you helped me learn as well. Thanks for all your support.

As ever, when it comes to mistakes, I am an island. Any errors or omissions are mine alone.

David Powell
Chicago, IL
September, 2014

Tullahoma
June 24—July 4, 1863

At 3:00 a.m. on Wednesday, June 24, 1863, reveille sounded across the vast camps of the Army of the Cumberland, awakening 65,000 men. Little else would be ordinary that morning. After six months of garrison duty in and around Murfreesboro, Tennessee, Maj. Gen. William Starke Rosecrans's army was at last on the move.

The offensive was much anticipated by Union authorities in Washington, including President Abraham Lincoln, Secretary of War Edwin M. Stanton, and Maj. Gen. Henry W. Halleck, the overall commander of the Union armies. For two months these men had been prodding Rosecrans to take the field in support of other Federal forces fighting in Virginia and Mississippi. Rosecrans's planning had been as meticulous as his objective was ambitious: the entrapment and destruction of the Confederate Army of Tennessee.

As Rosecrans saw it, the key to success was to swing around the flank of the enemy army and, via a sudden descent, capture the Army of Tennessee's supply railhead at Tullahoma, Tennessee. Doing so successfully would require surprise, lest Confederate Gen. Braxton Bragg, commanding the Rebel army, discovered the maneuver too soon and simply retreated. In order to distract Bragg, Maj. Gen. Alexander McDowell McCook and his Union XX Corps, supported by the bulk of the Federal cavalry under Maj. Gen. David Sloane Stanley, marched south on June 24 astride the direct road to Tullahoma toward Shelbyville, Tennessee, the location of the Confederate Army of Tennessee's left flank. Another segment of the army, Maj. Gen. Thomas L. Crittenden's XXI Corps, protected the flanking force by marching first east toward the small hamlets of Bradyville and Lumley's Stand, and then south to seize Manchester. This route would carry the XXI Corps well clear of Bragg's right flank at Wartrace, but place Crittenden's men far beyond any immediate support should the Rebels suddenly discover the move and turn on them. In order to provide that support, Maj. Gen. George Thomas led his XIV Corps southeast on the pike from Murfreesboro to Manchester with orders to push quickly through to a place called Hoover's Gap.

Speed and surprise were essential. General Bragg had arrayed his weaker force behind the Highland Rim, a series of ridges and hills demarcating the low terrain around Nashville from the higher plateau surrounding it. The rim was pierced only by a few gaps, each capable of being manned by a smaller force sufficient to indefinitely hold off a much larger one given enough time to prepare for the onslaught. Stanley's and McCook's Federals were headed for Guy's and Liberty gaps, while Thomas's troops moved to seize Hoover's Gap. Crittenden's men had the farthest to march, up through the steep and narrow valley of Dug Hollow toward Bradyville and Lumley's Stand, and from there turning south toward Gilley's Gap and Manchester beyond. McCook's movement was a feint, intended to fool Bragg into thinking the Yankees were willing to launch a frontal attack on his defenses, while Crittenden's men delivered the real blow. Thomas's mission was also critical, for if he did not quickly seize Hoover's Gap and open direct communications with Crittenden, the Union XXI Corps would be exposed to piecemeal destruction—and Bragg was an aggressive commander.

The tone of the campaign was set early, on June 24, at both Liberty and Hoover's gaps when it was discovered that each place was but lightly defended. At Liberty Gap, two Union brigades in Brig. Gen. Richard W. Johnson's division of McCook's XX Corps roughly handled the pair of Arkansas regiments defending the entrance and occupied most of the gap that same day, completing the task by the morning of the 25th. At Hoover's Gap, Col. John T. Wilder's brigade of Indiana and Illinois Mounted Infantry, armed with their newly acquired Spencer seven-shot repeating rifles, brushed aside a Confederate cavalry regiment to seize the entire gap by mid-afternoon. Wilder's men beat back a two-brigade Rebel counterattack, inflicting sizable losses on their desperate opponents. The ease and speed of these significant successes surprised and delighted the Army of the Cumberland's high command. That evening, as more Federals arrived to hold Wilder's hard-won prize in greater strength, General Thomas congratulated Wilder fulsomely: "You have saved the lives of a thousand men . . . today. I didn't expect to have this gap for three days."[1] The only ominous note was the rain, sometimes driving, that began to steadily fall at about midday.

The Confederate response at both gaps was feeble largely because General Bragg's mounted arm failed to alert him to the developing crisis. At the beginning of May, Bragg's cavalry numbered more than 17,000 men in five divisions divided into two corps commanded by Maj. Gens. Joseph Wheeler and Earl Van Dorn, respectively. By the end of June, that force had been reduced to 11,000 troopers in three divisions when Bragg was ordered to transfer one to Mississippi and allowed another under Brig. Gen. John H. Morgan to raid into Kentucky—an order Morgan promptly exceeded by crossing into Ohio in a grandiose and ultimately futile effort to snatch an extra bit of glory to burnish his fading luster. Worse still, the capable Van Dorn was dead, shot by a jealous husband and his corps reduced to the single division of newly promoted Nathan Bedford Forrest. Wheeler's two-division corps was stationed on Bragg's right, charged with watching for any move toward Manchester, while Forrest's men guarded Bragg's left.

Forrest was relatively new to the regular duties of cavalry. His steady stream of successes thus far had come as a raider and leader of irregulars. McCook's and Stanley's feint toward Shelbyville, of which the action at Liberty Gap was a part, fooled Forrest, who reported the movement to Bragg as a major effort. Far worse was what happened with Wheeler. On the morning of June 23, just one day before Rosecrans's grand movement began, Wheeler decided to stage a raid of his own. Intending to damage the rail line north of Nashville, down which virtually all of Rosecrans's supplies flowed, Wheeler began transferring most of his cavalry from the Confederate right to the left where, in conjunction with Forrest, he intended to strike northward. Blinded on his right as a result, Bragg was oblivious to the Federal effort that began the next day and culminated in the seizure of Hoover's Gap.

One thing all of Rosecrans's meticulous planning could not control was the weather. The intermittent rain of June 24 had, by the next day, become a steady downpour. It would continue, noted a frustrated General Crittenden,

---

1   James A. Connolly, "Major James Austin Connolly," *Transactions of the Illinois State Historical Society for the Year 1928* (Phillips Brothers, 1928), 268.

"incessantly for fifteen days," turning roads to quagmires.[2] After making more than a dozen miles on the 24th, Crittenden's progress toward Manchester slowed dramatically. "At seven o'clock," noted the 58th Indiana regimental history, "we were again on the march. The rain was now coming down in torrents. About ten o'clock we passed through Bradyville, a miserable, dilapidated town. . . . Here the turnpike ended and we had to take the dirt road, which was now almost impassible." Two Union divisions next snaked their way toward Gilley's Gap on a country road so choked with traffic that the 58th "could only make four miles today."[3] Despite Rosecrans's careful planning, uncooperative weather threatened to unravel the entire operation.

Always seeking a way to strike the enemy, Bragg turned his attention to Guy's Gap, yet another passage through the Highland Rim roughly five miles east of Liberty Gap. Bragg wanted Lt. Gen. William J. Hardee's infantry corps to hold Rosecrans in place around Wartrace while his other corps under Lt. Gen. Leonidas Polk marched north from Shelbyville through Guy's Gap to strike the Union army in the rear. The plan shocked both Hardee and Polk, who protested that the Confederate army was heavily outnumbered and that Bragg's plan would only further divide their forces into more easily digestible fragments. The issue would not be resolved until the night of the 26th, when Bragg finally realized the impractical nature of his plan and called instead for a retreat to Tullahoma.

The distance from Shelbyville to Tullahoma was just short of 18 miles, and from Wartrace a little more than 19. In good weather this was but a solid day's march. By the morning of June 27, when the Confederates began their muddy trudge southward, the weather and the roads were anything but good. The next two days witnessed a slow motion race between Bragg's men, trudging for Tullahoma, and Rosecrans's troops slogging their way toward Manchester. After a grueling stop-and-go march through mud that topped out at six inches deep on the best roads, Bragg's army finally reached the relative safety of Tullahoma on the afternoon of June 28.

---

2   U.S. War Department. *The War of the Rebellion: A Compilation of the Official Records of the Union and Confederate Armies*, 128 vols. (Washington, D.C., 1880-1901), Series 1, vol. 23, pt. 1, 521. Hereafter cited as *OR*. All references are to Series 1 unless otherwise indicated.

3   John J. Hight and Gilbert R. Stormont, *History of the Fifty-Eighth Regiment of Indiana Volunteer Infantry. Its Organization, Campaigns and Battles from 1861 to 1865* (Press of the Clarion, 1895), 147.

The only comfort the Rebels could take was that the Federals fared no better. Rosecrans, along with the lead elements of both Crittenden's XXI Corps and Thomas's XIV Corps, reached Manchester on the afternoon of the 27th, about the same time Bragg arrived in lightly garrisoned Tullahoma a mere dozen miles away. The bulk of each corps, however, was still miles behind. The XIV Corps at least had the advantage of using the pike from Hoover's Gap to Manchester, but a few miles south of the gap the road entered a two-mile stretch of gorge as it climbed out of Matt's Hollow, a slope that slowed Thomas's trains to a crawl and so jammed the road that Rosecrans directed some of McCook's men—who had by now departed Liberty Gap and were headed toward Manchester via Hoover's Gap—to seek alternate routes.

The XXI Corps had by far the worst of it. Crittenden's troops found the going to be little short of nightmarish. Just ascending the road up Dug Hollow to Gilley's Gap took Brig. Gen. Thomas J. Wood's division an astounding 11 hours, and these foot troops did not get to halt until four miles north of Manchester on the afternoon of the 28th. "It has scarcely ever been my ill-fortune, in eighteen years of active service . . . to have to pass over so bad a road," Wood reported.[2] In all, it would take the XXI Corps four days to march just 21 miles, much of the delay, fumed Crittenden, resulting from wagons overloaded with "unauthorized baggage."

June 27 produced another bright spot for Union arms. Confederate cavalryman Joe Wheeler and his troopers held the town of Shelbyville that afternoon, protecting the retreat of the Confederate main body and also waiting for General Forrest's division to arrive from Spring Hill. Union cavalry charged into town, overrunning Wheeler's lines and thundering through the town square, routing the Rebels and netting 400 prisoners. Spearheading that attack were Federal regiments of Col. Robert H. G. Minty's brigade, soon to catch Rosecrans's eye for other missions.

Throughout June 28 Rosecrans waited for his various columns to straggle into Manchester. By the night of the 27th the Federal commander knew Bragg had discovered the flank movement and was reacting by falling back to the trenches of Tullahoma, leaving Rosecrans to contemplate his next step. He had eschewed a frontal assault once, favoring the flank march over a direct fight at Shelbyville, and he was no more inclined to try such an attack now against the fully manned defensive works at Tullahoma.

---

2   OR 23, pt. 1, 524.

In fact, both sides needed a breather. June 29 saw little marching on either side. The Confederates worked on improving their defenses, while the Yankees inched cautiously forward, feeling out Bragg's lines. This was another deception, however. Turning to Wilder's newly christened "Lightning Brigade," on June 28 Rosecrans ordered Col. Wilder to move south across the Elk River. If possible, Rosecrans wanted Wilder to destroy the rail bridge over the Elk near Dechard, Tennessee, or at least damage the depot at Dechard as best he could. If the bridge could be brought down, Bragg would be cut off and nearly out of supplies. Wilder departed on the 28th, leading his main column into Dechard that night while sending the 123rd Illinois to destroy the bridge at Allisonia. As it turned out, the troopers of the 123rd found the Tullahoma road crowded with Rebels, which prevented them from taking the Elk River Bridge (though Wilder's men did inflict some damage at Dechard). Wheeler's Confederate cavalry pursued Wilder and forced him to abandon Dechard sooner than he otherwise would have, but Wilder's command successfully evaded pursuit and headed back to Manchester on the 30th.

Initially, Bragg had no intention of retreating another step. His two corps commanders, however, were less sanguine about making a fight of it at Tullahoma. Wilder's sudden descent on Dechard, even though the damage inflicted was light enough to be repaired within a few hours, demonstrated that a large Union force might easily follow to seize the rail line in strength. And indeed, once his supplies were replenished (admittedly a difficult prospect given the rain-sodden roads) Rosecrans was set on implementing exactly that strategy. Accordingly, on June 30 Bragg abruptly decided on retreat. His reversal of opinion was so sudden that it caught his own generals by surprise. By that night a thoroughly dispirited Rebel army, fractious generals and all, was in full retreat. This time the Rebels would not stop short of Chattanooga and the Tennessee River. The Federals pursued during the first few days of July, rounding up stragglers and abandoned Confederate stores.

While Tullahoma was not the decisive master stroke Rosecrans envisioned (because Bragg's army had escaped intact), it was, thought Rosecrans, a masterpiece of strategy marred only by the rain. The Army of the Cumberland suffered fewer than 600 casualties. The Confederates lost at least 2,000 men, including 1,600 prisoners, with the suggestion of many more who simply deserted the colors. On July 4, at Winchester, Tennessee, General McCook hosted a celebratory dinner party for Rosecrans and a host of lesser officers. Over the next few days, the Federals's mood was further enlivened by the news of Lee's retreat from Gettysburg and the surrender of an entire Confederate army at Vicksburg.

Rosecrans was soon stunned to discover that Washington did not share in his exultation. On July 7, Edwin Stanton seemed to dismiss the achievement when he wired: "We have just received official information that Vicksburg surrendered. . . . Lee's army overthrown; Grant victorious. You and your noble army now have the chance to give the finishing blow to the rebellion. Will you neglect the chance?" "You do not appear to observe," Rosecrans frostily replied, "the fact that this noble army has driven the rebels from Middle Tennessee. . . . I beg on behalf of this army that the War Department may not overlook so great an event because it is not written in letters of blood."[3]

Now, Chattanooga loomed in the distance.

---

3 Ibid., pt. 2, 518.

Chapter One

Molding an Army:

Summer 1863

Major • General William Starke Rosecrans was a frustrated man in the late summer of 1863. Other Union commanders had won great victories or fought tremendous battles that summer. Grant had taken Vicksburg. Meade defeated Lee in Pennsylvania. From Washington President Abraham Lincoln, Secretary of War Edwin M. Stanton, and Maj. Gen. Henry Wager Halleck all prodded Rosecrans to end his inaction and accomplish something of like stature in Middle Tennessee. Rosecrans, a perfectionist, refused to move before he was ready. "General Halleck is very urgent," he complained to his chief of staff, Brig. Gen. James A. Garfield on June 12, "and thinks that I am the obstinate one in this matter." At the end of that month Rosecrans answered his critics with what he regarded as a campaign of brilliant maneuver by marching his Army of the Cumberland across a broad front on several axes. The operation outflanked and outfoxed Confederate Gen. Braxton Bragg's outnumbered Army of Tennessee from its stronghold at Tullahoma. Outgeneraled, Bragg retreated without a major battle, arriving at Chattanooga in the southeast corner of the state, on July 3.[1]

---

1   William Starke Rosecrans, "The Tullahoma Campaign," *National Tribune,* March 11, 1882.

Rosecrans's triumph was overshadowed by the electrifying news of the twin Union victories at Gettysburg and Vicksburg during the first week of July. Even though both successes came burdened with heavy casualty lists, they also defeated enemy armies in the field. The Army of the Cumberland's feat was accomplished with minimal loss, but Bragg's Confederates escaped largely intact. Rosecrans's protests fell on deaf ears. Sensing a potential end to the long and bloody rebellion, Washington politicians urged him to press on. The Tullahoma campaign might have been technically brilliant, but Washington also had a point: Bragg's army had escaped intact and would still have to be defeated, likely several times, before a decision could be reached.

Unlike the Federals in Virginia and Mississippi, whose supply lines were short and waterborne transport rendered them essentially unbreakable, the Army of the Cumberland was forced to depend almost entirely upon long and vulnerable railroads for its lifeline. The point of origin for supplying the army was Louisville, Kentucky. From there, the tracks of the Louisville & Nashville road snaked south through central Kentucky and northern Tennessee to terminate at Nashville. A critical rail bridge at Munfordville, Kentucky and the "Big South" Tunnel at Gallatin, Tennessee, demonstrated the vulnerability of these rail lines. Damage to track could usually be repaired quickly, but bridges and especially tunnels represented critical choke points that could not be replaced or re-bored easily. In August 1862, as the Confederates invaded Kentucky, Confederate raider John Hunt Morgan and his men caved in the tunnel at Gallatin by ramming a burning train into it at full speed. The tunnel was out of service for more than three months, leaving the Army of the Cumberland bereft of much-needed supplies for weeks on end.[2]

From Nashville, the supply line was taken up by the Nashville & Chattanooga Railroad, which curved southeast to Stevenson, Alabama, before crossing the Tennessee River at Bridgeport and entering Chattanooga from the west. The N&C had its share of bridges (notably over the Elk, Duck, and Tennessee rivers), as well as at least two more important tunnels. Bragg

---

2   In Mississippi, Ulysses S. Grant initially attempted to rely on rails for his advance south to Vicksburg, from Memphis, Tennessee, but a successful raid on his main supply depot at Holly Springs in December 1862 put an end to that line of approach. Grant thereafter relied on the Mississippi River as his line of supply for the next six months of operations against Vicksburg. See Michael B. Ballard, *Vicksburg: The Campaign that opened the Mississippi* (University of North Carolina Press, 2004).

destroyed the bridges during his retreat, but he wasn't as creative as Morgan had been: instead of blasting the tunnels he filled them with debris that left them largely undamaged. Within a couple of weeks, Federal army engineers restored the road to operating condition as far south as Bridgeport.

With the head of his army at Bridgeport, Rosecrans was forced to expend a considerable amount of time and resources to protect nearly 350 miles of vulnerable track and infrastructure. One reason the Yankees could not simply press on after the Tullahoma operation was because the Army of the Cumberland needed to stockpile mountains of supplies at forward bases in order to be prepared for anticipated interruptions of its tenuous logistical lifeline. Those bases, along with the rails themselves, had to be protected with garrisons, blockhouses, and patrols. A huge base was established at Murfreesboro, Tennessee, near the old battlefield of December 1862. "Fortress Rosecrans" was intended to hold a permanent garrison of several thousand men and supplies for 100,000 troops in the field for as long as three months.

Fortunately, the Department of the Cumberland did not have to bear alone the entire responsibility for defending the line. Most of the Louisville & Nashville Railroad fell under the jurisdiction of the Union Department of the Ohio, currently commanded by Maj. Gen. Ambrose Burnside. Burnside replaced Maj. Gen. Horatio G. Wright, who was transferred to the Army of the Potomac in May 1863. The Department of the Ohio was charged with defending Kentucky and ensuring the security of the L&N, and, after Burnside's arrival, was given the mission of invading East Tennessee. Lincoln had long cherished the liberation of that region since it was a hotbed of pro-Unionist sentiment deep in Secessia, and those Unionists had suffered at the hands of Rebel authorities intent on cracking down against anti-Confederate resistance. Rosecrans also endorsed the idea, for he thought his own plans would materially benefit from the strategy. Earlier that March he had urged Wright that "the way to stop the raid into Kentucky is to prepare to invade East Tennessee; threaten in several directions and you will scare them." He was no less enthusiastic about Burnside's proposed operations.[3]

---

3 *The War of the Rebellion: A Compilation of the Official Records of the Union and Confederate Armies*, 128 vols. (Washington, D.C., 1890-1901), Series 1, vol. 23, pt. 2, 148. All subsequent references refer to Series 1 unless otherwise indicated.

Because it wasn't on the front lines, however, the Department of the Ohio was often called upon to shift troops to other theaters. Many of the forces in Rosecrans's growing command came from Kentucky. Burnside had no sooner arrived in the department with two divisions of his IX Corps when he was called upon to forward many of these troops to General Grant operating against Vicksburg. As a result, the department's strength wildly fluctuated. On March 31, 1863, Burnside's strength amounted to slightly more than 22,000 men present for duty. By April this number had swelled to nearly 33,000, and by May Burnside had 38,000 troops. After reinforcing Grant, the department's June strength fell to 32,000, and by August 10 peaked at nearly 40,000 troops. From this last total, however, Burnside needed to organize a field force for the move into East Tennessee, which amounted to nearly 28,000 men. Of the remaining 12,000, roughly 7,000 of those were stationed in or still forming in the states of Illinois, Indiana, Michigan, and Ohio; leaving only 5,000 Federals to protect the vital rail lines through Kentucky. It was hoped that with Union troops occupying Knoxville and Confederate cavalry raider John Hunt Morgan captured and imprisoned in Ohio, this paltry force would be sufficient to maintain the security of the exposed line.[4]

During the two months following Tullahoma, Rosecrans carefully assembled the supplies and troops he would need for the next great leap southward. Chattanooga sat across the Tennessee River embedded in the mountain fastness of the southern Appalachians. Wresting it from the Rebels would be no easy task.

Although enthusiasm for Rosecrans was waning among many key Federal politicians, such was not the case within the Army of the Cumberland. Rosecrans assumed command of what was to become one of the three great Federal armies of the war when he replaced Don Buell at the head of the Army of the Ohio on October 27, 1862. Buell had recently fought the battle of Perryville to an unsatisfying result, and when the Rebels escaped Kentucky without further damage, the Lincoln administration decided Buell simply had to go. The job fell to Rosecrans only after Maj. Gen. George H. Thomas turned down the appointment in what Thomas apparently hoped would be a gambit to retain Buell. Instead, the administration moved on to find someone else, and that someone was Rosecrans. The decision angered Thomas, at least initially, but his personal friendship with Rosecrans smoothed over whatever frustration

4 Ibid., 198, 299, 379, 489, 604.

he felt, as did a re-shuffling of dates of rank so that Rosecrans was now the senior officer. The end result was that what could have been a troubling relationship with his senior subordinate became instead a solid working partnership.[5]

The Union Army of the Ohio grew dramatically during Buell's tenure. His command, organized into five divisions, was spread across Middle and West Tennessee in the summer of 1862, until the Confederate incursion into Kentucky brought Buell racing north in pursuit. Once at Louisville, Buell incorporated a host of new regiments—some of which had been in uniform only a few days—and reinforcements arrived from other theaters to coalesce into a massive new command of 11 divisions informally divided into three corps-sized "wings." The necessarily rapid command changes and reassignments did not always work to the benefit of crafting an effective, cohesive organization. In the wake of the disappointing stalemate that was Perryville, the army's structure stabilized into multi-division commands led by Maj. Gens. George Thomas, Thomas L. Crittenden, and Alexander McDowell McCook. However, when Rosecrans took the reins the entire army was still officially designated as the "XIV Corps," with each of the aforementioned officers leading only an ad-hoc wing.

Rosecrans set about to immediately reorganize and train his command. Given the recent influx of thousands of new men, he spent a considerable amount of time on drill and discipline. The last two months of 1862 were spent putting the command in fighting trim, but he had little time to accomplish much before pressure from above demanded he take the field against the Confederates gathered around Murfreesboro, Tennessee. Near the end of December Rosecrans felt he was ready to advance. The resultant battle of Stones River (also known as the battle of Murfreesboro) was a hard-fought contest among the cedars and rock outcroppings along the banks of that stream. Both sides planned to attack, but the Rebels struck first. The early morning assault routed Rosecrans's right wing and nearly collapsed his army on December 31. The Yankees grimly hung on, and eventually the Confederate army and its commander Braxton Bragg fell back, yielding the field and the chance to claim victory to Rosecrans and his men.

---

5 Larry J. Daniel, *Days of Glory: The Army of the Cumberland, 1861-1865* (Louisiana State University Press, 2004), 191-192.

William Starke Rosecrans in the Spring of 1863.

Tennessee State Library and Archives

The margin of success was a narrow one. Both sides lost about equally in the fight, and though exhausted by the bloody slugfest, neither army was destroyed.Further stalemate was the result. Rosecrans's first offensive managed to gain only about 30 miles before grinding to a halt as he dug in around Murfreesboro. Bragg fell back to the next defensible terrain, near the towns of Shelbyville and Wartrace. Neither army enjoyed a significant advantage in numbers. As a result, this near-parity produced an inactivity that lingered far longer than either commander intended—much to the dismay of their respective governments in Washington and Richmond.

Rosecrans used this time to plan, re-forge the army into a war-fighting machine of his own creation, and become better acquainted with his commanders. Likewise, the pause also allowed his men to become more comfortable with their new commander.

$*$ $*$ $*$

The man now steering the helm of the Army of the Cumberland was a member of the West Point class of 1842, which produced 17 Civil War general officers. Though both men were West Pointers and professional soldiers, Rosecrans was Buell's opposite in many ways: boisterous and outspoken where Buell was "cold and formally polite." The two men shared at least one characteristic —"unflagging in energy." Rosecrans lacked prewar combat experience, having missed the Mexican conflict, but had done well so far in this struggle. He had played an instrumental role in early successes in West Virginia, which helped propel George B. McClellan to such heights in Virginia in 1862, and since then led semi-independent commands at Iuka and Corinth. His successful defense of Corinth, coming just a week before his orders to replace Buell, contributed favorably in his getting tasked for the new command.[6]

William Starke Rosecrans was born on September 6, 1819, in Sunbury, Ohio, just north of the state capital at Columbus. His family was prosperous. His father Crandall Rosecrans was a farmer, a businessman and a pillar of the community. Though many Confederates would later refer to Rosecrans as "Dutch" or "German," mistaking him for an immigrant soldier like Franz Sigel or Carl Schurz, in fact Rosecrans was a sixth generation American, baptized in

---

6   Daniel, *Days of Glory,* 182.

the Church of England, of mixed Dutch and English descent. The first 'Rosenkrantz' arrived in New Amsterdam in 1651. William's great-grandfather fought in the Revolution, and his father served on the Canadian frontier in the War of 1812. Soldiering and patriotism were imbued in the new arrival almost from birth.[7]

Rosecrans's family couldn't afford to pay for his education, and so what learning he did acquire was haphazard, and amounted to less than a year's formal schooling. Instead, Rosecrans read, sought out tutors, and where possible, taught himself. He worked as a clerk in his father's and others' business ventures. In 1837 he successfully applied for an appointment to the Military Academy at West Point, entering as a member of the class of 1842. One might expect him to struggle with the rigors of academia, given his lack of classroom experience, but instead William Rosecrans flourished.Always in the top ten percent , he graduated fifth in a class of 51. Fellow classmates included James Longstreet, Alexander Peter Stewart, Earl Van Dorn, and Daniel Harvey Hill. William T. Sherman, George H. Thomas, and Bushrod Rust Johnson were two years ahead of him; Ulysses S. Grant, a year behind. Simon Bolivar Buckner was two years behind, in the class of 1844. The careers of all these men would be intertwined in the years to come.[8]

While West Point was primarily an engineering school during the nineteenth century, the young Ohioan found time to pursue two outside interests: religion and military history.All cadets were required to attend weekly church services, which at the time were Episcopalian. In his reading, however, Rosecrans developed an interest in Catholicism so intense that he not only converted to the religion of Rome three years after graduation, but he also convinced his younger brother Sylvester to follow suit. William must have been very persuasive; Sylvester became a priest, and eventually, bishop of Ohio.[9]

William's other passion, military history, led him to the Napoleon Club, which was an extracurricular group founded by famed West Point professor Dennis Hart Mahan, because there wasn't enough time in the regular

---

7   William M. Lamers, *The Edge of Glory: A Biography of William S. Rosecrans, U.S.A.* (Louisiana State University Press, 1999), 8-9.

8   Civil War Generals from West Point, http://sunsite.utk.edu/civil-war/wpclasses.html, accessed 8/14/2013.

9   Lamers, *Edge of Glory,* 14.

curriculum to devote to the purely military arts. Under Mahan's tutelage, Rosecrans became a lifelong student of the two giants of grand strategy in the eighteenth and early nineteenth centuries: Frederick the Great and Napoleon Bonaparte.[10]

However, military life in the decade following his graduation proved uneventful, so Rosecrans left the regular army in 1853 to pursue engineering and business interests, among which were co-founding a kerosene refinery in Cincinnati. In 1857 he suffered an industrial accident while experimenting to develop a better product, becoming badly burned when a lamp exploded. He was 18 months recuperating, and the resultant "distorting, livid scars gave a permanent 'smirk' to his face." The accident did nothing to detract from his energy, however, and he returned to his ventures with zeal, only to see his life disrupted by a new calamity: war.[11]

The firing on Fort Sumter in Charleston stirred both his patriotic and his military juices. On April 26, 1861 Rosecrans joined the staff of Brig. Gen. George B. McClellan, who had just accepted command of Ohio's military forces from Governor William Dennison. Rosecrans would not linger long as a staff officer. In June he was promoted to colonel and given command of the 23rd Ohio (which included future presidents Rutherford B. Hayes and William McKinley in its ranks), and, simultaneously, given a commission as a Brigadier General of U.S. Volunteers.[12]

His first action came at the battle of Rich Mountain, commanding a brigade under McClellan, and fighting against a badly overmatched Lt. Col. John Pegram and his brigade of Virginians. Rosecrans proposed a bold flanking move, which, when combined with McClellan's main assault, would assure the Rebels' complete defeat. Rosecrans executed his part of the plan well enough that, even though McClellan failed to move at all, Pegram's Virginians were still badly defeated.[13]

Nevertheless, McClellan got most of the credit, hailed as a military genius. In the wake of the Union disaster at Bull Run, McClellan was given command

---

10 Ibid., 15.

11 Ibid., 18.

12 Ethan S. Rafuse, *McClellan's War: The Failure of Moderation in the Struggle for the Union* (Indiana University Press, 2005), 95; Ezra J. Warner, *Generals in Blue: Lives of the Union Commanders* (Baton Rouge, Louisiana State University Press, 1991), 410.

13 Rafuse, *McClellan's War,* 114-115.

of the main Union army in Virginia, the force which would eventually become the Army of the Potomac. There McClellan experienced the highs and lows of a political whirlwind; hailed as a savior in 1861, given command of all the Union armies by early 1862, his political fortunes were laid low and he was sidelined by the beginning of 1863. Rosecrans's career track was less spectacular. He served in West Virginia for a time, commanding that department after McClellan's elevation. In the spring of 1862 he played a peripheral role in opposing Confederate Maj. Gen. Thomas Jonathan "Stonewall" Jackson during that commander's famous Valley Campaign in the Shenandoah Valley. Jackson was able to move against, fight, and defeat various baffled Union opponents largely because the Union command structure was fragmented. The campaign is notable also because it marks the one time that President Abraham Lincoln and Secretary of War Edwin M. Stanton attempted to direct operations themselves. That attempt was a notable failure. It also brought Rosecrans into direct conflict with the irascible, opinionated Stanton. Rosecrans, hot-tempered himself, was soon at loggerheads with Stanton over troop movements and virtually everything else; their bickering carried out over the telegraph as Jackson's Rebels waltzed through the Valley seemingly at will. The enmity between the two men would become a permanent dislike.[14]

Following the mess in the Shenandoah, Rosecrans was ordered west to join Maj. Gen. Henry Wager Halleck's growing concentration of force outside the town of Corinth, Mississippi in the wake of the bloody (and controversial) battle of Shiloh. Corinth held a Rebel army under Gen. Pierre Gustave Toutant Beauregard, while the Union forces attempting to capture Corinth included Union Maj. Gens. Ulysses Grant and George Thomas. Beauregard eventually abandoned Corinth rather than be trapped there. He was soon replaced by Confederate Gen. Braxton Bragg, who promptly took his new command on a bold move into Kentucky, culminating in the Perryville campaign that fall. Part of Halleck's grand force followed Bragg. The rest, including Grant and Rosecrans, remained in West Tennessee and northern Mississippi as an occupying force.

Here Rosecrans served as a district commander, his headquarters in captured Corinth, under Grant's overall direction as departmental commander. Again, it would be a difficult relationship.

---

14 Lamers, *Edge of Glory*, 68-82.

In the fall of 1862, another Rebel force, this one led by a former classmate, Maj. Gen. Earl Van Dorn, attempted to re-take Corinth. Van Dorn had between 20,000 and 30,000 men; and while Grant's command was stronger, it was also dispersed in various garrisons across West Tennessee. In September, at Iuka (a few miles east of Corinth) Grant attempted to trap Van Dorn's small army between two Federal converging columns. Rosecrans led one such pincer, with Maj. Gen. E. O. C. Ord commanding the other. Grant provided overall direction, riding with Ord's column. Coordination proved difficult, the timing inexact. Rosecrans arrived later than promised, but Ord never attacked at all, leaving Rosecrans, with 7,000 men, to fight more than double his numbers. The Confederates slipped away, and Grant blamed Rosecrans for the failure.[15]

Rosecrans had his partisans, especially among Ohio newspapermen, and they were quick to point out that the real failure was Grant's. Especially outspoken in Rosecrans's favor was the Cincinnati Commercial, which carried several articles bluntly accusing Grant of inattention during the campaign. This partisan war of words, carried out mainly by proxy, permanently soured relations between Grant and Rosecrans. While Rosecrans might have had more of the right of things on his side, he was proving to have a knack for alienating his superiors. Whitelaw Reid, one of those newspapermen and subsequently a chronicler of Ohio's wartime exploits, identified this flaw early in Rosecrans's career. At Rich Mountain, noted Reid, Rosecrans's planning and conduct were outstanding. "But," Reid cautioned, "he already exhibited symptoms of the personal imprudence which was to form so signal a feature in his character . . . dissatisfaction with the conduct of his superior - a dissatisfaction which he afterword expressed officially"[16]

Next came the battle of Corinth, fought on October 3-4, 1862. This fight marked Van Dorn's second attempt to retake the town, leading 22,000 men against Rosecrans's garrison of roughly 20,000 troops. Van Dorn was successfully rebuffed, and Rosecrans's victory came as part of a pattern of Rebel defeats that helped magnify its significance: Lee had been driven out of Maryland at Antietam by September 19, Van Dorn's army limped back south on

---

15 Frank P. Varney, *General Grant and the Rewriting of History: How the Destruction of General William S. Rosecrans Influenced Our Understanding of the Civil War* (Savas Beatie, 2013), 31-79, covers the battle of Iuka and the ensuing recriminations between Grant and Rosecrans in detail.

16 Lamers, *Edge of Glory,* 120-122; Whitelaw Reid, *Ohio in the War: Her Statesmen Generals and Soldiers,* in 2 vols. (Robert Clarke Co., 1895), vol. 1, 316.

October 5, and Bragg's army was driven out of the Blue Grass State by October 9. Despite his earlier travails with Stanton, when the time came to replace Buell for perceived slowness in chasing Bragg, Rosecrans seemed a natural choice for the new command.[17]

Rosecrans's elevation to army command met with general approval in the ranks, where the men compared him favorably to the stodgy Don Buell. Newspaper correspondent William Shanks, who, as a Radical Republican was no great admirer of conservative Democrats like Rosecrans, was forced to admit that "the army threw up its hat in delight" at his assumption of command. Col. Benjamin F. Scribner, a brigade commander in Lovell H. Rousseau's division thought Rosecrans impressed the troops "by his open and genial manner, contrasting agreeably with the taciturn exclusiveness of . . . Buell."[18]

Rosecrans was not without his detractors. To the dismay of some, the new commander's vociferous Catholicism was a definite drawback. This was an anomaly in largely Protestant nineteenth century America. Rosecrans often waxed enthusiastic about his newfound faith, to the point that Brig. Gen. Milo S. Hascall, who served with Rosecrans in the old army, regarded him as "most emphatically a crank on that subject," and predicted that the fortunes of a number of Catholic officers would rise with Rosecrans's arrival simply because the new man was such "a narrow-minded bigot."[19]

Major General John M. Palmer, an Illinois politician who had developed into an effective soldier, was another skeptic. In addition to religious issues, like many volunteers, Palmer resented the regulars. He viewed them as cautious careerists, and far too willing to steal the plaudits of other men in order to further their own military ambitions. Volunteers, thought Palmer, would revert back to civilian life once the war was won, making them less likely to be jealous of rank, position, or battlefield acclaim. His division did not receive the credit it was due for "saving the army" at Stones River, wrote Palmer, due to "regular

17 David J. Eicher, *The Longest Night: A Military History of the Civil War* (Simon and Schuster, 2001),374-378.

18 Shanks, *Personal Recollections*, 258; Benjamin F. Scribner, *How Soldiers Were Made; Or The War As I Saw It Under Buell, Rosecrans, Thomas, Grant, and Sherman*(Blue Acorn Press, 1995), 64.

19 Milo S. Hascall, "Personal Recollections and Experiences Concerning the Battle of Stones River," *Military Order of the Loyal Legion of the United States, Illinois, in Papers of the Military Order of the Loyal Legion of the United States,* 70 vols. (Broadfoot Publishing, 1993), vol. 13, 152-154. Hereafter MOLLUS.

army and Catholic influences" at headquarters. "In the battle some fifteen or twenty brigadier-generals were employed and only four or five major-generals [will be appointed] and Rosecrans will have his friends fill the few chances, and his friends are regulars and Catholics."[20]

Other critics of Rosecrans focused on his abundant energy. William Shanks held strong opinions about many Federal officers, and Rosecrans was no exception. The biggest problem with the new man, as Shanks saw it, was nerves. Shanks described Rosecrans's constant activity as "nervousness." He became so agitated at times, recalled Shanks, as to become "incoherent. . . . I have known him, when merely directing an orderly to carry a dispatch from one point to another, grow so excited, vehement and incoherent as to utterly confound the messenger."[21]

Rosecrans could be hot-tempered, quick to anger, and equally quick to lash out verbally at the target of his rage. He was also, in at least equal measure warm and charismatic. Brig. Gen. John Beatty encountered both aspects of the general's personality in April 1863. Beatty was a citizen-soldier, and despite Rosecrans's West Point background, was favorably disposed toward the new general when he took command. Rosecrans, Beatty concluded, "has been long enough away from West Point, mixing with the people, to get a little common sense rubbed into him." That high opinion was momentarily shaken by an encounter with Rosecrans's famous temper. The new commander subjected Beatty to a humiliating public tongue-lashing for failing to move his command promptly when ordered. Beatty, however, thought the order to move was destined for the other General Beatty serving in the same army. The chastened Beatty hurried to army headquarters the next day to explain the problem in person. Rosecrans, in full view of staff and orderlies, cut him off with a thunderous, "Why in hell and damnation did you not mount your horse and come to headquarters to inquire what [the order] meant?" Beatty tried again to explain, to no avail. Rosecrans's "face was inflamed with anger, his rage uncontrollable, his language most ungentlemanly, abusive, and insulting," was

---

20 George Thomas Palmer and Lloyd Lewis, *A Conscientious Turncoat: The Story of John M. Palmer 1817-1900* (Yale University Press, 1941), 100.

21 William F. G. Shanks, *Personal Recollections of Distinguished Generals* (Harper and Brothers, Publishers, 1866), 258.

how Beatty later recalled the encounter. Furious and humiliated, he departed with the thought of resigning from the army.[22]

A few days later, however, Beatty shot off a letter demanding an apology. This time the army commander asked his subordinate to visit him again, and Rosecrans and the brigadier enjoyed a cordial private conversation during which Rosecrans made it clear that he valued Beatty's skills and services. On the way out, Rosecrans repeated as much in front of his staff (including Brig. Gen. James Garfield) and went so far as to inquire whether Beatty was satisfied. Indeed he was. "I expressed my thanks," explained the brigadier, "shook hands with him and left, feeling a thousand times more attached to him, and [filled with] more respect for him than I had ever felt before." Such was the power of William Starke Rosecrans's charm in a face-to-face setting.[23]

Rosecrans's detractors still included Edwin Stanton. This new command once again saw him reporting directly to Washington, and his tone-deafness to political nuance would again become his Achilles heel. In 1862 Stanton had resented what he viewed as Rosecrans's meddling "due to [Rosecrans's constant] suggestions." Stanton's animosity towards the Ohioan would only increase during the spring and summer of 1863, as Rosecrans sent a new and seemingly endless flow of "suggestions" over the telegraph wires from Nashville to the District of Columbia. Rosecrans's damaged relationship with Grant was at the moment less critical, since the two men were now commanding different departments and had little interaction, but Grant's opinion of Rosecrans was by no means improved. Neither Stanton's dislike nor Grant's subdued animosity blocked Rosecrans's promotion, but they would shadow him should he falter in his new position of high responsibility. He was being closely watched.[24]

Despite the lack of tactical success, Stones River was greeted as a victory in the North, especially coming as it did on the heels of the disaster at Fredericksburg on December 13, 1862. Congratulations flooded into Rosecrans's headquarters, and his stock in Washington soared. "There is

---

22 John Beatty, *The Citizen-Soldier: The Memoirs of a Civil War Volunteer* (University of Nebraska Press, 1998), 230, 256-257.

23 Ibid., 260-263.

24 George Hartsuff to Rosecrans, quoted in Varney, *General Grant and the Rewriting of History*, 36. Dr. Varney's book examines Grant's relationship with Rosecrans in exhaustive detail.

George H. Thomas, Rosecrans's second-in-command and his most
reliable subordinate. *Henry Fales Perry*

nothing you can ask within my power to grant to yourself or your heroic
command that will not be cheerfully given," telegraphed an unusually effusive
Secretary Stanton. This endorsement seemed to give Rosecrans carte blanche to
pursue a much more ambitious agenda with regard to making the army a more
effective and efficient command.[25]

25 Lamers, *Edge of Glory,* 246.

The first change came with the renaming of the army. The Army of the Ohio nomenclature had been left behind in Kentucky, and now the clumsy XIV Corps designation, with its three sub-corps, was also scrapped. Going forward, Rosecrans would command the Army of the Cumberland. Thus was created, along with the armies of the Potomac and the Tennessee, one of the three great Union commands of the War of the Rebellion, a brand with which the veterans would identify for the rest of their years. The Center, Right, and Left Wings were changed to the XIV, XX, and XXI Corps, respectively. Divisions and brigades were also renumbered. The reorganization created a more logical and coherent command structure.

Along with Buell, one other general who departed the army was Brig. Gen. Charles C. Gilbert. Gilbert was an acting general, his appointment an interim one subject to the approval of Congress, which had not been in session at the time. He commanded one of Buell's corps at Perryville, and fumbled badly. On the afternoon of October 8, 1862, Braxton Bragg's much smaller Confederate army attacked Union Maj. Gen. Alexander McDowell McCook's Corps, and nearly routed it. The other two thirds of the Union army looked on, and the huge Federal advantage in numbers was negated. Gilbert, despite the fact that he could personally witness much of this fight, recalled that he had strict orders from General Buell not to attack until the next day, and did nothing. Buell, through a trick of atmospherics, knew nothing of the fight, and no one thought to tell him until the battle was almost over. In the subsequent investigation, Gilbert was relieved, much to the joy of many of the soldiers in his command who viewed him as an incompetent martinet. His general's straps lapsed when Congress failed to approve his appointment, and he reverted to his Regular Army rank of captain. No one was sorry to see him eventually depart the army.

Beyond removing Gilbert, Rosecrans's reorganization of his command structure did not extend to replacing any of his other existing corps commanders. George Thomas, who under Buell had been kicked into an upstairs limbo as second-in-command of the army (with no direct authority over any troops) replaced Gilbert in commanding what would become a much reorganized four-division XIV Corps—the largest in the Army of the Cumberland. Alexander McCook and Thomas Crittenden headed up the XX Corps and XXI Corps, respectively.

Thomas's changed responsibilities were not a demotion. Far from just being the army's senior corps commander, Thomas was the second most important man in the army. The stocky southern Virginia native was born in 1816 and graduated from West Point in 1840 two years ahead of his new boss.

The newly-commissioned second lieutenant of artillery experienced infantry duty in Florida during the Seminole crisis, and served valiantly with his guns during the Mexican War. Thereafter, Thomas spent years on the plains as a prewar cavalryman, serving under Robert E. Lee and Albert Sidney Johnston in Texas. When war came he rejected sectionalism and remaining staunchly Unionist even though many Northerners questioned his loyalty early in the conflict. His distinguished combat record (with rare experience in all three branches of the army) had long since quashed any whispered backbiting and concern about his loyalty.[26]

Given the manner of Rosecrans's arrival, Thomas's relationship with his new boss could have been enormously awkward. Instead, it blossomed and the two officers quickly developed a powerful working relationship. Behind Thomas's deliberate manner lurked deep intelligence and bedrock-solid dependability. It helped that Rosecrans took Thomas fully into his confidence, and he usually heeded the burly Virginian's advice.[27]

Personally, George Thomas was reserved and reticent, a man of few words. This measured manner was enhanced by his physical movement, for while Thomas was a big bulk of a man, tall and imposing, he also moved stiffly due to a back injury suffered while stepping off a train. Though he could appear deliberate, even slow, in movement and speech, he was not slow of thought. He was an effective logistician, a sound strategist, and he knew how to win the loyalty of green volunteers. His men would come to revere him.

Nothing exemplifies this loyalty better than that found in the ranks of his old division. In January of 1862, George Thomas, leading three brigades, marched to Logan's Crossroads in southeast Kentucky. Thomas's objective, in conjunction with another Union division en route, was to drive a similar-sized Confederate force under the command of Rebel Brig. Gen. George B. Crittenden out of the state. Crittenden, knowing he would eventually be outnumbered, attacked first. The battle, fought amid rain and mud, was a confused affair. Thomas was not initially present at the battle, but when he arrived on the scene, he orchestrated a spirited counterattack that broke the Rebel line and routed Crittenden's poorly equipped little army. Thomas's men

---

26 Francis F. McKinney, *Education in Violence: The Life of George H. Thomas and the History of the Army of the Cumberland* (Americana House, 1991), 93.

27 Freeman Cleaves, *Rock of Chickamauga: The Life of General George H. Thomas* (Greenwood Press, 1974), 119-20.

were delighted, and would later recall that final charge at Logan's Crossroads with great pride.[28]

While Thomas had few detractors in the army, the same could not be said for his two corps counterparts. Both McCook and Crittenden drew criticism aplenty. Each man attained his general's star early in the war, but for political considerations as much as military merit.

Ohioan John Beatty, whose sometimes-acerbic pen offered up opinions on nearly everyone in the army via his private journal, famously described the portly Alexander McCook as "a chucklehead," with a "grin which excites the suspicion that he is either still very green or deficient in the upper story." Radical journalist Shanks regarded him as having the sense and manners of "an overgrown schoolboy." Unfortunately for McCook's reputation, these characterizations have largely defined him and his place in Civil War history. It didn't help that McCook also had the dubious distinction of having his men crumble under Confederate attacks at both Perryville and Stones River, which in turn caused other parts of the army to speculate that things weren't quite up to snuff in the XX Corps—charges the men of that corps hotly contested. Rosecrans, however, was favorably disposed to both men and made no effort to have them replaced.[29]

McCook was born in 1831, and entered West Point at the age of 16. He graduated in 1852, 30th in a class of 42. Fellow classmates included Philip Sheridan, George Crook and David Stanley. Assigned to the 3rd Infantry, over the next five years McCook served mainly in the American southwest, on active duty fighting the Apache. He proved to be a capable soldier, entrusted with increasing responsibilities. In 1857, he served as Chief of Guides for what came to be known as the Bonneville or Gila expedition, a punitive campaign against Apaches in present-day New Mexico and Arizona. In 1858, he was recalled to West Point as an instructor in infantry tactics.[30]

---

28 Eicher, *The Longest Night*, 161-163.

29 Beatty, *The Citizen-Soldier*, 235-236; Shanks, *Personal Recollections*, 249.

30 James H. Wilson, "Alexander McDowell McCook," *Thirty-Fifth Annual Reunion of the Association of Graduates of the United States Military Academy at West Point, New York, June 14th, 1904* (Seeman & Peters, Printers and Binders, 1904), 42. It took McCook an extra year to graduate (he was originally a member of the class of 1841). Whether he was deficient in academics or lost a year due to an excess of demerits is not explained by any of his biographers. Both McCook and Sheridan did not graduate with their original classes. McCook, who should have been in the class of 1851, graduated in 1852. Sheridan, who should have graduated in 1852, was kicked out

He arrived to take up his new duties at an interesting time in the Military Academy's existence; during a period when West Point was experimenting with a five year curriculum instead of the traditional four year course of study. The course of study was expanded in 1854, though it would be curtailed by the coming of the Civil War and never revived. The added year allowed primarily for more time to teach military tactics in the three branches: infantry, artillery, and cavalry; as well as introducing practical subjects like Spanish language courses (a very useful language skill to have in the American southwest at that time). With increased emphasis on tactics, the choosing of instructors in those subjects took on added importance. McCook had the proven skills and demonstrated ability to be a logical choice for this role.[31]

Despite his own struggles with academics as a cadet, McCook was a respected, popular instructor. He certainly applied himself, studying up on the science of war in order to better his instruction in the art. James H. Wilson, who was a cadet at the academy during McCook's tenure there, found the big Ohioan to be "generous, sympathetic, and outspoken, he gained both [our] respect and [our] confidence from the start and held them to the end." He would prove equally popular among his fellow officers. Loyal and faithful, McCook's friendships tended to be lifelong.[32]

His time at the Academy was cut short with the coming of the war. His family were prominent Ohio Democrats, and while not pro-slavery, took a dim view of abolitionists; an attitude which did not prevent a flood of McCooks into Union service upon secession. Alexander was the only West Pointer, but in all the McCook family sent 17 members to war, six of whom became generals and several members died during the conflict.

Immediately after the firing on Fort Sumter McCook offered his services to the governor of Ohio, who appointed him colonel of the newly forming 1st Ohio, a three month regiment that was rushed to the Federal capital. He and his men took part in the first major engagement of the war at Bull Run, and though his command was not initially engaged, McCook and his command drew praise

---

for a year because of his involvement in a fight with a fellow cadet; he graduated in 1853. Wayne Fanebust, *Major General Alexander M. McCook, USA: A Civil War Biography* (McFarland & Company, 2013), 10.

31 *Official Register of the Officers and Cadets of the U.S. Military Academy, West Point, New York* (James F. Baldwin, Printer, 1858), 17-18.

32 Wilson, "McCook," 40.

for maintaining their discipline and withdrawing in good order, even "saving" their brigade from disaster as they did so. He was promoted to brigadier general and transferred to Ohio, serving under William T. Sherman and subsequently Don Carlos Buell. He commanded a division in Buell's army, and led that command into combat on the second day of the battle of Shiloh, April 8, 1862. Here he had his best day in the war. His division was instrumental in driving the Rebels from the field, recapturing many Union camps, and winning significant praise from his superiors. Even Grant, who criticized McCook for failing to pursue the retreating Confederates at the battle's close, in his memoirs later apologized to the Ohioan and admitted that McCook's troops had done all that could be expected on the 8th. On the basis of his role at Shiloh, McCook was promoted again, to major general, in July 1862. Just 31 years old, he was a full decade younger than most of his similarly ranked peers.[33]

Then came Perryville. Now in command of a corps, his career so far had been meteoric. By the fall of 1862, with Buell obviously out of favor in Washington and likely to be replaced, some even thought McCook might get the job. Brigadier General William P. Carlin, West Point class of 1850, later reflected that "at that time some of [McCook's] friends desired to see him elevated to command of the Army of the Ohio, and it was pretty evident that nothing but a victory . . . under Buell's command could save the army from supersedure. It is not going beyond the probabilities . . . to say that McCook's ambition accorded with the view of his friends." This sort of talk must have been heady stuff to the young Ohioan: Even George B. McClellan, the "Young Napoleon" himself, was 35 when he was given command of the Army of the Potomac. That talk quickly subsided after October 1862. While no one doubted McCook's courage at Perryville, his corps was nearly routed.[34]

Physically, Beatty described McCook as "young, and very fleshy," clean shaven, and with "a weak nose, that would do no credit to a baby." Beatty also noted that McCook "swear[s] like [a] pirate, and affects the rough and ready style." He certainly was a large man. Former cadet Wilson, in his obituary of his good friend, described McCook as "powerful in build, rotund in person, ruddy in complexion, active and energetic of habit. [H]e was capable of every exertion

---

33 Fanebust, *McCook*, 52, 95-96, 98.

34 Robert I. Girardi and Nathaniel Cheairs Hughes, Jr., Eds. *The Memoirs of Brigadier General William Passmore Carlin, U.S.A.* (University of Nebraska Press, 1999), 66.

that the vicissitudes of a soldier's life could make necessary or advantageous."
He was certainly not graceless. William P. Carlin, was riding next to McCook at
Stones River when the latter's horse was suddenly shot. "McCook was a large
and fleshy man," recalled Carlin, "but the agility he displayed in leaping from
that wounded horse was truly wonderful to behold."[35]

Stones River raised another question mark concerning McCook's ability to
manage a corps when his command was surprised and again all but routed by a
Confederate assault on December 31. In fact, there was plenty of blame to go
around for this fiasco, starting with Rosecrans himself, who seemed
overconfident on the eve of that battle. Rosecrans's battle plan for the fight was
actually predicated on McCook being attacked; indeed, Rosecrans counted on it
to divert Bragg's attention away from Rosecrans's own roundhouse punch,
which was going to be delivered by Thomas Crittenden's corps against Bragg's
right flank. That punch never landed because McCook's corps couldn't hold
their own, but to be fair, no one expected Bragg to use nearly his whole army to
overwhelm the Union right. As a result, while Rosecrans expressed
disappointment with McCook's tactical acumen privately in a communiqué to
General Halleck, he made no public criticism of the XX Corps commander, and
did not relieve him.[36]

Rosecrans's XXI Corps commander was the only non-West Pointer in the
group. Tall and courtly, Tom Crittenden belonged to a prominent Kentucky
family and had a reputation as a hard drinker. Born in May 1819, Crittenden was
44 years old in the fall of 1863. He was the second son of the very powerful U.S.
Senator John J. Crittenden (of Crittenden Compromise fame) under whom he
studied law and passed the bar in 1840. His older brother, George B., eschewed
the law and chose soldiering, graduating from West Point in 1832. George
served in the Black Hawk War and on the frontier thereafter, doubtless bringing
home tales of breathless adventures.[37]

When the United States declared war on Mexico in 1846, Thomas tossed
aside his law books and followed brother George into the army. Thomas
secured an appointment to the staff of fellow Kentuckian Zachary Taylor, then

---

35 Beatty, *The Citizen-Soldier,* 235; Girardiand Hughes,*Carlin Memoirs,* 79

36 Fanebust, *McCook,* 158-159.

37 Daniel, *Days of Glory,* 190-191; Ezra J. Warner, *Generals in Gray: Lives of the Confederate Commanders* (Louisiana State University Press, 1991), 65.

commanding the U.S. forces on the Texas-Mexico frontier. The next year, Thomas was appointed lieutenant colonel of the newly-raised 3rd Kentucky, serving in that capacity until the unit was sent home in June 1848 during the general demobilization at the end of the conflict. The 3rd performed occupation duties, having arrived in Mexico too late for the main fighting.[38]

Upon his return from the military, Thomas Crittenden prevailed upon the newly-elected President Taylor for an overseas appointment, serving as the U.S. Consul in Liverpool, England from 1849 to 1853. Thereafter he returned home to Frankfort until the next war called him again into uniform.

Secession split not just the country, but the Crittenden family as well. George B. Crittenden joined the Confederacy, though he fared poorly. He was soundly defeated by George Thomas at Mill Springs in January 1862 and shelved thereafter, as much for his drinking problem as for tactical incompetence. The senior Crittenden and younger son Thomas remained loyal to the Union. Thomas L. Crittenden was commissioned a brigadier general of volunteers in September 1861, as much for his political influence in the all-important border state of Kentucky as for any military skills.

Like Alexander McCook, Tom Crittenden commanded a division during the second day's fight at Shiloh, and did well. He and his corps were not engaged at Perryville, kept out of the fight by outdated orders and the general confusion prevailing at Buell's headquarters during that battle. Crittenden did earn praise at Stones River from Rosecrans: "[his] heart is that of a true soldier and patriot," effused the army commander. Whatever was to come for the Army of the Cumberland, Crittenden would have a part in those events.[39]

In addition to the three-wing command structure inherited from Buell, Rosecrans also created two new corps. A top priority was to augment his weak and inefficient cavalry, and the new commander devoted his full attention to improving his mounted arm. In addition to a paucity of numbers, the few mounted men in the army he inherited were scattered among the infantry corps as escorts or separate brigades. This changed during the spring of 1863, when the Army of the Cumberland's cavalry command grew from a series of scattered fragments into a full corps under the guidance of Maj. Gen. David S. Stanley.

---

38 William Hugh Robarts, *Mexican War Veterans: A Complete Roster of the Regular and Volunteer Troops in the War Between the United States and Mexico, From 1846 to 1848* (Brentano's, 1887), 52.

39 OR 20, pt. 1, 198.

One of Rosecrans's trusted subordinates, Stanley was a classmate and fellow Catholic with prewar cavalry experience. Despite Palmer's suspicions, Stanley had won over Rosecrans in large part for his performance at the battles of Iuka and Corinth. When Rosecrans ascended to Buell's spot, David Stanley came along to help organize the Army of the Cumberland's mounted arm.

Rosecrans viewed his cavalry—or more specifically, the lack thereof—as his Achilles Heel in the summer of 1863. When the army marched on Murfreesboro back in December, Stanley commanded only 3,000 horsemen. By March of 1863, the Confederate mounted forces facing the Federals in Middle Tennessee amounted to nearly 17,000 men, with a more usual strength ranging between 12,000 and 15,000 troopers. Even after Rosecrans consolidated all available mounted troops, Federal numbers were still only about one-half of those arrayed against him. As a result the Federal army holding Nashville and Murfreesboro felt somewhat besieged, able to venture out from its fortified camps only in large well-escorted columns.

This state of affairs appalled Stanley. "The cavalry had been badly neglected," he complained. "It was weak, undisciplined, and scattered around, a regiment to [each] division of infantry. To break up this foolish disposal . . . to form brigades and eventually divisions, was my first and difficult work." As might be expected, infantry commanders resisted the idea of giving up their mounted forces, recalled Stanley, but "General Rosecrans sustained me." Once gathered, Stanley was able to form three "pretty substantial brigades" with a combined force of roughly 5,000 men. It was a good start, but a lot more needed to be done before Stanley could face his opponents on anything resembling equal terms.[40]

To offset the Rebel mounted advantage, Rosecrans and Stanley assiduously worked not only to have more cavalry sent their way, but to ensure that the troopers they did have carried the best arms and equipment. Rosecrans favored repeating weapons and breechloaders of all sorts and demanded them in such numbers that he soon exasperated the authorities in Washington. "You cannot expect to have all the best arms," snapped General in Chief Henry W. Halleck, after one such telegraphic exchange.[41]

---

40 David S. Stanley, *Personal Memoirs of Major General D. S. Stanley, U.S.A.* (Harvard University Press, 1917), 120.

41 *OR*, 23, pt. 2, 51.

Interestingly, Stanley still favored the saber, a weapon largely abandoned by the Rebels and most Federal troopers. Carbines had their place, but Stanley thought that over-reliance on firearms sapped a cavalryman's confidence. He insisted that each squadron receive training in edged-weapon use and that they keep their swords sharp. He even ordered up grindstones for that very purpose.[42]

A second approach to improving his cavalry arm involved mounting infantry. Rosecrans's concept was to create a series of elite battalions, one for each infantry brigade. Each battalion would recruit the best men in each regiment, arm them with repeaters, mount them, and use them in a dual role for scouting and as battlefield skirmishers. Captain Joseph T. Patton of Company A, 93rd Ohio, described how the battalions were formed:

> Soon after the battle of Stone River, Gen. Rosecrans issued an order establishing a "roll of honor," to be selected from men whose conduct at that battle would entitle them to this distinction. Three privates were selected from each company, three corporals and two sergeants from the regiment, and one officer, elected by the officers of the regiment. I was elected to command the company from the 93d. The several companies from the four regiments of the brigade formed a "light battalion." It was proposed to mount the battalion for special service. We bought Henry rifles and devoted our time to special drill, being relieved from all duty except guard at Corps headquarters.

This idea was quickly dismissed by Washington. Rosecrans's "Elite Battalions" trespassed on legal boundaries that the War Department was unwilling to cross. Only Congress could authorize the creation of new units. As a result, noted Captain Patton, "we returned to our respective commands." However, the idea was not entirely shelved. Even after disbandment, added Patton, "the men of 'the light battalion,' with their Henry rifles, did valiant service in every battle until the close of the war." [43]

As a compromise, the War Department did allow Rosecrans to convert existing units. The most famous of these was Col. John T. Wilder's brigade of two Indiana and three Illinois regiments. Wilder, aged thirty-three, was an accomplished millwright and business owner from Greencastle, Indiana,

---

42 Stanley, *Memoirs*, 121.

43 J. T. Patton, "Personal Recollections of Four Years in Dixie," *MOLLUS*, vol. 50, 418.

already very successful and modestly wealthy when the war commenced. He tried to raise an artillery battery, equipped with guns cast at his own foundry in Greencastle, but the unit was instead accepted into service as Company A of the 17th Indiana. Wilder rose to regimental command and saw action in western Virginia and in the aftermath of Shiloh. His most notable moment on the battlefield prior to Tullahoma arrived in September 1862 when he was commanding a garrison of largely untried troops defending the Louisville & Nashville Railroad Bridge spanning the Green River at Munfordville, Kentucky. His valiant defense lasted three days, during which time Wilder traded command with another officer who arrived with reinforcements. In the end Wilder was forced to surrender his 4,000 men to a Confederate force numbering more than 25,000. Exchanged and paroled, he returned to brigade command in the spring of 1863.[44]

Wilder and his command were an anomaly in the ranks of the Union army. By Civil War standards his command of 2,283 men in five regiments—the 92nd, 98th and 123rd Illinois, 17th and 72nd Indiana, as well as Capt. Eli Lilly's 18th Indiana battery of artillery—was superbly equipped. All but five companies of the infantry carried seven-shot Spencer repeating rifles instead of muzzle-loading rifle-muskets, and Captain Lilly's battery upped the ante by adding four light 12-pound mountain howitzers to his normal complement of six 3-inch rifles. Nominally speaking Wilder's was just another brigade in George Thomas's XIV Corps, part of the 4th Division under Maj. Gen. Joseph J. Reynolds. In the spring of 1863, however, as Rosecrans cast about for ways to augment his outnumbered Federal cavalry, Wilder's scheme to arm his brigade with repeaters and mount it on seized horses came to Rosecrans's attention.[45]

Wilder had approached his superiors with the idea of impressing local livestock to mount some or all of his command as best he could. This dovetailed nicely with Rosecrans's intentions, and Wilder was allowed to proceed with his plan. There was some initial reluctance to issue non-standard arms to the brigade, but the Indiana colonel, whose peacetime success had made him financially secure, arranged to privately equip his men with Spencers. The men agreed to sign loans for the weapons and Wilder guaranteed the notes

---

44 Richard A. Baumgartner, *Blue Lightning: Wilder's Mounted Infantry Brigade in the Battle of Chickamauga* (Blue Acorn Press, 2007), 20-26.

45 David A. Powell, "Numbers and Losses in the Chickamauga Campaign," unpublished manuscript at Chickamauga-Chattanooga National Military Park.Hereafter CCNMP.

through his hometown bank. In the end, the War Department relented and paid for the rifles. The incident highlighted Wilder's can-do, independent streak. The result was everything Rosecrans could have wished for: mobility and firepower that no Confederate force of equal numbers could match.[46]

Their first test as mounted infantry came at Hoover's Gap on June 26, 1863, followed a few days later by their raid on Dechard, Tennessee. In each case Wilder's men achieved solid results and both Rosecrans and Thomas praised their actions. Thereafter Rosecrans was wont to issue orders directly to Wilder, treating his command as an army asset rather than as just another brigade in a division. Thomas was not particularly pleased with this arrangement, but it was division commander Reynolds who most felt the slight of protocol. It didn't help that the men of the brigade had become accustomed to living off the land, and in late summer reports of indiscriminate plundering began working their way up the chain of command. Wilder's men viewed the reprimands that followed as little more than manifestations of the rest of the army's jealousy toward their newly won status. On August 1, 1863, Lt. Col. Henry Jordan of the 17th Indiana wrote a carping letter to Wilder, who was at home on leave and recruiting. Jordan described the tension within the ranks and attributed the problems to Reynolds. "[T]he truth is that old Joe Reynolds is the very same old counterfeit I always told you he was, and is head over heals into the conspiracy against us," wrote Jordan. "He openly expresses his dissatisfaction at your practice of skipping him in your communications with Dept. Head Qtrs. and is determined to raise merry hell with everybody in the brigade on that account." Wilder's men were coming to regard themselves as a breed apart. Little came of either the thievery complaints or Reynolds's dissatisfaction. Wilder's men were too valuable for Rosecrans to ignore, and he continued treating them as an independent strike force.[47]

Other mounted efforts were less successful, in part because those parts of Middle Tennessee that could be foraged for suitable livestock were already depleted or fast becoming so. A second brigade under Col. Abel Streight of the 51st Indiana was recruited, intended for use on a raid against the Confederate

---

46 Baumgartner, *Blue Lightning*, 38. Baumgartner provides a detailed look at the mounting and equipping of Wilder's brigade. The 75th Illinois elected not to convert, and was eventually replaced by the 92nd Illinois.

47 "Dear Col." Henry Jordan to John T. Wilder, August 1, 1863, Wilder Papers, Indiana State Library. Hereafter InSL.

rail line serving Bragg's Army of Tennessee. Unfortunately for Union arms the effort failed and Streight and most of his command were captured. The result put a damper on further such efforts. Only one more regiment, the 39th Indiana, would be mounted and armed on the Wilder model.

By the late summer of 1863, Rosecrans had materially augmented his mounted force to about 10,000 cavalry and mounted infantry. Even better, almost all of his cavalry, while not armed with Spencers, had largely been equipped with either breech-loading carbines or multi-chambered Colt revolving rifles, which greatly augmented their effectiveness. The Army of the Cumberland's mounted arm was now a formidable force capable of meeting the Rebel cavalry on a more equal footing.

General Stanley, meanwhile, looked beyond merely augmenting the cavalry's numbers to improving its leadership. Here he enjoyed less success. Stanley formed his 9,000-man Cavalry Corps in June of 1863 into two divisions. While he was able to choose brigade commanders with some freedom, he later lamented that the divisional commanders "were dictated by [army chief of staff James A.] Garfield, and worse could not be found. [John Basil] Turchin, a fat, short-legged Russian, who could not ride a horse, and Robert [B.] Mitchell, a politician, always thinking of the votes he could make in Kansas."[48]

Despite his dumpy appearance and Stanley's disdain for his riding skills, Turchin (born Ivan Vasilievitch Turchaninov) was the son of a Russian cavalryman serving with the Don Cossacks, some of the most feared horseback fighters in Europe. His father was a major in a Cossack regiment (though not ethnically a Cossack himself), and Ivan was destined for a military career at an early age. He spent five years at a military school in St. Petersburg, where, unlike cadets at West Point, he received a comprehensive education in warfare and tactics as well as mathematics and engineering. Commissioned as an artillery officer in 1841, by 1844 he was serving in the Tsar's Imperial Guard and continued doing so when revolutionary fervor swept across Europe. Turchin was called upon to put down many bloody revolts. He did well, and went on to the General Staff School to study logistics and graduated with honors. More combat experience came with the Crimean War, where Turchin fought the British and French at Sevastopol.[49]

---

48 Stanley, *Memoirs*, 135.

49 Stephen Chicoine, *John Basil Turchin and the Fight to Free the Slaves* (Praeger Publishers, 2003), 1-3, provides a summary of Turchin's Tsarist experience.

At heart, however, Cossacks were free men and not subjects, and Turchin identified more with the revolutionaries he was battling than with his fellow officers. Despite his favored status and a promising career, Turchin grew disillusioned by the inequities inherent in Imperial Russia. In 1856 he and his wife Nadine fled, first to London, and eventually to America. They settled in Chicago, where he put his engineering skills to use with the Illinois Central Railway. He and his wife both had a burning hatred of slavery; whether their abolitionist bent stemmed from the serf system in Russia or chattel slavery in the American South is unknown, but by 1861 Turchin could hardly remain on the sidelines as his new country prepared for war.[50]

Turchin trained and commanded the 19th Illinois until August 1862. During the war's early years, the former Tsarist officer came to scorn what he viewed as the coddling of secessionists, dismissing early Federal efforts at prosecuting a kinder form of warfare as the "guarding-potato-patches policy." Things came to a head at Athens, Alabama, where, in response to a bushwhacking incident, Turchin unleashed his men on the town. The subsequent looting outraged senior commanders and resulted in his court-martial and dismissal. Turchin, who believed (with some justification) that he was better skilled and more qualified to command men on campaign than most of the generals he served under, managed with the help of his wife to overturn the result and finagle a reinstatement. His new assignment was to command one of Stanley's two new cavalry divisions.[51]

Stanley's frustrations with Turchin boiled over in May 1863, the result of an action at Middleton, Tennessee, where Stanley planned an attack against a Rebel camp. According to Stanley, Turchin was late, took a wrong turn, and "spoiled my well-planned expedition." Stanley kicked the matter upstairs to Rosecrans with an ultimatum: "If he stays then relieve me." Rosecrans eventually mollified Stanley in an unusual way by having Turchin exchange commands with Brig. Gen. George Crook, who was then commanding an infantry brigade in Reynolds's division of the XIV Corps.[52]

50 Warner, *Generals in Blue*, 511.

51 John B. Turchin, *Chickamauga* (Fergus Printing Co., 1888), 11.

52 Stanley, *Memoirs*, 137; Martin F. Schmitt, ed. *General George Crook: His Autobiography* (University of Oklahoma Press, 1946), 103. Stanley was much happier with Turchin's replacement, fellow West Pointer and classmate George Crook. Crook was like-minded in his contempt for politicians-turned-general.

In truth, Stanley harbored prejudices against not only politicians, but "the foreigner and the radical." Turchin almost certainly reciprocated his superior's disdain. The Russian-born officer was often contemptuous of native-born American soldiers, whom he regarded as his military inferiors. Rosecrans understood that Turchin, despite his un-martial appearance and his insistence on bringing Nadine everywhere with him, even on campaign, was a solid soldier. Before the upcoming campaign was over, Rosecrans would have reason enough to be thankful Turchin was still with his army.

The object of Stanley's and Crook's mutual dislike was Stanley's other "problem," Brig. Gen. Robert B. Mitchell. Like Turchin, Mitchell returned the disdain in spades. A volunteer like Palmer, he loathed West Pointers, whom he also considered far too cautious in battle. Mitchell had Mexican War experience serving in the 2nd Ohio. In the 1850s he moved to Kansas, becoming embroiled in that bloody conflict on the abolitionist side, and by 1861 was serving as the new state's adjutant general. He entered the war as colonel of the 2nd Kansas and received a dangerous wound at Wilson's Creek. After he recuperated Mitchell recruited a regiment of Kansas cavalry and in the crisis that was Bragg's invasion of Kentucky, Mitchell rose to lead a division under Buell. He and most of his men watched the battle of Perryville, for much to Mitchell's frustration they were not committed to action. This frustration led him to be one of General Buell's chief critics in the court of inquiry that followed that disjointed battle, and fueled his dislike of West Pointers in general.[53]

As befitting a politician, Mitchell was a shameless self-promoter. The ever-observant Gen. John Beatty had dinner with Mitchell in November 1862, right after Buell was relieved of command: "Blows his own trumpet, as of old," noted Beatty, who went on to add that Mitchell "expects a division will be given to him soon." Instead, for the first half of 1863 Mitchell served as commander of the post of Nashville. To Stanley's great dismay, Mitchell was given command of the 1st Cavalry Division in June 1863 in time for the Tullahoma campaign.

---

53 *OR* 16, pt. 1, pp. 92-98. During the Kentucky campaign, Mitchell commanded an infantry division under Maj. Gen. Charles C. Gilbert, another academy graduate, with whom he clashed repeatedly. Gilbert was criticized for his failures to act at Perryville, largely as a result of Mitchell's testimony. Mitchell was particularly incensed because Gilbert detached one of Mitchell's brigades and sent it off to help McCook's corps, leaving Mitchell to watch helplessly. This brigade, the only one of Gilbert's command to see serious action, suffered nearly 500 casualties in the fight.

Thus far, however, Mitchell had served effectively and had given Stanley no overt reason to demand his removal.[54]

In addition to rectifying his cavalry concerns, Rosecrans decided to centralize control of the men guarding his line of communications. On June 8, 1863, Maj. Gen. Gordon Granger was assigned to command the newly crafted Reserve Corps, brought into being to take control of the large number of garrison troops strung out along the railroad and garrisoning important posts like Nashville. Protecting his precious logistical lifeline was critical, and Rosecrans had no intention for these men to forsake their guard duties and serve as a new field force. Heretofore, however, all of these detachments were reporting directly to Rosecrans's own headquarters. Uniting these defenders under a single subordinate commander allowed Rosecrans to exert greater control and flexibility over the myriad of regiments and independent posts, as well as making the shifting of them as needed to meet changing threats much easier. Equally important, the administrative burden for these many outposts and detachments would fall to Granger, freeing Rosecrans's staff from spending hours of time sorting through mind-numbing paperwork, time which could be better spent focusing on the business of waging offensive war.

Granger was a 41-year-old New Yorker and West Pointer (class of 1845) with meritorious combat service in Mexico (winning two brevets) and on the frontier. He had seen more recent combat at Wilson's Creek in August 1861, and led a brigade during the siege of Corinth following the Shiloh operation. He was an Old Army man with Old Army ways, and like the now-departed Gilbert, not popular with the troops. One of the men who served under him that spring was Pvt. John M. King of the 92nd Illinois, who held Granger in no high esteem. King regarded Granger as an officer "destitute of brains" who probably owed his appointment to West Point to political influence. This type, sneered Private King, "manages to commit his lessons to memory and mumbles them over to his teacher. After four years of training of this sort he graduates, becomes a lieutenant or captain of the regular army, and in the case of war, if he has strong political friends, he becomes a Major General of Volunteers. Such a man is General Granger, stylish, haughty, and indignant." King further dismissed Granger as a "granny," full of "red-tape foolishness." To King, Granger seemed fascinated with endless parades and capable of capricious orders issued merely to assert his martial authority. As commander of the Reserve Corps, however, Granger's duties were mostly administrative. His command was not intended to take the field as a combat unit.[55]

Another key officer who joined the army at this time was the object of much of General Stanley's displeasure. James A. Garfield, simultaneously a sitting Ohio congressman and a brigadier general, was eager to further his combat experience, which in turn could only help fuel his political ambitions. He was not completely green. He served as both a regimental and brigade commander, seeing action in eastern Kentucky and at Shiloh. In the summer of 1862 he became ill, and took an extended leave to recuperate. During that time he was recruited to run for Congress in the elections of 1862, and won. Upon the recovery of his health, he traveled to Washington to await further assignment.

In Washington he sat on the court-martial of Fitz-John Porter, then being tried for disobedience of orders during the Second Battle of Bull Run. Porter was found guilty, an outcome Garfield, who was friends with one of Porter's chief accusers Gen. Irvin McDowell, found very satisfactory. By this time Garfield's opinion of West Pointers (at least as reflected in the characters of men like McClellan, Halleck, and Porter) was similar to Palmer's; dubious to say the least. While in the national capital, Garfield also cultivated another important political connection, Salmon P. Chase, Secretary of the Treasury. Despite his access to the nexus of power, however, Garfield hoped to obtain a field command. In January 1863, with the completion of the Porter court's work, that wish was fulfilled: Garfield was ordered to report to the Army of the Cumberland for assignment.[56]

He spent three weeks with Rosecrans awaiting a position with the Army of the Cumberland. The two got along well. Rosecrans was so impressed with him that he offered Garfield the job of chief of staff instead of a line command. An artillery round at Stones River had decapitated Julius P. Garesche, the previous occupant of that office, and Rosecrans needed a first-rate replacement. The offer was unexpected and ran contrary to Garfield's initial expectations. The Ohioan was hoping not for a staff appointment but for command of a brigade

---

55 Warner, *Generals in Blue*, 181. Claire E. Swedberg, ed. *Three Years With the 92nd Illinois: The Civil War Diary of John M. King* (Stackpole Books, 1999), 64, 66, 68.

56 Garfield would continue to correspond with Chase during his time with the Army of the Cumberland, a fact which would both help and ultimately hinder Rosecrans.

or even a division. After some soul-searching, however, Garfield accepted. The assignment would have a significant impact on the army's future operations.

Professional soldiers dominated the top command of the Army of the Cumberland down to the divisional level. In addition to Rosecrans and four of his five corps commanders, nine of the 13 men commanding divisions during the campaign and battle of Chickamauga were professionals. From brigade leaders on down, however, it was very much a volunteer army. There were a small number of academy graduates commanding brigades, but they formed a distinct minority. Of the 34 infantry and five cavalry brigades comprising the army, only about a half-dozen were led by West Pointers. A few more commanders had foreign military experience, including one Russian (Turchin) and several Germans. The overwhelming majority were simply citizen-soldiers—bankers and businessmen, not a few lawyers, a number of politicians, and some Mexican War veterans among them. Each learned his trade the hard way in that most brutal of all classrooms: the battlefield.

By the fall of 1863, most of them had learned their trade well, as had the men in the ranks. While no one would ever mistake them for professionals in the European or Old Army sense—their informal sense of discipline and easy manner between officer and enlisted man proved that—they understood war and were good at it. In the face of adversity, Rosecrans could rely on the resilience of these men, especially the brigadiers and colonels. The great hidden strength of the Army of the Cumberland was in the essential competence of these officers and the men they led.

*   *   *

And to what use would Rosecrans turn his now-finely honed, well trained and well organized military machine? For more than a year, the army's primary objective had been the city of Chattanooga. The Army of the Potomac marched "on to Richmond." The Army of the Tennessee marched south along the Mississippi River, to let "the father of waters" once again "flow unvexed to the sea." The troops marching under Buell (and later under Rosecrans) might not have had a catchy newspaper slogans or poetic imagery to spur them on, but that did not make Chattanooga any less of critical objective. "Much as the American people of a later generation would dread the ghastly sacrifice of life they believed would inevitably be extracted at the crossing of the Rhine," wrote historian Glenn Tucker in his seminal work on the battle of Chickamauga, "or in storming the Japanese mainland, so had the North come to look with terror toward the impending battle for the heart city of the South."[57]

Chattanooga first loomed large in Federal plans shortly after the capture of Nashville in February 1862. Initially, Lincoln wanted Buell to move directly into East Tennessee after Nashville but Buell, with a better grasp of the logistical constraints, understood that he must first capture Chattanooga and its vital rail connections before he could move on Knoxville. Henry Halleck, who was not yet general in chief, wanted Buell to support his own movement towards Corinth, Mississippi; requesting that Buell both reinforce him directly and also capture Florence, Alabama, another important rail point.[58]

Halleck's strategy prevailed. Eventually most of Buell's force was diverted to Mississippi, fighting at Shiloh on April 8, and then joining in the month-long campaign towards Corinth that May. Only after the Confederate evacuation of Corinth did Halleck (who by now had been promoted over Buell) order the Army of the Ohio to march towards Chattanooga, moving westward from Corinth and repairing the badly damaged Memphis & Charleston Railroad along the way.

Buell again objected. Instead of moving laterally across northern Alabama he preferred to return to Nashville and then march his army southeast along the Nashville & Chattanooga Railroad, which he felt was less vulnerable to raids. Halleck again insisted. Buell was proven correct. Progress was slow, with Buell not reaching the towns of Stevenson and Bridgeport —both towns on the N&C Railroad—until July.[59]

In the meantime, the Confederates took a hand. General Braxton Bragg, newly promoted to command the Army of Tennessee, transferred his men to Chattanooga, arriving in time to thwart Buell's attempted seizure. Then Bragg marched into Kentucky, in conjunction with Kirby Smith's small army from East Tennessee, and all Union thoughts of Chattanooga were again forgotten. Buell chased Bragg into Kentucky, fought the battle of Perryville, and was replaced. When Rosecrans inherited Buell's command, he also inherited its objective: Chattanooga. Stones River and Tullahoma were merely stepping-stones along the way.

---

57 Glenn Tucker, *Chickamauga: Bloody Battle in the West* (Morningside House, Inc., 1961), 15.

58 Daniel, *Days of Glory,* 74-75.

59 Ibid., 93-96.

In 1861 the budding industrial center of Chattanooga, with its important and expanding rail connections, numbered about 2,500 residents. A veritable web of tracks converged here. The Nashville & Chattanooga tracks connected the city to the Tennessee capital, and from there, all the way to Louisville. The Memphis and Charleston connected at Stevenson. The Western & Atlantic ran south to Atlanta. The East Tennessee & Georgia line ran to Knoxville, and from there all the way to Virginia. Because of Muscle Shoals in north central Alabama, the Tennessee River was not navigable from Chattanooga's docks all the way to the Ohio, the Mississippi, and beyond; but with the advent of the railroads, Chattanooga's place as a transportation hub was assured.

Those tracks all led to Chattanooga because, even if the river wasn't navigable, millennia of erosion meant that the Tennessee had carved an important valley through the southern end of the Appalachian mountain chain. Behind the shield of those mountains, the new Confederacy established budding war industries: foundries, powder and clothing mills, and other vital manufactories. Alabama, Georgia, and the Carolinas were all critical to the Southern war effort, especially after the loss of Nashville, Memphis, and New Orleans. Once Chattanooga was in Union hands, Federal armies could directly threaten those new industries.

Thus far Rosecrans had achieved significant tactical success using wide envelopments. He conducted his first army-sized maneuver in December 1862 when he departed Nashville on a wide front that culminated in the battle of Stones River. His second envelopment was aimed farther south at Tullahoma, a movement that was both larger and much more successful. Part of the reason for that success was its scope. The advance to Stones River was limited to a front of about 25 miles, during which Rosecrans's separate columns were never more than about 20 miles apart. While the tight frontage reduced the Federal army's potential risks of being defeated in detail, it also limited Rosecrans's chances of catching Bragg out of position and mauling him piece by piece. The much more ambitious Tullahoma operation carried the Union army nearly 50 miles closer to Chattanooga. At the height of the movement, the Federal columns were 40 miles apart. Marching on such a broad front expanded Rosecrans's risk, but confused the Confederates as to his ultimate objective.[60]

Rosecrans's new mission was to capture Chattanooga, and, if possible, advance beyond it toward Atlanta. It was by far his most difficult and dangerous task to date. His first obstacle was not Bragg and his Confederates but the Tennessee River, which nature had made too wide and too deep to ford at most places. Because Bragg had destroyed all the bridges and any boats he could find when he fell back beyond that waterway after being turned out from his Tullahoma defensive line, Rosecrans would have to force a crossing with his own pontoons.

Rosecrans's next obstacle was also geographic in nature. The mountains surrounding the city took the form of long and imposing ridges that ran generally southwest to northeast, one behind the other and each essentially perpendicular to the Union army's intended avenue of advance. Once across the Tennessee River, the Army of the Cumberland would have to climb each of these ridges in turn. Nor could the mountains be scaled easily. Eons of erosion meant that for much of their length, the heights were marked by steep palisades that precluded passage. The limited number of gaps piercing these mountain walls dictated that the blue columns would be spread even farther apart, with only limited access to lateral communication roads should they need to concentrate quickly.

Despite the inherent risks involved Rosecrans promptly decided on another wide envelopment. This time, however, he could rely on Maj. Gen. Ambrose E. Burnside and his nearly 30,000 men stationed in Kentucky to help further the deception. A move against Knoxville by Burnside, who was charged with capturing Knoxville and East Tennessee while Rosecrans moved on Chattanooga, would implant Bragg on the horns of a thorny strategic dilemma. The Rebels were strong enough to oppose one advance but not both, and so would have to choose which city to defend. In order to derive maximum mutual benefit, however, both Federal armies would need to advance simultaneously.[61]

On paper, it made sense for Rosecrans to approach Chattanooga first by moving east to Cookeville and McMinnville, before turning south to march on the city. Doing so would allow him to remain on Burnside's strategic right flank, and allow either Federal force to come to the other's aid if the need arose. Logistically, however, moving into that part of Tennessee was not possible for a large army. No rail line ran east beyond McMinnville to carry supplies in quantity, which meant that wagons would have to haul everything from

---

61 OR 30, pt. 2, 545-552.

ammunition and uniforms to food, forage, and nails. Worse yet, the region immediately east of Manchester was called "The Barrens" for good reason. This sparsely settled area of rough hills and forest offered few roads and narrow valleys, and thus little chance for the Federals to live off the land. Once through The Barrens the Yankees entered the equally sparsely settled Cumberland Plateau with its difficult mountain crossings. The road to Chattanooga was clearly not a move east. Further study of the terrain and logistical issues convinced Rosecrans that the natural gateway into Chattanooga was to first advance south into Alabama and then turn east, following the course of the Tennessee River Valley. This was the same course the Nashville and Chattanooga Railroad took through Stevenson, Alabama, before crossing the river at Bridgeport. This route also incorporated difficult terrain and presented limited opportunities for forage, but the presence of the railroad would allow Rosecrans to stockpile supplies and establish advanced depots. Both Stevenson and Bridgeport were on the north bank of the Tennessee, only some 30 miles downstream from Chattanooga.[62]

With his general course of operation decided upon, Rosecrans decided to feint north with limited infantry and cavalry to fool Bragg into thinking that the main Federal army would move in conjunction with Burnside. After a few days of conspicuous activity to the north baited the trap, Rosecrans would send his three infantry corps across the Tennessee River between Chattanooga and Stevenson. Crittenden's XXI Corps would move directly against Chattanooga to pin Bragg's attention in place. Thomas's XIV Corps and McCook's XX Corps, meanwhile, would cross the river as quickly as possible and slip through the mountain ridges into northern Georgia with the intention of cutting the railroad between Chattanooga and Atlanta somewhere east of Rome, Georgia. As Rosecrans saw it, at the very least Bragg would have no choice but to retreat once again as he had at Tullahoma. He could not survive around Chattanooga without his rail connection with Atlanta. If all went exactly according to plan, however, the wide envelopment offered a reasonable chance of trapping Bragg's army in the mountains, where it could be destroyed. The plan was a mirror image of the Tullahoma move. In the former operation, Rosecrans feinted right and moved left. This time he intended to feint left and move right.

---

62 Good descriptions of this terrain can be found in both Rosecrans's official report, *OR* 30, pt. 1, 48-49, and Thomas L. Connelly, *Autumn of Glory: The Army of Tennessee, 1862-1865* (Louisiana State University Press, 1986), 138-145.

This new movement was also his most ambitious to date, for it required at one point that his right and left flanks be separated by almost 60 miles.[63]

Preparing for such a grand move required a great deal of work. At the conclusion of the Tullahoma campaign, Union forces seized both Stevenson and Bridgeport. On July 29, a Union infantry division under Maj. Gen. Philip H. Sheridan of McCook's corps occupied both towns. Rosecrans ordered the railroad repaired all the way back to Nashville. Once the line was in working order, he established depots to accumulate supplies for the next move. The stockpiling would take weeks, and the effort was not lost on local observers.[64]

Knowing that he could not keep the preparations for a river crossing below Chattanooga entirely secret, Rosecrans relied upon a combination of stealth and misdirection to deceive Bragg, with spies and Confederate prisoners planting false stories. When a captured Rebel lieutenant was brought to Union headquarters after he slipped across to the north bank of the Tennessee River to visit his family near Winchester, Rosecrans offered to let the officer go— provided he told Bragg all he saw and heard while in Federal hands. Ostensibly, the officer was to report that Rosecrans was planning to cross the river at Bridgeport. Rosecrans, however, also contrived to let the Rebel "overhear" a conversation during which Rosecrans ordered the establishment of a depot at McMinnville, Tennessee, with 100,000 rations "immediately [once] the road is in order." Part of the real plan was offered openly to the gullible young Confederate in hope that Bragg would assume it nothing more than an obvious trick; the cover story of the McMinnville depot, however, was offered up as a careless error Rosecrans hoped Bragg would assume to be legitimate. A spur of the Nashville railroad ran to McMinnville, and any move toward Knoxville or the upper Tennessee crossings would have to depart from that point. Rosecrans hoped these stratagems would keep Bragg guessing about which threat was real and which was the feint. In order to preserve this uncertainty as long as possible, Rosecrans planned to advance on a broad front. On August 15 he issued orders that would define the opening phase of the campaign and concentrate his army along the banks of the Tennessee.[65]

63 John Fitch, *Annals of the Army of the Cumberland* (Stackpole Books, 2003), 458.

64 Philip H. Sheridan, *Personal Memoirs of P. H. Sheridan, in Two Volumes* (Broadfoot Publishing, 1992), vol. 2, 272.

65 William Starke Rosecrans, "Rosecrans's Accounts of Tullahoma and Chickamauga," *National Tribune,* March 25, 1882; *OR* 30, pt. 2, 35-38.

To further deceive Bragg, Rosecrans intended to shove Crittenden's XXI Corps east from McMinnville into the Sequatchie Valley, mimicking the early stages of an advance along the northerly route. Seizing this terrain would also give Rosecrans another strategic advantage. The valley was a long narrow gorge that, from its origin point on the north bank of the Tennessee near Jasper, ran northeast for about 60 miles with a width of only two to four miles. Walden Ridge formed the southeastern wall, separating the valley from Chattanooga, and like the rest of the mountains in the region could only be traversed at a few points. Control of the valley would give Federal troops an easy lateral route across Bragg's front, while seizing the few gaps in Walden Ridge would allow the Federals to prevent Rebel cavalry from observing their activities. If it worked, Bragg would only catch glimpses of Union troops when and where Rosecrans chose to send men across Walden Ridge to appear suddenly in front of the Rebel army picketing the south bank of the Tennessee. Each of the XXI Corps's three divisions would enhance the deception by advancing on a different axis, entering the valley at three widely scattered points.

There were still details to be addressed. Part of a Rebel cavalry brigade under Col. George G. Dibrell occupied the area around Sparta, Tennessee, sent there to recruit and keep an eye on the Yankees. For now, Rosecrans was content to let them be since their reports of extensive Union activity at McMinnville only reinforced Rosecrans's ruse. The advance of XXI Corps would deal with them accordingly, though Brig. Gen. Robert H. G. Minty's Federal cavalry brigade would have to drive them away ahead of the corps' infantry before Dibrell's troopers could discern Crittenden's real routes and objectives.[66]

Since McCook already had one of his divisions at Stevenson, the rest of the XX Corps would join it and cross there. With Sheridan already guarding the river keeping unwanted Rebel scouts on the far bank, McCook's headquarters moved to Stevenson in early August. His remaining two divisions followed suit with orders to "select a convenient camp, concealed from the observation of the enemy," and prepare to cross once Rosecrans was sure Bragg had taken the bait.[67]

66 Ibid., 36.

67 Ibid., 37.

Thomas's XIV Corps was the fulcrum of the advance. Rosecrans intended for his four divisions to cross the river between Bridgeport and Jasper at the lower end of the Sequatchie Valley. From there, Thomas's men could either move north up the valley to support Crittenden or southwest along the Tennessee to reach McCook. In either case, if Crittenden's columns were not to become bottled up in the narrow confines of the Sequatchie, Union control of the town of Jasper was critical. Rosecrans wanted all these movements accomplished quickly. His August 15 orders called for Thomas's initial movement to be finished by August 19.[68]

The first two weeks of August were marked by extensive preparations, primarily in accumulating supplies. The country ahead offered but sparse pickings for an army on the move, leaving Rosecrans with no choice but to haul with him as many supplies as possible during the initial advance until he could reach more densely settled country. Crittenden's men, who would be farthest from the railroad, had orders to carry 10 days of rations and eight days of forage with them into the Sequatchie Valley. Thomas's troops, with better access to the advanced depot at Bridgeport, would take with them rations for eight days and five days' forage. The XX Corps would initially advance along the railroad, and so could draw supplies directly from both depots. Once they struck eastward, however, each man would need to carry at least a week's provisions. As a result, hundreds of carloads of supplies would have to be pushed forward to these various points before a man could take a step.[69]

Once these preliminary movements were completed, intelligence reports and reconnaissance missions would determine whether Bragg had shifted his forces to resist a crossing below Chattanooga. If the way was open, Rosecrans could begin the next stage of his plan: a fast passage across the Tennessee River. The XXI Corps would move southwest to Jasper while sending a limited force across Walden Ridge to continue the plan of deception. Conversely, if Bragg anticipated this move below Chattanooga, Rosecrans could still funnel troops and supplies up the Sequatchie and let Crittenden seek a crossing north of town in conjunction with Burnside's movements. While this option was clearly the less desirable of the two choices, it was a useful option to leave open, and, depending on Bragg's response, might offer a viable alternative for occupying

---

68 Ibid., 35-36.

69 Ibid.

Chattanooga. In either case, after a second pause of a few days to accumulate more rations in the forward depots, Rosecrans would be ready to enter Georgia.

Chapter Two

The Army of Tennessee:
Summer 1863

The Confederate Army of Tennessee was a deeply flawed organization by the summer of 1863. Like their Federal counterparts, after two long years of war the men in the Southern ranks were competent and effective combat soldiers. The ranks of the commanders, however, were rent with dissention.

At the army's head was Gen. Braxton Bragg, a tall, spare man with dark looks, prominent eyebrows, and a short-trimmed salt-and pepper-beard. Born in North Carolina, Bragg was 46 that year, a West Pointer of the class of 1837. He did well at the Academy, graduating fifth in a class of 50; fellow classmates included William W. Mackall and W. H. T. Walker, both now in gray, as well as Joseph Hooker and John Sedgwick, both wearing Union blue. His first active duty was in Florida, fighting Seminoles, assigned to the 3rd U.S. Artillery. His name would become a household word thanks to the Mexican War, the battle of Buena Vista, and Zachary Taylor. In February 1847 Taylor's small American force was attacked by a much larger Mexican army. Bragg commanded a battery of artillery there, a so-called "flying battery" because it was equipped with lighter, more maneuverable guns pulled by horses. Bragg was seemingly everywhere that day, using his mobility to break up attack after attack. In a widely circulated (and highly romanticized) newspaper story, at one point Taylor, witnessing one such attack, supposedly exhorted: "A little more grape, Captain Bragg!" While in reality, if "Old Rough n' Ready" Taylor said anything

Braxton Bragg, beleaguered commander of the Army of Tennessee.
Library of Congress

at all, it was likely to have been: "Give 'em hell, God damn them!" The phrase struck a chord. It made Bragg's name a catchword and propelled Taylor into the White House.[1]

Catchphrase notwithstanding, Bragg's performance at Buena Vista was unquestionably excellent. Among those who fought alongside him was future Confederate President Jefferson Davis, commanding the 1st Mississippi Rifles.

Bragg returned to the United States in 1848 amid much hoopla. He was feted and dined repeatedly by an excited public, a fame which eventually wore thin. It also brought him to meet Eliza (or to friends, Elise) Ellis, a Louisiana planter's daughter, beautiful and wealthy in her own right since she inherited a portion of her father's estate. The two were married in 1849.[2]

Bragg spent the next few years in uniform, serving at various posts. In 1853 Jefferson Davis was appointed Secretary of War, and immediately commenced a series of military reforms aimed at improving all aspects of the army. The artillery branch received much attention, bringing Bragg into contact with Davis again. Bragg was vociferously in favor of army reforms, which naturally aligned him with Davis, but the two did not see eye-to-eye when it came to the artillery. Both men could be obdurate, and this impasse over artillery organization and assignments eventually led Bragg to resign his commission in 1856. After all, he was wealthy, the owner of a sugar plantation in Louisiana courtesy of his bride; Bragg did not need the army to prosper. He left the service harboring enmity for Davis, and convinced that Davis bore a grudge against him. When Davis did not stand for president of the United States in 1856, Bragg was relieved. "He could drive me from the army but not from my party," wrote Bragg to a friend.[3]

Bragg prospered in civilian life, but secession found him back in uniform, first as a Louisiana Militia officer, then as a Confederate brigadier general. Again, the presence of Davis—this time as President of the Confederacy— caused him problems. Bragg was jealous that Pierre G. T. Beauregard, another Louisianan, West Pointer, and former United States officer, was ranked higher than Bragg on the list of new generals, and Bragg felt he knew why.

---

1   Grady McWhiney, *Braxton Bragg and Confederate Defeat, Volume I* (University of Alabama Press, 1991), 90-92.

2   Ibid., 118.

3   Ibid., 140.

Bragg and his wife were friends with William T. Sherman, and at a dinner in New Orleans held to say goodbye to Sherman who was headed back north, Elise confided: "you know that my husband is not a favorite with the new president."[4]

Originally assigned to Pensacola, where the Federals still occupied Fort Pickens, Bragg spent 1861 in what amounted to a backwater. He was a good organizer. He raised and trained a corps of 10,000 troops during this time, demonstrating martial skills far beyond a mere artillery captain's sphere of responsibility. Those troops fought well at Shiloh, when called upon to reinforce Albert Sidney Johnston's army after the disasters of Forts Donelson and Henry. Bragg, commanding a corps in Johnston's army, did less well. In fact, all the senior Confederate officers soon lost control of the battle, meaning that most of the fighting deteriorated into individual brigade and sometimes regimental assaults. The result was a bloody but disjointed contest that ultimately fell short of Johnston's goal: destroying Ulysses S. Grant's army. Johnston himself was killed on the field, leading a charge.[5]

After the battle, command of the Rebel army fell to P. G. T. Beauregard, Bragg's rival from Louisiana. Beauregard had his own difficult relationship with President Davis, however, and within two months, was relieved of command. Bragg, the next ranking man present, was appointed in Beauregard's place.[6]

Bragg inherited a crisis. In June 1862, Federal armies were deep in Mississippi, and threatening Chattanooga. The Rebels abandoned the fruitless siege of Corinth and retreated to Tupelo, seemingly powerless to stop the much larger Union forces. Assessing his responsibilities, Bragg orchestrated one of

---

4   Samuel J. Martin, *General Braxton Bragg, C. S. A.* (McFarland & Company, 2012), 89.

5   Bragg has drawn harsh criticism over the years for his performance at Shiloh, especially for launching a repeated series of fruitless attacks on the position known as the "Hornet's Nest." Over time it has become clear that much of that criticism is overblown; since many of those attacks did not take place, or did so without Bragg ordering them. See Larry J. Daniel, *Shiloh: The Battle that Changed the Civil War* (Simon and Schuster, 1997), 214; Timothy B. Smith, *The Untold Story of Shiloh: The Battle and the Battlefield* (University of Tennessee Press, 2006), 29-31; O. Edward Cunningham, with Gary D. Joiner and Timothy B. Smith, eds., *Shiloh and the Western Campaign of 1862* (Savas Beatie, 2007), 259-60.

6   General Beauregard's replacement was controversial. Beauregard abandoned Corinth and retreated, when Davis wanted a renewed offensive. Beauregard then took sick leave, a move which further annoyed Davis, who charged Beauregard with abandoning his command. Bragg, who had been appointed a full General of the Confederacy to date from April 6, the first day of Shiloh, took command.

Leonidas Polk, Bragg's chief adversary within the Army of Tennessee's command ranks.
William Polk

the more impressive logistical and strategic feats of the war: he took 40,000 men to Chattanooga, arriving ahead of Buell's ponderous advance, and then launched an invasion of Kentucky in conjunction with Kirby Smith's forces from East Tennessee. By September, 50,000 Rebels were occupying central Kentucky, the North was in a panic, and the threat of further Union advances into the deep south curtailed. It was an impressive achievement.

Unfortunately for Confederate fortunes, the Kentucky campaign ended with the battle of Perryville. Buell's much-reinforced and greatly expanded army marched out of Louisville in early October to drive Bragg out of the Bluegrass state. Bragg, misreading the tactical situation completely, ordered 16,000 of his own troops to attack what he thought was a diversionary column, but turned out to be Buell's main body of 55,000 men. Amazingly, the Rebels prevailed, mainly due to an excess of caution and some extreme bumbling on the Union side of the line; but when Bragg realized he faced Buell's whole army, he retreated. This disappointing denouement to what just a month ago appeared to be a brilliant exploit of strategic acumen, worthy of a great captain of old, would touch off a cancer of rancor within the Army of Tennessee's leadership ranks that would never fully heal.[7]

Despite Bragg's manifest abilities in terms of training, discipline, logistics, and strategic insight, he was also possessed of some significant negative attributes as a leader. He was short-tempered, swift to find blame, quick to take credit for success, but slow in recognizing the achievements of others. He was also often physically ill, which only made him more irascible. His biographer Grady McWhiney summarized him thusly: "Bragg was courageous, and at times imaginative, resourceful, and bold. But he was never patient, either with his men or with the enemy, and he lacked that imperturbability and resolution so necessary in field commanders. Handicapped by poor health, he had no real taste for combat. And he was not lucky. Nor did he have the ability to inspire confidence in his subordinates. Notoriously inept at getting along with people he disliked, he simply could not win the loyalty of his chief lieutenants."[8]

For much of 1863, his failing physical condition was especially bad, which exacerbated his prickly personality quirks. Colonel John H. Savage of the 16th Tennessee described Bragg as "mentally and physically, an old, worn-out man, unfit to actively manage an army in the field." "Bragg," noted medical historian Dr. Jack Welsh, "was very thin, stooped, and had a sickly, cadaverous appearance. He had chronic migraine headaches, stomach trouble, and generally poor health, in part due to chronic dystentery." He took "a mercury preparation each summer" due to "liver problems" contracted in Florida. Things came to a head in the summer of 1863. In May, "he was bothered by a

---

7   Eicher, *The Longest Night*, 367-370.

8   McWhiney, *Braxton Bragg*, 390. McWhiney's comment about Bragg having "no real taste for combat" is interesting. Bragg certainly conducted a number of hard-fought actions while in command of the army, but he was rarely at the forefront. As army commander, he remained in the rear, where his generals could find him, and where he felt he could exercise the most control. Too often, this meant he was out of touch with what was happening on the field. He was not a coward, having proven his courage in battle at Buena Vista and again at Shiloh, where he repeatedly exposed himself; but the main lesson he took away from Shiloh was how confused things became after Johnston's death. As a result, if anything, Bragg remained too far back from the front in subsequent fights.

boil on his hand," which over the next two months became "a siege of boils and chronic diarrhea." This ordeal, Bragg admitted, "culminated in 'a general breakdown.'"[9]

For the past year, Lt. Gens. Leonidas Polk and William J. Hardee had served as Bragg's two principal subordinates. Like Bragg, both were West Pointers. Polk, however, resigned his commission immediately upon graduation to take orders as an Episcopalian priest (he eventually rose to the rank of bishop), having never served a day of active military service. His principal military qualification was that he was a friend and classmate of Jefferson Davis. With the war's arrival, President Davis offered his former friend a general's commission; Polk temporarily set aside his churchly duties for those of the sword. It was one of Davis's more unfortunate decisions.

Hardee was at least a professional army officer with long service on the frontier. A small dapper man with carefully groomed mustache and goatee, he was also the author of the ante-bellum army's newest tactics manual, translated from the French in 1855 and adapted to accommodate the new rifled muskets that were then entering service. He was not brilliant, but he was a capable soldier. Both he and Polk would have troubled relationships with Bragg.[10]

The root of the army's command problems is traceable to the disappointing conclusion of the Kentucky campaign. The movement north had begun well, raising hopes both within the army and across the Confederacy. The climax of the campaign at Perryville was a confused affair. Bragg was heavily outnumbered and confronted the entire Federal army with just a portion of his own, but he badly misread the situation and contemptuously overrode the objections of his two principal subordinates to order an attack against desperate odds. Only Federal blunders saved Bragg from a serious disaster. Although arguably a Confederate tactical success, nearly two-thirds of the Union army didn't fight at all. When Bragg finally realized he was outnumbered almost four to one, he affected a successful withdrawal from the battlefield. Unable to

---

9 John H. Savage, *The Life of John H. Savage* (Nashville, 1903), 137; Jack D. Welsh, M.D. *Medical Histories of Confederate Generals* (Kent State University Press, 1995), Kindle edition; McWhiney, *Braxton Bragg*, 389.

10 William J. Hardee was competent, but not much more than that. He disliked serving under Bragg, but when he transferred to Mississippi later in 1863, he was not happy in that assignment, either. He shied away from larger responsibility when it was offered to him at the end of 1863, leaving the question of how he would perform at army command forever unanswered.

remain in Kentucky, the high hopes of the South ended in retreat from the state and bitter recrimination, much of which was leveled against Bragg.[11]

A second disappointment came at Stones River (Murfreesboro) at the turn of the year. Bragg attacked early on December 31 and once again achieved a measure of tactical success, but not enough to drive the Union army from the field and back into its Nashville defenses. After a day's uneasy pause followed by a poorly executed assault on January 2, 1863, Bragg had shot his bolt and retreated. His withdrawal conceded defeat in both the minds of his army and the citizenry of the South.[12]

Stones River became an especial focal point of enmity between Bragg and infantry division leader John C. Breckinridge, the former United States vice President serving in Hardee's Corps. Breckinridge blamed Bragg for the slaughter of his division, sent forward in the useless January 2 attack. Bragg, meanwhile, blamed Breckinridge for providing bad intelligence on Union movements, for failing to attack on December 31, and for losing control of his own command during the January 2 assault. Bragg firmly believed Breckinridge lied about these matters in his official report. Affairs were made immeasurably worse when Col. Theodore O'Hara, a member of Breckinridge's staff, planted fraudulent stories in Southern newspapers about Bragg's decision to retreat after the battle. Bragg opted for withdrawal only after consulting with his generals, all of whom agreed a retreat was necessary. O'Hara's leaks, however, suggested Bragg withdrew despite his subordinates' desire to stay and fight. More than any other single event, these anonymous information leaks, mostly from O'Hara's poison pen, set off a chain reaction of disaster within the Army of Tennessee's officer corps.[13]

The six months of relative quiet during the first half of 1863 gave everyone time to brood over insults real and imagined. Disagreements festered into quarrels, which broke into open feuds. The stress did nothing for Bragg's

---

11 When viewed objectively, the campaign was not a complete failure. It did restore a measure of Confederate fortunes in the Western Theater after a disastrous spring in 1862.That mattered little, however, when expectations for a more lasting success had been so high.

12 For the latest scholarship on Stones River and Bragg's role therein, see Larry J. Daniel, *Battle of Stones River: The Forgotten Conflict Between the Confederate Army of Tennessee and the Union Army of the Cumberland* (Louisiana State University Press, 2012).

13 See Martin, *General Braxton Bragg, C.S.A.*, 252-253; Peter Cozzens, *No Better Place To Die: The Battle of Stones River* (University of Illinois Press, 1990), 210-216. For more detail on the state of affairs within Bragg's command, see Thomas L. Connelly, *Autumn of Glory*, 75-76, 81-84.

health, which continued to deteriorate. A full airing of the failings of the Kentucky campaign, coupled with controversies over the retreat from Murfreesboro, led to a near-mutiny in the army.

Bragg exacerbated his problems with his subordinates by singling out the Kentuckians within his army for special approbation. Bragg entered into the Kentucky campaign with the mistaken idea that the state's citizens were anxious to throw off the yoke of Yankee oppression, and he hauled wagonloads of weapons with him to arm the expected thousands of new recruits waiting to swell his ranks. Kentucky, however, was at heart a Unionist state, and by the fall of 1862 most of the pro-Southern Kentuckians were already wearing Confederate gray. Few rallied to the Confederate colors. Disgusted and harboring feelings of being misled, Bragg blamed prominent Bluegrass Rebels like Simon Bolivar Buckner, John Hunt Morgan, William Preston, and John Breckinridge for deceiving him. Proud men all, Breckinridge and company resented Bragg's acerbic criticism of them and their native state. Buckner would eventually become one of Bragg's bitterest foes within the Army of Tennessee.

Matters came to an ironic head in early 1863 when Bragg did something very odd for a commander: He solicited opinions from his subordinates on his own fitness to command. What he was expecting from such a plebiscite is unknown, but what he heard stunned him: resign. Bragg of course had no intention of relinquishing command of the army. The whole embarrassing mess culminated in March 1863. Alarmed at the command crisis spilling over into the public sphere, President Davis sent theater commander Joseph E. Johnston (with whom Davis had his own difficult relationship) to examine the situation and take charge, if necessary. Johnston offered no substantive help. In fact, Johnston refused Davis's explicit order to take command of the Army of Tennessee and send Bragg to Richmond, where he could be used much more effectively in a staff role. When Davis issued that order in early March, Bragg's wife was dangerously ill and Johnston seized upon that fact as a pretext for refusing to follow it, arguing it was a bad time to add to Bragg's burdens.[14]

In reality, health had nothing to do with it. Johnston didn't want to assume the responsibility of army command, especially in a situation where it might be perceived that he worked behind Bragg's back to further his own ambitions. This did nothing to help resolve the army's problems. In fact, Johnston made them worse by wholeheartedly endorsing Bragg and praising the latter's

---

14 *OR* 23, pt. 2, 674; McWhiney, *Braxton Bragg*, 387.

handling of affairs. Johnston's affirmation simultaneously reassured Davis in faraway Richmond while doing nothing to resolve the core problem festering in Tennessee. The net result was the creation of a simmering long-term resentment between Bragg and his senior commanders. As bad as it was, it was about to get much worse.[15]

In April 1863, another officer was introduced into this unsettled mix of command personalities. Brigadier General William Whann Mackall assumed the position of Bragg's chief of staff. Although a West Point classmate (Class of 1837), Mackall was not a close friend of his new boss. He did, however, have a very close relationship with Joseph E. Johnston, and it is possible that Mackall got the job at Johnston's recommendation. Mackall had a solid career before secession. The native Marylander was wounded in the Seminole War, earned two brevets in Mexico, served on the Pacific Coast in 1861, and resigned and hurried home to accept a Confederate commission as a lieutenant colonel. His first posting was with another Johnston—Albert Sidney—as chief of staff of the Army of Mississippi. Before the battle of Shiloh, however, Mackall was promoted to brigadier and reassigned to command the post of Island Number 10. Unfortunately, he did not fare well in that position. Outmaneuvered and besieged, Mackall surrendered his entire force of 7,000 men in April 1862. Exchanged, he returned to duty that August. From there he held a series of staff jobs through the fall and winter until joining the Army of Tennessee.[16]

Mackall found his new commander wanting. His private letters excoriated Bragg, itemizing numerous failures. "He is very earnest at his work," admitted Mackall, and "his whole soul is in it, but his manner is repulsive and he has no social life. He is easily flattered." Mackall despaired at Bragg's indecision and lamented that his own advice was rarely heeded. Bragg "has more than once issued orders for the movement of the army—would scarce listen to my objections, and yet I have gone to bed perfectly satisfied that the movement

---

15 Craig L. Symonds, *Joseph E. Johnston: A Civil War Biography* (W. W. Norton, 1992), 197. Bragg has often been described as one of Jefferson Davis's close friends, and this was the primary reason Davis kept Bragg in command for so long. This is not true; Davis made the decision to relieve Bragg that spring.

16 OR 8, 804. Mackall later asserted that Beauregard give him this post with the understanding that it was a "forlorn hope," and there never was much chance of a good outcome, but public opinion failed to understand that nuance. For more information on Mackall's prewar years and early Civil War experience, see Richard M. McMurry, "William Whann Mackall," in *The Confederate General*, 6 vols. (National Historical Society, 1991), vol. 4, 126-127.

would never be made. . . . If he doesn't want news to be true, he will listen to nothing. . . . [H]e has not genius, and . . . he will fail in our hour of need. His mind is not fertile nor is his judgment good."[17]

Mackall's resentments ran deeper than just a dislike of Bragg and a distain for his lack of abilities. In point of fact, the Marylander thought he should be holding a much higher rank. He had resigned to go South even though his native state did not leave the Union. Based on his prewar record, Mackall expected to be warmly received and offered a general's wreath. Instead, he recalled that Jefferson Davis treated his arrival "coldly." As a result, he disdained most of the men who now ranked him within the Army of Tennessee. One particular character flaw probably held him back: Mackall tended to be a pessimist. "He was always opposed to fighting," lamented diarist and fellow staff officer Col. Taylor Beatty, and was "always predicting disaster." His letters to Joseph Johnston, who was then serving in Mississippi, reflected a growing disillusionment with Bragg and the state of affairs generally. Johnston reciprocated with his own pessimistic view of the progress of the war, as well as a preoccupation with self-justification over the loss of Vicksburg in early July 1863. Their mutual negativity served to reinforce one another's sense of gloom. To quote Bragg's most recent biographer, "Mackall was not the stalwart subordinate that Bragg so desperately needed." While Mackall fretted and the army command structure splintered, troops were being transferred away from the Army of Tennessee to other theaters where Federal armies were more active.[18]

Jefferson Davis understood that the Confederacy had too few troops to defend simultaneously the entire Western Theater, and was forced to rely upon interior lines to shuttle Rebel troops from point to point to meet various Union thrusts. In late 1862, after Joseph Johnston recovered from his Seven Pines wound, Davis sent Johnston west to act as that department's overall commander, with authority to shift troops at will as he saw fit. Johnston, however, fundamentally disagreed with Davis' concept. On paper it looked like Middle Tennessee and Mississippi were close enough for this strategy to work. In reality, the lack of both direct rail lines and convenient rivers meant that the Confederates, and not the Federals, had the longer lines of communication. For

---

17 William W. Mackall, *A Son's Recollections of his Father* (E. P. Dutton & Co. 1930), 178-179.

18 "Entry for February 2, 1864," Taylor Beatty Diary, Southern Historical Collection, University of North Carolina; Martin, *General Braxton Bragg*, 277.

example, even though Jackson, Mississippi and Shelbyville, Tennessee were less than 400 straight line miles apart, troops sent from Jackson had to first travel south to Mobile on the Gulf coast, across the bay on ferries, and then north to Atlanta before moving up the railroad to Tennessee—a distance of nearly 800 miles along existing transportation lines. The two men would never see eye-to-eye on how best to defend the West. Each grew increasingly disenchanted with one another. Davis didn't help matters when he overrode Johnston's refusal to exercise his discretion and ordered troops sent elsewhere.

The first such transfer came in December 1862, just before Stones River, when a Union move threatened Vicksburg. Davis ordered Bragg to send Maj. Gen. Carter L. Stevenson's large division of 10,000 troops to reinforce the Mississippi bastion. This detachment stripped Bragg of fully one-fifth of his combat power just a couple of weeks before a major battle, but arrived in Mississippi too late to have any influence on affairs at Vicksburg. Stevenson's division was never returned to Bragg, becoming instead a part of the Army of Mississippi. The next crisis erupted in May 1863. As Middle Tennessee settled into what looked to be a quiet front, two more infantry divisions and a cavalry division followed, all sent to Jackson, Mississippi where they became part of Johnston's short-lived Army of Relief, so-named as the force that was supposed to lift the siege of Vicksburg. Over the course of six months Bragg lost the use of more than 20,000 infantry and 4,000 cavalry, or 40% of his entire strength.[19]

Then came Tullahoma. Bragg, with fewer than than 50,000 men, barely 30,000 of them infantry, was heavily outnumbered by Rosecrans's 65,000 troops. He was also outgeneraled. To some observers he appeared demoralized and displayed a mercurial changeability. After falling back to the defenses of Tullahoma, on the night of June 28 Bragg gave every impression of being determined to fight there, asserting as much to Brig. Gen. St. John Liddell in a discussion that evening. Others, who knew Bragg better, told Liddell that they doubted he would make a stand. They were right. Two days later on June 30 Bragg issued orders to retreat, and the army fell back to Chattanooga.[20]

---

19 These troops included Maj. Gens. John C. Breckinridge's and J. P. McCown's infantry commands, as well as Brig. Gen. William H. Jackson's two-brigade cavalry division. McCown's division was initially returned to East Tennessee, not Mississippi, and reorganized there.

20 Nathaniel Cheairs Hughes, Jr. ed. *Liddell's Record: St. John Richardson Liddell Brigadier General, CSA Staff Officer and Brigade Commander, Army of Tennessee* (Louisiana State University Press, 1985), 128.

The abandonment of Middle Tennessee without a major battle was a severe blow to the Army of Tennessee's morale in general, and especially to the thousands of native Tennesseans that made up so many of the rank and file. Discontent spread deep and wide; desertion spiked. Even Bragg's own assessment of the miserable affair was stark: "This is a great disaster," he confided to Dr. Charles T. Quintard during the retreat.[21]

By July 7, the army was across the Tennessee River. For the next six weeks, while the Federal army shifted supplies forward and planned the next move, Bragg concentrated on restoring the Army of Tennessee to fighting condition. Just a week later, however, yet another call was made on the Army of Tennessee and General Hardee was transferred to Mississippi to help organize and command troops in that state. Despite the ongoing friction between Bragg and Hardee, the latter's transfer was a real loss to the army. If not a brilliant general in his own right, Hardee was an excellent trainer, a firm disciplinarian, popular with the troops, and a solid combat officer—all skills Bragg sorely needed. To replace him, Bragg received newly (and temporarily) promoted Lt. Gen. Daniel Harvey Hill, who arrived in Chattanooga on July 19.[22]

Bragg and Harvey Hill were old acquaintances, having served together in the Regular Army. Along with George Thomas, Hill had served in Bragg's battery in 1845, where all three men (along with John F. Reynolds, who had been killed leading the Union First Corps at Gettysburg barely a fortnight previous) messed together. Hill had not seen Bragg since the days in Mexico, however, and was shocked at Bragg's careworn appearance. "He . . . seemed gloomy and despondent," Hill recollected years later. "He had grown prematurely old since I saw him last, and showed much nervousness." Hill had already heard something of the army's troubles, noting that Bragg's "relations with his next in command (General Polk) and some others of his subordinates were known not to be pleasant. His many retreats, too, had alienated his rank and file from him."[23]

---

21 Judith Lee Hallock, *Braxton Bragg and Confederate Defeat, Vol. II* (University of Alabama Press, 1991), 23.

22 Nathaniel Cheairs Hughes, Jr. *General William J. Hardee: Old Reliable* (Louisiana State University Press, 1992), 157. D. H. Hill's promotion was provisional, made by Davis while the Confederate Congress was in recess and thus subject to Congressional approval when their session resumed.

23 Daniel H. Hill, "Chickamauga: The Great Battle of the West," in *Battles and Leaders of the Civil War*, 4 vols. (Thomas Yoseloff, Inc., 1956), vol. 3, 638.

If Hill had his doubts about Bragg, Bragg had reason to reciprocate. D. H. Hill had served his entire Civil War career in the Eastern Theater, mostly in Virginia. His first action came at a large skirmish at Big Bethel in June 1861, where he served as a colonel commanding the 1st North Carolina. Hill was one of the first officers to see real combat in this new war. He served with the force that eventually became the Army of Northern Virginia under Joe Johnston and then Robert E. Lee up through the Maryland campaign of 1862. His best moment came when he commanded the over-matched Confederate force defending South Mountain on September 14, 1862, rendering what Hill considered his most important service of the war to date when his division held firm in a day-long battle against two Union infantry corps before finally being driven back early that evening. Hill's tenacious defense gave Lee the time he needed to gather in scattered segments of his army, but his command lost some 2,500 men in the ultimately losing effort. Lee would fight the Federals under McClellan to a stalemate on the banks of Antietam Creek at Sharpsburg three days later, but the campaign ended in disappointment and an early retreat into Virginia.

Hill's solid battlefield accomplishments notwithstanding, Lee transferred Hill well away from the main stage of the war to command the Department of North Carolina. The reason he did so was simple: in Lee's view, Hill "croaked." Hill was "often gloomy," given to pessimism and finding fault with others, especially superiors. He was also acerbic. One contemporary described him as "harsh, abrupt, [and] often insulting in the effort to be sarcastic." Hill's normal approach to life was in decided contrast with Lee's, who tended to be much more optimistic; it is not surprising that Lee would want him gone. Like Bragg, Hill was also often in poor health. He had chronic pain from a spine injury and suffered accordingly, especially when the weather turned cold or wet. "I often shiver in bed like a man in an ague," he once informed his wife. "When once chilled, I have not vitality enough to react and a mountain of blankets would not warm me." His many physical limitations only added to his sharp, sardonic tongue. In an army that already included the constant pessimism of men like William Mackall and Braxton Bragg, Hill's arrival could only be considered icing on a very bitter cake.[24]

24 Douglas Southall Freeman, *Lee's Lieutenants: A Study in Command*, 3 vols. (Charles Scribner's Sons, 1971), vol. 3, 721; Hal Bridges, *Lee's Maverick General: Daniel Harvey Hill* (McGraw Hill, 1961), 147, 149.

Worse yet, not everyone saw Hill's performance at South Mountain in a positive light. Some Lee loyalists blamed Hill for the disappointing conclusion to the Maryland campaign, a factor Hill deeply resented. When Lee began to think about expanding his army by creating a third infantry corps, another Hill—Ambrose Powell—was favored over Daniel Harvey. D. H. nearly resigned over the perceived slight, and only grudgingly assumed the appointment to command in North Carolina instead. For the first six months of 1863 Hill held that largely backwater post until President Davis rode up to Hill's lodgings in "the suburbs of Richmond" one July morning and offered him a combat command in the Western Theater. To Hill the offer represented vindication and a second chance to prove himself on the field. And so Hill, the difficult subordinate, found himself under the command of Braxton Bragg, an even more difficult commander. The two difficult personalities were bound to clash.[25]

Another new arrival appeared a few weeks later. Major General Thomas Carmichael Hindman arrived in Chattanooga on August 13 from Richmond, bearing orders authorizing him to take command of Maj. Gen. Jones M. Withers's division in Leonidas Polk's corps. Withers was a capable combat officer who had seen plenty of service—when healthy. Unfortunately, as the war continued he grew increasingly less so. He was absent for much of 1863, his division left in the hands of its senior brigadier, J. Patton Anderson of Florida. Withers submitted his resignation that July, but agreed to stay on with the condition that he could assume a less active role. He was promptly transferred to district command in Mobile. Hindman, who was then on detached duty in Richmond, was sent as his replacement.[26]

Hindman was a firebrand: short of statue, flamboyant in appearance, and contentious. Though born in 1828 in Knoxville, Tennessee, his family soon traveled west and he grew up as a Mississippi planter's son. His first great adventure in life was the War with Mexico. He enlisted in the 2nd Mississippi Rifles as a lieutenant, but saw only disease and dusty occupational duties instead

---

25 Originally Hill was slated to go to Mississippi and Hardee to remain with Bragg. Instead, Hardee departed for Mississippi and Hill arrived to take his place. Hardee's departure seems to have been at the behest of influential Mississippians seeking to enhance the state's defenses in the wake of the Vicksburg disaster, with Hardee being held in high regard there.

26 OR 30, pt. 4, 495.

of combat.[27] He studied law when he returned home and eventually turned to politics. Hindman served a term in the Mississippi state legislature and campaigned vigorously for various pro-slavery, States' Rights candidates, among them Jefferson Davis. In 1854, however, drawn by burgeoning opportunity, Hindman moved across the Mississippi River to Helena, Arkansas.

Once in Arkansas he formed a law partnership with a prominent local attorney, but his real passion continued to be the political arena. His knack for politics proved successful and he rose to prominence in the local and state Democratic scene. His proclivity for confrontation, however, challenging the established "old guard" of the Democratic party machine in Arkansas, led to several instances of gunplay. "Hindman had a wonderful talent to get into fusses," observed one contemporary, "from which he always came off either victor or with credit." Fortunately for Hindman's survival, he befriended Patrick C. Cleburne, an Irish immigrant and fellow Helena resident. Cleburne was also a budding lawyer, having first worked as a storekeeper and as a druggist. More than once Cleburne's negotiating skills smoothed over violent confrontations, but Cleburne couldn't be everywhere. In June 1855, a quarrel on the floor of the State House ended in a shooting when two political rivals attacked Hindman. The native Tennessean managed to shatter one of his attacker's arms and escape the return fire, but had to hide behind the speaker's podium to avoid an angry mob. He was eventually cleared of any charges.[28]

As Cleburne discovered, a friendship with Hindman could be downright dangerous. They weathered a yellow fever epidemic and emerged as heroes for tending the ill when most fled, and Cleburne was nearly killed during a second gunfight in May 1856 when he backed up his friend in the hard streets of Helena. Hindman emerged only lightly wounded, but one of their assailants fell dead. Cleburne was seriously injured and spent months recovering.[29]

Hindman went on to serve in the U.S. Congress in 1858. He did not return to take his seat in 1860 because secession was erupting across the South. An

---

27 Diane Neal and Thomas W. Kremm, *The Lion of the South: General Thomas C. Hindman* (Mercer University Press, 1997), 10-12.

28 Charles Edward Nash, *Biographical Sketches of Gen. P. C. Cleburne and Gen. T. C. Hindman* (Press of Morningside Bookshop, 1977), 150; Neal and Kremm, Lion of the South, 26.

29 Craig L. Symonds, *Stonewall of the West: Patrick Cleburne & The Civil War* (University Press of Kansas, 1997), 40-41.

ardent Fire Eater and secessionist, Hindman played an instrumental role in taking Arkansas out of the Union. He raised his own regiment for the war, was appointed colonel of the 2nd Arkansas, and led a brigade at Shiloh. He fought well there and earned praise from none other than Bragg himself. From that point on however, his military career followed a more difficult path.

Hindman was wounded at Shiloh and returned home to Helena to recuperate. While there, he learned that his conduct in that battle had garnered him a promotion to major general. At the end of May 1862 he also received a wide-ranging new command in the form of the Department of the Trans-Mississippi, which was just then threatened with invasion. A month earlier its previous commander, Maj. Gen. Earl Van Dorn, had been called east to join the Confederate army at Corinth; Van Dorn took most of the troops slated to defend Arkansas with him.

Hindman's new task was vastly more complicated than leading a brigade, which thus far had been his most important military duty. In Arkansas he would need to recruit, arm, and train an entire new army out of virtually nothing, and with scant attention from a much-stressed Confederate War Department in far-off Richmond. Moreover, his position required working with civilian authorities and thus a deft diplomatic touch he did not possess. His combat experience, political skills, and network of contacts in his adopted state may have seemed the perfect match for the job, but his confrontational style suggested otherwise.

Despite his abrasive personality, Hindman achieved some notable success in Arkansas by raising a new field force of nearly 30,000 men. In doing so, however, he ruled via fiat and martial law, enforcing sometimes draconian measures and earning the enmity of his political counterparts. Richmond responded by sending Maj. Gen. Theophilus H. Holmes west to take overall command of the Trans-Mississippi Department, a move demoting Hindman to a more limited district command that Richmond hoped would insulate him from the political facet of the job. When an opportunity beckoned to defeat his Union counterparts in detail, the aggressive Hindman pushed out his small and under-equipped army in early December. On the 7th, in northwest Arkansas, Hindman waged a hard-fought battle at Prairie Grove. It was a close-run affair, but by dusk the Confederates had clearly gotten the worst of it. Out of reserves, low on ammunition and food, and with his artillery severely battered, Hindman withdrew under cover of darkness, handing the field and the victory to his enemy. Though a tactical draw, Hindman's retreat provided the Union with a solid strategic victory in that part of the state. Southern morale plummeted and the response was predictable: the entire Arkansas political delegation in Richmond paid a visit to President Davis to demand that Hindman be relieved. Faced with political unanimity, Davis agreed.

Hindman hoped for another field command and asked to be sent to Bragg's Army of Tennessee. He was instead assigned to head up a Board of Inquiry investigating Maj. Gen. Mansfield Lovell's conduct in the loss of New Orleans. This duty consumed most of the spring and summer of 1863 before finally clearing Lovell of all charges that July. With the shackles of administrative work loosened, Hindman finally got his desire for a fighting position and was sent to Bragg's army to replace Jones Withers.

In theory, assigning Hill and Hindman to the Army of Tennessee made sense. Both men were experienced combat officers of demonstrated ability, and their assignment pumped new blood into the veins of an army that desperately needed an infusion of fresh, capable officers who might be able to change the toxic high-level relationships within the army's command structure. Reality was an altogether different matter. Neither of these men had been successful team players in previous command positions, which was the reason they were available to join Bragg in the first place. Could they now restrain the more difficult aspects of their personalities and work well with a man whose temperamental quirks were as equally problematic as their own?

There existed within the Confederate western command structure yet another oddity that could only complicate matters. The Department of East Tennessee was officially a separate command reporting to Richmond—or Joe Johnston, once the latter was installed as commander in the Western Theater. In 1862, when Bragg left Mississippi to move into Kentucky, he left the jurisdiction of his own department and entered the command sphere of Maj. Gen. Edmund Kirby Smith, who was then heading up East Tennessee. Although Bragg was Smith's senior it was Smith's department, so they worked out an agreement that Bragg would command their combined force only after the two armies joined together in Kentucky. As might be expected, this divided command structure caused problems in Kentucky, where Bragg and Smith nominally cooperated with one another, but with neither man fully in charge of the Confederate forces.

In fact, East Tennessee had always been in some sort of turmoil. "Between August of 1862 and July of 1863," no less than "nine men commanded the department," noted historian Thomas Connelly. The lines of command remained murky, and the continuous change in commanders confusing. Eventually Smith moved on to the Trans-Mississippi, and Maj. Gen. Simon

Bolivar Buckner was given the job of pulling rein on the difficult region. The terrain and thrust of the Union advances, however, made it inevitable that Bragg's and Buckner's forces would have to work together in any upcoming campaign, and it was apparent to everyone that informal arrangements such as had prevailed in Kentucky would not be sufficient.[30]

President Davis, who had never been satisfied with Joe Johnston's understanding of his role as a theater commander, ended that position when he sent Johnston to Mississippi in May to take charge of affairs there in a last-ditch effort to save Vicksburg. Thereafter, Johnston became commander of the Department of Mississippi and Alabama, and thus no longer Bragg's direct superior. On July 25, Davis made Bragg's command "separate and independent, reporting directly to" the office of the Secretary of War. At the same time, Davis merged the Department of East Tennessee into Bragg's larger Department of Tennessee. This latter decision returned Maj. Gen. Simon Bolivar Buckner to Bragg's sphere of command and re-established a relationship that was anything but a cordial one.[31]

Like most of the generals of his rank, Simon B. Buckner was a West Pointer, having graduated from the academy in 1844. He was also the recipient of a pair of brevets earned during the Mexican War. Tired of army life, Buckner resigned his commission in 1855 to pursue a business career. His journey took him north to Chicago, where his wife had real estate interests, and he remained there for several years. He was successful in business, unlike his friend and former colleague Ulysses S. Grant, to whom he once loaned money.

Buckner was a native Kentuckian from a prominent Bluegrass family. When war broke out in 1861 he was serving as adjutant general of the state militia, charged with the impossible task of keeping Kentucky neutral in the rapidly expanding civil war. Both sides courted his services but his heart was with the South. He turned down a Union commission and accepted a Confederate brigadier generalship in September 1861.

The importance of Kentucky and Buckner's central role as the state's highest military officer, coupled with a solid military reputation earned in Mexico, gave him an early prominence in the Confederate army. His record since between his commission and the summer of 1863, however, was distinctly

---

30 Connelly, *Autumn of Glory*, 107.

31 *OR* 24, pt. 1, 235.

uneven. His first chance to display his abilities in combat came at Fort Donelson in February 1862, where he faced off against his old friend Grant. As ill-luck would have it, a strange series of events conspired to put him in command of the doomed post, which Buckner ultimately surrendered together with nearly 13,000 Confederate troops after more senior officers fled in disgrace.

Since his two senior officers had abandoned Donelson Buckner escaped censure for the disaster, but his performance there left much to be desired. Throughout the siege he was pessimistic to the point of defeatism, and he allowed personal enmity between himself and fellow Confederate Gideon J. Pillow (a rivalry dating from prewar political affairs) to interfere with sound military decisions. The result was a muddled breakout effort that ended in confusion and failure largely because Buckner refused to advance at the agreed-upon time. His capture there meant that Buckner missed an opportunity to demonstrate higher command abilities on the field at Shiloh two months later. He returned to field duty in time for the Kentucky campaign in the fall of 1862.[32]

Kentucky was the first time Buckner experienced campaign service under Braxton Bragg. It was not to his liking. The Kentuckian led a division at Perryville, where both he and his men performed well. Larger questions, however, permanently damaged Buckner's relationship with his commanding officer. Bitterly disillusioned by the disappointing turnout of the citizens of that state, Bragg spoke despairingly about the feckless Bluegrass region and its people; and blamed notable Kentuckians like Buckner and Breckinridge for misleading him about the true sentiments of the native population. Once the failed invasion ended Buckner left the Army of Tennessee for an assignment to improve the defenses of Mobile, Alabama. He was out from under Bragg's command and happy to have escaped. The following May of 1863, however, Richmond transferred Buckner again, to assume command of the Department of East Tennessee. This new post brought him back into direct contact and inevitable conflict with Bragg. In August, after Bragg's retreat from Middle Tennessee following the Tullahoma disaster, Buckner found his independent East Tennessee command virtually subsumed into Bragg's sphere of authority. His complaints to the Confederate War Department fell on deaf ears.

---

32 Kendall D. Gott, *Where The South Lost The War: An Analysis of the Fort Henry-Fort Donelson Campaign, February 1862* (Stackpole Books, 2003), 276.

Richmond settled on a cumbersome arrangement whereby Buckner continued to exercise nominal administrative responsibility over his department, but for all practical purposes it functioned as one of Bragg's infantry corps.[33]

Administrative squabbles notwithstanding, Buckner did an excellent job reorganizing his new command. East Tennessee was always intended to be a source of reinforcements for the Army of Tennessee if Bragg was threatened, but in the past most of the force was parceled out to various garrisons and so not easily or readily available for prompt field duty with the Army of Tennessee. His department numbered about 16,000 men, with nearly half of that in cavalry. The whole force was organized into seven brigades, five of mixed command and two of horse. By August, Buckner had shuffled his various units about to create an effective infantry division of three brigades, and merged his two cavalry brigades into a second division under command of the senior brigadier, John Pegram. If needed, he could take the field with about 11,000 men, leaving the remainder to provide nominal garrisons for strategic points such as the Cumberland Gap. With his recent grant of authority over East Tennessee, Bragg on August 6 re-designated Buckner's command as "Third Corps, Army of Tennessee." Buckner would be needed.[34]

It takes more than a mere shuffling of regiments and commanders, however, to create an effective combat unit. Leadership and morale were important factors in forging motley formations into cohesive units. Despite Buckner's efforts, not all problems could be simply smoothed away. Leadership problems were most apparent in the new cavalry command. It consisted of two brigades, one led by Col. John Scott and the other by Brig. Gen. John Pegram. Unfortunately, relations between Scott and Pegram were not amicable.

Pegram was a native of Virginia. Though he grew up in genteel poverty after his father died unexpectedly, his family was always socially well connected. (His younger brother was William R. "Willie" Pegram, the 'boy artillerist' of Army of Northern Virginia fame.) John won an appointment to West Point, Class of 1854, where he graduated tenth in his class of 46. He served most of his time on the frontier, though an extended leave of absence in 1859 allowed him to take a trip to Europe. He was in New Mexico in 1861 when the war came, and he resigned to offer his services to Virginia. Appointed lieutenant colonel of the

33 William C. Davis, *Breckinridge: Stateman, Soldier, Symbol* (Louisiana State University Press, 1992), 328; Hallock, *Braxton Bragg*, 36-37.

34 *OR* 23, pt. 2, 855, 954.

20th Virginia, he served without distinction in Western Virginia in 1861, and along with his regiment was captured by the Federals at the battle of Rich Mountain. Once exchanged, the regiment was re-organized and the men refused to vote Pegram back into a command position. Among other reasons, "he did not win his command's confidence because of his constant vacillation."[35]

Stripped of command, Pegram sought other duties. When Gen. Pierre G. T. Beauregard applied to Richmond for engineers, no less a figure than Robert E. Lee (who knew Pegram from Lee's time as commandant of West Point) recommended his fellow Virginian for the job. He spent much of 1862 in staff duties for Beauregard, Kirby Smith, and Bragg. Finally, that fall, Bragg selected Pegram for command of a cavalry brigade.

His tenure with Bragg proved less than successful. At Stones River on December 30, 1862, Pegram provided Bragg with intelligence that the Union army was crossing Stones River early that morning. This, in turn, caused Bragg to hold an entire infantry division out of the first day's fight on the 31st. What Pegram failed to report was that the Federals almost immediately turned around and crossed back in response to Bragg's own attack, and so were no longer a threat. The second bit of news was vital because it would have allowed Bragg to use the withheld division to support his main attack on the west bank. The withholding of that division could have turned the battle decisively in Bragg's favor. Both Bragg and divisional commander Breckinridge were critical of Pegram in their reports. When Bragg consolidated his mounted arm by forming Maj. Gen. Joseph Wheeler's cavalry corps in January, Pegram left the Army of Tennessee to command the scattered cavalry forces dotting East Tennessee.[36]

Once in East Tennessee Pegram developed problems with Col. John Scott, a wealthy planter and recruiter of the 1st Louisiana Cavalry from the best of Pelican State society. Arrogant and headstrong, Scott could be a difficult subordinate. He too had performed poorly with the Army of Tennessee, and now found himself serving Pegram as a regimental commander. The two clashed almost immediately.

---

35 Walter S. Griggs, Jr. *General John Pegram, C.S.A.* (H. E. Howard, 1993), 37.

36 Ibid., 61. As earlier noted, Bragg also blamed Breckinridge for failing to report these Union movements. *OR* 20 pt. 2, 503. The exact order transferring Pegram has not been found. However, the January 20, 1863, returns for both the Army of Tennessee and the Department of East Tennessee clearly show that Pegram was now serving in the latter command.

The men quarreled over an improperly delivered order during an action at Somerset, Kentucky, on March 30, and Scott lost his temper. Pegram arrested and court-martialed Scott in April 1863 for insubordination. The court-martial found Scott guilty and referred him to General Buckner for punishment. Much to Pegram's disgust, Buckner issued nothing more than a verbal reprimand and returned Scott to duty. Relations remained distant between Pegram and Scott. Scott proved no more successful when trusted with independent brigade command. In June 1863, Scott led his mounted men on an unsuccessful raid through East Tennessee. The expedition did little harm to the Federals, but cost many Southern casualties (including significant desertions) and led to a drop in morale among Scott's men. "My loss will not, I think, exceed 350 men, very few of whom were killed," Scott admitted in his report. "The straggling of men to their homes is, however, very great, as it was impossible for me to protect the rear and at the same time guard the front, owing to the very small assistance I received from field and company officers of the several commands."[37]

Scott's report touched upon a problem that plagued most of the troops from East Tennessee, whether infantry or cavalry. Many units in Buckner's command were locally recruited mountaineers—East Tennesseans, Kentuckians, North Carolinians, and Georgians who all shared common roots in Appalachia. Slaves were few, Unionist sentiment strong, and many of the men in the ranks were forced into service by the draft or the threat of it. They often served but grudgingly, or with the tacit belief that they would fight to defend their own homes. They were not happy about leaving those homes to go fight elsewhere in a war they regarded as not of their making. Desertion was a plague on Buckner's house and a steady drain on his regiments. He and others knew that problem would spike if and when his command was called to leave East Tennessee.

A lack of discipline was not just confined to a few mountain men. If Bragg possessed any singular advantage over Rosecrans, it was in cavalrymen, a fact Rosecrans repeatedly rammed home to Washington that year. Even without Pegram's 5,000 troopers, on August 20, 1863, the Army of Tennessee boasted 11,018 officers and men present for duty in three cavalry divisions. Joe Wheeler's Cavalry Corps, with two divisions under John Wharton and William T. Martin, numbered 7,142; Nathan Bedford Forrest's separate division

37 Nelson Gremillion, *Company G, 1st Louisiana Cavalry, CSA: A Narrative* (University of Southwestern Louisiana, 1986), 30; OR 23 pt. 2, 842.

contained 3,876 more. The Southern cavalry, however, was no less rent with command difficulties than was Bragg's infantry.[38]

Joe Wheeler was young, just twenty-six years old. He hailed from Georgia, though he spent a considerable amount of time with family in the North. Short, barely five feet tall, and ungainly looking, one member of his escort described him as "a very small man . . . [who] looks just like a monkey or a ape." Though his appearance was unprepossessing, Wheeler was an 1859 graduate of West Point, part of the academy's first expanded five-year curriculum. He had served as both a cavalry instructor and on the frontier, and on paper should have been an ideal candidate for melding Bragg's mounted arm into an effective force.[39]

And perhaps he might have been, except for the fact that Wheeler proved unable to enforce discipline. His command would become notorious for casual looting, for chronic absenteeism, and for a general lack of military skills. In January 1865, after the disastrous campaign across Georgia, a general outcry against Wheeler's corps forced Confederate authorities to thoroughly inspect all aspects of his command, including training, equipment, and discipline. Colonel Alfred Roman's lengthy damning report found his cavalry deficient in virtually every area.[40]

In addition to the lack of discipline in the ranks, Wheeler also had trouble with some of his fellow generals. His senior divisional commander, Brig. Gen. John A. Wharton, did not get on well with the bantam Georgian. Wharton was a wealthy Texan with no previous military experience who nonetheless had risen rapidly by dint of his performance in battle. He fought very well at Perryville and Stones River, where he led an oversized brigade. After that battle Bragg formed the cavalry corps and promoted Wheeler to lead it. Wharton was given a division in the corps, but was not promoted. This state of affairs rankled the Texan, who felt that he deserved to be leading the corps. At the very least, he felt he should be bumped up to major general, the normal rank for an officer in charge of a division.

Wheeler might be excused some of the responsibility for not getting along with fellow general Nathan Bedford Forrest. During the course of the war more

---

38 *OR* 30, pt. 4, 518.

39 Charles F. McKay to "Dear Mother," Atlanta History Center, Atlanta, GA.

40 See David A. Powell, *Failure in the Saddle: Nathan Bedford Forrest, Joseph Wheeler, and the Confederate Cavalry in the Chickamauga Campaign* (Savas Beatie, 2010), 12-16, for a detailed analysis of the problems inherent in this command.

than one Rebel officer found Forrest a difficult subordinate to manage. In the postwar era Forrest would rise to become one of the South's larger-than-life legends. He joined the army as a private and rose to the rank of lieutenant general. A planter, slave-dealer, and self-made businessman, Forrest made his home in the Mississippi Delta Country south of Memphis, where he was active in southwest Tennessee politics. He was also a man accustomed to violence from an early age. In September 1863, however, most of his greatest wartime feats were still ahead of him and he was still feeling his way forward as a cavalry corps commander. As recently as August he was commanding a mere brigade, but abrupt steps up to divisional and, with the merger of Simon B. Buckner's department into Bragg's army, corps responsibility soon followed.

The root of Forrest's animosity towards Wheeler stemmed from a poorly conducted attack in February 1863 when Forrest joined with the Georgian in a winter raid against a Union supply depot at Dover, Tennessee. Forrest's brigade led the assault against the enemy garrison and attacked early and unsuccessfully. The botched action cost Forrest a quarter of his men and he was quick to find fault. His reaction was both fiery and characteristic. In his usual outspoken manner, the Tennessean unequivocally stated that he would never again serve under Wheeler's command.[41]

Bragg's solution was to keep them apart. Forrest was assigned to Earl Van Dorn's Cavalry Corps and stationed on the Army of Tennessee's left flank in Middle Tennessee, while Wheeler's newly organized corps was sent to the army's right. While the army lay quiescent during the spring of 1863, there were always missions for the cavalry. Forrest was detached to chase down Union raiders in Alabama, and numerous small fights and skirmishes in Middle Tennessee marked the months of March, April, and May.[42]

The death of Van Dorn at the hands of a jealous husband that May briefly elevated Forrest to corps command, but just as quickly his corps was dismantled when one of his divisions was sent to Mississippi. Early the next month Forrest was temporarily incapacitated when he was stabbed during a quarrel with a junior officer. Just two weeks later Rosecrans launched his Tullahoma operation. Tullahoma revealed that Forrest, a highly skilled raider

---

41 John W. Morton, *The Artillery of Nathan Bedford Forrest's Cavalry* (R. Bemis Publishing, 1995), 77.

42 Thomas Jordan and J. P. Pryor, *The Campaigns of General Nathan Bedford Forrest and of Forrest's Cavalry* (De Capo Press, 1996), 249.

and determined fighter, did not yet grasp more traditional cavalry operations. The intelligence Forrest relayed to Bragg was incomplete and helped convince the army commander that the Union advance of Forrest's front was the main effort. Even worse, Wheeler failed to detect Rosecrans's real main advance against his own front. As a result, Bragg was badly misinformed and eventually outmaneuvered.[43]

Still, both men retained Bragg's confidence. In August, Forrest applied to leave Tennessee to return to Mississippi, where he thought he could make the lives of the Union occupying troops there miserable through partisan action. Bragg denied the request, noting that Forrest was one of the army's greatest strengths. At the beginning of September Bragg reaffirmed that opinion when he returned Forrest to corps command, assigning him Pegram's newly formed mounted division from East Tennessee.

Bragg trusted Wheeler for reasons more personal than military. Wheeler might have had faults as a disciplinarian and cavalryman, but he was loyal. He remained a pro-Bragg man through all the army's upper-ranks turmoil during the first half of 1863. The payoff was that Bragg retained him in command. Within just a few weeks, Bragg would have cause enough to regret that decision.

Braxton Bragg made a fundamental mistake as he looked over his situational maps and pondered Rosecrans's next move. From his vantage point in Chattanooga, Bragg was experienced enough to have realized that the size of Rosecrans' army dictated only one possible avenue of advance, and that was along the Nashville & Chattanooga Railroad. Union Maj. Gen. Ambrose Burnside's Army of the Ohio, only 30,000 strong, might be able to draw enough supplies over lengthy wagon roads from Kentucky as it plodded toward Knoxville. Rosecrans's Army of the Cumberland, however, was more than twice as strong as Burnside's command and did not have that luxury. This meant that Rosecrans would have virtually no choice but to cross the Tennessee River below Chattanooga, not above it in the direction of Burnside and Knoxville. Perhaps overestimating the Federals' admitted wealth of transportation assets, Bragg anticipated that Rosecrans would try and operate in tandem with Burnside for as long as possible. He was wrong.

---

43 For more on Van Dorn's career and information on his death, see Edwin C. Bearss, "Earl Van Dorn," in William C. Davis, ed., *The Confederate General*, 6 vols. (National Historical Society, 1991), vol. 6, 70-75. The division sent to Mississippi belonged to Brig. Gen. William H. "Red" Jackson, whose departure in early June effectively dismantled Van Dorn's corps.

Still, Bragg was not about to neglect any stretch of the riverbank, upstream or down. Forrest was responsible for screening the crossings on the Tennessee between Kingston and the mouth of the Hiwassee River, 30 miles upstream from Chattanooga. Between the Hiwassee and Bridgeport, Alabama, Bragg relied on his infantry to patrol the south bank of the river. Downstream, Wheeler's cavalry was deployed as far south as Gadsden, Alabama, nearly 80 miles to the southwest. Bragg extended his force along a front stretching more than 150 miles, a decision that reflected his uncertainty about where the Federals would appear. And over most of that vast stretch of riverbank he would be wholly dependent upon his cavalry to provide early warning of any attempted crossing.

After the retreat from Tullahoma, Wheeler established his headquarters at Gadsden. Once there, he concentrated more on refitting his cavalry than on patrolling the Tennessee. Only two regiments were detailed to watch the extended river line. The 3rd Confederate Cavalry was assigned the vital 50-mile stretch between Bridgeport and Guntersville. The 8th Confederate Cavalry patrolled the next 40 miles of riverbank from Guntersville to Decatur, Alabama. All told, Wheeler dispatched barely 500 troopers to watch 90 miles of riverbank.[44]

The rest of Wheeler's command was sent to the rear. John Wharton's cavalry division was ordered to Rome, Georgia, where it spent the month of August in comparative comfort, holding barbeques and "living high on Peach Pie." The end of August found Wharton's horsemen still there, some 50 miles due south of Chattanooga and at least that far from the river Bragg believed they were patrolling. They were in no position to watch for or contest a Union crossing. William T. Martin's division was even more out of position. Martin's camps were located near Alexandria, in Calhoun County, Alabama. Alexandria was almost 100 miles southwest of Chattanooga, 45 miles southeast of the nearest point on the Tennessee at Guntersville, and approximately 60 miles from Stevenson. These deployments would have fatal consequences for Bragg's plans.[45]

44 OR 23, pt. 2, 912, 930; Ibid., 923; George Knox Miller letter, September 15, 1863, UNC.

45 John McGrath Papers, Louisiana State University, Baton Rouge. See also J. K. P Blackburn, L. B. Giles, and E. S. Dowd, *Terry Texas Ranger Trilogy* (State House Press, 1996), 208; I. B. Ulmer Reminiscences, 3rd Alabama Cavalry file, Alabama Department of Archives and History. Montgomery, Alabama. Hereafter ADAH.

Chapter Three

A River to Cross:
August 16 to September 8, 1863

"Having put the railroad in condition to forward supplies, Rosecrans, on the 16th of August, commenced his advance across the Cumberland Mountains, Chattanooga, and its covering ridges on the southeast being his objective point. . . . [T]he front of his movement extended from the head of Sequatchie Valley in East Tennessee, to Athens, Ala., thus threatening the line of the Tennessee River from Whitesburg to Blythe's Ferry, a distance of over 150 miles." Thus summarized Maj. Gen. Henry W. Halleck in describing the scope of Rosecrans's complex operation. It was the Army of the Cumberland's most ambitious effort to date, and into the most forbidding terrain yet faced.[1]

In the last two weeks of August, however, these initial moves were designed to close the Federal army up to the banks of the Tennessee River in preparation to crossing in strength, while still deceiving Bragg as to when and where those crossings would come. One of the leading elements of this movement was Col. John Wilder's Lightning Brigade. On the 16th, Wilder was called to army headquarters at Dechard to meet with Generals Rosecrans, Thomas, his own divisional commander, Joseph J. Reynolds, and chief of staff James Garfield. There, recalled Wilder, "I was informed that the Army of the

---

1 OR 30, pt. 1, 33.

Cumberland was to move on Chattanooga. . . . [My] role was an independent one, leading the advance across Walden's Ridge, and then, from the north bank of the Tennessee opposite Chattanooga, to make an active demonstration on that place."[2]

Though he would be detached from the army to act independently, Wilder was not going it alone. Brig. Gen. George D. Wagner's brigade (First Division, XXI Corps) was tasked to provide support. A movement by Col. Robert H. G. Minty's cavalry brigade—similarly supported by Brig. Gen. William B. Hazen's brigade (Second Division, XXI Corps)— was tasked with the same mission as Wagner and Wilder, even farther north, coming down the Sequatchie Valley from Sparta, Tennessee. Collectively these 7,500 troops were to convince Bragg the entire Union army was about to cross at or above Chattanooga.

Wilder was still preparing when Minty set out on August 15, opening the campaign by attacking Confederate cavalry under Col. George Dibrell near Sparta, the latest in a series of ongoing skirmishes with those Rebels. Minty's thrust cleared Dibrell's troopers out of Sparta and the rest of White County, then continued riding on to Pikeville, Tennessee. That skirmishing with Dibrell would be the only significant action prior to reaching Chattanooga. Neither of Bragg's cavalry commanders (Forrest or Wheeler) made any real effort to control or even contest the terrain beyond the Tennessee River.[3]

Wilder spurred his men out of camp on August 18. Aside from rounding up a handful of inattentive Confederate guerrillas more focused on hanging Unionist civilians than in watching for the Federal army, Wilder reached Poe's Tavern without incident. There, he efficiently snapped up a Confederate picket post, which in turn prevented Bragg from learning of his presence. At nine in the morning on Sunday, August 21, Wilder's men appeared on Stringer's Ridge opposite the city's riverfront prepared to deliver a nasty surprise.[4]

That Sunday had been set aside as a day of fasting and prayer by the Confederate government, but Chattanooga still bustled with activity. While the Southerners prayed, fasted, and worked, Capt. Eli Lilly unlimbered his four 3-inch ordnance rifles from the 18th Indiana Battery opposite the town and

---

2 John T. Wilder, "Preliminary Movements of the Army of the Cumberland Before the Battle of Chickamauga," in *MOLLUS*, vol. 7, 263.

3 Powell, *Failure in the Saddle*, 36-38.

4 Wilder, "Preliminary Movements of the Army of the Cumberland Before the Battle of Chickamauga," 264.

opened fire. His gunners worked over the waterfront and arced their shells into the town itself. Among other damage, Lilly reported that he sank one steamboat and "wrecked" another, both tied up at the city docks. As might be expected, the sudden shelling threw the townspeople into a panic. "The streets are always crowded," observed Col. Newton Davis of the 24th Alabama, and when the shells fell "you never saw such skidadling in all your life. Shop keepers, peach & apple vendors, and speculators of all descriptions . . . commenced running in every direction."[5]

The deception operation was off to a splendid start. Hazen and Wagner quickly moved their infantry up to support the mounted forces and battery, staging an elaborate show in the effort. "Our purpose was to watch the crossings . . . and to make the enemy believe that the entire army was going to cross there," explained Hazen, who employed "a series of show-marches, camps with fires, and martial music of fifteen regiments, so disposed as to completely deceive our friends on the opposite side."[6]

This ongoing bit of trickery included almost daily bombardments by Lilly's guns, often to the great amusement of the Union troops. "The other day," wrote one Indiana Yankee, "a deserter pointed out . . . the headquarters of Gen. Bishop Polk . . . and the Captain was not long in sending two or three shells through the building. The old sacrilegious reprobate vamoosed the ranch on double quick."[7]

Braxton Bragg reached Chattanooga on August 22 to take stock of the unfolding situation after convalescing with his wife in Cherokee Springs (near Ringgold). Bragg understood that he was being played, but on some level the deception still worked because it catered to his underlying assumptions. At the same time reports began to flow in from Simon B. Buckner in Knoxville. General Burnside's advance into East Tennessee had begun, threatening the small garrison at Cumberland Gap and other points. As far as Bragg was concerned, Rosecrans would "sever himself from Burnside," so the Federal activity opposite Chattanooga could only be tactical in nature. In response and

---

5 Baumgartner, *Blue Lightning*, 129; Davis to Wife, August 22, 1863, Newton H. Davis Letters, ADAH.

6 Hazen to Mr. Benson H. Lossing, August 23, 1866, William P. Palmer Collection, Western Reserve Historical Society, Cleveland OH.

7 "From Chattanooga," *La Fayette Daily Courier*, September 14, 1863.

as previously agreed, Buckner began shifting his main forces toward Kingston and points south in preparation to join with Bragg at Chattanooga.[8]

Although he was secure in his knowledge that the shelling and martial pomp was a tactical distraction, Bragg also believed he would have to give up Chattanooga at some point lest it become a trap. This understanding ran counter to President Davis's expectations, but as early as August 23 Bragg began preparing Richmond for the worst. "We have our batteries in all suitable positions," he wired Davis, "but cannot save this town." The news alarmed Davis, who the next day ordered his personal aide, Col. James Chesnut, to leave Camden, South Carolina, and "go to Chattanooga and report by letter."[9]

Downstream from Chattanooga, meanwhile, quiet reigned. Small parties of Federals appeared on the riverbanks as far south as Caperton's Ferry (near Stevenson), but activity was minimal. The dearth of Rebel cavalry here was sorely felt. With only two regiments to cover 90 miles of riverbank, Bragg remained woefully blind in exactly the spot Rosecrans needed him to be sightless. Infantry from Polk's Corps guarded some of the closer ferries and likely bridge sites, but they reported only negligible Yankee activity. Confederate intelligence identified some larger bodies of Federal troops around Jasper, at the mouth of the Sequatchie Valley, but their presence wasn't regarded as significant.

Bragg's most pressing concern was for more men. On August 20, the Army of Tennessee mustered but 44,000 troops, 10,000 of them cavalry. Buckner might add another 10,000, half of which were more cavalry and many of them suspect. If he was going to face Rosecrans in a stand-up battle, Bragg needed good infantry and a lot of it. At Tullahoma, his depleted army had no choice but to retreat or risk battle on the enemy's terms. The troops dispatched by Richmond to Mississippi—some 19,000 foot and 3,000 horsemen during the last 10 months—neither saved Fortress Vicksburg nor returned to Tennessee. The lengthening odds only made holding the important city of Chattanooga that much more difficult.[10]

---

8   OR 30, pt. 4, 526; William Brent Journal, Bragg Papers, WRHS.

9   OR 52, pt. 2, 517.

10   OR 30, pt. 4, 518-519. These troops included Maj. Gen. Carter L. Stevenson's large division of four brigades, 10,000 strong, transferred in December 1862 and now part of the captured Vicksburg garrison; the 5,000 men of Maj. Gen. John C. Breckinridge's three brigades, and roughly 3,500 men in two brigades of what was once Maj. Gen. John P. McCown's division,

Bragg appealed for reinforcements during the waning days of August. Joe Johnston wired back on the 24th, though his offer of help came with conditions. "[I am sending] 9,000 infantry and artillery. This road works so wretchedly," he cautioned, "that it will take five days, including yesterday, to get them off. This is a loan, to be promptly returned." Johnston did not want these troops to move any farther than Atlanta, where they could replace Brig. Gen. Edward C. Walthall's brigade of Mississippians who Bragg had also recalled to the front. Johnston was well aware that any troops that moved north of Atlanta would likely be absorbed into Bragg's army, with a very diminished chance of ever returning to Mississippi. Bragg, however, needed combat power and not garrison troops. No one would be stopping in Atlanta except to change trains.[11]

One other potential source of additional manpower lay in the paroled prisoners from Vicksburg. Most of the troops from that lost city were assembling at camps in Mississippi, but the paroled Tennesseans were ordered to report to Chattanooga, or, in the case of one brigade, to East Tennessee. By the end of the month they were reporting in, but they needed arms and re-organization. Bragg estimated they would require 10,000 weapons to be rendered combat effective. There was also the matter of proper exchange. Returning these troops to duty without being duly exchanged for similarly captured and paroled Federals would violate the terms of the prisoner of war cartel. Despite Bragg's urgent need, for the moment these troops would not take the field lest the Federals retaliate in kind. Other sources of manpower would have to be found. President Davis turned to the governors of Georgia and Alabama for state militia and local defense forces to help Bragg. He diverted Chesnut to this task, and even asked for help from Confederate Vice President Alexander Stephens of Georgia, who was in the state recuperating from an illness.[12]

Back in Richmond, meanwhile, an old idea was being dusted off and discussed anew. A few months earlier in May, before the fall of Vicksburg,

---

now all serving with Johnston's "Army of Relief." Brigadier General William H. Jackson's cavalry division was also part of the transfer.

11 OR 30, pt. 4, 541.

12 For years, some Federals believed Bragg's army included illegally rearmed parolees. Writing in 1882, Henry M. Cist, a former staff officer under Rosecrans, would state as much in his history of Rosecrans's Army of the Cumberland. Henry M. Cist, *The Army of the Cumberland* (Charles Scribner's Sons, 1882), 228; OR 52, pt.2, 520.

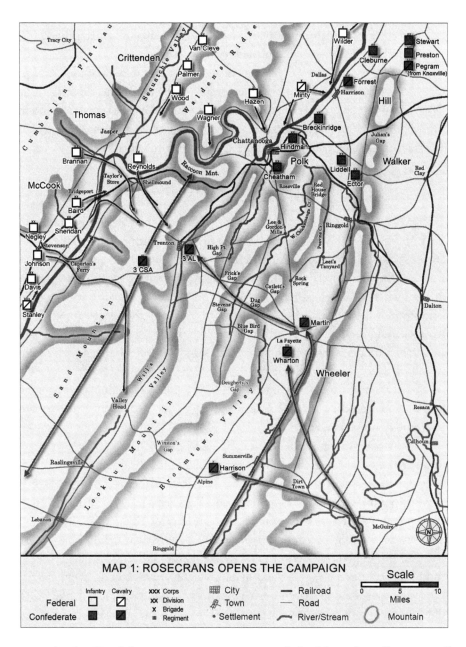

MAP 1: ROSECRANS OPENS THE CAMPAIGN

some in the Confederate government proposed the idea of sending part of Lee's Army of Northern Virginia—or perhaps even Lee himself—west to the Army of Tennessee. The idea died on the altar of Pennsylvania and Lee instead invaded the North a second time. Now, with affairs in Virginia locked in a tight stalemate, the idea found new life. Two crack divisions of Lt. Gen. James

Longstreet's First Corps might be spared. If so, they would add another 9,000 veteran infantry to Bragg's diminished rolls.

Even if Bragg received everything promised or possible, all of these troops would take time to arrive wherever their origin. In the meantime, there was little he could do but determine what Rosecrans intended. Bragg's own strategy was simple: "to await developments of the enemy and when his point of attack is ascertained, to neglect all smaller affairs and fall on him with our whole force."[13]

*   *   *

By August 28, Rosecrans had successfully closed the bulk of his infantry to the north bank of the Tennessee. Union army headquarters was established at Stevenson five days earlier on the afternoon of the 23rd. Over the next few days Rosecrans personally reconnoitered the various crossing sites, alarming junior officers when he did so. Brig. Gen. William H. Lytle's brigade had charge of Bridgeport, where the railroad bridge crossed the Tennessee until burned by the Rebels during their retreat in July. On the 25th, Lytle led Rosecrans, McCook, and Stanley on one such reconnoitering mission. "I never felt half as nervous in a battle as I did that day," Lytle confessed. If the Confederates had somehow slipped a cavalry patrol across the river, "Rosey & McCook & Stanley [might] be *bagged*. . . . I would be censured for not bringing along a stronger escort and catch the d—l generally!"[14]

Lytle's fears proved groundless. The vast bulk of Joe Wheeler's troopers were far away, and Rosecrans laid his plans unhindered. Beginning the next day, he intended to rapidly throw most of his army across the river at a number of crossing points. Two divisions of McCook's XX Corps received orders to cross at Caperton's Ferry, near Stevenson, and another at Bridgeport. Two more divisions under Brig. Gens. Jefferson C. Davis and Richard W. Johnson were assigned the Caperton's Ferry site. Davis's mission was to immediately climb Sand Mountain and clear that dominating height of any lurking enemy, while Johnson's men were to march north along the river and establish contact with Phil Sheridan's division, which was spearheading the Bridgeport crossing.

13 OR 30, pt. 4, 531.

14 Connie Schein, *Diary of Nicholas Hiegel 1857-1863* (n.p. 2001), 24; Ruth C. Carter, ed., *For Honor Glory & Union: The Mexican & Civil War Letters of Brig. Gen. William Haines Lytle* (University Press of Kentucky, 1999), 199.

Sheridan's instructions were to secure the town of Trenton, in Wills Valley, on the far side of Sand Mountain.[15]

George Thomas's XIV Corps was slated to make simultaneous crossings in three places. Brig. Gen. Absalom Baird's division was to support Sheridan at Bridgeport while Brig. Gen. John M. Brannan's division crossed at the mouth of Battle Creek and moved up through Taylor's Store. Maj. Gen. Joseph J. Reynolds's division was assigned a crossing at Shellmound. Both Brannan's and Reynolds's men were to then join the general move eastward into Trenton. Maj. Gen. James S. Negley's division was tasked with bringing up the corps' supply trains. Negley would wait in his camp near Stevenson for the other Union columns to clear the bridges before crossing.[16]

Leaving the deception force under Wilder and others in place opposite Chattanooga, the rest of Maj. Gen. Thomas L. Crittenden's three divisions had already marched south through the Sequatchie Valley to Jasper, Tennessee. This column was meant to be discovered by Bragg's scouts, at least as far as Jasper, but then instead of doing as Bragg expected and crossing Walden's Ridge at its southern end to join the force in front of Chattanooga, Crittenden's men had orders to follow Thomas's XIV Corps across the Tennessee River.[17]

In a move rather unusual for Civil War armies, Rosecrans decided not to jab with his Union Cavalry Corps. Instead, he elected to cross the wide Tennessee with his foot soldiers in an effort to get as much of his most powerful arm across as possible during those critical first few days before Bragg could react. The mounted arm would follow the XX Corps when traffic allowed. The corps trains, in turn, would follow their respective commands with the cavalry protecting them and the army trains during this initial phase of operations. The cavalry would also be expected to escort supply wagons to and from the primary depots as the army moved deeper into Georgia, securing them from guerrillas or raiding Rebel cavalry. Once past Sand Mountain, however, Rosecrans intended to throw the bulk of Stanley's cavalry corps forward on a raid of its own.

---

15 *OR* 30, pt. 1, 485.

16 Ibid., 245-246.

17 Ibid., 52.

Alexander McDowell McCook and his XX Corps, along with the Union cavalry, would lead Rosecrans's far-flung right wing. *William Sumner Dodge*

To secure the critical depots at Bridgeport and Stevenson once the first line infantry and cavalry were across the river, Rosecrans intended to bring up elements of Maj. Gen. Gordon W. Granger's Reserve Corps. Granger's men could be brought forward as needed as the Federals advanced, precluding the need to keep detaching elements of the main body to guard rear areas.[18]

Two targets in particular, Dalton and/or Rome, Georgia, offered worthwhile objectives for the Union mounted arm. The former was a depot

18 William S. Rosecrans, "The Chattanooga Campaign," *National Tribune*, March 25, 1882.

town 30 miles southeast of Chattanooga on the Western & Atlantic line. The railroad branched there, the west fork running to Chattanooga while the east fork carried traffic up into East Tennessee and, via Cleveland, on to Knoxville. Destruction of the railroad at or south of Dalton would sever Bragg's only supply line, making a retreat only a matter of time. While less critical, Rome was also an inviting objective. The city of workshops, foundries, and supply warehouses sat 70 miles due south of Chattanooga. Connected by a spur line to the main railroad via Kingston, Rome played an important part of Braxton Bragg's overall supply chain. While its loss would not immediately damage the Army of Tennessee, a threat to it could not be ignored. The loss of either place would greatly harm Bragg's ability to wage combat in North Georgia.

Getting into position to threaten or take both places was the key. Once the army was safely across the Tennessee, Rosecrans intended to send McCook's Corps and Stanley's cavalry toward Valley Head, Alabama, approximately 25 miles south of Trenton. From there they would turn east, crossing Lookout Mountain to move into Broomtown Valley. Once ensconced in the valley, both Rome and Dalton were accessible. If Bragg were already moving by this time, McCook could turn north toward La Fayette and join Rosecrans's main body as it intercepted the Confederates.

The crossing operations went surprisingly smoothly, virtually unhindered by enemy opposition. The first were made by boat and the rare ford. Once the south bank at each site was fully secured, pontoon bridges were quickly thrown down. Given the number of different sites Rosecrans intended to use simultaneously pontoons were in short supply, so the 1,200 foot bridge span needed at Bridgeport had to be partly improvised from local timber, including flooring stripped from local barns and houses.[19]

Despite the labor involved, not to mention the hazards of a river crossing if the enemy contested it, Union morale soared. "The rebels are decerting by whole regiments and by whole companies," marveled Pvt. Isaac Raub, a member of the Pioneer Brigade at Stevenson. "The rebs say as soon as our troops getts across the Tennessee River that there will be thousands of there men that decert and come to our side." Pvt. Helim Dunn of Company D, 74th Indiana observed the same phenomenon. "More than 1000 have come in," he informed his father on August 30. Dunn, a member of John Brannan's division

19 Mark Hoffman, *My Brave Mechanics: The First Michigan Engineers and Their Civil War* (Wayne State University Press, 2007), 162.

(XIV Corps), was to be one of the first troops across the river, and so had good reason to be on the lookout for positive signs.[20]

The next day, Dunn and his comrades began crossing the Tennessee at Battle Creek. The sparse Rebel pickets who until then had been watching the south bank, and who conversed often with the Yankees opposite, vanished. The Union troops crossed on rafts or swam and landed without opposition. A few miles upstream at Shellmound, Joseph Reynolds's division also made an easy passage. By mid-morning, Reynolds estimated that he could "cross 400 men per hour." To the surprise of many, the river itself posed the most danger. The 10th Kentucky recorded their only loss at Battle Creek as one man drowned. Sergeant Alanson Ryman of the 68th Indiana, Reynolds's division, recalled the crossing as a festive day's work: "The river is broad and still . . . [here] and the boats flying back and forth filled with men, horses, cannon, &c, made quite a lively scene, and to add to its charms we had good music from Turchin's Brigade band."[21]

Over the next several days, the Union army swarmed across the river almost without incident. Rosecrans must have been delighted; the potential hazardous crossings could not have gone better. The whole affair might have been a training exercise for the amount of enemy interference encountered. The biggest mishap occurred at Bridgeport, where on the afternoon of September 2 the pontoon bridge collapsed, sending several supply wagons tumbling into the river. The men of the 1st Michigan Engineers restored the span by the next day. A second washout was restored even more quickly. With something like half the army's trains slated to use the Bridgeport crossing, the time lost due to these washouts was potentially serious. The continued lack of Confederate resistance, however, rendered the setback moot. The eventual delay added up to little more than an extra 48 hours before the Army of the Cumberland was across and ready to move forward.[22]

More daunting than the river were the mountains. Two massive ridges now lay astride the Federal route: Sand and Lookout mountains. Each was a long,

---

20 "Mary Jane," August 21, 1863, Nesbitt/Raub Family Papers, WRHS; H. H. Dunn to father, August 30, 1863, Dunn Letters, IHS.

21 Near modern-day South Pittsburg, TN. Jack K. Overmeyer, *A Stupendous Effort: The 87th Indiana in the War of the Rebellion* (Indiana University Press, 1997), 70; OR 30, pt. 3, 233; "Dear Jane," Camp near Trenton, Geo. Sept 9th, 1863, Alanson R. Ryman Letters, IHS.

22 Hoffman, *My Brave Mechanics*, 163-164.

flat-topped ridge running dozens of—and in the case of Lookout Mountain, almost 100—miles along a northeast-southwest axis. The sides were steep, often sheer palisades hundreds of feet high. Only a few gaps in the palisade permitted passage, and negotiating them was both dangerous and time-consuming. Typically, each command required a full day to climb the mountain, another day to move the four or five miles across the top, and a third to conduct the equally difficult down-slope movement. Ascending or descending was very hazardous, and not to be attempted without full daylight. What would be a single day's march of 10 or so miles in less rugged country could easily consume half a week in northern Georgia, and forces that might appear to be within easy supporting distance on a map might in reality be several days apart.

Sand Mountain was the easier of the two heights to traverse. At its northern end, Running Water Canyon cut a water-level passage between Sand and Raccoon mountains, which extended to the south bank of the Tennessee. Union troops at Battle Creek or Shellmound could move via this passage into Wills Valley toward Chattanooga. While this route was easier for transportation reasons, the very narrowness of the gorge meant it could also be a perfect place for an ambush or a determined defense. It could not be Rosecrans's only approach. Other troops climbed directly over Sand Mountain to seize Trenton, and by doing so outflanked any potential defenders of the gorge.

Once in Wills Valley the Federals confronted looming Lookout Mountain. The valley (also called Lookout Valley at its northern end, as one approached Chattanooga) was also fairly narrow, only four to five miles in width in most places, with Lookout's forbidding ramparts looming as its eastern wall. Lookout was massive and unavoidable, running from the banks of the Tennessee River deep into northern Alabama. The only direct route into the city ran around the northern shoulder of Lookout on a narrow shelf squeezed in between the river and the crest, which carried both the railroad and a wagon route. "Overlooked by cliffs a thousand feet high," Rosecrans mused, "to have forced a passage at this point would have been obviously impossible."[23]

Rosecrans's solution to this dilemma was maneuver. His army would cross Lookout Mountain at points well south of the city and strike for Bragg's rear, its aim the severing of the Western & Atlantic Railroad. With Burnside's men

---

23 Rosecrans, "Chattanooga Campaign," *National Tribune*, March 18, 1882.

controlling East Tennessee and the Army of the Cumberland astride the Rebel supply line south of the city, the very terrain that made Chattanooga a natural fortress turned it into a trap. If Rosecrans managed his maneuver effectively, Bragg would have to retreat, starve, or surrender. And if the Federal army moved quickly enough, retreat might not be a viable option.

Sand Mountain had to be seized immediately, for from its heights Confederate observers could see every move the Yankees made. Fortunately for Union plans, only Col. William Estes's 3rd Confederate Cavalry, 550 men strong, guarded the area. Responsible for watching 50 miles of river bank, Estes was forced to disperse his command into small detachments, each much too weak to contest the vast enemy army now moving upon them. These men were all either captured or fled as the Federals swarmed across the river. Sand Mountain and Trenton were both soon in Union hands.

Anticipating the next stage of the advance, Maj. Gen. David S. Stanley pushed his Federal cavalry ahead through Wills Valley to the foot of Lookout Mountain. By the evening of September 3, Stanley established his headquarters five miles from Valley Head. From there he sent scouts over the mountain in the direction of Alpine and south towards Rawlinsville looking for the best route to Rome.[24]

While the infantry crossed quickly and the cavalry could now range ahead, the various trains and artillery took more time. The army's forward motion halted for a time, held up as the rest of the logistical tail snaked its way across the several bridges and strained to cross Sand Mountain. The process was indeed laborious. In Negley's division, the infantry lined the road from the bottom all the way to the top. "They stacked their arms and piled their equipment well off the road. Then the artillery and train began the ascent with doubled teams, while the foot soldiers . . . acted as a human conveyor, walking the spokes of each wheel and pushing on each vehicle as it came opposite their station." There were losses, with animals dropping dead from overstrain and the occasional wagon slipping over the edge to smash on the hillside below, but on the whole the army made it over safely, if slowly. Not until September 4 did Rosecrans feel ready for the next stage: crossing Lookout Mountain.[25]

24 *OR* 30, pt. 3, 331.

25 McKinney, *Education in Violence*, 223; *OR* 30, pt. 1, 52.

Shockingly, during this first critical week Bragg received only limited knowledge of all this activity. Staff officer Colonel Brent noted that word of the crossings at Shellmound and Bridgeport arrived at headquarters on August 29, but they were dismissed as "a feint." At 1:00 p.m. on the 29th, the 3rd Confederate Cavalry's Colonel Estes hastily dispatched a report of the crossing at Caperton's Ferry. His command, he added, was "gradually falling back on Trenton." However, since the message was routed first to Joe Wheeler all the way down at Rome, Estes's message probably did not reach Bragg's headquarters until the next day, August 30.[26]

Even if he had gleaned more details of the crossings, however, Bragg likely would not have reacted to them decisively. Small parties of Federals had been slipping across the Tennessee between Shellmound and Stevenson since the 22nd, sparring with Rebel outposts and rounding up partisans. Each incident had so far been dismissed as deception; these fresher reports were viewed as simply more of the same. Bragg's attention remained fixed on his right flank toward Knoxville. He was completely deceived by Rosecrans's diversions, as evidenced by Brent's casual dismissal of the Bridgeport crossing. D. H. Hill, whose corps defended the upstream portion of the river, was also fooled. Hill adamantly insisted that the main crossings would come on his front, between the mouth of Chickamauga Creek and Harrison, Tennessee.

It was not until August 29 that Bragg at least awoke to the fact of Wheeler's neglect. Once he realized that the existing Rebel screen was wholly inadequate, he ordered Wheeler to bring his entire cavalry corps forward. Still, even this order reflected Bragg's fixation with Hill's front. The Confederate commander was so convinced that the real threat loomed to the northeast that he ordered Wheeler to split his corps and send Wharton's division to help screen Hill's position instead of reinforcing the pathetically slim downstream force. Nathan Bedford Forrest's cavalry was already present with Hill. By moving Wharton to join Hill, Bragg was concentrating three of his four available mounted divisions on the Confederate right flank. This left only Brig. Gen. William T. Martin's small division of six regiments (some 2,500 troopers) to face nearly the entire Union army.[27]

---

26 Entry for August 29, 1863, Brent Journal. These reports came from Captain P. H. Rice, Confederate Signal Corps, commanding a detachment atop Lookout Mountain. OR 30, pt. 4, 564.

27 Entry for August 29, 1863, Brent Journal; OR 30, pt. 4, 563-564.

Another warning reached Confederate headquarters on the morning of the 30th. The 19th Tennessee, which included two companies raised locally, was picketing the road north of Trenton west of Lookout Mountain. Early that morning, the 19th Tennessee's pickets were assailed by 375 men from Col. Daniel M. Ray's 2nd Tennessee Cavalry (US), supported by Col. Edward King's brigade of Reynolds's division (IV Corps). Ray's men, King reported, drove the Rebels "handsomely." Once again Brent's journal speculated that the Federal force responsible for this dust-up was "probably not large," but Bragg could not afford to ignore this threat any longer. On August 30, Bragg diverted Wharton's cavalry, then en route to join Hill, to La Fayette, Georgia. He also ordered General Polk to send a full infantry brigade to reinforce the 19th Tennessee.[28]

Belatedly realizing that the beleaguered 3rd Confederate needed help and quickly, Wheeler made a stopgap effort to aid Estes by ordering Lt. Col. T. H. Mauldin's 300 men of the 3rd Alabama Cavalry to make a forced march northward. However, the 3rd was still 45 miles away, and it was August 31 before Mauldin reached Trenton. He stayed only long enough to fire off two dispatches that revealed the desperate nature of this state of affairs. In his first message, Maudlin reported that he could find no regiment to reinforce. The 3rd Confederate, he wrote, "have been scattered and the whole line is open." In his second missive, Mauldin reported his position as "picketing on the [east] side of Sand Mountain, endeavoring to protect my command." Worse yet, Union cavalry were in the valley around Trenton, some ranging as far as Lookout Mountain, giving Mauldin reason to worry about his line of retreat. The next day Mauldin abandoned Wills Valley altogether, falling back to establish a new picket line atop Lookout Mountain stretching from Chattanooga to Trenton. Some independent scouts and scattered local home guards remained behind Union lines, but they were unable to make regular contact with Bragg's headquarters. At best, their information was days late, and at worst, wildly inaccurate.[29]

28 S. J. A. Frazier, "Reminiscences of Chickamauga," Clipping from *The Lookout*, May 20, 1909, Hamilton County Library, Chattanooga, Tennessee. See also, *OR* 30, pt. 1, 469, 911; Entry for August 30, 1863, Brent Journal; Entry for August 30, 1863, Alfred T. Fielder Diary, 12th Tennessee Infantry, Tennessee State Library and Archives, Nashville Tennessee. Hereafter TSLA.

29 *OR* 30, pt. 4, 574; Holt, W. T. Army of Tennessee Scout Book, Museum of the Confederacy, Richmond, Virginia, entry for September 4, 1863, shows the report of one such scout named S. G. Ballard.

About 5:00 p.m. on September 1, Wheeler, with Wharton's troopers, arrived at La Fayette.[30] This town of several hundred residents, destined to become the focal point of Union and Confederate movements for the next two weeks, was 21 miles due south of Chattanooga and about 18 miles southeast of Trenton on the east side of Lookout Mountain. From La Fayette, Wharton could send troops west through the narrow valley of McLemore's Cove to reinforce Mauldin's thin line atop Lookout. The rest of Martin's division, however, would not arrive for several more days.

By September 2, Bragg finally grasped that Rosecrans's main force had crossed between Bridgeport and Stevenson, a crucial development he passed along to Richmond. The Rebel commander was still groping about largely in the dark, however. A tersely worded message to Wheeler, also sent on the 2nd, demonstrated how little information Bragg had at hand. That day, army chief of staff General Mackall wrote to Wheeler: "Dear General: I am uneasy about the state of affairs. It is so vitally important that the General [Bragg] should have full and correct information. One misstep in the movement of this army would possibly be fatal. Your line of pickets now occupy on Lookout Mountain about the same advantages they possessed on the river or Sand Mountain. The passage at Caperton's Ferry broke the line and a week has passed and we don't know whether or not an army has passed." It was a stunning, if artfully worded, rebuke.[31]

Martin's cavalry division had only reached Summerville, Georgia, a small hamlet 20 miles south of La Fayette by the 2nd. While there, Martin got wind of rumors placing Union troops within four miles of the village, and passed this word up the chain of command to Chattanooga. While no larger bodies of Yankees had yet crossed Lookout Mountain, these reports must have identified bodies of Union scouts, who in turn passed on accurate, detailed information about Martin's own column. Their commander, Brig. Gen. Robert B. Mitchell, identified five of Martin's six Confederate regiments by name, numbering "about 2,000 men, imperfectly armed, but well mounted."[32]

---

30 Entry for September 1, 1863, William B. Corbitt Diary, Emory University, Atlanta, Georgia.

31 *OR* 30, pt. 4, 583-584

32 William Robert Stevenson, "Robert Alexander Smith: A Southern Son," *Alabama Historical Quarterly*, Volume XX (1958), 43; *OR* 30, pt. 3, 332.

While all this was occurring, Bragg was also trying to reorganize his army so as to incorporate his arriving reinforcements. On August 2, the leading elements of Maj. Gens. John Breckinridge's and William H. T. Walker's divisions began arriving from Atlanta. Both divisions were attached to D. H. Hill. This was a natural fit for Breckinridge's men, since they had originally served in that corps (once William Hardee's, now Hill's) before being sent to Mississippi back in June. This assignment, however, threw the command structure out of balance. Hill now had four divisions (Patrick Cleburne, Alexander Stewart, John Breckinridge, and W. H. T. Walker) while Polk's Corps had but two (Ben Cheatham and Thomas Hindman). Simon Buckner's command from East Tennessee contained only William Preston's infantry division and about 5,000 cavalry in Pegram's and Scott's brigades. Accordingly, Bragg transferred Stewart's 5,000 men away from Hill and assigned them to Buckner. Since Stewart was Hill's northernmost division, the closest to Buckner's arriving command, this decision was based more on the convenience of geography than any other consideration.[33]

Nathan Bedford Forrest also returned to corps command at this time, with the accession of the new East Tennessee Cavalry division forged out of Buckner's department, now commanded by Gen. John Pegram. Pegram had been ordered to join Forrest at the end of August, though the formal order creating the corps would not be issued until September 3. As noted earlier, however, Pegram's command, while numerically the strongest of all four of Bragg's cavalry divisions, had significant problems. Not only did Pegram and Scott hate each other, but morale among the rank and file was at best an open question. Desertions spiked among Pegram's regiments when they were ordered to leave East Tennessee. Many of these men were reluctant Confederates, drafted or having enlisted to avoid that draft. Many viewed themselves as home guards with no interest in leaving to fight elsewhere.[34]

Captain Julius Gash commanded Company D of the 6th North Carolina Cavalry, one of the units most disaffected:

My company papers, receipts, muster rolls, and all gave up. I don't care a D—n. My company has about gone up too. All deserted or at home without leave. Twenty-five of

---

33 *OR* 30, pt. 4, 561; Hill, "Chickamauga," 641.

34 *OR* 30 pt. 4, 591; See Powell, *Failure in the Saddle*, 22-25, for discussion of the problems in Pegram's command.

our regiment started home about a week ago, but were nearly all apprehended! . . . General Buckner says he intends shooting every man of them, and I hope to God he will. . . . I have learned during this war that there is no confidence to be placed in white men. I'll swear men have deserted my company who I had the most implicit confidence in and men too who have been for near twelve months good soldiers as was in the Confederate army.[35]

The troop transfers from Mississippi were arduous affairs. Without a direct rail connection across central Alabama, most of Breckinridge's and Walker's men were routed south to Mobile first, then back north to Atlanta, and finally to Chattanooga. For all but the first arrivals, the journey took longer than the five days anticipated by Joe Johnston. Quartermaster Sergeant Washington Ives of the 4th Florida, one of Breckinridge's men, noted that his command left Morton, Mississippi, at 11:00 a.m. on August 26, arrived in Mobile on the 28th, and didn't detrain at Chickamauga Station 10 miles south of Chattanooga until September 4—an exhausting 10-day transit.[36]

Colonel Claudius C. Wilson of the 30th Georgia, who commanded a Georgia brigade in Walker's division, also led an organization plagued with absenteeism. Wilson's Georgians had been serving on the Atlantic Coast until transferred to Mississippi. Once back in their own state, Wilson noted, "many soldiers deserted their commands and went home." Wilson placed the losses in his brigade at no less than 500 men, 240 from the 30th Georgia alone since that regiment was recruited from regions directly along the route of the West Point and Atlanta Railroad. "I presume they will return after a short furlough," added Wilson, "but I was mortified at their conduct." Wilson was correct in that most his men wanted a visit with the home folks rather than a way out of the war, and some of them would return by the time the armies collided.[37]

Another important accession to the Army of Tennessee was the nearly 2,100 Mississippians of Brig. Gen. Edward Cary Walthall's brigade, who had spent most of August detached on provost duty at Atlanta. Walthall's infantry

35 Christopher M. Watford, *The Civil War In North Carolina: Soldiers' and Civilians' Letters and Diaries, 1861-1865* (McFarland & Co. 2003), 122-123.

36 Jim R. Cabaniss, Ed. *Civil War Journal and Letters of Washington Ives 4th Fla. C.S.A.* (Jim R. Cabaniss, 1987), 40-41.

37 "Dear Kate," September 3, 1863, Claudius Wilson correspondence, 30th Georgia file, Chickamauga-Chattanooga National Military Park. Hereafter CCNMP.

were also old hands with the Army of Tennessee and normally served with Hindman's division. When he returned, however, Walthall was directed to report to Brig. Gen. St. John Liddell, a brigade commander in Cleburne's division of Hill's Corps, with this new force now labeled Liddell's division.[38]

Bragg took steps to safeguard his rear. He detached Walker from Hill's corps and, with the attachment of Liddell's newly minted division, created a Confederate "Reserve Corps" to be used in a manner similar to how Rosecrans used Granger's command in the Army of the Cumberland. Brigadier General States Rights Gist's brigade, which had just de-trained at Chickamauga Station two days earlier, was sent south to Rome with 1,500 infantry and a battery of artillery.[39]

This constant shuffling and re-shuffling of his army in the face of an impending threat was not only time-consuming, but disruptive and bad for morale. Armies are not created simply by slotting units into tables of organization. Commanders function best when they have confidence in their men, and men fight best for officers they respect and trust. In addition, the creation of new corps and new divisions meant that a large number of officers would be stepping into new roles with expanded authority. It has always been a truism of war that not every promising regimental or brigade officer will be as effective at the next level of command. While these new troops needed to be integrated into the existing army structure, Bragg's changes were excessive and confusing. Unfortunately for the Army of Tennessee, this would not be the last time Bragg felt the need to reorganize his army.

With Buckner closing on the city from the northeast and at least some of the promised reinforcements on hand, Bragg began to explore the possibility of launching a counterattack. At midday on September 2, Bragg assembled his available divisional and corps commanders for a conference. The only detailed account of that meeting was left by Brig. Gen. St. John Liddell who was attending his first such assemblage. Military protocol in such affairs has always been for the most junior officer present to speak first, before his opinions can be influenced by his superiors. As the newest divisional commander, Liddell now took center stage. He viewed Rosecrans's dispositions as a great opportunity, especially if the Federals were bold enough to press on. Writing in

38 Hughes, *Liddell's Record*, 133.

39 Eugene W. Jones, Jr. *Enlisted For the War: The Struggles of the Gallant 24th Regiment, South Carolina Volunteers, Infantry, 1861-1865* (Longstreet House, 1997), 111.

1866, Liddell claimed (with the benefit of hindsight) that he argued the Army of Tennessee should feign ignorance of the Federal movements "until Rosecrans had fairly made his position inextricable . . . beyond support in the valley . . . near La Fayette. . . . In short, Rosecrans was making a hazardous movement, and we should not intercept him at this point." General Polk spoke next, asking Liddell if he thought "Rosecrans so incautious . . ." Liddell answered in the affirmative. Rosecrans was overconfident, he opined, "having lost all caution" after Tullahoma. The reference to a previous Bragg failure brought a smile to Polk's face, recalled a suddenly abashed Liddell, but no one really objected to the substance of the argument.[40]

Next to speak was D. H. Hill, who proposed that the Confederates "cross the river and move back into Middle Tennessee." Such a move was logistically impossible, and most everyone assembled knew it. Bragg dismissed the notion as "absurd . . . and not to be thought of for the present." Hill left no detailed account of this meeting, but he did record a general impression of Bragg's attitude at this time. Hill was struck by "the want of information at General Bragg's headquarters" as opposed to Robert E. Lee's, "and I was most painfully impressed with the feeling that it was to be a haphazard campaign on our part." Hill also found Bragg petulant. "It is said to be easy to defend a mountainous country," Bragg complained, "but mountains hide your foe from you, while they are full of gaps through which he can pounce upon you at any time. A mountain is like a wall of a house full of rat-holes."[41]

Though neither Liddell nor Hill noted it in their writings, Bragg was planning an attack, though of a much more limited scope than found in Hill's grandiose proposal. The Rebel commander wanted to lash out at Rosecrans's scattered forces on the north bank of the Tennessee. Realizing by this time that at least two Union corps had crossed the river to the southwest, Bragg proposed to send a Confederate column across the river north of Chattanooga to attack the Yankees now demonstrating in Sequatchie Valley. With the bulk of Rosecrans's army miles away, there was an opportunity to damage that portion

40 OR 30, pt. 4, 584; Hughes, *Liddell's Record*, 135. Writing in 1866, Liddell gets a number of details wrong. For example, he places this conference in the middle of August, well before Rosecrans crossed the river, and his assertion that Wheeler was present seems unlikely. His conclusions also seem a little too pat to be completely accurate, especially with his own prognosticating of Rosecrans's intentions and attitudes. Still, in other important regards it meshes closely with other known facts, and I have accepted it as generally accurate.

41 Hughes, *Liddell's Record*, 135; Hill, "Chickamauga," 641.

of the Federal force left behind. The problem, of course, was getting sufficient troops and guns across the river to do so. Bragg had one pontoon bridge emplaced at Chattanooga, but not enough transport to take it up and move it elsewhere. Using the pontoon bridge to cross at Chattanooga itself was not feasible because, without the element of surprise, the Federals could easily defend their side of the bridge. In fact, Captain Lilly and the enthusiastic gunners of the 18th Indiana viewed the bridge as a favorite target and shelled it repeatedly. How useful it would even be without extensive repair was an open question. Even worse, the Yankees had erected fortifications at likely crossing points and so were ready to oppose any such foray. Overcoming these challenges would be difficult, and perhaps impossible.

The third and fourth days of September were occupied with debating these thorny problems. Ever willing to support a bold attack, Nathan Bedford Forrest promised that he could find fords across the river and use his horsemen to help the infantry get across. D. H. Hill's Corps was selected for the task, but the infantry commanders worried about being able to cross their artillery, especially if they had to immediately storm Federal earthworks. Before it could be put into execution, the hazardous plan was overcome by events.[42]

While Bragg was planning Hill's cross-river offensive, a series of alarming reports began streaming into headquarters. One of the first was Martin's news of Federals at Summerville. A second, from Wharton, placed Federals at Cash's Store on Sand Mountain, 18 miles southwest of Trenton. Both of these reports reached Bragg on the 3rd, suggesting a much wider swing to the Union movements than just a direct flanking attack against Chattanooga. Worst of all, if Federals were indeed at Summerville, they were now east of Lookout Mountain and much closer to the Western & Atlantic Railroad than previously supposed. Bragg's logistical lifeline was in danger.[43]

While in fact these were only Yankee patrols, and the Federals had not yet crossed to the east side of Lookout in strength, they were very close to doing so. On September 5 a new report reached Bragg's headquarters corroborating the earlier information. This dispatch placed the Union XX Corps in Wills Valley with "10,000 [troops,] reported about 14 [miles] below Trenton." With these details in hand, and Martin's division now at La Fayette, Bragg dramatically

---

42 Ibid., 594. The dispatch from Bragg to Hill, dated 10:00 a.m. September 4, 1863, outlines Bragg's plan, the problems with the crossings, and Forrest's promise to find suitable fords.

43 Entry for September 3, 1863, Brent Journal.

shifted course. He ordered Wheeler to send Wharton south to Alpine, just six miles from Summerville at the eastern foot of Lookout Mountain. Wharton was ordered to block the pass there and hopefully prevent any further Union incursions.[44]

Bragg also intended to find out, once and for all, where Rosecrans was headed. Late on the 5th, he sent Wheeler an unequivocal directive to push a reconnaissance into Wills Valley. On the face of it, there seemed little room for argument or interpretation as the content of the directive was well stated. "The General commanding directs that you will, without delay, move with your command into the valley, drive in the enemy's pickets, and assail him so as to develop his designs, strength, and position. This must be done even at the sacrifice of troops. The General expects a rapid movement and prompt report."[45]

In response, Wheeler provided only excuses. Replying with a lengthy missive the next afternoon, Wheeler ticked off a laundry list of reasons why he could not obey Bragg's order. His troops were scattered over 40 miles. Felled trees blocked the gaps. He would not find out anything even if he went, he insisted, and going into Wills Valley would render his horses unserviceable. Such a move, he insisted, would leave Rome, Georgia, exposed. He would have to fight his way into the valley because Federals picketed the gaps on their side of the mountain. The information Bragg wanted could be discovered by "other means," insisted Wheeler, who assumed Bragg "would not desire great risks run or almost insuperable difficulties overcome."[46]

The most damning sentence in Wheeler's September 6 dispatch reveals a great deal about what the cavalier regarded as the proper role of cavalry on campaign—and where his understanding diverged from Bragg's. "I thought if General Rosecrans's Army was commencing a vigorous campaign upon us, it was of the first importance that our cavalry be kept in as good a condition as possible, as it would be indispensable to protect our lines of communication." Wheeler was wrong. It was of the first importance that his troopers discover what Rosecrans was up to, and then promptly inform his commanding officer. At this point, defending lines of communication could only be a secondary

---

44 Entry for September 5, 1863, Holt, Army of Tennessee Scout Book,; Entry for September 5, 1863, Brent Journal..

45 *OR* 30, pt. 4, 602.

46 Ibid., 614.

mission. This exchange reveals the wide cleave just between Bragg's and Wheeler's expectations.[47]

In short, Wheeler was not about to do what Bragg ordered done. Instead, he continued to forward intelligence of limited value, painting Union dispositions in sketchy and unclear terms. On September 4, Wheeler had informed Bragg that the Federals in Wills Valley amounted to no more than 4,000 or 5,000 men. Two days later on September 6 the cavalryman suggested they had been reinforced to a corps. If the former were true, there was probably no more than a division of cavalry in the valley—likely a feint or a raid. If the latter was accurate, however, a force of that size posed a real threat to Bragg's communications. Apparently Wheeler's "other means" were not sufficient to tell the difference with any degree of certainty. In fact, the Federal force was indeed substantial. By September 6, the little settlement at Valley Head (site of Winston's Spring, a major water source for upper Wills Valley), hosted 15,000 Yankees, including four brigades of Union cavalry and two infantry divisions of the Federal XX Corps, with another infantry division not far away.[48]

Finally, in the face of Wheeler's intransigence on the 6th, an independent scout named Davenport reached Bragg and confirmed some of the Wills Valley details, reporting the Union concentration at Valley Head. Among other things, he claimed to have counted 71 pieces of artillery descending Sand Mountain.[49]

While Bragg pondered this disturbing news, the Federal army moved with a newfound confidence. Overwhelmingly comprised of solders from Illinois, Indiana, and Ohio, these men were now entering a vast and scenic country, even more impressive than the Cumberland Plateau they had just crossed. For most of them it was a dramatic contrast with their native prairie. While the marches were arduous, there was still time to sightsee. Besides mountains, caves

---

47 Ibid., 615.

48 Ibid., 614; The four brigades of cavalry were the main body of Rosecrans's Cavalry Corps, 6,000 strong, while XX Corps's two infantry divisions numbered about 4,500 men apiece. The third division, when it joined, would add another 4,000 men. See RG 394, returns for XX Corps and Cavalry Corps, Army of the Cumberland, September 10, 1863, National Archives and Records Administration, Washington D.C, hereafter NARA. For the actual Union dispositions, see McCook's report, OR 30, pt. 2, 485; see also S. H. Stevens, "Second Division Itinerary," CCNMP.

49 Entry for September 6, 1863, Holt, Army of Tennessee Scout Book, titled "Davenports scout." Davenport was apparently Mountraville Davenport, a home guard captain who was a local terror to Unionist farmers in the area. As noted, however, his information was several days late: Union troops had reached Valley Head on September 2, 1863.

abounded. One of the prime attractions was Nick-a-Jack Cave in Sand Mountain near Shellmound. Thousands of inquisitive Yankees from the XIV Corps and XXI Corps, while marking time waiting for the crossings to be complete, found time to explore this grotto. Lieutenant Marcus Woodcock of the 9th Kentucky, in Horatio Van Cleve's division (XXI Corps), was one of the visitors. "I went in a little beyond the reach of daylight," because, Woodcock admitted, he didn't think to bring a torch. "There were scores of torches in the hands of soldiers going and returning." Sergeant Alanson R. Ryman of the 68th Indiana proved a little more adventurous. "[The] cave here . . . has been explored for miles underground," he noted, adding, "I myself went in a long way." The cave was a rich source of saltpeter, and had been being mined by the Confederates on "a large scale, [but] I don't think it will furnish any more material for Rebel gunpowder now," concluded the Hoosier.[50]

Generals were also not immune to playing tourist. On September 5, Rosecrans indulged his scientific proclivities to explore Hill's Cave (modern-day Cave Spring, Georgia). This small adventure included a bad moment when, "The General's rather bulky form became wedged in a narrow passage," reported an onlooker. "[F]or a few minutes it was a question whether the campaign might not have to be continued under the next senior general. . . . He seemed pretty well frightened." Fortunately, Rosecrans was extricated without harm and the campaign continued as intended. Supposedly, Rosecrans wrote his name on the wall.[51]

Also on the 5th, a party of officers from the XXI Corps, including the corps chief of staff Col. Lynn Starling and division leader Van Cleve made a point of visiting the cornerstone marking the boundaries of Alabama, Tennessee, and Georgia. At age 53, Van Cleve was one of the oldest generals in the army, but he took a boyish delight in recording his trip: "Sept 5th 12 M," he wrote. "I am now in the state of Georgia. Sept 5th, 12.2 M. Now in Alabama. Sept 5th 12.4 M. Now in Tennessee."[52]

50 Kenneth W. Noe, ed., *A Southern Boy in Blue: The Memoir of Marcus Woodcock 9th Kentucky Infantry (U.S.A.)* (University of Tennessee, 1996), 185; "Dear Jane," Camp near Trenton, Geo. Sept 9th, 1863, Alanson R. Ryman Letters, IHS.

51 Suzanne Colton Wilson, *Column South with the Fifteenth Pennsylvania Cavalry From Antietam to the Capture of Jefferson Davis* (J. F. Colton & Co., 1960), 85-86.

52 "My Darling Wife," Horatio Van Cleve Letters, Minnesota Historical Society, St. Paul, MN, hereafter MHS.

Freed from the earth's clammy grip, Rosecrans returned to duty. Intent on capitalizing on the success of the river crossing, the Union commander began pushing his army into a more aggressive posture. Buoyed by his success, Rosecrans was looking ahead even though his army's progress had slowed to a crawl. With the XIV Corps concentrated around Trenton, Crittenden's XXI Corps was in position to take the lead for a direct advance on Chattanooga. In the van was Thomas J. Wood's division. Wood had only two brigades on hand (Wagner's men were still north of the Tennessee as part of the diversion mission), and so moved rather cautiously into Running Water Canyon.

Wood left his camps near Shellmound on Saturday afternoon, September 5, with orders to proceed through the canyon as far as Wauhatchie, where a spur line from Trenton joined the main Nashville & Chattanooga tracks leading from Bridgeport. Securing Wauhatchie would open lateral communications with the XIV Corps in Trenton proper and allow Wood to execute his primary mission, a reconnaissance of the Confederate defenses astride the direct route into Chattanooga. The forbidding terrain, coupled with yet more delay while his supply train caught up (it had crossed at Bridgeport, and was lagging) meant that Wood only reached the hamlet of Whiteside halfway through the gorge before dark halted his progress. Palmer's division (also short one brigade—Hazen's) and Van Cleve's division followed closely behind Wood and reached Whiteside at 9:00 p.m. The corps had been promised a regiment of cavalry to aid in scouting, but none had yet arrived. The march itself was difficult. "We had some of the roughest roads I ever saw, noted 2nd Lt. Jason Hurd of the 19th Ohio, "over bluffs and ragged rocks into ravines and out again. It was so dark we could not see . . . and were compelled to take whatever of tumbling and thumping and bruising and bumping fortune dealt out to us, like blind men."[53]

With enough sunlight to move on, Wood pushed through the canyon the next morning and out into Lookout Valley. Colonel Charles Harker's brigade of three Ohio and one Kentucky regiments led the advance. Almost immediately, Harker reported, Rebel skirmishers contested their way, but both Wood and Harker were surprised that no more substantive opposition developed because

---

53 OR 30, pt. 1, 626, 710, 802; Diary transcript of Jason Hurd," 19th Ohio file, Combat Studies Institute, Fort Leavenworth KS, hereafter CSI.

the terrain was "most favorable to a prolonged and obstinate resistance by a small force."[54]

Wood reached Wauhatchie at midday. He dispatched couriers to Trenton and sent scouts eastward toward Chattanooga. All the while he found himself in full view of Confederate signalers atop Lookout Mountain, who could easily determine his strength and position to the last detail. A strong line of Rebel works barred the way into Chattanooga, and, of course, Wood had no way of knowing how many enemy troops lurked just out of sight, concealed around the shoulder of the imposing peak. His problems were further compounded when he was ordered to send one of his brigades forward to probe those Rebel works to determine the enemy's strength.

Instead of pushing out a brigade, Wood appealed for support from Crittenden, who along with the rest of the corps had marched south toward Trenton through Murphy's Hollow. Crittenden declined to send any help. Rosecrans had specifically ordered him not to send more than one division to Wauhatchie. Instead, Crittenden informed Wood that if attacked, he should fall back toward Trenton as well. That night, with the enemy active on his front, Wood did retreat a mile or more onto some higher ground he thought more defensible.[55]

Tom Wood was a professional soldier. He graduated from West Point in 1845, won a brevet in Mexico, served in the U.S. Cavalry on the frontier through much of the 1850s, and rose quickly to flag rank at the outbreak of the Civil War. He led a division at Shiloh, Perryville, and most notably, at Stones River, where he earned praise for his tenacious fighting style. The ever-opinionated journalist William Shanks thought Wood "a thorough and efficient disciplinarian," but he could also be "captious." Above all, Shanks regarded Wood, and not Crittenden, as the real soldier in the XXI Corps: "Tom Wood furnished [Crittenden] with all the military brains, and furnished for him all the military character he ever had." Shanks overstated the case, but precious few disputed that Wood was an effective fighter. Fellow brigadier John Beatty was a little more jaundiced. Wood "swear[s] like a pirate," observed Beatty, who went on to state that both Wood and Crittenden "know how to blow their own

---

54 *OR* 30, pt. 1, 626.

55 Ibid., pt. 3, 370; Ibid., pt. 1, 627.

horns exceedingly well." At Wauhatchie, Wood's captious streak rose to the fore.[56]

Something among the several messages that passed between Wood and Crittenden struck Wood as a rebuke of his performance, especially in falling back. Wood was sure he faced at least two Rebel divisions with at least 10,000 men, more than a match for his 3,000 troops. In one dispatch Wood bemoaned Crittenden's "blind obedience to orders" (in conjunction with not moving another division up to Wood's support), which in turn rankled Crittenden. When Crittenden passed the details of Wood's communications on to Rosecrans, he described Wood's retreat to higher ground and provided a copy of that dispatch to Wood, which the latter took as an implied rebuke of his decision to withdraw.

On the evening of September 7, Wood penned a remarkable missive several pages in length rebutting Crittenden's comments and defending his own actions. He sent the rebuttal to Rosecrans, via chief of staff Garfield. In it, Wood explained that he meant no disrespect to the army command when he used the term "blind obedience to orders," and took great pains to point out that he did not "fall back," but merely shifted his position to the rear. The difference, he explained, was that he never lost control of the critical Chattanooga-Trenton Road, making his redeployment merely a tactical maneuver and not a retreat.[57]

Rosecrans likely viewed this petty dispute with something approaching exasperation. Wood was feeling maligned, but his focus was misplaced. Rosecrans needed positive information about the real enemy, namely Bragg, and that officer's intentions. The Rebels were clearly stirring, and Rosecrans needed more intelligence on their activity. Dispatches from Wagner, Hazen, Minty, and Wilder all revealed a great deal of enemy activity, and to them it looked increasingly like Bragg's army was about to cross the Tennessee and attack them. They had clearly caught wind of Bragg's plans in that regard.[58]

Information received at Rosecrans's headquarters between September 5 and 7 painted a confusing picture. On the one hand, numerous reports from deserters, spies, and civilians suggested that Bragg would fight for Chattanooga

56 Shanks, *Personal Recollections*, 295; Beatty, *The Citizen-Soldier*, 234-35.

57 *OR* 30, pt. 3, 419-25.

58 Ibid., 371, 386.

rather than retreat as he had at Tullahoma. Bragg was said to have given a speech in the city insisting as much. In addition, reinforcements were arriving, including Buckner's troops from East Tennessee and, as some reports placed it, Joe Johnston from Mississippi with up to 30,000 men.

On the other hand, there was also information suggesting that Bragg would not stand and fight. On September 6, a citizen named Crow, "who is reliable" brought word that "Bragg has been ordered to retreat." A second report, obtained from three Rebel deserters, seemed to confirm this: "Yesterday morning (Sept. 5th) ten days rations were ordered into the wagons. The impression was . . . in view of an evacuation," claimed the men, "or a move into [Kentucky.]"[59]

Rosecrans also had past history to contemplate. Twice before Bragg had chosen retreat. After Stones River, his Confederates fell back and left Rosecrans the field and a rightful claim to a victory, however tenuous. Bragg didn't even try to give battle at Tullahoma. Rosecrans and many of his officers believed Bragg would now fall back yet a third time, despite boasting of holding Chattanooga; the risks of getting trapped in that place were too great. Accordingly, while Crittenden was knocking on the front door to the city, Rosecrans was pushing his other corps commanders to hasten forth and slam the back door closed.

Part of the back door effort, Thomas's XIV Corps was largely gathered around Trenton by September 5, except for Baird's division, which was still on the west side of Sand Mountain. Now it was time to ascend Lookout. Reconnaissance suggested that the easiest path up that mountain was via Johnson Crook, a dramatic valley that bit deeply into Lookout's western flank and angled northeast for several miles to Newsom Gap. Maj. Gen. James Scott Negley's division was there, having seized all the usable property of the Empire State Iron & Coal Mining Company as well as a sizable amount of wheat at Payne's Grist Mill.[60]

It would take the next two days to reach the top of the mountain. Most of the 6th was consumed working up the valley, which while it might be an easier way up than scaling a sheer cliff, was still no effortless route for an army. Late that afternoon, a patrol from the 42nd Indiana encountered Rebels near the top

---

59 Entries for September 4-7, 1863, "Summaries of the news reaching the headquarters of General W. S. Rosecrans, RG 393, NARA.

60 *OR* 30, pt. 1, 325.

at a spot where Newsom Gap breeched the palisade. Lieutenant Alfred Hough of Negley's staff recalled that the "road was barricaded by the enemy" and defended by "a heavy stone breast work." Here, no more than 100 Confederate cavalrymen held up the entire division, resisting "several attempts to dislodge them."[61]

Fortunately, a local civilian with Unionist proclivities showed up after dark offering to "lead a column by a secret path to the top" a couple of miles from the breastwork. A small force did so at dawn, neatly outflanking the defenders who immediately retreated across the plateau of the mountain top and down the eastern face. With the opposition so disposed, Negley's main body began the arduous climb. By 4:00 p.m. on the 7th, two of his three brigades were atop Lookout. It would be yet one more day, however, before the trains were up and the whole division ready to cross to the eastern side. In the meantime, the rest of the XIV Corps remained in Wills Valley.[62]

Far to the south, McCook's XX Corps had made the most promising progress. By the 5th, McCook was encamped at Valley Head with Davis's and Johnson's divisions at the foot of Winston's Gap. McCook lacked only Sheridan's division, plus the corps trains, to complete his assembly and begin his own move over Lookout Mountain. Unfortunately, Sheridan's men had been delayed, first by the traffic snarls with the bridges at Bridgeport, and then in waiting for Thomas's troops to clear the roads leading from the river before negotiating the passes over Sand Mountain. Still near Trenton, and enmeshed with Thomas's men, it would be several days before Sheridan was fully closed up on Valley Head.

Accordingly, between September 5 and 9, Davis's and Johnson's men enjoyed a comfortable break. They had been marching almost nonstop for two weeks, up one mountain and down the next, and needed the rest. Their camps clustered around a large spring that was the source of Wills Creek. Here sat the stately home of Col. William O. Winston. Born in Virginia, Winston was raised in Tennessee but immigrated to this corner of Alabama in the 1830s, building a fine brick mansion next to the spring on an estate of 3,000 acres. It was by far the grandest home the Federals had seen thus far—especially when contrasted

---

61 Robert G. Athearn, ed., *Soldier in the West: The Civil War Letters of Alfred Lacey Hough* (University of Pennsylvania Press, 1957), 137.

62 *OR* 30, pt. 1, 326.

with the subsistence-level, hardscrabble farms dotting Sand Mountain. As such, the Winston home acted like a magnet for the senior officers of the XX Corps; both Alexander McCook and Jefferson C. Davis made their headquarters there, with staffs and tents littering the sprawling yard.

Colonel Winston was a planter, lawyer, politician, and president of the Wills Valley Railroad, which owned the spur from Wauhatchie to Trenton. An extension planned to run all the way to Valley Head was interrupted only by the war. He also had two sons in the Confederate army. Like many others in the region, however, Winston opposed secession and had voted against it in the state convention of 1861. As a Unionist, his property was protected from many of the ravages that 20,000 hungry Federals otherwise might have visited on an aristocratic plantation. The presence of the assembled generals also helped his cause.[63]

The presence of two ladies also helped maintain proper decorum. Jefferson C. Davis was so certain that Braxton Bragg would not fight for Chattanooga that he had brought his wife Marietta on campaign with him. With her was her good friend Clara Horton Pope, the wife of Union Maj. Gen. John Pope (recently of Second Bull Run and "Headquarters in the Saddle" ignominy) and a distant relation, by marriage, to Mary Todd Lincoln. The women had no business being there. In fact, Rosecrans had explicitly ordered all wives, civilian visitors, and other hangers-on to the rear when the campaign kicked off on August 16. Moreover, with every draft animal and wagon needed to haul supplies, the army itself had been stripped to a minimum of transport for things like regimental needs and officer's baggage. Despite this strict injunction, Davis brought both women along. Being "on the side of easy and safe occupation, and as his wife was a somewhat delicate lady, but apparently a very refined one, he wanted her to sojourn in Chattanooga a while, or possibly he thought a little campaigning would be beneficial to her health." Davis, like many of his fellow officers, believed this would be another largely bloodless campaign.[64]

---

63 Thomas McAdory Owen, *History of Alabama and Dictionary of Alabama Biography*, 4 vols, (The S. J. Clarke Publishing Co. 1921), vol. 4, 1791. "Colonel" Winston's rank seems to have been purely honorary.

64 Charles Dennis Memoir, Rutherford B. Hayes Presidential Library, Fremont Ohio, hereafter RHB. This was an odd friendship. Clara's husband John was a Republican who believed blacks could be good soldiers, and was a strong supporter of civil rights for blacks after the war. Davis was a pro-slavery Unionist who distrusted abolitionism in the army.

For the men, the sojourn on the Winston grounds approached an idyllic pause. For one thing, they ate well. "[I] lend my revolver to the men to shoot hogs," recorded Lt. Chesley Mosman of the 59th Illinois on September 5. "Plenty of corn and apples. Boys begin to play cards as soon as we camp." Union sentiment was running high, even among the locals. The next day, at the site of the former Valley Head United States Post Office, Mosman noted that "seventeen civilians take the oath of allegiance and start north for Illinois. Some join the regiment here as soldiers." Patrols were turned into excursions. On the 8th, as a detail from the 59th worked to improve the "alleged road" up to the top of Lookout Mountain, others from the brigade climbed to the top for the view. Some "21st Ills. men pry loose great boulders and send them rolling and bouncing 40 to 100 feet at a jump down the mountains. It was glorious sport."[65]

Rosecrans expected more than sport. McCook's delay need not prevent Stanley's cavalry from executing its mission of raiding either Rome or toward Dalton. At 8:30 on the morning of the 5th, Garfield informed Stanley that the time for such a move was at hand, hoping "that your instructions in regard to the movement on Rome can be successfully carried out."[66]

Stanley was less optimistic. Rome was still 50 miles away, Dalton closer to 60, and the roads over the mountains were poor. He had with him only four brigades, some 6,000 troopers, and was tasked with multiple missions. In addition to raiding, he was supposed to protect the supply trains on their increasingly extended trips to and from the depots at Bridgeport, screen McCook's move when the XX Corps advanced, and maintain lateral communications with the XIV Corps to the north. At the very least, Stanley wanted Minty's brigade returned to him before detaching a large portion of his strength on such an extended raid. Even worse, he lacked the normal preparations for a raiding mission. An inquiry sent to Col. Edward McCook, temporarily commanding the First Cavalry Division (two-thirds of Stanley's strength) revealed a complete lack of tools suitable "for tearing up a railroad track," nor any explosives necessary for "blowing up railroad bridges, culverts, &c." Colonel McCook would immediately send back to Stevenson for the necessary equipment, but that would take some time to move forward, and

65 Arnold Gates, ed., *The Rough Side of War: The Civil War Journal of Chesley A. Mosman 1st Lieutenant, Company D, 59th Illinois Volunteer Infantry Regiment* (The Basin Publishing Co. 1987), 74-5.

66 OR 30, pt. 3, 374.

there was no point in launching any raid without them. This last oversight smacked of neglect.[67]

For his part, Alexander McCook was not inclined to move over Lookout Mountain until his entire corps had reassembled, which meant waiting for Sheridan's division to close up. Without McCook's support, Stanley feared that once he passed Winston's Gap, Rebels could simply reoccupy the pass and cut him off. "How far am I to regulate my movements by those of the infantry[?]" he demanded. Frustration was beginning to show.[68]

Rosecrans spent the next several days prodding Stanley to move, and Stanley kept finding excuses to wait. Headquarters directed McCook to send infantry over the mountain to Alpine to hold Winston's Gap and alleviate Stanley's fear of being cut off. Minty, however, would not ride to join Stanley as he was still north of the Tennessee River and needed there. Stanley was instructed not to wait for him. Making the raid was imperative; nothing else would so quickly stir Bragg out of his camps than severing his supply lines. And yet, none of these requests instilled any sense of urgency in the cavalry commander, who delayed his mission's departure until the morning of the 9th.

The truth was that Stanley didn't want to carry out the mission. He didn't think much of Rosecrans's idea for a deep raid, and he thought the commanding general was making a serious mistake. Despite Stanley's usually ardent admiration for his commander (Stanley thought that the war provided "no better example of successful strategy than the Tullahoma operation"), he believed that "Rosecrans had no idea of the use of cavalry." Instead of being sent off on raids, Stanley wanted to use his mounted men in close pursuit, harrying Bragg's columns as they retreated. Stanley chose not to blame Rosecrans for this lapse, transferring instead his resentment to Garfield, whom Stanley viewed as "everlastingly meddling." Stanley was also getting sick with a fever and dysentery, which within a few days would send him back to Stevenson in an ambulance.[69]

Because of Stanley's delays, the intended raid against Rome and/or Dalton never came off. On September 8, Rosecrans received the electrifying news that Bragg was abandoning Chattanooga. That afternoon, Rosecrans dictated a

67 Ibid., 375. Colonel Edward McCook was a first cousin to Maj. Gen. Alexander McCook.

68 Ibid., 374.

69 Stanley, *Memoirs*, 158.

blistering rebuke to Stanley. "I am sorry to say you will be too late," snapped the army commander. "It is also a matter of regret to me that your command has done so little in this great movement."[70]

70 *OR* 30, pt. 3, 468.

Chapter Four

Cat and Mouse in the Mountains:

September 8-11, 1863

By September 6, Braxton Bragg knew he would have to leave Chattanooga to avoid Rosecrans's planned entrapment. That day, the Confederate leader ordered his army to move south toward La Fayette, with his ultimate destination Rome. He also began to worry about the situation as far away as Atlanta. Having stripped that city of troops to augment his field strength, Bragg now appealed to Joe Johnston for another loan. "Hasten a division of infantry to Atlanta if you can spare it," he wired, further promising that the troops would only be needed for "a few days. It will save that depot and give me time to defeat the enemy's plans." Johnston agreed, albeit reluctantly, detaching two brigades under Brig. Gens. Matthew D. Ector and John Gregg, another 2,500 men. His understanding was firm however: these troops were not to go any farther than the designated city. Johnston did not want them to be absorbed into Bragg's army, even temporarily.[1]

The next day, September 7, Bragg postponed his planned move south. Indecision still ruled at headquarters. The problem of Joe Wheeler's vacillation concerning the size of the Union force gathering at Valley Head was seemingly resolved that morning when Maj. Pollack B. Lee of Bragg's staff expressed his own doubts that the enemy's move was anything more than a feint. Lee was

---

1 *OR* 30, pt. 4, 607-608.

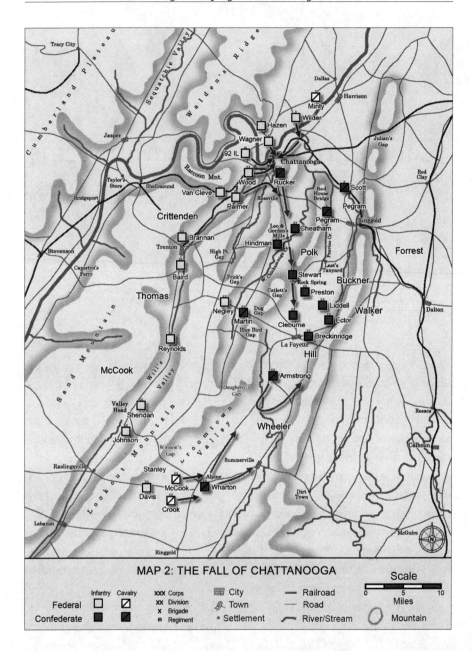

MAP 2: THE FALL OF CHATTANOOGA

	Infantry	Cavalry	XXX	Corps		City		Railroad
Federal	☐	☒	XX	Division		Town		Road
Confederate	■	◪	X	Brigade	•	Settlement		River/Stream
			III	Regiment				Mountain

Scale
0   5   10
Miles

present with Wheeler at Alpine, and so his opinion carried real weight even though it contradicted the scout Davenport's assertion that an entire corps was camped at Winston's Gap. Lee's conclusion was enough for both D. H. Hill and the Bishop Polk to counsel for a suspension of the withdrawal south, especially with Federal troops approaching the city from around the northern end of

Lookout Mountain. Still, no one was entirely satisfied with this unsettled state of affairs. "A restive feeling exists" among the generals, admitted Colonel Brent. The pause lasted barely half a day. Bragg reinstated the movement that afternoon, with orders that the army march at dusk. If Major Lee was wrong, waiting any longer could well be fatal. Chattanooga would have to be abandoned to the enemy.[2]

Bragg intended to concentrate his army between Lee and Gordon's Mills, 15 miles south of Chattanooga, and the town of La Fayette. Hill's Corps led the way and Polk's men followed, their column moving directly south on the La Fayette Road. Walker's and Buckner's troops were routed via Graysville, first onto the Summerville Road, then southeast via the Old Federal Road, and finally turning south toward La Fayette through Peavine Valley. Stores and sick men were sent south on the railroad. In an ominous note, Bragg ordered depots and hospitals as far south as Resaca—45 miles to the southeast—evacuated as well. Alarmed civilians moved quickly to jam the southbound trains. Bragg would move with his own headquarters to Lee and Gordon's Mills on the 8th and from there await developments, all the while looking for an opportunity to reclaim the initiative.[3]

Given the shuffling within the command structure and the army's fragile morale, yet another retreat was a hard thing for men to swallow. Expressions of dismay coursed through the ranks. Even many years later, Pvt. Marcus B. Toney of the 1st Tennessee recalled his sharp disappointment. Toney and his comrades had spent two months erecting defenses around Chattanooga. "I did not like to leave the forts upon which we had expended so much [effort], knowing that in a short while the enemy would be enjoying the fruits of our labor," complained Toney. Pvt. Thomas W. Davis of the 6th Tennessee Cavalry recorded his "mingled emotion of disappointment & vexation" at the news. "Found Gen. Brag on the Chickamauga at Lee & Gordon's Mill—Rosecranz has achieved a great victory without the loss of a man. It will cause a thrill of joy to vibrate through the entire Yankee nation."[4]

2   Entry for September 7, Brent Journal, WRHS.

3   *OR* 30, pt. 4, 611.

4   Marcus B. Toney, *The Privations of a Private* (Publishing House of the M.E. Church, South, 1907), 59; Entries for September 8th and 9th, "The Civil War Diary (June-November, 1863) of Thomas W. Davis," Hamilton County Library, Chattanooga, TN.

The army's leadership worked overtime to counteract this prevailing sense of disillusionment. This time they were going to fight, promised the generals, and fall on Rosecrans's dispersed columns one by one. One such cheerleader was Tennessee Governor Isham G. Harris, who for some months had been serving with the army as one of Bragg's volunteer aides since most of his state was now occupied by the enemy. Harris, noted 1st Sgt. Edwin H. Rennolds of Company D, the 4th/5th Tennessee, "addressed a large crowd of [Cheatham's] division" to explain matters to the men. "The enemy was reported crossing the mountain 12 miles off and that we would await him . . . [and] that we were equal to him in numbers. Tennessee was at stake," thundered Harris, but "he did not fear the result. He says we will fight in four days." [5]

Bragg left the city on September 8, but not without one last confrontation. Back in July, when he first arrived in the city, Bragg established his headquarters at the Brabson House, a two-story brick mansion on East Fifth Street. On September 7, the widow Brabson held a farewell tea for the departing general, whom she knew well; Bragg had also headquartered there in 1862. The party could only have been a rather gloomy affair, and one sparsely attended. Civilians had been leaving for days, with all the trains south to Atlanta crowded with refugees and their valuables.

One man who hadn't yet left town was Henry Watterson, the brash young editor of the *Chattanooga Daily Rebel*. Bragg had been much critiqued by Southern newspapers since the sputtered Kentucky combat at Perryville, and no one was more hostile than Watterson's *Rebel*. Worse yet, Watterson often published important details of troop strengths, movements, and intentions, all of which Bragg was sure Rosecrans was reading with great interest. For a time that summer Bragg banned the paper from being sold in military camps. The result was a financial disaster for Watterson, who was selling as many as 10,000 copies a day with the army in town. He appealed the decision. Watterson claimed to have served as a Confederate soldier under Leonidas Polk and Nathan Bedford Forrest. After the war he would boast of being a staff officer under Polk, of service with Forrest in 1862, and that he had been Joseph Johnston's "Chief of Scouts" in 1864. Almost certainly he was probably an imposter, since no Confederate records show him as serving. Physically

---

5   Entry for September 9, E. H. Rennolds Diary, TSLA.

Watterson was poorly suited for army life, weighing in at a slight eighty pounds and troubled with poor eyesight. [6]

Watterson was also an unusual sort of fire-breathing Rebel. The son of a Tennessee congressman, he spent much of his life and was schooled in Washington, D.C., lived in New York City, and stood on the inaugural platform with Abe Lincoln in 1861. He initially "believed that secession was treason" but when he returned to Tennessee in 1861, soon adopted the Southern side of the conflict as his own.[7]

The slightly built nearsighted young man, however, was a gifted writer and journalist who, by the age of 22, had already worked for major papers in the northeastern part of the country. He made contacts easily, which provided him with valuable sources inside the army. That inside information, presented with verbal flair and acid wit in the columns of the *Rebel* made the paper immensely popular with the troops. Faced with Bragg's ban, Watterson approached Col. Alexander McKinstry, who was positively disposed toward Watterson because of his claimed service with Forrest, and who was now heading up Bragg's Bureau of Intelligence. The pair struck a deal. Watterson agreed to let McKinstry approve what he printed, and further allowed McKinstry to use the paper to plant whatever false rumors Bragg wanted, in exchange for permission to keep printing. This arrangement apparently satisfied the irascible army commander, for the *Rebel* remained in circulation.

On the afternoon of September 7, at the Widow Brabson's farewell tea, Watterson ambled into the brick mansion on East Fifth Street. The latest retreat and the panic infecting Chattanooga were fuel for the young incendiary, who loudly lambasted "Bragg's almost supernatural ineptitude." Within feet of Watterson was Bragg himself. The pair had never met personally, and the newspaperman didn't recognize the general. Bragg confronted Watterson, and the two exchanged what one witness described as "pointed words." The embarrassed and likely well-chastised Watterson quickly made himself scarce. Shortly thereafter Bragg excused himself and set out with his headquarters for La Fayette.[8]

6   B.G. Ellis, *The Moving Appeal: Mr. McClanahan, Mrs. Dill, and the Civil War's Great Newspaper Run* (Mercer University Press, 2003), 601-603.

7   Ibid., 602.

8   Roy Morris, Jr., "That Improbable, Praiseworthy Paper: the *Chattanooga Daily Rebel*," *Civil War Times. Illustrated*, Vol. 23, No. 7 (November, 1984), 21.

The Confederates now began to experience some of the same miseries that had plagued marching Union columns. Chief among them was the unforgiving all-pervasive dust. Weeks of drought left the dirt roads bone dry. It didn't take long in such conditions for thousands of marching feet to grind those roadbeds into troughs of dust. Sergeant Rennolds, whose regiment was one of the last to leave town, suffered mightily. He found "the road was almost shoe-mouth deep in dust and nearly suffocating." As the leading elements of Bragg's command neared La Fayette, their appearance frightened the locals. La Fayette was filled with refugees fleeing the advancing Federals, and now the appearance of approaching troops—heard first, rather than seen, in what to some sounded like an approaching distant storm—triggered fears anew. "We could scarcely see the men for the dust," recalled one resident. As the head of the column drew near, one of these animated dirt-clouds inquired the name of the town. In return, recalled the civilian, "we asked him if they were Confeds or Yankees, and he laughingly replied, 'We are General Bragg's dust heap.'"[9]

During Bragg's initial shift southward he also expanded Nathan Bedford Forrest's responsibilities. Despite the fact that Wheeler's corps was already deployed in and around La Fayette, Bragg instructed Forrest to lead the advance with "Dibrell's brigade and such other cavalry as he may deem necessary." At the same time, however, the newly elevated corps commander must also "picket the river, bring up the rear . . . so as to cover all." Forrest had saved Rome once from Yankee marauders under Col. Abel Streight the previous spring; if necessary, Bragg wanted him in place to do it again.[10]

The expanded cavalry mission was a tall order. Not only did it divide Forrest's new corps over many miles and assign the army's entire security to one-half of his cavalry, but it did so with the least experienced part of his mounted arm. Forrest reacted promptly, riding south with not just Dibrell but Frank Armstrong's entire division, leaving Pegram and Scott to handle the retreat.

Accordingly, on September 6, Pegram's troopers burned the bridge over the Hiwassee River at Charleston and marched south to Philadelphia, Tennessee. The next day they moved farther south to Graysville, Georgia, on

9 Entry for September 9, E. H. Rennolds Diary, TSLA; Anonymous, "Reminiscence," *Confederate Reminiscences and Letters, 1861-1865, Volume X* (Georgia Division, United Daughters of the Confederacy, 1999), 10.

10 *OR* 30, pt. 4, 611.

the state line, where they remained for the next two days as a rear guard while Buckner's and Walker's infantry trekked past. In the meantime, Forrest directed Scott's brigade to Ringgold, Georgia, another dozen miles south along the railroad to secure that place. These moves left only one of Pegram's regiments, Rucker's Tennessee Legion, garrisoning Chattanooga. Another 75 men from Lieutenant Colonel Mauldin's detachment of the 3rd Alabama Cavalry also still held the northern tip of Lookout Mountain. These last two units represented the final vestige of Confederate strength in the city.[11]

Dibrell's men departed on the 7th, heading to Rome via Ringgold with instructions to establish contact with Wheeler. Forrest, Armstrong, and Armstrong's remaining brigade under Col. James T. Wheeler of the 6th Tennessee Cavalry (no relation to Gen. Joe Wheeler) quickly followed. After strenuous marching, the entire force reached Summerville, 45 miles south of Chattanooga, by September 8. There they found John Wharton, who informed Forrest that the Federals had just occupied the hamlet of Alpine, recently abandoned by Wharton and Wheeler. The always aggressive Forrest decided to probe these Federals the next day, with about 900 men.[12]

September 8 was a busy day for Rosecrans as well, who lost no time following closely on Bragg's heels. That day a Union patrol from Col. Smith D. Atkins's 92nd Illinois Mounted Infantry slipped past Mauldin's screen and climbed to the northern summit of Lookout Mountain. From there, the Illinois men could see the full extent of the Confederate retreat. Across the river, General Wagner also caught wind of the evacuation and promptly telegraphed the news to army headquarters. "I will occupy the town tomorrow," concluded Rosecrans. Crittenden was ordered to begin his advance before dawn.[13]

In fact, Rosecrans intended to do much more than just capture the city. The commanding general was already thinking of Bragg's army as a beaten foe, one that would run rather than fight. A strategic victory the likes of the capture of Chattanooga was indeed welcome, but it also posed a problem; William Starke

---

11 Jeffrey C. Weaver, *The Confederate Regimental History Series: The 5th and 7th Battalions North Carolina Cavalry and the 6th North Carolina Cavalry (65th North Carolina State Troops)*, (H. E. Howard, 1995), 103; *OR* 30, pt. 2, 523; Entry for September 8, 1863, Brent Journal, WRHS; Gustave Huwald Letter, Leroy Moncure Nutt Papers, UNC.

12 Jordan and Pryor, *Forrest's Cavalry*, 305.

13 Anonymous, *Ninety-Second Illinois Volunteers* (Journal Steam Publishing House and Bookbindery, 1875), 100-101; "Summaries of the news reaching the headquarters of General W. S. Rosecrans," September 8. NARA.

Rosecrans could not afford another bloodless victory that left his opponent alive and able to fight another day. He no longer had enough political capital for such achievements. He had to engage Bragg and destroy his army, or at least inflict a substantial defeat.

At 3:30 a.m. on September 9, the ever-nocturnal Rosecrans sent word for George Thomas to consult with him at headquarters "at once." Departmental headquarters was in Trenton, while Thomas's command tent was pitched a few miles south at Brown's Spring. Thomas met with Rosecrans early that morning to hash out the army's next move only to discover that the commanding general was already fixed on a plan of action: immediate pursuit. The cautious Thomas objected to the proposal. The army is dangerously exposed, he argued, especially with McCook's Corps so far to the south. Instead, the Virginian wanted to concentrate the entire army in and around Chattanooga, await the repair of the railroad, and prepare a renewed advance in a more measured fashion. Thomas's plan could take weeks, and even months, especially to rebuild the rail bridges. Rosecrans overruled him.[14]

At 9:00 a.m. on September 9, Rosecrans dashed off a series of orders to Thomas, McCook, and Stanley, which in essence converted the posture of the Army of the Cumberland from an advance to a headlong pursuit. Thomas's XIV Corps would move due east "as rapidly as possible to La Fayette and make every exertion to strike the enemy in flank." In similar language, McCook's XX Corps was urged on to Alpine and Summerville, to "attack him [Bragg] whenever you can reach him with reasonable success." Speed was so important that McCook was told he "need not wait for your trains, which can follow you under strong escort." Stanley, who doubtless still had the army commander's earlier rebuke ringing in his ears, was ordered to cut loose for Rome and also to cover the army's "extreme right flank." Rosecrans still retained enough confidence in his cavalry commander to "leave your operations to your own discretion," but in return, Stanley had better deliver: "If their retreat can once be turned into a rout, your command can do them immense injury."[15]

Later, and with the benefit of hindsight, a number of officers argued that Thomas had been right. In his memoirs, Maj. Gen. John M. Palmer of the XXI Corps recalled that when he received his copy of the orders outlining the

---

14 *OR* 30, pt. 3, 482; McKinney, *Education in Violence*, 225.

15 *OR* 30, pt. 3, 483, 488-489, 500.

pursuit, he found them "remarkable." Were the Rebels really retreating? "I knew," wrote Palmer, "that on that day a Rebel force was at Lee and Gordon's Mills, and that Bragg himself was at Lafayette." With the mills only six miles from Rossville, it did not seem that the Army of Tennessee was fleeing all that quickly. Writing in 1866, William B. Hazen, one of the army's more outspoken brigadiers, thought he knew the reason for Rosecrans's sudden recklessness: more newspaper foolishness, this time on the Union side. "Mr. Edmund Kirk of the N. Y. Tribune had visited our army at Murfreesboro and told Gen. R. that the country looked to him as our next president . . . [and] inflated the man until he was no longer the careful vigilant commander of the second great army of the nation. . . . He expected to drive Bragg into the sea."[16]

In reality, Thomas's cautious strategy was no guarantee of success, for Chattanooga itself was an equal opportunity trap. For one thing, McCook was at least several days' march away, 40 miles to the south—a march only made considerably longer if the corps could not come through La Fayette. Until the XX Corps closed up, Thomas's XIV Corps would have to remain stationary, or place McCook and the cavalry in even greater danger. This inaction would surrender the initiative. If Bragg's men were demoralized, the pause would give them time to recover. If they weren't, it would allow Bragg precious time to spring a trap. Either prospect was unpalatable. Additionally, if Rosecrans concentrated at Chattanooga, his supply line would not be behind him but extend parallel to his front, stretching back 20 miles to his right and connecting with Bridgeport. Bragg wouldn't be forced to come at the Federals in Chattanooga. Instead, he could simply operate against Rosecrans's supply depots at Bridgeport, Stevenson, or some point in between. The Army of the Cumberland would have to stretch itself out to defend this line, allowing the Confederates to pick and choose their desired point of attack. Even worse, instead of acting as blinds hiding Federal intentions both Sand and Lookout mountains would screen Rebel movements. If instead the Federals could advance as far as some secure point on the Western & Atlantic line—say Ringgold, Dalton, or even Resaca—the geography would favor the Federals.

Chattanooga's capture proved ridiculously easy. Early on the 9th, the 92nd Illinois Mounted Infantry led Maj. Gen. Thomas J. Wood's division of the

---

16 John M. Palmer, *Personal Recollections of John M. Palmer: The Story of an Earnest Life* (The Robert Clarke Company, 1901), 171; William B. Hazen to Mr. Benson H. Lossing, August 23d, 1866, WRHS.

The Crutchfield House, one of the most prominent buildings in Chattanooga,
was owned by prominent East Tennessee Unionists.
Chattanooga Public Library Collection

Union XXI Corps into the city after a short, sharp fight with the 3rd Alabama.
The Confederates left behind three men killed and 10 wounded. Both the
Alabamians and Rucker's troops were chased out of town at a trot. By 10:00
a.m. the flag of the 92nd Illinois floated proudly from the roof of the
Crutchfield House, Chattanooga's finest hotel. Members of Wilder's brigade
standing on the far bank cheered. With everyone eager to be in on the victory,
another flag had already been planted on what the Federals called the "Mound
Fort." A party from the 97th Ohio in Wagner's brigade, who watched the
Rebels clear out the previous day, decided they should be the first to have their
banner wave above the gateway city. Along with some members of the 40th
Indiana, Company C of the 97th crossed the river on "a horse boat," informally
skippered by Capt. Jack Caster of the 40th, to plant the 97th's colors on the
ramparts of the rebel earthwork atop Cameron Hill.[17]

---

17 OR 30, pt. 2, 71; Smith D. Atkins, *Chickamauga. Useless, Disastrous Battle: Talk by Smith D.
Atkins, Opera House, Mendota, Illinois, February 22, 1907, At Invitation Of Women's Relief Corps. (n.p.,
1907), 7. Atkins noted that his men were fired upon by Lilly's guns and it took a little while and a

Except for a smattering of Unionist sympathizers, the city of 2,500 was largely deserted. Two of the most prominent of these were Thomas and William Crutchfield, owners of the Crutchfield House hotel. Thomas Crutchfield was also a former mayor of the city and the prominent landowner of Amnicola, a large estate along the south bank of the Tennessee upstream from town. William, the more hotheaded of the two siblings, nearly dueled with Jefferson Davis in January 1861 after Davis left Washington to return to his own state of Mississippi. Davis delivered an inflammatory oration at the hotel, which prompted William to denounce him as "a traitor to his country and a perjured villain, and in most sarcastic, measured tones painted Mr. Davis out to the people as their future military despot." Thomas's restraint of his brother narrowly averted physical violence. Now, with the appearance of Federal troops and the city in Union hands, William volunteered his services as a guide and informant.[18]

That same afternoon, the 92nd Illinois continued through town and beyond, leading Maj. Gen. John M. Palmer's infantry division on to Rossville just a few miles south of town. There the infantry halted, but Atkins's Illinoisans weren't done for the day. The 92nd marched back north to the Tennessee River, where they helped bring the rest of Wilder's brigade across to the south bank near the mouth of Chickamauga Creek. Their labors finally complete, the Midwesterners bivouacked that evening in a grape arbor, where they discovered their just reward: 30 barrels of Catawba wine, every drop promptly confiscated for the Union. More importantly, all of Wilder's command was south of the Tennessee River by nightfall.[19]

Following Wilder's lead, that same day Hazen's and the rest of Wagner's infantry crossed at Frier's Island. Wagner's brigade rejoined Wood's division, now in the city with Wood installed as garrison commander. It took Hazen's

---

bit of impromptu signaling to convince Lilly to hold his fire. "From the 40th Indiana," *LaFayette Daily Courier*, September 25, 1863, and *OR* 30, pt. 1, 629. There are a number of competing claims concerning who was first into the city, and who planted the first flag. Dr. William Glenn Robertson gives the credit to Sgt. Andrew C. Hossum, Cpl. William C. Jackson, and Pvt. Jacob Kraps, all of Company C of the 97th. See William Glenn Robertson, "Chickamauga Campaign: The Fall of Chattanooga," *Blue & Gray Magazine, Vol. XXIII*, No. 4 (Fall, 2006), 50. The "Horse Boat" in question was a mule-powered ferry.

18 "William Crutchfield Biography, Hamilton County Genealogical Society Website, http://www.hctgs.org/Biographies/crutchfield_william.htm, accessed 10/29/2012.

19 *Ninety-Second Illinois Volunteers*, 102; *OR* 30, pt. 1, 446.

men six hours to make their crossing. The Tennessee was 800 yards wide here, but shallow enough that the men could wade. Hazen recalled the pomp and circumstance of a stunning martial scene: "The bright morning, the glistening of the arms, the orderly movement of the column crossing with buoyant spirits while the bands . . . played the national airs, made this one of the most wonderfully interesting spectacles I ever beheld." Once across, Hazen's men moved south to the railroad in the direction of Ringgold and fell into camp. With no need to fight for the city, Crittenden diverted Van Cleve to Rossville as well, five miles south of Chattanooga, in anticipation of a continued rapid pursuit. An elated Crittenden also relayed the heady report of "Mr. Thompson, said to be a very loyal citizen." Bragg, claimed the intelligence, was in full retreat, and "if we pursue vigorously they will not stop short of Atlanta. Troops badly demoralized; all feel that they are whipped; one-seventh of the troops mostly naked; the rations for three days would make one good meal." That information could only have delighted departmental headquarters.[20]

At 2:00 a.m. on the 10th, after the very full day's labors of the 9th were finally behind him, Crittenden sent an important communiqué to Ambrose Burnside, whose Federals were similarly overrunning East Tennessee. Sent at Rosecrans's direction, Crittenden informed Burnside that "the enemy has retreated in the direction of Rome, Ga. [and that] the general commanding [Rosecrans] requests that you move down your cavalry and occupy the country recently covered by Colonel Minty." This dispatch not only informed Burnside that Minty's brigade was being transferred across the Tennessee, but that as far as Burnside was concerned, his own southern flank was protected. With Bragg headed south, the only Confederate force left to dispute control of East Tennessee drew supplies from southwest Virginia, and after receiving this telegram, Burnside devoted most of his attention and troops to meeting that threat.[21]

The news was less satisfactory on Thomas's XIV Corps front. In van of the XIV, Maj. Gen. James Scott Negley's division was already atop Lookout Mountain, having ascended via the road up Johnson's Crook on the 7th. Two portals offered access down the west side of the mountain; Cooper's (also known as Frick's), and Stevens's Gaps. Negley sent troops to seize both on

20 As quoted in Joseph R. Reinhart, *A History of the 6th Kentucky Volunteer Infantry U.S.* (Beargrass Press, 2000), 207; OR 30, pt. 3, 481.

21 Ibid., 523.

Union Artillery climbing Lookout Mountain.
Charles Carleton Coffin

September 8. They found very few Rebels, but did have to clear their share of felled trees and other material obstructing Stevens's Gap. Brigadier General John Beatty and his brigade cleared Cooper's Gap, driving off a small picket of Confederates. From there, Beatty could view a vast panorama to the east, which revealed "long lines of dust trending slowly to the south." Beatty "inferred from this that Bragg had abandoned Chattanooga."[22]

As usual in this difficult country, it took Negley's men all day on the 9th to descend to the valley below, where he concentrated his command at the foot of Stevens's Gap that evening. Thomas ordered him to start for La Fayette the next morning. Behind Negley, and available for support if needed, was Absalom Baird's division, though short one of its three brigades. Brannan's and Reynolds's divisions of the same corps had orders to move via Cooper's Gap as soon as they could follow, though they would be at least another day, and maybe two, behind.[23]

22 Beatty, *The Citizen-Soldier*, 330.

23 *OR* 30, pt. 3, 485.

At the eastern foot of Lookout, Negley found himself in a constricted V-shaped valley called McLemore's Cove. Ahead, the much smaller Pigeon Mountain lay between him and his objective. At least the intervening spine was not nearly as daunting as the previous ridges over which his men had labored. Pigeon was some 11 miles south of Stevens's Gap, an eastern offshoot of Lookout Mountain projecting like an angled thumb from a left hand. Pigeon Mountain was pierced by four main gaps, south to north as follows: Blue Bird, Dug, Catlett's, and Worthen's. La Fayette lay 10 miles farther east across the cove, through Dug Gap by the most direct route. Pigeon also provided a modicum of cover to Rebel forces in La Fayette. As it stood, Negley could only guess about what enemy forces awaited.

The intelligence on the subject was mixed. At midday on the 9th, Negley sent back word that locals informed him as many as "three or four divisions . . . moved up to Dug Gap" and were "making preparations . . . to resist our advance." That same evening at 8:30 p.m., however, another citizen told him that Bragg's main forces had fallen back southeast through Ringgold to Dalton, which was another 15 miles to the east. "All the information I have received this evening . . . induces the belief that there is no considerable rebel force this side of Dalton." Thomas forwarded all this information on to Rosecrans and instructed Negley to move on La Fayette the next morning.[24]

George Thomas remained wary of a trap, and ordered up the rest of his corps. Baird's division was to follow Negley directly, down through Stevens's Gap, while Reynolds and Brannan, all under Reynolds's direction, would descend the mountain via Cooper's Gap. Thomas wanted all four of his XIV Corps divisions in McLemore's Cove and in position to take La Fayette by force should it come to a fight. However, assembling the entire corps would take time. Negley, meanwhile, would have to proceed cautiously, and much more slowly than Rosecrans expected.[25]

And what of Bragg? He spent the day with Leonidas Polk at Lee and Gordon's Mills awaiting developments. Early on the morning of September 9, Confederate pickets tumbled back from Cooper's and Stevens's gaps bearing word of Yankees at both places. Intelligence identified them as Thomas's XIV Corps troops. Immediately Bragg halted Polk's Corps at the mills, letting D. H.

24 Ibid., 484, 486.

25 Ibid., 485.

Hill's men go on into La Fayette. He also directed Lieutenant Colonel Mauldin to place his 3rd Alabama Cavalry across the mouth of McLemore's Cove. Simon Buckner's column was directed to Rock Spring Church, between Polk and Hill, while William Walker's men continued trudging on to La Fayette.[26]

Bragg also once again redeployed his cavalry. On the afternoon of the 8th, upon finding Wharton at Summerville, Forrest decided to lead a probe of his own toward Alpine. This decision induced a change in attitude on Wheeler's part. The thus-far indolent Wheeler reversed his earlier reluctance to close with the Federals and ordered Wharton to take 300 handpicked men from his own division and go along. Slated to depart on the morning of the 9th, this combined force, 1,200 troopers strong, was slated to depart from Alpine for a reconnaissance across Lookout Mountain. This order might have developed into a significant fight on September 9 had Forrest's missions not been abruptly changed late on the 8th with a sudden order to ride back north to La Fayette. With two divisions at Rossville, Crittenden's XXI Corps was within 10 miles of Ringgold, and John Pegram's thin Southern cavalry screen was not doing much of a job slowing them down.[27]

Bragg also ordered Wheeler to send the rest of Will Martin's small division into McLemore's Cove to reinforce Mauldin and extend the cavalry screen opposing the XIV Corps. Lieutenant Colonel Milton L. Kirkpatrick's 51st Alabama was also already in the cove screening Pigeon Mountain. They did their best to blockade Dug and Catlett gaps in the hope of keeping the Yankees at bay, but it would take more than one regiment—a lot more—to stop Negley.

Wheeler, however, was still not focused on the mission at hand. "Shall I pursue raids?" he queried. The question could only have frustrated an already exhausted Bragg. The answer came back quickly: "you will divert no force except to protect our rear," Brent replied.[28]

As for Bragg, it did not take long to appreciate the fact that Negley's appearance at the eastern foot of Lookout Mountain was perhaps the opportunity he'd been seeking. The exact size of the Union force in McLemore's Cove was unknown on the night of the 9th, but even if it were Thomas's entire command, Bragg had four corps of infantry of his own close at

---

26 OR 30, pt. 4, 627, 629, and September 9, Brent Journal, WRHS.

27 OR 30, pt. 4, 615, 627-628; Jordan and Pryor, *Forrest's Cavalry*, 305-306.

28 OR 30, pt. 4, 629-630.

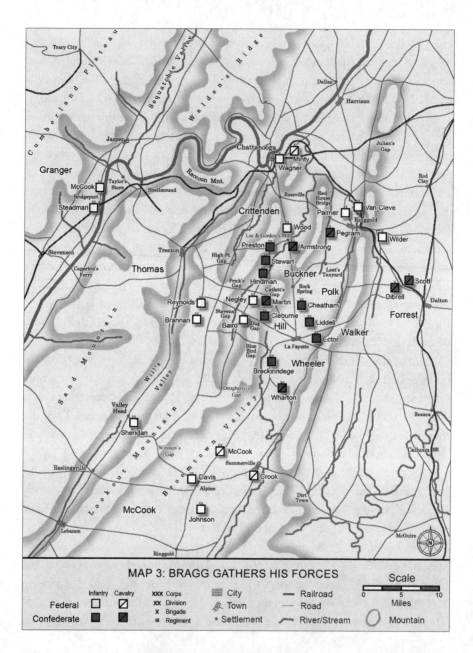

MAP 3: BRAGG GATHERS HIS FORCES

hand, or more than 40,000 men. This was more than enough to overwhelm a single Union corps. Instead of choosing one of these organizations to spearhead an attack, however, Bragg chose two divisions from two different corps to land his first blow against Rosecrans's over-extended army.

Close at hand as part of Polk's Corps was Thomas Carmichael Hindman's 7,200-man division formerly commanded by Maj. Gen. Jones Withers. Hindman joined the army in August, replacing the ailing Withers. In addition to losing Withers in the top slot, one of the division's best brigades under Walthall, five good Mississippi regiments, was on detached duty in Atlanta that summer serving as that city's garrison. As noted earlier, when Walthall returned, instead of rejoining his old command, his brigade was assigned to Liddell as part of the newly assembled Reserve Corps. Still, Hindman's command was one of the largest divisions in the army, and all of the men were well-seasoned veterans.[29]

At 10:00 p.m. on September 9, Hindman and Bragg met at army headquarters, where Bragg outlined his plans. Hindman was to move south toward Davis's Crossroads, where he would join with Pat Cleburne's division of D. H. Hill's Corps. Hill was already in La Fayette, and Cleburne deployed to watch the gaps in Pigeon Mountain, making Cleburne the obvious choice for the rendezvous. Once at Davis's Crossroads, the entire Confederate force, more than 12,000 strong, would turn west and "move on the enemy, reported to be 4,000 or 5,000 strong, encamped at the foot of Lookout Mountain at Stevens's Gap." While in Arkansas, Hindman had proven his offensive-mindedness. Hill had also already demonstrated a willingness to attack, as evidenced by his offer to cross the Tennessee River earlier in the week. In Bragg's eyes, Cleburne was one of the best divisional commanders in his army. The selection of these three men, thought Bragg, put the mission in the hands of the most aggressive officers available and ones who were recent enough arrivals to have not yet been infected with the recalcitrance that often seemed to affect senior officers in the Army of Tennessee. Hindman was to begin his movement at once, and establish contact with Hill once down in the cove.[30]

On the face of things, the orders were clear: move at once to pounce on whatever incautious Federal rats had poked their heads out of this particular hole and destroy them. Unfortunately for the Confederates, however, a number of factors complicated Bragg's instructions and a creeping confusion set into the otherwise promising operation.

The first was a report that another Union column of unknown strength descended Cooper's Gap, four miles north of Stevens's Gap, that same day.

29 August 31st, 1863, Field Returns of Hindman's Division, RG 109, NARA.

30 OR 30, pt. 2, 28.

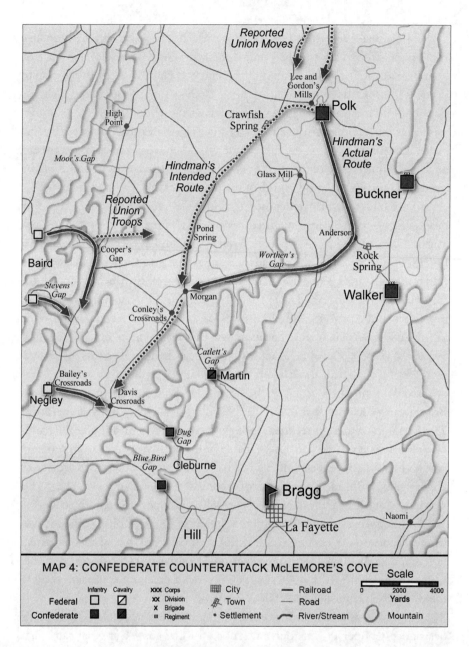

MAP 4: CONFEDERATE COUNTERATTACK McLEMORE'S COVE

Scale

	Infantry	Cavalry	XXX Corps	▦ City	— Railroad
Federal	□	◪	XX Division	🏛 Town	-- Road
Confederate	■	◪	X Brigade	• Settlement	〜 River/Stream
			III Regiment		◯ Mountain

0   2000   4000
Yards

The report was accurate and the column was John Beatty's brigade. Once down, Beatty marched to join Negley's main body. To the Rebels however, and especially to Hindman, the force at Cooper's Gap raised an ongoing concern about the security of Hindman's western flank. Accordingly, Hindman did not march directly south past Crawfish Springs and down into the cove; instead, he marched first to Dr. Anderson's house near Rock Spring before turning west through Worthen's Gap to enter the cove from the northeast. The route added several miles to the march.

A second complication was seeded inside the plan itself, which called for converging columns to join up en route to the enemy. Timing such affairs correctly was always tricky, as a fledgling Confederate army discovered at Shiloh in early April 1862. With imperfect communications, any one delay could be fatal to the entire plan.

A third hurdle arose because of the troops Bragg sought to employ. Instead of using a single cohesive corps for the job, Bragg pulled two divisions from two different corps, with overall authority given to a man new to the army. As noted above, Bragg had reasons for this decision, but it created both a conflicted chain of command and a new command relationship on the eve of what could well be a major battle.

Orders were issued for the operation and "Between 1 and 2 o'clock on the morning of September 10," Hindman noted, "I moved . . . from Lee and Gordon's Mills." Given the darkness the march was slow and fitful, with the dust and especially sketchy nature of the road through Worthen's Gap adding to the difficult movement. Hindman's column covered seven miles by dawn before halting near the Morgan farmstead at the mouth of the cove, "4 or 5 miles from Davis' [Crossroads.]" While the men slaked their thirst from the water of nearby West Chickamauga Creek, Hindman fretted. According to Bragg's plan, he should have heard from D. H. Hill by now, prior to their link-up at the Widow Davis's home. So far, no word from Hill had been received.[31]

Instead, Hindman was getting an earful from others, both from local citizens and some of Martin's cavalry scouts. Everything he heard troubled him. Reports now placed two Union divisions in the cove, one at Stevens' Gap and another already occupying Davis's Crossroads. If true, Federals were in force to both his front and right flank. Worse news was that Dug and Catlett's gaps to the east—the routes by which Hill was going to move to join him—were "so heavily blockaded as to be impassable." Hindman was beginning to feel like more like the prey instead of the predator.[32]

---

31 Ibid., 292-293.

32 Ibid., 293.

Bragg's orders to Hill went out at 11:45 p.m. on the 9th, at the same time Hindman's were issued. Hill, at La Fayette, was 13 miles away straight down the La Fayette Road. Davis's Crossroads was also 13 miles distant. Bragg expected Hill's orders to arrive well before Hindman's full column completed its march, allowing Hill more than ample time to either make the designated rendezvous on time or, if "unforeseen circumstances" delayed things, to "notify Hindman."[33]

Later, when describing the operation, Hill wrote that "Bragg's want of definite and precise information had led him more than once to issue "impossible" orders, and therefore those intrusted [sic] with their execution got in the way of disregarding them." In Hill's mind, the order to join up with Hindman was a perfect example of this phenomenon, and Hill treated it exactly as described.[34]

The order was nearly five hours in transit and did not reach Hill until 4:30 a.m. on the 10th, which meant that Hill couldn't keep Bragg's schedule even if he were of a mind to comply. However, that was only the first of many problems Hill foresaw. Cleburne's command was not concentrated and ready to move but scattered, with most of two brigades watching the southern approach to La Fayette. Additionally, Hill reported that Cleburne had been sick all day. Worse still, those same obstructions in Dug and Catlett's gaps that so worried Hindman also bothered Hill, and they would take hours to clear. In short, the movement Bragg planned was "impossible." Hill relayed all this back to Bragg and recommended that the operation be cancelled or at least postponed for 24 hours. Oddly, Hill failed to inform Hindman on the mistaken assumption that if the latter officer was already in the cove, there "could be no direct communication" with him now.[35]

By 8:00 a.m. Bragg had not only received Hill's reply but had also decided on an alternate course of action. Directly east of Hindman on the other side of Worthen's Gap at Rock Spring was Simon B. Buckner's entire corps, 9,500 men in two divisions. Bragg ordered Buckner to join Hindman as soon as he could, replacing Hill; the army commander also notified Hindman of the change,

33 Ibid., 28.

34 Hill, "Chickamauga," 646.

35 *OR* 30, pt. 2, 300.

enclosing a copy of Hill's reply. Despite Hill's difficulties, Bragg expected the attack to go on as ordered.[36]

Maj. Henry S. Foote of Buckner's staff was present at Bragg's headquarters that morning. On his way there, he fell in with an old friend, Nathan Bedford Forrest, who was also reporting to Bragg. Forrest was in an irritable mood. He "talked to me with much freedom," recalled Foote, "and said he was going to give the 'Gineral' a piece of his mind." Forrest, it will be recalled, had been sent dashing off to the south on September 7 to reinforce Wheeler, and then just as summarily ordered back north on the night of the 8th. Having force marched himself and Frank Armstrong's division 50 miles or more in the past two days, Forrest was doubtless annoyed and exhausted. Foote, however, counseled him "not to fool with Bragg."[37]

Bragg met with Forrest first and instructed him to "repair northward, to ascertain definitely the movements of the enemy in the direction of Chattanooga." McLemore's Cove was not the only place where Federals threatened, and Bragg needed better intelligence than he was getting so far from Pegram's cavalry. It was also apparent that Ringgold could not be held, and even Dalton was likely in danger. In response, Bragg ordered the Army of Tennessee's main depot to be moved back down the rail line to Resaca. Twenty-eight miles south of Ringgold, and about an equal distance east-southeast of La Fayette, Resaca should be safely beyond the enemy's immediate grasp. To be sure, Bragg also ordered half of the army's existing ordnance stores moved farther south, all the way to Atlanta.[38]

Bragg also took the precaution of sending an infantry brigade to Dalton. Brig. Gen. Bushrod R. Johnson's command of A. P. Stewart's division, Buckner's Corps, was a small one. It included four much-reduced Tennessee regiments and numbered only about 900 effectives, but it was all the force he could spare at the moment. Bragg's hope was that more reinforcements could be hurried up the railroad from Atlanta.[39]

---

36 Ibid.

37 Henry S. Foote, *Recollections of the Chickamauga Campaign* (n.p., n.d.), 3.

38 Jordan and Pryor, *Forrest's Cavalry*, 306; *OR* 30, pt. 4, 635.

39 Entry for September 10, Bushrod R. Johnson Diary, RG 109, NARA. Johnson's men were suffering greatly from the want of shoes. Colonel John Fulton would later report that no less than 225 men and two officers would be sent to the rear because they were barefoot.

Next came Major Foote of Buckner's staff. Once an admirer of Bragg's, Foote admitted that now "I did not like him" because "he had been unkind to some of my friends, and promoted incompetents." Foote delivered his own message, some matter of routine, and then hurried back to Buckner with the new orders. By 11:00 a.m. Buckner informed Hindman that he was en route, moving as fast as he could, but most of the afternoon would pass before Buckner could join him. During the agonizing wait Hindman inched his own force deeper into the cove, advancing a mile or so to Conley's Crossroads before again halting. Buckner reached Morgan's Crossroads at 4:45 p.m. and reported that fact to Hindman, who ordered him to stay put for the night; there was not enough water at Conley's for all three divisions. Besides, Hindman was still worried about the reputed Federal force at Cooper's Gap as a potential threat to his own right flank. With Buckner holding Morgan's crossroads, Hindman's own retreat route remained secure.[40]

Union division commander James S. Negley was no less cautious. He, too, felt as though he was putting his head in a potential trap. Despite the last intelligence he had received on the 9th suggesting the Rebels had evacuated La Fayette, Negley proceeded at a snail's pace across the floor of McLemore's Cove. His men moved out at 10:00 a.m. only to encounter William Martin's Confederate cavalry. Negley's advance skirmished with the Rebels more or less the entire way from Bailey's to Davis's Crossroads, where the main body of Federals halted. Negley pushed a reconnaissance toward Dug Gap. The patrol returned with unsettling news: the gap was "obstructed," recalled Brig. Gen. John Beatty, "and enemy in force on the right, left and front."[41]

Various sources were now suggesting that, far from retreating, the Rebels occupied La Fayette with most of their army. An indiscreet young Rebel lieutenant was the first to give the game away. The officer, captured that morning on the picket line, "was so defiant in his manner and boasted so loudly" that the Yankees were walking into a trap that Negley took heed. A little later, a young child strayed into the Union lines and revealed that a large number of Confederates were at his home only a mile distant. A friendly local slipped

---

40 Foote, *Recollections*, 3. Foote had served on Maj Gen. John P. McCown's staff, a senior officer Bragg had court-martialed for disobedience at Stones River (Murfreesboro), and who had been without a meaningful command since. Bragg's enmity toward McCown still rankled Foote. *OR* 30, pt. 2, 293.

41 Ibid., pt. 1, 326; Beatty, *The Citizen-Soldier*, 330.

into the Federal lines at 1:30 p.m. with word of "Buckner's Corps" approaching from the left. With his fears confirmed, Negley went over to the defensive and summoned help.[42]

Drawn by Negley's alarming reports, Thomas pulled up his mount at Negley's command post late on the afternoon of September 10 to confer with his subordinate. "An officer of the Thirty-Second Mississippi," recorded Thomas, blundered into Negley's lines while on picket. "He was not very communicative, but was generous enough to advise General Negley not to advance or he would get severely whipped." This and other information aroused Thomas sufficiently to ride back to his headquarters near Stevens's Gap and issued orders instructing all three of his remaining divisions to close up and be ready to support a concerted drive across Pigeon Mountain the following day. Absalom Baird's division, the closest of the trio, was ordered to descend the mountain that night and be ready to march to Negley's immediate support on the morning of the 11th. Thomas also noted that if Crittenden could move "one or two of his divisions" toward La Fayette, "it would very materially aid the advance of my corps." Finally, the burly Virginian lamented the lack of Wilder's mounted infantry brigade, "as I believe if I had it I could have seized Dug and Catlett's Gaps before the enemy."[43]

Baird's division was working its way down the east face of Lookout via Stevens's Gap, but would need all night to descend to the valley floor. At 9:00 p.m., with some of his force still descending, he responded to an inquiry from Negley by urging that general to consider falling back. Baird had only 2,800 men, being short not only one brigade but also a regiment each from his remaining commands, all of which were still back on the mountain or guarding trains. If Negley's fears were accurate, Baird reasoned, both divisions could easily be caught and crushed. As Negley understood it, however, Rosecrans remained in favor of pushing an advance and not falling back; nor would Thomas brook a retreat. Baird promised to depart at 3:00 a.m. on the 11th and join Negley in front of Dug Gap as soon as he could.[44]

---

42 Entry for September 10, Robert S. Dilworth Journal, Ohio Historical Society, Columbus, Ohio, hereafter Robert S. Dilworth Journal, OHS; Athearn, *Soldier in the West*, 138-139; OR 30, pt. 1, 326.

43 OR 30, pt. 3, 511.

44 Ibid., pt. 1, 271.

*   *   *

McLemore's Cove was not the only hotbed of activity. Rosecrans wanted all three of his corps pushed aggressively forward, and prodded each commander accordingly. While Bragg focused his efforts down in the cove, an entire Union corps was threatening his army from above, advancing south along the Western & Atlantic Railroad.

As he promised in his dispatch to Burnside, early on the 10th Tom Crittenden sent his XXI Corps south out of Chattanooga. Palmer's division, which was already at Rossville, led the way south by moving out along the Federal Road toward Ringgold southeast of Chattanooga. Van Cleve's division followed. This division was short Col. George F. Dick's brigade, which had been left behind as a garrison earlier in the campaign. Dick was now hurrying to catch up and that morning was on the far side of Lookout Mountain near Trenton, about 10 miles from Chattanooga. Tom Wood's division brought up Crittenden's rear, also moving with just two brigades after having left General Wagner's regiments to guard the Union's new prize of Chattanooga.[45]

Palmer was also short a brigade, for William Hazen's command was still en route to join him from Chattanooga after their crossing of the Tennessee the day before. Brigadier General Charles Cruft's brigade now led Palmer's column. Departing Rossville at 6:00 a.m., Cruft's advance was uneventful until it reached a ridge overlooking a narrow valley through which flowed Peavine Creek. He was about eight miles beyond Chattanooga and a bit less than three miles from the hamlet of Graysville, Georgia, the reported location of the nearest enemy forces. Palmer and Cruft could see Rebel cavalry across the creek. Cruft deployed four companies of the 1st Kentucky as skirmishers to lead the advance, and Palmer loaned him a small battalion of cavalry comprised of his own escort and some men from the 4th Michigan to help out. This combined force crossed the Peavine, driving back the Rebels. The rest of the brigade followed.[46]

The Rebel horsemen belonged to John Pegram's brigade, which had deployed across a wide front stretching from Lee and Gordon's Mills to Ringgold. Only the 6th Georgia and 6th North Carolina cavalry regiments were immediately available to oppose Cruft's push—far too few to hold off two

---

45 Ibid., 821.

46 Ibid., 723.

divisions of Yankees. When word of Cruft's advance reached Pegram, he rode his two regiments from Graysville to the Peavine Creek Bridge via an unfinished railroad bed unknown to Federal maps. Pegram sensed an opportunity. Most of his command was dismounted and deployed in a skirmish line astride the Ringgold Road, but part of the 6th Georgia remained horsed and in reserve. Pegram sent two companies of Georgians charging down the unfinished rail bed to strike the 1st Kentucky in flank. The result was all he could have hoped for: the tactical strike captured an entire company of bluecoats, 58 men, with scarcely a shot fired. The rest of the Federals quickly retreated across Peavine Creek.[47]

General Forrest arrived at the tail end of the action after having spent nearly three continuous days in the saddle. Ordered back to La Fayette late on September 8, he reached that place with his column the next day as Chattanooga fell into Union hands. After his interview with Bragg on the morning of the 10th, Forrest rode from that place to join Pegram. Initially he moved to Dalton, perhaps expecting to find Pegram falling back from Ringgold, but turned north just in time to witness the Graysville fight. Other than some escorts Forrest rode alone, for Armstrong's division had been diverted to help General Polk on the La Fayette Road. He arrived in time to see the Union prisoners being herded south. Forrest could be bloody-minded at times, a trait he exhibited now. "Shortly after Gen. Forrest came up," recalled a Rebel gunner, "and being told of the taking of the prisoners, he only regretted, in his blunt way, that they had not been killed in the fight." Pvt. John W. Minnich of the 6th Georgia Cavalry remembered that the prisoners were "*all Germans*, and they were a sulky set." Minnich tried repeatedly to converse with them, using "My Pennsylvania Saxon-Hollandic mixture, but all efforts to get a word from them were futile." At last Minnich gave up, contenting himself with a last, grumbled "*dumble kopf.*" Minnich and his fellow Georgians were happier with their captured rifles, Austrian muzzle-loaders of good quality, which nicely augmented their own motley assembly of weapons.[48]

The sudden reverse at Peavine Creek halted Palmer's advance for the day, and also enraged Cruft, who demanded to know how an entire company could be so easily captured. A flurry of explanatory reports over the next week would

47 Ibid., 723-725.

48 Gustave Huwald Letter, UNC; J. W. Minnich, "Unique Experiences in the Chickamauga Campaign," *Confederate Veteran,* vol. XXXV, No. 6 (June, 1927), 222.

attempt to explain just that, but in the meantime, Palmer was still poised to descend on Ringgold the next morning and there was nothing much to stop him beyond Pegram's cavalry. Even better (though he did not yet know it), Palmer's mounted strength was about to be significantly augmented: John T. Wilder's powerful brigade was now at hand. Wilder's men finished crossing the Tennessee at Friar's Island that morning and about 2:00 p.m. started moving south along the Western & Atlantic RR toward Ringgold, a track that paralleled Palmer's route. They pushed forward without any real opposition as far as Parker's Gap, three miles short of Graysville, and were now poised to threaten Pegram's flank when the advance resumed the next morning. While there, Wilder received a directive from Rosecrans ordering the Hoosier colonel to send the 92nd Illinois on a mission that revealed just how confident the army commander was feeling: the regiment was to report to Maj. Gen. Joseph Reynolds's division, Thomas's XIV Corps, "at La Fayette."[49]

Palmer's advance southeast from Chattanooga concerned Bragg because of its direct threat to his railhead if the Federals pressed as far as Dalton. The movement of Wood's division, however, proved even more immediately alarming. Wood left Chattanooga at 10:00 a.m. on September 10. "[We] started out to hunt the enemy, as he seemed at this time to be lost," came the wry observation of Lt. Col. Robert C. Brown of the 64th Ohio. Another Buckeye, Lt. Samuel Platt of the 26th Ohio, thought the march began well, noting "that a great many deserters [met] us on the road." Toiling along in the rear of the rest of the corps, the dust must have been terrific. Wood moved only a short ways past Rossville, halting east of Missionary Ridge. For the men of the 125th Ohio, it was a memorable camp next to "a large potato field. The boys dug up most of the crop inside of ten minutes," boasted the 125th's adjutant and future regimental historian, Charles T. Clark.[50]

The Federals were under the impression that Bragg was in full retreat. It came as a surprise, then, when Wood learned of "a considerable force on my right flank." He halted and sent word to Crittenden. The Southern force was reported to be at Lee and Gordon's Mills, no more than eight miles distant. As

---

49 Wilder Revised Report, November 26th, 1888, CCNMP; Baumgartner, *Blue Lightning*, 158.

50 Charles G. Brown, ed., *The Sherman Brigade Marches South: The Civil War Memoirs of Colonel Robert Carson Brown* (Charles G. Brown, 1995), 45; Entry for September 10, Samuel Platt Diary, Mahoning Valley Historical Society, Youngstown, OH; Charles T. Clark, *Opdyke Tigers: 125th O.V.I. A History of the Regiment and of the Campaigns and Battles of the Army of the Cumberland* (Spahr and Glenn, 1895), 85.

with Palmer's advance, Rebel cavalry, "in large numbers," seemed to be everywhere. Early that evening, observed the 64th Ohio's Lieutenant Colonel Brown, "two colored men came into camp" and confirmed the presence of Polk's Confederate infantry corps at the mills. The men were teamsters on their way back to Chattanooga and had unexpectedly run into the 64th Ohio, part of Charles Harker's brigade. "The negroes . . . seemed glad to see us," remembered Maj. Samuel L. Coulter of the 64th. They "had just been 'down to Massa Bragg's army with . . . supplies.'" When asked the location of Bragg's army, their answer proved a surprise. "Just down there three or four miles," came the answer, with "the old uncle . . . pointing to our right and rear." According to rumor, Bragg was there, too. Harker took the two men and their information to Wood, who doubted the claim but felt duty-bound to kick the news up the chain of command.[51]

The Rebel cavalry was indeed present, and more than a bit rattled by Wood's appearance. Initially, the roads leading out of Rossville were picketed by another of Pegram's regiments (Rucker's Legion). "At 8 a.m. one of Rucker's men came into camp with great haste, saying Rucker was being driven back and the enemy was only 1 1/2 miles off," noted Lt. William B. Richmond of Polk's staff. The news soon grew more alarming: "Rucker was in full retreat" and the enemy now only "three-quarters of a mile away." Polk put Frank Cheatham's infantry division on full alert and prepared to be attacked. No such blow landed. "The whole camp excited," wrote Richmond in disgust, "and all through the stampeding report of the cavalry." Polk appealed for a more sober-minded and reliable mounted force and was rewarded with the arrival early that afternoon of Frank Armstrong's entire division, diverted to the mills as Forrest was approaching the front.[52]

Armstrong soon set matters right, establishing an effective picket screen and providing a more accurate picture of the Union dispositions. While there was no immediate threat, he did discover the entire XXI Corps deployed between Peavine Creek and Rossville. In response, while operations in McLemore's Cove were running their course, Bragg decided that Polk, with

---

51 *OR* 30, pt. 1, 629; John J. Hight and Gilbert R. Stormont, *History of the Fifty-Eighth Regiment of Indiana Volunteer Infantry, Its Organization, Campaigns, and Battles from 1861 to 1865* (Press of the Clarion, 1895), 178; Brown, *Sherman Brigade*, 45; S. L. Coulter, "Taking of Chattanooga," *National Tribune*, November 12, 1885.

52 *OR* 30, pt. 2, 72.

only Cheatham at hand, should fall back to Dr. Anderson's where he would be less exposed, but still keep open a path of retreat for Hindman and Buckner should they need one. Frank Armstrong would remain in place, headquartered at the McDonald house on the La Fayette Road about five miles north of the mills, with instructions to fall back only if pressed.[53]

As far as Forrest was concerned, Bragg was being too cautious. After observing the check delivered to Palmer at Graysville, Forrest sent out a number of patrols to scout the Federal positions. He was sure that Crittenden's XXI Corps was vulnerable, strung out on the road between Rossville and Red House Bridge and well beyond any likely support from the rest of the Union army. "This intelligence he at once dispatched both to General Polk . . . and [Bragg]," at Lee and Gordon's Mills, "six miles distant." No reply was forthcoming. At midnight, Forrest and Pegram rode to the mills in search of Bragg to urge him to move against Crittenden's exposed columns. Bragg, however, was already gone, headed off to La Fayette to find D. H. Hill. Unaware of the larger movement drama unfolding in McLemore's Cove, and now thoroughly frustrated and tired, Forrest returned to his command believing a rare chance was slipping away. "Imagine Napoleon, Frederick, or the Duke of Wellington with such an opportunity," lamented the cavalryman's later biographers.[54]

Rosecrans was also bristling with impatience. His concern mostly focused on Negley's lack of progress toward La Fayette. "[T]his delay [is] imperiling both extremes of the army. . . . Your advance ought to have threatened La Fayette yesterday evening," he snapped at George Thomas in a dispatch the evening of September 10. Rosecrans also put little or no credence in Wood's reported Bragg sighting, informing Crittenden that "there have been several rumors within the last two days that General Bragg . . . [intends] to fight us between [Chattanooga] and La Fayette. These rumors, and particularly the story of the contraband, are hardly worth a moment's consideration." Though "they should be treated with total indifference if General Thomas' corps had reached La Fayette this morning," admitted the commander, these allegations could not be completely ignored. That night Rosecrans ordered Crittenden—who was also still in Chattanooga—to ride forward the next day and personally assess the

---

53 Ibid., 73.

54 Jordan and Pryor, *Forrest's Cavalry*, 307.

situation. If in Crittenden's judgment Bragg was in full retreat, his XXI Corps must press on to Ringgold, threatening Dalton or turn to La Fayette, depending on where the Rebels had gone. If Bragg was not in full withdrawal mode, Crittenden was authorized to "draw . . . back on Rossville." In the meantime, Wood was to keep one brigade at Rossville and send another to reconnoiter Lee and Gordon's Mills.[55]

Despite a difficult night ride from Chattanooga, Tom Crittenden saw no immediate need to break off his pursuit on September 11. Departing Chattanooga at 1:00 a.m., it took Crittenden five hours to traverse the roughly 10 miles to where General Palmer's division was camped along Peavine Creek—a delay Crittenden attributed to being "misled by the guide." When he reached the intersection of the Federal and La Fayette roads just beyond Rossville, Crittenden's guide took the right fork which led to La Fayette. They must have realized their mistake soon enough and reversed course, for Crittenden never made mention of encountering Armstrong's Confederate pickets who were only a short distance to the south.[56]

Captain John J. McCook and his small party, however, were not so lucky. McCook and a three-man escort left Chattanooga at 2:00 a.m. bearing written versions of the orders Rosecrans had already issued verbally to his XXI Corps commander. At Rossville, McCook was informed of Crittenden's wrong turn. Fearing the worst, the captain also hastened down the La Fayette Road to find him. Unlike his boss, he encountered Rebels. At 4:00 a.m., a quarter mile north of the small frame building known locally as Cloud's Store, McCook and his escort stumbled into Armstrong's pickets. Shots rang out in the darkness and the small party split, two men from the escort going to the left of the road while McCook and an orderly bore to the right. Assuming they had been fired on by mistake, the two men on the left pressed forward and were captured. McCook and the orderly turned tail and hastened away, reconnecting with Crittenden on the Federal Road after dawn.[57]

Crittenden's plan for the day was to continue on with Palmer and Van Cleve southeast to Ringgold. Palmer's division would move first to Graysville, with the trains of both divisions, and then turn south while Van Cleve would

55 OR 30, pt. 3, 511, 517.

56 Ibid., pt. 1, 603.

57 "First Firing On Chickamauga Battlefield," Interpretive Tablet, Fort Oglethorpe, GA.

take "the more direct route to Rossville over the hills." Tom Wood was ordered to send Col. Charles Harker's brigade over to the La Fayette Road and then south toward Lee and Gordon's Mills on a reconnaissance. Wood, meanwhile, was to take Buell's brigade and the divisional trains forward two miles to Peavine Creek in anticipation of joining the rest of the corps at Ringgold.[58]

If Crittenden was aware that Colonel Wilder was also about to move on Ringgold, the XXI Corps commander made no mention of it in his report. Nor did Wilder seem to be conscious that Crittenden's men were nearby. Wilder did send a strong patrol into Ringgold after dark on the 10th, four companies of the 72nd Indiana, who returned near midnight to report the town empty of Rebels. This was strange, for they should have encountered at least part of Confederate Col. John Scott's cavalry brigade (Pegram's division), which were charged with defending the town. Also present should have been some of Pegram's own mounted force, which of course had been opposing Critttenden's column at Peavine Creek. This was not the first time Scott's or Pegram's men would be lax in their picketing, and it would not be the last.[59]

Both Wilder and Crittenden's forces began marching shortly after sunrise, around 6:00 a.m. on September 11. Wilder placed Colonel Atkins's 92nd Illinois in the lead, reasoning that once through Ringgold, Atkins would be well-placed to break off from the main column and move toward La Fayette from the northeast, per their previous orders. About 8:00 a.m. they found the Rebels.

Atkins was advancing cautiously with two companies dismounted and deployed as skirmishers, so he was not overly surprised when he encountered Scott's Confederates a mile or so north of Ringgold. When the Confederate picket line fell back to its main body, Atkins dismounted the rest of the regiment and deployed in line of battle. "The Ninety-Second had scarcely formed," notes their regimental history, "when the enemy's line, about five hundred strong, moved out at a walk." Scott essayed a mounted charge, "but they were hotly received." The repulsed Rebels fell back leaving "thirteen of their dead upon the field." A second charge was equally unsuccessful. The sound of the fight quickly drew Wilder, who brought up a section of Capt. Eli Lilly's 18th Indiana Battery for support.[60]

---

58 *OR* 30, pt. 1, 711.

59 Ibid., 446.

60 *Ninety-Second Illinois Volunteers*, 102.

The two rifled cannon dropped trail in the road and began shelling the Confederates. Wilder ordered Maj. William T. Jones to bring up his 17th Indiana. "Our regiment dismounted and filed over to the left of the road," observed Assistant Surgeon George W. H. Kemper of the 17th, "passing over a large hill." Wilder, brash and aggressive by nature, was too impatient to wait for the 17th to come alongside Atkins's line. "Wilder ordered the [92nd] regiment forward, and forward it went, Wilder himself in the middle of the road, on the skirmish line, revolver in hand, and telling the boys on both sides of the road: 'Dress on me, boys.'"[61]

With a regiment moving in on their right flank and another advancing on them recklessly, Spencers barking, Scott's Rebels fell back. Wilder and the two companies astride the road moved forward so quickly that the rest of the regiment failed to keep pace, and Atkins ordered the rest of the command to remount and follow. As he did so, booming cannon fire from the southeast announced the arrival of the Union XXI Corps, specifically Col. Sidney M. Barnes's brigade of Van Cleve's division. The appearance of these Federals on Scott's left flank triggered an immediate retreat, which explains the abrupt collapse of resistance against Wilder's drive down the road.

Wilder's and Van Cleve's men swept into the streets of Ringgold, capturing the depot and a limited amount of commissary supplies; Forrest, Scott, and Scott's brigade managed to escape without serious loss. The Confederates recalled Scott's stand as "dogged," insisting that the fight north of Ringgold was "stubbornly maintained" for two hours. Scott only had 900 troopers and four cannon, however; Wilder's force alone outnumbered him twice over. The addition of Van Cleve's flanking column made any defense of the town impossible, and the Rebels fell back south of Tunnel Hill.[62]

The 8th Kentucky and 51st Ohio led the way into town, supported by the 35th Indiana and 99th Ohio, Van Cleve riding proudly in their midst. Surgeon Joseph T. Woods of the 99th Ohio witnessed the initial seizure of the town and the looting that followed. From "the little hill" that overlooked the village from the west, Woods could see the whole affair: "Women and children fled in terror. Many houses had been vacated their former occupants having gone south with

---

61 Entry for September 11, 1863, G. W. H. Kemper Diary, OHS; *Ninety-Second Illinois Volunteers*, 103.

62 Jordan and Pryor, *Forrest's Cavalry*, 307.

the Rebel army & our boys during the day pretty well cleaned out all that was eatable or destructable in that town."[63]

South of Ringgold, the Western & Atlantic tracks crossed Chickamauga Creek three times within a mile. The retreating Confederate cavalry stopped long enough to fire all three bridges, which were soon burning too steadily to be extinguished by the pursuing Yankees. Some of Barnes's men pursued as far as the second bridge before breaking off the chase. Though it was still well before noon Van Cleve halted his division there and went into camp near the Stone Church chapel. Corps leader Crittenden established his headquarters in town and ordered up Palmer's division, which was still en route from Graysville with the trains.

Crittenden and his two divisional commanders had reason to be optimistic. Both Palmer and Van Cleve had a detached brigade rejoin them this day, strengthening Crittenden's force in Ringgold by one-third. Palmer also recorded the heady news provided to them by Rebel prisoners and panicked locals: "a hundred sources . . . all pointed to Rome, Ga. as the point fixed for the concentration of the whole rebel army." The road to Dalton, some 15 miles to the south and just beyond the imposing edifice of Rocky Face Ridge, appeared to be completely open except for the same Rebel cavalry they had driven so handily from Ringgold.[64]

Once in Ringgold, John T. Wilder split his command. Colonel Atkins and his 92nd Illinois left the brigade to report to the XIV Corps, turning back up the Rossville Road to make the journey. Wilder's other four regiments pushed south as far as Tunnel Hill, two-thirds of the way to Dalton.

The only potential check to Crittenden's optimism came from his First Division commander, Tom Wood. That morning, one of Wood's brigades under Charles Harker left its camps along the Federal Road and marched southeast to the La Fayette Road. Harker's orders were to reconnoiter as far as Lee and Gordon's Mills. Major Coulter of the 64th Ohio brought along the two captured black teamsters who, despite having been taken into custody and lost their wagons to confiscation, seemed happy to help. Speaking to the oldest of the pair, "we gave him to understand in very positive terms that if his story was

---

63 "Dear Sister Sade & all at home," Sept 12, 1863, Joseph T. Woods Papers, Duke University, Durham, NC.

64 These were Brig. Gen. William B. Hazen's and Colonel George Dick's brigades, belonging to Palmer and Van Cleve, respectively. *OR* 30, pt. 1, 711.

not true the most terrible consequences would befall him. To this he replied, 'Take dis darkey along, and if what he say is not true, just cut his head off.'"[65]

The old gentleman's head was secure. Colonel Emerson Opdyke of the 125th Ohio described the movement to his wife the next day. From almost the moment they swung onto the La Fayette Road, "firing soon commenced, and our brigade drove two brigades of rebel cavalry for nine miles." Upon reaching Lee and Gordon's Mills about midday, Harker's men drove the Rebels back across West Chickamauga Creek, establishing a picket line on the far bank. They halted on the hill overlooking the crossing. Evidence of a large Confederate presence was everywhere. Major Coulter alertly noted the presence of "extensive camps which showed signs of recent occupation."[66]

In response, Rosecrans dashed off an order that afternoon sending General Wood and his remaining brigade to reinforce Harker. Wood wasted no time. Leaving the Federal Road, he moved south on a cross-path to the Reed's Bridge Road, where he could double back westward to the La Fayette Road. He met no opposition, though he did find yet more evidence of the Rebel presence: the remains of a large camp of five regiments of Confederate cavalry. At Reed's Bridge, the troops hastily re-floored the structure since the original planking had been torn up by enemy horsemen. Wood reached Harker about 8:30 p.m. "It seems the story of the contraband was not so far off the mark," Wood admitted. "Harker says that not only was General Bragg here yesterday, but also generals Polk and Hill, with a large force of infantry and cavalry."[67]

Wood's information confirmed similar intelligence from Thomas's XIV Corps operating farther west on the other side of La Fayette. The Rebels were not running south as fast as they could; they were in strength in and around La Fayette, although how strong remained to be determined. Whether they would stay there was another question. Other information, perhaps not as reliable, suggested Bragg was still in retreat mode. When Colonel Opdyke of the 125th Ohio, part of Harker's brigade, relayed word that "a bright mulatto" claiming to be one of Bragg's servants who "deserted him last night [and] says Bragg was

---

65 Coulter, "Taking of Chattanooga."

66 Glenn V. Longacre and John E. Haas, eds., *To Battle for God and the Right: The Civil War Letterbooks of Emerson Opdyke* (University of Illinois Press, 2003), 94; Coulter, "Taking of Chattanooga."

67 This would only be the first of several times the bridge would have to be re-planked. *OR* 30, pt. 3, 548. The camp remains were almost certainly from those of John Pegram's troops.

going to Rome and Atlanta with 25,000 men," someone at army headquarters shot back that Opdyke should "keep the bright mulatto and keep a bright look out for Bragg." Tongue-in-cheek humor aside, the Confederate force at La Fayette could no longer be ignored. September 12 would see Crittenden's advance down the rail line curtailed, and then diverted to join Wood at the mills.[68]

*   *   *

September 11 was a long and trying day for Nathan Bedford Forrest. He had only Scott's brigade with which to oppose the Union advance on Ringgold. John Pegram's brigade still stretched to the southwest, hanging onto the fringes of Van Cleve's columns and maintaining the picket line between Ringgold and Frank Armstrong's troopers at Lee and Gordon's Mills. Pegram's force numbered about 1,900 men, more than double Scott's estimated 900 troopers, but Pegram had to cover the 10-mile gap yawning between Armstrong and Scott. The result was that he could not concentrate a significant force to impede Horatio Van Cleve's advance. Pegram had to content himself with attempting several smaller raids against Union supply trains moving back and forth between Ringgold and Rossville.

Just before dark Forrest received welcome reinforcements with the arrival of Col. George Dibrell's 2,200 troopers. Detached from Armstrong, Dibrell led what the men styled "Forrest's Old Brigade." They were all Tennesseans, they were all veterans, they were well known to Forrest, and they were far more dependable in his mind than anyone riding with Scott's command. Sometime on the morning of September 11, Forrest ordered Armstrong to send Dibrell's brigade on a reconnaissance to Dalton. When he reached that place and found it quiet, Dibrell spurred his mounts north and joined Forrest just south of Tunnel Hill.[69]

With Wilder's Federals pushing close on his heels, after dark the impatient Forrest decided to head up a reconnaissance back into Tunnel Hill. Characteristically, Forrest chose to lead this mission himself, despite the fact that he was now a corps commander and responsible for the coordination of roughly 8,000 men. Leading his personal escort company, Forrest passed the

68 *OR* 30, pt. 3, 549.

69 Jordan and Pryor, *Forrest's Cavalry*, 307.

picket line of the 5th Tennessee Cavalry northward into Tunnel Hill, which was currently hosting Wilder's brigade. Lt. William G. Allen of the 5th Tennessee had an unfortunate encounter with the famous man. Allen had orders to let no one pass. He tried to stop Forrest until he was dressed down by the angry general. The experience rankled Allen, who bore a grudge thereafter: "I formed an unfavorable opinion of him [Forrest] because he rode rough shod over me while on duty." Forrest should have listened to Allen. A short distance beyond the general and his party rode into the Union picket line, which let loose a well-aimed volley that wounded Forrest and two of his escort. Another one of Forrest's staff officers, Lt. Matt Cortner, was captured by the 98th Illinois Mounted Infantry.[70]

The ball struck Forrest in his back within an inch of the old wound suffered just after Shiloh. Luckily for the Confederates it was not nearly as serious as his earlier injury. One account recalled that the general, "faint from pain and loss of blood . . . took a drink of whiskey at the surgeon's urging but did not leave the field." His earliest biographers, however, merely noted that he was "little disturbed" by the wound. Forrest also learned nothing from this affair that he did not already know: the Yankees held Tunnel Hill in force and showed no signs of withdrawing.[71]

*   *   *

Meanwhile, far to the south, McCook's XX Corps and Union cavalry were also still not making enough progress to suit Rosecrans. On September 9, goaded by Rosecrans's most recent missive, the cavalry descended to Alpine, the little village in Broomtown Valley at the eastern foot of Lookout. The cavalry was now in the hands of Brig. Gen. George Crook, since Stanley was increasingly incapacitated by dysentery. For the moment Stanley was still

---

70 William G. Allen Memoirs, TSLA; Entry for September 11, 1863, Edward Kitchell Diary, Abraham Lincoln Presidential Library, Springfield, IL, hereafter ALPL. Kitchell recorded Cortner's name as Lieutenant Cortue. Confederate documents show that Lt. Matthew Cortner was captured just before Chickamauga and later paroled and exchanged. Discussion with historian Michael R. Bradley, May 10, 2005.

71 By a Confederate, *The Grayjackets: And How They Lived, Fought, And Died, For Dixie* (Jones Brothers and Co., 1867), 356-357; Welsh, *Medical Histories*, 71; Jordan and Pryor, *Forrest's Cavalry*, 307.

nominally in charge, but it would be Crook who would exercise tactical command.[72]

Finding the main road through Henderson's Gap blocked with felled trees that morning, Crook's column detoured to a second road, which was similarly blockaded. These obstacles, which Wheeler had claimed would present an "almost insuperable difficulty" for his own troopers, were removed in short order by the Yankees. As one officer in the 4th Ohio put it, "Before we left camp, 20 men were detailed from each Reg't with axes & they did their work so well that the column was delayed only a short time." By noon, the Yankees had reached the eastern foot of Lookout Mountain and were skirmishing with the Rebels. Elements of two of Wharton's regiments, the 8th Texas and 4th Georgia Cavalry, contested the pass for a while, but were unable to stop a full brigade of Federals. That night the Rebels retreated northeast to Summerville, about half the distance to La Fayette. The Federal success was not without cost, however: the 1st Ohio Cavalry alone recorded 30 casualties in the engagement. Behind them came Davis's division, climbing the mountain's western face and halting up top, ready for their turn to descend and support the cavalry the next day on the 10th.[73]

Like Crittenden's men far to the north, Gen. Jefferson C. Davis was still clearly expecting Bragg to run and not fight. "Old Bragg has left Chattanooga and is coming down the valley. . . . We [will] have a pretty hot time over there," he informed Lieutenant Mosman of the 59th Illinois early that morning. Mosman was in Sidney Post's brigade and on picket when the general rode up. Belying these combative sentiments, however, Mrs. Davis and Mrs. Pope soon rode by: "These ladies must want to see a fight-fairly spoiling for it seems; to be riding to the front that way."[74]

---

72 Crook, *Autobiography*, 104. Crook noted that "General Rosecrans's letter would have made almost any officer ill."

73 Entry for September 9, 1863, James Thompson Diary, 4th Ohio Cavalry file, CCNMP; Entry for September 9, 1863, William E. Crane Diary, 4th Ohio Cavalry, George Thomas Papers, RG 94, NARA; Anonymous, *Proceedings of the Thirtieth Annual Reunion, 1st O.V.V.C.* (n.p. 1909), 16. Had General Forrest not been recalled northward the day before, this might have been a more substantial fight, as 900 men of Dibrell's Brigade would also have been present. Many of these thirty must have been lightly wounded, since official tallies of the fight recorded only four killed and six wounded in the action.

74 Mosman, *Rough Side of War*, 76.

There would be no fight that day, however, because McCook's men still had to get over Lookout Mountain. Brig. Gen. William Carlin's brigade led Davis's column, and the only action they saw was a minor fracas over some peaches. Capt. William C. Wheeler of Company C, 81st Indiana and some of his men were gathering the fruit when a party of Rebels found them. In the ensuing skirmish over the juicy northern Georgia delicacy, "there was . . . much strategy on the part of the captain," noted an amused Carlin. Otherwise, the advance was unopposed. By nightfall, McCook and Davis's men were at Alpine, Gen. Richard Johnson's division was close by, also in Broomtown Valley, while Phil Sheridan's division and Sidney Post's brigade remained west of the mountain with the corps trains.[75]

While the infantry were toiling up and down mountain gaps, Crook was ordering out patrols. Colonel Eli Long, with the Second Brigade of Crook's division, rode toward La Fayette; two brigades of Col. Edward McCook's First Division made a probe as far as the hamlet of Milville on the road to Rome. Colonel Louis D. Watkins's brigade, also of the First Division, headed for Summerville. That town was last reported as occupied by John Wharton's Rebels, but once again contact was sporadic and slight. Crook and Long saw no fighting at all. They did bring back word of the growing concentration of Confederates in La Fayette, including "all the cavalry force of Bragg's army." Watkins met and drove Wharton's pickets "through the town [Summerville] without serious resistance, while McCook discovered (via a captured dispatch) that Rome was garrisoned by an infantry division. On September 11th, with infantry support now close at hand, the semi-invalid Stanley prepared to make a further effort to uncover the Rebel positions and movements, sending out cavalry patrols to Summerville and toward Rome.[76]

In the meantime, Bragg sprang his trap in McLemore Cove.

---

75 Gerardi and Hughes, *Carlin Memoires*, 94; OR 30, pt. 1, 486.

76 Ibid., 889.

Chapter Five

McLemore's Cove:
September 11, 1863

James Negley's Union division was vulnerable in McLemore's Cove, and Braxton Bragg was determined to crush him.

Union activity in the form of Tom Crittenden's XXI Corps north of La Fayette and along the Western & Atlantic Railroad potentially threatened the viability of the counterattack in the cove, but it did not dissuade Bragg from the effort. Instead the hazard in his rear acted as a catalyst, spurring him into decisive action. The window for damaging the Federals in the cove was narrowing by the hour as Yankee activity along the railroad increased the threat against Bragg's own supply depot at Dalton. To lose Dalton was to lose La Fayette, and if that occurred Bragg would have no choice but to fall back on Resaca or risk being trapped and destroyed. Using interior lines to his advantage, he would quickly fall upon and crush Negley and then turn and deal with Crittenden before Dalton fell into enemy hands.

Given the approaching XXI Corps threat, the slow progress on September 10 made for a frustrating day. Still, Bragg managed to accept D. H. Hill's excuses with outward equanimity, and issue orders reinforcing Thomas Hindman with Simon Buckner. He did take a moment to warn Hindman that time was slipping away. Before leaving Lee and Gordon's Mills for La Fayette, Bragg dispatched a pair of messages to Hindman. The first, at 6:00 p.m., noted Crittenden's move south and the need for urgency: "It is highly important that you should finish the movement now going on as quickly as possible." Ninety minutes later, in a more encouraging tone, he added, "the enemy is now divided. Our force at or near La Fayette is superior. . . . It is important now to move vigorously and crush him." Immediately on the heels of that 7:30 p.m. missive, Bragg and staff decamped for La Fayette, there to confer with Hill and supervise what Bragg hoped would be a morning descent upon Negley's isolated Federals.[1]

From a distance, Hindman's aggressive attitude and reputation as a fighter, not as of yet poisoned by the discontent simmering in the Army of Tennessee, made him the logical choice to lead the attack in McLemore's Cove. In reality, Hindman's presence was not greeted with enthusiasm by at least two of his new subordinates, Brig. Gens. James Patton Anderson and Arthur M. Manigault. In addition, Bragg would soon have reason enough to call into question the division commander's field abilities in this first important operation undertaken at Bragg's direction.

Cracks in the Hindman competency portrait began to appear shortly after he assumed command. What had been a fine division was within a short time wracked with dissention. "[T]he change was truly an unfortunate one," lamented Manigault. "[Hindman] had a reputation of being a desperate fighter, good disciplinarian, but a scheming, maneuvering, political general, with whom it was dangerous to come in contact." The Arkansas transplant, thought the South Carolinian, "was certainly a man of talent," but he was also the "most slippery intriguer I ever met with. Our Division, from being the first in point of numbers, drill, efficiency, and discipline . . . sank to that of a third-rate one."[2]

None of Hindman's brigade commanders were professionals, though all had seen volunteer service in the Mexican War. Patton Anderson had the most varied antebellum career. He started as a doctor in Mississippi, raised a battalion for the Mexican War, served in the state legislature, and was appointed U.S. Marshal to the Washington Territory. At the outbreak of the Rebellion, Anderson was an enthusiastic delegate to the Florida secession convention and later appointed colonel of the 1st Florida. Both a Bragg loyalist (he and his wife

---

1   OR 30, pt. 2, 301; Entry for September 10, Taylor Beatty Diary, UNC. This was the same evening that Forrest came calling, near midnight, to outline his own observations about the vulnerability of Crittenden's position, only to find Bragg already gone.

2   R. Lockwood Tower, ed., *A Carolinian Goes to War: The Civil War Narrative of Arthur Middleton Manigault* (University of South Carolina Press, 1983), 78-79.

Thomas C. Hindman (right) along with Simon B. Buckner (facing page), were charged with delivering Bragg's masterstroke in McLemore's Cove.

Miller, The Photographic History of the Civil War

were friends of the Braggs) and a seasoned brigadier, having risen to that rank early in the war in February 1862, Anderson led his brigade well at Shiloh and then a four-brigade division in Kentucky at Perryville. When the army was reorganized in the fall of 1862, Anderson was shifted into Jones Withers's division, where he once again saw heavy action, this time at Stones River (Murfreesboro). Withers's frequent illnesses and absences meant that, for much of the time, Anderson had been acting as de facto division commander. He had every reason to expect to receive command of the division, but Hindman was inserted over him. This bit of restructuring could only have been a grave disappointment.[3]

Command rivalry was not confined to the top slot. There was trouble between Anderson and Manigault as well. The South Carolinian viewed Anderson as something of a competitor for his own ambitions. After the Perryville campaign, Bragg nominated Manigault along with a list of other colonels for promotion. When the new list of brigadiers came down a month later, Manigault's name was nowhere to be seen—a blow to the low country aristocrat's pride. Worse was to follow. "I was not a little mortified that a General Patton Anderson had been assigned to the command of our brigade," admitted Manigault. Withers, who was the division commander at the time, intervened and moved Anderson to another brigade whose commander was also absent, allowing Manigault to lead his brigade into action at Murfreesboro. Manigault was finally promoted to brigadier in April 1863. Both the sting and the stain remained, however, and he continued to bear a strong grudge against

---

3   Warner, *Generals in Gray*, 7; A. Ellarwell to J. Patton Anderson, Jan 31, 1864, J. Patton Anderson Papers, University of Florida, includes a discussion of Anderson's hopes for promotion and trouble finding an appropriate command.

the Floridian. While he blamed Hindman for many of the organization's ills, Manigault also believed that Anderson, as "senior brigadier . . . also had much to do with [the] deterioration" of the division.[4]

Men in the ranks echoed similar resentments when confronted with Hindman's dictatorial manner and lack of tact. Just two weeks after his assumption to command, Pvt. Tom Hall, a new recruit to the 24th Alabama, witnessed an unfortunate encounter at the end of August with the general and his staff. "All I have to fear now is our new general," Hall informed his father. "Hindman has proven himself to be a regular low life rowdy for what he done the other night. Our division was on the march until about two [a.m.] When we halted Gen. Hindman found Polk's staff camped on the spot [he picked] and he went up and roused them calling them . . . 'unprincipled curs.' To say the least he was challenged to a duel which he did not accept."[5]

The one exception to this brewing stew of resentment seemed to be Zachariah C. Deas. Born in South Carolina but by the war's outbreak a wealthy cotton broker in Mobile, Deas raised the 22nd Alabama for the war in the fall of 1861. Wounded at Shiloh, he returned in time to fight at Perryville and be promoted from the same list that included Manigault, though he was ill during the Murfreesboro combat.

Bragg, who had proven remarkably obtuse about his own level of popularity among his senior subordinates, was almost certainly oblivious to the discontent within Hindman's new command. That would soon change.[6]

The night before the planned McLemore's Cove counterattack was marked by two fateful councils, both of which revealed significant differences between Bragg and his commanders. The first occurred while Bragg was riding to La Fayette. Called into being by Hindman, this first conference included all three of Hindman's brigadiers (Manigault, Anderson, and Deas), Simon B. Buckner, and both of his divisional commanders (A. P. Stewart and William Preston). Once the talking started, Hindman's lack of confidence became apparent.

---

4 Tower, *A Carolinian Goes to War*, 53, 62, 79. One of Manigault's transgressions, apparently, was that he authored a letter critical of the Davis administration that inadvertently became public at about this time.

5 Charles T. Jones, Jr., "Five Confederates: The Sons of Bolling Hall in the Civil War," *Alabama Historical Quarterly*, Vol. 24 (1962), 179.

6 Bragg's genuine surprise that his ill-advised questionnaire of the previous spring found that a majority of his officers wanted him to step down captures this obliviousness perfectly.

Initially, Hindman showed the assembled officers a note he intended to send to D. H. Hill asking Hill to attack first, with his own force falling upon the Union flank once Hill had the enemy's full attention. It was about then that Bragg's two messages about Crittenden's movement arrived, and when they did Hindman's focus shifted. Crittenden's advance rattled the Arkansan, who now seemed to see enemies on all sides. If the Federals advanced via Crawfish Spring, he reasoned, they might bypass Benjamin Cheatham entirely and fall on Buckner at Morgan's farm. Additionally, "there was . . . an unknown force of the enemy within striking distance on our right, and another force in our front probably equal to our own." Even worse, "we were hemmed in by Pigeon Mountain," with Dug and Catlett's gaps still blockaded. This litany of dangers worried everyone and triggered what can only be described as command paralysis. The "unanimous" conclusion of all present was to do nothing without "more definite information." Hindman summarized the conference and its conclusion in a note to Bragg and asked for stronger assurance that Hill could indeed force Dug Gap.[7]

Unwittingly echoing Forrest, Hindman also included in this dispatch a proposal to turn and strike at Crittenden. Hindman reasoned that if the Rebels "crushed that corps . . . [we] would destroy one-third of the enemy's force and leave all of our own united to contend against the balance." Hindman envisioned making this move with his own men, Buckner's Corps, Cheatham's division, and possibly D. H. Hill's force. Once the dispatch outlining these factors was written, Hindman entrusted it to Maj. James Nocquet, Buckner's chief engineer, and sent him riding off to find Bragg at La Fayette. Once Nocquet set his spurs, Hindman dispatched a series of patrols to the north, south, and west. [8]

Hindman's sudden desire to turn on Crittenden's XXI Corps might have made sense if the army was not already committed to a major attack in the cove. It would take a great deal of time to reposition in essence three corps of Rebel infantry to accomplish the goal; there was no indication Rosecrans would sit idly by and let Bragg have his way. Crittenden's men, meanwhile, were at least 20 miles away. There was an equally or more vulnerable Federal column just

7   William Glenn Robertson, "The Chickamauga Campaign: McLemore's Cove," *Blue & Gray Magazine*, vol. XXIII, No. 6 (Spring, 2007), 42; *OR* 30, pt. 2, 294.

8   *OR* 30, pt. 2, 294.

Bragg's old messmate, Daniel Harvey Hill.
Miller, The Photographic History of the Civil War

three miles distant, outflanked and outnumbered if only the Rebels could lurch themselves into violent action. There was an additional advantage in striking Thomas first. A successful counterattack would crush or at least cripple the XIV Corps and perhaps drive it back across Lookout Mountain. A success in McLemore's Cove would leave Bragg's army directly between two wildly divided wings of the Federal army, and thus able to turn on either at will. For a number of reasons Bragg's desire to strike Negley first was the correct strategic choice.

While Hindman was taking counsel of his fears, Bragg reached La Fayette at 11:30 p.m. and conferred with Hill. Also present were Pat Cleburne, W. H. T.

Walker (commanding the newly formed Reserve Corps), and division commander St. John Liddell. Also expected but not yet present was Brig. Gen. William T. Martin, whose cavalry was the primary source of Bragg's information concerning the Federals in the cove.

Among them Bragg encountered Cleburne first. The Irishman was "surprised . . . that Hill should have reported him sick." In fact Cleburne was not ill at all, and had been active with his troops the entire day. Bragg apparently said nothing to Hill about this inconsistency, but it bothered him. He would later accuse Hill of deliberately lying about Cleburne's illness and see it as further evidence of Hill's "querulous, insubordinate spirit." For the moment, however, the officers got on with the important business at hand.[9]

Hill was still mostly concerned with Union General McCook's presence at Alpine and dismissed Negley's force at Davis's Crossroads as a feint. Bragg understood that Alpine was another 20 miles south, and there was still time to damage Negley, feint or not. At midnight he drafted another order to Hindman reiterating Crittenden's movements, Cheatham's deployment so as to protect Hindman's and Buckner's rear, and the need for all the involved commands to strike as early as possible. Shortly thereafter, staffer Nocquet arrived bearing Hindman's missive.

James Nocquet was known to Bragg—and not in a good way. A Frenchman, Nocquet's "disdain for Americans was notorious, and his English language skills were absymal." Before attaching himself to Buckner, Nocquet served as an engineer for Bragg for all of one month, which was all it took for Bragg to fire him as an incompetent. It is difficult to imagine anyone in the entire army who could have been a worse messenger selected to explain Hindman's and Buckner's views to their boss.[10]

Nocquet began detailing Hindman's fears and speculations. General Martin pulled up his mount soon thereafter. The cavalryman "found a major of engineers in broken English giving . . . a very incoherent report of the . . . situation." An exasperated Bragg cut Nocquet short midway through his effort, his anger at the entire sad state of affairs having reached the boiling point. The army commander spread a map of the area out on the table and instructed,

---

9 Bragg to E. T. Sykes, February 8, 1873, quoted in Edward T. Sykes, "Walthall's Brigade, A Cursory Sketch with Personal Experiences of Walthall's Brigade, Army Of Tennessee C.S.A. 1862-1865," *Mississippi Historical Society Publications, Centenary Series I*, (1916), 611.

10 Robertson, "Chickamauga: McLemore's Cove," 43.

"Major, I wish you to tell me nothing but what you know as a fact." It was a good question, but the answer could not have pleased Bragg: there was very little he knew as fact. Most of Hindman's information, stammered out Nocquet, "was only what he had heard and he could not say that it was reliable." Martin stepped forward at Bragg's request and refuted Nocquet point by point. Hindman's orders would stand. Bragg told Nocquet to return to Hindman at once bearing new instructions.[11]

"I was so greatly vexed," Bragg admitted later, "that my deportment toward General Hill and Major Nocquet during the conference was observed by my staff and intimation given me of some harshness." A snarling Bragg told his chief of staff Mackall to draft new instructions emphasizing Hindman "was to attack the enemy [even] if he lost his command in carrying out the order." Gloomy as ever, Mackall pointed out that Hindman had already been sent similarly peremptory orders. He nonetheless instructed Colonel Brent to draft the new note and then passed it to a courier. The wording of this midnight order would prove more controversial than any of the immediate participants could have imagined. It read as follows:

HEADQUARTERS, ARMY OF TENNESSEE,
La Fayette, Ga., September 10, 1863 - 12 p.m.

Major-General HINDMAN,
    Commanding, &c.
GENERAL: Headquarters are here, and the following is the information: Crittenden's corps is advancing on us from Chattanooga. A large force from the south has advanced to within 7 miles of this point. Polk is left at Anderson's to cover your rear. General Bragg orders you to attack and force your way through the enemy to this point at the earliest hour that you can see him in the morning. Cleburne will attack in front the moment your guns are heard.
    I am, general, &c.

GEORGE M. BRENT
Assistant Adjutant-General

For added emphasis, Bragg "verbally directed the major [Nocquet] to return to General Hindman and say that my plans could not be changed, and

---

11 William T. Martin to Bragg, 1867, William T. Martin Letters, CCNMP; *OR* 30, pt. 2, 311.

that he would carry out his orders." With that, the chastened Frenchman hurried away sometime after midnight. The orders of course encompassed rather then excused D. H. Hill, who would have to see that Cleburne's division was in position to attack by daylight on the 11th.[12]

Bragg's midnight order reached Hindman at 4:20 a.m. The division leader read the note and put a curious construction on it. To the Arkansan, the important part of the order was the repeated news of Crittenden. Read as a warning, this suggested to Hindman that "the general commanding considered my position a perilous one . . . [and he] expected me not to capture the enemy, but to prevent capture of my own troops." The attack toward Dug Gap was not aimed at crushing Negley; rather, it was designed at "forcing my way through to La Fayette, and thus saving my command." For Hindman, the note confirmed his view: the whole affair was now a desperate effort to save his command rather than crush an exposed enemy. Brent's poor wording opened the door to yet another major point of confusion and controversy.[13]

Over the next two hours Hindman's compass-point patrols returned bearing little useful information. The scout up the road to Crawfish Spring found nothing. From Davis's Crossroads, word returned to only confirm that Negley was indeed still there. About 5:30 a.m. the patrol sent west to find out what Federals were at Stevens's Gap returned empty-handed. The mounted men had spent the night detained by some of Martin's troopers who thought they were spies. Hindman dispatched a second party west with orders to return by 7:00 a.m., which was also the time set for the entire command to move south.

Nocquet reached Hindman at 6:30 a.m. bearing Bragg's verbal coda that his plans could not be changed, "and that he would carry out his orders." In keeping with the spirit of the night, the Frenchman garbled the message. "Hill expected me to make the attack and would co-operate," wrote Hindman, but claims Nocquet told him that Bragg said "I should execute my own plans and he [Bragg] would sustain me." This final sentence was nonsense, of course. Hindman was not to "execute his own plans" but instead carry out Bragg's very emphatic instructions "unchanged." In a comedy of errors that would have been difficult to script, Nocquet's extracurricular addendum served only to

12 Bragg to Sykes, February 8, 1873, in "Walthall's Brigade," 612; *OR* 30, pt. 2, 29. Note that the order found in the *OR* is timed 12:00 p.m. This is in error; the order should actually show the time as 12:00 a.m.

13 *OR* 30, pt. 2, 295.

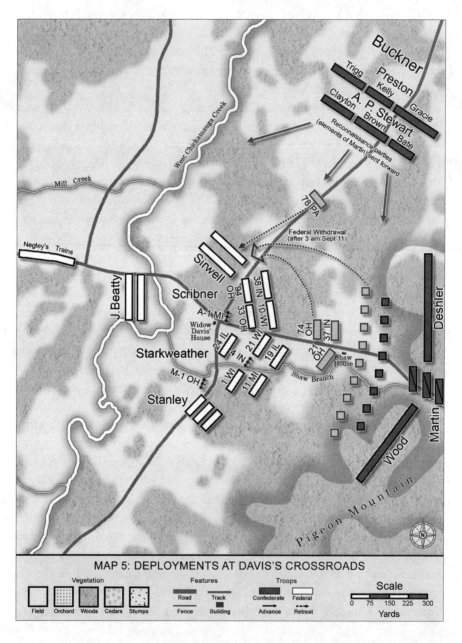

MAP 5: DEPLOYMENTS AT DAVIS'S CROSSROADS

reinforce Hindman's sense of imminent danger, while seemingly granting the latter officer permission to cancel the attack if he felt so warranted. Bragg's orders were cast aside.[14]

14 Ibid.

The 7:00 a.m. departure clearly indicated Hindman was in no hurry, and his order of march further confirmed that fact. Instead of leading with his own division, which at Conley's was already a mile closer to Davis's Crossroads than Buckner's men, Hindman directed that Buckner's corps, and specifically A. P. Stewart's division, lead the advance. While in normal circumstances the lead was routinely rotated for the comfort of the men (especially in dusty conditions), the urgency of Bragg's orders in this case should have dictated that Hindman's men go first. Because of this arrangement it would be 8:00 or as late as 8:30 a.m. before the Confederates gained a foot of new ground in Negley's direction. Hindman also warned Buckner "to move with caution, and not to hazard an engagement until some reliable information was obtained of the strength and position" of the Yankees, orders that all but guaranteed the movement would proceed at a snail's pace.[15]

Throughout the movement, Hindman and Buckner remained focused more on retreat than on attack. Buckner's engineer company was dispatched to clear Catlett's Gap of the previously felled trees. It reported back at 10:00 a.m. with an estimate that the task would be finished by noon; neither general wished to press much farther south while that gap was still impassable. 2nd Lt. George W. Dillon, of Company I, 18th Tennessee, recorded the painfully slow progress that morning. The men left their camps about 8:00 a.m., "ready and equipped for a general engagement." Three hours and a little more than three miles later, they "formed a line of battle at 11:00 o'clock." Federals were ahead.[16]

Little happened between 11:00 and noon. In keeping with his orders, Buckner's first move was to send out reconnaissance parties, leaving the bulk of his infantry to halt and mass near the road about two and one-half miles short of Davis's Crossroads. Stewart's division deployed astride the road. With 4,400 men, Stewart's line stretched more than half a mile; Buckner spent a great deal of time arranging his overall deployment.

Union Gen. James S. Negley got little if any sleep on the night of September 10. His division numbered just 4,476 officers and men, far less than the 10,000 or 15,000 Confederate estimates gave him. He was feeling dangerously exposed, and for good reason. Hoping to bluff the enemy until help arrived (successfully, as it turned out), Negley aggressively shoved his pickets forward

15 OR 30, pt. 4, 632; Simon B. Buckner, "Report of Operations" September 16, 1863, Bragg Papers, Tulane University, New Orleans, LA.

16 OR 30, pt. 2, 295; Entry for September 11, George W. Dillon Diary, TSLA.

Colonel Benjamin F. Scribner,
First Brigade, Baird's Division.
From Henry Fales Perry, History of the Thirty-Eighth Regiment
Indiana Volunteer Infantry

on the 10th. Colonel William Sirwell
and three of his regiments—the 37th
Indiana, and 21st and 74th
Ohio—pushed right up to the foot of
Dug Gap, taking up a line near the
Shaw House on the road leading
through the gap. Stanley's and Beatty's
brigades remained in position in and
around the Widow Davis home.[17]

At 2:00 a.m., Sirwell's men were
shaken awake "by the Col, instead of
the bugle note," noted Lt. Robert Dilworth of the 21st Ohio. Leaving their
pickets in place to disguise the movement, the regiments quietly withdrew
nearly a mile before taking up a position just north of Davis's Crossroads facing
in the direction of the Conley place. Lieutenant Colonel William D. Ward had
his Hoosiers of the 37th Indiana in line "at daylight to meet an expected attack,"
but when dawn arrived nothing happened. It was not "until 10 AM when a
strong skirmish line advanced and attacked us but we held our ground." Sirwell
reported these facts to Negley, adding that the Confederate line extended well
beyond both of his flanks. Beyond Sirwell's right lay only Pigeon Mountain,
Dug Gap, and more Rebels, but if the enemy turned his left they would cut off
Negley's only retreat route across the valley.[18]

It was with no little relief, then, when Baird's 2,800-man division joined
Negley by 8:00 a.m. Negley, Baird explained, wanted to shift Stanley's brigade
over to extend Sirwell's right, and wanted Baird's two brigades to take up
Stanley's current position fronting the gap. This was a remarkable decision, in
effect swapping out almost Negley's entire line of battle. Simply placing all or
part of Baird's two brigades on Sirwell's left would have accomplished the same

17 Strength Returns for September 10, 1863, RG 94, NARA.

18 Entry for September 11, Dilworth Journal, OHS; William D. Ward journal, 136, DePauw
University. Greencastle, IN; *OR* 30, pt. 1, 384.

task, and with much less danger, but Negley's plan prevailed. It "was an operation of some delicacy," admitted Baird.[19]

Somehow these complex maneuvers were completed without any real enemy interference, although firing along the skirmish line remained lively. Col. Benjamin F. Scribner commanded Baird's First Brigade, and his worst moment of the morning was not the result of Confederate activity. Scribner suffered from hay fever and wore "dark goggles to protect my eyes, as the glare of the light without them was unendurable. My horse disturbed a hornet's nest in front of my lines and became unmanageable," he later recalled, "and so slashed me about . . . that my glasses were lost." Losing the goggles was a "disaster," for without them Scribner was effectively blind. "I called to my men with much earnestness to find them for me, which they soon did, to my great relief." The soldiers chortled about the event, then and later, telling "with decided relish" the story of how Scribner "stopped the fight to find my spectacles."[20]

Spectacles or not, the Federals were sure a desperate battle was at hand. Less sure was an ever more frustrated Braxton Bragg. At 4:00 a.m. that same morning, Bragg, D. H. Hill, and their respective staffs rode to join Patrick Cleburne, whose division was now concentrated on the east side of Dug Gap and ready to support Hindman when he arrived. Cleburne had begun moving his infantry through the gap well before daylight and well before the gap was cleared of Hill's feared obstructions. Private William Preston of the 33rd Alabama recalled the difficult journey through Dug Gap in the pre-dawn gloom, the men moving "in Indian file, one behind the other, crawling under around or over trees, logs and brush that had been cut and fell on the road, at times . . . with high walls on each side that . . . gave the impression that we were in a hole in the ground." Once the bulk of the infantry was through and deployed in the woods on the western face of the gap, Cleburne set details from Sterling A. M. Wood's brigade to clearing those obstructions in order to push through his artillery and ammunition trains.[21]

Daylight found Bragg, Hill, and Cleburne waiting for Hindman's gunfire. Only silence greeted them. Cleburne had sent a staff officer with several couriers north along the top of Pigeon Mountain "to send him instant

---

19 OR 30, pt. 1, 271-272.

20 Scribner, *How Soldiers Were Made*, 141.

21 William Preston Memoir, ADAH.

intelligence of Hindman's first gun," but the effort proved wasted. Hindman, of course, was hours away. Bragg stewed, "restless[ly] walking back and forth . . . occasionally he would stop and irritably dig his spurs in the ground," recalled Capt. Irving Buck, one of Cleburne's staff officers. As the hours slipped away, Bragg sent Hindman a series of new dispatches in an effort to goad things along; they only made the problem worse.[22]

The first message was sent at 11:00 a.m., and probably arrived around noon—just as, Hindman later claimed, his "whole line was about to advance." The content was astounding: "If you find the enemy in such force as to make an attack imprudent, fall back at once upon La Fayette by Catlett's Gap, from which obstructions have now been removed."[23]

Fall back at once? What happened to Bragg's injunction to attack at once even if it cost Hindman his entire command? Now it appeared as though Bragg was losing his nerve. Quite reasonably, this missive (which seemed to confirm all their earlier worst fears), sparked a new round of concerned and animated discussion between Hindman, Buckner, and Patton Anderson. Capt. Milton P. Jarnagin, a member of Buckner's staff, later recalled this hasty conference. "A courier from Gen. Bragg arrived, and told the generals that . . . Bragg wanted them to attack the enemy at once . . . unless something had happened to make it unadvisable. They said, 'We do not know whether anything has happened or not.' So they halted . . . [and] sent a courier back . . . to inquire of Gen. Bragg the meaning of his order."[24]

Other messages soon followed. About 1:00 p.m., Captain S. W. Presstman arrived, again inquiring whether Hindman felt certain he could retreat via Catlett's if necessary. By now the gap was clear, and Hindman was certain he could do so, but he must have further wondered why the commanding general was so concerned about a retreat. A final message from Bragg, once again penned by Mackall, arrived an hour or so later. This note placed the Federal strength at 12,000 to 15,000 men, demanded that Hindman report in via courier every hour, and concluded with this ominous note: "The enemy are advancing

---

22 Anonymous, "Major General Patrick R. Cleburne. A Biography, Chapter V," *The Kennesaw Gazette*, March 15, 1889; Irving A. Buck, *Cleburne and His Command* (Press of Morningside Bookshop, 1982), 139n.

23 *OR* 30, pt. 2, 296.

24 Milton P. Jarnigan Reminiscences, TSLA.

from Graysville to LaFayette. Dispatch is necessary to us." There was no mention of an assault in McLemore's Cove against Negley's isolated Federals.[25]

This chain of communiqués convinced Hindman there was now no course but retreat. At 2:45 p.m. he sent word to Bragg that he appeared to be outnumbered, and with Crittenden's Federals bearing down from the north, an immediate retreat back through Catlett's Gap was in order and would begin immediately.[26]

Bragg later roundly condemned Hindman for this decision, but in fact his own dispatches strongly suggested Bragg was himself having second thoughts. He might well have initiated matters on his own front by ordering Cleburne to attack first in an effort to pull Hindman and Buckner into the growing fight per their previous orders. The risk of doing so wasn't that great. Cleburne numbered 5,400 men, and so was strong enough to hold his own for at least a short while. Besides, at least part of Walker's Reserve Corps had closed up to the east side of Dug Gap in case they were needed. And in fact around noon Bragg started to do exactly that by ordering Cleburne to strike. Once again he had second thoughts and, before Cleburne's men could close with Baird's Yankees, Bragg ordered them to halt. He would wait for Hindman and stick with the original plan.[27]

About 2:00 p.m., before Hindman had conclusively decided to withdraw, Bragg sent yet another courier. Captain and Judge-Advocate Taylor Beatty, who acted as a field aide when he was not exercising martial justice, carried word "that the attack which was ordered at daybreak must be made at once or it will be too late." Beatty arrived sometime around 3:00 p.m., only to discover that Hindman "had [already] made preparations to withdraw." Hindman explained to the astounded Beatty that he had forgone attacking earlier because "his information was of so various a character that he had vacillated." Clearly sensing Captain Beatty's dismay, Hindman insisted that his earlier orders were discretionary, not peremptory.[28]

Before Hindman's column could begin its retrograde move, Federals beat them to the punch. Word filtered back from A. P. Stewart's skirmish line that it

25 OR 30, pt. 2, 296.

26 Ibid., pt. 4, 636.

27 Symonds, *Stonewall of the West*, 142.

28 Entry for September 11, Taylor Beatty Diary, UNC.

was the Yankees who were retreating. The news stopped Hindman and Buckner in their tracks. Beatty rode off to find Bragg again and relay these latest developments.

As the morning wore into afternoon, Negley and Baird decided they had little choice but to retreat. Menaced by as many as 30,000 Confederates, Negley could not explain why the enemy hesitated so long, but he knew every minute was a gift. Most of Baird's trains had been left at Stevens's Gap, but Negley's wagons were still present and had to be extricated first. Negley directed John Beatty to march his brigade back to Bailey's Crossroads, and there take up a defensive position to let the "immense train . . . near four hundred wagons" pass to the rear.[29]

In the meantime, Negley proposed to fall back behind the Widow Davis house to a ridge 500 yards to the west, with good fields of fire overlooking the crossroads. His two remaining brigades would retreat first and establish new lines as Baird's men followed. Baird's two brigades would then fall back to Missionary Ridge, about a mile west of the Davis house, and establish a third line with less-exposed flanks; Negley's command would join them there. It was a perilous venture. An enemy attack mid-move would spell disaster.[30]

But there was no disaster because there was no Rebel attack. To Lieutenant Colonel Ward of the 37th Indiana, the affair seemed like a giant game of leapfrog. "They sent a large force to our left flank," Ward noted, "but their line of march was easily traced . . . by the dense cloud of dust. . . . As soon as the dust indicated the point of place they intended striking us, a brigade would be posted to meet them, and as soon as they would become engaged we would rapidly fall back." Though the skirmishing was lively, the fact that Hindman and Buckner were preparing to retreat themselves allowed Stanley's and Sirwell's brigades to retire virtually unscathed. Once atop the ridge with artillery planted, Negley informed Baird to commence his own movement.[31]

Scribner's men led the way. Posted on the left of Baird's line, Scribner's regiments were deployed facing northeast, with the 38th Indiana's left anchored on the Chattanooga Road and the 10th Wisconsin's right edging the Dug Gap

29 Beatty, *The Citizen-Soldier*, 330-331. John Beatty was no known relation to Taylor Beatty, above.

30 *OR* 30, pt. 1, 272.

31 Entry for September 11, Ward Journal, DePauw University.

Road. They faced Texans from James Deshler's brigade of Cleburne's division, and by mid-afternoon it had become apparent Rebels were working around Baird's left flank. Scribner ordered the 38th Indiana to extend its skirmish line as far left as possible. As additional companies of Hoosiers double-quicked across the Chattanooga Road to reinforce and extend the picket line, reported the regimental historian, they "were exposed to a heavy fire . . . but the movement was so rapid that there were very few casualties."[32]

Baird was on edge and restlessly active. Companies A and K of the 10th Wisconsin, on the 38th Indiana's right, were deployed as skirmishers. While so engaged, Lt. Lucius D. Hinkley of the 10th looked up to see the division commander and three or four staffers ride up. This portion of the skirmish line was in "thick brush," recalled Hinkley, with no field of fire, though enemy rounds were "periodically singing through the bushes in a lively way." Snapped Baird, "Lieutenant, what are you doing here?" With Hinkley's skirmishers hidden in the brush just ahead, to Baird's eye the lieutenant seemed to be all alone. The surprised Wisconsinite pointed out his men. "'Why don't you move your line forward?'" further demanded the general.

"I don't command the line," came the reply. "My captain is down to the right, and our major . . . is somewhere down that way." Baird, continued Hinkley, "looked as if I merited some further remarks, but instead he rode off to the right." Baird must have located the major, for soon Hinkley and his men were advancing, moving up to a fence line overlooking an open field . . . "twenty-five or thirty rods" wide.[33]

From this vantage the enemy was more visible, and the Badgers traded fire with the Rebels for some time until word came to retreat. When Hinkley and his fellow skirmishers reached the regiment's former location, they found instead that the 10th Wisconsin—indeed the entire brigade—was gone. "We hunted back through the woods for two miles or more before we overtook it," recalled the officer. Lieutenant Colonel John H. Ely was delighted to see them. So quickly had the orders come to fall back that Ely feared both skirmish companies might be captured. The warm welcome startled Hinkley into fully

32 Henry Fales Perry, *History of the Thirty-Eighth Regiment Indiana Volunteer Infantry: One of the Three Hundred Fighting Regiments of the Union Army* (F. A. Stuart, Printer, 1906), 83.

33 Lucius Dwight Hinkley Recollections, Wisconsin Historical Society, Madison, WI. Hereafter WHS.

realizing the peril he had just escaped: "We had been having a quiet, easy time of it in the bushes without a thought of any special danger, but higher officers, better informed of the situation, had given us up for lost."[34]

Brigadier General John C. Starkweather, also a man of Wisconsin, followed suit. Only three of Starkweather's regiments were present: the 24th Illinois, and the 1st and 21st Wisconsin. The remaining unit, the 79th Pennsylvania, had been detailed earlier to help improve the road through Stevens's Gap and was still in the vicinity of Lookout Mountain. Despite their paucity of numbers (short the 79th, the brigade numbered only about 1,100 men), the troops remained confident, even cocky. "It was an exciting experience of alternate fighting and retreating," recalled 2nd Lt. James M. Randall of Company G, the 21st Wisconsin. "To hold a position until nearly surrounded, then retreat at double-quick time back to a new line. Not only exciting but hazardous." "We all retired rapidly, but in splendid order," reported Starkweather. "My command formed lines of battle at every point where ground would permit. . . . I feel prouder than ever of my brave men. Great praise is accorded to them for the masterly manner in which they covered the retreat."[35]

The Confederates opposite the Federal retrograde realized only too late the nature of the opportunity slipping through their fingers. General Will Martin was perhaps the most frustrated man on the field next to Bragg himself. Martin had begun the promising day with Bragg and Hill watching Cleburne's infantry file through Dug Gap and deploy. Then, he recalled, given "unlimited discretion in the use of my" division, the Confederate cavalryman rode north to Catlett's Gap and then west to join Hindman. "I reported to him for duty . . . and gave [him] what information I possessed about the cove and the object and importance of the presence of our large force." Martin fully expected action, but was gravely disappointed when "hours were lost in consultation." When word came of the Union retreat, Hindman canceled his own withdrawal and instead ordered Stewart's infantry forward at the double-quick. He also ordered Martin to "charge the enemy's rear."[36]

---

34 Ibid.

35 James M. Randall Diary, ehistory online, http://ehistory.osu.edu/osu/sources/letters/randall/index.cfm, accessed 3/4/12; General Starkweather to his wife, reprinted in newspaper, found in Quiner Scrapbooks, WHS.

36 William T. Martin to Bragg, 1867, CCNMP.

This order resulted in the most sizable action of the day, though it can hardly be called a battle. Martin sent about 150 Alabama cavalrymen thundering down the Dug Gap Road, where they met elements of the 19th and 24th Illinois infantry in line behind a convenient stone wall. These two regiments were supported by two batteries, the 4th Indiana and M, 1st Ohio Light, both stationed on Negley's pre-selected ridge 500 yards to the west. Martin's cavalry were repulsed "after sharp loss." Lieutenant Eben P. Sturges, who commanded a section of the Ohio battery, dismissed the encounter as another skirmish, noting that he only "fired three rounds," though one of his men was wounded in the thigh. Negley observed the brief fight and told Sturges, "You handle your artillery very gallantly." Sturges, who was not one of Negley's admirers, only grudgingly acknowledged the praise in a letter to his family: "I do not, as you perhaps imagine, value a compliment from him very highly. Please say nothing of this." While the fight was a minor affair, Lt. John V. Patterson of the 21st Ohio took it as an omen of future Rebel intentions: "Our division (Neglies) got a little too fast . . . ran into Bragg's whole army and we got back 5 miles right soon . . . I rather think we will have to fight him they appear to be stubborn and not inclined to travel any further southward just now."[37]

By 5:00 p.m. the Federals were all falling back to Negley's third line on Missionary Ridge. They did so without further mishap. There, Negley received welcome news that reinforcements were at hand. The first of these was Brig. Gen. John Turchin's brigade, part of Reynolds's division, XIV Corps. General Thomas, well aware of Negley's exposed position in McLemore's Cove, had been hastening both Reynolds's and John Brannan's divisions across Lookout Mountain. Turchin led the way, his men roused from their sleep at 6:00 a.m. on the 11th to reach the western foot of the mountain two hours later. It took Turchin's trains the next eight hours to fully ascend, reaching the summit at 4:00 p.m. His leading infantry crossed and then descended Stevens's Gap by nine that night, although his wagons would remain on top of Lookout for now.

---

37 William T. Martin to Bragg, 1867, CCNMP; "Dear Folks," Sept 12, 1863, Eben Sturges Diary and Letters, U.S. Army Heritage and Education Center, Carlisle, PA. Hereafter AHEC. Sturges disliked Negley in part because he found the General "a man very fond of style," always putting on a show, with his staff "dressed up as if on parade," even in the hottest weather; all of which struck Sturges as the hallmark of a martinet. See his letter to "Dear Mother," Aug. 24, 1863; Paul C. Tremewan, ed., *As Near Hell as I Ever Expect To Be* . . . (Xlibris, 2011), 137.

Behind them toiled Reynolds's other brigade under Col. Edward A. King, followed by John Brannan's men, who would be marching through the night.[38]

With Turchin was his wife, Nadine. Against all orders and regulations, Nadine accompanied her Russian-émigré husband everywhere, even on campaign. Through the day the Turchins could hear the cannon fire of Negley's fitful fight, and Nadine recorded that her husband's troops were "'welcomed' by the bullets of enemy patrols." Nadine, however, was angry over issues unrelated to the coming fight. She was fuming at a recently departed hanger-on to her husband's military family named Boland, who, for some time had been hoping Turchin would secure him a commission. When the Russian was unable to do so, "this narrow-minded fellow, exceedingly vicious and no less conceited, took it as a personal offense." The Turchins had just received an angry letter from Boland that Nadine would stew over for days. She was a devoted wife who jealously guarded her husband's good name and career while he took care of the fighting.[39]

There was, as might be expected, more than simmering anger on the Confederate side of the line. By 5:00 p.m., most of the Rebels knew a tremendous opportunity had been lost. Captain Jarnagin was riding toward Davis's Crossroads in the wake of General Preston's advance when he came upon fellow staffer Capt. Isaac Shelby, who told Jarnagin that "a great blunder has been made, which will carry a great responsibility with it." The disgusted Jarnagin concurred with the captain's conclusion. Shortly thereafter he met Bragg and D. H. Hill riding down from Dug Gap and guided his horse along with them until they all met General Buckner. Buckner was approaching the group when "Bragg sternly demanded: 'Gen. Buckner, where are the enemy?' [Buckner] replied, 'they have escaped through Stevens' Gap.'"[40]

Martin also rode back to Davis's Crossroads after his troopers were checked at the stone wall. There he met Bragg, who was "indignant and excited at . . . that utter disregard of [his] orders." Bragg quizzed Martin about what had gone wrong, and Martin described the afternoon's missteps, which only made

---

38 Entry for September 11, Diary of Lieutenant Thomas L. Steward, printed in *Chattanooga New Free Press*, September 21, 1938; Clipping found in Hamilton County Library, Chattanooga TN.

39 Entry for September 12, Nadine Turchin Diary, ALPL.

40 Jarnagin Reminiscences, TSLA.

Bragg angrier. Next into this knot of discontent rode Hindman. Bragg's "greeting was by no means cordial," recalled Martin.[41]

Frustration was not confined to the generals. Plenty of Hill's troops also understood that a tremendous opportunity had been squandered. Captain Buck of Cleburne's staff waxed poetic (or perhaps not) when he observed that Cleburne's men were "In ecstasies of grief," adding that "men and officers swore, some were almost in tears, many were in despair." Grief, tears, or cursing notwithstanding, a golden moment to knock part of Rosecrans's Army of the Cumberland back on its heels and seize the initiative had slipped away.[42]

Despite the frustrations of the day, Bragg had no intention of hurling his men against Negley's new position at the foot of Lookout. Remaining in the cove would only reverse the circumstances and place Bragg's forces in danger of being trapped. Accordingly, he ordered everyone back across Pigeon Mountain to La Fayette. Hill's troops would retrace their steps through Dug Gap, followed by Buckner's divisions. Hindman, meanwhile, would utilize the newly cleared Catlett's Gap for his own movement.

By this time it was also dawning on some of Hindman's men that a tremendous opportunity had been lost. September 11th had done nothing to improve Hindman's reputation with his command. General Manigault concluded that "the opportunity offered General Hindman for distinguishing himself and striking a terrible blow was favorable in the extreme, but he was not up to the work, it being far beyond his capacity as a general." Overlooking his own cautious role in the drama, Patton Anderson offered similarly negative commentary. "The fact is Hindman was ordered to attack the enemy . . . at daylight. He did not do it," he wrote his wife on October 5. The brigadier grudgingly admitted there were "perhaps good reasons" for the delay, but lamented that when the attack did come off by 4:00 p.m., "it was too late—the bird had flown."[43]

Lieutenant William B. Richmond of Polk's staff observed a still-simmering Bragg that night and echoed Patton Anderson's opinion. Richmond accompanied Polk in a ride south from Dr. Anderson's house in search of new orders for September 12. They met Bragg at General Walker's headquarters

---

41 Martin to Bragg, 1867, CCNMP.

42 Buck, *Cleburne and His Command*, 140.

43 Buck, *Cleburne and His Command*, 93; James Patton Anderson to wife, October 5, 1863, Anderson Papers, University of Florida, Gainesville FL. Hereafter UF.

well after nightfall. "General Bragg and all his staff returned, having been clear through the gap to Hindman and Buckner, and no enemy there. The bird had flown and the farce was complete," explained the lieutenant. "Forty [thousand] men to catch two brigades—those in a trap, it was supposed, impossible for them to escape from; and when search was made they were like the Irishman's flea. Comment, pooh!"[44]

44 *OR* 30, pt. 2, 74.

Chapter Six

A Second Frustration:

September 12-15, 1863

The 11th of September was a wake-up call for William Rosecrans. Until that evening the Union commander harbored the illusion his opponent was in full retreat, and the moment was ripe for an unrestrained pursuit. Davis's Crossroads largely disabused him of that belief. More caution might be in order. Rosecrans, however, was not quite ready to admit that Braxton Bragg had completely turned the tables on him.

At 10:00 p.m. on the night of the 11th, Rosecrans turned to Brig. Gen. Robert B. Mitchell to carry an order to Alexander McCook's XX Corps that the Rebels might be concentrating at La Fayette. Rosecrans "suggest[ed] that [McCook] close up toward General Thomas." The order wasn't "peremptory," noted Rosecrans, and McCook could use his own discretion "if you find the facts different from what is now supposed." Mitchell was assigned to command the First Cavalry Division of Stanley's Corps, but had been absent until now on sick leave. He had just arrived in Chattanooga and was about to head south to rejoin his men when the army commander tasked him to carry the message. Rosecrans explained to Mitchell the situation as he knew it, and asked him to also visit the XIV Corps on his way south to convey Rosecrans's intentions to Thomas.[1]

---

1   OR 30, pt. 3, 541. Mitchell's presence at headquarters is unexplained in the *Official Records*. He was apparently with his command during the early stages of the campaign, as evidenced by

Mitchell wasted little time. His first stop on his way south was at General Negley's headquarters, which he reached by 1:00 a.m. on September 12. The news Mitchell bore alarmed the latter officer, who in turn sent word to Thomas that "from the remarks General Rosecrans made to General M, [Rosecrans] is totally uninformed as to the character of the country in this vicinity, and of the position, force, and intentions of the enemy." Negley urged Thomas to communicate with army headquarters immediately and impress upon Rosecrans the very real nature of the threat they all faced.[2]

Thomas didn't need Negley to tell him that Rosecrans was out of touch. A message directly from Rosecrans to Thomas, written at 11:15 a.m. on the 12th, contained Rosecrans's surprising conclusion that "Negley withdrew more through prudence than compulsion." This dispatch must also be seen as an implied rebuke of Thomas, for it directly contradicted the XIV Corps commander's own views, as expressed at dawn on the 12th, that "Negley and Baird were attacked . . . with an overwhelming force." Now Thomas fired back. In dispatches sent at 3:30 p.m. to Chief of Staff Garfield, and at 8:30 p.m. directly to Rosecrans, George Thomas reiterated that Negley was attacked by "the whole of D. H. Hill's corps and a part of Buckner's force, [supported by] 2,000 cavalry." Behind them, Thomas insisted, "a large force is concentrated at La Fayette." The threat was real, and Rosecrans should not ignore it any longer.[3]

Assistant Secretary of War Charles C. Dana, who arrived at Rosecrans's headquarters the night before, summarized the thinking at army headquarters about this same time, which still differed from Thomas's conclusions. "Last night it seemed probable that Bragg had abandoned his retreat on Rome and returned with the purpose of falling upon the different corps and divisions of our army, now widely separated," wired Dana in a dispatch to Edwin M.

---

orders issued to him. He later reported that he did not officially return to duty until September 14, but on September 10 Rosecrans issued a very curious order to Mitchell instructing him to "send General Crook's division . . . to . . . Bridgeport to protect [against] . . . a heavy force of rebel cavalry . . . reported moving in that direction." OR 30, pt. 3, 521. In that order, which was apparently never acted upon, Mitchell is addressed as "commanding cavalry," which suggests Rosecrans was already aware that David Stanley was unable to physically continue in active command. It is possible Mitchell was summoned to army headquarters in Chattanooga so Rosecrans could personally discuss future operations with him before heading back to his corps.

2 *OR* 30, pt. 3, 567.

3 Ibid., 564-566.

Stanton in Washington. However, "the indications of this morning are that he was merely making a stand to check pursuit."[4]

Neither Rosecrans nor those in his immediate military family viewed Dana's arrival with enthusiasm. The assistant secretary of war had spent much of the summer in Mississippi with Gen. U. S. Grant. By trade Dana was a newspaperman, the managing editor of Horace Greeley's *New York Tribune* before the war. He was a strong anti-slavery man and, as it turned out, harbored equally strong opinions on how the war should be waged. In 1862, those opinions clashed with Greeley's and he resigned. Stanton offered Dana the chance to serve as a sort of informal Inspector General. He remained a civilian with no military rank, but reported directly to Stanton, and through him, had Lincoln's ear. Many Federals viewed Dana as little more than Stanton's spy in the field.

Dana arrived in Chattanooga with a letter of introduction from Stanton. Among other things, Stanton asked Rosecrans to show Dana every courtesy, and that Rosecrans could "explain to [Dana] fully any matters which you may desire . . . to bring to the notice of the [War] department." Rosecrans read the letter and then stunned the new arrival with an outburst of his own complaints against Gen. Henry Halleck and Secretary Stanton, including the familiar litany of a lack of support, the need for more cavalry, and the like. It was both an awkward moment and an ill-advised start of their relationship. Dana explained to Rosecrans that he had no authority to deal with such problems, but was there to provide whatever help he could. Quieted if not fully mollified, Rosecrans accepted Dana as a member of headquarters.[5]

"Thus began a peculiar relationship," was how Rosecrans's chief biographer William Lamars termed it. "Dana ate, slept, poked around with the staff, and gossiped. Each evening he reported to Stanton. The army received him as if he were 'a bird of evil omen.'" Rosecrans's partisans were sure he was there only to find an excuse by which Stanton could relieve their boss. His daily telegraphic updates, however, provide an excellent narrative of how Rosecrans viewed the ongoing campaign as it was unfolding, untainted by hindsight.[6]

---

4   Ibid., pt. 1, 185.

5   Charles A. Dana, *Recollections of the Civil War* (Collier books, 1963), 107.

6   Lamers, *Edge of Glory*, 312.

Meanwhile, far to the south at Alpine, and as yet unaware of the orders Mitchell bore, Alexander McCook and George Crook were still acting on previous instructions. In ignorance of what was transpiring in McLemore's Cove, a Union cavalry reconnaissance on the 11th informed McCook of three things: "Bragg has not gone to Rome; that none of his force has passed over the Dalton road, and that there is but a small infantry and cavalry force in Rome (10,000 to 11,000 men)." There was instead a great deal of evidence that the Rebels were holding La Fayette in strength. McCook knew that if these facts were true, his XX Corps was precariously situated—a "false position" as he termed it. The next day, September 12, he decided that all of the cavalry must turn north toward La Fayette to determine once and for all who held that city.[7]

A pair of roads led north from Alpine to La Fayette. The first ran straight up Broomtown Valley west of the Chattooga River and entered the town from the southwest. The second ran east to Summerville before turning north to cross the Chattooga a few miles up and then on into La Fayette from the south. George Crook divided his force to cover both approaches. He personally led two brigades north while Col. Edward McCook (commanding the First Division in Mitchell's absence) moved the other two brigades via the Summerville approach.

Neither effort produced significant contact. Crook, leading Col. Eli Long's Second Brigade of his own division and Col. Archibald P. Campbell's First Brigade, First Division, ventured within 10 miles of La Fayette before halting for the night at Valley Store, "having met no resistance whatever." Along the way Crook overtook Col. Thomas Harrison's 39th Indiana Mounted Infantry, which had also been heading to La Fayette the previous day as ordered by General McCook to make contact with Thomas's XIV Corps. Harrison halted his Hoosiers when it became apparent no Federals were in La Fayette. His trip proved so uneventful that Harrison, who had been up all night, managed "a fine sleep this afternoon under a fine shade made by a Hawthorn" tree.[8]

Colonel McCook's column had just returned from its previous scout toward Rome that morning of Saturday the 12th and was settling into a well-deserved feed when the order came down to saddle up. "At 10:00 a.m. we started for Summerville, and six miles beyond," wrote Cpl. George W. Baum of

7   OR 30, pt. 3, 569.

8   OR 30, pt. 1, 891. "Dear Wife," Sept 12 1863, Thomas J. Harrison Papers, InHS.

the 2nd Indiana Cavalry.[9] McCook, with the brigades of Col. Daniel M. Ray and Col. Louis D. Watkins, both of Second Division, advanced to Trion Factory, where the Summerville Road crossed the Chattooga River. There, McCook tersely reported, we "encounter[ed] Wheeler's cavalry [and] drove them some distance." The scrimmaging produced a handful of Rebel captives, "one Captain . . . and nine privates," noted Hoosier John A. Mendenhall of the 2nd Indiana, but little else. The Union column returned "to Summerville after dark, tired and hungry and almost suffocating with dust."[10]

Alexander McCook, meanwhile, prepared for the worst. All of the supply trains that had just descended the eastern face of Lookout Mountain into Alpine were ordered to turn around and go back up in case a retreat order was issued. For the time being, however, his infantry would remain at Alpine ready for a move in either direction. Late that afternoon Mitchell arrived bearing Rosecrans's latest dispatches. McCook drafted a reply at 4:45 p.m. outlining his own situation. "There is a great commotion at La Fayette today," he reported, "judging from the clouds of dust . . . appearing to extend from La Fayette north. Whether this is dust made by the enemy's or Thomas' column coming into La Fayette I cannot say." As McCook saw it, he had two options. If the Rebels did not retreat, McCook would move to join Thomas via Lookout Mountain. If they did abandon La Fayette, he would move to Summerville since from there he could threaten both Resaca and Rome. Before making that choice, however, McCook determined to try one final time to confirm what Bragg was up to. He ordered Crook to take all his cavalry into La Fayette the next day, September 13. He concluded his dispatch on an optimistic note: "I think Crook will find La Fayette abandoned by their infantry; in my judgment, Resaca is their point."[11]

Bragg wasn't abandoning anything, but McCook was right about one thing: Resaca was important to the Confederates. Although established as Bragg's main supply depot, as of the 12th it was still effectively unguarded except for a motley collection of state troops under Georgia militia officer Maj. Gen. Henry C. Wayne. Alarmed at the rapidly deteriorating situation in North Georgia, Governor Joe Brown ordered General Wayne to "fight for Resaca Bridge and

9   Entry for September 12, George W. Baum Diary, InHS.

10   OR 30, pt. 1, 895; Entry for September 12, John A. Mendenhall Diary, Morrison Reeves Public Library, Richmond, IN.

11   Alexis Cope, *The Fifteenth Ohio Volunteers and Its Campaigns: War of 1861-5* (published by the author, 1916), 306; OR 30, pt. 3, 571.

never surrender it . . . while possible to hold it." All Wayne could count on to execute Brown's order were the 1st and 2nd Regiments of the Georgia State Line, various companies of the Georgia State Guard (the latter was specifically raised for railroad duty, and was maintained as a separate organization from the State Line), and a number of Georgia state and Confederate batteries. The whole force numbered just 1,000 to 2,000 men, with perhaps two dozen cannon of mixed types, the whole shielded behind entrenchments. Wayne also ordered Col. Edward M. Galt of the 1st Regiment State Line to "rally the reserve Home Guards," but the local lack of arms prompted Galt to reply that he might "as well summon the Jay Birds."[12]

Substantially more and better troops would be needed to hold Resaca, and fortunately for the Confederates, they were available. The 3,400 men of Brig. Gens. Matthew D. Ector's and Evander McNair's brigades were now at Atlanta, on grudging loan from Joe Johnston, having just arrived on the 11th. Immediately, Bragg ordered both brigades to roll north to Resaca. That order was received in Atlanta at 1:00 p.m. on the 12th, and by 9:30 p.m. both Ector's and McNair's men left for that place. The two commands spent barely 24 hours in Atlanta before being shanghaied. [13]

On the 13th, upon hearing that the first of the reinforcements from Virginia were also arriving in Atlanta, Johnston immediately sent a wire to Bragg: "McNair's and Gregg's brigades are therefore, I suppose, no longer required: please send them back." He had dispatched Ector and McNair with the understanding they would go to Atlanta and no farther. Bragg broke that promise, though his need for them was indeed great. Still, Johnston was unhappy with the turn of events; on September 16th he attempted to go over Bragg's head and appeal directly to the War Department in Richmond for the return of those brigades. He was ignored. Johnston would have been further angered had he known Crittenden's XXI Corps was already turning aside from the railroad to head back toward La Fayette.[14]

Crittenden received new instructions at 8:30 p.m. on September 11. In light of the information provided by Gen. Tom Wood, of Rebels recently occupying Lee and Gordon's Mills and still in force near Rock Springs, Rosecrans directed

---

12 William Harris Bragg, *Joe Brown's Army: The Georgia State Line, 1862-1865* (Mercer University Press, 1987), 74.

13 *OR* 30, pt. 4, 643.

14 Ibid., 645, 653.

Union XXI Corps Commander Thomas L. Crittenden.
Wilbur F. Hinman

Crittenden to move back toward La Fayette and connect with Wood's division now at Lee and Gordon's Mills. From there, Crittenden could defend the direct approach to Chattanooga if Bragg struck northward, or support Thomas in an attack on La Fayette should a Union offensive still be possible. Crittenden affirmed that he would march at daylight. Now it was Van Cleve's turn to take the corps trains, moving via the Reed's Bridge Road to Peeler's Mill, where there was a good lateral road to use toward either La Fayette or back to Chattanooga. Palmer moved via a secondary road "south a short distance of Van Cleve . . . without baggage." Wilder's mounted infantry needed to be recalled first from Tunnel Hill. They would ride down the Ringgold-La Fayette Road via Leet's Tanyard armed with instructions "to attack boldly, and report often."[15]

Nathan Bedford Forrest's Confederate cavalry opposed this multi-pronged advance as best they could, though with varying degrees of tenacity. There was a great deal of Union wagon activity in the area, with supply convoys moving rations to the front or starting their return journey to Bridgeport via Chattanooga for the next load. Because each leg was a multi-day trip, small columns of wagons could be found everywhere, each one an attractive target for Forrest's cavalry patrols. That morning Tom Wood informed departmental headquarters that Rebel horsemen were "an abundant force" locally, easily able to slip past Union pickets (especially given the density of the morning fog). In a second missive, Wood added that "the whole country . . . is cut by parallel and cross roads which would readily facilitate the passage . . . of small bodies . . . of rebel cavalry to our rear."[16]

Colonel Atkins and the 92nd Illinois Mounted Infantry discovered the truth of Wood's assertions well enough on the evening of the 11th as they approached Rossville from Ringgold. As the 92nd crested a ridge just short of Rossville, Atkins spotted both a Union wagon camp laagered up by the side of the road and a column of enemy cavalry approaching that camp from the south. Atkins later counted the Rebel force at 700 men—an overly generous estimate—but the feisty former lawyer and newspaperman did not hesitate to pitch in with his own men. The Rebels were driven off without loss to either the 92nd or the teamsters, but the incident was a graphic warning of the porous nature of the Union lines.[17]

Rosecrans was fully aware of the dangers posed by the Rebel horsemen, but was simply too short of cavalry to do much about it. The decision to

15 Ibid., pt. 3, 546, 574.

16 Ibid., 579.

17 *Ninety-Second Illinois Volunteers*, 103.

concentrate all but one of his cavalry brigades on the southern flank with McCook was understandable given the missions he wanted Stanley to undertake and the far-flung nature of the XX Corps's movement. This decision, however, left only two brigades—Wilder's and Brig. Gen. Robert H. G. Minty's commands—for his myriad other needs. Rosecrans's decision to place the majority of those two brigades on the Union northern flank as part of the deception operation opposite Chattanooga left barely a regiment to cover Crittenden's and Thomas's advance. Shifting Wilder to join Crittenden met one critical need, but George Thomas was still without an adequate mounted screen. Nothing highlighted this problem more than the near-disaster in McLemore's Cove.

Thomas recognized his plight and appealed for help at 6:30 a.m. on the 12th: "I am greatly in want of cavalry," he wrote, "and would respectfully ask that if Wilder's brigade . . . is not on special duty, to have it sent to me at once. . . . The information I desire, and which is all important, is beyond my reach."[18]

Minty's First Brigade, Second Division, was still north of the Tennessee River on September 10, deployed upstream from Chattanooga in an effort to maintain a communications link with Maj. Gen. Ambrose Burnside's force in East Tennessee. That mission had by now assumed a secondary importance. Rosecrans had already recalled Minty from that duty on the 11th, and decided now to let Thomas have Wilder after Minty joined Crittenden. Minty's troopers spent September 12 crossing to the south bank with orders to join Crittenden's column, but they would be at least one more day arriving. In the meantime, Wilder was the extent of the mounted force Crittenden had at his disposal.[19]

The roving Rebel mounted patrols did not bother Crittenden's divisional and corps trains, however, guarded as they were by Brig. Gen. Van Cleve's three brigades. By midday Van Cleve's division reached Peeler's Mill without incident and halted to rest the men. Stripped down to fighting trim, Maj. Gen. John Palmer made rapid progress with his division toward his final objective, Lee and Gordon's Mills. Palmer halted at midday near the Gilbert farm on Peavine Creek to allow Van Cleve to close up. While there, Palmer interviewed locals who told him that "a heavy cavalry force" had moved on to La Fayette the night before, doing what damage they could in their passing. At 1:00 p.m., however,

18 OR 30, pt. 3, 564.

19 Ibid., pt. 1, 925.

"firing . . . heard toward Gordon's Mills" stirred Palmer into motion, with William Hazen's brigade leading the way.[20]

The gunfire emanated from a skirmish between Brig. Gen. Frank Armstrong's Southern cavalry and Tom Wood's Federal infantry. Hazen's brigade, leading Palmer's division, also encountered enough opposition to suffer a handful of casualties. The regimental history of the 41st Ohio dismissed these Rebels as merely "detachments for observation, giving little trouble." More immediate trouble, at least from an infantryman's point of view, was found in "a shed by the roadside, the ground within covered with bark and [wood] chips." Seeking shelter and perhaps provender, Yankees unwise enough to venture into the shed "went away loaded with vermin."[21]

Hazen's van pushed south along the east side of West Chickamauga Creek toward the Mills, where the fighting had commenced around 11:00 a.m. when a Confederate force attacked the pickets of the 3rd Kentucky and 125th Ohio, both of Harker's brigade (Wood's division). "The rebels opened upon us with artillery and small arms," wrote Col. Emerson Opdyke of the 125th. Opdyke rode forward to investigate: "To my pleasant surprise I came among Hazen's skirmishers after the same game." Prior to his colonelcy in the 125th Opdyke had been a company commander in the 41st Ohio, and an impromptu reunion occurred after the Confederates disengaged.[22]

With Palmer and Wood united, Crittenden ordered Van Cleve forward, thus concentrating his entire corps around Lee and Gordon's Mills. Though the mill machinery was destroyed, an ample store of wheat remained undamaged and appropriated in the name of the Federal government. The general mood was ebullient. "This is a grand time for military operations," penned Opdyke. "Roads good—that is dry —and an abundance of corn forage wherever we go: the rebels seem dispirited and fleeing and our triumph seems sure."[23]

Colonel Wilder and his Lightning Brigade saw the most action that day. Wilder pulled out of Tunnel Hill before dawn. Forrest's men were also up early. Major James Connolly of the 123rd Illinois was assigned rear guard duties,

---

20 Ibid., 711.

21 Robert L. Kimberly and Ephraim S. Holloway, *The Forty-First Ohio Veteran Volunteer Infantry in the War of the Rebellion, 1861-1865* (W. R. Smellie, Printer and Publisher, 1897), 48.

22 Longacre and Haas, *To Battle for God and the Right*, 94.

23 Ibid.

commanding three companies who skirmished with Scott's and Dibrell's Confederates. "[I] had to cover the retreat of the brigade . . . for some six hours before we got to a safe place," Connolly wrote home on September 16. Despite some nervous moments, Connolly escaped without loss.[24]

That safe place was Ringgold, where at 9:00 a.m. Wilder paused for two hours to issue rations and feed the horses. With orders in hand to strike for La Fayette, Wilder headed out of town southwest in the direction of Leet's Spring. The spring was named for and home to Arthur I. Leet, an English immigrant and Methodist minister who in addition to his religious calling had established a tanyard and milling operation there.[25]

This movement placed Wilder's command on a collision course with Brig. Gen. John Pegram's mounted brigade of Rebels, who had spent the night near Peavine Church just a mile or two west of Leet's. Having less distance to travel, Pegram's men arrived first and halted for a leisurely rest stop, drawn by the "cool, clear waters that gushed out" by the side of the road. Some men bathed in the spring or did their laundry, hanging it out to dry in the warm morning sun. Fodder was gathered for the horses. Not completely unmindful of the risks of being surprised while engaged in these domestic chores, Pegram sent 15 men out to scout the road in the direction of Ringgold. However, the patrol blundered into Wilder's Yankees and were all killed or captured before any warning could be sent back to their comrades. A short time later, when the rest of Pegram's men saddled up and rode up the Ringgold road, they were completely unaware they were riding into deadly trouble.[26]

Alerted to the Rebel presence after capturing Pegram's patrol, the 17th Indiana and 98th Illinois, Wilder's two leading regiments, deployed a sizable mounted skirmish line to their front. Pegram's first warning of trouble arrived when his lead regiment, the 6th Georgia Cavalry, spotted a line of horsemen in the woods atop a ridge on their flank. The two lines were "within easy rifle range," recalled Pvt. John Minnich of the 6th Georgia, but the caked dust concealed the color of their uniforms. After a few moments of uneasy silence, one of Minnich's comrades shouted, "by ——! Colonel. They are Yankees!"

24 James A. Connolly, *Three Years in the Army of the Cumberland* (Indiana University Press, 1987), 280.

25 http://www.chickamaugacampaign.org/pdfs/LeetsSpring.pdf, Accessed 3/27/2012.

26 Minnich, "Unique Experiences," 222; Huwald letter, Nutt papers, UNC.

When fighting erupted, Pegram's men fell back in some disorder to the clearing around Leet's Tanyard.[27]

Once at Leet's the 6th North Carolina Cavalry and a single gun from Capt. Gustave Huwald's Tennessee Battery deployed on a ridge overlooking the spring in an effort to hold off the Yankees while Pegram tried to form the rest of the brigade in line about half a mile farther south. Wilder pushed upon the scene, unhorsed the 17th and 72nd Indiana Mounted Infantry, and sent them forward against the North Carolinians. A brisk fight developed. Rather than risk a frontal attack, four companies of the 72nd Indiana diverted east in an effort to flank the Rebel line. This sharp bit of tactics prompted the 6th North Carolina to retreat to Pegram's main line.[28]

Even armed with their Spencer repeating rifles, Wilder's men approached this new line with caution. Now abreast, the 17th and 72nd Indiana prepared to advance with the 98th Illinois coming up behind them in support. Once again Col. Abram Miller of the 72nd eschewed a frontal attack for another outflanking attempt against Pegram's right. The same four companies of Hoosiers started to work their way around to the east a second time. This effort proved less successful. The 120 or so men of the flanking party shifted into the woods on the left only to discover they were confronting two full regiments of Rebels (the 6th Georgia and Rucker's Tennessee Legion). Comprised of some 600 men, the Confederate line was longer than the Indianans expected and much stronger. Far from turning the Rebel flank, the Hoosiers found their own left considerably overlapped by the 6th Georgia. John Bernard, a member of the 72nd, noted that "the fight proved disastrous for some of our boys." A tough engagement resulted, with the Hoosiers very much in danger of being surrounded. The four companies lost 16 killed and wounded including Capt. W. H. McMurtry of Company I, who was hit by three bullets and expired almost instantly.[29]

While the men of the 72nd's flanking force were fighting for their lives, Wilder, the 17th Indiana, and the balance of the 72nd engaged the rest of

27 Minnich, "Unique Experiences," 222.

28 Ibid.; and Pegram's Report, OR 30, pt. 2, 528. Pegram claimed his new line was only 400 yards to the rear, but Minnich disputed that distance. Entry for September 12, 1863, William H. Records Diary, InSL.

29 OR 30, pt. 1, 451; Powell, "Numbers and Losses," CCNMP; John M. Bernard to his wife and children, September 15, 1863, InHS; Baumgartner, *Blue Lightning*, 168.

Pegram's line. They, too, were feeling outnumbered. Their anxiety heightened considerably when the swell of sound rose from the right. "I never heard such firing," marveled Cpl. Ambrose Remley of Company E, 72nd Indiana. "I could hear them cheering as they advanced. . . . I never wanted to go help anybody so bad in my life. I was afraid they would all be killed or taken prisoners." Remley and his comrades had enough Rebels to deal with on their own front, however. Assistant Surgeon Kemper of the 17th thought it "a severe little battle," adding the 17th suffered three wounded and two captured. "We were almost completely surrounded," noted Kemper. "Pegram's strong cavalry force was in sight."[30]

Forrest added to Colonel Wilder's woes by pressing the 123rd Illinois, which was still on rear guard duty, from the direction of Ringgold. Retreat back the way they had come was now impossible. Kemper was right—the Lightning Brigade was "almost completely surrounded." Short the 92nd Illinois, Wilder's brigade numbered only about 1,900 men. If Forrest could deploy his available strength of Scott's, Pegram's and Dibrell's brigades, he could bring to bear more than 5,000 troopers. Those long odds, however, were largely offset by Wilder's devastating Spencer-armed firepower and the difficulty the Rebels faced in coordinating their actions from converging directions without direct communication.

The fighting lasted about two hours. Wilder's initial advance drove Pegram's force far enough south to open the road leading west toward Peavine Church. Since that road also led to Lee and Gordon's Mills, Wilder decided to use that route to disengage, though he waited until dark to do so to utilize the added cover of night to conceal his movement. Carrying their casualties with them, "the wounded were loaded into ambulances and wagons" while the dead were laid out on the porch of Leet's white frame house. Sergeant Benjamin Magee of the 72nd Indiana later recorded that indeed the Rebels seemed to be everywhere—front, rear and sides. He also claimed that "Col. Wilder was much confused and did not know what to do." After extensive consultation, wrote

---

30 Dale Edward Linville, *Battles, Skirmishes, Events and Scenes: The Letters and Memorandum of Ambrose Remley* (Montgomery County Historical Society, 1997), 81; "Dear Cousin Hattie," Sept 27, 1863, G. W. H Kemper Letters, Ball State University; and "entry for September 12," Kemper Diary, OHS.

Magee, Col. Abram Miller in command of the 72nd "got us mounted on the road leading west."[31]

Given the extent of the fighting, Union losses, estimated between 23 and 35, were surprisingly light. Pegram reported 50 Confederates lost to all causes, while another source recorded as many as 82. Regardless of how many Rebels fell, the affair gave them a healthy respect for repeating rifles; they let the Federals fall back unmolested. Wilder's dead, which Private Minnich of the 6th Georgia counted at 13, were buried in Leet's orchard along with a dozen Georgians.[32]

The retreating Federal column did not get far before running into a new problem. Musician Henry Campbell, the 18th Indiana Battery's 17-year-old bugler, captured the events that afternoon in his journal:

> [We] moved down the right hand road about 1 mile, where the road entered the main La Fayette Road. Here we halted to find which road the main body of rebels had gone, as all the roads were dusty; and had the appearance as if a large force of troops had been over them. Col. Wilder seeing a column of troops moving south, way over to the right, sent a scout over to them with dispatches—supposing they were part of Crittenden's Corps—Scout never returned, it was Pegram's Division of rebels and we were ahead of them. Way over to open fields to the left of us could be seen a long dark line of battle, arms glistening in the setting sun.[33]

Wilder halted and deployed the brigade to receive an attack from what appeared to be a superior force. Sergeant Magee (who remembered this happening after dark) recalled that it was a captured Confederate picket who identified this force as a Confederate division. The "long dark line of battle" turned out to be Maj. Gen. Benjamin F. Cheatham's 7,000-man Confederate division, which had fallen back to Rock Springs from the Mills the day before.[34]

31 Baumgartner, *Blue Lightning*, 174; Benjamin F. Magee, *History of the 72nd Indiana Volunteer Infantry of the Mounted Lightning Brigade* (S. Vater and Co., 1882), 160.

32 The higher estimate comes from Connolly, *Three Years in the Army*, 119, and likely also includes the rear guard casualties. Baumgartner, *Blue Lightning*, 175; John W. Minnich, "Reminiscences of J. W. Minnick," *Northwest Georgia Historical and Genealogical Society Quarterly*, vol. 29, no. 3 (Summer, 1997), 20.

33 Entry for September 12," Henry Campbell Journal Transcript, Ramsey Archival Center, Wabash College, Crawfordsville, IN.

34 Magee, *History of the 72nd Indiana*, 160.

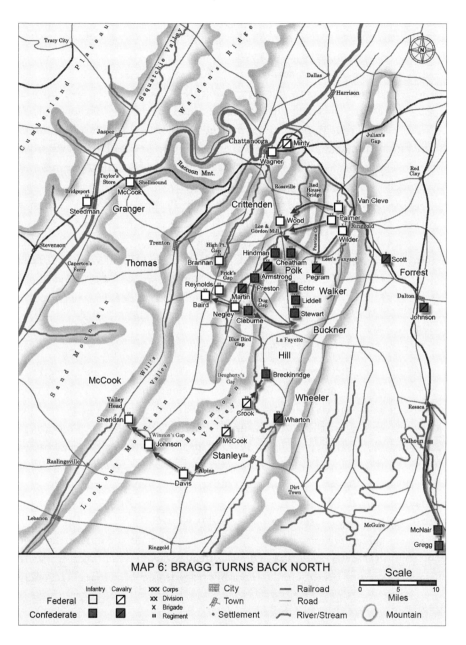

MAP 6: BRAGG TURNS BACK NORTH

With darkness almost completely covering the landscape, Wilder once again sought some means of escape. This time he turned to the locals for assistance. "The 17th [Indiana] press[ed] in all the old inhabitants . . . to act as guides, threatening them with instant death if they failed." They soon found one suitable fellow. "[We] pressed . . . an old citizen to pilot us out," recalled Magee. The old man protested that he wanted no part of such a hazardous undertaking, but the Federals insisted. He eventually agreed to guide them. Before they left, however, Wilder engaged in a bit of trickery. In an effort to misdirect the Confederates, he ordered Capt. Lawson S. Kilborn of the 72nd to set up a false camp on a nearby hill complete with campfires. The deception worked well enough for Wilder's force to slip away unmolested. As the fires burned the local led the Federals though fields and farm lanes back to Lee and Gordon's Mills. The column "crossed and re-crossed roads, followed cow paths &c," recorded Campbell the bugler, "and after marching about 8 miles we reached Crittenden's Corps with greatly relieved minds."[35]

Wary of following Wilder's men too closely, Pegram reported the action at Leet's to Bragg and outlined the Union dispositions as he understood them: "Van Cleve's division . . . said to be advancing on the Gordon Mills Road, Palmer's division . . . on the Pea Vine Church Road, and Wood's division . . . on [the] Ringgold and Lafayette Road." Bragg quickly grasped that he had been handed another opportunity to strike, assuming Pegram's details were correct.[36]

*   *   *

At 7:00 a.m. that morning, while Crittenden's men were converging on Lee and Gordon's Mills and before Wilder had even left Ringgold, Maj. Gen. Frank Cheatham's division of Polk's Corps began marching north out of La Fayette. As noted earlier, on the 11th Cheatham's men were at Doctor Anderson's house guarding Worthen's Gap and Hindman's line of retreat should he need one. After the disappointing conclusion in McLemore's Cove, Cheatham was ordered to La Fayette with the rest of the army, which turned out to be a mistake, given the Union XXI Corps's movements. Bragg soon ordered Cheatham to change destinations and head back to Rock Springs. Cheatham's division covered the intervening 10 miles at a halting pace, the intense dust and long column slowing progress to a crawl. Private Edwin H. Rennolds of the 4th Tennessee, part of Brig. Gen. Otho Strahl's brigade, recorded that his regiment

---

35 Campbell Journal, Wabash College; Magee, *History of the 72nd Indiana*, 160. Several Federals recounted with glee the extent the Rebels were taken in by this decoy camp, going so far as to describe a dawn attack launched by Pegram and part of Cheatham's division. No Confederate accounts corroborate such an action. There was a renewal of picket firing at dawn, which might well explain the Union accounts of the supposed "fight."

36 *OR* 30, pt. 2, 76.

did not depart La Fayette until 10:00 a.m. Polk and his corps headquarters waited until 4:00 p.m. to ride out, arriving at Rock Springs around 7:00 p.m.[37]

Bragg also turned to Walker's Reserve Corps to support Cheatham. A Georgian by birth, Maj. Gen. William Henry Talbot Walker was a graduate of West Point (class of 1837) and Old Army professional. His predilection for collecting enemy lead during the Seminole and Mexican wars earned him the nickname "shot-pouch." Walker's peers respected him and recognized his abilities as a fighter. His short, slight stature belied his combative nature both on and off the battlefield. He was in his element leading troops in combat, but he could be a contentious man, opinionated and argumentative to a fault.

Walker served under his old classmate Bragg at Pensacola in 1861, where he fumed at everyone and about everything due to his dissatisfaction at the slow pace of events in that secondary theater. Claiming ill health, Walker arranged for a transfer and spent the next two years in various commands in Virginia, on the Atlantic Coast, and most recently under Joseph E. Johnston in Mississippi until Johnston sent him to Chattanooga.[38]

A potential organizational disaster loomed when Brig. Gen. St. John Liddell was dropped into Walker's Reserve Corps. Liddell had recently commanded a brigade in Pat Cleburne's division until, just before the evacuation of Chattanooga, Bragg elevated Liddell to lead a new division comprised of his own and Brig. Gen. Edward C. Walthall's brigades. That order also assigned the new division to Walker's scratch corps, which dismayed Liddell. A man who could take the least implied slight as a grave personal insult, Liddell was certain the assignment was punishment for having referred to Tullahoma as a "disaster" during Bragg's September 2 council of war.[39]

Born in Mississippi in 1815, Liddell turned 47 on September 6. Unlike Bragg and Walker, he did not graduate from West Point. Although he won an appointment to the academy in 1833, he was discharged after only a year for unspecified "conduct highly subversive to good order and discipline." (Rumor had it he fought a duel and wounded a fellow cadet.) One of his classmates that

37 Entry for September 12, E. H. Rennolds Diary, TSLA; OR 30, pt. 2, 76.

38 Stephen Davis, "A Georgia Firebrand: Major General W. H. T. Walker, C.S.A.," *Confederate Historical Institute Journal*, vol. II, no. 3 (Summer, 1981), 4.

39 Hughes, *Liddell's Record*, 136-137. Liddell was friends with General Mackall, and later asked that officer for an explanation for the transfer. Mackall, said Liddell, would only say, "It was done contrary to my wishes."

year was his new commander, William Walker. Denied a military career, Liddell pursued a plantation life in Louisiana. In 1847 he became embroiled in a real estate feud with his neighbor, the exact origins of which remain murky. What we do know is that it lasted beyond the Civil War, was known locally as the Black River War, and ultimately claimed 14 lives including Liddell's. Liddell, wrote historian and biographer Nathaniel Cheairs Hughes, "hated well, and never apologized for it." When civil war arrived in 1861, Liddell left his plantation to return to uniform. He served briefly in Virginia before landing positions on the staffs of Gens. William J. Hardee and Albert Sidney Johnston. After Shiloh, he managed a brigadier general's commission and led his brigade into stiff fights at Perryville and Murfreesboro. He was not popular, especially with Walthall's recently transferred Mississippians. One of them found Liddell "ill-fitted, by reason of undue excitability, to personally command troops in time of action." Ironically, that was essentially the same complaint Liddell lodged against Walker.[40]

Walker's men filed back from Dug Gap on the 11th and fell in behind Cheatham's column. "Ordered to move on the Snow Hill Road 12 miles," recorded Maj. Alfred L. Dearing of Walker's staff, "as the enemy are reported in force. Polk's Corps and Walker's ordered to meet them." Walker's temper, never far from boiling over at the best of times, was tested by all this back and forth movement. His corps had become a "shuttlecock concern," he complained to his wife, shifted to and fro each time Bragg planned an attack.[41]

While Walker marched and fumed, Bragg pondered Pegram's electrifying dispatch concerning the engagement at Leet's and Union dispositions. At 6:00 p.m., he ordered Polk to attack what was supposed to be a single division (Palmer's) "at daylight" on September 13. "This division crushed," Bragg exhorted, "and the others are yours." A second order, sent at 8:00 p.m., emphasized again the need for a dawn attack and added more detail concerning Palmer's location, "three quarters of a mile beyond Peavine Church on the road to Graysville."[42]

---

40 Hughes, *Liddell's Record*, 8, 13; Warner, *Generals in Gray*, 187; Sykes, "Walthall's Brigade", 597.

41 Entry for September 12, Alfred Long Dearing Diary, Hargrett Library, University of Georgia, Athens GA, hereafter UGA; Russell K. Brown, *To the Manner Born: The Life of General William H. T. Walker* (University of Georgia Press, 1994), 164.

42 OR 30, pt. 2, 30. This location actually pinpoints Wilder's brigade, not Palmer's division.

Once Walker's troops deployed on Cheatham's right, Walker and Liddell rode to see General Polk. Liddell was still taking the measure of his new commander and former West Point classmate, a man he had not seen in many years. The evening conference he witnessed between Walker and Polk inside Rock Springs Church did nothing to reassure the Louisianan of "Shotpouch's" qualifications for high command. The aggressive Walker responded to Bragg's attack order with enthusiasm. Polk, on the other hand, saw nothing but peril and so deployed Liddell's and Walker's men in a defensive posture astride the roads to both Ringgold and Rossville until the rest of the force could come up.

Walker and Polk quarreled; Liddell observed. The defensive disposition made sense to Liddell, but not to Walker, who "found fault with 'Old Polk's' dispositions, one after another, until the General seemed greatly perplexed in trying to explain and alter them to suit Walker." Nothing satisfied the Georgian. The argumentative general continued objecting until, noted Liddell, one of "Polk's staff officers appealed to me to get Walker off." Liddell had maneuvered Walker almost out the door when "something occurred to him, he went back to the General, determined to settle it or have the last word." The frustrated Liddell appealed for Frank Cheatham, who was also present, to intercede. Cheatham, too, had been observing the unsettling exchange. "Suddenly, Cheatham turned around to me, saying with an oath that he would not serve two hours under Walker to save his life. Walker stayed until he had pretty much exhausted rhetoric and expletives, until finally he and Polk ran out of things to argue about." Lamented Liddell, "This was the man Bragg had placed over me."[43]

Had Bragg been present, he undoubtedly would have taken up where Walker left off. With Walker's departure, Polk sent to Bragg informing him that the Yankees outnumbered him, and of the decision to go over to the defensive. In fact, added Polk, "the enemy is moving with steady step on my position—it is a strong one—and will no doubt attack early in the morning. My troops I cannot get into position to attack myself at so early an hour as day-dawn. If I find he is not going to attack me, I will attack him without delay." When Bragg read this dispatch an hour before midnight, he may well have been moved to "rhetoric and expletives." To Bragg, Polk's foot-dragging looked like more of the stalling that had foiled his plans in McLemore's Cove. Bragg dashed off a quick reply. Polk must "not defer his attack, his force being already numerically

43 Hughes, *Liddell's Record*, 140.

superior to the enemy, and . . . success depended on the promptness and rapidity of his movements." Polk must strike at dawn, Bragg insisted. To allay Polk's fears, Bragg also promised him reinforcements, turning once again to Simon Buckner's Corps, which would march to join Polk from La Fayette first thing in the morning.[44]

*   *   *

Bragg's attack orders were based on two false assumptions: the first a result of a miscalculation on Bragg's part, and the second predicated on a blunder by Pegram. Bragg's error was his assumption that Polk would have his entire corps in place for the attack. Hindman spent most of the night extracting his division out of McLemore's Cove and marching 13 difficult miles to La Fayette, where his men spent the day resting and cooking another three days' rations. Hindman would not be able to resume his march to join Polk until 10:30 p.m., and getting there would require another all-night march. The bishop-turned-general was thus less than certain he would be ready for a dawn attack, and why he believed he was outnumbered. Bragg assumed Polk would have 25,000 troops to fall on Palmer's Yankees; Polk understood that when he received the attack order he had only Cheatham's 7,000 men plus Walker's roughly 6,500 immediately available. This was still a sizable force if he was in fact only facing Palmer.[45]

The second blunder was Pegram's. His dispatch outlined the movements of Crittenden's XXI Corps during the day, but did not inform Bragg that all of Crittenden's troops had reached Lee and Gordon's Mills by nightfall. Instead of leaving three divisions scattered across 20 miles of northern Georgia, Crittenden's entire command of 15,000 men (less the brigade garrisoning Chattanooga) was now concentrated and ready for a fight.

Another dawn arrived without a Rebel attack. This time Bragg was not immediately on the scene, but he was hastening to reach it. He departed La Fayette at 5:00 a.m., ahead of Buckner's Corps, and likely reached Polk shortly after 6:00. Disappointing news awaited. Hindman's command was up but not yet in place, Polk's "line of battle had not yet been formed," and word from

---

44 William M. Polk, *Leonidas Polk, Bishop and General,* 2 vols. (Longmans, Green and Co. 1915), vol. 2, 241-242; *OR* 30, pt. 2, 30-31.

45 Entry for September 12, Joseph Miller Rand Diary, Mississippi Department of Archives and History, Jackson, MS. Hereafter MDAH.

Cheatham (via Pegram's cavalry) was that "the enemy had disappeared from our front."[46]

Hindman was sick, so Patton Anderson once again assumed command of that division. The troops were tired, having made a second night march in a row. Nor was the break during the day in between all that restful. According to Lt. James Fraser of the 50th Alabama, on September 12th the division was "halted in an open field and left to melt until 2 o'clock p.m. (I think the most refined manner of cruelty.)" Sunset march orders were cancelled, and the division did not move until midnight. It was sunrise before the column reached Rock Springs Church, where they discovered, according to newspaperman Felix G. de Fontaine who rode with the division, "the wary enemy had changed his position . . . and was not to be found."[47]

As was now a refined tradition within the Army of Tennessee, an argument ensued. According to Polk, Bragg initially insisted the enemy must still be somewhere on the Graysville Road, and should be attacked there—even though no one could find them. At 7:00 a.m. Polk issued a preliminary attack order, almost certainly at Bragg's insistence. Ninety minutes later, a second order converted this effort into a reconnaissance, with Cheatham, Hindman, and Walker directed to "push forward a brigade each on the Gordon's Mills [La Fayette] Pea Vine [Graysville] and Ringgold Roads, respectively, following the cavalry, in order to develop the enemy." The Federals intervened before the issue was resolved.[48]

Polk was not altogether wrong in supposing that he might be attacked. So far, Tom Crittenden's portion of the campaign had consisted of one easy success after another, and his attitude remained buoyantly optimistic. If the Rebels wouldn't come to him, he would go find them. Having reassembled his corps, he was ready to bring on a fight. That morning, Crittenden ordered a series of probes. The newly arrived 4th U.S. Cavalry was sent to the right, via Crawfish Spring, to make sure no Rebels had slipped between Crittenden and Thomas's XIV Corps in McLemore's Cove. Horatio Van Cleve made a similar

46 Entry for September 13, Brent Journal, WRHS. This last was clearly a reference to Wilder's escape the night before, and perhaps the discover y of the false camp.

47 Entry for September 12, Extract from Civil War Diary of James H. Fraser , 50th Alabama file, CCNMP; Tower, *A Carolinian Goes to War*, 104.

48 Polk, *Bishop and General*,vol. 2, 242. Polk's son and biographer recorded that Bragg did not arrive until 9:00 a.m., but that is clearly much too late. *OR* 30, pt. 4, 645.

reconnaissance down the La Fayette Road, with Wilder moving to Van Cleve's left toward Leet's Tanyard, close enough to screen Van Cleve's flank.[49]

Van Cleve moved out about 9:00 a.m. with Samuel Beatty's brigade of infantry in the lead. Beatty placed his 19th Ohio in line to the left of the road, the 79th Indiana and 17th Kentucky on the right and, with the 9th Kentucky and a battery of artillery in support, set off. "Our brigade was sent out to feel the enemy," recorded 2nd Lt. Marcus Woodcock of the 9th Kentucky. "We had scarcely cleared the picket line ere the skirmishing began with considerable warmth on both sides." Initial contact was with more Rebel cavalry, this time from Frank Armstrong's division. The Confederate horsemen fell back a mile or so to Cheatham's picket line. There, resistance stiffened when Beatty met Strahl's Tennessee brigade moving north on the same misson. The Confederate foray was an effort, supposed Pvt. Van Buren Oldham of the 9th Tennessee, "to bring on the attack."[50]

Despite the potential for a serious infantry clash, the engagement instead turned into a long range artillery duel, more noisy than bloody. Captain Lucius Drury commanded both the 3rd Wisconsin Battery and served as Van Cleve's divisional artillery chief. Drury was an able and aggressive officer with more to his resume than just gunnery. At McMinnville during the summer of 1863, the multifaceted officer had served as chief of Van Cleve's scout. In that capacity he had led a number of far-ranging patrols across Middle Tennessee. As the action developed, Drury was again in the forefront, positioning the guns and overseeing their activity. "Our battery . . . charged ahead of our skirmish line and getting in a very advanced position, poured out our shells as rapidly as possible," noted the 3rd Wisconsin's historian. The Confederates responded in kind, the opposing guns thundering on for about 30 minutes. The noise was significant enough to draw the attention of Union signalers atop Missionary Ridge near Rossville, who reported up the chain of command to Rosecrans's headquarters. The fighting broke off before the action could become general.[51]

49 James Larson, *Sergeant Larson, 4th Cav.* (Southern Literary Institute, 1935), 173.

50 Noe, *A Southern Boy in Blue*, 191; Entry for September 13, Van Buren Oldham Diaries, University of Tennessee at Martin. Oldham's regiment was in Brig. Gen. Maney's Brigade, not Strahl's, and thus not directly engaged.

51 Hiram H. G. Bradt, *History of the Services of the Third Battery Wisconsin Light Artillery in the Civil War of the United States, 1861-65* (Courant Press, 1902), 25; OR 30, pt. 3, 597.

Van Cleve reported only four casualties for the entire affair. Two were from the 19th Ohio, and a lieutenant from the 79th Indiana. The fourth was Captain Drury, a man Van Cleve regarded with fondness. The aggressive captain paid for his boldness by being picked off by a Rebel skirmisher. The round pierced his liver, the diaphragm, and his right lung. Nearly everyone assumed Drury was done for. Hauled back "more than two miles over the roughest of roads" to the Mills, the surgeon who treated him gave the wounded officer ten to one odds that he would die. "I'll take the odd chance and live," came the whispered willful reply. He would return to duty within six months, but for now he was out of the war.[52]

About 12:30 p.m. on the 13th, as Van Cleve's dust-up was winding down and the troops falling back to the Mills, Rosecrans sent two communiqués to Crittenden. The first was a lengthy missive dictating the XXI Corps's next moves. Leaving Wood's division to hold the Mills, Rosecrans wanted Crittenden to take his other two divisions east to Missionary Ridge, where they could cover the several roads running north out of the valley of Chattanooga Creek. The move was intended to block any effort by Bragg to insert a force between Crittenden and Thomas, which would block Thomas's best line of retreat up that same valley. Wood might be vulnerable at the Mills, but he could retreat toward Rossville and find reinforcements from Gordon Granger's Reserve Corps if the Confederates attacked. The second communiqué, a direct response to Van Cleve's noisy artillery fight, directed Crittenden "to move back to Gordon's Mills . . . in case you have advanced beyond that point."[53]

Having promised Crittenden aid from Granger in exchange for Wood's exposure, Rosecrans took steps to make sure that aid was forthcoming. Granger was still at Bridgeport guarding the Army of the Cumberland's supply line. His Reserve Corps of seven brigades was organized in three divisions, but only three brigades were close at hand. Colonel Daniel McCook's large Illinois and Ohio brigade was at Shellmound and already moving to Chattanooga. Brigadier General James B. Steedman's two-brigade First Division had also been summoned from Bridgeport. In response to Rosecrans's query, Granger, who had been diligent in pushing his troops forward, could happily report that McCook's brigade would be in Chattanooga by the end of the day on the 13th,

---

52 *Society of the Army of the Cumberland, Seventeenth Reunion* (Robert Clark & Co. 1886), 253. Information first provided by Louis Mosier, via email, on 6/21/2011.

53 *OR* 30, pt. 3, 607-608.

and that Steedman "will be in Chattanooga by noon tomorrow." All told, another 6,000 troops would be available to backstop Wood at Rossville sometime on September 14. Shortly after these instructions were dispatched, Rosecrans left Chattanooga to ride south and join Thomas. Chattanooga was now too far from the scene of action. For the time being, army headquarters would remain in the city and serve as the clearinghouse for all information. Rosecrans, however, wanted to be up at the front to monitor the action more closely.[54]

Rebel losses from the Gordon's Mills fight passed unrecorded, but they could not have been considerable. The effect of this skirmish on Confederate commanders, however, was more significant. There was no longer any doubt as to the enemy's location. Even though Colonel Brent dismissed the short fight as a "slight cannonade," Bragg took precautions nonetheless. As Brent recorded in his journal, "Orders were given for our right to swing around toward the La Fayette and Chattanooga Road." The shift might have turned into an opportunity to strike Van Cleve in the flank if he had ventured far enough south, but instead the Yankees fell back. By midday Bragg concluded there was no chance of catching the XXI Corps divided, and reluctantly called off Polk's previously ordered assault.[55]

Despite Van Cleve's encounter with a strong force of Rebels, Crittenden remained naively optimistic, largely because neither the 4th U.S. probe nor Wilder's efforts encountered any threat. From this Crittenden concluded, "there is no considerable force of [enemy] infantry near me at this time. . . . I am satisfied they are not about to attack me. . . . Indeed I think I can whip them if they do—all of them."[56]

Ironically, it was now Polk who wanted to attack. Buckner's column had arrived and taken up position behind Cheatham's division. With more than 30,000 men on hand, Polk argued that Crittenden "was only five miles away, and the creek was easily fordable at many points both below and above his position." Launching a large-scale attack, however, would take time. All three corps—Polk's, Buckner's, and Walker's—would have to take up new positions, crossing the creek would be necessarily slow, and the likelihood of

---

54 Ibid., 613.

55 Entry for September 13, Brent Journal, WRHS

56 William Glenn Robertson, "The Chickamauga Campaign: The Armies Collide," *Blue & Gray Magazine*, vol. XXIV, no. 3 (Fall, 2007), 21.

accomplishing all of this and still attacking before dark was very small. At least another day would be required, but Bragg no longer believed that he had that day to spare. Word from La Fayette suggested that Federal forces were now advancing on that town from both the south, where McCook's XX Corps threatened, and from the west, where Thomas's XIV Corps had reentered McLemore's Cove.[57]

The threat from the west turned out to be minimal, though initially it seemed substantial enough to once again alarm D. H. Hill. With Cleburne's division still holding the gaps in Pigeon Mountain and John C. Breckinridge's three brigades deployed south of town, Hill's infantry was the only force left in La Fayette. Joe Wheeler's cavalry corps was screening each force, with Will Martin still in the cove and John Wharton's two brigades spread out ahead of Breckinridge's infantry line. On the afternoon of the 12th, while Bragg's focus was to the north, D. H. Hill's was zeroed in on another column of Yankees pushing their way into McLemore's Cove. George Thomas was indeed pushing Federal skirmishers forward, but not for aggressive purposes.

* * *

Thomas's XIV Corps spent September 12 moving the last of its troops and trains down into the cove, where Thomas had selected the line of Missionary Ridge upon which to establish a defensive line. There his four divisions could deploy abreast covering both Cooper's and Stevens's gaps, "behind which our trains can be parked and securely guarded . . . when a forward movement is determined on." In order to cover this movement, at 2:00 p.m. Thomas ordered John Brannan to take his Third Division on "a reconnaissance to the front."[58]

"We proceeded . . . to where the engagement took place yesterday, but found no enemy in force," recorded Capt. John D. Inskeep of Company C, part of the 17th Ohio of Brannan's command. The movement covered about six miles, with Brannan's men probing only as far as Davis's Crossroads before returning to take up their place in Thomas's new line after dark. This activity, however, was enough to briefly worry D. H. Hill, who asked Cleburne to find out if it signified a renewed threat to La Fayette. Cleburne's reassuring reply

---

57 Polk, *Bishop and General*, vol. 2, 244.

58 *OR* 30, pt. 3, 600; Entry for September 12, John D. Inskeep Diary, OHS. Brannan also borrowed a brigade from Baird for this mission.

arrived about midday on the 13th. "I have delayed in answering your note for the purpose of getting more information," explained Cleburne. The Federals advanced to within "1 mile from the foot of the mountain . . . [but] I am led to believe that they do not intend anything very serious at this point."[59]

Thomas also sent another probe into the cove a couple of miles farther north, this one conducted by Joe Reynolds's Fourth Division. It was, if anything, even less exciting than Brannan's patrol. The command, Lt. Thomas Stewart of the 11th Ohio noted in his diary, "changed camp and went out on a scout, coming back, Company 'I' was put on picket." A fellow Buckeye in the 68th Ohio, Cpl. Alanson Ryman, merely noted that they moved about three miles "and lay down for the night."[60]

In Hill's view, the threat of Union cavalry on the south road was much more worrisome. On the night of the 12th, it will be recalled, McCook ordered George Crook to make a strong movement toward La Fayette the next day to determine once and for all how many Confederates occupied the place.

Crook still had troopers on both of the main roads leading to La Fayette, with two brigades camped at Summerville and two more at Valley Store on the Alpine Road. The cavalry commander (who would personally accompany the latter, or left-hand, column) intended to advance on both roads to converge his troopers on La Fayette. Both columns started early, both covered the first few miles in uneventful fashion, and once they reached the Chattooga River, both found Rebels.[61]

Colonel Edward McCook commanded the force that set out from Summerville with Ray's and Watkins's brigades, all told about 2,700 sabers. After a comfortable breakfast the troopers approached the Chattooga Bridge at 10:00 a.m., where they found Col. Thomas Harrison's Confederate cavalry brigade deployed in opposition. With five regiments and a battery Harrison officially mustered nearly 2,300 men, though detachments almost certainly had considerably weakened his command. Backstopping Harrison, however, was

59 Entry for September 12, John D. Inskeep Diary, OHS; Moses B. Walker Report, 31st Ohio, Thomas Papers, RG 94, NARA; OR 30, pt. 4, 646

60 Entry for September 13, Thomas L. Stewart Diary, Hamilton County Library, Chattanooga TN; "Dear Jane," September 15, 1863, Alanson R. Ryman Letters, InHS.

61 Crook was still in command of the cavalry. Robert Mitchell arrived in Alpine on the night of September 12, too late to assume command over operations on the 13th.

Brig. Gen. Benjamin H. Helm's infantry brigade of Breckinridge's Division, Hill's Corps.[62]

The fighting that followed was severe enough to be notable, with both sides claiming a victory. "We here met with a considerable force of rebel infantry and some cavalry," admitted John Mendenhall of the 2nd Indiana Cavalry, "after considerable maneuvering and some skirmishing we were ordered back . . . . Our reconnaissance seemed to prove that Bragg's main army was moving down the Chattooga Valley." His advance blunted, Colonel McCook fell back and sent word to General Crook. As far as the Rebels were concerned the Union withdrawal was evidence of a sound thumping. "We had quite a brush with the enemy," Adjutant George Guild of the 4th Tennessee Cavalry reported, "driving him from the field."[63]

The second column riding out of Valley Store that morning with Crook at its head was accompanied by Col. Archibald Campbell and led by companies A, C, and E of the 9th Pennsylvania Cavalry.[64] At 3,200 sabers, Crook's column was slightly stronger than McCook's, but it too, would be overmatched. When long range artillery fire dropped amongst the Keystoners near the Chattooga crossing Crook aggressively responded. "It was the evident intention of General Crook to dash in as near the center of the rebel army as possible," admitted Lt. (and later historian) Marshall Thatcher of the 2nd Michigan Cavalry.[65]

Crook ordered the lead battalion of the 9th to charge up the road. The bold effort foundered when it "run [upon] a masked bat[tery] of three pieces . . . they cut loose," recorded participant Capt. Thomas McCahan of Company M. A number of men and horses went down. Undaunted, Crook ordered a second charge, and away the Pennsylvanians thundered again. "This was in a lane," wrote McCahan, "the dust so thick [we] could not see a regiment of rebel infantry on either side in the woods." Someone, however, spotted that infantry

62 Entry for September 13, William E. Corbitt Diary, EU; see also George W. Baum Diary, InHS; George B. Guild, *A Brief Narrative of the Fourth Tennessee Cavalry Regiment, Wheeler's Corps, Army of Tennessee* (n.p. 1913), 23.

63 Entry for September 13, John A. Mendenhall Diary, Morrison Reeves Library, Richmond, IN; Undated clipping from "The Tennessee Farmer," George B. Guild Scrapbook, TSLA.

64 Marshall P. Thatcher, *A Hundred Battles in the West* (published by the author, 1884), 141; John W. Rowell, *Yankee Cavalrymen: Through the Civil War with the Ninth Pennsylvania Cavalry* (University of Tennessee Press, 1971), 144.

65 Thatcher, *Hundred Battles*, 141.

just in time to avert disaster and allow McCahan's battalion to break off the assault. They were in the process of doing so when they swept up a portion of the Confederate skirmish line—"18 rebel prisoners all Irish," McCahan marveled, "the sauciest men I ever saw." The "all Irish" captives were Louisianans from New Orleans, part of Brig. Gen. Daniel Adams's brigade of Breckinridge's division.[66]

Adams's 1,600 infantry were supported by about 2,200 men from Col. C. C. Crews's mixed Georgia and Alabama cavalry brigade—far too many men for Crook to simply brush aside. When word arrived from McCook reporting similar opposition on the Summerville Road, Crook ordered McCook to abandon his approach and join him. Late that afternoon, the entire Union cavalry force fell back toward Alpine. La Fayette was still in Confederate hands.

Crook's retreat did nothing to allay D. H. Hill's fears. While Crook's cavalry was probing, Hill sent word to Bragg at Rock Springs that "Yankees, McCook's Corps, [were with]in four miles of La Fayette and that Breckinridge was engaged." It was alarming news. The loss of La Fayette would cost Bragg his forward supply dumps and cut him off from the most direct route to Resaca. The army commander promptly decided to return to La Fayette and ordered Buckner's Corps back south. W. H. T. Walker would follow Buckner, as would at least part of Polk's command. By dawn on September 14, virtually the entire Confederate army would be back in the same place it had occupied 24 hours earlier, in the fields around La Fayette. No wonder "Shotpouch" Walker called his new command a "shuttlecock."[67]

*   *   *

Neither Bragg nor Hill knew it, but the threat from the south had already evaporated by the time Hill's report reached Bragg's field desk. Early on the morning of the 13th, XX Corps commander McCook received new orders that dramatically changed his mission. Crook's probes on the 13th were no longer aimed at a reconnaissance to determine if La Fayette was vulnerable, but now designed to cover a retreat. McCook's new orders were to march his XX Corps north with all possible speed.

66 Entry for September 13, Thomas S. McCahan Diary, Historical Society of Pennsylvania, Philadelphia, PA. Hereafter HSP.

67 Entry for September 13, Brent Journal, WRHS.

McCook received two orders early on the morning of September 13. The first, from Rosecrans, reached him 30 minutes after midnight. The second, from Thomas, arrived about mid-morning. Circumstances had changed; Bragg was definitely not retreating. "It is of the most vital importance," stressed Rosecrans to his corps leader, that "[you] get within supporting distance of General Thomas at the earliest moment." Thomas's order also instructed McCook to "move immediately with two divisions" to support his XIV Corps near Stevens's Gap. One division would cover the corps trains, while Stanley's cavalry (neither Rosecrans nor Thomas was yet aware of Stanley's incapacitation) covered the movement. McCook sprang into action. At 8:30 a.m. he replied that his men were already en route, and that he should "be with General Thomas tonight, or very near him."[68]

McCook also took a moment to justify his actions to the departmental commander. Rosecrans was growing increasingly short-tempered as the hunt for Bragg metamorphosed from an aggressive pursuit into a need to gather in his own scattered forces. The delays in communications between his headquarters in Chattanooga and McCook's at Alpine frayed Rosecrans's nerves, and his dispatches to McCook and Stanley took on an increasingly peevish tone. Rosecrans worried that this lack of timely communication on McCook's part could be "classified by the commanding general as the next worst thing to running from the enemy" and was endangering the army. While Rosecrans never communicated this directly to McCook, Maj. Frank Bond overheard the comment and included it in a dispatch, perhaps in an effort to spur the recipients into more frequent communication. As might be expected, McCook took offense. Such was not the case, protested the XX Corps commander. He had maintained a courier line as best as he was able since the movement began. Sloppy staff work was more to blame, said McCook, for Rosecrans twice had moved his headquarters (from Stevenson to Trenton, and then from Trenton to Chattanooga) "without my knowledge." Moreover, he continued, "I cannot be responsible for the courier line of the Anderson Cavalry" who carried most of these dispatches. The Anderson Cavalry (15th Pennsylvania) belonged to army headquarters, not the XX Corps, and the horsemen were frequently slow, at least in McCook's estimation.[69]

68 OR 30, pt. 3, 570, 602-603.

69 Ibid., 603.

Rosecrans was being unreasonable. A brilliant man, he often didn't understand why everyone else couldn't live up to his own high personal expectations. His natural impatience didn't help matters, and he failed to account for how his own actions sometimes placed him incommunicado. The very day McCook was bridling at these insinuations of personal failure, Rosecrans took himself off of what passed for the nineteenth century's communications network for nearly 10 hours by moving his field headquarters from Chattanooga at 1:00 p.m. on September 13. The army leader was relocating to General Thomas's position, but the only secure way of doing so was by climbing Lookout Mountain at its point overlooking Chattanooga, riding south for more than two dozen miles to Cooper's or Stevens's gaps, and descending the mountain again behind the XIV Corps line in McLemore's Cove. According to Maj. Frank Bond, the headquarters party did not reach Thomas until "ten thirty P.M."[70]

McCook was about to once again be assailed for being too slow. His initial time estimate for joining Thomas—"[I will] be with General Thomas tonight, or very near him"—was optimistic under the best of circumstances. By the afternoon of the 13th, those circumstances looked considerably less rosy.

McCook had a choice of three routes by which to move his XX Corps north. All three required ascending Lookout Mountain at Alpine. From there, however, the most direct route lay via Dougherty's Gap, which descended the mountain at the head of McLemore's Cove where Pigeon Mountain split off from the main summit of Lookout. Once in the Cove, it was a march of about a dozen miles to Davis's Crossroads, and just a bit farther to Stevens's Gap. If the Cove was not firmly held by Union troops, however, McCook could be exposing his column to the same sort of trap Thomas had just barely avoided.

The second route was to retrace his path across Lookout, descend the mountain at Winston's Gap, and move north to Johnson's Crook. There he would have to climb Lookout a second time and cross and descend a second time, using either Stevens's or Cooper's gaps. This route was twice as long in road distance and required two complete crossings of Lookout Mountain

---

70 Charles H. Kirk, *History of the Fifteenth Pennsylvania Volunteer Cavalry Which Was Recruited and Known as the Anderson Cavalry in the Rebellion of 1861-1865* (n.p., 1906), 231; Extract of Diary for September 13th, Bond to Rosecrans, August 24th, 1891, Cist Family Papers, Cincinnati Historical Society. Hereafter CincHS.

instead of one. As noted earlier, each ascent and descent of Lookout added at least a full day to any movement.

The third option was along a road across the top of Lookout directly to Stevens's Gap, obviating the need for the second ascent and descent. This road was still longer than the one via Dougherty's, but it did not involve a second complete passage of the mountain. By that fact alone it suggested a faster path.

In this regard, however, the Army of the Cumberland's usually superb intelligence-gathering and map-making skills failed. While the roads were shown on Federal maps, the quality of the road to Dougherty's Gap and the other across the top of the mountain was unknown. No one had thought to scout them. The Union courier line from Chattanooga to McCook's headquarters still ran via Trenton and down Lookout Valley to Valley Head, not across the top of Lookout; it would not be shifted until September 15. Colonel Thomas Harrison's 39th Indiana Mounted Infantry was active on both sides of the mountain, but not, apparently, atop it. On September 13, McCook sent most of the Hoosier regiment across to Valley Head and then up Lookout Valley as part of that courier line. Only two companies were tasked with scouting the top of the mountain.[71]

McCook turned instead to local residents for information about the quality of those roads and the ease of passage down through Dougherty's Gap. What he learned alarmed him: "No good road" led to Dougherty's, and the paths were no better in the direction of Stevens's Gap. Perhaps just as alarming, the gap itself proved elusive. "It is impossible to learn anything from the citizens on the mountain of any gap of that name," bemoaned a frustrated (and bedridden) General Stanley, when he was ordered to scout for it the next day.[72]

McCook's overriding concern, however, remained the threat to his two lead divisions once they were down in the Cove. At midday, McCook admitted he was already running behind, delayed by Johnson's and Davis's ammunition wagons. He would not even reach the head of Dougherty's before nightfall. Lack of specifics concerning Thomas's position added to his worries, so much so that by 5:00 p.m. he sent word to Stanley, "I now have but one route to pursue, and that is by Winston's." Stanley concurred, and then both McCook and Stanley sent dispatches, via McCook's courier line, to Thomas informing him of this fact, sent down the east side of Lookout via Winston's. This decision

71 Kirk, *Fifteenth Pennsylvania Volunteer Cavalry*, 231; Entry for September 13, William J. Ralph Diary, InHS; OR 30, pt. 3, 605.

72 Lamers, *Edge of Glory*, 318; OR 30, pt. 3, 637.

would delay the full concentration of the Army of the Cumberland for at least 48 hours, or until September 16 at the earliest.[73]

Fortuitously for the Federals, Bragg's decision to move back to La Fayette meant he could do little to exploit McCook's delay. His own men were already jaded from the constant marching, and many of them needed to replenish their rations. Buckner's men had returned to their old camps on the night of the 13th, and Bragg ordered Polk and Walker back south as well. That movement, executed the next day, marched Bragg's troops in exactly the opposite direction of McCook's moving column.[74]

For another 24 hours, Hill remained convinced the Federals were concentrated at Alpine and an attack could be expected at any hour. Joseph Wheeler, who had Wharton's cavalry division watching those same Yankees, was unable to discern any retreat. Crook's cavalry remained on the west side of Lookout all day on the 14th covering the last of McCook's movement out of Broomtown Valley, leaving Wheeler's scouts unable to penetrate this screen or get atop Lookout anywhere else to observe McCook's infantry columns toiling westward. "Reports are conflicting," lamented Colonel Brent in his journal that afternoon. "McCook's Corps and a large force said to be at Alpine."[75]

While Bragg's army spent the next two days resting and refitting at La Fayette, its commander passed much of his time exploring why things had gone so wrong in both McLemore's Cove and with Polk's intended attack at Lee and Gordon's Mills. On the 14th, Bragg demanded explanations from Polk and the ill Hindman. No immediate reply was forthcoming from the latter, but Hindman did begin soliciting reports from the parties involved, including Buckner and Patton Anderson. Polk answered more promptly with what amounted to a rehash of his dispatch of the night of September 12. Both subordinates understood Bragg's displeasure had not abated, and that these issues would be revisited at a more proper time. The groundwork for inquiries and courts-martial were being laid, a dark shadow that would affect future decision-making. Everyone clearly understood the undercurrents of tension rippling through the Army of Tennessee's senior command. "It is impossible

---

73 OR 30, pt. 3, 603; ibid., 332. Note that the dispatch is misdated September 3. Ibid., 615

74 Ibid., pt. 4, 648.

75 Entry for September 14, Brent Journal, WRHS.

that this farce can continue much longer," wrote a disgusted William H. T. Walker in a letter to his wife on September 15.[76]

Rosecrans was also fretful, though for different reasons. He had no way of knowing that Bragg's army would remain inactive for the next few days. McCook understood that the choice to go by way of Winston's Gap rather than directly across the top of the mountain would upset his boss, and at 4:30 a.m. on September 14 dispatched a lengthy missive outlining his reasoning. This dispatch essentially provided a more detailed explanation of his 5:00 p.m. communiqué the night before: bad roads and the unknown dangers of the Cove dictated prudence. At 6:30 a.m., George Thomas responded to McCook's and Stanley's messages of the night before with approval, noting that "the route by Winston's Gap, I should think, is the only practicable one for you."[77]

By now Rosecrans was close by, also having arrived late the night before. As was his custom, he stayed up late and slept late. When he arose the next morning and read the news of McCook's route he was, unlike Thomas, displeased. Just before noon on the 14th Rosecrans sent his own message to McCook, with a strikingly different tone: "The general commanding regrets that you are moving back through Winston's Gap. . . . He directs you to turn around at once to the head of McLemore's Cove."[78]

Rosecrans was reacting instead of thinking things through. Given the time-lag that each dispatch required for delivery, this one (sent at noon) would take about five hours to reach McCook. Since Rosecrans was responding to McCook's dispatch from the night before, the XX Corps would have been on the road nearly a full 24 hours before it could even begin to reverse course. Vacillation would be the greater danger now. McCook understood this and protested—but in his reply at 5:30 p.m. on the 14th he also informed Rosecrans he would "suspend the movement until I hear from you." At 9:00 p.m., once Rosecrans digested McCook's reply, he realized it was too late to backtrack. Small garrisons would still have to be left at Dougherty's Gap and Valley Head to prevent Rebel cavalry from interfering with the XX Corps rear and supply lines, but the bulk of the corps must come on as quickly as possible via

76 OR 30, pt. 2, 307; Brown, *To the Manner Born*, 167.

77 OR 30, pt. 3, 628.

78 Ibid., 629.

McCook's original route. Rosecrans's snap decision had added at least another half-day's delay to the march.[79]

The upshot was that the XX Corps would not be closing up with Thomas's line until either late on September 15 or early on the 16th (although McCook himself rode ahead and would be present early on the 15th). Fortunately for the Federals the added delay proved of little consequence because the Confederates remained ensconced in La Fayette and would not move out again for several days.

The next few days saw little action. Rosecrans shifted troops from both Thomas and Crittenden to cover the gap between the XIV Corps and XXI Corps. On the 14th, Joe Reynolds's Fourth Division moved to Pond Spring, where, reunited with the 92nd Illinois and the rest of Wilder's brigade, undertook patrols in the direction of Catlett's and Worthen's gaps without any significant enemy contact. "Our scouts saw the rebel pickets but we passed along without interruption," observed Pvt. William Boddy of the 92nd. It seemed more like a pleasure outing than a military mission: "[We] spent a beautiful day and traveled about 20 miles."[80]

Crittenden, together with Palmer's and Van Cleve's infantry divisions, moved west to the hills of Missionary Ridge early on the 14th as ordered. The XXI Corps commander found little to do there. There were no Rebels in sight, and certainly none trying to interpose themselves between his and Thomas's corps. A lack of water meant he could not camp two divisions where he was (atop the ridge at the cabin of a man named Henson). After a series of inquiries to Rosecrans, Thomas, and via army headquarters still in Chattanooga, Crittenden moved off the hills and into Chattanooga valley, where he could at least find sufficient water.[81]

Realizing that there was no threat for Crittenden to counter, that same afternoon Rosecrans ordered Crittenden back almost where he had begun the march that morning. Rosecrans intended that Crittenden's three divisions be dispersed along a several mile front, with Wood remaining at Lee and Gordon's Mills, Palmer's three brigades sent to cover Glass Mill, and Van Cleve stationed as a reserve at Crawfish Spring. This activity wore on Van Cleve, who at just a

---

79 Ibid., 630.

80 Robert E. Berkenes, ed. *Private William Boddy's Civil War Journal: Empty Saddles . . . Empty Sleeves . . .* (TiffCor Publishing, 1996), 76.

81 *OR* 30, pt. 3, 631-632.

month shy of 54 was the oldest division commander in the army and feeling every year of his age. "After this campaign is over I expect to feel the effects of sleepless nights, irregular meals, and hard bread and bacon. I am standing it thus far very well," he believed, "but cannot be expected to stand it long." As to the elusive nature of the Rebels, Van Cleve added, "We have been beating about here seven days looking for the enemy, but as yet do not find them in heavy force."[82]

82 Ibid., 632-633; "My Darling Wife," September 14, 1863, Horatio Van Cleve Letters, MinnHS.

Chapter Seven

Bragg Essays a New Plan:

September 15-17, 1863

By the second week of September, most of the rank and file of the Army of the Cumberland understood that Braxton Bragg's army had been heavily reinforced. It was common knowledge that Simon Bolivar Buckner had evacuated East Tennessee, and the steady influx of tired and homesick deserters brought rumors of more Rebels arriving daily via the rails. Most seemed to be from coming from Joseph E. Johnston's army in Mississippi, and there were even several purported sightings of Johnston himself. One deserter from Forrest's cavalry claimed to have seen the famous Confederate general at Dalton on September 11. A lieutenant of the Rebel 3rd Kentucky Cavalry who was more or less captured voluntarily placed Johnston at La Fayette on the 9th amid a host of other Rebel generals. While General Rosecrans's headquarters generally disregarded sightings of Johnston, no one could deny that significant elements of his command were now arriving in North Georgia.[1]

Even more troubling were similar rumors of troops en route from the Virginia theater. If true, the Confederacy was making an epic effort to defend Chattanooga and defeat Rosecrans. Was the Army of the Cumberland about to find itself heavily outnumbered? Rosecrans was convinced no such large scale

---

1   *OR* 30, pt. 3, 582, 604.

movement could be undertaken without ample warning from General Halleck in Washington. Surely the Confederacy could not transfer an entire army corps (or more, by some of the rumors) across the country without Union intelligence catching wind of it. In fact, that was exactly what the Confederates were doing. On September 8, Lt. Gen. James Longstreet and the leading elements of his First Corps of Lee's Army of Northern Virginia marched away from their camps near Orange Court House destined for Georgia. Their departure was the result of prolonged deliberation and was too late to prevent Bragg from having to abandon Chattanooga, but they were on their way now.

Longstreet's detachment was the culmination of a debate that commenced in May, well before either the fall of Vicksburg or the invasion of Pennsylvania. A number of Confederate political and military leaders were growing increasingly concerned about the deteriorating nature of the military situation west of the Appalachians. Every Yankee offensive had been ably rebuffed in Virginia thanks to Robert E. Lee's leadership, but the war was being lost bit by bit in the western states. The Confederacy did not survive long enough to form distinct political parties, but a loose amalgam of politicians and military officers did coalesce for the purpose of opposing President Davis and his military strategy. By 1863 this group, dubbed the "Western Concentration bloc" by historian Thomas L. Connelly, pushed hard for more resources for western operations. During the spring of 1863 the interest group prodded the president for major reinforcements, and perhaps even Lee himself, to be sent west to redress the situation. Their pleas passed unheeded, and Lee instead marched north into Pennsylvania.[2]

That early July Lee was sharply defeated at Gettysburg and Vicksburg surrendered. By the end of August, the impending threat to Chattanooga revived Western Bloc arguments to shift assets west. The decision was put off until the first week of September, by which time both Chattanooga and Knoxville had fallen. Their loss meant the Confederacy lost its most direct route linking east and west via rail from southwest Virginia through East Tennessee. Troops bound for Bragg would now have to travel 900 miles, or

---

2   For a full discussion of the "Western Concentration bloc," see Thomas L. Connelly and Archer Jones, *The Politics of Command: Factions and Ideas in Confederate Strategy* (Louisiana State University Press, 1973), 49-86. The Western Concentration bloc included notable politicians, such as Texas Senator Louis T. Wigfall, generals on the outs with President Davis, including Joseph E. Johnston and P. G. T. Beauregard, and also James Longstreet from the Army of Northern Virginia.

more than twice the original distance. The convoluted journey across much of the Confederacy's deteriorated and mismatched rail system involved multiple routes and changes of trains. Even the exact composition of the force was debated. Longstreet commanded three divisions, but only two would accompany him to Georgia. Major General George Pickett's depleted command had not yet recovered from its bloody Gettysburg ordeal and would be left in Richmond. Brigadier General Micah Jenkins's large 2,000-man brigade went in its place. An active Union threat to Charleston, South Carolina, also served to trim down the reinforcement pool and a pair of brigades would be dropped off there to defend the region. Longstreet tapped Georgians for the effort, at least in part because he feared many might desert if they reentered their home state.[3]

When finally established, the plan called for the large scale movement of nearly 15,000 infantry, three battalions of artillery, plus the horses and baggage of an entire infantry corps. Brigadier General Alexander Lawton, the Confederacy's quartermaster, and Maj. Frederick W. Sims, who headed up the Confederate Bureau of Railroads, coordinated the complex operation. Sims bore the central role, speeding telegrams to stations all across the South, alerting locals and arranging for rolling stock. The loss of Knoxville early in the effort complicated his work and required a complete rerouting of the entire affair. It soon became apparent that moving Longstreet's 15,000 men might be too much for the rails to bear. "Three thousand troops per day is the utmost that can be transported," Sims wired Lee on September 7, and so were given top priority. Wagons, artillery, and horses were more cumbersome then men and would be inserted later into the rickety pipeline. Most units moved without their customary supply trains or even officers' mounts. Bragg would have to meet their needs out of his own already slim resources once they arrived. Longstreet's artillery was reduced to a single battalion of six batteries commanded by Lt. Col. Edward Porter Alexander, his ablest gunner.[4]

The bulk of Longstreet's veterans were issued new uniforms before leaving. Most drew clothing while in camp along the Rapidan River at the end of

---

3   OR 29, pt. 2, 704. Brigadier Generals George T. Anderson's and William T. Wofford's brigades were chosen for the duty, although both would be sent on to Chattanooga that October.

4   Frederick A. Eiserman, *Longstreet's Corps at Chickamauga: Lessons in Inter-Theater Deployment*, Master's Thesis, U.S. Army Command and General Staff College, Ft. Leavenworth, KS, 1985, 22.

August in a general issue to the entire army, but some received their new clothes while on the move." We drew new uniforms as we passed through Richmond en route to Atlanta," recalled Capt. George Todd of the 1st Texas. "These, especially the pants, were almost blue." In fact, these uniforms were made from imported British wool, dyed a dark steel gray, and were very different than the usual uniforms found in Bragg's army. They would prove both distinctive, and sometimes confusing, in the dust and smoke of the battle to come.[5]

The early stage of the trip out of Virginia was smooth enough, but troubles arose after crossing into North Carolina. About 9:00 p.m. on September 9, leading elements of Brig. Gen. Henry L. Benning's brigade (2nd, 15th, 17th, and 20th Georgia regiments) detrained in the state capital at Raleigh. Benning spent some time "procuring transportation" for the next leg of the journey before laying down by the siding to catch some sleep. Other Georgians, however, decided to head into town. Some made for the home of the editor of the *North Carolina Standard*, widely viewed as a disloyal publication for its ongoing criticism of President Davis and the progress of the war. Not finding the editor at home, the mob moved on to the *Standard's* office and sacked it. By then it was approaching 11:00 p.m. and Benning's brigade was boarding trains to move on. The incipient mob was quelled and the troops rounded up and returned to their ranks. The damage, however, was done.[6]

The citizens of Raleigh were enraged. The next day, a counter-mob attacked the pro-government *State Journal*, doing even more damage. Feelings ran high against the soldiers—any soldiers—unlucky enough to follow Benning's men; Raleigh's residents seethed over the vandalism for the next two days. The day after the initial destruction, North Carolina Governor Zebulon Vance telegraphed Richmond, "Soldiers now on the road from Weldon have indulged in threats of further violence when they arrive here." Davis must do something, insisted Vance. In a panic, the governor finished with a melodramatic flourish: "If you wish to save North Carolina to the Confederacy, be quick." On the 11th, a mob of Alabama troops "entered the city and spread terror . . . by threatening murder and conflagration." Vance was especially angry at the regimental officers, who seemed unwilling to stop the trouble. He

---

5   George T. Todd, *First Texas Regiment* (Texian Press, 1963), 17.

6   OR 51, pt. 2, 770; Alexander Mendoza, *Confederate Struggle for Command: General James Longstreet and the First Corps in the West* (Texas A & M University Press, 2008), 32-34.

threatened to recall North Carolina troops from Lee's army in order to defend the state.[7]

Order was restored by that evening, with provost troops guarding the rail depot to ensure that no more of Longstreet's men entered the city. Ill-feeling persisted on both sides. Word of the vandalism followed Benning all the way to Georgia, where more than two weeks later he wrote a report of the affair denying responsibility on the part of his men and officers. The guilty, he claimed, were a party of North Carolina provost guards who had hitched a ride with his Georgians. No culprits were ever caught or prosecuted for the short-lived riots.[8]

The rest of the expedition proved less unruly, but progress was at times painfully slow. Years later, John Coxe of the 2nd South Carolina recalled, "Our own brigade . . . went via Petersburg, Weldon, Wilmington, Florence, Charleston, Savannah, Millen, Macon, and Atlanta." The state of the equipment was uncertain. On the leg south from Wilmington, Coxe remembered, "the engine drawing our train was in bad order, and slow progress and many stops to allow the engineer to 'tinker' with his machine greatly delayed us. . . . We found we had progressed only about forty miles that entire night." The faulty engine was replaced with another, but the second locomotive proved an even worse mechanical specimen. This locomotive was "old, wheezy, and leaked steam in many places, while the water gushed from the tender in several streams." Coxe's experience was common, for the rolling stock all along the Southern railroads was in bad shape. Inadequate machinery slowed progress to a crawl for most of the troops at various points along the circuitous route.[9]

Once out of North Carolina, relations between soldiers and citizens improved. In fact, for most of the men the move reminded them of happier times earlier in the war, when every train was greeted with crowds and food. "The reception of the troops all along the route was enthusiastic in the extreme," recorded Maj. Gen. Lafayette McLaws, Coxe's division commander.

---

7   OR 51, pt. 2, 763-765. These Alabamans belonged to Evander M. Law's brigade.

8   Ibid., 770.

9   John Coxe, "Chickamauga," *Confederate Veteran*, vol. XXX, no. 8 (August, 1922), 291. Coxe also noted that at one halt, troops descended on a turpentine factory near the tracks and set barrels of the stuff alight to keep warm. The fire soon spread out of control and burned the entire place to the ground, which did nothing to help relations between the troops and North Carolina citizens.

"Dinner and supper for all comers were provided with the greatest liberality." As a native Georgian, McLaws was petitioned to "show myself [repeatedly] as the ladies wished to see the Georgia General." "I was sick during our journey," wrote Capt. Joab Goodson of the 44th Alabama some two weeks later, "and, of course, didn't enjoy it much. Large crowds of ladies were assembled at different points, who greeted us with sweet smiles, kind words, and frequently with quantities of nice 'rations'. . . . The boys amused themselves by writing billet deaux, and throwing them to some young ladies as they passed." One young woman wrote back, much to Goodson's amusement, prompting the lucky private to respond in kind. "I saw him earnestly engaged writing yesterday; so you may look out for a bit of romance."[10]

With so many troops converging on Atlanta, bottlenecks were inevitable. Everything, both reinforcements and supplies, had to be shuttled up the Western & Atlantic line to Resaca, Dalton, or eventually (once it was reoccupied by Forrest's men), Ringgold. Some regiments spent several days in Atlanta awaiting their turn to move north. A train wreck at Cartersville on September 13 compounded the delay and closed the road for more than a day. At 9:00 p.m. that night the northbound locomotive *Senator*, hauling a train loaded with Tennesseans belonging to Brig. Gen. John Gregg's brigade from the Mississippi army, collided head-on with the southbound *Chieftain* hauling sick men from Bragg's army. "The number killed on the *Senator* was 12 or 14," recorded Cpl. Jackson Sanders of Company K, 30th Tennessee. "The number of wounded is about between 60 and 70. The 14th we was engaged in getting the broken fragments of the cars off the road, which took near all day."[11]

How closely Bragg was apprised of this movement is hard to know. No surviving dispatch from Richmond specifically alerting him to the fact that Longstreet was on the way has been found. On September 12, Atlanta's commander Col. Marcus H. Wright informed Bragg that the first of Longstreet's men had arrived. "Benning's Brigade here with no orders," he

---

10 John C. Oeffinger, ed. *A Soldier's General: The Civil War Letters of Major General Lafayette McLaws* (University of North Carolina Press, 2002), 202; Stanley Hoole, ed., "The Letters of Captain Joab Goodson, 1862-64," *The Alabama Review*, vol. 10, no. 1 (April, 1957), 149-50.

11 William G. Robertson, "Chickamauga: The Armies Collide," *Blue & Gray Magazine*, vol. 24, no. 3 (Fall 2007), 22; "Entries for September 13 and 14," L. Jackson Sanders Diary, 30th Tennessee Infantry file, Stones River National Battlefield, Murfreesboro, TN. Hereafter SRNB.

wired, providing Bragg with the first confirmed details of the reinforcements. Joe Johnston had wind of the movement the next day and immediately demanded the return of Gregg's and McNair's troops, to no avail. If Bragg even saw the request, he ignored it. He needed every bayonet now. Also by the 13th, Longstreet's next brigade under Brig. Gen. Jerome B. Robertson detrained in Atlanta. Everyone would be forwarded north once the track was cleared.[12]

Longstreet remained in Richmond until September 14 coordinating the movement of his corps and arranging for suitable campsites for those waiting for their turn or, like much of the artillery, not sure if they would go at all. Most of the corps artillery entered camps around Petersburg, Virginia. Longstreet's staff remained with him except for Maj. Osmun Latrobe, who left the Confederate capital on the 12th and arrived in Atlanta four days later with orders to report to Bragg as soon as he could find him. One of Longstreet's senior commanders, Maj. Gen. John Bell Hood, also left Virginia before his superior.[13]

Hood was in Richmond recuperating from his Gettysburg arm wound when his division boarded the cars north of Richmond for the long trip to Georgia. His arm was still in a sling, but with his troops moving out he refused to be left behind. A number of "brigade and regimental officers came to Hood in a delegation and appealed to him to lead them again. . . . Hood agreed immediately." These officers might have had an ulterior motive in mind. If the gangly and now almost gaunt Kentuckian did not make the trip, command of the division would fall to the newly attached Micah Jenkins, who ranked every other brigade commander. An outsider, Jenkins's ascension to divisional command rankled the existing brigadiers and would be a source of friction later in the campaign. Hood was game, however, and departed on the 14th, making only one stop along the way. In Petersburg, he detrained briefly to visit a young woman with whom he had become enamored: Sally Buchanan "Buck" Preston. Miss Preston was popular on the Richmond social scene, and Hood had fallen in love during his recovery. She, however, did not reciprocate his feelings. When Hood pressed his case in Petersburg, a strange scene ensued. Hood asked for her hand. She "half-promised me to think about it. She did not say yes, but

12 *OR* 30, pt. 4, 643.

13 Entries for September 12-15, Osmun Latrobe Diary, Maryland Historical Society.

she did not say no, that is not exactly." Just before he departed Hood declared, "I am engaged to you." "I am not engaged to you," retorted Preston.[14]

The initial destination for all these troops was the Army of Tennessee's depot at Resaca, established when it appeared that neither Ringgold nor Dalton could be successfully defended. However, when Tom Crittenden's movement turned aside to head back to Lee and Gordon's Mills, the destination changed. When John Pegram's cavalry reported Ringgold abandoned by the Yankees on the morning of September 13, Bragg started thinking of reoccupying the place. Bushrod Johnson's brigade was still at Dalton after returning from its brief reconnaissance to Tunnel Hill on the 12th and was available to make the move. So were Brig. Gen. Evander McNair's brigade and that part of Brig. Gen. John Gregg's brigade that had escaped the train wreck at Cartersville and was now at Resaca—and for the time being beyond Joe Johnston's recall. So too would be the new arrivals of Longstreet's Corps as soon as the tracks were reopened.[15]

Bragg issued Special Orders No. 244 on September 15 shifting his depot back to Ringgold, "or as near thereto as possible," and moved all these troops to that place. The orders included not only Johnson's, McNair's and Gregg's commands (close to 4,000 men), but the 4,500 troops comprising the first three brigades of Hood's division (Brig. Gens. Evander Law, William Benning, and Jerome Robertson) reported as having departed Atlanta the previous day, and another 1,400 men of Brig. Gen. States Rights Gist's brigade previously detailed to defend Rome. As the ranking brigadier, Bushrod Johnson was the overall commander of this motley force until Hood or another senior officer arrived.[16]

Thanks to the Rebel cavalry's overzealous destruction of the three rail bridges across meandering East Chickamauga Creek south of Ringgold, Bragg's "as near thereto as possible" proved to be an open field near the Stone Church two miles south of town soon designated as Catoosa Platform. The platform consisted of hastily constructed wooden walkways lining the tracks. Despite its

14 Richard O'Connor, *Hood: Cavalier General* (Prentice-Hall, Inc., 1949), 158; Richard M. McMurry, *John Bell Hood and the War For Southern Independence* (University of Nebraska Press, 1982), 76. Even worse, Jenkins and the next ranking brigadier general, Evander Law, were intense rivals with no love lost between them.

15 Entries for September 12 and 13, Bushrod Johnson Diary, NARA. Johnson would soon be elevated to lead a new division, with Col. John S. Fulton assuming command of the brigade.

16 Folder 10, Bragg Papers, WRHS; *OR* 30, pt. 4, 649, 652.

makeshift nature, Catoosa would soon become the major supply and reinforcement terminus for Bragg's Army of Tennessee.

The sudden shift of his supply base back north signaled that, despite the twin frustrations of McLemore's Cove and Polk's failure to attack at Lee and Gordon's Mills, Bragg was not ready to abandon offensive operations. Rosecrans's Army of the Cumberland was still scattered and thus still vulnerable—but only if the Rebels could coordinate an effective strike.

On the morning of September 15, a host of Confederate commanders assembled at Bragg's headquarters in La Fayette to discuss how to accomplish that. D. H. Hill, Polk, Walker, and Buckner were present at the conference, as were a number of staff officers and others unnamed. The meeting was neither relaxed nor cordial. Bragg, who one participant described as "sick and feeble," was upset with several of his generals. His demeanor and appearance made a lasting impact upon Colonel Brent. "[T]he responsibilities of his trust weigh heavily upon him," concluded the army's assistant adjutant general. Despite his apparent infirmity, Bragg presented a new plan to the assembled corps commanders. He intended to strike directly for Chattanooga and, in doing so, turn Rosecrans's northern flank. There was still an opportunity to cut the Federals off from the city, Bragg explained, and trap them deep in the north Georgia mountains. "Something . . . more promising of success might have been devised," wrote a skeptical Brent, but most of the assembled generals agreed with Bragg's plan.[17]

By shifting what amounted to another infantry corps to Ringgold via railroad, Bragg could regain the positional advantage he previously held a week earlier *vis-à-vis* Rosecrans's scattered Federal army. If properly executed, the bulk of the Army of Tennesee would once again be farther north and thus closer to Chattanooga than the majority of Rosecrans's command. Only a single 1,800-man Yankee brigade garrisoned Chattanooga, and Maj. Gen. Gordon Granger's small Reserve Corps (fewer than 6,000 men) protected the Rossville Gap through Missionary Ridge. There was still time to cut Rosecrans off from his base. Special Orders No. 244 was not in itself an order for an attack, but it was clearly issued in anticipation of one.[18]

---

17 Connelly, *Autumn of Glory*, 189; Entry for September 15, 1863, Brent Journal, WRHS.

18 This was George Wagner's brigade, Thomas Wood's First Division, Crittenden's XXI Corps, reinforced by some extra infantry and a battalion of cavalry.

*   *   *

For most of Rosecrans's army, the few days between September 13 and 17 were marked by inactivity. The XIV Corps and XXI Corps could do very little until McCook's XX Corps reached them. With the exception of daily patrolling, Thomas's and Crittenden's men spent these days in camp awaiting developments. McCook's men and the Cavalry Corps had no chance to rest as they toiled up and down Lookout Mountain in their haste to move northward. Rosecrans, meanwhile, contemplated Bragg's next move. He also received some unsettling information concerning the flow of Rebel reinforcements.

On September 9, the day Longstreet's troops boarded trains in Richmond, the *New York Herald* ran a lengthy story summarizing the Army of Northern Virginia's strength and probable intentions. The story proved remarkably accurate, so much so that it caused General Lee considerable distress. "It appears that some of Lee's best regiments, horse, foot, and artillery, have been sent southward," reported the paper, "but whether to Charleston or to Chattanooga, we have yet to learn."[19]

Lee was alarmed at how quickly this news reached Northern sources. Luckily for the South, the Federal high command initially took little notice of the story because the Union Army of the Potomac had not detected any such movement from the Army of Northern Virginia. On September 6, General Halleck wired Maj. Gen. George Gordon Meade, "Rosecrans seems apprehensive that reinforcements to Bragg have been sent from Lee's army to East Tennessee by Lynchburg. Employ every possible means to ascertain if this be so. If [true] . . . I must reinforce Burnside." Because the movement had not yet begun, Meade's scouting efforts discovered nothing. In fact, rumor ran in the opposite direction. "It is reported here by deserters that a part of Bragg's army is reinforcing Lee," Halleck telegraphed Rosecrans on September 11. The Washington-based general urged Rosecrans to find out if this were the case.[20]

19 Eiserman, *Longstreet's Corps*, 44. The *New York Times* story was not the result of a leak, but merely speculation on the paper's part. It was an uncanny guess, however, as to Confederate operational intentions.

20 *OR* 29, pt. 2, 158; ibid. 30, pt. 3, 530. Ironically, had Burnside not overrun East Tennessee and captured Knoxville so quickly, or if Lee and Davis had not debated the merits of the reinforcement quite so long, it is very likely that Meade's efforts would have uncovered an earlier movement.

During the next week, however, circumstances changed. Information arrived, first in a trickle and then in a flood, describing Longstreet's redeployment to the Western Theater. On September 12, Maj. Gen. John J. Peck, the Union commander at New Berne, North Carolina, listened as a civilian named "Mr. Clements"—a native Pennsylvanian and former railroad man—reported the transfer. Some 13,000 troops were en route to Bragg, he insisted, and he had counted them personally. Peck informed both his superior, Maj. Gen. John G. Foster at Fort Monroe, Virginia, and Rosecrans. Foster relayed the report to Halleck in Washington on the 14th. By that time Halleck had a sheaf of reports in hand from Meade confirming the same information from various probes conducted by the Army of the Potomac. [21]

Halleck's initial reaction to this credible news was curious. Instead of informing Rosecrans immediately, his first thought was of East Tennessee. At 3:00 p.m. on the 14th, Halleck wired Ambrose Burnside in Knoxville the following cryptic order: "There are reasons why you should reinforce General Rosecrans with all possible dispatch. It is believed the enemy will concentrate to give him battle. You must be there to help him." He did not send word of Longstreet's impending arrival to Rosecrans for another 24 hours. At 4:30 p.m on the 15th, Halleck wired Rosecrans, "It is very probable that three divisions of Lee's army have been sent to reinforce Bragg." Halleck promised Rosecrans reinforcements from other theaters, a pledge left unfulfilled when solicitations to Maj. Gen. John Pope in Milwaukee and Maj. Gen. John M. Schofield in St. Louis yielded no immediate help. Both departments were hundreds of miles away and had few if any troops to spare. Similar entreaties to Mississippi were potentially more fruitful since large numbers of troops sat idle around Vicksburg and much of the corresponding Confederate strength had already been siphoned away from Joe Johnston. Low water and lack of transport, however, meant any available Federal troops would be weeks in arriving.[22]

Later, after the Union loss at Chickamauga, much of the blame for failing to reinforce Chattanooga would fall on Ambrose Burnside. He deserves a share of it, but not the full measure. Based on earlier triumphant messages from Thomas Crittenden (sent upon the capture of Chattanooga) and the urgings of the

---

21 Ibid. 29, pt. 2, 173, 186. Peck's effort to warn Rosecrans directly was a good thought, but of little use since the dispatch in question did not arrive in Chattanooga until October 16, 1863. Fortunately for the Union cause, not all such warnings were so untimely.

22 OR 30, pt. 3, 638, 644.

government in Washington to secure East Tennessee, Burnside's small army was concentrated north of Knoxville when Halleck's first dispatch arrived. Burnside's available field force numbered only 15,000 of all arms, with which he had to secure a wide swath of territory. His main threat was from southwestern Virginia, where a small Rebel force of about 6,000 men under Maj. Gen. Samuel Jones blocked any Federal advance. Here, too, rumors abounded. Word of the original Confederate plan to reinforce Bragg via East Tennessee found new root when a report that Lt. Gen. Richard S. Ewell's Second Corps, Army of Northern Virginia, was being sent to reinforce Jones in a do-or-die effort to retake Knoxville. If true, Ewell's 20,000 troops would give the Rebels a powerful numerical advantage over Burnside. Accordingly, Burnside planned to attack and crush part of Jones's force at Jonesborough, Tennessee, just a few miles south of the Virginia border, before Jones could receive reinforcements from Lee.[23]

Burnside's relative isolation in East Tennessee and the lack of a direct telegraph link meant that any communication between himself and Halleck was subject to a time lag of between two and three days. Burnside did not receive Halleck's cryptically urgent dispatch of September 14 until at least two days later, on the 16th, while the bulk of his small army was still sparring with Rebels around Jonesborough. Given Halleck's lack of detail, Burnside had to make a decision. Now that he had already embarked on an attack against Jonesborough, the portly Rhode Islander reasoned he should finish that effort and then, "with all possible dispatch," hurry south to help Rosecrans. Although understandable, it was the wrong decision. Even if he had started moving reinforcements toward Chattanooga immediately, he almost certainly would have been too late to reinforce Rosecrans. In addition, the Rebels did reinforce Jonesborough with troops from Lee's army (though only a brigade of Pickett's men, rushed over from Richmond, and not an entire corps) that both negated Burnside's small numerical advantage and foiled his attack. Burnside's dispatches back to Washington didn't help make his case. While he was repeatedly promising to rush south as soon as possible, his missives were dispatched from locations farther and farther north and east. On September 19, the first day of large-scale battle between Rosecrans and Bragg, President Lincoln read with dismay a week-old dispatch from Burnside detailing the

23 William Marvel, *Burnside* (University Of North Carolina Press, 1991), 280-282.

intended attack against Jonesborough. "Damn Jonesborough!" erupted the president.[24]

Despite his status as the commanding general of the entire Federal army, Halleck's unwillingness to issue clear and direct orders to generals in the field was the primary cause of the problem. He neither gave Burnside a direct order nor outlined the reasons for his concerns. Instead, Halleck equivocated, his language couched in terms of discretion and, as previously seen, cryptic intent. Halleck had exhibited similar traits in his dealings with Meade. In June 1863, Halleck wasted no time urging Rosecrans to attack Bragg in Middle Tennessee to prevent Bragg from sending reinforcement to other theaters. Now, in mid-September the same situation was playing out in Virginia. Meade was reluctant to attack, and Halleck acquiesced. On September 14, Meade wired that "if Lee's army is as much reduced as the intelligence . . . would lead us to believe," once his own detached troops were returned, Meade should be able to "require [Lee] to fall back." However, "at the same time, I see no object in advancing" without substantial reinforcements. Halleck, in an odd twist of logic, suddenly agreed. "I think preparations should be made to at least threaten Lee," suggested Halleck, who added, "I do not think the exact condition of affairs is sufficiently ascertained to authorize any very considerable advance."[25]

President Lincoln saw through all this equivocation, and his increasing frustration with his generals was on full display in a pair of terse communications. The first, sent to Halleck on the 15th as Halleck and Meade were fussing over an advance, was straight to the point: "My opinion is that he [Meade] should move upon Lee at once in a manner of general attack." This might have prodded Meade into action had the president not added the caveat that his "opinion is not to control you and General Meade." The second communication, written on September 21, abandoned any pretense of a hands-off posture when Lincoln bypassed Halleck with an order to Burnside to "go to Rosecrans at once with your force, without a moment's delay." The order reached Burnside on the 22nd—too late to influence the outcome of Rosecrans's campaign.[26]

---

24 Ibid., 283, 286.

25 *OR* 29, pt. 2, 180, 186.

26 Ibid., 187; Marvel, *Burnside*, 285.

Rosecrans's own scout and spy network also provided some warning of Longstreet's impending arrival. The huge increase of traffic in and around Atlanta and along the overburdened Western & Atlantic Railroad did not go unnoticed. Starting on September 15, intelligence summaries recorded at army headquarters mentioned Longstreet (and a few even Ewell's corps) involved in the Atlanta and north Georgia rail movement. One report from "a person . . . who left Atlanta last Friday" (September 11) was recorded on the 16th and identified the troops as belonging to Ewell. The same source listed the Confederate strength between "30,000 to 32,000 men."[27]

Rosecrans remained cautiously skeptical about all this information, but he could not afford to completely ignore it. Nor, unfortunately, could he do much about it until McCook closed up with his other two corps. Fortunately for the Army of the Cumberland, Bragg was largely inactive as well; only minor skirmishing marked the passage of what would otherwise be perfect fall days and cool nights in the mountains and valleys of north Georgia.

*   *   *

On September 13, Joe Reynolds's division of Thomas's XIV Corps occupied Pond Spring, several miles south of Lee and Gordon's Mills and situated in the mouth of McLemore's Cove, finding enemy troops in proximity. Matters remained mostly quiet. The next day, September 14, Reynolds greeted his long-detached First Brigade under John Wilder, which arrived that afternoon. Thomas sent Wilder to Reynolds so his mounted infantry could patrol the gaps in Pigeon Mountain. Thomas may have been thinking of Wilder's daring action at Hoover's Gap during the Tullahoma campaign when the XIV Corps commander ordered Reynolds to push Wilder, "if not too much

---

27 Entry for September 16, "Summaries of the news reaching headquarters of General W. S. Rosecrans," RG 393, NARA. This "person" may have been sent by Henry Greene Cole, proprietor and owner of the Marietta Hotel in Marietta, Georgia. A staunch Unionist, Cole was later imprisoned by Confederate authorities. In an 1873 claim for damages, Cole testified, "by accident I got hold of the news that Longstreet was going to . . . reinforce Bragg . . . before the next day I had sent that news to Gen. Thomas. . . . The General always gave me a great deal of credit for that act . . . I headed off Longstreet by three days." George Thomas supported Cole's testimony in an 1869 letter in which he noted that Cole "rendered the government most valuable assistance by sending information through the lines of movements of the enemy, which movements might not have been known but for . . . Mr. Cole." See "Testimony of a Union Spy That Lived In Marietta," pamphlet, Marietta Museum of History, Marietta, GA.

fatigued . . . in the direction of Dug and Catlett's Gaps, both of which he will seize (if not defended by a strong force) and hold if possible." Reynolds, however, concluded that Wilder's men and horses were too jaded for such an effort.[28]

A brief ripple of excitement coursed through Pond Spring on the 15th when "some troops made their appearance, coming down the mountain from the north . . . Col. King orderd out the 68th Ind[iana] and 105th Ohio to ascertain who they were." The troops proved to be Federals from Palmer's division, returning from a largely pointless expedition to Missionary Ridge the day before. They moved to a position just north of Reynolds to cover Gower's Ford on Chickamauga Creek.[29]

The rest of the time passed quietly enough, recalled Sgt. William Miller of the 75th Indiana of Col. Edward King's brigade, part of Reynolds's division. "I had plenty of Sweat [sweet] Potatoes," wrote Miller," but no coffee and very poor water." Pond Spring "is a curiosity," he continued. "It appears to rise out of the hills and appears to be grown up with moss or weed . . . that gives it the appearance of a 'Frog Pond' in Indiana. There is a bench walk constructed from the north bank to the center about a hundred feet long" to where the clear water of the spring bubbled up. Colonel Lane, commanding the 11th Ohio of Turchin's brigade, also part of Reynolds's division, recalled difficult work during this uneasy respite. "Here the brigade had a hard service . . . on picket two days without relief and continually fired upon." On September 16, in place of Wilder, Reynolds sent Turchin's men to scout toward Dug and Catlett's gaps, "only to find the enemy in them and determined to stay." This minor probing and skirmish fire was the only contact between the two armies.[30]

Like his opposite, Rosecrans also moved his headquarters. On September 15, he transferred everything to Crawfish Spring, including the main command group he had left behind in Chattanooga. Also like Bragg, the usually hardy Ohioan was not feeling well that day, although the cause of his specific discomfort remains unknown. Rosecrans took up residence in the James Gordon mansion while his escort and headquarters personnel spilled out upon the surrounding lawns and fields. "The spring here is a magnificent one," wrote

28 OR 30, pt. 3, 626.

29 Entries for September 15 and 16, William Bluffton Miller Diaries, InHS.

30 Ibid.; William Forse Scott, *Philander P. Lane: Colonel of Volunteers in the Civil War Eleventh Ohio Infantry* (privately printed, 1920), 212.

Col. John P. Sanderson of Rosecrans's staff, "affording an abundant supply, for man & beast, of the entire army, of cool, soft, delicious water." Sanderson described the main building as a "very large, double, two-story brick house." The elder Gordon had died the previous February, but his widow was at home, "and is the most frightened creature imaginable," recorded the colonel. "Two of her sons are in the rebel army, her grown daughter ran off on the appearance of our army, and the old lady, to believe her, is pitifully poor and almost starving . . . . All this, I am satisfied, is pretense. The poor people around here are for the Union, and they tell a different tale."[31]

Rosecrans's decision to transfer his headquarters on the morning of September 15 meant he missed meeting Alexander McCook that afternoon at Thomas's headquarters. McCook had ridden ahead of his men, who were still working their way over Lookout Mountain, to report in person and determine what was next for his XX Corps. He informed both Thomas and (via courier) Rosecrans that at least two of his divisions would be on hand by the night of the 16th, and the rest up no later than the following day. Even better, General Stanley reported that Crook's division of cavalry occupied Dougherty's Gap and was ready to descend into the south end of McLemore's Cove. In this same message, Stanley admitted, "I am so prostrated that I am not able to [even] sit up," and relinquished command of the cavalry to General Mitchell.[32]

There was still the matter of the thinly held country between the main body of the Army of the Cumberland at Lee and Gordon's Mills and the base of operations being established in Chattanooga. Rosecrans had already done what he could to move up troops to reinforce the town by deploying Granger at Rossville, but he needed a stronger presence closer to Ringgold. For that mission, he turned to Colonel Minty.

---

31 "Regret to learn of General Rosecrans's indisposition," wrote General Crittenden that evening while asking for the whereabouts of departmental headquarters. Whatever ailed Rosecrans must have been minor, for the matter was not raised again. OR 30, pt. 3, 650; "Sep 16, 1863," John P. Sanderson Letters, OHS. Whatever Sanderson's suspicions, the family's son-in-law, James M. Lee (married to the fleet of foot daughter) was a Unionist and would be of some help to the Federals in the coming days. Sanderson was a Pennsylvania lawyer and influential politician. He was head of that state's branch of the Know-Nothing Party. His friendship in 1861 with then-incoming Secretary of War Simon Cameron (also a Pennsylvanian) resulted in his appointment as lieutenant colonel of the 13th U.S. Infantry. Sanderson served on Rosecrans's staff until his death in the fall of 1864 from illness.

32 OR 30, pt. 3, 653.

Minty's cavalry was reassigned to Crittenden to replace Wilder, who had been sent back to rejoin Thomas per the Virginian's earlier request. On September 15, Crittenden sent Minty into Peavine Valley with instructions to establish a cavalry screen covering the XXI Corps's left flank in the direction of Ringgold. Minty pitched his main camp at Peeler's Mill on Peavine Creek and immediately dispatched regular patrols toward Ringgold and Leet's Tanyard. Minty was feeling a bit undermanned because about half his brigade was absent on other duty. The 3rd Indiana Cavalry was in Chattanooga on courier duty, and Crittenden retained the 7th Pennsylvania Cavalry at Crawfish Spring. Information harvested during his patrolling only added to his worries. "I have strange reports from the citizens," reported Minty. "They say positively that Forrest is at Ringgold, Pegram at Leet's, Buckner at Rock Spring, Cleburne and Longstreet at Dalton."[33]

The mention of Longstreet's name was particularly alarming. On the 16th, additional patrolling confirmed that Rebels were all around; Minty appealed for reinforcements. With Confederates threatening him from both Leet's and Ringgold, he feared being cut off because he didn't have enough troopers to simultaneously cover both avenues of advance. The cavalryman appealed for the return of the 3rd Indiana and 7th Pennsylvania and asked Crittenden to backstop him by posting "a brigade of infantry at Reed's Bridge. As I am now situated I may be forced to retreat at any moment." Finally, Minty concluded, "I think, without doubt, that Longstreet is in this part of the country." Concerned, Crittenden sent the 7th Pennsylvania to Minty but could spare no infantry for Reed's Bridge.[34]

Despite Minty's alarming dispatches, Rosecrans had reason to be satisfied. By September 16, he believed his army was substantially out of danger, or nearly so. It was time to start thinking offensively once again. The ever-present Assistant Secretary of War Charles Dana relayed the army commander's latest thoughts to Washington at 1:00 pm on the 16th: "Sheridan's division got down into the valley [McLemore's Cove via Stevens's Gap] yesterday, and the others will get down today. The concentration of the army will then be perfect. . . . The present plan . . . is to hold gaps in Lookout Mountain . . . and seem to threaten the gaps . . . in Pigeon Mountain, and then, taking care to show campfires . . . to

---

33 Ibid., 651.

34 Ibid., 679.

march by night . . . taking the road which lead's around its northern extremity and surprise the rebels at La Fayette." Despite Minty's warnings, Dana informed Washington that "no reinforcements from Virginia have yet arrived here" or in Dalton. If Rosecrans could resume the offensive, perhaps there was still time to defeat Bragg ahead of the full Rebel concentration.[35]

* * *

Braxton Bragg was also thinking of attack. At his direction, George Brent drafted Special Orders No. 245 on September 16. Simon Buckner's and W. H. T. Walker's combined force of about 16,000 was ordered to march at dawn the next day for Peavine Church, and take up a position there facing west along the creek of the same name. Leonidas Polk's 13,000 men were to follow at 8:00 a.m., thus allowing enough time for the roads to clear, and take up a position on Buckner's left, holding the banks of West Chickamauga Creek as far upstream as Glass Mill. D. H. Hill's two divisions, 9,000 strong, would leave their positions south of La Fayette and return to the gaps in Pigeon Mountain west of town, falling in on Polk's left. The orders sent the Confederates gathering at Ringgold in several directions. Bushrod Johnson's brigade could now be returned to Buckner's Corps while the brigades under Gregg and McNair, together with the Virginia arrivals (under an unspecified senior brigadier) marched toward Reed's Bridge. After leaving men to picket the roads south to Alpine and Summerville to ensure the Federals did not suddenly reappear there, Joe Wheeler's cavalry would press the flanks of the Union columns cover any gaps between Polk's left at Glass Mill and Hill's right at Dug Gap.

The most critical mission of all was given to Brig. Gen. Nathan Bedford Forrest. His troopers were to screen Buckner's and Polk's columns as they marched north, and capture four critical crossings over Chickamauga Creek. Dalton's Ford, Alexander's Bridge, Bryam's Ford, and Reed's Bridge all needed to be in Rebel hands if Bragg was going to rapidly insert his army between Rosecrans and Chattanooga. Unfortunately, Forrest's best troops—Armstrong's division—were still busy screening Polk's front, which left only Pegram's men available for this new mission. If Wheeler moved promptly,

---

35 Ibid., pt. 1, 187-188.

taking over Armstrong's duties south of Lee and Gordon's Mills in a timely fashion, Armstrong could rejoin Forrest.[36]

If properly executed, these instructions would place Bragg's entire army in line facing west from Reed's Bridge to Dug Gap by the afternoon of September 17, with three-fifths of his strength concentrated north of Lee and Gordon's Mills (Rosecrans's left flank). From there, Bragg could maneuver south against an exposed Federal flank, or turn north and threaten Chattanooga. Moreover, each corps could use a different road for its advance, eliminating the possibility of congestion and delays.

A flurry of directives flew out of Bragg's headquarters at 3:00 a.m. on September 17 suspending the entire movement. At least some of Bragg's officers greeted this last minute hang-fire with misgivings. Brent bemoaned the army's continued "uncertainty and vacillation." Years later, when D. H. Hill recorded his impressions of the campaign, he thought the hesitation disastrous. A strike on the 17th, Hill later argued, "must have been fatal to Rosecrans in the then huddled and confused grouping of his forces." Bragg never explained in writing why he ordered the suspension. However, Bragg's headquarters received a significant visitor in the predawn hours that morning in the form of Maj. Osmun Latrobe, the first of James Longstreet's staff officers to reach Bragg in person. The news he carried with him presumably included details on the size of Longstreet's force and a better idea of how soon it would arrive and be ready for action. Whatever information Latrobe shared was significant enough for Bragg to modify his plan.[37]

With the marching orders now suspended, Bragg called another conference for 8:00 a.m. that morning. The second meeting changed very little, and by noon army headquarters was issuing orders resuming the march. The most significant modification was that Bushrod Johnson would not return to A. P. Stewart's division, but would instead remain part of the Ringgold column; by

---

36 Ibid., pt. 4, 657; Original copy in Folder 10, Braxton Bragg Papers, William Palmer Collection, WRHS, has more detail on the movement. All numbers taken from Powell, "Numbers and Losses," CCNMP. Note that Special Orders No. 244 does not specify which of Bragg's cavalry should seize the crossings, but Forrest's troopers were the obvious choice since all of Wheeler's men were more than 20 miles away, south of La Fayette.

37 Folder 10, Bragg Papers, Palmer collection, WRHS; Entry for September 17th, Brent Journal, WRHS; Hill, "Chickamauga," 649; Entry for September 17th, Osmun Latrobe Diary, Maryland Historical Society; William Glenn Robertson, "The Chickamauga Campaign, The Armies Collide," 40. Robertson offers a detailed analysis concerning the ramifications of Latrobe's arrival.

the default of his seniority, Johnson would assume command of the force until such time as Hood or Longstreet arrived in person. In addition, Johnson's new command would not depart Ringgold until September 18 in order to allow time for the rest of the army to redeploy northward from La Fayette. This temporary arrangement, and Johnson's impromptu command, were designated "Johnson's Provisional Division." Another change involved Hill, who was to turn over the defense of the Pigeon Mountain gaps to Wheeler's cavalry on the night of the 17th and shift his corps north as far as Glass Mill. When all was ready, Bragg planned to move against the Federals on September 18.[38]

While their generals conferred that morning, the rank and file of the Army of Tennessee prepared for battle. Issued rations were cooked and in some cases, already eaten. Transportation except ammunition wagons and ambulances had been sent to the rear to free up the roads as much as possible. In order to steel his men for the coming fight, Bragg issued a general order to be read to everyone signifying that the supreme moment of decision was at hand: "Heretofore you have never failed to respond to your general when he asked sacrifice at your hands. Relying on your gallantry and patriotism, he asks you to add the crowning glory to the wreath you wear. Our cause is in your keeping. . . . You have but to respond to assure us a glorious victory over an insolent foe." Once the orders were read and the troops prepared, Walker, Buckner, and Polk marched their infantry north once more up the same dust-choked roads that had marked the limits of their existence for the past week. Thick brown plumes drifted lazily into the Georgia sky, remarked by friend and foe alike.[39]

Corporal Augustus P. Adamson of the 30th Georgia, Walker's Corps, was ready. "It is very likely that the coming struggle is to be a bloody one and I need not say I do not dread it . . . but I feel confident we will be successful," he wrote his sister the next day. "I have great confidence in General Bragg, and all the abuse that has been heaped upon him was ill-timed and unwise. There is no doubt of his being the best disciplined General in the service," added the Georgian, "[though] he is indeed, a rough-looking old fellow."[40]

---

38 *OR* 30, pt. 4, 660-661.

39 Louis R. Smith and Andrew Quist, eds., *Cush: A Civil War Memoir by Samuel H. Sprott* (University of West Alabama, 1999), 46.

40 A. P. Adamson, with Richard Bender Abell and Fay Adamson Gecik, eds., *Sojourns of a Patriot: The Field and Prison Papers of an Unreconstructed Confederate* (Southern Heritage Press, 1998), 190-191.

* * *

By mid-morning on the 17th, Alexander McCook reported that Phil Sheridan's and Jefferson C. Davis's divisions were "down [Lookout] mountain" and moving to replace Thomas's divisions in front of Pigeon Mountain, so that Thomas's own troops could sidle farther north and close up with the XXI Corps. That morning, in a circular to his corps commanders, Rosecrans directed them "to post officers of intelligence on all available high points . . . to watch the valley and surrounding country closely." Those observers soon had much to see.[41]

Rebel movements were first interpreted as a renewed movement down into McLemore's Cove, but it soon became apparent that that effort was cavalry replacing Hill's infantry garrisons in Dug and Catlett's gaps. With McCook at hand, Rosecrans now initiated a slow and cautious leap-frogging of divisions from the various corps northward, moving his own army closer to Chattanooga. Crittenden was to shift Palmer and Van Cleve downstream, taking position on Wood's left, north of Lee and Gordon's Mills. Thomas was directed to move his XIV Corps out of the cove and take up a position between Owen's Ford and Pond Spring, replacing Palmer. McCook's two leading divisions moved to Pond Spring to connect with Thomas's right. Everyone kept a wary eye on Pigeon Mountain, from which Rebels could issue forth through the gaps without much warning. Thomas left Reynolds's division at Pond Spring throughout the day to watch Dug Gap, which caused a bit of a traffic jam with McCook's troops that evening. McCook, meanwhile, advanced Colonel Harrison's 39th Indiana Mounted Infantry to Davis's Crossroads in case the Confederates moved off Pigeon Mountain in that direction.[42]

Rosecrans also cast an increasingly nervous eye north of Lee and Gordon's Mills to where Minty's cavalry maintained their lonely vigil. Minty, it will be recalled, asked for infantry support on the 16th, but Crittenden had none to send. Rosecrans, however, could do better. Having just returned Colonel Wilder's "Lightning Brigade" to George Thomas a day or so before, he snatched Wilder away once more. On the morning of September 17, Rosecrans summoned Wilder to Crawfish Spring and told the cocky Hoosier colonel to shift his command to Alexander's Bridge to fill in part of the gap yawning

---

41 *OR* 30, pt. 3, 702.

42 Ibid., 701-707.

between Minty and Crittenden's flank. Wilder moved promptly and his men would be in place by dusk.[43]

That morning, minor skirmishing looked to be turning into something more significant at Owen's Ford, where Brig. Gen. William B. Hazen's brigade of Palmer's division was camped. "A regiment of rebel cavalry made a charge on the outpost pickets at daylight," recorded Col. Isaac B. Suman of the 9th Indiana. " Hazen was nearly captured: "I, with a single aid," explained the brigadier, "was on the Lafayette Road at the picket post. The attack was so sudden that the horsemen were upon us, and some passed us and were captured before they could check their horses." Fortunately the crops there had not been harvested. "The pickets instantly took cover," recalled Hazen,"while I sought the friendly shelter of a field of high corn." The Southern prisoners included a captain and a few others from the 4th Georgia Cavalry. Company F of the 4th were local boys, some recruited in the shadow of Cooper's Gap. Years later, one old Georgian recalled the incident: "Our good brave Captain Helvingston . . . was shot dead . . . and at the same time Private Jack Boss' horse became uncontrollable in the charge and he was killed."[44]

The most significant action that day occurred near Ringgold, well north of where the two armies were maneuvering. Unlike the other small action, this fight was triggered by Yankees, or more specifically, the restlessness of Union Maj. Gen. Gordon Granger, who now occupied Rossville with three brigades of the Union Reserve Corps. Granger was a professional, a graduate of the West Point class of 1845 with extensive Mexican War and frontier service. He was also a bit of a martinet. His men had been holding Rossville since September 14, but supplies were only intermittently arriving from the depots at Bridgeport and Stevenson. To compensate for food shortages, a number of men slipped beyond the picket lines for some unauthorized foraging. The news put Granger in a furious temper. As punishment, the general "had a number of men stripped of their coats and shirts and tied by their thumbs. Granger might be a Regular with Regular Army ways, but his men were volunteers and deeply resented being treated like criminals for the "crime" of going hungry. Officers from several regiments gathered to confront their angry commander. "Gen. Granger was profane and made terrible threats," wrote Sgt. Maj. Charles A. Partridge of

43 Ibid., 703; Baumgartner, *Blue Lightning*, 191.

44 *OR* 30, pt. 1, 768; William B. Hazen, *A Narrative of Military Service* (Ticknor & Co. 1885), 120; Anonymous, "My Experiences," *Walker County Messenger*, April 3, 1902.

James B. Steedman, who led two brigades of
the Union Reserve Corps on a
September 17th reconnaissance.
Battles and Leaders of the Civil War

the 96th Illinois, "but . . . he could not
misuse intelligent volunteers . . . and he
slunk away into his tent, damning
everybody." With Granger gone, Brig.
Gen. James B. Steedman, who
commanded Granger's First Division
and had been a politician before the
war, smoothed things over and averted a potential mutiny by releasing the
prisoners.[45]

Granger was also not very popular with some of the senior officers.
Brigadier General William B. Hazen regarded him as a "plotting, ambitious"
man. Thomas, too, seems not to have liked him much, but Rosecrans held
Granger's combat record in high regard: "You think he is a blatherskate,"
Rosecrans once told Thomas, "and in one sense he is . . . but you will find him a
great man in battle." Perhaps Granger's greatest problem was his lack of tact.
He had strong opinions and he voiced them when he would have been better
off remaining silent. According to the *New York Herald's* field correspondent
William Shanks, Granger "never disliked a man without showing it." Lieutenant
James H. Wilson, an engineering officer who would later rise to fame leading
cavalry, met Granger shortly after Chickamauga and found him a curious
mixture of ability and arrogance. The corps leader, wrote Wilson, was
"Imprudent and reckless in behavior . . . [Granger] would do himself more
harm by a day of senseless braggadocio than he could repair by a month of
irreproachable conduct."[46]

45 Warner, *Generals in Blue*, 181; "Entry for September 15, 1863," William Galways Journal,
InSL; Charles Partridge, *History of the Ninety-Sixth Regiment Illinois Volunteer Infantry* (Brown,
Pettibone and Company, 1887), 167.

46 Hazen to Benson H. Lossing, August 23, 1866, William P. Palmer Collection, WRHS; Peter
Cozzens, *This Terrible Sound: The Battle of Chickamauga* (University of Illinois Press, 1992), 93;
Shanks, *Personal Recollections*, 271; James H. Wilson, *Under the Old Flag: Recollections of Military
Operations in the War for the Union, the Spanish War, the Boxer Rebellion, etc.* (D. Appleton and Co.,

Granger was nervous on the morning of September 17. Aside from Minty's cavalry screen, his Reserve Corps of 6,000 men comprised the only force of significance standing between Rosecrans's main body at Lee and Gordon's Mills and Brig. Gen. George Wagner's understrength garrison at Chattanooga, a distance of 12 miles. Aware of the growing Confederate concentration at Ringgold, Granger ordered Brigadier General Steedman to take a reinforced brigade and battery of artillery down the Federal Road "for the purpose of making a reconnaissance . . ."[47]

Steedman's First Division included two brigades. He tapped Col. John G. Mitchell's brigade of four regiments for the expedition, augmented by the 22nd Michigan and 89th Ohio, both commanded by Michigan Col. Heber Le Favour. These last two units belonged to other commands, but had been detached on various guard duties during the course of the campaign. As additional Reserve Corps units arrived to take their place, the two orphaned regiments had been bundled along to the front as part of Steedman's command until they could rejoin their own outfits. Artillery support for the movement consisted of the six guns of Battery M, 2nd Illinois Light Artillery.[48]

"Up at 2:30 [a.m.] and off at 4:30," journaled Illinois artillery sergeant George E. Dolton. "The road is very hilly, but not rocky." The morning passed uneventfully. "There are several creeks on the way," he noted, and given the recent drought, the men took each opportunity to collect water. Dolton marveled when he set eyes on a peanut field, "as I had never seen any growing before, I was surprised to find the nuts in the ground." Of Rebels that morning, however, the column saw not a one.[49]

1912), 306. Wilson was the only officer from Gen. U. S. Grant's staff to be promoted to command troops in the field.

47 *OR* 30, pt. 1, 853.

48 The 22nd Michigan normally belonged to Second Division, Reserve Corps, and was stationed in Nashville until September 5th, when it was ordered to Bridgeport. Once there, it was attached to Steedman's command. The 89th Ohio normally belonged to Turchin's Brigade of Reynolds's Fourth Division, XIV Corps. On August 16th, the regiment was sent to garrison Tracey City, Tennessee, where it remained until September 1st, when it was ordered to Bridgeport. The 89th escorted trains as far as Bridgeport, where it arrived on September 12th. The next day it, too, was attached to Steedman's division, until such time as it could rejoin Turchin. It would remain a part of Steedman's command until after the battle of Chickamauga.

49 George E. Dolton, with Theodore A. Dolton, ed., *The Path of Patriotism: The Civil War Letters of George Edwin Dolton* (Booksurge, LLC, 2005), 75.

Steedman finally found the enemy about a mile short of Ringgold, where the Federal Road crossed East Chickamauga Creek. "A portion of our forces crossed the creek and took one piece of the battery and planted it on a hill and commenced shelling them out," recalled Sgt. David H. Clifton the next day. The bombardment shocked Ringgold's defenders, who swarmed about like a kicked-over anthill. Captain William H. Harder of the 23rd Tennessee was coming up from Catoosa Platform when he met "our scouts and teamsters in a wild flight, having been set on by Federal cavalry." Frank T. Ryan of the 1st Arkansas Mounted Rifles, part of Brig. Gen. Evander McNair's brigade, was scrounging for vegetables when he and several comrades were surprised by the shelling. Hurrying back to his unit, Ryan found the brigade in line facing the hill where the Yankee gun was deployed. More troops were hustled up from Catoosa Station, billowing red dust with each quick step.[50]

Steedman's foray had come as a complete surprise because Louisianan John Scott had blundered. Colonel Scott's cavalry brigade was the first of Bragg's forces to reoccupy Ringgold after Crittenden and Wilder cleared out a week earlier. Scott's troopers should have been picketing all the roads leading into or out of Ringgold, but if they had to cover only one, the Federal Road was the most obvious and important route. Letting 2,500 Yankees and a battery of artillery approach undiscovered until the last minute amounted to negligence.

Steedman didn't linger long outside town. He could see well enough that Ringgold was swarming with Rebels, including a brigade of cavalry and thousands of infantry. He also took note of the dust rising from south of town; more Confederates were on the way. Steedman ordered his column to withdraw toward Rossville that afternoon. He made six miles before halting for the night at Battle Spring, near the crossing of Peavine Creek.[51]

Colonel Scott failed to mention in his after-action report that he had been surprised. "When the enemy again advanced upon Ringgold," explained the colonel, "I marched out to meet them and drove them back. That night the enemy encamped about five miles from Ringgold, on the Chattanooga Road. . . . About midnight, with four companies Second Tennessee Cavalry and one piece

---

50 *Delaware Gazette*, October 2, 1863; William Henry Harder Reminiscences, TSLA; Frank T. Ryan Reminiscences, Civil War Miscellany file, Georgia Department of Archives and History, Morrow GA. Hereafter GDAH.

51 *OR* 30, pt. 1, 859.

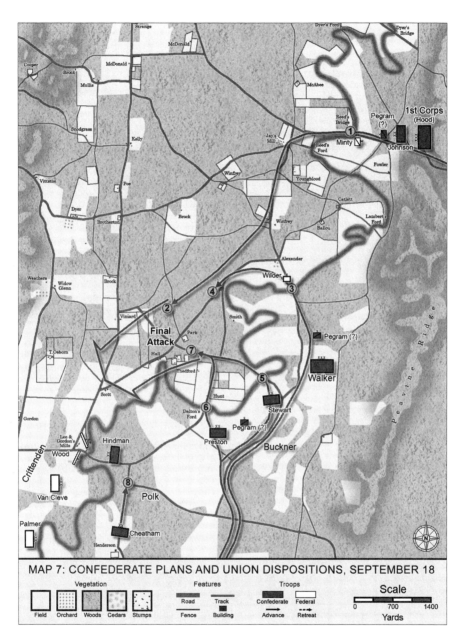

MAP 7: CONFEDERATE PLANS AND UNION DISPOSITIONS, SEPTEMBER 18

of artillery, I surprised their camp, throwing the whole force into confusion. After a sharp fight I retired . . . the enemy not following."[52]

52 Ibid., pt. 2, 531.

Scott's stealthy attack turned the tables and this time it was Steedman's pickets who weren't paying attention. Like Scott, Steedman was equally loath to admit it. About 11:00 p.m.," he noted, "the enemy . . . threw six shells into my camp, and then, under the cover of darkness, speedily retired." Sergeant Dolton's account of the brief affair was a little more frank. "They sent four shells into our camp, which caused us to put out our fires in a hurry. Had they [Union pickets] been put out as they ought," he admitted, "we should not have been fired upon." The incoming shells also caused a bit of a stampede, as Scott's report suggested. "Our infantry grasped their guns and began to retreat, officers and all" until Steedman put a stop to the spreading panic. The general stormed through the camps demanding to know "who had commanded them to fall back, & made them return . . . and go to sleep." Four of Steedman's six regiments were untried in combat, though all had been in service for at least one year. All of them, however, had spent most of 1863 on garrison duty, and were relearning the hard way the dangers of active campaigning. Somewhat embarrassed, they returned to their camps. Neither side suffered any losses during the nighttime dust-up, but Dolton took note that "Gen. Steadman [sic] put four officers under arrest for running." Steedman roused his command at 4:00 a.m., but didn't break camp for three hours, a bit of studied carelessness to show any Rebels who may be watching that he would not be hastened. The column returned to Rossville by noon.[53]

The entire affair would have been inconsequential except for the fact that a Union column had very nearly marched into Ringgold before being discovered. This unexpected threat triggered a series of changes to Bragg's overall plan. The Confederate leader immediately ordered Scott's division commander, John Pegram, who was then at Leet's, to send "a sufficient force at once" to Ringgold to ensure its defense. Bragg also revised Bushrod Johnson's orders once again, directing that the Ringgold column now heading for Leet's Tanyard instead make for Reed's Bridge. The change in Johnson's destination would position the Confederate right even farther north in relation to the Union left, and also place Johnson in a better position to intercept another such foray against the Confederate depot. Forrest's latest orders reemphasized the need to cover Johnson's "front and right flank." These last two orders, sent in a directive to

53 Ibid., pt. 1, 859; Dolton, *Path of Patriotism*, 75.

both Johnson and Forrest, were not written until after midnight (early on the morning of September 18), and would be late in arriving at Ringgold.[54]

Bragg now believed his army was ready for the grand movement. A circular to all the pertinent commanders, also issued sometime during the predawn hours of September 18, outlined Bragg's final concept:

[circular]   Headquarters, Army Of Tennessee
                                  In the Field, Leet's Tan-yard, September 18, 1863

1. Johnson's column (Hood's) on crossing at or near Reed's Bridge, will turn to the left by the most practicable route and sweep up the Chickamauga, toward Lee and Gordon's Mills.

2. Walker, crossing at Alexander's Bridge, will unite in this move and push vigorously on the enemy's flank and rear in the same direction.

3. Buckner, crossing at Thedford's Ford, will join in this movement to the left, and press the enemy up the stream from Polk's front at Lee and Gordon's Mills.

4. Polk will press his forces to the front of Lee and Gordon's Mills, and if met by too much resistance to cross will bear to the right and cross at Dalton's Ford, or at Thedford's, as may be necessary, and join in the attack wherever the enemy may be.

5. Hill will cover our left flank from an advance of the enemy from the cove, and by pressing the cavalry in his front ascertain if the enemy is re-enforcing at Lee and Gordon's Mills, in which event he will attack them in flank.

6. Wheeler's Cavalry will hold the gaps in Pigeon Mountain and cover our rear and left and bring up stragglers.

7. All teams, &c., not with troops should go toward Ringgold and Dalton, beyond Taylor's Ridge. All cooking should be done at the trains. Rations, when cooked, will be forwarded to the troops.

8. The above movements will be executed with the utmost promptness, vigor, and persistence.

By Command of General Bragg:

                                                    George Wm. Brent,
                                            Assistant Adjutant-General.[55]

Taylor Beatty, who rode with General Bragg on the 17th while army headquarters was relocated to Leet's Tanyard, observed much of the day's

---

54 Bragg to Pegram, September 17, Bragg Papers, WRHS; Bragg to Johnson and Forrest, September 18, Bragg Papers, WRHS.

55 *OR* 30, pt. 2, 31.

discussion. That night, before he sought sleep, Beatty (with what must have been understated excitement), wrote, "We are advancing upon the enemy." Then, momentarily dwelling on his personal discomfort, he added, "Very cold tonight."[56]

Not far away, the excitement was more overt at the headquarters camp of Kentuckian William Preston, a brigadier commanding one of Buckner's divisions. There, officers and men alike were keyed for battle, and the proximity of so much of the army allowed more casual visiting among the officers than usual. That night, fellow Kentuckian Benjamin Hardin Helm dropped by. Helm led the Kentucky Brigade of Breckinridge's division, part of D. H. Hill's Corps. Helm and Preston were both part of the same social circle back home and members of a coterie of Kentuckians in the Army of Tennessee who loathed Bragg for the slaughter of Stones River. "Helm . . . was at our quarters," recorded a quartermaster on Preston's staff, "and in glorious spirits." The prospect of battle and of victory was palpable that night. Moved to poetry, at one point, Helm "repeated the couplet from our Kentucky song—

> We will drive the tyrant minions
> To the Ohio's beaming flood,
> And dip her waves in crimson,
> With coward Northern blood

and laughingly said he expected to see those words verified in sixty days."[57]

The Ohio River might be a long way off, but there would be blood enough to satisfy everyone within the next 72 hours.

---

56 Entry for September 17, Taylor Beatty Diary, UNC.

57 "Battle of Chickamauga—Interesting Letter," *Abingdon Virginian*, October 9, 1863. The lyrics are part of a stanza from "The Kentucky Battle Song," written by Charlie L. Ward of the 4th Kentucky Confederate Infantry.

Chapter Eight

Reed's Bridge:

Friday, September 18, 1863

Bushrod Rust Johnson was an unlikely choice to lead Bragg's army into battle. Born into an abolitionist family of Ohio Quakers, he charted his own course early in life. Obtaining what education he could afford, Johnson struggled as a part-time teacher until he finally decided to seek an appointment to West Point. Successful in his application, he graduated from the military academy as a member of the class of 1840 and commissioned a second lieutenant of infantry that July. As a later family descendent put it, Bushrod chose "a rather strange career for a Quaker."[1]

The military career he elected for proved unsuccessful. Johnson served in the Mexican War, but failed to win distinction. He was forced to resign his commission in 1847 when he foolishly became involved in a scheme to ship private goods on army vessels. Johnson returned to teaching at a series of military schools in Kentucky and Tennessee, and in 1852 married Kentuckian Mary E. Hatch. His misfortune continued when his son Charles was born in 1854 "sickly and retarded," and his wife died in the summer of 1858.[2]

---

1 Charles M. Cummings, *Yankee Quaker, Confederate General: The Curious Career of Bushrod Rust Johnson* (The General's Books, 1993), 60.

2 David S. and Jeanne T. Heidler, eds. *Encyclopedia of the American Civil War*, 5 vols. (ABC-CLIO, 2000). vol. 3, 1072; Cummings, Yankee Quaker, 134, 152.

Minty's Troopers retreating across Reed's Bridge.
Hamilton County Public Library, Chattanooga, Tennessee

A second chance at a military life emerged when the Civil War came. Johnson, who had spent the last decade and a half in the South, forsook his Northern abolitionist roots for a commission in the state army of Tennessee.

His early appointment to high rank in the state forces, however, did not translate immediately into similar rank in Confederate service. After some lobbying on his behalf in Richmond, Johnson was made a Confederate brigadier general in January 1862. Johnson commanded brigades in combat at Fort Donelson, Shiloh, Perryville, and Stones River, but promotion eluded him. When September 1863 arrived, he was still leading his brigade in Alexander P. Stewart's division of Simon Buckner's corps. Circumstance rather than design elevated the Quaker to greater responsibility.[3]

On September 15, Johnson's brigade was detached and sent to Ringgold to secure that town. As senior brigadier, he took charge of the forces gathering there, which included his own brigade (now led by Col. John S. Fulton of the 44th Tennessee) plus two others under Brig. Gens. John Gregg and Evander McNair. The three organizations were combined into what was officially designated "Johnson's Provisional Division." This new formation was one of the smallest in Bragg's Army of Tennessee, and would enter combat on September 18 with only 3,755 officers and men.

Johnson's three new lieutenants were all solid performers, though not professional soldiers. John Fulton was a 35-year-old lawyer born in Fayetteville, Tennessee in 1828. After enlisting at Bowling Green, Kentucky, as a private in Company F, 44th Tennessee, he proved his leadership and combat prowess on the field at Shiloh, after which he was elected colonel of the 44th by acclaim. He led his regiment successfully at Perryville in October 1862 and on the last day of that year at Murfreesboro, where he was wounded. His performance at Murfreesboro singled him out for inclusion on the Confederate Roll of Honor for that battle, a rare distinction for a regimental commander. Fulton was again with his regiment at Tullahoma in June 1863, when the army was turned out of its position and fell back to Chattanooga.[4]

John Gregg was also a lawyer. Born and bred in Alabama, he moved to Texas in the 1850s and became a judge. In 1860 he was a member of Texas

---

3 Warner, *Generals in Gray*, 157.

4 *OR* 20, pt. 1, p. 978. Authorized in October 1862, the Confederate Roll of Honor was a list, by regiment, of men who were "conspicuous for courage and good conduct on the field of battle." The list was to be read before every regiment in the army, published in newspapers, with a copy preserved at the War Department in Richmond. At Murfreesboro, only seven other field grade officers were so named. John Berrien Lindsley, *The Military Annals of Tennessee. Confederate. First Series: Embracing a Review of Military Operations, with Regimental Histories and Memorial Rolls.* 2 vols. (Broadfoot Publishing, 1995), vol. 1, 538.

Secession Convention, a prominent role he bootstrapped into a successful election to the new Confederate Provisional Congress in 1861. Manassas convinced Gregg that the war would be much longer than most people expected, so he returned home to raise the 7th Texas. His first action at the head of the regiment arrived in February 1862 at Fort Donelson, where he and his Lone Star State troops, along with the rest of the garrison, were captured by Ulysses S. Grant. He was not exchanged and paroled until August 1862, after which he was assigned a command in Mississippi. Gregg's biggest challenge came in May the following year when his heavily outnumbered brigade fought the battle of Raymond, once again facing off against troops belonging to an army led by Grant. An aggressive field commander, Gregg believed he outnumbered the Federals and launched an attack—only to discover his 3,000-man brigade faced several divisions of Grant's arriving Yankees. When the truth became apparent, Gregg managed a successful disengagement after a day's hard fighting, thus proving he could command ably in the face of adversity. Gregg and his troops had not previously served under Bragg.[5]

Johnson's final brigade commander was also well seasoned. Evander McNair was a businessman at heart. The North Carolina native, born in 1820, moved to Jackson, Mississippi, and launched a mercantile operation. He enlisted during the Mexican War and served in future Confederate president Jefferson Davis's own regiment, the 1st Mississippi Rifles. After moving to Arkansas in the 1850s, where he renewed his mercantile business, McNair raised the 4th Arkansas and was elected its commander. He handled his brigade exceptionally well at Richmond, Kentucky, in August 1862, charging and routing a green Union line of battle. He was promoted to brigadier that November just in time to lead his men at Murfreesboro, where his brigade helped rout the Union right flank at first light on December 31st. In the spring of 1863 McNair and his men were sent to Mississippi, joining in the failed Vicksburg relief effort, fighting at Jackson, and were now only recently returned to the Army of Tennessee.[6]

However temporary and expedient it might have been, Johnson's elevation to command this new force was the promotion he had long craved. He was also

---

5 Warner, *Generals in Gray*, 119; Timothy B. Smith, *Champion Hill: Decisive Battle for Vicksburg* (Savas Beatie LLC, 2004), 72.

6 Warner, *Generals in Gray*, 205; Kenneth A. Hafendorfer, *The Battle of Richmond, Kentucky: August 30, 1862* (KH Press, 2006), 250-253; OR 20, pt. 1, 944.

given temporary authority over the three brigades of John Hood's division (Robertson, Law, and Benning) just then arriving from Virginia, which doubled the size of his command, if only for a short while. The ambitious Buckeye-turned-Confederate general was determined to make the most of the elevated responsibilities that had essentially fallen into his command lap.

As was so often the case in Bragg's Army of Tennessee, organization and structure often changed without much warning, and Johnson's transient command was nearly snatched away from him at the last minute. Bragg's original attack orders (Special Orders No. 245, dated September 16) directed Johnson to return to A. P. Stewart's division. Had they not been suspended, it is likely that Johnson would have reverted to brigade command in the coming fight. On September 17, however, Special Orders No. 246 directed him to take his new division to Leet's Tanyard, southwest of Ringgold. His star appeared ascendant once again. Although Johnson was unaware of it, the latter order was also already out of date. As noted earlier, Federal James Steedman's probe against Ringgold on the afternoon of September 17 forced Bragg to revise his plans yet again. Bragg's last-minute change of Johnson's destination to Reed's Bridge, however, was not written until early on the morning of the 18th, and had not yet reached him. Bragg's evolving concept of the mission sowed confusion amongst his field commanders.[7]

At 5:00 a.m., Johnson departed Ringgold with his own three brigades and Brig. Gen. Jerome B. Robertson's Texans in tow. Brigadier General Henry L. Benning's Georgians remained behind to guard the depot. The third of Hood's brigades, Brig. Gen. Evander M. Law's Alabamians, had just arrived and was allowed to cook breakfast before following. Johnson should have had cavalry leading his column, since Bragg's orders included instructions to Nathan Bedford Forrest to do just that.[8]

This new mission fell to John Pegram's cavalry division of two brigades, since Forrest's other division under Frank Armstrong was still at least a dozen miles to the southwest, guarding Bishop Polk's left flank near Glass Mill. However, Forrest was at Dalton, Georgia, roughly 16 miles south of Ringgold, and Pegram's division was widely scattered. Colonel John L. Scott's brigade was at Ringgold, having returned there after their scrap with Steedman the day

7   Robertson, "The Chickamauga Campaign: The Armies Collide," 43.

8   *OR* 30, pt. 2, 451.

before. Divisional commander Pegram and his old brigade were at Leet's Tanyard, eight miles southwest of Ringgold, maintaining a cavalry screen between that town and the Rebel force assembled near Rock Spring (which included Cheatham's Division, Buckner's and Walker's Corps). Given Bragg's urgent order to send troops in response to Steedman's Union reconnaissance, Pegram and at least some of his horsemen should also have been at Ringgold, instead of passing the night at Leet's. Pegram, however, acting as both divisional and brigade commander, was overly focused on his old brigade.

Pegram also had orders to provide troopers to lead both Buckner's and Walker's columns during their march north and decided that mission took priority. Given Forrest's location at Dalton, this left the inattentive Colonel Scott as the senior cavalryman in Ringgold. Scott should have reported to Johnson, or at least assigned a cavalry regiment to the infantryman. On the morning of the 18th, however, Scott pushed his entire brigade up the Federal Road, retracing his pursuit of Steedman the night before. In the wake of his previous embarrassment, Scott was more focused on Rossville than on Johnson's needs.

Why Forrest kept his headquarters in Dalton during this period remains a mystery. He knew as early as the 16th, given Bragg's orders of that date, that it would fall to his corps to lead the advance and seize the critical crossings along West Chickamauga Creek. His presence in Ringgold could have ensured that Bragg's intentions were carried out. Instead, Forrest began the day far to the rear, and would play no role in the important events of the morning of September 18.

Forrest's absence was not the only broken link in the chain of command. By now, the confusion piled up by the accumulated orders of the past several days was beginning to have an impact. Bragg's on-again, off-again planning and steady stream of modified orders from September 16-18 left Johnson a full step behind. According to the circular issued just that morning, Johnson's column was to head for Reed's Bridge, a bit more than six miles due west of Ringgold. Johnson, however, had yet to receive that set of orders, so when his column began marching that morning, it headed for the destination previously specified: Leet's Tanyard. Leet's was well south of both Reed's and Alexander's bridges. If this march continued without interruption, Johnson would end up behind Buckner's and Walker's corps, not abreast of them on their right.[9]

9   Ibid., 451.

Three miles down the road a courier found Johnson and informed him of the changed orders. Johnson would have to retrace his steps to reach the proper route. Part of these new instructions tasked Forrest with supplying cavalry to screen this movement, but there were no troopers in sight. This mistake in destination doubled the length of Johnson's march. It was only six and one-quarter miles from Ringgold to Reed's Bridge, but the extra three miles each way due to the countermarch put the day's total at more than 12 miles. It was 10:00 a.m. before the head of Johnson's column approached Peeler's Mill on Peavine Creek. Bragg's intended early start was already derailed. [10]

*   *   *

Colonel Robert H. G. Minty was not a man to be unnerved by being outnumbered or by operating alone. Hailing from a long military tradition, he had proven himself to be a capable officer in his own right. Minty's father was a British army officer stationed in County Mayo, Ireland, when the future Civil War general was born there in 1831. He saw much of the world growing up, for he and his brothers often accompanied their father from duty station to duty station. In 1849, Minty was commissioned in his father's former unit, the First West India Regiment of Foot. He served nearly five years until disease forced him to sell his commission and emigrate. He moved to Canada, where he took up railroading before eventually ending up in Michigan. When sectional war erupted in 1861, Minty tendered his services, first as a major in the 2nd Michigan Cavalry and then as lieutenant colonel in the 3rd. He proved to be an excellent cavalry officer—aggressive, bold, and competent. In 1862, Minty returned home to recruit the 4th Michigan Cavalry, and by the spring of 1863 was leading a mounted brigade. Further proof of his ample talent was on display when he served as part of Rosecrans's deception force pretending to threaten Chattanooga from the north. Minty was used to operating independently, and he excelled at it.[11]

Minty was well aware of Bushrod Johnson's presence at Ringgold, and he expected a fight. By 4:00 a.m. he had his entire command saddled up and ready

---

10 Ibid., 467. Distances are taken from Henry V. Boynton, *The National Military Park, Chickamauga-Chattanooga: An Historical Guide* (The Robert Clarke Co., 1895), 12.

11 Rand K. Bitter, *Minty and his Cavalry: A History of the Saber Brigade and its Commander* (Self-published, 2006), 2-5, 11-13.

to move. As he had the previous day, Minty dispatched at dawn two strong patrols, each of 100 men, south toward Leet's Tanyard and east toward Ringgold to scout for Confederates. Both sent back word by 7:00 a.m. that the enemy was stirring. Captain Heber S. Thompson of the 7th Pennsylvania Cavalry led the patrol on the Ringgold Road. Thompson's command was a mixed force drawn from both the 4th Michigan and 7th Pennsylvania. The captain cautiously approached Peavine Ridge, halted his command, and sent out a patrol of four men under Cpl. John Williams, which took up a position around a house about 100 yards west of the creek. It was about 7:00 a.m. when Corporal Williams's men opened fire on a Rebel patrol, triggering a brief skirmish.[12]

In later years, Minty and some other members of the brigade would recall a solid day's fighting that began about 6:30 a.m. Reality was something different, for Johnson's countermarch slowed things down considerably. Thompson's initial clash that morning was not with any of Johnson's Confederates, but with a handful of Scott's troopers out on a routine patrol. Minty sent couriers to General Granger at Rossville and General Crittenden at Lee and Gordon's Mills to inform them of the enemy activity, but then most of the Federal cavalry returned to normal duties. Wolverine Capt.Henry A. Potter of the 4th Michigan recorded that at 7:00 a.m., the brigade buglers sounded "stable call," allowing the troopers to dismount, unsaddle, and feed their animals. Sergeant James Larson of the 4th U.S. Cavalry also recalled a leisurely morning. One of Larson's messmates "got hold of a nice fat sheep" late the day before, and Larson's squad planned an elaborate feast for the 18th—tasty mutton stew cooked up in a large camp kettle. The excess meat was passed out to other squads, who set to frying up their unexpected bounty. They "soon had finished their breakfast and even had time to take a little smoke," recalled the hungry cavalryman. It was about 10:00 a.m. when, in response to a renewed fusillade of gunfire, buglers sounded "boots and saddles." Larson and his mates had to go without, for unfortunately their more elaborate meal was not ready to eat. With no time to wait, Larson vowed that in the future, he would adhere to the

---

12 Entry for September 18, 1863, Henry Albert Potter Diary, Bentley Historical Library, University of Michigan, Ann Arbor, MI; *OR* 30, pt. 1, 922; George W. Skinner, ed. *Pennsylvania at Chickamauga and Chattanooga: Ceremonies at the Dedication of the Monuments Erected by the Commonwealth of Pennsylvania to mark the positions of the Pennsylvania Commands engaged in the Battle* (William Stanley Ray, State Printer of Pennsylvania, 1897), 309.

"soldier's first rule of eat what you can get when you can get it, and as soon as you get it."[13]

By 10:00 a.m. Johnson's brigades were finally on the right road and moving ahead in strength. He called a halt about 1,000 yards short of Peavine Creek. Lieutenant Colonel Watt W. Floyd, commanding the 17th Tennessee, took Capt. George W. McDonald's Company K forward about 700 yards to deploy a picket line. Once established, Floyd and regimental adjutant James B. Fitzpatrick stole forward the remaining 300 yards to the creek. When their appearance drew fire from Corporal Williams's squad, the pair of officers fell back. Captain Thompson reinforced Williams's post with 16 more men, and together the entire group launched a mounted charge. Within a short time they ran up against Captain McDonald's Rebel pickets, whose fire killed Pvt. John Ward and wounded Williams. Lieutenant Colonel Floyd merely noted that the Federal probe was easily repulsed with several casualties. That probe, however, caught sight of Johnson's column. Captain Thompson deployed the rest of his battalion along Peavine Ridge overlooking the creek and sent a rider hustling back to inform Minty that "the rebels were coming in bunches." Unbeknownst to either side, the battle of Chickamauga had begun.[14]

This small clash brought Johnson's entire column to a halt. As recently as the day before, Peeler's Mill had been the site of Minty's brigade camp. Evidence of recent Federal visitation was abundant. When his regiment stopped, a member of the 3rd Tennessee infantry of Gregg's brigade recalled seeing a 10-year-old girl crying by the side of the road. Her home had been plundered by Union foragers, the fences destroyed, and one "great big dead Yank" was lying on his back in the middle of her yard. Reed's Bridge was about two miles distant, but Peavine Ridge loomed in the immediate front. According to the locals it was swarming with Federals who, unlike their unfortunate comrade in the farmyard, were very much alive.[15]

---

13 In his report, found in *OR* 30, pt. 1, 922 Minty gives no sense of the timing, other than to mention that he fought all day. In the *National Tribune*, however, Minty suggests that the first fighting began at 6:20 a.m. and continued without letup. See Robert H. G. Minty, "Minty's Saber Brigade: The Part They Took in the Chattanooga Campaign," *National Tribune*, March 3, 1892. See Also Joseph G. Vale, *Minty and the Cavalry* (Edwin K. Meyers, 1886), 225; Potter Diary, Bentley Historical Library; Larson, *Sergeant Larson*, 175.

14 *OR* 30, pt. 2, 479; Skinner, *Pennsylvania at Chickamauga and Chattanooga*, 309; *OR* 30, pt. 2, 479; "My Dear Davidson," October 20th, 1863, Robert Burns Letters, MnHS.

15 J.C. M. "A Story of the War," *The Sunny South*, August 15, 1896; *OR* 30, pt. 2, 451.

Johnson was contemplating his next move when additional word from Bragg arrived. Floyd was away scouting, trying to determine the extent of the Union opposition, when Captain R. H. S. Thompson arrived from army headquarters with a fresh dispatch intended to goad Johnson into more rapid action. The division leader was to "push on . . . vigorously and engage the enemy regardless of the force in your front." Bragg stressed the need for speed: "The army is now waiting on your movement."[16]

Now Forrest's troopers were sorely missed. Johnson needed mounted troops for reconnaissance. He had no idea how many Federals he was facing, or where they were deployed. A small patrol might be swept aside, but if the Yankees were present in any strength, a hasty advance could result in bloody failure. Johnson erred on the side of caution and put his entire division into line. Three brigades abreast formed his first line, while Robertson's Texans remained behind in reserve. Johnson would use his full strength to drive the Federals from the ridge ahead. He was still deploying his division when Forrest finally made his appearance.

Thus far, September 18 had not been one of Forrest's better days. Despite Bragg's repeated and detailed instructions, his troopers were not in position to accomplish any of the assigned missions. At dawn that Friday, Colonel Scott's brigade rode west along the Federal Road toward Rossville and reached Red House Bridge sometime around mid-morning. There, Scott's 1,100 cavalrymen bumped into Union Reserve Corps troops and halted for the rest of the day. John Pegram's brigade began its day at Leet's, where it waited with Buckner for Walker's Reserve Corps to file past. Frank Armstrong's cavalry division was still being retained by Polk near Glass Mill because Wheeler was slow in shifting his own troopers to replace Armstrong. When Forrest belatedly joined Johnson on the Reed's Bridge Road, he brought with him all he had—his own escort and Lt. Col. Robert M. Martin's battalion of survivors from John Hunt Morgan's command, roughly 350 mounted men.[17]

Forrest's escort was a hand-picked unit used by the general as shock troops and a reserve of last resort. Lieutenant Colonel Martin's battalion, on the other hand, was a scratch force of Kentuckians who had either missed Morgan's disastrous raid into Northern states or had escaped disaster in Ohio and

---

16 Brent to Johnson, September 18th, Folder 10, Bragg Papers, Palmer Collection, WRHS. Thompson was appointed as Bragg's Acting Chief of Artillery in August.

17 Entry for September 18, 1863, William E. Sloan Diary, TSLA.

returned to East Tennessee on their own. That August, Morgan's survivors were formed into an ad-hoc regiment with Col. Adam R. Johnson appointed as commander. Stragglers flocked in, and by early September Johnson had accumulated nearly 1,200 men, 700 of whom were more or less mounted. Much to the dismay of the troops, various Confederate authorities argued over whether the entire force should be dismounted and turned into infantry. Eventually the command was divided and the mounted portion assigned to Forrest. On September 15, these 240 troopers joined him at Dalton.[18]

At first blush few would have mistaken them for soldiers. They lacked virtually every accoutrement of war, and were so ill-equipped they resorted to twisted tree-bark rope instead of leather for bridles. But they had weapons and cartridge boxes, and that was enough. Bragg was unimpressed and once again suggested dismounting them, but Forrest insisted they remain cavalry and assigned Lieutenant Colonel Martin to command them. It was a sound choice. Martin was a fighting commander known for his often reckless courage. He had recently returned to duty after suffering a severe wound that spring at McMinnville, inflicted by Yankees of the 7th Pennsylvania. Now, here in North Georgia, Martin would get a chance to extract a little revenge.[19]

Bushrod Johnson had about 5,000 infantry supported by 20 pieces of artillery at Peeler's Mill. In opposition Minty could mass 973 Federal troopers and one section (two guns) of artillery. The arm Johnson lacked was cavalry, which he sorely needed to scout the Union position, seek possible outflanking routes, or closely pursue the enemy when they retreated. Forrest's arrival should have remedied Johnson's needs, but his first reaction was to dismount Martin's battalion and send it forward to reinforce Johnson's infantry skirmishers, despite the fact that foot soldiers were a commodity Johnson already had in abundance. Once these dispositions were made, around 11:00 a.m. the Rebel line advanced against the Union positions on Peavine Ridge.[20]

---

18 Dee Alexander Brown, *The Bold Cavaliers: Morgan's 2nd Kentucky Cavalry Raiders* (J. B. Lippincott & Co., 1960), 247-248. Johnson and the dismounted elements of Morgan's men remained in the rear, awaiting horses and guarding trains.

19 Ibid., 249.

20 All numbers taken from Powell, "Numbers and Losses," CCNMP. Johnson had three artillery batteries with him, and was joined by two more just at this time. See OR 30, pt. 2, 451; OR 30, pt. 1, 922. Minty's numbers were greatly reduced by extensive detachments made for picket duties. OR 30, pt. 2, 524.

When Union Capt. Heber Thompson reported renewed Rebel activity near Peeler's Mill, Minty reinforced his pickets on the La Fayette (Leet's) Road, and took the balance of the 4th Michigan, one battalion of the 4th U.S., and 1st Lieutenant Trumbull D. Griffin's two-gun section of the Chicago Board of Trade battery forward to join the fight at Peavine Ridge. The Union troops deployed on the crest of the ridge on either side of the road, where Minty obtained his first good look at the size of the Confederate troops tramping in his direction. The cavalryman estimated Johnson's command at 7,000 infantry, with at least 13 Confederate regimental flags waving above the ranks of gray and brown. The Rebels pressed Captain Thompson's skirmishers back to the foot of the ridge, where Griffin's guns opened with the first artillery rounds of the day. Minty knew he could not hold his position long, but he had the satisfaction of watching Johnson undertake the time-consuming task of forming his brigades into lines of battle.[21]

Less satisfying was the sight of a large dense plume of dust rising farther northeast. Was Johnson flanking him, or was another Rebel column marching from Graysville to Dyer's Ford, a mile north of Reed's Bridge? A Confederate crossing at Dyer's Ford would outflank Minty's position. Lieutenant and Brigade Inspector Joseph G. Vale of Minty's staff later painted a vivid, if imaginary, picture of the threat when he described the force as "a column of infantry, miles in length." In reality, none of the Union defenders knew what the plume signified, but its presence alarmed Minty enough to appeal to the only other Federal force he knew to be within supporting distance: Colonel Wilder at Alexander's Bridge. Even though he was having his own problems with Rebel infantry, Wilder cooperated by sending the 72nd Indiana, seven companies of the 123rd Illinois, and two guns from Capt. Eli Lilly's 18th Indiana Battery. As it turned out, the threat to Dyer's Ford proved nonexistent. There was no Rebel infantry column moving in that direction, nor would there be at any time that day. Exactly what kicked up the dust is unknown, but it was likely the result of Colonel Scott's Rebel cavalry working their way up the Federal Road toward Red House Bridge.[22]

With Wilder's reinforcements on the way, Minty focused his attention on the Confederates pressing his immediate front. The heavily outnumbered

---

21 Ibid., pt. 1, 922. D. H. Haines, "Record of the Fourth Michigan Cavalry," Bentley Historical Library.

22 *OR* 30, pt. 1, 922; Vale, *Minty and the Cavalry*, 225; *OR* 30, pt. 1, 447.

colonel knew a static defense would not work, so he intended to fall back slowly, concealing his main strength and giving ground grudgingly where needed in the hope of delaying the enemy as long as possible. He had already achieved some success by forcing Johnson to deploy his entire division, but that same act also meant that Johnson's line overlapped both his own flanks atop the ridge. In a strong show of bluff, Minty decided to push aggressively with his skirmishers while pulling his main line back to the next defensive position. He sent two companies of the 4th Michigan forward to reinforce Captain Thompson's small force, and then ordered Thompson to move down into the valley, to advance and drive the Confederate skirmishers back onto their main line. Minty reformed the balance of the brigade in line west of Peavine Ridge out of direct view of the enemy. "The Seventh Pennsylvania [was] on the right," recalled Minty, "the Fourth Michigan in the center, two battalions of the Fourth Regulars on the left, and one battalion [of Regulars] with the section of artillery in the orchard behind the Reed house." Every man was on the east bank of the Chickamauga. "The artillery was masked along the east bank . . . on the right of the bridge near the ford," noted Chicago artilleryman Lt. Sylvanus Stevens. Concealed in the orchard, Minty hoped his guns could fire from ambush and cover his retreat across the creek. If necessary, they could make their own escape via the ford just behind them. He also sent Vale back to camp with orders to pack up and fall back across the creek.[23] Vale and the brigade trains were to fall back towards the Union XXI Corps at Lee and Gordon's Mills.

Captain Potter's 4th Michigan company was one of the two sent to reinforce Thompson. Dispatched to the right of the Union line, Potter moved his troopers toward Peeler's Mill near their campground of two nights past. It was there that Potter caught his first glimpse of Confederate infantry. "They were in strong force," he recorded that evening, with "artillery plainly visible." It was also at that time he noticed "a strong flanking party of the rebels moved to our right."[24]

23 Haines, "Record of the Fourth Michigan Cavalry," Bentley Historical Library; R.H.G. Minty, *Remarks of Brevet Major General R.H.G. Minty made September 18th, 1895 At the Dedication of the Monument Erected to the Fourth Michigan Cavalry at Reed's Bridge, Chickamauga National Park.* (n.p. 1896), 4; Undated postwar statement of Sylvanus H. Stevens, Chicago Board of Trade Battery file, CCNMP; Minty was taking a bit of a chance relying on this ford. In his own report, he described the crossing as "bad," OR 30, pt. 1, 923; and Vale stated that the creek was "supposed to be uncrossable" here. Vale, *Minty and the Cavalry*, 226-227.

24 "Entry for September 18, 1863." Potter Diary, Bentley Historical Library.

This flanking party marked Forrest's entry into the fight. Replying to the Federal cannon, two of Johnson's artillery batteries were soon firing with vigor at the Yankees in an attempt to discourage both the Union cannon and the Federal skirmishers from pressing forward too closely. Meanwhile, as the big guns barked back and forth, Forrest led his own command and about 60 more men from the 17th Tennessee forward to join the fight. Largely reinforced, Rebel skirmishers drove back Thompson's outnumbered Federal line by holding in front and working around their flanks. The Yankees withdrew across the ridge. Lieutenant Colonel R. B. Snowden, commanding the 23rd Tennessee, mistook this Fabian strategy for "feeble resistance." As he saw it, "our skirmishers, with Forrest's cavalry, made short work of the enemy's strong position, he falling back in some confusion." Snowden found the terrain here more trouble than the defenders: "The difficulty now was to march . . . over the very rough and uneven ground, passing briar thickets, many of the men being barefooted." The Confederate deployment and advance took considerable time. It was at least 12:30 p.m. and possibly as late as 1:00 p.m. before the last Yankees abandoned Peavine Ridge.[25]

The ridge towered over the surrounding terrain, and it was now the Southerners' turn to get a good look at their opponents. For the first time, Johnson realized he faced only a brigade of horsemen. It was at this time that Forrest made a curious request. He wanted to take his cavalry and the entire 17th Tennessee Infantry on another, larger flank move to the left, toward what he thought was Minty's main camp. Perhaps Forrest was looking to turn the Federal line, or perhaps his background as a raider drove his decision to strike at a supposedly vulnerable Yankee baggage train. In any case, Johnson let him go but the movement proved fruitless. According to Lieutenant Colonel Floyd, the combined command shifted "about a half mile to the left . . . but before we got in range the enemy fled." Floyd, the 17th Tennessee, and virtually all of Forrest's men, however, had taken themselves out of the fight. They would not rejoin the main attack until after the Rebels had forced the creek crossings later that day.[26]

While Forrest moved to the left Johnson pushed forward with the rest of his command, following the road through the gap in the ridge. When his leading

25 Harder Reminiscences, TSLA; *OR* 30, pt. 2, 488.

26 *OR* 30, pt. 2, 452, 479.

infantry burst into view, Minty's men engaged them. Griffin's two guns opened fire from their orchard ambush. Their shots, wrote Lieutenant Stevens, "threw the head of the [rebel] column into confusion and a continued concentrated fire held the enemy in check." Minty was a firm believer in the effectiveness of mounted cavalry and he displayed that confidence now, ordering squadrons of the 4th Michigan and 7th Pennsylvania forward at the charge. This moment offered Lieutenant Vale another chance to wax dramatic in describing the moment. The two regiments, he wrote, "delivered a terrific saber charge, riding into the thronging masses of their infantry and hewing them down by the score." The Confederates were less impressed. Not a single Confederate report mentions the charge, and no Southern outfit suffered any significant losses from this attack. In reality, the mounted thrust forced the Rebels to be more cautious with their skirmishers, but achieved little else.[27]

It was at some point during this first engagement west of Peavine Ridge that Wilder's reinforcements finally appeared on the scene. Colonel Abram O. Miller arrived at the head of his own 72nd Indiana, seven companies of the 123rd Illinois, and a pair of guns. The small column halted west of Chickamauga Creek to await more detailed instructions from Minty. From that point they watched the fighting develop, Confederate artillery shells screeching overhead from time to time. The only serious discomfort for the men of the 72nd Indiana was when someone's horse stirred up a large hornet's nest underfoot. As Hoosier Ambrose Remley put it, "the rebels' shells bursting over us and the Yellow Jackets stinging our horses and us made it anything but comfortable."[28]

Fortunately, those Federals did not have to mark time for long. Miller reported around 1:00 p.m., and Minty wasted little time assigning him a mission. With fresh orders in hand, Miller deployed his command northward about two miles to cover several important crossings. The 72nd covered Dyer's Ford and bridge, while Col. James Monroe took his 123rd Illinois farther downstream to Dalton's Ford. Monroe was further instructed to send a patrol as far as the Red House Bridge, where it should find men from the Union Reserve Corps. By

---

27 Stevens's Statement, Chicago Board of Trade Battery Unit file, CCNMP; Vale, *Minty and the Cavalry*, 226. Vale did not personally witness this charge: he had already been sent back to orchestrate the retreat of the brigade wagons.

28 Linville, *Battles, Skirmishes, Events and Scenes*, 81.

1:30 the Union men were off and trotting, still chasing a phantom Rebel infantry column supposedly threatening Minty's flank.[29]

Back at Reed's Bridge, meanwhile, Minty was preparing to fall back across the creek. However effective his artillery and cavalry charge might have been, Minty knew he could not stand east of the creek without eventually being trapped and destroyed there. After buying as much time as possible with his aggressive stance west of the ridge, Minty began withdrawing his command to the west bank to assume his next line of defense. The two battalions of the 4th U.S. fell back with orders to form on a slight elevation west of the creek while a squadron of Regulars commanded by Lt. Wirt Davis remained behind to cover the withdrawal. Sergeant Larson recalled the maneuver with evident pride: "Company A moved slowly toward the bridge as though there were nothing whatever to hurry about, crossed over by twos and at once formed line . . . close to the bank of the Chickamauga. . . . The movement was beautifully executed, and although under fire continually it was done as slowly and steadily as if on drill or parade." Now it was the 4th Michigan's turn. Captain Potter fell back with his Wolverines, passing through their campsite of that morning and behind Davis's remaining Regulars to cross the creek "without loss." From there, the Michiganders dismounted and established a line "toward & along the river" in order to cover the 7th Pennsylvania and Davis's squadron of Regulars as they took their turn evacuating the east bank.[30]

Thus far the crossing at Reed's Bridge had gone off without a hitch, but the remaining Federals east of the waterway found it more hazardous. Robert Burns, also in the 4th Michigan, witnessed nearly the entire passage. "At one time nearly our . . . whole brigade had to cross the Chickamauga over a narrow bridge, two abreast. I stood there a long time, directing them, and seeing that the shaky planks were kept in their places." Minty personally led the 7th Pennsylvania across. By this time, however, Confederate pressure increased as

---

29 OR 30, pt. 1, 464. Miller noted the time as just before noon, but this was probably too soon, given that the Federals were still on Peavine Ridge at that time. Note that the "Dalton's Ford" specified in these orders is a different Dalton Ford than the one used by the Confederates to cross Chickamauga Creek south of the Hunt house.

30 Minty, *Remarks*, 4. Union cavalry regiments were organized into three battalions, each comprised of four companies or troops. Each battalion was further subdivided into two squadrons, each with two companies. In modern usage, the terms 'squadron' and 'battalion' have become interchangeable. Larson, *Sergeant Larson*, 177-8; Potter Diary, Bentley Historical Library.

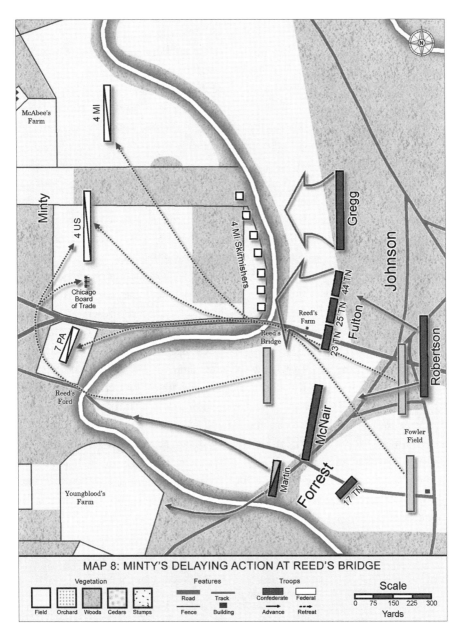

MAP 8: MINTY'S DELAYING ACTION AT REED'S BRIDGE

Johnson's infantry pressed closer to the creek and Southern artillery unlimbered to engage the retreating Federals. Worried that the Pennsylvanians could not get safely across, Lieutenant Davis ordered another charge with his squadron of Regulars. The mounted thrust checked the Rebel infantry in his front for a time, but did nothing to stop the Confederate cannon fire. Sergeant James Shuster of

Company M, 7th Pennsylvania, described "crossing the bridge under a heavy infantry and artillery fire," but the Keystone soldiers of the 7th managed to finish their crossing. Lieutenant Davis paused long enough to tear up the bridge flooring (those same "shaky planks" described by Wolverine Burns) and toss the timber into the water. Fortunately for the Federals, Southern gunners were still trying to obtain the range, and casualties remained light. It was now 2:00 p.m. or a little after; Minty had once again safely extricated his brigade from a potentially lethal trap.[31]

Years after the fight, Minty wrote that the artillery and its escorting battalion of Regulars crossed without incident. While true, not every Federal unit escaped via the bridge, and some had a more difficult time of it than others. When Minty ordered the main body of the 4th U.S. to fall back, he also sent word to Griffin's guns to retreat via the ford behind the Reed house. Before the battery could cross, recalled Lieutenant Stevens, "a detachment of the enemy, by a flank movement through a thicket, reached the battery and were entertained by a hand-to-hand contest while the guns were limbered to the rear and run across the ford." The Rebel foray into the path of the guns was launched by Capt. William Henry Harder's Company G of the 23rd Tennessee, part of Fulton's brigade. Company G, wrote Harder, "advance[d] rapidly and after some delay cutting through the briars and vines[,] emerged to the open ground on the flank of the battery . . . opened fire on it . . . and charged it, but the federal[s] had done limbered up and moved."

With the successful extrication of his artillery, all of Minty's command was safely across the Chickamauga. Once across the cavalryman ordered his brigade to fall back to a second rise about 700 yards farther west. His skirmishers fell back about half that distance and took up whatever cover they could in the flat open fields stretching east and sloping down to the creek bank.[32]

---

31 "My Dear Davidson," October 20th, 1863, Robert Burns Letters, MinnHS; Minty, *Remarks*, 4; James H. Shuster, "Holding Reed's Bridge," *National Tribune*, August 11, 1919; Vale, *Minty and the Cavalry*, 227. Removing the flooring and rails was probably all the damage the Federals could realistically inflict. Civil War armies lacked reliable explosives that could be rigged to destroy structures at a moment's notice. Dynamite would not be invented until 1866, and it took a great deal of black powder, concentrated in the right places, to inflict even minimal damage on an open structure like a bridge. Burning was the best option, but that took time, and Minty needed to use the bridge up until the last minute. Enough artillery solid shot would do the trick, again a time consuming process, especially since he only had two cannon.

32 Minty, *Remarks*, 4; Stevens's Statement, CCNMP. Harder Reminiscences, TSLA. Harder's company was changed from D to G earlier in the war. His description of it is markedly similar

Without orders, Harder and the rest of the 23rd Tennessee made for the de-planked bridge.[33] The Tennesseans lost several men during their approach including their color bearer, but it was not Federal fire that stopped them but the abrupt banks of the watercourse. Within minutes the rest of Fulton's brigade was crowding along the east bank. Captain Potter of the 4th Michigan watched the arrival of the Rebels, "three separate lines of their infantry mov[ing] from the left & swing towards the bridge. I sent word to Major [Horace] Gray to that affect and he moved the regiment back once more . . . skirmishing all the time." Rebel skirmishers crossed the creek by various means to follow the Union retirement as quickly and closely as possible. The 23rd's skirmishers picked out a precarious path across what was left of the bridge. Behind them, Captain Harder ordered Company G to hastily re-floor the skeletal structure using siding torn from the nearby Reed barn. The Union fire, which continued unabated, "splintered with grape shot" the timbers of the bridge while the Rebels worked to re-plank it.[34]

One of the casualties inflicted here did not wear a uniform. According to Lieutenant Vale of Minty's staff, a woman and her two small children occupied the Reed house throughout the fight. The woman, who Vale naturally assumed was part of the Reed family, refused to evacuate when the Yankees warned her that morning that a fight was likely. Frustrated by her intransigence, Minty ordered her to at least "stay inside the house." The deep booming of artillery and sharper explosions of rifle fire proved too attractive to ignore, however, and she was "continually out viewing the scene" as the battle unfolded. During the 23rd Tennessee's rush toward the bridge, the woman "ran out to the road, shouting 'You Yanks are running!' . . . seemingly crazed with excitement," wrote Vale. Unfortunately, she ran into the line of fire of a Confederate artillery battery, "and at the first discharge . . . their missiles . . . laid her a mangled corpse in front of her door." Minty forever deeply regretted her death and lamented that he had failed to forcibly remove her and her children from the home when

---

to Stevens's. One major difference is that Harder indicates that it occurred later in the fight, after the Rebels crossed the creek. Based on other inconsistencies of timing in Harder's account, I have decided that it happened as described above.

33 OR 30, pt. 2, 484.

34 Potter Diary, Bentley Historical Library; Harder Reminiscences, TSLA.

she refused to leave of her own accord. She remains one of the battle's many unknown dead.[35]

There was no time to mourn the death of an unknown woman, however. Captain Harder's men were finishing the new bridge floor when General Forrest appeared. The general complimented Company G's quick work at the bridge and, as Harder watched with both amazement and admiration, Forrest calmly rode across the structure toward the Yankees. "I cautioned him to be careful," remembered the captain, but "he only laughed and rode forward. . . . He rode to within 100 yards of the Federal [line.] He halted with his accustomed attentive . . . manner . . . and took in the situation . . . while discharge after discharge of grape and canister dashed by him." Colonel Fulton, commanding Johnson's brigade that day, sent the 23rd, 25th, and 44th Tennessee regiments across the bridge after the cavalry general. The infantry crossed smartly and shifted to the right nearly 400 yards in order to allow the rest of the division to cross and deploy in turn.[36]

The action, which had been brisk, now intensified. One section of Bledsoe's Missouri Battery advanced again and dropped trail near the Reed House to engage the Chicago Board of Trade's guns that were still launching iron at the bridge. A Mexican War veteran, Capt. Hiram Bledsoe raised and equipped his battery to serve in the pro-Confederate Missouri State Guard back in June 1861. He led his guns in Missouri and Mississippi with distinction, and Chickamauga would be no different. Under the cover of Bledsoe's fire, Brig. Gen. John Gregg decided to forgo using the bridge, which by now was a focal point of a great deal of enemy fire, and ordered his brigade to wade the creek upstream.[37]

The 17th Tennessee found its way back into the action about this time. When Lieutenant Colonel Floyd discovered that the rest of Fulton's brigade

35 Vale, *Minty and the Cavalry*, 234. The woman was not Mrs. Reed. In fact, none of the Reed family was present during the battle. According to a local historian, the "woman was probably a refugee, possibly a relative, from Tennessee," E. Raymond Evans, *Chickamauga: Civil War Impact on an Area: Tsikamagi, Crawfish Springs, Snow Hill, and Chickamauga* (City of Chickamauga, 2002), 68; Vale, *Minty and the Cavalry*, 234. It is possible that Vale was mistaken. No Rebel account mentions her death, and Vale himself did not witness the incident, though in his history he wrote that a number of eyewitnesses attested to the veracity of the tale.

36 Harder Reminiscences, TSLA; OR 30, pt. 2, 472.

37 William Terrell Lewis, *Genealogy of the Lewis Family in America* (Courier-Journal Job Printing Co., 1893), 139; John T. Goodrich, "Gregg's Brigade In The Battle of Chickamauga," *Confederate Veteran*, vol. XXII, no. 6 (June, 1914), 264.

was across the creek and deployed for action, he hurried his regiment across the bridge. All the while, reported Floyd, the bridge was "under a heavy fire from the enemy's artillery." Heavy the Chicago Board of Trade fire might have been, but effective it was not. Floyd reported only one casualty during this operation. Once across, the 17th joined the rest of Fulton's men in line of battle. Once across the stream, Gregg's command fell in alongside Fulton's men. Bushrod Johnson now had 10 regiments in two brigades drawn up to oppose Minty's thin cavalry line. Unfortunately for the Confederates, however, more precious time had been lost. It was now nearly 3:00 p.m.[38]

The delay frustrated the already unwell Bragg. By midday, he had expected to hear that Johnson was across the creek with his division and moving rapidly toward the Union left flank near Lee and Gordon's Mills. When no word to that effect reached army headquarters (at Leet's Tanyard), Bragg decided to goad his subordinate into more aggressive action. During the crossing, Johnson received the following terse note from Colonel Brent, written about 2:00 p.m.: "The Gen'l C'mdg directs me to say that you endanger the left by the delay. He therefore wishes you to press forward with the utmost vigor and dispatch."[39]

Bragg was not the only aggravated Rebel that afternoon. Fulton's brigade and, to a lesser extent, Gregg's regiments, had seen some action, but for the troops farther back in Johnson's column, the day had been one of frustration. Frank Ryan of the 1st Arkansas Mounted Rifles, Evander McNair's brigade, found the first half of the day exceedingly exasperating. "We would move along for a short distance and halt, and about the time you had fairly sat down . . . the order would be given—'fall in, forward' and then move up a short distance and halt again," he complained. "[A]nd so it would go, consuming an hour or two, in making a mile or two. . . . Of all the disagreeable and perplexing things every old soldier knows that such marching . . . is the most vexatious."[40]

Johnson, wary of the damage Minty could inflict upon his command and unfamiliar with the terrain, prepared carefully each time he confronted the enemy. Once across the creek it took time to get the long Confederate lines ready for a general advance. This time, the Rebels expected the Federals to stand and fight. McNair moved his brigade up and into line supporting Fulton

38 OR 30, pt. 2, 479.

39 Folder 10, Bragg Papers, WRHS.

40 Frank T. Ryan Reminiscences, Civil War Miscellany file, GDAH.

and Gregg. The brigade surgeon, W. L. Gammage, recalled they stood waiting for about half an hour. Gammage and his staff used the time to establish a field hospital to receive the casualties everyone expected would follow the sharp engagement about to open.[41]

Just prior to the advance, Maj. Gen. John Bell Hood arrived on the scene. Although still recovering from a severe arm wound suffered at Gettysburg 11 weeks earlier, Hood refused to remain in Virginia when his troops were selected to reinforce Bragg's Army of Tennessee. After traversing the same arduous route as the rest of Longstreet's men, Hood detrained at Catoosa Station around midday. An order from Bragg awaited him there, instructing Hood to catch up with Johnson and assume command of the column. Hood's unexpected appearance, his arm still in a sling, created a stir within the ranks of Jerome Robertson's Texans, who raised their hats in lieu of cheering as the wounded general trotted past. Hood found it a "touching welcome."[42]

Hood and Johnson briefly conferred while the infantry finished forming. While Hood later took credit for deploying the infantry, reinforcing Forrest's cavalry, and extending the battle line to threaten both of Minty's flanks; both he and Johnson place Hood's arrival at 3:00 p.m., and by that late in the day these events were well underway. Moreover, Johnson had already reported his success in forcing the crossing to Bragg, who relayed the information to W. H. T. Walker and Simon Buckner. Bragg's message identified the column's commander as Johnson, not Hood, which suggested the latter had not yet appeared on the scene when that note was dispatched.[43]

Whoever set the ball in motion for this final attack, the effort proved to be more of the same. Minty had no intention of mounting a last-ditch defense, and remained wedded to his Fabian strategy. His men had thus far performed well, holding up the Rebels for hours without being drawn into a close-quarters fight they could not win. Accordingly, when a Yankee courier arrived bearing a

---

41 W. L. Gammage, *The Camp, the Bivouac, and the Battlefield* (Arkansas Southern Press, 1958), 90; Robertson, "The Chickamauga Campaign: The Armies Collide," 45.

42 John Bell Hood, *Advance and Retreat* (Blue and Grey Press, 1985), 61; and Bragg to Hood, September 18, Folder 10, Bragg Papers, WRHS; J. B. Polley, *Hood's Texas Brigade* (Press of the Morningside Bookshop, 1988), 199. The brigade officers suppressed any cheers in the mistaken belief that the Federal cavalry were not aware that Rebel infantry was present, and did not want to ruin any surprise. Hood, *Advance and Retreat*, 61.

43 Hood, *Advance and Retreat*, 61; *OR* 30, pt. 2, 452; Bragg to Buckner and Walker, September 18, Folder 10, Bragg Papers, WRHS.

message from Lieutenant Vale, who by this time had reached Lee and Gordon's Mills with the brigade baggage train, Minty was ready to give more ground. Vale's news was alarming. Colonel Wilder had been standing off another Rebel column more than a mile south at Alexander's Bridge, but was outflanked and forced to fall back southwest toward the Union XXI Corps. Rebels in large numbers were crossing the creek at various points upstream. Minty's line of retreat was in jeopardy.[44]

Wilder's retreat, justified as it was, rendered Minty's defense untenable. Minty recalled Colonel Miller's force, which was still picketing the downstream crossings, and ordered his entire command to fall back. The troopers executed a short stand near Jay's Mill to help cover the retreat. A shell from one of Bledsoe's Missouri guns shattered a wheel on one of the Chicago Board of Trade battery's pieces, but, noted Lieutenant Stevens, the sergeant commanding the piece "limbered up and dragged the gun from under a running fire" until it was out of range and could be temporarily repaired.[45] Colonel Abram Miller and his 72nd Indiana, seven companies of the 123rd Illinois, and section of guns had a largely uneventful afternoon guarding the downstream crossings, despite the action raging to their south. The sound of fighting all around them, however, was unnerving. To Pvt. Jerome Stubbins, the gunfire was "intense, causing considerable confusion among our troops." The men witnessed the beginning of Minty's fight, and they knew Wilder was being menaced at Alexander's Bridge. To their north, Company F of the 123rd Illinois expected to find other Union troops at Red House Bridge, but was instead ambushed by Rebel cavalry. The Illinoisans beat a hasty retreat, losing six men captured in the scuffle, including Lt. James Biggs. When Minty's retreat order arrived, Miller lost no time in withdrawing. Miller's detachment quickly fell back at the "trot to keep them from cutting us off," wrote Hoosier private Alva C. Griest of Company B, 72nd Indiana. Not everyone slipped away with ease. "I had to run for it," admitted Maj. James Connolly to his wife. "I lost my hat in the race—that wretched hat I told you about in my last letter." Corporal John Rippetoe of Eli Lilly's battery remembered he and his fellow gunners "came very near to being trapped and had to get out of that in a hurry." The confusion led to several men becoming lost in their efforts to escape. Joshua Foster and

44 OR 30, pt. 1, 923; Vale, *Minty and the Cavalry*, 228; Minty, *Remarks*, 5.

45 Stevens's Statement, CCNMP.

three comrades, all of Company I, 72nd Indiana, were unable to rejoin their command until the next day, while Pvt. Robert Alexander of the 123rd Illinois was unable to reach his horse before falling into Rebel hands. Alexander's fate would be a difficult one that included a series of Rebel prison camps with a final destination of Andersonville.[46]

Minty formed his troopers into a final line of battle some distance southwest of Jay's Mill and waited there for Miller's men to arrive. When they finally reported in about 4:30 p.m., Minty ordered the entire force to fall back to the La Fayette Road, and from there join Tom Crittenden's corps at Lee and Gordon's Mills, "making a circuit round the Confederates who had crossed near Alexander's Bridge." They were joined en route by Lt. John H. Simpson's detachment, which had been all but given up for lost. Simpson's squadron of the 4th Michigan had been sent out that morning to picket the road to Leet's Tanyard, but had been cut off when Reed's Bridge fell to the Rebels. Somehow, Simpson's men managed to swim the creek and rejoin the brigade without loss.[47]

Minty's departure left the field to Bushrod Johnson's command (now under John B. Hood). John Pegram's brigade of Forrest's cavalry arrived as the fight was winding down, too late to play any significant role. Pegram's 2,200 troopers had begun their frustrating day near Leet's Tanyard, delayed by narrow roads crowded with Walker's and Buckner's infantry before spending more time as spectators to the fight at Alexander's Bridge between Wilder's Federals and Brig. Gen. Edward C. Walthall's Mississippians of the Confederate Reserve Corps. When Walthall's repulse foiled Pegram's intention to cross Chickamauga Creek at that point, he rode north and crossed at Fowler's Ford to finally join Forrest near Jay's Mill about dusk. The upshot was that Pegram's troopers played no role in the fighting at either bridge, failed to lead any of the

---

46 Entry for September 18th, Jerome K. Stubbins Diary, OHS; Baumgartner, *Blue Lightning,* 199; Entry for September 18, Alva C. Griest Journal, InSL. Griest was a Quaker who abandoned his pacifistic faith to join the fight against slavery and rebellion; "Dearest Mary," October 5th, 1863, John Rippetoe Letters, Indiana State University, Terra Haute, IN; Baumgartner, *Blue Lightning,* 199-200. Alexander did not survive his imprisonment. He died on September 8, 1864, and is buried at Andersonville National Cemetery, Grave 8127.

47 Vale, *Minty and the Cavalry,* 228; Minty, "Minty's Saber Brigade;" Minty, *Remarks,* 5-6; Vale, *Minty and the Cavalry,* 227.

Rebel columns as specified in Bragg's orders, and consumed more than 10 hours to travel fewer than 10 miles.[48]

Bushrod Johnson's tribulations were not quite at an end. Two roads branched off from Jay's Mill toward Lee and Gordon's Mills, the Brotherton Road to the southwest and the Jay's Mill Road to the south. The former intersected with the La Fayette Road two miles distant; following it would place his entire division astride Rosecrans's main line of retreat to Chattanooga, and squarely on the flank of the Crittenden's XXI Corps. The smaller track on the left ran due south toward the Alexander farmstead before ending at Alexander's Bridge Road—the most direct route to Walker's troops. Johnson wanted to move down the Brotherton Road, but Hood had other ideas. Bragg's orders to Hood, which he received when he stepped off the train at Catoosa, directed the general "open communications with General Walker, who will cross at Bryam's Ford on your left."[49] The quickest way to fulfill these orders lay due south, toward the Alexander's Bridge Road. Hood ordered Johnson to march in that direction. With one of Gregg's regiments in line screening the movement, the rest of the division formed up in column of companies and followed. For reasons that remain obscure, none of Pegram's men led this advance. Instead, the Rebel cavalry scouted to the north and to the west, protecting the rear of Hood's infantry column.[50]

The choice of the Jay's Mill Road would have significant consequences on the course of the fighting to come.

---

48 J. W. Minnich, "Unique Experiences in the Chickamauga Campaign, *Confederate Veteran*, vol. XXXV, no. 10 (October, 1927), 381. Minnich, "Reminiscences of J. W. Minnick," 20.

49 Bragg to Hood, September 18, folder 10, Bragg Papers, WRHS.

50 *OR* 30, pt. 2, 452.

Chapter Nine

Alexander's Bridge:

Friday, September 18, 1863

The vicinity of Peavine Creek between Leet's Tanyard and Rock Spring buzzed with activity when the sun rose on September 18. Two corps of Confederate infantry were encamped there, and they were now preparing for what promised to be a long day with an uncertain end. Each corps consisted of two infantry divisions and supporting artillery, some 17,000 men all told. Each corps had a specific role to play in the Army of Tennessee's grand design to move into position and crush the Army of the Cumberland. The timetable was tight, the roads narrow, and the routes limited. These four infantry divisions, their artillery and other impedimenta occupied a great deal of road space. The congestion soon to begin would be but one reason they would arrive late at their designated jump-off points.

General Bragg's September 18 circular spelled out W. H. T. Walker's and Simon Buckner's roles with specificity. Walker was to cross his men at Alexander's Bridge, connect with Johnson's left flank, and "push vigorously on the enemy's flank and rear." Once Walker was across and in contact with Johnson, Buckner would cross at Thedford's Ford, "join in the movement to the left, and press the enemy up the stream." If properly executed, Bragg would have nearly 25,000 men across the Chickamauga by nightfall on the 18th, all drawn up in a massive line of battle facing southwest toward Lee and Gordon's

Mills, astride Rosecrans's line of communications and poised to roll up and crush the Union left flank.[1]

Once again, Walker and Buckner were to set out at 6:00 a.m. to allow ample time to cross the creek by early that afternoon. Drawn up on paper the plan looked more than feasible. Problems, however, immediately became evident when viewed from ground level and put into motion. The initial part of the march required Walker and Buckner to share a single road. The inevitable congestion that followed triggered one delay after another, not only for the two infantry corps but for Pegram's cavalry as well, which was supposed to provide escorts for all three (Johnson's, Walker's, and Buckner's) columns. Only Buckner left an account of the jam, a tersely worded but understated observation that his "march was somewhat retarded by the encounter." If Bushrod Johnson had received the correct orders for the 18th and not lost so much time counter-marching, this delay might have been much more significant. As it turned out, both Walker and Buckner would find themselves waiting at the end of the day for Johnson's division to arrive.[2]

Walker and one of his division commanders, St. John Liddell, rode at the head of the column alongside Walthall's Mississippians. Liddell was a seasoned combat officer by 1863 leading his largest command to date. His two brigades numbered 4,031 men in 10 regiments and two batteries of guns. Both Walker and Liddell knew their objective was Alexander's Bridge, but they began the day's march uncertain which side controlled it. Bragg's previous orders directed Forrest to seize all the required crossings before the infantry arrived, but the earlier suspension and subsequent changes to the orders left the infantry generals uneasy about whether that objective had been accomplished. As they would soon discover, it had not. Late that morning just before he reached the bridge, reported Walker, "I was informed that I would have to fight for it."[3]

*   *   *

Like Minty, Col. John Wilder was prepared for an early fight but did not know when or whether the enemy would materialize. The previous afternoon

---

1   OR 30, pt. 2, 31.

2   Ibid., 357.

3   Powell, "Numbers and Losses," CCNMP; OR 30, pt. 2, 239.

he had been ordered to move to Alexander's Bridge to watch it and other crossings over West Chickamauga Creek. By the morning of the 18th his Lightning Brigade was spread over a wide area. While at army headquarters, Wilder acquired some knowledge of the area he was to picket. James M. Lee, son-in-law of the recently deceased James Gordon and co-owner and business manager of Lee and Gordon's Mills was a stout, if secretive, Union man. Lee's loyalty had been affirmed by several other Chattanooga region residents, and the Federals turned to him for local intelligence. Wilder was impressed. "He told me very frankly of all he knew, but cautioned me not to let it be known that he had given me the information, as everybody could not be trusted, and it was as much as his life was worth to have it known," explained the colonel. "I asked him then about the movements of the troops to see how accurate his knowledge was and how truthful it might be, and I found him very correct [as] it corroborated the information I already possessed." In addition to his duties at the mill, Lee also rented a number of local farming tracts including the 120 acres of the Alexander farmstead where Wilder established his headquarters. The Alexander farmhouse was at the time unoccupied.[4]

Wilder's task was a tall one, and his brigade was already short one regiment. The 92nd Illinois had been detached yet again, this time to establish a courier line for General Thomas and his XIV Corps miles away at Pond Spring. As Wilder soon discovered, defending the bridge site with his under-strength command would not be enough to prevent the enemy from crossing the creek. A large military force could only cross at a few points, but enemy skirmishers could slip over almost anywhere, and there were numerous fords both upstream and down that would allow formed infantry and artillery access to the west bank. Wilder had no choice but to disperse his regiments over several miles, establishing picket lines and garrisoning likely fording points. Upstream, about one-half of the 123rd Illinois was assigned to cover potential crossings toward Lee and Gordon's Mills, nearly five miles distant as the creek meandered. Nearer the bridge and downstream, he posted several companies from the 17th and 72nd Indiana along the creek's north bank.[5]

4 Francis A. Green, *The Witness of a House* (Gordon-Lee House, 1984), 53-54. According to the 1860 census, owner John J. Alexander was the county's second largest slaveholder. For reasons that remain unknown, however, he left the area in 1861.

5 *Ninety-Second Illinois Volunteers*, 107-108; J. N. Abbott, "Opening of Chickamauga Fight," *National Tribune*, April 9, 1914. Exact dispositions on the night of September 17 are unclear, but

These detachments left Wilder with about 1,400 men on hand. His disposable force included the 17th and 72nd Indiana (less the companies sent forward as pickets), as well as Lilly's battery, the 98th Illinois, and the remaining half of the 123rd Illinois. From the brigade camp and command post at the Alexander house, situated on a rise of ground overlooking the eponymous bridge about 650 yards to the south, Lilly's guns could dominate both the bridge and its approaches. Wilder kept his remaining infantry there as well, where they could support the battery or shift to threatened locations as needed.[6]

As the battery made camp that night, a number of men slipped away to do a little impromptu foraging despite standing orders to the contrary. The battery bugler, Henry Campbell was among those digging up some of James Lee's potato crop when he was caught in the act by the brigade provost marshal. The provost ordered the scroungers to fall in under arrest, while "a big Corpl of the 72nd was ordered to tote the sack [of potatoes] to headquarters." The arrest was more for show than anything else. During the march back the transgressors slipped away by ones and twos until the guard detail had only one or two prisoners left in tow. Nor were the men willing to give up their potatoes. Once back in camp, Campbell informed 1st Sergeant Martin Miller about the loss. The sergeant set out to retrieve their intended supper and "marched boldly up to the sack just as if he had been ordered, shouldered and marched off with it." Embarrassed, the provost marshal dropped the matter and no one was punished.[7]

The next morning, when action did not immediately develop on their front, Wilder's men returned their attention to food. "The morning . . . opened clear and beautiful, and men from the Seventy-Second [Indiana] were soon in the country foraging," recorded the regimental historian. The haul was plentiful, and "a hearty and quiet breakfast was enjoyed." At 10:00 a.m., some Hoosiers decided to repeat their success to garner provisions for future meals. A number of men crossed the creek to the south, but a short time later "came back like

Abbott places his own location as Dalton's Ford. As noted in the previous chapter, there were two Dalton's Fords over the Chickamauga: one north (downstream) and one south (upstream) from Reed's Bridge.

6   The looping nature of the creek meant that while Reed's Bridge Road crossed the West Chickamauga on an east-west axis, Alexander's Bridge Road did so from north to south.

7   John W. Rowell, *Yankee Artillerymen: Through the Civil War with Eli Lilly's Indiana Battery* (University of Tennessee Press, 1975), 111.

flying birds" hotly pursued by Rebel cavalry. Cut off from the bridge, several Yankees "plunge[d] into the creek and swam across," covered by the fire of their comrades. Company A of the 72nd tore up the bridge flooring and threw together a "lunette fort" with the planks in the road just north of the bridge, "determined to hold it at all hazards." A Rebel cavalry patrol tried to rush the bridge, only to be brought to a halt by well-aimed fire from behind the crude breastwork. The Confederates withdrew.[8]

The Rebel cavalry thrust alerted the rest of Wilder's brigade that the enemy was on hand; just about the same time as, three miles downstream at Reed's Bridge, "Boots and Saddles" called Minty's troopers to formation, interrupting their late breakfast and other camp duties.[9] As activity coursed through Wilder's camps, word arrived from Minty about 11:00 a.m. that his flank was threatened. Could Wilder send help? Even though his own front was thinly manned, the Hoosier general dispatched seven companies of the 72nd Indiana and the entire 123rd Illinois, nearly 750 men, or more than one-half of his manpower then on hand, to Minty's relief. Wilder also ordered Lt. Col. Edward Kitchell and part of the 98th Illinois out to replace the dispatched 123rd regiment. Kitchell and two companies rode to what he called "Smith's Ford" while additional detachments covered other crossings. This left only the 17th Indiana and about one-half of the 98th ready to support the picket companies should they be pressed. The decision displayed Wilder's confidence in the abilities of his men. [10]

The first Rebel probe that withdrew in the face of the crude lunette consisted of cavalry from John Pegram's brigade either en route to join Forrest or screening General Walker's advance. The troopers yielded to St. John Liddell's infantry, who were ordered by Walker to clear the way. Leading Liddell's column were the men of his former brigade, seven Arkansas regiments and one from Louisiana under Daniel C. Govan. Six of the seven Arkansas

---

8 Magee, *History of the 72nd Indiana*, 167.

9 Ibid.

10 "Entry for September 18th," Edward Kitchell Diary, ALPL. There is no "Smith's Ford" in the area to which Kitchell was assigned. By the fall of 1863, however, many refugees had moved into the area and sometimes squatted in abandoned houses, so the potential for confusion was great. See the discussion in the previous chapter about the unidentified woman who was living in the Reed home with her children during the fighting on Minty's front. It is also unclear when the 98th Illinois replaced the 123rd Illinois. It is possible it did so that morning as part of a normal relief, but Kitchell's diary suggests he was not sent to the fords until noon, well after the 123rd Illinois was sent to reinforce Minty at Reed's Bridge.

commands had been consolidated into three tactical units because of heavy losses after two years of war and their inability to receive a steady flow of replacements. The 1st Louisiana Regulars, which had also suffered heavy casualties as well as leadership problems at the battle of Murfreesboro nine months earlier, had been similarly consolidated with Lt. Col. George F. Baucom's 8th Arkansas Regiment.[11]

The brigade's commander was a man of varied background. Daniel Govan was born in North Carolina, raised in Mississippi, and schooled in South Carolina. He hurried out to California for the gold rush in 1849, returned three years later, and moved to Helena, Arkansas in 1861. Along with Thomas C. Hindman, Govan helped raise the 2nd Arkansas infantry and led that regiment as its colonel. When Liddell was elevated to division command, Govan stepped up to lead the brigade. As his men approached the Alexander Bridge, Liddell ordered Govan to halt and deploy his regiments into line, supported by Liddell's second brigade under Brig. Gen. Edward C. Walthall. It was now well after lunch, and according to Bragg's timetable Walker and Buckner were supposed to be across the creek.[12]

While Govan and Walthall deployed, Liddell rode forward to reconnoiter. "The reconnaissance I made was a very hasty and imperfect one," he lamented, which in turn forced him to rely "chiefly upon the information obtained from General Pegram." Liddell moved Govan to the left of the Alexander Bridge Road and brought up Walthall's men on Govan's right. Once the realignment was complete, Liddell directed Walthall to advance his Mississippians directly against the bridge while Govan's Arkansans swung to the left and moved to the creek bank farther upstream.[13]

Edward Cary Walthall was a 32-year-old Mississippi lawyer whose energy and intelligence had caught the eye of his superiors. Born in Virginia, he moved as a youngster to the Magnolia state, was admitted to the bar in 1852 and lived and practiced in Coffeeville. He began the war as a lieutenant, saw combat at

11 Arthur W. Bergeron, Jr., *Guide to Louisiana Confederate Military Units, 1861-1865* (Louisiana State University Press, 1989), 71. Almost certainly it was this discovery of Wilder's men that provided General Walker with the first intimation that he would have to fight for the crossing. However, the lack of official reports and paucity of other accounts regarding Pegram's activities make tracking the movements of his cavalry on September 18 rather difficult.

12 Heidler and Heidler, *Encyclopedia of the American Civil War*, vol. 3, 856; OR 30, pt. 2, 257.

13 Ibid., 251. While Liddell gives the time as 2:00 p.m., the reports of the brigade and regimental commanders mark the time between 12:00 noon and 2:00 p.m.

Mississippian Edward C. Walthall,
a postwar image.

Battles and Leaders

Mill Creek in early 1862, and endured much hardship after that Confederate disaster. His strong leadership helped hold the 15th Mississippi regiment together during a long and arduous retreat. Four days after fighting at Shiloh he was elected captain of the 29th Mississippi. Steady promotions followed and Walthall was given a brigade in the fall of 1862. Sickness, however, kept him out of action at Murfreesboro. He returned to the army the following spring and soon proved to be a practical, effective, and determined brigade commander.[14]

Walthall's five regiments went into line on September 18 with the 34th Mississippi on the left, aligning on the road, followed by the 30th, 29th, 27th, and 24th Mississippi extending the front to the right. They had yet to see their objective, since the brigade deployed on the reverse slope of a low ridge out of sight of the creek and the Federals on the opposite bank. With 1,827 men in the ranks, Walthall's line stretched roughly 600 yards in "dense thicket," which posed a challenge to effective command. The Mississippians would have to move through this brush for some distance before they could see their objective. A quarter mile ahead, the Mississippians encountered Union skirmishers, whose prompt withdrawal revealed a new problem: the road did not run straight to the bridge, but instead took a 90-degree turn that forced Walthall to change guide from the left, where it aligned on the road, to the center. He ordered the 29th Mississippi to head straight for the crossing while the rest of the brigade aligned accordingly. The heavy thickets, Federal

14 Dunbar Rowland, *Mississippi, Comprising Sketches of Counties, Towns, Events, Institutions, and Persons, arranged in Cyclopedic Form*, 2 vols. (Southern Historical Publishing Association, 1907), vol. 2, 896.

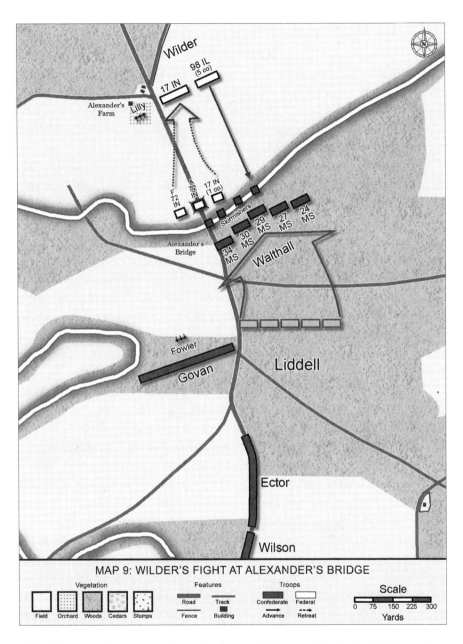

MAP 9: WILDER'S FIGHT AT ALEXANDER'S BRIDGE

Vegetation: Field, Orchard, Woods, Cedars, Stumps

Features: Road, Track, Fence, Building

Troops: Confederate, Federal, Advance, Retreat

Scale: 0 75 150 225 300 Yards

skirmishers, and unexpected turn in the road disrupted the brigade's formation and highlighted the incomplete nature of Liddell's reconnaissance.[15]

15 Powell, "Numbers and Losses," CCNMP: OR 30, pt. 2, 272, 281.

Walthall attempted to wheel the entire brigade to the left and reorient his line on the stream, but his five regiments quickly lost track of one another. The 34th and 30th Mississippi moved across the road into an open field under enemy fire and broke contact with the 29th Mississippi on their right. Taking cover behind an "abrupt hill," Col. Junius I. Scales of the 30th Mississippi took charge of his own and the 34th regiment and sent his adjutant to find Walthall and inquire about what to do next.[16]

Walthall's right flank fared even worse. The 24th and 27th Mississippi had trouble almost from the moment they stepped off. Within a short time they found themselves all but running in an effort to execute a left wheel on the fly. Captain J. D. Smith of the 24th later admitted that "in this movement the regiment became much confused and scattered, and did not arrive on the line at the river in time to take any part in the engagement." Colonel James A. Campbell's 27th regiment performed a little better. Although his command was equally scattered, he managed to get his men to the bank of the creek and join in the action. Once there, however, the Mississippians discovered that "the banks of the creek were very abrupt on both sides, and not knowing the depth of the water," explained Campbell, "I ordered my regiment to lie down . . . and hold their position."[17]

Federals near the Alexander house watched Walthall's approach, which one described thusly: "a column of infantry issued from the woods, passed across the fields on our front, and formed line of Battle reaching from the road on the left to the woods on the right." Wilder ordered Lt. Joseph A. Scott's section of Eli Lilly's battery to open fire on a pair of Rebel guns belonging to Capt. William A. Fowler's Alabama battery, which were unlimbering to support Walthall's attack. The Southern gunners barely managed to get off four rounds, reported bugler Henry Campbell, who was also serving one of Lilly's three-inch rifles. The gray gunners fell back because "we made it too hot for them." The Rebel gunners may have only fired a few rounds, but they too had the range. "The first shell came very close to gun No. 2—it struck the ground out in front—ricocheted and struck the corner of the log house, in front of which the gun was standing—falling down among the cannoneers with the fuse still burning," Campbell recorded that night. "Sidney Speed seeing the

16 Ibid., 283.

17 Ibid., 277, 279.

danger—with great coolness picked the shell up and threw it away before it exploded. I don't think I will ever forget the awful, unearthly screeching that shell made." Fowler's Alabama guns were joined by Swett's Mississippi Battery, commanded that day by Lt. Harvey Shannon. Their fire set the Alexander house aflame, but they were unable to silence Lilly's guns.[18]

Their advance may have been a disorganized struggle, but the Mississippians looked imposing enough to the Federal skirmishers near the bridge. "They came up in splendid style," related Sgt. James H. Barnes of the 72nd Indiana, "lines well dressed . . . bayonets fixed and gleaming in the sun." Those few Federals holding to the east bank fired a round or two and retreated before the Rebel skirmishers, scrambling across the floorless bridge or wading to reach the relative safety of the far side of the creek, where they fell in behind the impromptu dirt and wood lunette.[19]

The Union defenses here were extremely thin. Company A of the 72nd Indiana, with but 37 men, manned the small fort blocking the road. Downstream just to their left, the 72nd's Company F lined the creek's bank. Until mid-morning, companies from the 123rd Illinois guarded Company A's right, but when that regiment departed to help Colonel Minty farther north, five companies of the 17th Indiana moved down to take their place, covering the west bank from Alexander's Bridge to "Smith's" (probably Dalton's) Ford several miles upstream. As previously discussed, Lt. Col. Edward Kitchell had already deployed one-half of his 98th Illinois at various points upstream as far as the Union XXI Corps at Lee and Gordon's Mills. The remaining half, under Maj. David D. Marquis, remained under Wilder's direct control at the Alexander house as a reserve. Alongside Marquis's detachment stood the other half of the 17th Indiana, supporting Lilly's guns. In all, only three of Wilder's companies—A and F of the 72nd Indiana and the company of the 17th Indiana nearest the bridge—were available to confront Walthall's entire brigade.[20]

Colonel William F. Brantley's 29th Mississippi was the first of Walthall's regiments to become fully engaged as it rushed directly toward the bridge. They

---

18 "Three Years in the Saddle," Entry for September 18th, Henry Campbell Journal Transcript, Wabash College; Joseph A. Scott Reminiscences, InHS; Rowell, *Yankee Artillerymen*, 113; "Three Years in the Saddle," Henry Campbell Journal Transcript, Wabash College; *OR*, 30, pt. 2, 270; Baumgartner, *Blue Lightning*, 205-206.

19 Magee, *History of the 72nd Indiana*, 168.

20 Entry for September 18th, Kitchell Diary, ALPL.

moved against the rapid fire of Federal Spencer rifles and Lilly's blasts of shell and canister in what their commander called a "fierce engagement." The Mississippians struggled through the storm of lead and iron to reach the bridge, only to discover it was unusable. Falling back wasn't a viable option, so they spread out along the south bank and returned the Union fire. The 29th lost 56 of their 368 men killed and wounded on September 18—a down payment on what would be a grim butcher's bill by the end of the battle.[21]

About halfway through the fighting both sides added reinforcements. Major William G. Pegram worked his 34th Mississippi down to the creek bank, a move that added 307 rifled muskets into the fighting. Some of Govan's skirmishers reached the bank farther upstream, colliding with more of the 17th Indiana. Two companies of the combined 5th/13th Arkansas also advanced in open order to brace the 34th Mississippi's left, losing two killed and four wounded.[22]

Wilder countered the increased pressure by ordering forward Major Marquis and the remaining half of the 98th Illinois—more than 200 additional Spencers—into the escalating combat. Marquis placed his men west of the road to support the beleaguered companies of the 72nd Indiana. The firepower brought to bear by the Union repeaters was staggering. Sergeant Barnes of Company A, 72nd Indiana, who was fighting in the middle of the road inside the small lunette, described the effect: "The company held its fire until the advancing enemy were so close we could see their eyes bat, then opened upon them with our Spencers, which belched such a constant and awful stream of well-aimed balls that the rebels were completely surprised, faltered, wavered, and then retreated." St. John Liddell witnessed this devastating fire firsthand and agreed with Barnes. "Our loss was 105 killed and wounded," wrote Liddell, "and I can only account for this disproportion from the efficiency of this new weapon."[23]

Colonel Brantley reported the bridge's stripped condition and the stubborn enemy resistance to Walthall, who relayed the dismaying report up the chain of command through Liddell to Walker. Stymied in front of the bridge, Walker ordered Liddell to move his command northeast about a mile and a half to

---

21 OR 30, pt. 2, 281.

22 Ibid., 285; and ibid., 263. In addition to the losses on the skirmish line, the 5th/13th Arkansas also reported two wounded in the rest of the regiment, the result of Lilly's shells.

23 Magee, *History of the 72nd Indiana*, 168; OR 30, pt. 2, 251.

Bryam's Ford in an effort to get around Wilder's left flank. Walthall recalled most of his men and, with a local guide leading the way, found the ford undefended and crossed without incident. Govan's Arkansans followed, with Walker's remaining two brigades under Brig. Gen. Matthew D. Ector and Col. Claudius Wilson in tow.[24]

Walthall's withdrawal from Alexander's Bridge and shift northward brought about a lull in the action. The bulk of the fight had consumed the better part of an hour, and it would take at least another hour for the Rebels to find and cross Bryam's Ford. For the moment, Wilder's front was quiet again. His losses thus far had been light, his men largely protected from distant fire, and few Rebel skirmishers had managed to cross the creek and engage at close range.

Neither Wilder nor any of his subordinates ever explained why they did not defend Bryam's Ford. It and Fowler's Ford, a little farther downstream, offered the Rebels access to Wilder's left flank and an opportunity to thrust troops between his and Minty's commands. The simplest explanation is also probably the best: Wilder ran out of troops. When he sent Colonel Miller to help Minty, his brigade was deployed along nearly 15 miles of creek bank attempting to guard crossings from Red House Bridge in the north all the way south to Lee and Gordon's Mills. The portion of Wilder's brigade patrolling in the area (possibly the company of the 72nd Indiana not engaged at Alexander's Bridge, or perhaps some of the brigade's handpicked scout detachment) soon sent word that the Rebels had crossed. "At 5 p.m." wrote Wilder, "a picket . . . reported a strong force of rebel infantry in my rear."[25]

In reality it was probably closer to 3:30 p.m. than 5:00 p.m., but in any case the Confederates had finally managed to reach the far bank via maneuver after failing to do so by direct assault. Wilder had no choice but to begin the complicated process of disengaging his scattered command. Orders went out for his troops to "fall back up the creek if possible." Forming "column by regiments," Wilder withdrew his command by the right flank, moving southeast

24 Ibid., 251, 272. The brigades of Matthew D. Ector and Claudius Wilson comprised Walker's other division, which Ector commanded at this time because he was its senior brigadier. Command of the division would change hands again when Brig. Gen. States Rights Gist and his brigade reached the field on September 20, 1863. Gist ranked Ector.

25 William E. Doyle, "Chickamauga," *National Tribune*, June 6, 1901; OR 30, pt. 1, 447. The Confederates consistently refer to this crossing point as Bryam's Ford, but the official battlefield atlas maps, prepared in 1896, also call it Lambert's Ford.

with the artillery in the center. While he was doing so, Walker's Rebels quickly re-floored Alexander's Bridge and hurried artillery across the span to unlimber and shell the retreating enemy. "[We] had to fall back four miles," Assistant Surgeon C. W. H. Kemper of the 17th Indiana informed his cousin, "the rebels shelling us all the while." Henry Campbell of Eli Lilly's battery agreed: "We had hardly gone ½ mile before [they] . . . opened a furious cannonade. . . . Lt. [John T.] Drury of Wilder's staff . . . had his foot shot away by a shell."[26]

Other Confederates crossing upstream from Alexander's Bridge also played a role in Wilder's decision to retreat. About 2:00 p.m., Simon Buckner's two divisions under Maj. Gen. Alexander P. Stewart and Brig. Gen. William Preston approached their assigned objectives. Bucker's troops were supposed to cross the stream at Thedford's and Dalton's fords once Walker and Bushrod Johnson had crossed farther north, and then move up to connect with those two columns. Buckner's was a supporting role, so he waited for Walker and Johnson to report their success to him.[27]

Although Buckner's role in the failed effort to attack Negley's Federals in McLemore's Cove just more than a week earlier was a secondary one, he was well aware that Bragg had already demanded a full accounting of that failure from Thomas Hindman. The fiasco would not be brushed aside once the campaign ended. Bragg intended to find a culprit. Hindman had also asked Buckner for his own report of the affair to use as evidence in his defense. The disappointment and simmering tempers cast a dark shadow over the coming battle, and only served to add to the climate of mutual recrimination that had pervaded much of the army's senior command from the origins of the Army of Tennessee. Only the ongoing campaign set aside Bragg's determination to extract retribution from those who had disobeyed his orders—a fact Buckner fully understood. He would take no chances now.

Despite his column's slow progress, Buckner took every precaution as he advanced his corps toward the creek. Alexander P. Stewart's division, advancing on Thedford's Ford, halted a mile short of the crossing. After Maj. James Nocquet conducted a reconnaissance, Stewart brought forward two

---

26 Kitchell Diary, ALPL; Magee, *History of the 72nd Indiana*, 170; "Dear Cousin Hattie," September 27, 1863, G. W. H. Kemper Letters, Ball State University, Muncie, IN; "Three Years in the Saddle," Henry Campbell Journal Transcript, Wabash College. John Drury was no known relation to Lucius Drury of the 3rd Wisconsin Battery.

27 *OR* 30, pt. 2, 357.

brigades under Brig. Gens. William B. Bate and Henry D. Clayton. Each took up a position overlooking the crossing. Bate reported that his orders were "to advance, take possession, and hold Thedford's Ford, but not to bring on a general engagement," so he sent only the 4th Georgia Battalion of Sharpshooters down to the creek. The Georgians found some of Kitchell's 98th Illinois men there and a skirmish broke out. Some of Stewart's artillery unlimbered and engaged the Federals along the creek and lobbed a few shells toward the Alexander cabin, but it wasn't a vigorous fight. When Kitchell's Yankees departed, Clayton advanced three companies of the 38th Alabama to picket the far bank. Once darkness fell, Stewart ordered Clayton to push his entire brigade across. Edgar Jones of the 18th Alabama recalled that once over, the night grew "quite cold, and though the men were wet," fires were prohibited.[28]

Buckner's other division, under William Preston, was tasked with securing Dalton's Ford farther south and had a similar experience. Preston deployed his command and pushed Col. John H. Kelly's brigade forward to the creek. Kelly's skirmishers found Federals on the opposite bank, but that seemed to be the limit of Preston's aggressiveness. The Federals soon disappeared, no doubt recalled by Wilder, but it was not until about 10:00 p.m. that evening before Preston sent Archibald Gracie's brigade across the ford with orders to "protect the crossing should the enemy advance." The fords were finally secured, but only one brigade from each division was across Chickamauga Creek. Buckner, however, was content to wait for morning when he would, hopefully, make contact with the other columns.[29]

Walker's progress wasn't much better. Bryam's Ford proved to be "rocky and uneven," an unfortunate circumstance that slowed the march, especially for the ammunition wagons. Liddell's two brigades moved to the Alexander cabin and halted for the night, camping on the same ground used by the Yankees. Many of the wagons didn't pass over the stream at all that night. Wilson's regiments had orders to "remain with the train . . . until it had crossed."[30]

---

28 Nocquet, it will be recalled, was the French engineering officer serving on Buckner's staff who so badly mangled Bragg's orders on the night of September 11th, in McLemore's Cove. *OR* 30, pt. 2, 361, 383, 401; "History of the 18th Alabama Infantry Regiment," by Rev. Edgar W. Jones, 18th Alabama file, CCNMP.

29 *OR* 30, pt. 2, 413, 428.

30 Ibid., 239, 251, 347.

Bragg, meanwhile, passed the anxious hours waiting at Leet's Tanyard for reports from his lieutenants. Urgent dispatches flowed throughout the day from army headquarters to both Walker and Buckner. That afternoon, Bragg reiterated to Walker that a "junction tonight with General Johnson is of vital importance." A second directive soon thereafter from Colonel Brent prodded Walker to "effect a junction . . . which . . . no doubt . . . you have already done." At 7:30 p.m., with full night nearly upon the field and now informed that neither Walker nor Buckner was entirely across the creek, Bragg snapped out a final order that brooked no uncertainty: "The Commanding General directs that you effect the passage in force at daylight tomorrow morning."[31]

At least Bushrod Johnson's men were on the move. While Bragg was fuming at Walker and Buckner, Johnson's command (at Hood's direction) moved south on the Jay's Mill road until it reached the Alexander house, still aflame from the earlier fight. There, the head of the column turned west onto the Viniard-Alexander Road, bypassing Liddell's troops and marching in Wilder's wake toward Crittenden's XXI Corps lines. The Rebels moved cautiously, with the 41st Tennessee feeling the way as skirmishers. The column continued on this path for several miles, the gloom of evening deepening with each passing minute until they again encountered resistance.[32]

Wilder's earlier withdrawal carried him southwest about a mile and a half to where the tracks leading from Thedford's and Dalton's fords met the Viniard-Alexander Road. There, he established a mounted picket line with the 17th and 72nd Indiana, waiting for Major Marquis's half of the 98th Illinois, serving as his rear guard, to catch up. When Marquis failed to show, Wilder dispatched aides to find him. Marquis, however, had led his portion of the 98th out of danger via an alternative route, so the messengers seeking him nearly stumbled into Johnson's oncoming Rebels. The 41st Tennessee came upon Wilder's new line well after nightfall. Private Theodore Petzoldt, deployed on the 17th Indiana's mounted skirmish line, recalled how skittish his horse proved each time he fired, and how by that time it was so dark "I could see the fire stream from the muzzle of my gun each time I shot." Sergeant George Wilson, also of the 17th, was frustrated that he and his fellow Hoosiers had no time to dismount. "We needed to be on the ground to properly get in our work," was

---

31 Brent to Walker and Brent to both Walker and Buckner, September 18, 1863, Bragg Papers, WRHS.

32 Goodrich, "Gregg's Brigade," 264.

how he later put it. He also thought the Rebels were pressing on with "indecent haste." They were near enough that Wilson could hear their officers barking commands. Years later he recalled that they were "a fearfully profane set" of men.[33]

The profane Confederates moving with "indecent haste" belonged to John Gregg's brigade. Perhaps Wilson was right and they did need to be on the ground to "properly get in [their] work," as Federal bullets wounded but three Rebels. He and his fellow Hoosiers, however, did force Johnson to deploy the entire division, a very difficult task in the dark. Gregg's men hustled into the first line, while Evander McNair's and John Fulton's regiments closed up behind them in support. As a precaution, Johnson also directed Jerome Robertson's brigade into line as a rear guard, facing northwest—the direction from which his column had just come. Once in place the main line stepped off to drive the Yankees once more.[34]

True to form, however, Wilder had no intention of making a prolonged stand and fell back to the east edge of Viniard Field, where he finally received some welcome support. Another of Wilder's couriers had found Brig. Gen. Horatio P. Van Cleve, commanding the Third Division of Crittenden's XXI Corps, and passed along word of Wilder's fight. In response, Van Cleve ordered Col. George F. Dick to take two regiments from his brigade to help the mounted infantry. Dick had just finished deploying the 59th Ohio and 44th Indiana along the east edge of Viniard Field, about 500 yards east of the La Fayette Road, when Wilder's mounted skirmishers retreated past his line.[35]

As he fell back, Wilder was no doubt delighted and relieved to find not only Marquis and his part of the 98th Illinois present, but also Colonel Miller and his demi-brigade, loaned to Minty earlier that morning. After pulling back from Dyer Ford earlier that day, Miller formed his two regiments on Brig. Gen. Thomas J. Wood's left and informed General Crittenden of the Rebel movements to the northeast. The rest of Wilder's men fell in alongside. Soon thereafter Minty joined the reunion. "Where do you want me?" Minty inquired.

33 Wilder Revised Report, CCNMP; Baumgartner, *Blue Lightning*, 210; Theodore Petzoldt, "Recollections," 17th Indiana file, CCNMP; George S. Wilson, "Wilder's Brigade," *National Tribune*, October 26, 1893.

34 *OR* 30, pt. 2, 452.

35 Ibid., pt. 1, 803.

Wilder directed him to form up on his own brigade's right. With his headquarters established in the Viniard house, Wilder ordered the entire line dismounted to prepare to receive Johnson's Rebels.[36]

In later years, Minty, Wilder, and their men would all recall that the Union infantry commanders remained skeptical that Confederates were really across the creek in force. According to Minty, General Wood had already informed Crittenden that Minty's troopers had been cut off and captured. Minty added that Wood seemed shocked when informed that Minty had been fighting a Confederate infantry division all day. "Do you mean on our side of the creek?" demanded Wood, who immediately set off for Wilder's line. "Where are they, Wilder?" asked Wood when he arrived. "Ride forward a dozen paces, General, and you will see them," replied Wilder. Major Connelly of the 123rd Illinois recalled a similar unwillingness to believe the danger. Despite repeated messages to Crittenden, claimed Connelly, "[our] reports were pooh-poohed. It was intimated at the corps headquarters that there was nothing but cavalry and that we shouldn't be frightened."[37]

Captain Joseph Vale offered up the most critical portrait of Wood and Crittenden. Vale found Crittenden shortly before Minty reported in, conferring with Wood and Wilder at the Viniard cabin. When Vale reported that Minty had been engaged with Rebel infantry all day, "Crittenden scoffed at the idea," recorded the captain, "and said 'Wilder here . . . has come in with the same outlandish story; there is nothing in this country . . . but . . . [enemy] cavalry.'" Next, according to Vale, Crittenden and Wood decided to conduct their own reconnaissance with Colonel Dick's pair of newly arrived infantry regiments. Addressing Dick, Crittenden said, "We expect to hear a good report from you, Colonel," which drew laughter from Wood. At this, "Wilder swore in an undertone, and Minty [who had just arrived] gritted his teeth."[38]

Whatever Crittenden and Wood initially believed, within minutes of the two generals' arrival there was proof enough of the enemy's presence when, out of the darkness, Johnson's front line stumbled into the prone 59th Ohio. "When he advanced within 50 yards, reported the 59th's commander, Lt. Col.

---

36 Ibid., 451; Minty, "Minty's Saber Brigade;" Baumgartner, *Blue Lightning*, 214.

37 Minty, "Minty's Saber Brigade;" Anonymous, *Dedication of the Wilder Brigade Monument on Chickamauga Battlefield* (The Herald Press, 1900), 12.

38 Vale, *Minty and the Cavalry*, 230.

Granville A. Frambes, "I gave the order to rise, fire, and charge, cheering loudly, the effect of which threw him into confusion." Having checked the enemy, Frambes ordered his Ohioans to fall back.[39]

In the ranks of the 44th Indiana on the 59th's left, Company H's 1st Sgt. Silas K. Freeman listened to sharp musketry fire with growing concern. "We could plainly hear the rebs cheering when our men run—they came down and outflanked the 59th who fell back after giving them a volley or two, and we were left there in the woods alone," wrote Freeman. "We fixed our bayonets and peered out into the darkness, expecting to see [them] dashing down on us. If they had known that we were there they could have taken us all prisoners." Fortunately for Freeman and his fellow Hoosiers, the 44th was soon ordered back as well, falling in alongside the reformed 59th Ohio and Wilder's exhausted mounted infantry.[40]

The shooting wasn't finished, however. Many of Wilder's troops blazed away as the action became general—at least briefly. Sergeant Magee of the 72nd Indiana recalled that when Wilder's men fell back behind the infantry, he and his fellows dismounted and "within a few minutes [we] threw up a line of works of old logs and rails." From behind this hasty rampart, he recorded, "a single volley from the whole line closed the work for the day, and the enemy ceased firing."[41]

Despite this multi-regiment fusillade, Rebel casualties proved minimal. It was simply too dark to fire effectively. One of the unfortunate few was Lt. Theodore Kelsey, who was cut down when the 10th Tennessee's Col. William Grace sent him back to report the details of the new resistance to Gregg. Word of the Federal opposition spread up the Confederate chain of command and, despite Hoosier fears, Johnson did not order a full attack. In fact, he was thinking defensively. As he later noted, "the whole Yankee army was in our front . . . while [most of] our [own] . . . was still on the east side of the Chickamauga." Johnson ordered his brigades back a short distance with instructions to pile up hasty breastworks of their own. Despite the evening's

39 OR 30, pt. 1, 832.

40 "Ed. Standard," S. K. Freeman Letter, Chattanooga, Sept. 23d, 1863, *Lagrange Standard*, October 10, 1863.

41 Magee, *History of the 72nd Indiana*, 170.

unseasonable chill, fires were prohibited, and one of every three men in each regiment was ordered to remain awake and under arms at all times.[42]

Years later, Minty recalled the look of "blank astonishment" on General Wood's face as he witnessed this final encounter and "exclaimed: 'By ____, they are here!'" While Wood may have been startled by the proximity of the night action, he was not unaware of the larger danger. Crittenden and Rosecrans were also alert to the threat. Steady reports from both Minty and Wilder had detailed the scope of their actions throughout the 18th. The left (northern) flank of the Army of the Cumberland was vulnerable, but its commander was already taking steps to rectify the dangerous situation.[43]

---

42 Ed Gleeson, *Rebel Sons of Erin: A Civil War Unit History of the Tenth Tennessee Infantry Regiment (Irish) Confederate States Volunteers* (Guild Press of Indiana, 1993), 218; OR 30, pt. 2, 453; Goodrich, "Gregg's Brigade," 264.

43 Minty, "Minty's Saber Brigade."

Chapter Ten

Night Moves:

Night of September 18-19, 1863

Despite later recollections penned by Cols. Minty and Wilder, Union infantry commanders were well aware the Army of Tennessee was on the move on September 18. What they were unsure about for most of the day was whether Braxton Bragg was positioning his army for a major offensive or a simple demonstration.

At 11:00 a.m. on the 18th, Minty sent a dispatch to Maj. Gen. Thomas Wood outlining the extent of his fight against Bushrod Johnson's division. By 2:00 p.m., Wood confirmed the fighting to his superior, corps commander Maj. Gen. Thomas Crittenden: "the enemy appears to have a heavy force of infantry opposite my right and center," and that he was receiving artillery fire. Another of Minty's missives informed Maj. Gen. Gordon Granger at Rossville of the Rebel activity. At 4:00 p.m., Wilder sent a more detailed message directly to Crittenden that the Rebels were advancing on multiple fronts and had crossed the Chickamauga in several places. Forty minutes later, and independent of Wilder's communiqué, Crittenden heard from Wood once again: "The enemy [facing Minty] apparently outnumber our troops 4 to 1 . . . [including] infantry, artillery, and cavalry." Wood's source was Father Jeremiah Trecy, a Catholic priest serving as chaplain to the 4th U.S. Cavalry who was also a close confidante of (and sometimes confessor to) General Rosecrans. Trecy had been with Minty earlier in the day, long enough to observe the initial fighting. He also carried word of Minty's and Wilder's retreat. Additional reports from the other divisions in Crittenden's XXI Corps corroborated Wood's information. There was ample evidence that Bragg's Rebels were indeed moving against them with "indecent haste," as one Union soldier on the receiving end of the advance described it.[1]

The intelligence was clear and Rosecrans believed it. His problem was that he could not afford to overreact. By September 18 he had managed to avoid the very real danger of defeat in detail that had so concerned him all of the previous week. Major General George Thomas and his XIV Corps defended the west bank of the Chickamauga south of Crittenden's line, holding open the door for Maj. Gen. Alexander McCook's XX Corps, which was now only a few miles south of Thomas's right flank. Rosecrans's original plan, once all three of his corps had reunited, was to leapfrog each organization northward one at a time, continually extending his line until the Army of the Cumberland was safely concentrated around Rossville. If he simply ordered the entire army to march to Rossville at once, he would once again expose the XX Corps to piecemeal destruction as it struggled to close up.

Thus, for most of the afternoon of the 18th Rosecrans eschewed any bold moves. At 3:45 p.m.—before he was aware that Minty was withdrawing—Rosecrans ordered Granger to reinforce the cavalry with a brigade taken from his Reserve Corps at Rossville. This decision did nothing to help Minty, who was apparently unaware of it, but it would have profound repercussions on Bragg's plans later that night. At 5:00 p.m., Assistant Secretary of War Charles T. Dana outlined the current thinking at army headquarters in a telegraph dispatch to the War Department in Washington: "Rebel demonstration today proves to have been a reconnaissance in force." Dana closed by adding, "Rosecrans has not yet determined whether to make a night march and fall on them at daylight or to await their onset."[2]

George Thomas and his powerful XIV Corps would play the central role in any Union response. That morning, Thomas's four divisions had begun shifting north to replace General Palmer's division of Crittenden's XXI Corps at Glass Mill. The move was designed so that Palmer could pass behind the rest of the

---

1   OR 30, pt. 1, 109, 112, 116; Ibid., pt. 3, 728.

2   Ibid., pt. 1, 66, 116, 190. Note the timing of the various orders and replies contains discrepancies. For example, at 4:30 p.m. Granger informed headquarters the brigade left "an hour ago," or fifteen minutes before army headquarters had even sent the order. This conflict was because of a lack of synchronization on the part of the various participants, who dated orders with whatever time their own watches showed.

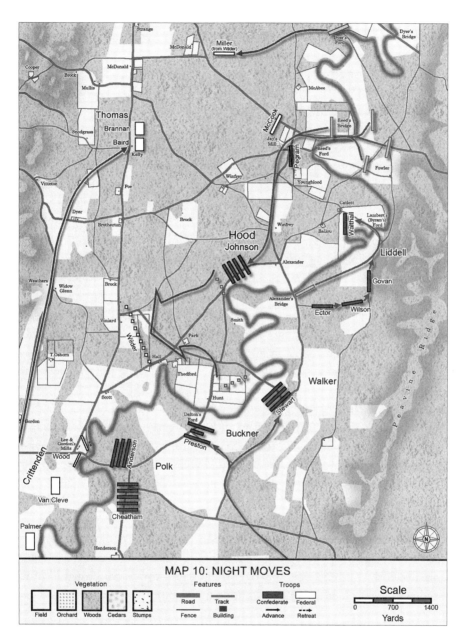

MAP 10: NIGHT MOVES

Vegetation					Features		Troops		Scale		
Field	Orchard	Woods	Cedars	Stumps	Road / Fence	Track / Building	Confederate / Advance	Federal / Retreat	0	700	1400

Yards

XXI Corps and extend Crittenden's left flank. Thomas's command was ideally situated to continue that movement much farther north, if necessary. At 4:00 p.m., Thomas and the first of his men arrived at Crawfish Spring. At 5:40 p.m., shortly after Dana's communiqué was sent off to Washington, Rosecrans called Thomas to the Gordon mansion for a conference.[3]

Despite the near-disasters of the past week, Rosecrans was not thinking about retreat and safety. He had been caught flat-footed by not realizing that, instead of retreating, Bragg was concentrating his army at La Fayette. That mistake forced the Federal army to spend five days (September 12-16) scrambling its way out of danger. The Union army commander, however, was also not about to just fall back into the relative sanctuary of Chattanooga and declare his campaign at an end. As early as midday on the 16th, Dana telegraphed Washington that Rosecrans intended to "surprise the Rebels at La Fayette."[4]

By the time Thomas arrived and dismounted for his meeting Rosecrans had reached a decision. Bragg, he explained to his corps leader, could not be allowed to interpose his Confederates between the Army of the Cumberland and Chattanooga. The basic outline of the scheme Dana detailed on the 16th still held—even if it needed to be modified. Clearly much of Bragg's army was no longer at La Fayette, but a night march could still shift a sizable Union force north of Bragg's right flank with the same chance of surprise. Accordingly, Thomas's three XIV Corps divisions (Negley's Second Division was already in the process of exchanging positions with Palmer's men and would have to remain behind for the moment to defend Glass Mill) would continue north to the Kelly farm on the La Fayette Road. Kelly's acreage was 3.5 miles north of Lee and Gordon's Mills, and 4.5 miles south of Rossville and Granger's Reserve Corps. Not only would this move turn the tables on Bragg, but it would also block an alternate route to Chattanooga via McFarland's Gap, which was currently unprotected.[5]

While Thomas and Rosecrans conferred, a detail from Company L, 1st Ohio Cavalry, Thomas's escort, waited for the XIV Corps commander outside the mansion. During the wait, Lt. Samuel H. Putnam recorded an unsettling conversation with a Rebel prisoner who had just been brought in to headquarters. "If General Bragg did not have our army all captured by Sunday

---

3 Robertson, "The Chickamauga Campaign: The Armies Collide," 48; *OR* 30, pt. 1, 248.

4 Ibid., 188. See Chapter 7.

5 Boynton, *Chickamauga-Chattanooga*, 12; Robertson, "The Chickamauga Campaign: The Armies Collide," 49. Robertson provides an excellent discussion of Rosecrans's thinking and decisions throughout September 18, 1863.

night," boasted the Rebel, "we might cut his head off with a cleaver, as General Bragg had just made them a speech and told them that he had four men to our one and he intended to capture Rosecrans's whole army, trains and all."[6]

Thomas's night march promised to be a difficult one. While the days were still warm, the temperature at night in North Georgia plunged, and water was scarce. Several weeks without rain had left the roads with a layer of thick choking dust, and most small streams and creek beds were dry. Drinking water could be had only in the larger creeks, such as the Chickamauga, or from the upwelling of mountain springs, which were fortunately common in that part of the state. Crawfish Spring, with its cold, clear, and plentiful water, drew soldiers like a magnet. One Union private remembered that just after his regiment halted and stacked arms along the road next to the spring, the troops plunged into the water wholesale. "[It] was filled to its banks by the tired hot and dusty men. . . . [A]s every man struck the water, he let out an unearthly yell and scrambled back on the banks there to roll on the grass, and shout and cut-up more monkey-shines than a schoolboy."[7]

Most of the men of the XIV Corps were unable to get in a cool swim, but they were thankful to establish camp for the day—that is, until new orders arrived to "get ready to move with three day's rations." Brigadier General Absalom Baird's division would lead the way north. It departed Alley's Spring before dark and reached Crawfish Spring about 2:00 a.m., where it paused briefly for rest and water. While there, Lt. Angus Waddle of the 33rd Ohio recalled an encounter with Capt. James P. Drouillard, one of Rosecrans's aides. Drouillard was acquainted with the 33rd's commander, Col. Oscar F. Moore, and filled the regiment in on the reason for the night move, making Waddle and his comrades singularly well-informed about their undertaking.[8]

Brigadier General John Brannan's division tramped north at dusk behind Baird. Shambling along in the ranks of the 17th Ohio was a newly promoted captain named John D. Inskeep. The Company C officer found the experience

6   "Dear Father," Samuel H. Putnam to Douglas Putnam, Sr., Sept. 26, 1863, Samuel Hildreth Putnam Papers, Marietta College, Marietta, OH.

7   Nathan Salisbury Reminiscences, New York Public Library, Theater Division Archives, New York City.

8   Entry for September 18th, Samuel F. Thompson Diary, WHS; Perry, *History of the Thirty-Eighth Regiment Indiana*, 87; Angus L. Waddle, *Three Years with the Armies of the Ohio and the Cumberland* (Scioto Gazette Book and Job Office, 1889), 50.

little short of exasperating. "We were continually starting and halting and it is impossible to estimate the distance correctly," he scribbled in his diary. "The whole country is alive with soldiers pushing forward as rapidly as the narrow roads would permit." Small roadside fires had been kindled intermittently along the road. Some had jumped to include nearby fence rails, which burned along the route as if to mark the way. The scene impressed Capt. I. B. Webster of the 10th Indiana, who would one day recall that at the time, it seemed as if "the whole heavens were lighted up." Except for a two-hour pause to allow the men to doze with their arms along the roadside, Thomas pushed his corps all night and reached the Kelly farm about dawn.[9]

Thomas's third and last division under Maj. Gen. Joseph Reynolds was still en route, having halted for breakfast at Osborn's several miles to the south. The division's 20-wagon ammunition train, guarded by Companies C and H of the 105th Ohio, brought up the rear of Reynolds's column. Reynolds had ordered Maj. George T. Perkins, commanding the 105th, to detail his two largest companies to guard the valuable wagons, and Perkins put Company C's Lt. John C. Hartzell in charge. The night march left an impression on the lieutenant, who recalled the "glowing beds of coals on each side of the road . . . casting weird, uncanny shadows all around." With Hartzell rode Nadine Turchin, who even now, with the armies on the verge of combat, refused to be separated from her general-husband.[10]

The men in the ranks were unaware of the reason for the rigorous night march. Rumors, as they always did, swept through the ranks, fueled by snippets of overheard comments uttered by staff officers and rife with speculation. Sergeant William B. Miller of Company K, 75th Indiana, was one of the thousands of men slogging along in Reynolds's command. "I find all our troops on the move," he wrote in his diary after the 75th finished its exhausting if fitful tramp along the overcrowded roads. "We marched all night but could not move very fast. There is Something up. . . . I think we will see the Elephant before

9   Entry for September 18, John D. Inskeep Diary, OHS. Inskeep was promoted to captain on September 9, 1863; Perry, *History of the Thirty-Eighth Regiment Indiana*, 87; I. B. Webster, "Chickamauga," *National Tribune*, July 2, 1891; Entry for September 18, John D. Inskeep Diary, OHS.

10   OR 30, pt. 1, 440; Charles I. Switzer, ed., *Ohio Volunteer: The Childhood & Civil War Memoirs of Captain John Calvin Hartzell, OVI* (Ohio University Press, 2005), 122.

many hours. Brannan's Division is in advance of us. There has been no firing during the night but things look suspicious."[11]

Thomas spent his long night gathering information. By the early hours of the morning, Wilder and his men could hear the "rumble of Thomas's march" as the infantry, artillery, and divisional wagons passed behind them up the La Fayette and Dry Valley roads. It was also a cold and mostly sleepless night for Wilder's and Minty's men. Captain Henry Potter of the 4th Michigan Cavalry remembered those dark hours as a miserable experience. "We remained as pickets during the night [and] the men suffered from cold & hunger—not a mouthful since breakfast—such a cold night is seldom felt at home in Sept[ember.]" Sergeant James Larson of the 4th U.S. Regulars recalled that the Rebels were so close that "when they spoke a little loud, we could hear them quite plainly." The men had no overcoats and few blankets, fires were prohibited, and any unnecessary movement was discouraged. Even though the officers gave "the usual order to keep awake . . . there was really no necessity [for it] . . . that night," observed Larson, "because the men were all too busy shaking with cold to find time or inclination to sleep."[12]

Dawn was just breaking on September 19 when the indefatigable Colonel Wilder reported to Thomas along the La Fayette Road "between Brotherton's and Kelley's." After Wilder detailed the situation and proximity of his own line to that of the Rebels, Thomas ordered Wilder to fall back several hundred yards to a small rise west of the Viniard house on the La Fayette Road. From there, his mounted infantry could easily control the road and the approaches to Lee and Gordon's Mills without being as exposed should the Confederates initiate an early-morning attack.[13]

There was plenty of other Union activity that night. At Rossville, Gordon Granger was on the alert and a bit edgy. By midday on the 18th, Brig. Gen. James Steedman, Col. John Mitchell's brigade, and various attachments had returned from their foray to Ringgold the day before. Granger wanted the

---

11 Jeffrey L. Patrick and Robert J. Willey, eds. *Fighting for Liberty and Right: The Civil War Diary of William Bluffton Miller* (University of Tennessee Press, 2005), 143.

12 "Address of Gen. John T. Wilder," *Indiana at Chickamauga: 1863-1900, Report of Indiana Commissioners, Chickamauga National Military Park* (Sentinel Printing Company, 1900), 110; "Account of the Battle of Chickamauga and Wheeler's Raid," unpublished manuscript, Henry Albert Potter Diary and Papers, Bentley Historical Library; James Larson, *Sergeant Larson*, 180.

13 Wilder Revised Report, CCNMP.

Federal Road watched closely now that he knew Ringgold was jammed with Rebel troops. The Reserve Corps leader ordered Steedman, one of Granger's division commanders, to send Brig. Gen. Walter C. Whitaker's brigade toward Red House Bridge. Whitaker's men were well-rested after spending the night in their camps around Rossville. Their commander had just arrived two days earlier to resume his place at the head of the brigade. The Kentucky attorney, state senator, and ardent Unionist had demonstrated ample bravery at Stones River, where he led the 6th Kentucky on January 2, 1863, against a failed major Confederate attack that included his fellow Kentuckians.[14]

Whitaker and his regiments moved out at 4:00 p.m., marching along as if the likelihood of finding danger was remote. It wasn't, and it would arrive in the form of Colonel Scott's Confederate cavalry, which had been dispatched from Ringgold to Red House Bridge earlier that day to prevent any more surprise Federal appearances there. Whitaker's troops collided with them a mile or so west of the bridge. Charles Partridge of the 96th Illinois described the advance as curiously incautious. With the men of the 96th leading the column, "the First Brigade marched forward at a good, swinging gait, not apprehending any danger, and chatting merrily as they passed along." When the head reached a tributary called Spring Branch, Whitaker and his staff splashed into the water to allow their horses to drink while the infantrymen broke ranks in an effort to cross without getting their feet wet." A Confederate picket fired two rounds, scattering some Yankees while others moved up to deploy as skirmishers.[15]

Once companies from the 96th and 40th Ohio deployed as skirmishers, the Federals crossed the shallow stream and pushed ahead until they reach a fence line. Beyond lay "an open field with stumps every few minutes, from behind which the Johnnies were firing salutes in honor of our arrival," recalled an Ohio sergeant named Isaac C. Doan. The Yankees rushed forward and cleared the field, driving Scott's dismounted Confederates back before going to ground on the far side of the field while the 18th Ohio artillery fired rounds over their heads. The shadows were lengthening; darkness would not be long in coming. Whitaker halted his command and dispatched a report: "[The enemy] has more than one brigade and a battery that I know of. How far shall I feel him in the

14 OR 30, pt. 1, 860-861; Reinhart, *6th Kentucky*, 150-153.

15 Partridge, *Ninety-Sixth Regiment Illinois*, 169.

morning? Have had 1 killed and 4 wounded. We have killed several of them. . . . Do not know where McCook is?"[16]

The McCook in question was not Alexander leading the XX Corps but his brother, Col. Daniel McCook Jr., commander of the Second Brigade, Second Division, Granger's Reserve Corps. His was the only brigade of that division present in Rossville (the rest being stationed back along the rail line to Nashville) and he lacked a division commander, who was still back in Tennessee. As a result, Colonel McCook operated as either an attachment to Steedman's division or as Granger directed. That same afternoon, while Whitaker was moving out on the Federal Road, McCook was making a similar march toward Reed's Bridge.

Two days earlier, on September 16, Minty had appealed to Crittenden to dispatch a brigade of infantry to Reed's Bridge as a backstop for his own cavalry. At the time, Crittenden had no one to spare. But on the 18th, when Rosecrans learned Minty was engaged with what appeared to be a division of enemy infantry, he ordered Granger to send one of his Reserve Corps brigades to serve in the same capacity. Granger was a man with many missions that day, but not sufficient troops to accomplish them. Mitchell's men needed to rest and eat after their expedition to Ringgold, and Whitaker was already tasked with replacing them on the Federal Road, which left only McCook's brigade available for this new mission. Granger issued the necessary orders, even though McCook's departure left Rossville significantly weakened. Other elements of the corps had been ordered to the front, but the closest, Brig. Gen. James G. Spears's brigade of loyal East Tennesseans, was still at Battle Creek on the Tennessee River. It would be at least two days before they could reach the field.[17]

Dan McCook was a member of one of the nation's most famous military families—the Fighting McCooks of Ohio. He stood in the shadow of many of those family members, and he was acutely aware of it. His brother Alexander commanded the XX Corps, while a cousin led a division of cavalry. Seventeen McCooks would eventually wear the Federal uniform, including a small galaxy

---

16 Isaac C. Doan, *Reminiscences of the Chattanooga Campaign: A Paper Read at the Reunion of Company B, Fortieth Ohio Volunteer Infantry, at Xenia, O., August 22, 1894* (J. M. Coe's Printery, 1894); OR 30, pt. 1, 120. Oddly enough, Steedman reported that Whitaker suffered 60 casualties in this fight.

17 Ibid., 853.

of stars that would include three major generals and three brigadier generals. Daniel burned to be one of them. He was described as "twenty-nine years old, six feet tall, and razor thin." When he left for the army he made his ambitions clear with a bold toast: "Here's for a general's star or a soldier's grave!" He had a tendency toward impetuousness, and desired to be where the battle roared the loudest, since success and glory in combat was the surest path to promotion. But in mid-September 1863 he was stuck in the rear with the Reserve Corps, the last place on earth Dan McCook wanted to be. It was with pleasure, then, when orders reached him to make for the front with a march toward Reed's Bridge. To him, the mission sounded like action at last.[18]

McCook and his five regiments marched down the Reed's Bridge Road and arrived just short of Jay's Mill at sunset. Colonel Minty and his troopers were gone, and except for a few stragglers so were the Rebels. McCook deployed his men about 300 yards short of the intersection of the Reed's Bridge and Jay's Mill roads and sent the brigade scouts forward as far as the mill. It was there that Sgt. Eli Shields of the 85th Illinois nearly gave the game away. "Shields was in the lead when we ran into the rebel army and had the nerve to sing out . . . 'Halt!'" recalled Pvt. Joseph Shawgo, also of the 85th. "To this some thoughtful Johnny replied 'Keep your dam mouth shut!'" With some haste the Federals pulled back, dismounted, and stole forward again, sensibly leaving Shields behind this time around. No sizable Rebel units were found, but the road was active with intermittent parties of Confederates passing along it, following in the wake of Bushrod Johnson's infantry column. The Union scouts quietly collected 22 prisoners including a band complete with instruments, various medical personnel, and a well-mounted major and his "very fine" horse, which was turned over to General McCook. Every prisoner belonged to Evander McNair's brigade.[19]

Sometime before midnight McCook received reinforcements. Colonel John Mitchell's brigade, deemed as being sufficiently rested, arrived and took

---

18 Charles and Barbara Whalen, *The Fighting McCooks: America's Famous Fighting Family* (Westmoreland Press, 2006), 257-8.

19 Entry for September 18, Levi Ross Diary, ALPL; Henry J. Aten, *History of the Eighty-Fifth Regiment, Illinois Volunteer Infantry* (Regimental Association, 1901), 103. McCook's brigade, like many other Federal brigades by this time, had a hand-picked band of mounted scouts drawn from regiments in the brigade available to perform local reconnaissance. Shawgo claimed 37 Rebels were captured. Levi Ross, in his diary, puts the number at 40. However, in his report McCook corroborated the official number as 22. See *OR* 30, pt. 1, 871.

up a supporting position. Thus reinforced, McCook now led nine regiments and two batteries: 3,129 men and a dozen cannon, or roughly one-half of Granger's entire corps. Granger was of two minds about ordering Mitchell to join McCook. Whitaker's clash with Scott's Confederate cavalry had produced a lively, if short-lived fight while McCook's tramp had thus far struck nothing but air. As a result, Steedman had urged that Mitchell reinforce Whitaker, not McCook. Granger overruled Steedman and passed off responsibility for the decision up the chain of command, noting that "Mitchell's brigade was sent on General Rosecrans's orders." At this hour, given the day's news concerning Bragg's movements, Reed's Bridge took priority.[20]

Not a man in Whitaker's brigade saw another Rebel that night and passed the hours quietly and in relative comfort. The reason was simple. Scott's men hadn't merely conducted a tactical retreat in the face of an aggressive Union probe; they had departed the scene entirely. Scott retreated across the Red House Bridge and then upstream (south) along the West Chickamauga for several miles. Later that night he joined up with Forrest, and then with Pegram's brigade near Alexander's Bridge. His withdrawal was as inexplicable then as it is today; a bad decision that once again exposed Ringgold. The small station on the Western & Atlantic line was rapidly becoming the critical supply point for the Army of Tennessee as it shifted north from La Fayette. It was also completely open to another raid by Granger's Federals—if they had but known it.[21]

Scott was not the only Rebel cavalryman making questionable decisions. Forrest failed to utilize Pegram's men any more judiciously. McCook's presence at Jay's Mill and the capture of those stragglers in the wake of Bushrod Johnson's column also represented a threat to Rebel communications with Ringgold. All the supplies for Hood and the rest of the arriving First Corps from Virginia had to move down the Reed's Bridge Road from Ringgold. To protect this vital lifeline, Hood gave the cavalry specific orders to "move out on my right and protect my right flank and ordnance train."[22]

Forrest, however, ordered Pegram's brigade to re-cross the Chickamauga at Alexander's Bridge and go into camp. The choice of this campsite was an odd

20 Powell, "Numbers and Losses," CCNMP; *OR* 30, pt. 1, 120.

21 Entry for September 18, 1863, William E. Sloan Diary, TSLA.

22 H. B. Clay, "On the Right at Chickamauga," *Confederate Veteran*, vol. XXI, no. 9 (September, 1913), 439-440.

one, for it was several miles south of where his troopers needed to be, and was on the wrong side of the creek to boot. Instead of pushing patrols aggressively up the Reed's Bridge and Brotherton roads with the intent of obstructing or at least observing the La Fayette Road, Forrest's pickets were poorly sited and posted well short of covering Hood's vulnerable flanks. The 1st Georgia Cavalry established its picket line along the Jay's Mill Road, about halfway between the Alexander house and the mill site. Cavalryman W. F. Shropshire later wrote that the 1st Georgia cautiously moved up the road "leading by Reeds Steam saw mill, seeking as advance position as possible . . . [when] reaching some 300 yards from the saw mill . . . [we were] fired into by the enemy from ambush." With that, the Georgians fell back out of range, leaving the crucial intersection and Reed's Bridge in Federal hands.[23]

Admittedly, Forrest was also short of troops. Frank Armstrong's division was not yet present, held up by a series of exasperating delays. That left the gruff Memphian only the two underperforming horse outfits of Scott and Pegram upon which he had to rely. Still, Forrest had roughly 3,000 cavalrymen—more than enough to post an effective screen and cover the front and flank of Hood's column. Wilder and Minty accomplished much the same mission, covering more than a dozen miles of rough terrain with not much more horseflesh. The truth was that Forrest was showing his roots as a raider, and his limitations with regard to regular cavalry work.

Confederate Brig. Gen. John Pegram substituted a patrol for a picket line. Well after dark (and probably after McNair's stragglers fell into Yankee hands), Pegram personally led a mounted scouting party up the Reed's Bridge Road. He didn't get very far. "During the night of the 18th," wrote an eyewitness,

> our Gallant General Pegram, wishing to reconnoitre, crossed [Alexander's] bridge accompanied by his staff and bodyguard, and to his surprise found himself in a lane between two large camps. He addressed a party of soldiers inquiring the name of the command, and was informed that an Ohio regiment occupied one side of the lane, while an Illinois regiment camped on the other side. Without showing alarm or surprise, he turned his horse's head, and recrossed safely Alexander's Bridge.[24]

---

23 Curtis Green, "Sixth Georgia Cavalry at Chickamauga," *Confederate Veteran,* vol. VIII, no. 7 (July, 1900), 324; W. F. Shropshire, "Reminiscences," *Confederate Veteran Papers,* Duke University, Durham, NC.

24 Gustave Huwald Letter, October 7, 1866, Leroy Moncure Nutt Papers, UNC.

Pegram had stumbled into McCook's and Mitchell's Federals. All of these important tidbits of information—the capture of McNair's stragglers, the 1st Georgia's brief skirmish, and Pegram's personal encounter—eventually reached Bragg's headquarters at Leet's Tanyard.

September 18 had been a long and frustrating day for Braxton Bragg. Making sense of the myriad of intelligence reports was difficult, and the army's progress had been dangerously slowed by the unexpectedly fierce resistance at Reed's and Alexander's bridges. Bragg was also distracted for a time by a renewed concern about his own left flank, stemming from a foolish and needless contretemps between Frank Armstrong and Joe Wheeler. Armstrong was still struggling to comply with his orders directing him to move north and cover Leonidas Polk's Corps, which he could not do until his picket posts were relieved by Wheeler's troopers. The afternoon dragged on, however, without any appearance by either Wharton's or Martin's cavalrymen. Finally, at 5:30 p.m., Polk informed Gen. D. H. Hill that he could wait no longer, and called Armstrong to join him. The shift should not cause a problem, thought Polk, because as his chief of staff informed Hill, "you are amply covered by General Wheeler's corps of cavalry, [and] he [Polk] does not feel at liberty to release any part of General Armstrong's command." Given Bragg's orders for his mounted arm this indeed should have been the case, but Polk had assumed that orders issued equaled orders promptly executed. He of all people should have known better. [25]

In fact, Joe Wheeler was not covering D. H. Hill's Corps. Earlier in the day, Wheeler visited Bragg and came away with an unusual interpretation of his mission. "All my command should be used to guard the left flank of the army," he informed Polk, "and it will be therefore impossible for me to relieve General Armstrong." This confusing dispatch is not timed, nor did Wheeler explain what he meant by the army's "'left flank," but presumably he was still thinking in terms of protecting La Fayette. The army, however, was no longer at La Fayette. Even then, Armstrong was screening crossings over the Chickamauga on Hill's left with no infantry south of him. It should have been obvious that in replacing Armstrong's brigades, Wheeler would be guarding the army's left as Bragg (and everyone else) now understood it. Certainly Armstrong thought so. In a 5:00 p.m. note tinged with frustration, he informed Polk that "General Wheeler is immediately in rear of General H.'s left, and has orders from General

25 *OR* 30, pt. 4, 664.

Bragg to protect the left flank of the army. My brigade is not needed there, whilst one of Wheeler's divisions is lying one mile west of Anderson's [house] doing nothing."[26]

Finally, with peremptory orders from Polk in hand, Armstrong left 60 men to screen his former position and departed without waiting for Wheeler. His departure left Owen's Ford across the West Chickamauga abandoned. At 8:40 p.m., D. H. Hill issued an alarming report that Federal troops had immediately crossed and were threatening his own flank. This would not do, for Bragg intended Hill to shift north and replace Polk opposite Lee and Gordon's Mills. Polk, in turn, had already been ordered to shift both his divisions across the Chickamauga at dawn and close up behind Buckner, adding more weight to the intended attack column. At 11:00 p.m. Bragg intervened to put an end to this bickering by issuing a direct order to Wheeler. "General: The enemy have crossed at Owen's Ford in force," explained the army commander. "Place yourself across their line of march and retard their movement, covering General Hill, until the movement on our right . . . is completed."[27]

Despite his understandable aggravation with the Confederate cavalry, Hill was overreacting. No Union report mentions a crossing at Owen's Ford on the 18th. Palmer's division of the XXI Corps defended that site on the 17th, where Hazen's brigade had a dust-up with members of the 4th Georgia Cavalry, but this scrap barely qualified as a skirmish. By the morning of the 18th, Palmer's Federals were moving north, replaced by Sheridan's men at Pond Spring; neither officer made mention of the ford. Perhaps a few Yankee pickets stole across the creek there that evening, but certainly there was no "crossing in force." Hill, true to form, was jumping at shadows.[28]

Despite Wheeler's incompetence, Bragg soon realized the threat to the army's left flank was not serious. Once the Army of Tennessee unleashed its own attack in the morning, that threat would be even less significant. The intelligence from Forrest's front, however, was more alarming. By the time the sun went down Bragg was convinced he had maneuvered all or part of three corps—Hood's, Walker's, and Buckner's, more than 20,000 men—on Rosecrans's left flank and in a perfect position to fall upon the Union XXI

26 Ibid., 666.

27 Ibid.

28 Ibid., pt. 1, 768.

Corps at dawn. Once Polk completed his movement, another 13,000 Rebels would be available to strengthen the surprise attack.

Word from Forrest, however, that Federals in unknown numbers were operating on Hood's right and rear potentially upset his entire scheme. Before any major attack could begin, Bragg had to have better information from Forrest. Accordingly, he instructed the cavalry commander to advance up the Reed's Bridge Road early in the morning and investigate. All other activity would await further word from Forrest.[29]

In the Federal headquarters, few people slept. A man of excitable temperament even under normal circumstances, Rosecrans spent a fidgety and irritable night. With Thomas on the march, all Rosecrans could do was wait and hope that he had guessed right. After all, in addition to the reports from Wilder, Minty, and Wood, the rest of the XXI Corps had also reported activity on their fronts. Many thought that in all likelihood this commotion was but a demonstration on Bragg's part, designed to capture Federal attention while the flanking movement unfolded. But there was no way to be sure.

One of the men present that night at Rosecrans's headquarters was Senator James W. Nesmith, the junior Senator from Oregon. Though Nesmith was a Democrat he worked well with the Lincoln administration, serving on various war committees; he also had some military experience as a militia officer in the decades before the war, which is where he met and became friends with Maj. Gen. Gordon Granger. Nesmith had just arrived at the front a couple of days earlier on an inspection tour, and spent much of the next three days in Rosecrans's company. "The enemy is now in our front and skirmishing . . ." wrote Nesmith in a letter to his wife Pauline that afternoon. "I can hear their guns plainly as I write. There may be a battle at any moment, though I hardly think that Bragg will attack our present positions, and the present firing I imagine is only to feel our lines. In this however," the Senator concluded, "I may be mistaken."[30]

The XXI Corps's position was a good one. Wood's two brigades held Crittenden's center, occupying sharply rising high ground on the west bank of the Chickamauga directly overlooking Lee and Gordon's Mills. Any Rebel attack here would face rough going. Van Cleve's division started the day in

29 Ibid., pt. 2, 524.

30 "Dear Pauline," Headquarters, Army of the Cumberland, Crawfish Spring Georgia, September 18th, 1863, James W. Nesmith Papers, Oregon Historical Society, Portland, OR.

reserve at Crawfish Spring, but shifted north at midday "and thrown into position near too and facing the river just below the mills" in support of Wood's right flank. As described earlier, Palmer's division left the vicinity of Owen's Ford during the night of the 17th and moved to guard the crossing at Glass Mill a little less than three miles southeast of Crawfish Spring. Palmer's line lacked dominating hills, but he did have excellent fields of fire across the flat, cultivated bottomland just west of the creek. Any attacker would have to first pass over the stream and then form up for an attack while completely exposed to Yankee artillery and musketry.[31]

This did not mean the day passed quietly, however. Troops from all three divisions reported Rebel activity on their front. Skirmishers and intermittent artillery fire punctuated the entire day. In Van Cleve's ranks, Lt. Marcus Woodcock of the 9th Kentucky was growing increasingly anxious as the minutes ticked past. When a Rebel artillery shell tore a hole in Col. Sidney M. Barnes's tent, it seemed to Woodcock "that our commanders didn't know exactly what they were at or where the Rebels were at." Dr. William Blair, the chief surgeon for Wood's division, knew what was up: "It became very manifest that a battle was soon to take place, and I without delay selected a location for a field hospital . . . 1/3 of a mile from [Crawfish] Spring." In the 100th Illinois, George Woodruff looked on as, about midday, "a brigade of four regiments [of Rebels] came out of the woods in front of our division, apparently intending to cross the creek at the ford near the mill . . . our artillery soon made them take . . . cover . . . again."[32]

The Rebels turned out to be Brig. Gen. Zachariah C. Deas's Alabama brigade, part of Thomas Hindman's division. The Alabamians were doing their best to fix Yankee attention here rather than farther downstream where Minty and Wilder were engaged. Captain Hubert Dent's six Napoleons supported them in their unenviable task. Yankee iron, however, inflicted but one casualty to a soldier in the 50th Alabama, a slight hand wound. Deas made no effort to cross the creek.[33]

31 Noe, *A Southern Boy in Blue*, 193; "Dear Sister," Chattanooga Tennessee, September 22, 1863, John J. McCook Letters, Gilder-Lehrman Collection, New York Historical Society.

32 Noe, *A Southern Boy in Blue*, 193; Report, October 3, 1863, William Blair Papers, Smith Memorial Library, InHS; George H. Woodruff, *Fifteen Years Ago: Or, the Patriotism of Will County* (Joliet Republican Book and Job Steam Printing House, 1876), 283.

33 *OR* 30, pt. 2, 338.

Crittenden still desired to shift Palmer's division from his right to his left, now more than ever since so many reports placed large concentrations of Rebels opposite that flank. Rosecrans had been using this slow side-step north technique to extend his line before he committed Thomas to the night march, and the Federal commander still regarded it as important enough to retain one of Thomas's divisions—the Second under Maj. Gen. James S. Negley—and have them replace Palmer's men as originally intended. The tension and uncertainty of the past week, however, were taking a toll.

When Negley and Brig. Gen. John Beatty reached Palmer's position, however, the division commander wasn't there. Palmer was at Rosecrans's headquarters receiving orders to shift to Crittenden's left, and the instructions had not yet reached Palmer's brigade commanders. When Negley and Beatty informed Brig. Gen. William B. Hazen that they were there to replace him, the mystified brigadier replied that he had no such directive, and couldn't leave his position without positive orders to do so. Taken aback, Negley ordered the troops to hold fast while he rode back to Crawfish Spring for clarification. He got little help. Instead of clarifying the situation with Palmer's men, Rosecrans ordered Negley to bring one of his brigades to Crawfish Spring. The Pennsylvanian had just departed to execute this new directive when Thomas further muddied the waters by sending an order for Negley to move up his entire division and encamp.[34]

The confusion was only beginning. Shortly thereafter, Rosecrans countermanded both his own and Thomas's instructions and sent Negley back with verbal orders to relieve Hazen's and Col. William Grose's brigades so they could execute Palmer's original instructions. Negley returned, but neither Hazen nor Grose had received their orders, and both men insisted they could not move without clear direction. Major James A. Lawrie, one of Negley's aides, recounted the mess in detail. "After about half an hour's delay General Beatty reported to me that General Hazen . . . refused to move. I rode forward to find General Negley for instructions," continued Lawrie, "and learned that he had gone down to Colonel Grose's position." After some delay, Lawrie found Grose who also refused to move. Riding on, Lawrie finally found Negley, who sent him back to Rosecrans's headquarters. There, Lawrie described the night's activities so far: "General Palmer's brigades refused to be relieved [and] . . . that the troops (General Negley's) . . . had been marched back and forth until they

34 Ibid., pt. 1, 328.

were almost exhausted." Rosecrans, Thomas, and Palmer were all present. Palmer explained that he had already sent orders to his brigades before dark, but would send them again immediately. Lawrie rode off once more, but was soon back. Negley couldn't move his troops to replace Palmer's because the roads were jammed with other Federals—the balance of Thomas's corps, starting their night march—and his men wouldn't be in place "much before daylight." Lawrie reported this last bit of unfortunate news about 10:30 p.m. Not surprisingly, Major Lawrie remembered that both "Rosecrans . . . and . . . Thomas were very much annoyed at the delay."[35]

Hazen was an Old Army Regular, a West Pointer in the class of 1855. Active service in Texas against the Comanche earned him a wound in 1859. He was scrupulously honest and a strict disciplinarian, but his recalcitrance over the issue of being replaced in line did not just stem from an overly officious attitude or a Regular's disdain for volunteers. Just the day before, Rosecrans had ordered Lt. Col. Arthur Ducat to make the rounds of the army picket lines to ensure all was in order. In fact, all was not in order. Among other things Ducat discovered "large gaps" in the pickets between divisions, and specifically noted that he "did not like the position" of Palmer's men, including Hazen's front. Palmer quickly rectified his divisional line. Hazen would not have forgotten this criticism by the time Negley's men appeared, unlooked for, intent on replacing his command—especially with Rebels right across the creek in obvious force.[36]

By this time Rosecrans was in full temper. When Hazen finally moved, he passed Crawfish Spring and stopped by Rosecrans's headquarters to pay his respects and visit his boyhood friend, army chief of staff James Garfield. To his dismay, "he was roundly and publicly castigated" by the commanding general for his role in the delay. Lieutenant Colonel Robert Kimberly of the 41st Ohio witnessed the unpleasant encounter. Rosecrans "was not in the best of humors, as some of us discovered upon riding up to see friends on his staff," remembered Kimberly, "In his petulance and excitability the commanding

---

35 Ibid., 336-337.

36 Warner, *Generals in Blue*, 225-226. Hazen would later earn fame as "the best-hated man in the army" when he incurred the wrath of senior commanders for his unflinching condemnation of unscrupulous post-traders cheating the Indians during the U. S. Grant presidential administration. Janet B. Hewitt, Noah Andre Trudeau, and Bryce Suderow, eds., *Supplement to the Official Records of the Union and Confederate Armies*, 100 vols. (Broadfoot Publishing Co., 1995), vol. 5, 78, Hereafter OR *Supplement*.

general forgot to be gentlemanly, some of them said; and [we] left him not at all relieved of any doubts [we] had concerning our sudden and forced march."[37]

The confusion, coupled with the traffic now jamming the few roads as several Union divisions attempted to pass through or near Crawfish Spring simultaneously, meant that few of Palmer's or Negley's men took up their assigned positions before dawn. One of those tasked to man Beatty's picket line was Sgt. Francis M. Carlisle of the 42nd Indiana. Carlisle and his comrades picked their way across to the east bank of the Chickamauga on an improvised log footbridge and up a slope to a log house, where the sergeant found members of the 17th Indiana and a dead civilian sprawled on the porch of the cabin. When the Hoosiers arrived in the farmyard the day before, they explained, "the man of the house ran out and said that no 'Damned Yankee' could come in his house. He was ordered to surrender. . . . He refused. . . [and] one of the 17th boys fired, killing him instantly." The sudden death of the patriarch caused the rest of the family to pack and flee with some haste. Shortly before dawn the men of the 17th departed as well, called in to rejoin their regiment. They left Carlisle and his fellow pickets to contemplate the sprawled corpse on the north porch of the cabin as the sun rose on the morning of September 19, 1863.[38]

---

37 Robertson, "The Chickamauga Campaign: The Armies Collide," 49; Robert L. Kimberly, "At Chickamauga," *Lippincott's Magazine*, vol. XVII (June, 1876), 715. Hazen would continue to stew over this public reprimand even after the battle of Chickamauga, and call on some of those present to provide evidence of his humiliation in an effort to get Rosecrans to formally apologize. Senator Nesmith was one such witness.

38 Francis M. Carlisle, Autobiography, 42nd Indiana Infantry, http://freepages.history. rootsweb.ancestry.com/~indiana42nd/fcarlisleauto.htm, accessed August 14, 2013.

Chapter Eleven

Opening Guns at Jay's Mill:

Saturday, September 19: Dawn to 10:00 a.m.

"**On** the morning of the 19th, I was ordered to move with my command down the road towards Reed's Bridge and develop the enemy, which was promptly done." With these few words, Nathan Bedford Forrest reported the opening of the large-scale fighting at Chickamauga. His bland language also masked any hint of reprimand General Bragg may well have delivered concerning the unexpected appearance of Federals on his front during the night.[1]

A new arrival reached North Georgia to join Forrest's command. After a journey lasting more than two weeks from his previous post at Staunton, Virginia, newly commissioned Brig. Gen. Henry B. Davidson finally arrived on the field to assume command of John Pegram's brigade. Davidson's arrival should have allowed Pegram to more fully exercise his duties as a division commander. In fact, Davidson would play almost no role in subsequent events. He was too new to the fluid situation and to the command to exercise effective control, and few of his men even knew he was on the field during the battle. Captains Henry B. Clay and Theophilis Brown were assigned to act as Davidson's staff, but as Clay later noted, because Davidson "was handicapped by his want of knowledge of the command," Pegram continued to exercise

---

1 OR 30, pt. 2, 524.

Nathan Bedford Forrest, who found Federals where Bragg least expected them.
Tennessee State Library and Archives

direct control of the brigade. Private J. W. Minnich of the 6th Georgia Cavalry, who would write extensively about the battle after the war, remembered that "although we called ourselves Davidson's Brigade, we often forgot that it was no longer Pegram's."[2]

2   Theophilis Brown, "What a Solder Saw and Knows," *Southern Bivouac, September 1882-August 1883*, 6 vols. (Broadfoot Publishing, 1993), vol. 1, 357; Clay, H. B. "Concerning the Battle of Chickamauga," *Confederate Veteran*, vol. XIII, no. 2 (February, 1905), 72; Minnich,

Forrest's first act was to order Colonel Scott's brigade back to Red House Bridge, correcting the latter's error in leaving that crossing uncovered the night before. To William Allen in the 5th Tennessee Cavalry, it seemed as if the marching and counter-marching consumed the entire night. When they reached Forrest's camp, he recalled, "we sat on our horses some two hours [before we] were ordered back." Nimrod Porter remembered that the brigade "was ordered back again in double-quick time," only to find the Federals in possession of the abandoned crossing.[3]

Back at Jay's Mill, the 1st Georgia Cavalry was stirring well before dawn. Colonel James J. Morrison sent out a mounted patrol to seek out the Union line. When there was light enough to see a man 50 yards away, Sgt. J. B. Walker and six others from Company K picked their way forward to the "top of a small hill." From there, they observed a number of shivering Yankees who, in spite of instructions not to kindle any fires, were clustered around a large campfire near the sawmill. The Georgians delivered a fusillade into the huddle and fell back to report their findings.[4]

The volley opened tired eyes on both sides, and before long the "pop-pop-pop" along the picket line meant work for Captain Clay. Shaken awake by one of Pegram's couriers, the staff officer mounted his horse and rode forward to see what the shooting signified. He discovered that the Yankees had aggressively responded to Sergeant Walker's fire, and that the 1st Georgia's pickets were being pressed by a long line of Federal skirmishers who overlapped both Rebel flanks. Clay ordered up a squadron of the 1st Georgia to reinforce the line. Clay dismounted the reinforcements on "the picket company's right, [and] we went at them, but," admitted Clay, "they didn't drive very well." Clay's subsequent call for the rest of the 1st Georgia drew Pegram's personal interest as well as the additional reinforcements.[5]

Clay intended to advance with the entire 1st Georgia, but Pegram postponed the advance long enough to add some artillery and the 12th

---

"Reminiscences of J. W. Minnick," 21. For consistency's sake, this narrative refers to this command as "Pegram's brigade" throughout the fight on September 19.

3 William Gibbs Allen Memoirs, TSLA; Entry for September 18, Nimrod Porter Diary, TSLA.

4 W. F. Shropshire Reminiscences, "First Gun at Chickamauga," *Confederate Veteran* Papers, Duke University.

5 Clay, "On the Right at Chickamauga," 329.

Tennessee (mounted) Battalion. "We went in strong, the battery opening as we charged," recalled Captain Clay. "The force in our front gave way before us, with some loss in men and prisoners." The captives, as Clay's inquiries soon revealed, belonged to Dan McCook's brigade.[6]

Thirty minutes before daylight, McCook had shifted his line slightly to better cover the Reed's Bridge Road. Two companies each from the 85th and 86th Illinois covered McCook's front as skirmishers while a company from the 52nd Ohio screened the 86th's left. A water detail from the 86th was busy filling scores of canteens in a spring near Jay's Mill when Pegram's line attacked. One of those captured there was an Illinois private named Andrew Peters, doubtless one of the Yankees questioned by Clay.[7]

McCook reasoned that if he could destroy Reed's Bridge, he could isolate and kill or capture all the Rebels opposing him on his side of Chickamauga Creek. Without much evidence to go on, McCook had somehow reached the conclusion that he faced only a single Confederate brigade (perhaps because he had captured men from McNair's command during the night). The 69th Ohio was tapped to knock out the bridge. The 69th was not formally a part of McCook's brigade. It had been part of Negley's Second Division of Thomas's XIV Corps until just the previous month, when it had been left behind at Cowan, Tennessee, to guard the Union supply line. When Rosecrans called for more troops from the rear area, the Buckeyes found themselves temporarily attached to McCook until their regiment could rejoin Negley's division. Exactly why McCook selected the 69th is not known, but it may well have stemmed from the one of the oldest of Old Army adages—likely true since the days of the Roman Legions: "If there is a dirty job to be done, let the new guys do it."

None too keen about this solo mission, Lt. Col. Joseph Brigham led his men cautiously forward, accompanied by an equally reluctant civilian guide. A mile short of the bridge, the regiment turned off the road and approached the crossing through an "old deadening," where Brigham posted them on line with a fence overlooking the bridge. Once the handful of Confederates guarding the structure were captured, Brigham sent a detail forward to pile brush on the planking and set it aflame to ignite the supporting timbers. Once the flames

6 Ibid.

7 *OR* 30, pt. 1, 875.

were truly alight, the Ohioans hurried back to McCook's line amid growing Confederate shouts of alarm.[8]

The Buckeyes ended their mission convinced they had destroyed Reed's Bridge, and continued to assert as much for many years. In reality, however, they had not. More Rebels, perhaps from Brig. Gen. Evander Law's Alabama brigade which was en route from Ringgold and had camped somewhere east of Chickamauga Creek the night before, extinguished the fires. Bragg's army also had several companies of pioneer troops fully capable of quickly repairing any damage. Despite the best efforts of the Buckeyes, Reed's Bridge would continue to carry Confederate traffic to and from Ringgold.[9]

Excited by what appeared to be the very real prospect of trapping a sizable Rebel force, McCook sent a dispatch addressed to "General Thomas (or any other U.S. General)" that Reed's Bridge was burning, and "a rebel force of one or more brigades had crossed to this side of the creek." McCook might have wanted to stay and fight, but orders to the contrary arrived almost immediately. Neither star nor grave awaited this day. At 7:00 a.m. a dispatch from Granger arrived, recalling McCook's ad hoc division to Rossville. Pausing only long enough to secure the return of the 69th Ohio, McCook reluctantly started his men westward. Unlike their commander, many in McCook's ranks felt their departure came not a moment too soon. Private Levi Ross of the 86th Illinois believed "the Rebel lines were rapidly closing in on our flanks, and soon we would have either been prisoners of war or in eternity." McCook's men fell back along the Reed's Bridge Road and turned north onto the La Fayette Road, where they found troops from the XIV Corps "covered with dust" filing into the surrounding fields for breakfast. A visibly excited McCook detoured to touch base with General Thomas. As he passed Brig. Gen. John C. Starkweather's brigade, its commander called out and inquired about the earlier

---

8 L. E. Hicks, "The Capture of Reed's Bridge," 69th Ohio unit file, CCNMP; Gam Pease, "Chickamauga: The Part Taken by the 69th Ohio and McCook's Brigade," *National Tribune*, July 3, 1890; "Dear Sir," Letter of December 6, 1901, L. E. Chenoweth to Col. J. H. Brigham, Brigham Family Papers, Bowling Green State University, Bowling Green, Ohio. Hereafter BGSU. The civilian guide is unidentified. The "deadening" refers to a field in the process of being cleared, with a number of standing dead trees waiting to be felled.

9 John T. Wilder believed the 69th Ohio burned another bridge where the Jay's Mill Road crossed a small stream feeding into Chickamauga Creek, and that Colonel McCook was mistaken about which bridge was destroyed. See Wilder Letter to Ezra Carman, November 19, 1908, Carman Papers, NYPL.

firing. "We have got a brigade of them in the woods," McCook replied, "and we will capture every one of them."[10]

Major Michael H. Fitch of the 21st Wisconsin, part of Thomas's XIV Corps, was also close at hand. Fitch recalled that the head of the column reached the Kelly farmstead

> about daylight. There was an inferior looking log house on the opposite side of the road, and here General Thomas halted under a spreading tree. . . . Thomas lay down on some blankets, saying to his aide not to let him sleep more than an hour. He had not been lying more than fifteen minutes when . . . McCook . . . rode up. . . . [He] reported that he had burnt a bridge after a brigade of rebels had crossed . . . [and] . . . that this brigade could be captured if enough troops were immediately sent to that point.[11]

According to the corps commander, McCook informed George Thomas that only one Confederate brigade lay on this side of the creek, was now cut off thanks to the 69th Ohio's successful expedition to Reed's Bridge, and this act forced them to retreat towards Alexander's Bridge. McCook wasn't fully aware of the size and scope of the Confederate crossings on the 18th, but Thomas certainly was. Not only had Thomas conferred with Rosecrans at length the previous evening, where he had certainly been briefed on Minty's and Wilder's reports, but Thomas had just come from a face-to-face meeting with John Wilder sometime before dawn. Wilder, reported Thomas, "informed me that the enemy had crossed the Chickamauga in force at these two bridges the evening before." Moreover, even if Reed's Bridge were now in ruins Alexander's Bridge was intact, presumably re-floored. In addition, numerous fords provided ample access for either retreat or reinforcement.[12]

Despite this other reliable information, Thomas gave McCook's report enough credence to act upon. Eager for action, McCook asked Thomas to override his own orders (directing him to return to Rossville) and let his men join in, but Thomas, unsure of the situation farther north and the reasons for

---

10 OR 30, pt. 3, 743; Ibid., pt. 1, 871; Entry for September 19, Levi Ross Diary, ALPL; Aten, *History of the Eighty-Fifth Regiment*, 104; Edward McGlachlin. "Reminiscences of Two Days at Chickamauga and Fifteen Months in Rebel Prisons," *Pedigree Pointers: Newsletter of the Historical and Genealogical Society of Steven's Point, Wisconsin*, vol. 12 (Fall, 1989), 23.

11 Michael H. Fitch, *Echoes of the Civil War as I Hear Them* (R. F. Fenno & Company, 1905), 136.

12 OR 30, pt. 1, 249.

McCook's recall, demurred. A crushed McCook returned to his command and resumed the trek back to Rossville.[13]

On the face of it, Thomas's decision to shift from a defensive to an offensive posture in pursuit of a lone enemy brigade flies in the face of both his character as a soldier and seems contrary to Rosecrans's orders. One historian of the battle noted that "the wisdom of sending a single brigade into dense woods on the strength of an excited colonel's report is clearly open to debate," but that Thomas's decision was "the first tentative step towards seizing the initiative from Bragg." In fact, George Thomas was thinking in much bigger terms than bagging a single brigade, and very likely had Rosecrans's full approval in doing so. As Assistant Secretary of War Charles Dana's report from the evening before demonstrated, Rosecrans was keeping his offensive options open.[14]

By 6:30 a.m., Thomas had two full divisions on hand. Absalom Baird's division reached Kelly Field probably an hour earlier and went into position astride the La Fayette Road just south of the Kelly cabin. Baird's men busied themselves after their long and difficult night with a welcomed rest and breakfast. John Brannan's troops filed in behind Baird's and were faced east along the eastern edge of Kelly Field at a right angle to Baird's line. Thomas was not going to move west with only a single brigade; he intended to use both of his available divisions.[15]

Sometime before 7:00 a.m., after sending the sulky Dan McCook back toward Rossville, Thomas ordered Brannan to "post a brigade . . . on the road to Alexander's Bridge, and use his other two brigades to reconnoiter the road leading to Reed's Bridge." The division leader's instructions were straightforward: "To capture, if possible, a rebel force represented by Colonel Dan McCook to be a brigade cut off on the west side of the Chickamauga Creek; failing in this, to drive it across the creek." Unwilling to thrust Brannan into the unknown without support, Thomas also ordered Baird to cooperate with and support Brannan's movement by throwing "forward his right wing so as to get in line . . . with Brannan, but to watch well on his right flank."[16]

13 Daniel, *Days of Glory*, 316.

14 Cozzens, *This Terrible Sound*, 123.

15 *OR* 30, pt. 1, 275.

16 Ibid., 400, 249.

About this same time, Thomas also sent couriers to XXI Corps commander Tom Crittenden asking for the use of a division, and to XXI Corps division commander John Palmer, who was just completing his own night march designed to extend Crittenden's left flank. These dispatches to the XXI Corps outlined the big Virginian's aggressive objectives in a little greater detail: "Major General Palmer—The Rebels are reported in quite a heavy force between you and Alexander's Mill. If you advance as soon as possible on them in front, while I attack them in flank, I think we can use them up."[17]

A short time later, the roads were alive with more couriers. One ride carried a message from Thomas to Rosecrans to inform the army commander of the concept he had proposed to Crittenden and Palmer, and to note that he had two divisions ready to go and a third due to arrive momentarily. Another courier, this one from Crittenden, pounded the road back to Thomas with agreement to the combined advance once Col. William R. Grose's brigade completed its morning reconnaissance.[18]

Rather than conducting an expedition to find and capture a few stray enemy regiments, the XIV Corps commander was proposing nothing less than a corps-sized enveloping attack against the Confederate right flank, coupled with the simultaneous advance of another corps (Crittenden's) in support. Unsure of exactly what he would find, the cautious-by-nature Thomas would move Brannan and Baird forward in search of "a rebel force," and if the situation developed as he hoped, fall upon Bragg's right and "use them up."

The division leading Thomas's movement was in the hands of Brig. Gen. John Brannan, who though a relative newcomer to the Army of the Cumberland was well thought of by his fellow West Pointers. The class of 1841

---

17 Ibid., 124; Palmer, *Personal Recollections*, 175. There are several unusual things about this message. First, Palmer reprints it from a Confederate newspaper, which printed a captured copy of it a few days after the battle. This copy was carried by Lt. Col. Alexander Von Schroeder of the 74th Ohio who was then serving on Thomas's staff, and described as very nearsighted. He apparently rode into an enemy battle line without realizing it and was captured. Second, the date and time are shown as October [September] 19, at 9:00 a.m.; two hours after I attribute it here. However, as we will see throughout the text, Thomas's headquarters was often a couple hours ahead of the rest of the army in terms of timing; synchronizing clocks was still largely a thing of the future. In his own report, Thomas claims Brannan began his advance at 9:00 a.m.—the same time as on this note—while everyone else agrees Brannan set off much closer to 7:00 a.m. Finally, the term "Alexander's Mill" is ambiguous. Thomas could have meant either Jay's Mill or Alexander's Bridge (or the newspaper could have quoted it wrong), but in any case, Thomas was clearly relying on more information than just McCook's sketchy outline.

18 OR 30, pt. 1, 124-125.

John M. Brannan. His division, advancing east
from Kelly Field, was ordered to capture an
isolated Rebel brigade.

Battles and Leaders

graduate had seen extensive service in
the Old Army. He fought Seminoles in
Florida, logged years of service on the
western frontier, and saw combat in
Mexico under Gen. Winfield Scott,
where he was wounded and won brevet
promotion. When the current war
began, however, Brannan was stationed
at one of the nation's remote corners,
an artillery captain commanding the small garrison of Fort Taylor in Key West.
Through the fall of 1862 his service was all on the Atlantic coast where, upon
the death of departmental commander Maj. Gen. Ormsby Mitchell, Brannan
assumed command of the Department of the South.[19]

Brannan had not been forgotten. Always hungry for experienced officers,
generals in more active theaters requested his services. Major General George
McClellan wanted him for the Army of the Potomac in October 1862, but he
could not be transferred at that time. The following spring, however, Brannan
was assigned to the Army of the Cumberland and William Rosecrans, who was
needful of capable professionals. Originally assigned to Crittenden's XXI
Corps, on May 13, 1863, Brannan assumed command of the Third Division in
Thomas's XIV Corps to replace Maj. Gen. John M. Schofield, who had been
promoted and sent farther west to Missouri. Brannan led the division through
the nearly bloodless Tullahoma campaign and had conducted a number of
complex coastal operations, but thus far he had not been involved in a single
major battle.[20]

Just before the war, Brannan lived through an unusual personal tragedy that
resolved itself in a rather bizarre twist. In 1850, he married Eliza Crane and the
couple had a daughter the next year. On July 20, 1858, his wife "mysteriously

19 Heidler and Heidler, *Encyclopedia of the American Civil War*, vol. 1, 275.

20 *OR* 23, pt. 2, 322.

disappeared from the residence of her mother." A distraught Brannan spent the next two years searching for her. In the spring of 1860, he finally discovered what happened: she had eloped with a fellow officer, Powell T. Wyman, and the duo fled to Paris and opened a brothel. Eliza married Wyman, despite her already-wedded status.[21]

A newspaper explained the tragic case:

> It appears that General Brannan—and this is the most painful feature of the whole case—regarding his wife with confidence and affection, and supposing her to have committed suicide in a paroxysm of insanity, or to be wandering about in a demented state, exhibited the greatest anxiety and agony at her mysterious disappearance and expended his time and money in raking the lakes and advertising in the highways to ascertain her whereabouts, and if possible, recover her. . . . During all this time, it appears she was coolly speculating in prostitution on the other side of the Atlantic; that knowing of this great anxiety and agony on the part of her kindred and husband, she refused to disclose her whereabouts.[22]

When these shocking circumstances came to light, Brannan was granted a divorce and retained custody of his daughter. Wyman and Eliza returned to the United States in time for the war, and despite his carryings-on overseas, Wyman received a commission as a volunteer colonel of the 16th Massachusetts and was killed early in the war at Glendale on June 30, 1862.

Eliza's family sympathized with Brannan and cared for his daughter while he was in the army fighting the Rebels. Eliza's brother, Dr. C. H. Crane, went to war alongside Brannan and was by September 1863 the chief surgeon of Brannan's Third Division.

Colonel John T. Croxton's Second Brigade led Brannan's advance eastward that morning. On the way Croxton passed a disgruntled Dan McCook on his way back to Rossville. McCook expressed his frustration to Croxton, whose brigade McCook was convinced would now reap the glory he believed was rightfully his. When he had been placed under Steedman's command, lamented McCook, he "supposed . . . that he had been placed under a fighting officer." Instead, circumstances had "just plucked from his shoulder a star." Captain Charles B. Mann of the 74th Indiana, a member of Croxton's staff, recalled

---

21 *Beaufort Free South*, Beaufort, South Carolina, June 13, 1863.

22 Ibid.

seeing "General McCook riding up. . . . He had a brigade of rebels cut off from [the] Chickamauga and that if we would move right down we could capture that brigade."[23]

Croxton was a good choice for the job. A Kentucky lawyer and Yale graduate, the 27-year-old had served under Thomas since the battle of Mill Springs in 1861, and was a rising star in the Army of the Cumberland. The five regiments in his command made his brigade of 1,998 bayonets one of the largest in the army. The six guns of Battery C, 1st Ohio, followed in support.[24]

For the men in the ranks, there was little time to fix and eat their breakfasts that morning. Captain I. B. Webster of the 10th Kentucky recalled that he and his comrades were just starting to boil coffee and roast slabs of bacon when orders to fall in rang out. The men snatched up whatever they could. "Many among our regiment went into the Chickamauga battle with both hands full of something to eat or drink," explained Webster.[25]

Croxton's column followed a logging path toward Jay's Mill and not too far inside the trees formed line of battle. From left to right, Croxton placed the 4th Kentucky, 10th Indiana, and 74th Indiana in his front line, with the 10th Kentucky and 14th Ohio in support. He also ordered his men to drop their knapsacks and left behind a detail to guard the baggage. Once the regiments were aligned, Croxton ordered Maj. Job H. Van Natta of the 10th Indiana to take charge of the skirmish line, two companies each from the 4th Kentucky and Van Natta's own regiment, and advance.[26]

In order to mass firepower, Civil War armies massed men. Frontage was critically important. The side with the longer frontage not only had more firepower, but by overlapping an opposing line could turn a flank. Formed in a textbook two-rank formation, with officers and NCOs file-closing, a Civil War regiment was a close-packed entity. Men stood shoulder to shoulder with elbows touching; each man in line required about 24 inches of space. The distance between the back of the man in the front rank and the breastbone of the rear rank private was supposed to be no more than 13 inches. The density of

23 Joseph T. Woods, *Steedman and his Men at Chickamauga* (Blade Printing Co., 1876), 26; Charles B. Mann, "Anniversary of Chickamauga," *Muskegon Daily Chronicle*, September 19, 1908.

24 Warner, *Generals in Blue*, 104; Powell, "Numbers and Losses," CCNMP.

25 I. B. Webster, "Chickamauga," *National Tribune*, July 2, 1891.

26 *OR* 30, pt. 1, 415, 422; G. W. Haigh, "Chickamauga," *National Tribune*, January 15, 1915.

a standard battle line was about one man per foot, or three men per yard (not counting the file closers, who made up between seven and 15 percent of a regiment's strength). On parade, a regiment of 400 men in line of battle would form a front roughly 125 yards wide. Battle was a different matter entirely. Maneuvering over broken ground and through brush and woods disrupted the ranks and made control difficult, while casualties thinned ranks. Still, regiments remained surprisingly tightly packed under most circumstances, especially whenever they halted to reform.[27]

At the brigade level, there was more variation in how a commander deployed his troops. Croxton's double line formation was standard practice within the Army of the Cumberland by the fall of 1863, and in distinct contrast to how most Confederate brigades entered combat. During that third summer of the war, the Yankees adopted Brig. Gen. Silas Casey's newly published revised tactical manual, superseding William J. Hardee's 1855 work. Southern troops still relied upon Hardee's book, the author of which was now a Confederate lieutenant general. The major difference between the two works was that Casey's Manual called for a brigade's regiments to deploy in two lines instead of one. Using this new scheme of maneuver, the supporting line could move to protect a flank, extend a front, or relieve the battered front regiments as needed. However, it also meant that a Union brigade of four regiments would only occupy about half the frontage of a Confederate brigade of similar size, which typically deployed in one long line. Unless other Federals were on hand to form on the right and left, the Rebels could more easily envelop a flank. Conversely, a shorter battle line was easier to control. Rebel brigadiers, with their regiments in a single line, struggled to coordinate their commands over a much longer frontage. Wooded or uneven terrain exacerbated this problem. Much of the terrain at Chickamauga was both wooded and uneven. Which form of deployment would prove most effective remained to be seen.[28]

---

27 William J. Hardee, *Hardee's Rifle and Light Infantry Tactics* (J. O. Kane, Publishers, 1862), 3-6. Hardee discusses the details of forming a company. In a full strength regiment, seven of each company's 100 men served as file closers. Most regiments at Chickamauga had fewer than one-half of the 1,000 men they were supposed to have, so with that as a percentage, the ratio of officers and NCOs to privates in the line was much higher than called for in the drill manual.

28 U.S. infantry drill and tactical manuals from this period can be confusing. *Hardee's Tactics*, published in 1855, was intended to replace and update General Winfield Scott's 1835 manual of three volumes. However, Hardee only revised the first two volumes of Scott's work, addressing drill and tactics up through the regimental level. Scott's third volume, which dealt with brigade and divisional deployments, was left as is.

To watch Croxton's left, Brannan sent Col. Ferdinand Van Derveer's Third Brigade up to the Reed's Bridge Road, retracing McCook's footsteps of the night before. Van Derveer's brigade was a crack outfit. In 1861, when Thomas assumed command of Camp Dick Robinson and the 6,000 disorganized state levies gathered there, two of the brigade's four regiments, the 9th Ohio and the 2nd Minnesota, had its original members within the ranks of that mob. Thomas trained these men and taught them how to be soldiers. In January 1862, he took them into action at Mill Springs, winning one of the early Union victories of the war. The 9th Ohio, the Union's first all-German regiment recruited with immigrants from Cincinnati, had a special reputation for aggressiveness. It was their bayonet charge that had cleared the field at Mill Springs and drew the admiration of every Federal who witnessed the event.[29]

Van Derveer was another citizen-solder of some distinction. He joined the 1st Ohio during the Mexican War and led one of the storming columns into Monterrey. Since then he'd worked as a lawyer, county sheriff, and newspaper editor in Butler County. A staunch Democrat, he had no use for Lincoln, was good friends with the now-exiled Clement Vallandigham, and actively supported John C. Breckinridge in the 1860 election. Vallandigham was being called a traitor back home because he was running for governor of Ohio from exile as a 'Peace Democrat,' Breckinridge was commanding a division in Bragg's army, and Van Derveer was a pro-Union War Democrat. Against his wife's wishes, the colonel went to war with his young son Harry by his side, despite agreeing to send the boy home back in August when active campaigning began. With a fight pending, Van Derveer dispatched an aide to escort Harry to the divisional field hospital being established well to the rear at Cloud Church, with instructions to keep the lad safe.[30]

Van Derveer was short Col. Gustave Kammerling's 9th Ohio, which had been detailed the night before to escort the divisional ammunition train. The wave of German immigration starting in the early 1850s, in the wake of the failed revolution of 1848, triggered a powerful ethnic backlash. Most Germans were acutely aware of this discrimination. Since their arrival in the United States,

---

29 McKinney, *Education in Violence*, 109-111, 127-128; Kenneth A. Hafendorfer, *Mill Springs: Campaign and Battle of Mill Springs, Kentucky* (KH Press, 2001), 396-398.

30 Van Derveer Family History and Letters, Smith Library of Regional History, Lane Library, Oxford, OH; "My Dear Wife," Chattanooga, TN, Sept. 23rd, 1863, Ferdinand Van Derveer letters, Smith Library.

nativist groups (especially the Know-Nothing political movement of the 1850s) had been trying to deny them voting rights and other privileges of citizenship. Kammerling was a touchy man, sensitive to any slight. He regarded the assignment in the rear guarding wagons as a suggestion that his men weren't up to the fight. For the time being, however, orders were orders.[31]

Without a local guide or a good sense of what lay ahead, Van Derveer's three remaining regiments proceeded with due caution. A half-mile down the logging path the road crested a ridge, which Van Derveer thought was an ideal place to deploy his brigade. The veteran 2nd Minnesota and 35th Ohio took the lead on the right and left, respectively. The 87th Indiana, which had been in service for a year but had not yet fought in a battle, formed in support. When all was ready Van Derveer resumed his advance, but more slowly than before.[32]

Brannan held his First Brigade in reserve, well-positioned both to guard Croxton's right by covering the Alexander's Bridge Road and in position to provide reinforcements should either Croxton or Van Derveer run into trouble. A recent dispute had roiled the brigade and disrupted its chain of command. The brigade lacked a permanent brigadier, and its senior colonel, Edward H. Phelps, was off with his regiment guarding part of the divisional wagon train. To further complicate matters, Phelps had placed the next ranking colonel, Moses B. Walker of the 17th Ohio, under arrest over a minor protocol issue. Walker couldn't exercise his duties while under arrest, so Brannan made him a supernumerary aide until the issue could be resolved. This left Col. John Connell of the 31st Ohio in charge of the brigade, third in line of command and untested in that position. Walker later noted with perhaps just a touch of sour grapes that Connell's health was "very poor," and that there was "a general bad feeling" in the brigade over these command arrangements.[33]

While Brannan's division was uncoiling, forming, and moving slowly east, Nathan Bedford Forrest and the troopers of Pegram's brigade were taking a break at Jay's Mill. Part of the 1st Georgia was sent out on Reed's Bridge Road to make sure McCook did not return, while the rest of the brigade halted for a coffee boil. Here Forrest held a quick conference with Pegram. Captain Clay was summoned to the meeting and given orders to take another detachment of

31 Albert Dickennan, "The 9th Ohio at Chickamauga," *National Tribune*, October 18, 1906.

32 The 87th Indiana was at Perryville, but only suffered two wounded in skirmishing during that battle. They saw no fighting at Stones River.

33 Moses B. Walker Report, Thomas Papers, RG 94, NARA.

Jay's Mill, looking north. The field in view was filled with the 1,600 men of
Davidson's Brigade, dismounted and resting.

Henry Scarborough

the 1st Georgia west and patrol into the woods. Clay and his party
reconnoitered about three-quarters of a mile through the timber, with early
morning birdsongs the only sign of life. Clay returned to report the woods
empty and stretched out with his head on a tree root for a quick nap.[34]

Private W. R. Shropshire recalled a general sense of relaxation. "A large
portion of each regiment had dismounted, lying, standing or sitting, awaiting
orders . . . [for] . . . perhaps a half an hour." Pegram later reported that he and
Forrest "were in front examining the roads" during this lull. During their
absence, either General Davidson or Col. J. J. Morrison of the 6th Georgia
dispatched the 10th Confederate Cavalry into the forest just scouted by Clay to
establish a security screen as a well-considered precaution. The 250 troopers of
the 10th followed their Col. Charles T. Goode into the woods, picking their way
through the saplings at the edge of the logged field.[35]

34 Clay, "On the Right at Chickamauga," 329; and "Concerning the Battle of Chickamauga,"
72.

35 Shropshire Reminiscences, Duke University; *OR* 30, pt. 2, 528; Minnich, "Reminiscences of
J. W. Minnick," 21. "Minnick" is the same person as J. W. Minnich, quoted extensively earlier.
Davidson was the brigade commander, but in his account Minnich suggested Davidson was
not present yet and Morrison ordered the 10th out in Davidson's absence. Given how little
Minnich remembered about Davidson, it is possible he is mistaken in this regard.

Within a short time the Rebel cavalry collided with Maj. Van Natta's Federal skirmish line fronting Croxton's advancing brigade. Corporal W. H. Wiley, in company A of the 10th Indiana, was back with Croxton's main line when the Rebel cavalry appeared. "The firing commenced," he recalled, "at first a few scattering shots, then faster and faster until our entire skirmish line seemed to be engaged." The Yankee skirmishers tumbled back, pursued by the mounted Rebels. Colonel Goode of the 10th Confederate had ordered a charge, similar to the first action that morning. This time the Confederates were in for an unpleasant surprise.[36]

When the picket firing erupted, Croxton ordered his brigade to halt. The 10th Indiana was "lying behind the brow of a piece of rising ground," noted Sgt. Samuel Thompson of Company I, who watched as the Rebel horsemen closed to within "80 yards [then] we rose and poured such a volley . . . among them, that they wheeled their horses" and fled. "Many of the cavalry and their horses were killed."[37]

The sound of renewed fighting carried back to the Jay's Mill clearing. The first volley awoke the now confused Captain Clay, who had personally reported that very area devoid of Yankees not 20 minutes before. The 6th Georgia was called to attention and made for the crest of the hill just west of the clearing. These Georgians dismounted and were forming into line with their right flank refused when Goode's Confederates burst out of the trees in wild disorder. A trooper from the 6th Georgia described the scene this way: "Wild-eyed, hatless, horseless, without guns . . . wounded and bleeding . . . men yelling at the top of their voices, 'Git Boys. The woods are full of Yankees.'" With the 10th riding wildly for safety through his ranks, the trooper jumped up and headed for the rear as well, shouting, "Boys, this is Hell! I am going for cover!" In the 1st Georgia, Private Shropshire heard a number of Confederates yelling "Don't shoot, they are Longstreet's men," a notion quickly discarded as the firing grew more intense. The rest of the brigade fell in alongside the 6th and prepared to hold the ground.[38]

---

36 James Birney Shaw, *History of the Tenth Indiana Volunteer Infantry* (Burt-Haywood Co., 1912), 228.

37 Entry for September 19, Samuel F. Thompson Diary, WHS.

38 Clay, "Concerning the Battle of Chickamauga," 72; Minnich, "Reminiscences of J. W. Minnick," 21, 23; Shropshire Reminiscences, Duke University.

As ordered, Croxton found Confederates west of Chickamauga Creek. He advanced his men cautiously, content with driving the 10th Confederate back through Pegram's line. Then Croxton halted again, maintaining a continuous fire on the distant enemy. With Van Derveer converging on Croxton's left, the Federals were ideally situated to outflank the surprised enemy. Croxton had no need to press home a frontal assault before Van Derveer made his appearance on his left.[39]

It was Forrest who made the next critical decision. He could have disengaged, maintained a screen against this new threat, and reported the circumstances to Bragg. There was no pressing need for Pegram's much weaker cavalry force to slug it out with 2,000 Yankee infantry. Falling back, however, would also surrender control of Reed's Bridge and potentially expose Ringgold. Besides, Nathan Bedford Forrest was a fighter, not a screener. It is unlikely that disengaging ever crossed his mind. Instead, he ordered the cavalry to dismount and hold their ground while Forrest sought support. After deciding to stand and fight, he sent a courier to General Polk to once again request the return of Frank Armstrong's much-delayed division. Armstrong's men were still on duty opposite Lee and Gordon's Mills, however, so even their immediate release would not help Forrest in time to change the odds. Closer at hand were the infantry of W. H. T. Walker's Corps, camped in the fields around the remains of the Alexander cabin. In another dispatch Forrest alerted Bragg to the Union advance and also asked for some of Walker's men to assist him.[40]

The Rebel horse soldiers were ill-equipped to match Croxton's firepower. They were not only heavily outnumbered but indifferently armed, with both shotguns and smoothbore muskets mixed in with more modern rifled muskets. Forrest quickly moved to bolster the line in any way he could. Huwald's battery came forward at the trot and unlimbered on "a rocky ridge in a piece of woods between saplings so thick that it was difficult to see far forward." The battery only dropped trail with three pieces because one of its howitzers had been stationed the night before to guard Alexander's Bridge; Huwald sent a runner to collect the wayward gun. Huwald remembered the early fighting as seesaw action, with Croxton's Federals pushing forward several times, close enough that "canister was used with good effect." Forrest asked Huwald several times

39 Shaw, History of the Tenth Indiana, 229.

40 *OR* 30, pt. 2, 524.

whether the gunner could hold his ground, and each time he assured the cavalry general he could. The Federals were less impressed. "They run out a section of a battery (two guns) about 100 yards to our front," wrote Corporal Wiley of the 10th Indiana. "They did little harm, as their range was bad, their shells passing [a] considerable distance above our heads."[41]

Desperate for men to add to his firing line, the newly arrived Davidson sent an aide to Forrest requesting reinforcements. "You go right over there," Forrest barked to the aide, "tell the holders to hold ten or twelve horses, and *fetch* the balance right here." Reducing the number of horse-holders wouldn't do for long. Forrest continually rode the line and encouraged his men to hang on: "This . . . is an infantry fight . . . I am going for them myself, and they'll soon be here."[42]

Forrest in a fight was a fury to behold. As he galloped back and forth, recalled his aide-de-camp, Capt. Charles W. Anderson, Forrest "was ready to threaten, or do more than threaten, any who dared to give back to rapidly. At one moment . . . a private soldier, having parted company with his courage, cut loose from his place . . . and broke at top speed for the rear." The man had poor timing. "Forrest whipped out his six-shooter, ordered the man to halt, and was in the act of making an example of him" when Anderson exclaimed, "'Oh, general, think!'" That plea saved the man's life. Forrest, "lowering his pistol, let the unhappy mortal go in peace."[43]

At some point during this fighting Forrest's horse fell mortally wounded. The animal was a gift to the general by the grateful citizens of Rome, Georgia, after he captured Union Col. Abel Streight's raiding force outside the city that May. Forrest remounted another horse and rode through the fire to find Pegram: "Hold this position . . . until I can bring up reinforcements." Pegram's response was a little less certain than Huwald's, but perhaps more realistic: "I'll

41 Captain M. V. Moore, newspaper clipping, undated, Martin Van Buren Moore Papers, Southern Historical Collection, UNC; Huwald Letter, UNC; Shaw, *History of the Tenth Indiana*, 229.

42 W. M. Marriner, "Chickamauga: The Opening," *Southern Bivouac, September 1882-August 1883*, 6 vols. (Broadfoot Publishing, 1993), vol. III, no. 1, 11; Minnich, "Reminiscences of J. W. Minnick," 24.

43 John Allen Wyeth, *That Devil Forrest: Life of General Nathan Bedford Forrest* (Louisiana State University Press, 1989), 226.

hold it if I can, General."[44] With that, the corps commander struck out south in search of gray infantry.[45]

Braxton Bragg and his headquarters group left Leet's Tanyard early that morning and headed for Thedford's Ford. He was likely still en route when he received Forrest's dispatch. Bragg quickly sent Forrest's courier on to Walker, with orders directing Walker to send Forrest a brigade. A sizable grouping of the Army of Tennessee's senior officers formed at the ford. Bragg arrived around 8:00 a.m., recalled Col. Thomas Claiborne, and "nearly all his commanders" gathered round. "There was a big crowd of Staff." For the moment, however, all action was suspended as Bragg waited to see what developed to the north.[46]

General Walker tapped Col. Claudius Wilson's brigade to march to help the cavalry, sending Forrest's man on to locate Wilson. Like Brannan's Federals, Wilson's men had already had a long night. Both his and Matt Ector's regiments spent nearly every dark hour crossing the Chickamauga, and both brigades were just preparing breakfast when word arrived that Forrest was hard-pressed. Here, at the intersection of the Alexander's Bridge and Viniard-Alexander roads, Forrest's much-traveled officer found Wilson and handed the latter "an order . . . directing me to go with General Forrest and obey his orders."[47]

Wilson quickly put his brigade in motion, marching up the Alexander's Bridge Road before turning onto the Jay's Mill Road, retracing the cavalry's earlier route. Somewhere along the march Forrest rode up, briefed Wilson of the nature of the fight, and requested that his troops go into action on Pegram's left. The brigade formed a line on a low ridge south of Jay's Mill. Wilson posted his own 25th Georgia on the brigade right, with the 29th and 30th Georgia and 4th Louisiana Battalion extending the line to the left. The 1st Georgia sharpshooters probably led the initial advance as skirmishers, and soon formed on the left of the Louisianans. A brief pause followed before Forrest, who had ridden ahead, sent word to Wilson to attack. "The brigade was marched rapidly by the right flank for about five-eighths of a mile westward," reported Wilson,

44 Ibid.

45 Clay, "On the Right at Chickamauga," 329.

46 Brent Journal, WRHS; *OR* 30, pt. 2, 240; Thomas Claiborne Letter, Nashville, Tennessee, April 16, 1891, Eyewitness Accounts file, CCNMP.

47 Major Joseph B. Cumming War Recollections, Southern Historical Collection, UNC; *OR* 30, pt. 2, 248.

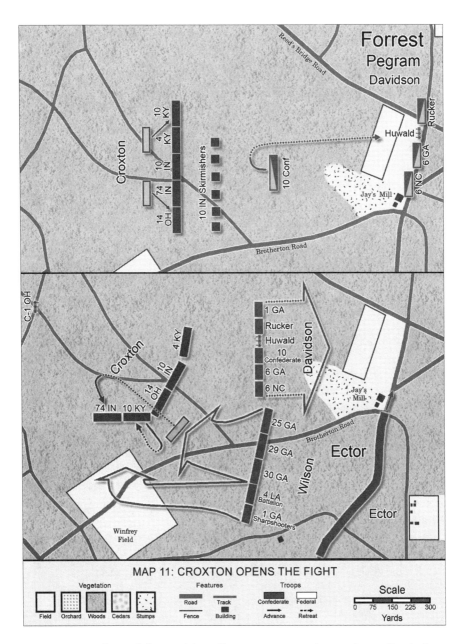

MAP 11: CROXTON OPENS THE FIGHT

"when it was formed forward into line on a run, and went immediately into battle." Just before going in, Wilson sent Lt. Rufus E. Lester down the line to alert the men of the impending action. When he reached Col. Thomas

Mangham, commander of the 30th Georgia, Lester told him, "Colonel, we are going to have hot times over yonder, get your men ready."[48]

Wilson's 1,200 men left the Jay's Mill Road at an angle, advancing northwest in an effort to strike Croxton's flank. The terrain here was mostly wooded except for the rectangular patch of Winfrey Field off to Wilson's left front; the new Rebel line overlapped Croxton's right by a considerable margin. During the fight with the cavalry Croxton brought forward both rear-rank regiments to extend his front. The 10th Kentucky formed on the extreme left of the line and the 14th Ohio on the right. The 14th bore the brunt of Wilson's initial blow. An Ohio private named Benjamin B. Jackson of Company G was in the thick of this new burst of fighting. "They marched up on us . . . 8 ranks deep," he wrote in a letter home, "& at the same time began to outflank us . . . [they opened] fire with awful effect, cutting down our men at an awful rate."[49]

Croxton was already aware of the threat developing on his right, and sent Captain Mann back to find John Brannan and bring up support. Mann missed Brannan somehow, but quickly came upon George Thomas, who was monitoring the developing action. When Mann explained his mission, Thomas sent him back to Croxton with word that Baird's division would come forward to help.[50]

Croxton had already begun forming a new line at right angles to his original position. The 74th Indiana was plucked from its place on the left of the 14th and sent angling to the right, executing "the movement under a sharp fire from the rebels."[51] Farther left, Croxton ordered Col. William H. Hays to pull his 10th Kentucky from that flank and double-quick the length of the Federal line to brace the 74th. Before Hays could fully traverse the length of the brigade line, however, the 74th Indiana, its flank overlapped and its front taking heavy firing, broke.[52]

---

48 *OR* 30, pt. 2, 248; Report of Lieutenant Colonel James S. Boynton, 30th Georgia file, CCNMP; A. P. Adamson, *Brief History of the 30th Georgia Regiment* (The Mills Printing Company, 1912), 34; Report of Lieutenant Colonel James S. Boynton, 30th Georgia File, CCNMP; Adamson, *30th Georgia*, 34.

49 *OR* 30, pt. 1, 422,424; "Dear Wife and Family," September 27, 1863, B. B. Jackson Papers, BGSU.

50 *Muskegon Daily Chronicle*, September 19, 1908.

51 *OR* 30, pt. 1, 418.

52 Ibid., 422.

Wilson entered the fight with some reason to be concerned about the performance of his mostly Georgia brigade. His troops had not been back to Georgia for more than a year, and during the trip through the state more than 500 men left the ranks to temporarily visit their homes. The young lawyer from Savannah "was mortified by their conduct." Many of absentees rejoined the ranks before the fighting. Any uncertainty Wilson may have felt that morning ended as he watched his Georgians tear into the Yankees with a will. In the center of his line, the 30th Georgia passed to the left of the Winfrey cabin and scrambled over the fence into Winfrey Field. The Hoosiers of the 74th spotted the move and opened fire on the Rebels mid-field. In response, Lt. Col. James S. Boynton reported, the 30th Georgia "moved briskly forward and charged in good order."[53]

Colonel Charles W. Chapman of the 74th tried to pull the right half of his regiment back at an angle to refuse the line and meet the 30th's charge, to no avail. Chapman's order was "misunderstood for a command to retire the whole line, and the regiment was momentarily thrown into confusion." Within seconds, the Hoosiers were scrambling to the rear, all order lost. Colonel Hays of the 10th Kentucky appeared, sized up the crisis at a glance, and ordered his regiment to charge. And charge they did, recalled Pvt. Henry G. Davidson, "driving them back about a quarter of a mile." Colonel Hays reported the distance as only 200 yards, but it was enough. Having temporarily checked the Georgians, Hays led his men back to the brigade and took up position on the 14th Ohio's right.[54]

This respite allowed the Hoosiers time to rally. Captain Mann rode up in time to witness the 74th "scattering." The mortified Mann, who had formerly commanded Company G, rode into the broken ranks of his old regiment. The captain seized one of the flags and, elevated on horseback and holding the banner aloft, offered the enemy a perfect target. When a bullet plowed a furrow along the inside of his arm, lodging "in the pit of his left elbow," members of the 74th reformed around him. Order restored, Mann headed back to have a surgeon look at his wound while the Indiana regiment fell in alongside the

---

53 "Dear Kate," Letter of September 3, 1863, Claudius Wilson correspondence, CCNMP; Report of the 30th Georgia, CCNMP.

54 OR 30, pt. 1, 419; "My Dear Aunt," Chattanooga, Tennessee, February 19, 1864, Henry G. Davidson Letters, ALPL.

Buckeye 14th. Thus repositioned, Croxton's brigade faced more south than east, engaging Wilson's Rebels all along its front.[55]

About this time, Wilson received word from Forrest "not to press the enemy farther." That was just fine with Wilson, who by now had taken Croxton's measure: the Federal brigade clearly outnumbered his own by a wide margin. The Georgian sent a courier to Matt Ector seeking help on his vulnerable left, only to find the Texan's brigade was not available. With no help forthcoming and the Yankees starting to push back, Wilson slowly began to give ground. At the head of the 14th Ohio, Lt. Col. Henry Kingsbury eschewed an officer's sword for a musket and cartridge box, proving, according to one correspondent, that "his heart and his musket were in the right place." Once order had been restored, "we formed & turned on them," wrote Private Jackson, "& drove them back nearly as far as we had retreated." The Georgians rallied and made a second effort, driving back Croxton in turn. Neither brigade was able to drive the other more than a short distance, carpeting the woods in between them with the wounded and the dead.[56]

Brigadier General Ector's brigade was unavailable because General Forrest had already made use of it. After placing Wilson, the cavalry commander had ridden off in search of more help for his pressured front. Within a short time he encountered Ector's mixed command of Alabamians, Mississippians, North Carolinians, and Texans. In the hasty expansion of Walker's division into the Reserve Corps during the last few days, Ector's, Wilson's and Brig. Gen. States Rights Gist's brigades were combined into a division with the senior Gist as its commander. Gist, however, was still en route from Rome, Georgia, where his command had been sent to defend that city against Yankee marauders. His absence left Ector in nominal command of the new division, but he would have little chance to do more than direct his own brigade.

Ector's brigade numbered 1,199 men, with one regiment each of Texas and North Carolina infantry, three regiments of dismounted Texas cavalry, and two scratch battalions—one from Alabama and another from Mississippi—drawn from troops whose parent regiments had been trapped inside Vicksburg back in July. The brigade bore an unusual nickname of mysterious origin: The Chubs. The troops had recently returned to the Army of

---

55 *Muskegon Daily Chronicle*, September 19, 1908; *OR* 30, pt. 1, 422.

56 *OR* 30, pt. 2, 248; "Account of the Battle of Chickamauga," *Toledo Blade*, October 2nd, 1863; "Dear Wife and Family," September 27, 1863, B. B. Jackson Papers, BGSU.

Tennessee, being one of the brigades Walker brought with him from Mississippi. They were transferred to the Magnolia State during the summer in the ill-fated effort to relieve Vicksburg. Like many Texans, Ector's troops had a freewheeling attitude toward army discipline, which outraged Walker. When they were assigned to his command in June, Walker thought they ought to be discharged instead. They would soon prove their fighting qualities to everyone, the martinet Walker included.[57]

With Wilson going into action on Pegram's left, Forrest intended to send Ector into action on the cavalry's right. Ector's troops met the first of the wounded coming out of the fight during their march up the Jay's Mill Road. "Some were hobbling along supported by some friend," recalled one eyewitness, "others were holding shattered arms, and among the number . . . [was] a fine looking officer sitting on his horse pressing his hand to his chest while the blood was trickling down his body." When they reached the Reed's Bridge Road, Ector formed his regiments into line and advanced northwest. Several hundred yards up the road, Ferdinand Van Derveer's three Federal regiments waited to receive them.[58]

Van Derveer had thus far erred on the side of caution. When the skirmish fire marking Croxton's initial encounter with the 10th Confederate broke out, the brigade "moved off the road to the right about a hundred yards" and halted. Lieutenant Frank G. Smith's Battery I, 4th U.S. Artillery, unlimbered astride the road behind the infantry. Van Derveer believed his line outflanked the Rebels confronting Croxton, and "began feeling his position with my skirmishers." The Rebels began to fall back. Van Derveer's only opposition came in the form of whatever scratch force Pegram could detach to face him—probably still only those companies of the 1st Georgia deployed as skirmishers across the Reed's Bridge Road, but they proved enough. Colonel James George of the 2nd Minnesota reported that the Rebels approached "within about 300 yards and opened a heavy fire of musketry." The Minnesotans replied in kind, and according to George were repulsed within about 10 minutes.[59]

This initial clash occurred sometime after Croxton became engaged, but before Wilson's infantry appeared on Croxton's flank. Shortly after Wilson

---

57 J. G. McCown, "About Ector's and McNair's Brigades," *Confederate Veteran*, vol. IX, no. 3 (March, 1901), 113.

58 Smith and Quist, *Cush*, 49.

59 Judson W. Bishop, *Van Derveer's Brigade at Chickamauga* (n.p., 1903), 7; OR 30, pt. 1, 428, 432.

struck, however, Van Derveer received word from Brannan that "The Second Brigade [Croxton] was . . . giving back and . . . I should at once make an attack."[60]

Before Van Derveer could do so, however, Ector's men appeared. Urgency, not caution, dictated Ector's movements as he replaced the 1st Georgia and prepared to attack—even though the brigadier was concerned about his flanks in general, and his right flank in particular. Pegram's cavalry still held their line around Jay's Mill, but farther north across the Reed's Bridge Road there were no Confederates for miles. The men in the ranks were acutely aware of this fact. Private Whittsett later recalled with great pride that the 9th Texas of Ector's brigade "was the extreme right regiment and Co. H. was the extreme right Co. of infantry in Bragg's Army."[61] Ector dispatched Capt. C. B. "Buck" Kilgore to find General Forrest and ask the cavalryman to watch his right closely. "I'll take care of it," was Forrest's gruff reply.[62]

Once his front was arranged the Texan led his brigade in a charge. Standing in the ranks of Company G, 2nd Minnesota, Capt. Jeremiah Dunahower watched the approaching enemy, "a solid line of men in gray coming towards us in something like a rush . . . we greeted them with a telling volley . . . followed . . . by firing at will." "They opened a murderous fire upon us," admitted Alabamian Sam Sprott, "and we in turn upon them." The Federal artillery proved equally deadly. In the 29th North Carolina, Lt. Joseph H. Stradley led Company H straight for Smith's guns and suffered severely for the effort. "In the beginning of the charge our captain was killed, and the command . . . devolved upon me," Stradley penned many years after the war. "The guns were well served, and their fire destructive. Four of my men fell in one pile." For all its fury, the assault was repulsed and Ector's riddled ranks fell back to regroup.[63]

A second effort only added to the casualty list. "We charged twice and were driven back," recalled Pvt. William Whitsett of the 9th Texas. Losses among the

---

60 *OR* 30, pt. 1, 428.

61 "Dear Brother," July 13, 1900, William E. Whittsett Letter, 9th Texas website: http://9thtexas.tripod.com, accessed 07/16/2008.

62 John Allen Wyeth, *The Life of Lieutenant General Nathan Bedford Forrest* (Harper & Brothers, Publishers, 1908), 250.

63 Jeremiah Dunahower Papers, "The Chattanooga Campaign," unpublished manuscript, 111, MinnHS; Smith and Quist, *Cush*, 50; J. H. Stradley, "Ector's Brigade at Chickamauga," *Confederate Veteran*, vol. XIII, no. 7 (July, 1905), 308.

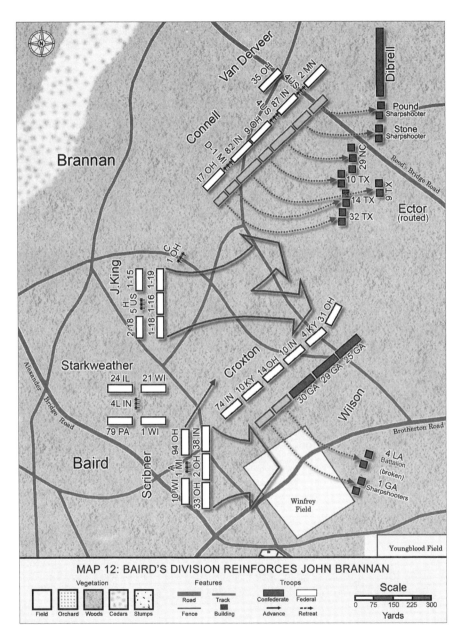

MAP 12: BAIRD'S DIVISION REINFORCES JOHN BRANNAN

officers were especially severe, including their animals. Ector "was slightly wounded four times and had two horses shot under him. . . . Every member of his staff . . . lost at least one horse, and every mounted officer in the brigade had

Matthew D. Ector. His brigade bore an unusual nickname—Ector's Chubs.

Miller: The Photographic History of the Civil War

his horse killed or severely wounded." In total, the brigade lost 527 men at Chickamauga, most of them falling in these two brief charges.[64]

Fortunately for Forrest and Ector, additional troops were just then coming up as his men were engaging Van Derveer's Federals. Colonel George Dibrell's cavalry brigade reached Jay's Mill probably just after Ector's first repulse. Dibrell dismounted his troopers and hurried them across the Reed's Bridge Road to form up on Ector's right.[65]

Sometime during Ector's second charge, the Federals got some help of their own. Brannan was still holding back Connell's three regiments as a reserve, and they shifted position several times while listening to the fight on their front. Ohio Pvt. Sam McNeil concluded that Connell "was uncertain about where he should move his command," but in reality, Brannan was still exercising control. With both Croxton and Van Derveer under attack, Brannan finally elected to break up Connell's brigade by sending the 31st Ohio southeast to help Croxton while he took the 17th Ohio, 82nd Indiana, and Battery D of the 1st Michigan northeast to support Van Derveer.[66]

Van Derveer's hard-pressed men were near the end of Ector's second assault when Brannan arrived, and Col. Van Derveer had just sent the 87th Indiana forward to replace the Buckeyes of the 35th Ohio, who were running

64 Whittsett Letter, 9th Texas website; "Ector's Brigade in the Battle of Chickamauga," *Mobile Daily Register*, October 14, 1863; Powell, "Numbers and Losses," CCNMP.

65 Letter from OSCEOLA, "Forrest's Old Brigade in the Battle of Chickamauga," *Memphis Appeal*, October 21, 1863.

66 Samuel A. McNeil, *Personal Recollections of Service in the Army of the Cumberland and Sherman's Army from August 17, 1861 to July 20, 1865* (n.p. 1910), 9; OR 30, pt. 1, 407-408.

low on ammunition. Neither of Ector's attacks came close to breaking the Federal line, and the 87th's involvement was limited to seeing off the last of the Rebels after that second effort. A Hoosier sergeant named Benjamin Brown of Company D described the moment: "We . . . relieved the 35th, and went into it with good spirits. I had fired eleven rounds at them when we were ordered to cease firing." By the time Connell's reinforcements came up the action was all but over. The new arrivals fell in on Van Derveer's right and connected to the 87th Indiana but had no one to engage.[67]

Connell's reinforcements were not the only Federals coming to help Van Derveer. At Thomas's order, Baird's First Division was moving east to support Brannan, and some of Baird's men would get a crack at Ector's retreating line. Baird advanced with Brig. Gen. John H. King's brigade of Regular Army battalions formed on the division's left. Alert to Thomas's warning, Baird ordered Col. Ben Scribner's five regiments in on the right, "bent to the rear so as to march by flank in rear of [King's] right, and be ready to front in that direction . . . should it be required." Brigadier General John Starkweather brought up the division's rear, acting as Baird's reserve. The artillery, Baird noted, "could not advance with the infantry" and was not much use in the wooded terrain, so he ordered the gunners to bring up their pieces as best they could.[68]

Brannan's brigades had not advanced on a united front, so there was already a gap between Van Derveer and Croxton. That space widened considerably when Croxton was forced to reorient his line to face Wilson's approaching Confederate brigade. Van Derveer's line also shifted to face southeast when they engaged Ector's men. Baird's brigades were ideally situated to take advantage of these deployments. Brigadier General John King's Regulars were heading due east, directly between Van Derveer and Croxton, while Scribner's brigade moved southeast on Croxton's right. In each case, a fresh Union brigade was poised to strike a Confederate brigade's exposed left flank.

Ector was not unaware of larger forces stirring around him. Just as he had been concerned earlier about his exposed right flank, he was now acutely aware that there was no support on his left. Davidson's cavalry was still off to the southeast near Jay's Mill, regrouping after their morning's fight, while Wilson's

---

67 "From the 87th Indiana Vols." *Rochester Chronicle*, October 15, 1863.

68 *OR* 30, pt. 1, 275.

Georgians were too far distant to connect with his flank. The Texas brigadier was growing increasingly uneasy concerning his isolated tactical situation. Alone in the woods and watching the repulse of his second charge, Ector again sent Kilgore back to find Forrest. The aide found the cavalryman in the same spot, near Huggins's battery. General Ector was "now uneasy about his left flank," Kilgore relayed. Forrest, never a patient man, became "furious," recalled the captain. "He turned around on me and shouted, loud enough to be heard above the terrible din . . . . 'Tell General Ector that, by God, I am here, and will take care of his left flank as well as his right!' It is hardly necessary," concluded Kilgore, "to add that we were not outflanked on either side." This story first appeared in print in 1908 and has been faithfully related in every work about Forrest since that time. However, most of those accounts fail to note that Kilgore, his memory clouded by either time or admiration for the great man, was mistaken: Ector's men were about to be outflanked from the left.[69]

Despite their designation as regiments in the U.S. Regular Army, the bulk of King's troops had no more military experience than the volunteer soldiers in the Army of the Cumberland. Unlike their compatriots in the Old Army, the regiments in King's brigade only came into being as part of the "new army" authorized by adding 11 new Regular regiments to the rolls in May 1861. The new units were different than the Old Army in organization, too. Instead of mustering 10 companies to form a regiment (as was done in both existing Regulars and in the state volunteer units), the newly raised 11th through 19th Infantry Regiments would instead each be organized into three battalions, each battalion comprising eight companies. Thus, in theory these new units were much larger than the original commands, numbering a total of 24 companies instead of the traditional 10. In practice, the new regiments rarely reached their fully authorized strength, usually fielding only one or two battalions.[70]

Some things remained the same, however. Old Army discipline prevailed within these new Regulars, much to the disgust of volunteers who chanced to witness such displays. In March 1862, a confrontation erupted between the officers of the 18th U.S. Infantry and a mob drawn from the ranks of the 9th Ohio and 2nd Minnesota who witnessed a couple of Regulars undergoing physical punishments for infractions. The resultant riot was quelled just short

69 Wyeth, *The Life of Lieutenant General Nathan Bedford Forrest*, 250.

70 Mark W. Johnson, *That Body of Brave Men: The U.S. Regular Infantry and the Civil War in the West* (Da Capo Press, 2003), 7.

of gunfire, and the incident left the volunteers with a lingering distaste for Regular Army officers and their stern ways.[71]

King's brigade took its current form in the spring of 1863. The Regulars fought well at Stones River on December 31, 1862, and Rosecrans wanted them brought up to strength and concentrated in a single unit. As a result, the new brigade included 38 companies in five formations: the 1st and 2nd Battalions of the 18th U.S., and the 1st battalion of each of the 15th, 16th, and 19th Regulars. King was promoted to brigadier general in April 1863 and assumed command.[72]

With the 1/18th, 1/16th, 1/19th in his front line, King advanced at Baird's order. The Regulars could clearly hear all the noises of a large fight, and as they drew near, the "shrill cheers or yells of the advancing confederates piercing through the roar of battle." Before long Lt. Henry B. Freeman, adjutant for the 1/18th, could see the enemy as well as hear them. Ahead was Ector's serried left flank; the Rebels were falling back from their second effort against Van Derveer. Seizing the opportunity, King "wheeled the brigade to the left in double time, then forward, striking the enemy in the flank and rolling him up like a curtain."[73]

Already disordered, the twice-repulsed Confederates routed when these new Yankees appeared. "[We] found [we] were flanked on the left & commenced falling back in confusion," wrote Pvt. C. B. Carlton of the 10th Texas, writing home to explain how his friend John Templeton ended up a Yankee prisoner. "The boys were scattered pretty badly," Carlton admitted, and when Ector ordered the brigade to march by the right flank the confusion only increased. Lieutenant Robert Ayres of the 19th U.S. reported that the 9th Texas "passing along our front from left to right, received our fire, which caused them to break and run and many came into our lines as prisoners." Exuberantly, Adjutant Freeman explained that the brigade advanced "nearly a mile and captured more prisoners than we had either time or means to care [for.]" Ector reported 138 men missing; his hardest hit regiment, the 32nd Texas, alone

71 Ibid., 133-137.

72 Warner, *Generals in Blue*, 268.

73 Henry B. Freeman Papers, "At the Battle of Chickamauga," 2, Wyoming Historical Society, Cheyenne, Wyoming.

accounted for 40 of those. The heavy losses, two repulses, and slashing attack against its exposed flank rendered Ector's brigade *hors de combat.*[74]

King's three front-line battalions pursued the routing Confederates with wild abandon, so much so that Capt. George W. Smith, heading up the 1/18th U.S. drifted far to the right (east) and for a time lost track of the rest of the brigade. Smith's battalion ended up engaging men from Wilson's brigade (probably from the 25th or 29th Georgia), which was also retreating at this time. When the Georgians finally fell back out of sight, Smith halted "in dense woods and hilly ground" to await developments. The rest of the brigade also stopped to reform at the rise of a wooded ridge. Lieutenant Howard M. Burnham unlimbered the six guns of his Battery H, 5th U.S. Light Artillery there, supported by the 1/15th, while King recalled and reorganized his wayward front line.[75]

While King was pummeling Ector, Col. Benjamin Scribner's five regiments were similarly savaging Wilson. Scribner's advance did not keep pace with King's, mostly because of Baird's warning to watch his right flank. More by chance than by design, his brigade was now sweeping directly toward the 1st Georgia Sharpshooter Battalion's naked left. Scribner's command was another large brigade numbering 1,730 men. The 2nd and 33rd Ohio comprised the first line with the 10th Wisconsin and 94th Ohio in support. Scribner's own regiment, the 38th Indiana, had initially been left behind with Battery A, 1st Michigan Light Artillery, but both were ordered to follow in the brigade's wake. Like all the artillery on this part of the field, the woods slowed the movements of the Wolverine battery.[76]

While Scribner and King advanced, Croxton and Wilson waged a bloody back-and-forth fight in the woods north of Winfrey Field. Despite his advantage of numbers, Croxton's need to reorient to the south had also forced him to give ground in the face of Wilson's aggressive charge, and the fight had moved roughly 400 yards north. This retreat left a number of Croxton's

74 "D. G. Templeton, Sir," Oct. 13th, 1863, C. B. Carlton letter, J. A. Templeton Papers, Simpson History Complex, Hill College, Hillsboro, Texas; *OR* 30, pt. 1, 322; Freeman, "Chickamauga," 2; *Mobile Daily Advertiser*, October 10th, 1863.

75 *OR* 30, pt. 1, 319.

76 Ibid., 285.

casualties behind enemy lines, including the mortally wounded Col. William B. Carroll of the 10th Indiana; little could be done for them now.[77]

The woods were hampering more than the artillery. As Scribner advanced, General Baird pulled up next to Maj. Rue P. Hutchins, commanding the 94th Ohio on the left of Scribner's second line. The 94th was angling too far to the right. Hutchins pointed out that he was following the 2nd Ohio, per orders, but Baird insisted the entire brigade was off course. Baird reoriented the 94th (which promptly moved to the left and thus diverged from the rest of the brigade) before presumably riding on to find Scribner to redirect the rest of his regiments. In the meantime Hutchins plunged on, slipping out of position on a course that would ultimately place him several hundred yards beyond Scribner's front.[78]

Now without the 94th Ohio, the rest of Scribner's men continued on their original course. Within minutes the front line struck Wilson's Georgians and routed them handily, uncovering Croxton's front as they did so. None of Scribner's regiments recorded this initial collision as anything other than an easy affair. "We were soon driving him before us and capturing many prisoners," noted Lt. Angus L. Waddle, adjutant of the 33rd Ohio. The 4th Louisiana Battalion, adjacent to the Georgia sharpshooters, suffered the worst with an overall loss of 60 percent, with 68 men (30 percent of their engaged strength of 228) missing. The sharpshooters suffered fewer losses, including only four missing, but were equally disrupted. Both units broke to the rear, exposing the left flank of the surprised 30th Georgia. The surprise appearance of another Federal line on their left, admitted James Boynton of the 30th, "compelled [us] to retire a short distance." However, he added, "The men were promptly reformed." Private Adamson remembered that the 30th "pressed forward until the terrible firing from both front and flank tore [our] ranks to pieces." Colonel Thomas Mangham fell here, leaving Boynton in charge, but with his loss the 30th Georgia dissolved into chaos.[79]

Scribner's regiments swept forward and swung to the left. Lieutenant Colonel Daniel F. Griffin of the 38th Indiana reported that his command

---

77 Entry for September 19, Thompson Diary, WHS.

78 *OR* 30, pt. 1, 297. In fact, Baird did not order a similar change of course for the rest of Scribner's men. Scribner's line was engaged before Baird reached him.

79 Waddle, *Three Years with the Armies of the Ohio and the Cumberland*, 51; Powell, "Numbers and Losses," CCNMP; Report of the 30th Georgia, CCNMP; Adamson, *30th Georgia*, 35.

conducted "a very rapid movement . . . for three fourths of a mile" until the line "halted on the crest of a hill, with a cornfield on our left and front." From the far side of that field, Confederate artillery threw shells in their direction. Captain Evan P. Howell's Georgia Battery, with two outmoded six-pounders and four 12-pound howitzers, had been struggling along in the wake of Wilson's infantry without a good opportunity to engage the Federals until Scribner's men arrived. Grasping the need to bolster Wilson's collapsing flank, Howell ordered his gunners to deploy one section into action on the east side of Winfrey Field to cover the brigade's retreat. Their stand was a brief one. Within minutes a deadly fire from the 2nd Ohio killed all the horses serving one of the pieces and dropped a number of the crew, forcing Howell to abandon one gun as he departed. "Our regiment charged on a battery," exclaimed Cpl. Charles E. Brown of the 2nd Ohio, "and killed all the horses, took the men prisoners, except them that was killed or run away."[80]

Wilson, meanwhile, found himself caught up rallying the 30th Georgia and lost track of his other regiments. He later reported that the 25th and 29th fell in with Ector, while the two battalions (1st Georgia Sharpshooters and 4th Louisiana) were only rallied back near Jay's Mill behind other reinforcements (perhaps Dibrell's cavalry) then arriving near that point. Fortunately for the Confederates, the Federals were not interested in a strong pursuit; both Wilson and Ector fell back unmolested and began reforming their broken commands.[81]

Croxton's men suffered significant losses and shot away most of their ammunition in repulsing Wilson's attack. Accordingly, when King's Regulars appeared Croxton took the opportunity to disengage and fall back, reforming around Battery C of the 1st Ohio posted on a ridge some 300 yards to the rear. His men refilled their cartridge boxes with another 60 rounds and awaited further orders.[82]

So far, aside from setting the original forces in motion, neither Thomas, Brannan, nor Baird had much luck controlling the developing fight. Both Croxton and Van Derveer had largely operated on their own hook, while chance more than planning placed King and Scribner on exposed Rebel flanks. The four Federal brigades fought four small independent battles while

---

80 OR 30, pt. 1, 290; Tablet, Brotherton Road near Winfrey Field, CCNMP; "My Dear Father," September 23, 1863, transcript from Ebay auction, copy in author's possession.

81 OR 30, pt. 2, 249

82 Ibid., pt. 1, 416.

Connell's and Starkweather's troops spent a fair amount of time either waiting in the woods or marching back and forth while their commanders tried to decide where best to commit them.

Just as Baird had interfered with Scribner's command to send the 94th Ohio off on a tangent, so had Thomas interfered with Starkweather. At 10:00 a.m. Baird ordered Starkweather to move up behind King and Scribner, connecting their lines and supporting their attack where needed. Thomas almost immediately countermanded this directive. Unaware that they had already been relieved by King, Thomas wanted Starkweather to replace Croxton's men.[83]

A Milwaukee attorney with spectacular facial hair including an elaborate mustache and sideburns in the style of Union Maj. Gen. Ambrose Burnside, Starkweather marched around in the woods for awhile, discovered that King and Croxton had already sorted things out, and finally halted his command in an open stand of cedars on a rise about a third of a mile northwest of Winfrey Field. Despite this small confusion, Thomas's foresight had placed Baird's division where it was needed most when they departed Kelly Field, and they played the decisive role in the initial action.[84]

Until 10:00 a.m., the Confederates lacked even that amount of tactical control. Forrest fed troops into the fight one brigade at a time, managing each crisis in the moment but without much regard for a larger battle plan or for Bragg's overall strategy. Wilson and Ector were each asked to fight larger enemy forces without support, and suffered accordingly.

The increasing volume of the fight to the north, however, was drawing more attention from Bragg and his other commanders.

83 Ibid., 299.

84 Tablet for Starkweather's Brigade, near Winfrey Field, CCNMP.

Chapter Twelve

Slugging It Out in Winfrey Field:

Saturday, September 19: 9:00 a.m. to 11:00 a.m.

Despite earlier orders to loan a brigade to General Forrest, William H. T. Walker apparently expected nothing much to develop in that direction beyond a little skirmishing. Thus, when the noise of heavy battle swelled as Claudius Wilson's brigade slammed into Croxton's men, and rose to an entirely different level in a second crescendo when Matt Ector went in, Walker was caught off-guard. Captain Cumming recalled that Walker was sitting with General Hood, the latter's arm in the sling from his Gettysburg wound, when "great was our astonishment . . . to hear the outbreak of heavy firing . . . on our right." Thomas Claiborne, on Simon Buckner's staff, recalled the same moment. Breaking off his conversation in mid-sentence, Walker exclaimed, "By God! They are attacking my division!" A hurried discussion with General Bragg produced an order for Walker to "attack with all the force I had" should the need arise. Walker and Cumming mounted their horses and rode north as the various other generals in attendance dispersed to attend to their respective commands.[1]

The astonished Walker reined in his horse at the front only to be greeted with the news that Forrest had commandeered Ector without asking, the Federals were present in large numbers, and both Wilson and Ector were now

---

1 Cumming Recollections, UNC; Thomas Claiborne Letter, CCNMP; *OR* 30, pt. 2, 240.

retreating. Despite a legendary temper that verged on "volcanic rashness," there was no time for recriminations. Walker did what any good leader would do: he assessed the unfolding situation and assumed command of his troops. After a short reconnaissance, the Reserve Corps commander rode back the mile or so south to bring Liddell's division forward.[2]

Ector and Wilson combined had numbered some 2,500 bayonets with six cannon before being pitched into the nascent battle. Nearly half of those men were already down, and one of the artillery pieces abandoned on the field. Liddell's division, also comprised of but two brigades, brought considerably more firepower onto the field with its 4,031 men and eight pieces of artillery. This time, the Confederates would not be fed piecemeal into action one brigade at a time.

Liddell's troops were lying along the Viniard-Alexander Road, stacked up behind Hood's Corps in a column nearly a mile long. Word from Walker put the two brigades into line of battle facing north, with Daniel Govan's Arkansans and Louisianans on the left and Edward Walthall's Mississippians on the right. Leaving the troops to pick their way north through the timber, Walker and Liddell rode ahead so the latter could get a look at the Federals he would be engaging. The sight that greeted both officers from their vantage point in the woods somewhere south of Winfrey Field was alarming. "A corps of the enemy was about being thrown forward to turn our right wing," Liddell reported, "which it was absolutely necessary to meet promptly." Walker concurred and ordered Liddell to attack. He sent word of his decision to Bragg.[3]

For the Federals, the battle had settled into a fitful lull. Baird's division (Scribner, Starkweather, and King) replaced Croxton's brigade, but did not form an organized line. Absalom Baird was a professional, a West Point graduate in the class of 1849. He had seen active tours against the Seminoles and on the Texas border, but had spent most of his time in the Old Army as a professor at the academy. Since the war broke out he had led a brigade and then a division in Kentucky for the better part of a year, but thus far had not commanded at either level in battle. On August 4, 1863, General Rosecrans

---

2 Walker's irritation with Ector's seizure is evident in his report: "(Ector having also been taken . . . without any authority from me . . . .)" See *OR* 30, pt. 2, 240. As for "volcanic rashness," see Davis, "A Georgia Firebrand," 1.

3 *OR* 30, pt. 2, 261. Captain Meek's report, commanding the combined 2nd and 15th Arkansas, makes it clear that the two brigades formed line immediately. *OR* 30, pt. 2, 251.

Absalom Baird, postwar photograph. His division moved up to support John Brannan's troops.

Albion W. Tourgee

ordered Baird to report to George Thomas for an assignment at the head of the First Division, XIV Corps, temporarily replacing Maj. Gen. Lovell H. Rousseau, who was on detached duty. Rousseau was a tough act to follow. The aggressive and immensely popular Kentucky lawyer-turned-soldier had performed well at both Perryville and Stones River, and was regarded by both Thomas and Rosecrans as one of the better division commanders in the Union Army of the Cumberland. But that September Rousseau was absent in Washington, lobbying for mounting his division in an effort to meet the unceasing Federal demand for more cavalry. He was due back any day, but had not yet returned. For the time being, Rousseau's division remained in the hands of a former professor who had never led a large organization under fire, and who had only assumed command on August 28, on the very eve of the new campaign.[4]

After their initial clash, Baird's three brigades came to rest more or less haphazardly. General King pulled four of his battalions back onto the ridge around Burnham's cannon, but left 1/18th U.S. a couple of hundred yards off to the right, down the slope and in the woods—apparently lost for the moment. Colonel Scribner's 94th Ohio, equally wayward, halted nearby. Both units were flushed with easy success after tangling with and chasing off part of Wilson's brigade (probably the 25th and 29th Georgia), and awaited further instructions.[5]

---

4 Ibid., pt. 3, 4; William L. Johnson, "Diary of Sergeant W. L. Johnson, of Company C, 33d Regiment, Ohio Volunteer Infantry," *Fifth Annual Report of the Chief of the Bureau of Military Statistics* (Van Benthuysen & Sons, 1868), 685.

5 Entry for September 19, James E. Edmonds Diary, AHEC.

Scribner formed the rest of his regiments along the north side of Winfrey Field, facing southeast. The 2nd Ohio held the brigade's left, the 33rd Ohio the center, and the 38th Indiana the right. Battery A, 1st Michigan Light Artillery, unlimbered on the 38th's right in the woods just behind the northeast apex of the field, with the 10th Wisconsin deployed in its right rear in support. Little concern was paid to the brigade's right flank, though negligence had nothing to do with the oversight. Both Baird and Scribner thought that flank was secure because Thomas had sent word that John Palmer's division of the XXI Corps was moving up to support them from that direction. Indeed, Scribner's 38th Indiana reported that the regiment's skirmishers had moved through Palmer's advance, thus confirming Thomas's assertion. Baird passed word down the ranks warning his men not to fire into them by mistake. Sergeant William L. Johnson in Company C of the 33rd Ohio noted that soldiers had a particular fear of friendly fire: "It makes a person tremble with horror to think he may be shot by his own men;" such cautions were "continually the cry of our officers in battle." The men from Palmer's division, however, had moved on and were no longer there.[6]

Expecting to be outflanked at any moment, Maj. Gen. Tom Crittenden had ridden to the left of his line at 7:40 a.m., where the regiments of Col. William Grose's brigade, part of Palmer's division, were deploying. When he did not spot any enemy activity to his front, Crittenden ordered Grose's brigade to "make a reconnaissance" up the La Fayette Road "to ascertain if [it] . . . was clear and . . . if Colonel McCook . . . held the bridge at Reed's Mill." Grose's men set off a short while later, and sometime after 9:00 a.m. made contact with Baird's right and part of the 38th Indiana. Naturally enough, Thomas and Baird assumed Grose's men had arrived in response to Thomas's request (sent shortly before Grose appeared), for support for his own attack. Grose, of course, knew nothing about Thomas's request or plans and had departed on his mission well before that message reached Palmer. Grose arrived just as Baird's men were going forward, the din of Brannan's battle fully audible. Grose formed his own regiments in line on Baird's right, facing east, but did not advance. A few minutes later Baird's division easily routed Forrest's impromptu offensive, and the noise subsided. Matters on that part of the field seemed well in hand, so

---

6 OR 30, pt. 1, 290, 293, 295; and sketch map, Scribner Papers, InHS; OR 30, pt. 1, 275, 290; Johnson, "Diary of Sergeant W. L. Johnson," 684.

Grose retraced his steps south to report back to Crittenden. His departure seems to have passed unnoticed by any in the XIV Corps.[7]

The mood of the men in the ranks of Scribner's command soared after their easy victory. "They can't fight us; the bloody First [Division] is too much for them!!!" exclaimed Col. Oscar Moore of the 33rd Ohio. In the 2nd Ohio, Sgt. Samuel B. Price marveled at how neatly the enemy had been routed. "They seemed to be glad of a chance to get to surrender," observed Price. Even when a section of Capt. Evan P. Howell's Georgia Battery dropped trail 150 yards distant in an attempt to cover Wilson's retreat, scattering "shell, grape and canister among us," continued Price, the fire served to only further tempt the ebullient Buckeyes. "Why in the name of God don't we take that piece?" Price heard an officer exclaim. Before anyone could organize a charge, however, Scribner's fire forced Howell to limber and withdraw, leaving one gun on the field. The general hilarity and buoyant atmosphere was cut short when the brigade surgeon arrived with startling news: "The enemy is in your rear and on your right," he informed Scribner. "They have taken my field hospital with all the wounded! They have captured Capt. DeBruin, the provost guard, and all the prisoners and are coming down upon you like a pack of wolves."[8]

Scribner cut no great martial figure, and thus far the campaign had been rough on him. His hay fever remained unabated, and he still wore his "goggles," the same accoutrement that had caused such frantic searching while under fire in McLemore's Cove the week previous. Fortunately for Scribner and his men he hung onto his makeshift spectacles this time around, for there was no time to stop the action now. The alarmed Scribner sent aides scuttling in every direction to inform the rest of the division of the impending blow, and dispatched Lt. George Devol to warn Palmer's division. What Scribner didn't know, of course, was that Palmer's men (Grose's brigade) weren't where he supposed them to be. Instead of blue uniforms Devol found only Rebels, who he somehow managed to elude before making haste to find General Thomas.[9]

7   OR 30, pt. 1, 606; Ebenezer Hannaford, *The Story of a Regiment: A History of the Campaigns, and Associations in the Field, of the Sixth Regiment Ohio Volunteer Infantry* (published by the Author, 1868), 462.

8   Richard A. Baumgartner, ed. *The Bully Boys: In Camp and Combat with the 2nd Ohio Volunteer Infantry Regiment 1861-1864* (Blue Acorn Press, 2011), 404; Scribner, *How Soldiers Were Made,* 145.

9   Scribner, *How Soldiers Were Made,* 140-141, 146.

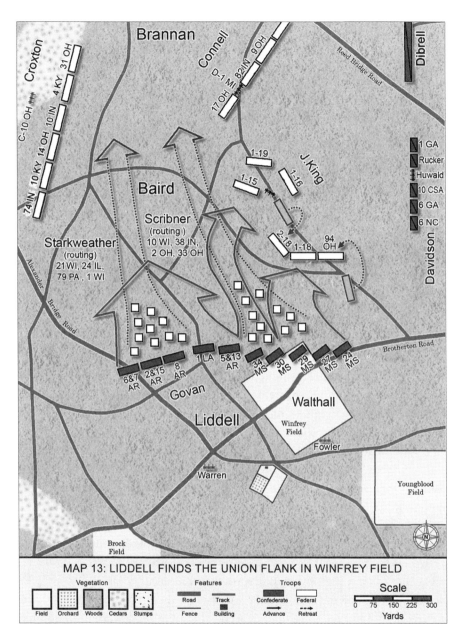

MAP 13: LIDDELL FINDS THE UNION FLANK IN WINFREY FIELD

The cause for the unrest on the Union side of the front was owing to St. John Liddell. The Confederate division commander had deployed the regiments of both of his brigades abreast in a line extending nearly three quarters of a mile. He now overlapped both of Scribner's flanks. Walthall's skirmishers on the right front were the first to engage, bursting into the

Winfrey Field, looking southwest. Walthall's men crossed this field from left to right, using the Brotherton Road as a natural trench. The original dirt roadbed was much lower at the time of the battle. *Harvey Scarborough*

southern end of Winfrey Field while the main line was still passing the Winfrey cabin several hundred feet behind them. Within minutes Walthall's wall of men stepped into the open and made for the surprised Federal line. The 34th, 30th, and 29th Mississippi, left to right, tramped through the open field while the 27th and 24th on their right skirted its eastern edge.

Walthall's advance did not end up as a single impetuous rush, though it began that way. Private James Brewer of the 34th was in that main line of the assault. "We had gone but a little ways before our skirmishers laid down and the line passed over them," noted Brewer. The Brotherton Road bisected the field about midway across, and the eroded nature of the roadway proved an irresistible lure for the Mississippians. Colonel William F. Brantley, leading the 29th Mississippi along the eastern edge of the field, was startled to see his entire regiment suddenly lie down in the depression as if on cue, without any orders to do so. Over on the right flank in the woods with the 24th Mississippi, Lt. Col. Robert P. McKelvaine thought the abrupt stop was intended and followed suit by ordering his men down into the roadway. The timing could not have been better. The Rebel line went to ground just as a Federal volley ripped out, saving the lives of many a Mississippian. Captain J. D. Smith reported that despite "the enemy's fire at . . . not more than 50 yards . . . [we] did not suffer much."[10]

Despite their surprise, Scribner's men initially reacted well. Their fire might not have dropped as many Rebels as intended, but its severity impressed Walthall. "My line was checked for a moment by a heavy artillery and musketry fire," reported the Mississippian. Years later, Captain Smith recalled this dive into the ditch as a carefully pre-arranged tactic, but if so, none of the official reports at the time took note. Pre-planned or not, the initial heavy advance followed by the pause at the road disconcerted the Federals. Within minutes "the order was given to charge," reported Col. James Campbell of the 27th Mississippi. "The men of my regiment with a shout rose and drove the enemy in their front."[11]

On Liddell's left, Govan advanced his brigade on the west side of the Winfrey Field. Govan's right flank also took heavy fire, but without the benefit of the same impromptu cover of the roadbed enjoyed by the Mississippians. As the skirmishers engaged fire, Walthall briefly conferred with an old friend, Col. Lucius Featherston of the 5th Arkansas, who was commanding both his own 5th and the 13th Arkansas regiment adjacent Walthall's left. The 5th/13th "advanced but a short distance when we received the enemy's fire," recalled Sgt. John T. Rone of Company C, who went on to note that Federal artillery fire "made [a] great opening" in their ranks. Featherston was cut down in the first rush. He snatched up the regimental flag when the color guard was decimated, but caught a bullet in the hip. The wound bled profusely and he died shortly after reaching the field hospital.[12]

Walthall, who had just started to advance his own brigade again, witnessed Featherston's difficulties. He galloped over, rallied the Arkansans, and led them forward. Walthall cut an imposing figure. One Rebel described him as "about three inches [over] six feet high, 175 pounds, and one of the finest looking men in the Confederacy." He rode "a superb charger," though the observer thought

10 James I. Brewer, Oct 2nd 1863, http://www.rootsweb.com~mscivilw/brewerletters.htm, accessed 8/16/2013; OR 30, pt. 2, 281; Ibid., 278.

11 OR 30, pt. 2, 273; J. D. Smith, "Walthall's Brigade At Chickamauga," Confederate Veteran, vol. XII, no. 10 (October, 1904), 483. Colonel Brantley's report makes it clear that the men went to ground without orders. OR 30, pt. 2, 280.

12 John T. Rone, "First Arkansas Brigade At Chickamauga," Confederate Veteran, vol. XIII, no. 4 (April, 1905), 167; OR 30, pt. 2, 263.

he sported a "peculiar mustache." Union artillery blasts scoured the field, and one of the rounds brought down the crown of a black-jack scrub oak, snaring Walthall and his mount in its grasp. While the Mississippi brigadier struggled to free himself, the Razorbacks of the 5th/13th streamed past and crashed into waiting Scribner's 10th Wisconsin.[13]

The Federals fought hard, but did so at a grave disadvantage no one could have seen coming. Lieutenant George W. Van Pelt's 1st Michigan Battery was well known as a prewar militia unit. The outfit, initially named the Coldwater Light Artillery, and then Loomis's Battery after its first commander, earned a full measure of fame at Stones River. Even their opponents were aware of its outstanding reputation. Assailed front and flank, the Wolverine gunners swung their pieces to the right and opened fire. The belching pieces failed to check the attack. "Van Pelt fired sixty-four rounds of double-shotted canister right into their faces without seeming to disturb the enemy," reported a stunned Scribner.[14]

The 10th Wisconsin began this stage of the fight in reserve, slightly behind and to the right of Van Pelt's battery. When the guns turned to fire into the charging Confederates, the Badgers found themselves prone in front of the firing guns, head forward on a downward slope. To stand risked being blown apart, and remaining prone meant they couldn't easily reload if they could reload at all. Before the Wolverines could engage the enemy, however, someone yelled for the men to get to their feet and open fire, recalled Lt. Lucius Hinkley of Company K, "but Van Pelt's gunners, with lanyards ready to pull, shouted: 'Lie down!' 'Lie down!' which for a moment kept our boys flat, while the canister from the guns hissed over them."[15]

Badger Augustus Bratnober of Company F watched the seemingly unstoppable Confederates sweep through their own skirmishers. "After the front line fired the next line passed through them, the first line reloading as they came on," recalled Bratnober, "our fire fairly stunned them but we could not reload without rising up." Situated in such an awkward and dangerous position, the 10th broke. "Somehow," marveled Lieutenant Hinkley, the men "got from

---

13 "Dear Cousin," John D. Williams to Julia Williams, September 28, 1863, Tennessee Civil War Records typescripts, vol. 3, 44, TSLA; Rone, "First Arkansas Brigade," 167.

14 Scribner, *How Soldiers Were Made*, 147.

15 Lucius Dwight Hinkley, *Fourth Annual Reunion of the Tenth Wisconsin Infantry Held at Tomah, Wis., July 21 and 22, 1898* (Oliver Brothers, Printer, 1898), 33.

under the muzzles of the cannon and to the rear." Amid the artillery, "horses and men were falling; Van Pelt was killed. His gunners attempted to limber . . . but with wounded men . . . and horses entangled in the harness, they were unable to clear the guns, and two pieces fell into the hands of the enemy." Van Pelt died slashing at the Rebels with his saber as they closed in around him. Three more guns were overrun as they started to retreat. Only one piece was salvaged by the crew.[16]

When the storm broke, Scribner attempted to pull the 38th Indiana back at right angles to the 33rd Ohio to face this outflanking onslaught. Indiana Lt. Col. Daniel Griffin, the commander of the 38th, reported that his fire initially checked the Rebels, but when they renewed their advance, "raking both fronts of the brigade with an enfilading fire of musketry" the 38th's left gave way. Only the 33rd and 2nd Ohio were left to stem the advance. Concentrating on the Mississippians to their front, Pvt. McLain Montgomery in the 33rd noted that he and his comrades held their first volley until Walthall's line was just 75 yards away. "Being flanked, [our] line gave way," recalled Capt. Joseph Hinson, the commander of Company D of the 33rd. In the retreat that soon followed Hinson took a wound that cost him an arm. The retreat of the 33rd left the 2nd Ohio alone, forlornly clinging to the original line that was no longer there. "The right of the brigade gave way by regiments, successively, until the Second Ohio retired." Lieutenant Colonel O. C. Maxwell of the 2nd fell here, "pierced through by two minie balls." His crippling wounds forced him out of the service. Within minutes of assuming command, the 2nd's Maj. William Beatty was down as well. Like the rest of the brigade, the 2nd gave way and fell back in "considerable disorder." Scribner's collapse was complete.[17]

Somehow the entire disaster missed the 94th Ohio. The first Major Hutchins knew of any threat beyond and behind his right flank was when he heard the noise of battle erupt in that direction. Hutchins dispatched a staff officer to investigate the meaning of the firing. The officer, explained Hutchins, "returned and reported that the enemy were in our rear, and that we were to fall back to the support of the regulars." The Buckeyes of the 94th were so far east

---

16 August Bratnober, "Extracts from diary" 10th Wisconsin file, CCNMP; Hinkley, *Fourth Reunion of the Tenth Wisconsin*, 32-33; Waddle, *Three Years*, 51.

17 OR 30, pt. 1, 290; As quoted in Lois J. Lambert, *Heroes of the Western Theater: 33rd Ohio Veteran Volunteer Infantry* (Little Miami Publishing Co., 2008), 175; Joseph Hinson, "Kicked With Artillery," *National Tribune*, March 26, 1896; Waddle, *Three Years*, 52; Johnson, "Diary of Sergeant W. L. Johnson," 684; Reid, *Ohio in the War*, vol. 2, 973; OR 30, pt. 1, 293.

that Walthall's right flank passed entirely to the west of them before the Rebels turned and broke the 2nd Ohio's left flank.[18]

The Rebel assault may have missed the 94th Ohio, but it didn't spare Starkweather's brigade or its supporting artillery. The noise of Scribner's engagement to the northeast drew Starkweather's attention, and before long he discovered enemy troops turning his own right flank. Like Scribner, he hurriedly ordered his brigade to wheel and meet the onslaught. Barked commands rang out, and his four regiments began their evolutions.[19]

Starkweather's brigade was facing east when the Confederate attack began. The 1st Wisconsin held the left and 79th Pennsylvania the right of the first line, while the 21st Wisconsin and 24th Illinois comprised the second, in the same order. Lieutenant David Flansburg's 4th Indiana battery was in the center of the formation, though still limbered. With this new threat, Starkweather intended to move the front line forward and to the right, facing south to meet the oncoming Rebels head on and support Scribner's endangered flank.[20]

To the men in the ranks, the enemy's attack seemed like a bolt from the blue. "While advancing, and just as the crest of a little hill had been reached, the brigade received a volley that it would have taken something higher than human courage to face," wrote Sgt. Edward McGlachlin of Company K, 1st Wisconsin. To German-born Cpl. John Eicker in the 79th Pennsylvania, it seemed as if "the brigade was pounced upon by the enemy laying in ambush." Caught in the very center of this maelstrom, Joseph C. Haddock of the 4th Indiana battery resorted to the supernatural to explain the appearance of the enemy: "While moving at a right oblique though a dense forest of saplings, the rebel infantry arose as if by magic, & poured in a fire that threatened to annihilate us."[21]

Captain William S. McCaskey was a strongly opinionated young Pennsylvanian from Lancaster. The staunch Republican and Unionist enlisted as a private in April 1861 before reenlisting as a sergeant in Company B of the 79th Pennsylvania that same September. McCaskey was in charge of the

18 Ibid., 297.

19 Ibid., 300.

20 Ibid., 303-305, provide a series of sketches illustrating Starkweather's intended deployments.

21 McGlachlin, "Reminiscences," 23; John Eicker Memoir, 14, Harrisburg CWRT Collection, AHEC; Joseph C. Haddock, "Historical Sketch of the 4th Indiana Battery," InHS.

regiment's skirmish line at the moment of contact, and was just deploying his men when the blow landed. "I . . . had not gotten them into position before they received a murderous fire from the enemy," explained the captain. The skirmishers bolted, falling back behind the regiment. McCaskey was trying to rally them when the entire brigade unraveled around him: "The line had broken, all confused, and in every continuance you could see dispair [and] surprise."[22]

Some of the Federals halted and attempted to return fire, but the sudden shock of being attacked without warning had men already breaking ranks. A Pennsylvania lieutenant named John Johnston, also in the 79th, remembered the increasing panic and breaking of the brigade: "Starkweather's voice can be heard, but the rattle of the musketry renders his commands too indistinct to be understood. . . .There is a buzz and confusion on the right of the regiment—it wavers, it breaks. 'Steady boys, steady, for God's sake don't run away!' says Captain Heidigger, and almost the same instant he falls to the ground mortally wounded. . . . [Then] the whole brigade is in confusion and running to the rear."[23]

Johnston was wrong. The entire brigade was not yet "running to the rear," though it soon would be. The routed front line, Johnston included, crashed into and through Starkweather's supporting 21st Wisconsin and 24th Illinois. Lieutenant John Otto, commanding Company D of the 21st, watched in horror as "the battery horses fell like flies," dropping with many of the crew still mounted upon them. Among them fell the 4th Indiana's Lieutenant Flansburg, which passed command to Lt. Henry J. Willits. Meanwhile, the Badgers of the 21st struggled to return fire, going to one knee and fixing bayonets. To Samuel H. Fernandez, a sergeant on the regimental staff, it was as if "thousands of perfect demons let loose on us, in the dark and thick wood." Lieutenant Otto was standing behind a thin chestnut tree when he spotted one of the battery animals tearing through the line in a panic, its hooves striking Pvt. Maurice Grunert and "sending him spinning, heels over head, backwards like a little rubber ball." It would be three days before the dazed Grunert recovered enough to return to the ranks.[24]

22 Hank Chapman, ed. *The Letters of William S. McCaskey* (Infinity Publishing Group, 2008), 35.

23 John M. Johnston, "At Chickamauga, A Soldier's Story of the Battle," *The Lancaster New Era*, September 10, 1892.

24 "From the 21st Regiment," *Wisconsin State Journal*, October 5, 1863; John Henry Otto Memoir, 243, WHS.

The 24th Illinois, a mixed German and Hungarian outfit from Chicago holding the right-rear of Starkweather's line, enjoyed a measure of fame in the army. Comprised largely of exiled European revolutionaries fleeing from the 1848 uprisings, it claimed to be the first ethnic German unit raised for the war. Many of the officers and men had military experience in Europe, a fact that greatly contributed to Gen. Ulysses S. Grant's 1861 assessment that the 24th was the best-drilled unit under his command. In 1862, under Brig. Gen. John Turchin, the regiment was involved in the infamous sacking of Athens, Alabama, an act of retribution for local partisan activity that earned Turchin and a number of others a courts-martial.[25]

Now these Germans and Hungarians found themselves deep within the woods of Georgia struggling to hold a crumbling line of battle. Colonel Goza Mihalotzy was shot through the right wrist in the first volley, but refused to leave the fight. Mihalotzy sheathed his saber and, with his reins clutched in his teeth, wrapped a handkerchief around the wound and set about holding his men to their task. Starkweather attempted to withdraw what was left of his brigade slowly to the left rear, but with only limited success. "I halt a moment in rear of the 24th Illinois," recounted Lt. John Johnston of the 79th Pennsylvania, "and do all I can to check the retreating fugitives—but it is only for a moment. . . The rebels fiercely attack the second line in overwhelming numbers, and . . . after a very few volleys, [we] waver, break and run."

Captain McCaskey, also of the 79th, despaired anew. "The second line had stood only until we had passed them," he lamented, "and [then] they broke indiscriminately, firing upon our own men & etc. Here is where the majority of our brave boys fell."[26]

Private Alfred Galpin of the 1st Wisconsin was detailed to Flansburg's 4th Indiana battery when the Rebels attacked that morning. "We unlimbered and limbered up twice," he recalled, "but could not get in a single shot." Three other guns managed to get off a round of canister or two each, but could not prevent the Confederates from sweeping over their position. Galpin was one of those overrun. "We all very wisely dropped to the ground at the first volley (which took a button off my blouse)." He and several companions played dead as the

---

25 For a more detailed look at this incident, see Roy Morris, Jr., "The Sack of Athens," *Civil War Times Illustrated*, vol. 25, no. 2 (February, 1986), 26-32.

26 John Henry Otto Memoir, 244, WHS; Johnston, "At Chickamauga;" Chapman, *William S. McCaskey*, 35.

Rebels ran through, over, and around them. When they deemed it safe to do so, Galpin and his mates scrambled to their feet and, using an "empty infantry musket," promptly captured a Confederate laggard. Somehow they managed to take their "Johnny" to the rear. Once there, they treated him to a "very fair dinner. He was much surprised and said 'Well! Boys, you treat a feller right.' [He] enjoyed the coffee tremendously." On that civilized note, the prisoner was sent into captivity.[27]

For the moment, the rout was complete, with the men of both Scribner's and Starkweather's brigades fleeing hundreds of yards through the woods toward Kelly Field. Some of them came upon George Thomas and his escort, a detail from Company L of the 1st Ohio Cavalry. Sergeant Edward P. Burlingame of the escort dryly noted, "there was evidently a slight panic & the movement to the rear was being made in confusion and haste. Officers and men were mixed indiscriminately and they rushed by the General paying no heed to the injunction, 'Look behind you.' Had they done so," continued Burlingame, "they would have stopped, for the rebels had ceased to advance." Thomas ordered "the detail under Sergeant [Daniel W.] Dye . . . to stop those who were fleeing but it was some time ere they could be convinced that they were out of danger." The panic was only a momentary aberration, for these same men, noted Burlingame, would later prove to be "faithful and courageous."[28]

For McCaskey, the catastrophe in the woods only affirmed his low opinion of the 79th Pennsylvania's commander, Col. Henry A. Hambright. McCaskey, zealous Republican that he was, had spent much of the past few months talking up emancipation and negro recruitment among the ranks of the 79th, winning over not a few converts in the process. To McCaskey's disgust, fellow Republican Hambright was less enthusiastic on the subject. That spring, noted the young firebrand, "when we got up those petitions denouncing Copperheadism, [Hambright] refused to sign them, saying that it would injure his friends at home." His colonel, concluded McCaskey, "is a two faced deceitful pimp." Now McCaskey added "coward" to that list, charging in a letter that "Hambright was in the rear and came up like a skiddelling after we reformed our line." McCaskey's charges were unfair, based more on their differences in politics and that Hambright previously favored other officers

---

27 Entry for September 19, Alfred Galpin Letters and Diary, WHS.

28 E. P. Burlingame to William Rufus Putnam, August 4, 1865, Samuel Hildreth Putnam Papers, Marietta College, Marietta, OH.

over McCaskey for the promotion to captain. Starkweather, by contrast, later noted that Hambright was among those "entitled to great praise for their coolness and bravery" during the fight.[29]

Meanwhile, Liddell's Confederate regiments moved on to their next target: John King's Regulars. Lieutenant Colonel Murray of the 5th/13th Arkansas reported that after Colonel Featherston's fall, "I immediately assumed command of the regiment and ordered it to press forward on the enemy's second line, which was done in gallant style, and this line . . . was soon broken and scattered as the first had been. . . . My command . . . soon engaged a third line." Murray's men and most of Walthall's Mississippians were about to crash into King's position.[30]

Like Starkweather, King had but the barest of warnings that hell was about to descend upon him. He was still busy positioning his lines after routing Matt Ector's brigade when Absalom Baird arrived and breathlessly ordered King "to make a new front at right angles with the other. I only had time, however, to get the Sixteenth Infantry and battery in position before being assailed by an overwhelming force." Once again the Federals were flanked and soon routed. Lieutenant Henry Haymond of the 18th Infantry described the abrupt reverse to his father: "Suddenly it was discovered that the enemy in fact was advancing up the ravine directly in our rear—We at once changed front to the rear . . . and formed a hasty line. We had scarcely got into position before a Division of Texas and Arkansas troops advanced upon us on the run, rushing over and capturing the battery before it could fire half a dozen rounds."[31]

King wrote too optimistically about getting the 16th turned and in line in time to face this new threat. Captain Robert Crofton, the ranking survivor in the battalion, related that "without any warning whatsoever, the rebels came up on our right flank and got right up on us before any disposition could be made to meet them. Consequently," he continued, "nearly the entire battalion was killed, wounded or captured." Only 62 of the battalion's 308 officers and men escaped. Battery H suffered a similar fate. Early in the engagement the battery's commander, 1st Lt. Howard M. Burnham fell with a mortal wound. "The battery was exposed to a most murderous fire of bullets; it was almost

---

29 Chapman, *William S. McCaskey*, 23, 35; *OR* 30, pt. 1, 302.

30 Ibid., pt. 2, 263.

31 Ibid., pt. 1, 309; "Dear Pa," Thursday night, September 24, 1863, Henry Haymond Letters, Navarro College, Corsciana, TX.

immediately taken by the enemy," noted 2nd Lt. Joshua Fessenden, one of the battery's two remaining officers. Lieutenant Fessenden and 2nd Lt. Israel Ludlow were also both wounded, Fessenden slightly and Ludlow severely enough to incapacitate him, resulting in his capture. A dozen more enlisted men were killed, 16 wounded, and another 13 captured. Sixty-five horses were also killed or wounded.[32]

The gun crews had only managed to fire four rounds of canister before being swept away, but one of the rounds created havoc within the Rebel ranks. A week after the battle, Lt. Augustus B. Carpenter of the 19th Infantry vividly recalled a desperate and defiant Union gunner standing by his double-shotted piece. The approaching Rebels just paces away informed him that "if he fired that gun they would kill him," Carpenter recounted. "'Kill and be damned,' said the sergeant, and jerked the string. The grape mowed a lane through the rebel ranks. The next moment the brave sergeant was pinned to the ground with rebel bayonets." Robert A. Jarman of the 27th Mississippi may have witnessed the same incident: "In our excitement and charge we ran through part of a line of Federal infantry in front of the guns, and I thought our time then had about come, but they surrendered to us and we pushed on to the battery that was just beginning to pay out grape and canister on the brigade . . . [we] killed the last gunner. . . . Each of us bounded astride of a gun and yelled our loudest, then we turned the loaded guns on the Yankees and gave them their own grape."[33]

All six guns and more than 400 Yankees were captured. King's overwhelmed survivors fled. Brief stands marked the scene as pockets of Regulars tried to rally, to no avail, bolting northward toward Col. Ferdinand Van Derveer's line of Federals deployed along the Reed's Bridge Road.[34]

Once away, all three of Baird's brigades gathered to reconstitute, discouraged and heartsick about what had so suddenly befallen them. Sergeant

---

32 OR 30, pt. 1, 318; *Memorial of Lieutenant Howard M. Burnham, United States Army, Who Fell in the Battle of Chickamauga, Tenn., September 19th, 1863* (Samuel Bowles And Company, Printers, 1864), 30; OR 30, pt. 1, 171, 324. Ludlow was a brother-in-law to Secretary of the Treasury Salmon P. Chase. Ludlow would be exchanged, but not recover; he would die of his wounds in a hospital in Cincinnati.

33 "Dear Uncle," Chattanooga, Tenn, Sept. 29th, 1863. A. B. Carpenter Letters, Yale University, New Haven, CT; Robert A. Jarman, "The History of Company K, 27th Mississippi Infantry," 17, MDAH.

34 Johnson, *That Body of Brave Men*, 387-391 provides an excellent, detailed description of the disaster.

Johnson of the 33rd Ohio took a few moments to scribble an assessment of General Baird's leadership in this, his first action as their division commander: "He appears brave on the battlefield, but he lacks confidence in himself—he lacks energy—he would do better to command an army of old women than an army of men."[35]

Thus far, Liddell's Rebels had achieved a stunning reversal of fortune. By 10:00 a.m., Matt Ector and Claudius Wilson had lost 50% of their complement and been all but routed off the field. By 11:30 a.m., Baird's Federals had suffered nearly the same fate, their batteries wrecked, and 1,200 prisoners were in Rebel hands. Smaller booty was also collected. "Some of the boys secured some such things as oilcloths canteens & a few blankets, but the only thing I got was a small steel watch key which one of the boys handed me after the fight," lamented James Brewer of the 34th Mississippi. Fellow Mississippian Capt. Joseph W. Ward of the 24th's Company L fared better, grabbing the sword of a first lieutenant. "The regulars thought it was a disgrace to them to be driven back and captured by volunteers," Ward chortled in a letter home.[36]

Baird's division had been wrecked, but the Confederates had shot their bolt and their own losses were not insignificant. Baird's Yankees might have been surprised, flanked, and driven back, but as Sgt. David R. Childers of the 34th Mississippi admitted, "We drove them for more than a mile, they shooting from behind trees—they fought well, yielded the ground very reluctantly." Moreover, both of Liddell's brigades were now disorganized, and Daniel Govan was well beyond any support and concerned about his own flanks. Liddell had warned earlier to be wary of his left, and Govan ordered Col. David Gillespie of the 6th/7th Arkansas to throw out a line of skirmishers to the west and prepare to change front quickly if threatened from that direction.[37]

When King's men fell back through the lines of the 2nd Minnesota and 87th Indiana, their sudden appearance with the Rebels hot on their heels could have caused similar consternation among Van Derveer's regiments. The

---

35 Johnson, "Diary of Sergeant W. L. Johnson," 685.

36 "Dear Mathilda," In front of Chattanooga, Oct. 2nd 1863, James I. Brewer letters, 34th Mississippi, http://www.rootsweb.ancestry.com/~mscivilw/brewerletters.htm, accessed 8/16/2013; "Dear Sister," Sept. 28 1863, J. W. Ward Letters, Barker Center for American History, University of Texas, Austin, TX.

37 "Dr Niece," 27 Septr/63, David R. Childers Letter, Sallie B. Veal Collection, GDAH; OR 30, pt. 2, 258.

pursuing Confederates, however, were no longer an unstoppable juggernaut because their own formations were disrupted and the men exhausted. The long-held disdain Van Derveer's volunteers felt for King's Regulars also served to fix the volunteers in place, lest they show fear in front of their rivals.

In later years, members of the 2nd Minnesota and 35th Ohio were highly critical of the Regulars' performance at Chickamauga. "I do not remember any more appalling spectacle," wrote Lt. Col. Judson Wade Bishop, "but our men took it with grim composure, lying down until the stampeded brigade had passed over our line." Captain Dunahower also recalled a great panic when he described in disgust how one Federal color bearer tossed his flag away just fifty yards shy of the 2nd's line.[38]

The 2nd Minnesota had no great respect for the Regulars since their encounter the year before, and it is possible these postwar accounts are exaggerated. Contemporary sources leave little doubt, however, that King's men were involved in an undeniable rout. Sergeant Brown of the 87th Indiana noted, "as we were lying down, they run over us . . . their officers . . . trying to rally their men, but they effected nothing." Private Peter Keegan, also of the 87th, recorded the scene in his diary: "Soon the Rebels rallied and came up in force, driving before them in disorder the Brig. of regulars. The 15th Reg. passed over us-87- in perfect rout. We remained still receiving this fire while the regulars passed . . . . [Then] we opened upon [the Rebels] pouring into them a deadly volley."[39]

This new Federal line, suddenly ablaze with fire, stunned Walthall's pursuing Mississippians. "A sharp contest with musketry followed," reported Colonel George of the 2nd Minnesota, "which resulted in a few minutes in the complete repulse of the late exultant enemy." Through the fortunes of war, Minnesota Pvt. Edgar Dickey temporarily found himself amongst the Mississippians and on the receiving end of this fire. Dickey's good friend, William S. Wells, had been shot in the thigh, and Dickey carried him about "fifty paces" off the firing line where the Rebel wounded were being collected to await the ambulances. It was at this time the Regulars came crashing through the trees, and "the doctors and all of them that were tending the wounded run

38 Bishop, *Van Derveer's Brigade*, 7-8; Dunahower, "The Chattanooga Campaign," 115.

39 Johnson, *That Body of Brave Men*, 391, 702, fn 24; Sgt. Benjamin F. Brown, "From the 87th Regiment, Indiana Vols." *Rochester Chronicle*, October 15, 1863; Entry for September 19, Peter Keegan Diary, InSL.

to save their lives." Dickey dragged Wells into a small hollow and, in a bout of quick thinking, feigned a wound himself. Confederates were all around him. As he lay there, he listened to "the groans and shrieks that came from the wounded . . . as the bullets would pierce them the second, third, fourth and even fifth time." Dickey was sure he would be killed by his comrades' fire, but within a few minutes Walthall's men began falling back and the firing abated.[40]

Their retreat spurred Colonel Kammerling into action. Kammerling, it will be recalled, was dismayed to be left behind guarding ammunition while there was a prospect of a fight. Aggressive to a fault, the German ex-revolutionary enlisted in the 9th Ohio during the early days of the war, and was in command of the regiment by August 1862. Kammerling and the 9th Ohio arrived too late for the first action, and so was more witness than participant in this fight since Walthall's front had narrowed considerably by the time his ragged line of Mississippians reached Van Derveer's position. Now, with the Confederates in retreat, Kammerling was more than ready to take the fight to them. "Chafing like a wounded tiger," marveled Van Derveer, Kamemerling "ordered his men to charge." The 9th, 502 men strong, took off at a run. The surprised 87th Indiana surged forward as well in an effort to catch up with the charging Buckeyes.[41]

The 9th came into the line between the 87th Indiana and Connell's brigade. Out on the Union right flank, the 82nd Indiana, 17th Ohio, and Battery D of the 1st Michigan added their fire to Van Derveer's. Like the 2nd Minnesota and 87th Indiana, Col. Morton Hunter had his 82nd Indiana hold their fire until the Regulars cleared their front, and then, "when within fifty yards of us, the battery and the Eighty-Second Indiana opened fire . . . the firing . . . was so sudden and so deadly that it gave them a check; in an instant, almost, they were on the retreat." With the 9th Ohio and 87th Indiana lunging forward, it seemed like a general counterattack was underway. Hunter also advanced with tight control,

---

40 *OR* 30, pt. 1, 433; "Dear Father and Mother," Camp Chattanooga, September 24, 1863, Edgar Van Buren Dickey Letters, Mankato State University, Mankato, MN. Dickey probably moved Wells to the brigade right, perhaps a bit to the south, instead of up the Reed's Bridge Road.

41 Constantine Grebner, with Frederic Trautmann, trans. and ed. *We Were The Ninth: A History of the Ninth Regiment, Ohio Volunteer Infantry April 17, 1861, to June 7, 1864* (Kent State University Press, 1987), 142; OR 30, pt. 1, 428; Peter S. Troutman, "From the 87th" *Rochester Chronicle*, May 19, 1864.

allowing his 82nd Indiana to go forward only far enough to clear "the enemy from our front."[42]

Not so with the 17th Ohio. "Bayonets were fixed and away we went with a yell," reported Capt. James W. Stinchcomb of Company A. With the combined weight of the 87th Indiana, and 9th and 17th Ohio bearing down upon them, the Rebels turned and fled. Rebel opposition was much lighter than anyone expected it might be. The 9th Ohio, at the forefront of this impromptu counterattack, lost 63 casualties, but neither the 87th Indiana nor the 17th Ohio lost a single man during this countercharge. By now, explained Sergeant Childers of the 34th Mississippi, "we had fought through 2 lines of the enemy—and had pierced the 3rd—when our men worn down and exhausted—thinned and riddled—we had to fall back." The Federal counterstroke quickly retook Burnham's Battery H, and the Yankees "hooted and yelled" when they did so.[43]

Van Derveer was as surprised as anyone when Kammerling tore off after the Rebels. He dispatched Capt. John R. Beatty, a Minnesotan serving on his staff, to race after the impetuous German. The hatless Beatty rode up just as the exuberant 9th milled around the guns in high excitement, "all talking at once." Beatty relayed Van Derveer's message for Kammerling to pull back his regiment. "I have gaptured a battery," replied the German, "Vot shall I do mit dis battery?" Beatty repeated the order for the exposed 9th to fall back; even now, another Rebel attack was materializing against Van Derveer's line. Stinchcomb and the rest of the 17th Ohio were out of breath, having "run them yelling like Indians, for three quarters of a mile . . . [now] we had to double quick about a half mile again."[44]

By now, many of the routed Regulars had rallied behind the 82nd Indiana. A detail from the 1/15th U.S., along with a limping Lieutenant Fessenden, returned to drag the guns off. The corpses of 45 artillery horses littered the ground, as did those of dead and wounded soldiers. The guns and four of the

---

42 Alfred G. Hunter, *History of the Eighty-Second Indiana Volunteer Infantry, its Organization, Campaigns and Battles* (Wm. B. Burford, Printer and Binder, 1893), 62-63.

43 "Letter from Captain Stinchcomb," *Lancaster Gazette*, October 8, 1863; September 19th, Peter Keegan Diary, InSL; Entry for September 19, John D. Inskeep Diary, OHS; "Dr Niece," 27 Septr/63, Childers Letters, Veal Collection, GDAH.

44 As quoted in A. H. Reed, "The Fourteenth Corps' Magnificent Stand Against Overwhelming Forces" *National Tribune*, September 21, 1916; "Letter from Captain Stinchcomb," *Lancaster Gazette*, October 8, 1863.

caissons were successfully retrieved, but the battery would not fight again at Chickamauga.[45]

Still concerned about the artillery pieces, Colonel Kammerling galloped ahead to find Van Derveer and when he did, he pulled his white mare up so hard that she nearly sat on her haunches. "'Colonel, Colonel, my Nint takes a battery. Vhat must I do mit him?' He was so excited and talking so fast that . . . Van Derveer said . . . 'speak slower; I can't understand a word you say.'"[46]

Van Derveer had no time to worry about Kammerling and his captured guns, and probably didn't appreciate the distraction. A few minutes earlier some of the 2nd Minnesota's skirmishers caught sight of a column of Rebels working their way across the Reed's Bridge Road moving north—an obvious threat to Van Derveer's own left flank. These Rebels were Col. George Dibrell's cavalry of Forrest's Corps, newly arrived and now dismounted. As Ector aptly demonstrated, a frontal attack was not likely to succeed. Instead, Forrest intended to feint against Van Derveer's front with some of his cavalry while the bulk of the brigade worked its way north of the road to descend on Van Derveer's left and rear.[47]

Each side left radically different impressions of this encounter. The Federals recalled it as an epic fight, the repulse of their fourth assault that morning that cut down the attackers in windrows. The paucity of detail from the Confederate side renders a clear picture difficult to ascertain, but Dibrell described the encounter as nothing more than a "heavy skirmish." His reported losses—about 50 men for the entire battle—support his version of the events and run contrary to Federals descriptions.[48]

Colonel George met this new threat by ordering his 2nd Minnesota to change front by companies successively to the left, first facing northeast and finally facing almost due north. There, according to George, "the enemy charged desperately, and were finally . . . repulsed and routed after a brief but bloody contest." Van Derveer supported the 2nd with a number of other commands, which extended the line left (northwest) several hundred yards. A section from Smith's Battery I, 4th U.S. was thrown across the road on the left

45 *OR* 30, pt. 1, 324.

46 Albert Dickennan, "The 9th Ohio At Chickamauga," *National Tribune*, October 18, 1906.

47 Dibrell Brigade Tablet, Intersection of Jay's Mill and Reed's Bridge Roads, CCNMP.

48 Lindsley, *Military Annals of Tennessee*, vol. 2, 660.

of the 2nd, and the 87th Indiana came up in a rush, hustling back at Beatty's recall to move up behind the guns and front on their left. Van Derveer added Capt. Marco Gary's Battery C, 1st Ohio on the left of the 87th, and finally dispatched the 35th Ohio to complete the new line. The new Federal line outflanked Dibrell and, according to Van Derveer, "a murderous and enfilading fire was poured into [the enemy's] ranks." Their ploy having failed, Dibrell's troopers withdrew.[49]

Away to the southwest, while Kammerling was leading his impromptu counter-attack and Dibrell was maneuvering north, the Confederate left suffered another reverse. Colonel John Croxton's brigade, reinforced by the 31st Ohio, was rested, re-supplied with ammo, and ready to rejoin the fight. Daniel Govan's Arkansans halted in the woods several hundred yards south of the Reed's Bridge Road. After routing Starkweather's Yankees, Govan's rightmost regiments joined with Walthall in taking on the Regulars, but the bulk of Govan's men simply ran out of obvious objectives.

With a remarkable grasp of situational awareness for such a fluid, tangled battle, Colonel Croxton sidled his command south about 300 yards and faced east, placing his line in perfect position to flank Govan. Augmented by the 31st, his front of six regiments was now too long for a single man to control. Croxton divided the brigade into two wings, with Colonel Hays taking charge of the left and Croxton the right. Passing scattered bands of Baird's survivors, the two wings soon drifted apart with a 300-yard gap opening between them and collided with Govan's left.[50]

Already warned to expect trouble from this direction, Colonel Gillespie turned his 6th/7th Arkansas to meet Croxton's assault. For a few minutes Gillespie's line held, but then, reported Lt. Col. Peter Snyder, who assumed command after Gillespie was wounded in the wrist, "they compelled us to fall back . . . about a half mile in [the] rear."[51]

To the Union 10th Kentucky's Maj. Henry Davidson, it seemed as if the Rebels were in a complete rout. "Col. Hays . . . ordered a bayonet charge, which was performed in a style never surpassed . . . .[We] charged Walker's whole Division of rebel Arkansians and Mississippians, driving them in the wildest

49 OR 30, pt. 1, 433; Peter S. Troutman, "From the 87th" *Rochester Chronicle*, May 19, 1864; OR 30, pt. 1, 429.

50 "A sketch of Chickamauga," *Louisville Daily Journal*, October 6, 1863.

51 OR 30, pt. 2, 267.

confusion, actually running clear through their lines, capturing many prisoners and light pieces of artillery." The rest of Govan's surprised brigade rapidly fell back toward Jay's Mill, crowding Walthall's Mississippians in their own retreat in the face of the 9th Ohio's charge. First Lieutenant Harvey Shannon had struggled all morning to get his battery into action and support Govan's infantry. His opportunity finally arrived when the Federals appeared out of the woods on their left. The Warren Light Artillery dropped trail and opened fire on the enemy "some distance to the rear," reported Shannon, "thus checking his advance."[52]

Croxton's and Hay's charge had once again reversed the tide in favor of Federal fortunes, recapturing Union cannon from both Van Pelt's and the 4th Indiana batteries before the Rebels could draw them off. His advance thoroughly disrupted W. H. T. Walker's last two engaged brigades, rendering the Confederate Reserve Corps combat ineffective, at least for the moment. The Yankees might have achieved more, but about this time Croxton discovered a new threat approaching along Alexander's Bridge Road. Confederate Brig. Gen. John K. Jackson's brigade, leading the advance of Maj. Gen. Benjamin Franklin Cheatham's division, was about to enter the evolving combat.

---

52 "My Dear Aunt," Chattanooga, Tenn., Feby, 19, 1864. Henry G. Davidson Letters, ALPL; *OR* 30, pt. 2, 270.

Chapter Thirteen

Bragg and Rosecrans React:

Saturday, September 19: 7:00 a.m. to Noon

Braxton Bragg listened throughout the morning with growing unease to the rumbling combat off to his north. Nathan Bedford Forrest's initial clash was not enough to interrupt his plan to mass his main force on the west side of Chickamauga Creek. W. H. T. Walker's troubling report, however, coupled with the commitment of St. John Liddell's division, gave Bragg pause.

While the fight to the north was drawing more of Bragg's attention, the remainder of the Confederate army continued to file into position. At dawn, both of Simon Buckner's divisions resumed crossing operations at Thedford's and Dalton's fords. Once over the stream, they marched northwest to link fronts with John Hood's Corps, which was formed on a long and low wooded ridge about three quarters of a mile east of the La Fayette Road. By about 7:00 a.m., both William Preston's and A. P. Stewart's divisions were formed in brigade column on Hood's left between the Viniard-Alexander Road and the Hunt house. It was not an ideal position. A sharp northward bend in Chickamauga Creek obstructed Preston's front and would complicate any attack. Maneuvering multiple brigades in the woods also took a fair amount of time. The only action that resulted from this deployment occurred when Stewart ordered the Eufala Artillery to open fire on some distant Yankees.[1]

---

1 OR 30, pt. 2, 357, 361.

Benjamin Franklin Cheatham
Battles and Leaders

To add even more weight to his main punch, Bragg intended to reinforce Buckner with Benjamin Franklin Cheatham's division of Polk's Corps. On the 18th, Polk's command tried to draw Federal attention to Lee and Gordon's Mills with a series of noisy but bloodless demonstrations designed to distract Rosecrans from the crossing operations downstream. At the same time, with the Federals largely gone from McLemore's Cove, Bragg directed Daniel Harvey Hill's Corps to move north and replace Polk's troops the next day. That swap (which was now underway) freed Polk's men to sidle north and join the main attack Bragg planned to deliver. Once Buckner's troops were clear, Frank Cheatham's five brigades (7,046 strong) of Polk's Corps began splashing across the Chickamauga at Dalton Ford at 7:00 a.m. By 9:00 a.m. they were deployed in two lines behind Buckner, where they would rest for the next couple hours.[2]

Frank Cheatham and the Army of Tennessee became inexorably intertwined during the army's difficult four-year existence. Appointed to brigadier general in the state forces before Tennessee even joined the Confederacy, Cheatham had led troops in every one of the army's battles to date. His varied career before the war included military experience in Mexico and with the state militia, running a store during the California Gold Rush, and a return to political and militia life back home in Tennessee during the 1850s.[3] This frontier life was a rugged one, and included a fair amount of drinking. Alcohol fueled one of the deepest rifts in the army's command structure when, at the battle of Stones River, Cheatham appeared to be drunk in action. One witness claimed he fell off his horse before going into the fight, while another

2   *OR* 30, pt. 2, 83.

3   Hiedler and Heidler, *Encyclopedia of the American Civil War*, vol. 1, 419.

recalled the intoxicated general leading a charge. There seems little doubt that he was impaired to some degree. Bragg censured him after the battle, and the affair became notorious within the army. Cheatham's men, virtually all Tennesseans, resented Bragg for what they came to see as undeserved attacks against their leader; their resentment deepened that summer when Bragg abandoned Middle Tennessee (and many of their homes) without a fight. Despite the controversy, Cheatham remained in command, and the Tennessee division remained a political thorn in Bragg's side. Neither man liked or trusted the other as the Confederate army coiled to strike Rosecrans in north Georgia that September.[4]

With a major battle about to break out, Bragg sought soldiers who knew the area to serve as guides for his commanders. The search bore considerable fruit in one of Cheatham's brigades. Within the ranks of the Second Battalion, First (Georgia) Confederate Regiment, Company I contained a number of familiar names: a Snodgrass, two Brothertons, a McDonald, a Kelly, a pair of Brocks, and two Dyers. All of them had originally enlisted in Company H of the 26th Tennessee, captained by James Clarke Gordon, son of local scion James Gordon whose house until that very morning had hosted General Rosecrans. Each had been sworn in by the younger Gordon while he stood on a rock in front of the mansion. Then they trooped off to Chattanooga to enroll in the 26th. The entire company was transferred to the 1st Confederate in 1862 in an effort to encourage more state homogeneity. James C. Gordon, by this time a major, commanded the five companies of the regiment now serving in John Jackson's brigade. As a result of Bragg's appeal, several Company I men stepped forward to form a pool of guides and lead the way.[5]

Moving Cheatham's men, however, split Polk's Corps. The shift north by the Tennesseans put distance between them and Thomas Hindman's division, which continued to cover the position across from Lee and Gordon's Mills. Polk remained with Hindman and detached Capt. John F. Wheless to survey his lines and report to Bragg. Unaware that Bragg was on the move that morning, Wheless rode to Leet's Tanyard only to discover the commanding general was already en route to the battlefield. The captain caught up with army

4   Christopher Losson, *Tennessee's Forgotten Warriors: Frank Cheatham and His Confederate Division* (University of Tennessee Press, 1989), 89-90.

5   James Alfred Sartain, *History of Walker County Georgia*, 2 vols. (Thomasson Printing, 1972), vol. 1, 109.

headquarters at Thedford's Ford. Bragg, he recalled, "was surrounded by a number of general officers with their staffs; and was rapidly dictating orders . . . he was self-possessed, bright, and confident." Wheless delivered the news "that the enemy had been moving . . . all night . . . towards our right," which confirmed that Walker was tangling with a sizable Federal force, and not just a brigade or two. Bragg sent Wheless back to Polk with orders "to come at once with the rest of his command" once the battle was fully joined.[6]

Meanwhile, problems on the Confederate left continued to demand some of Bragg's attention. Neither D. H. Hill nor Joe Wheeler was working well in harness, much to Frank Armstrong's disgust. Armstrong, it will be recalled, was supposed to have rejoined Forrest on September 18, turning over his responsibilities for screening the army's left flank to Wheeler. As of the morning of the 19th, that transition still had not happened. Pulled north by Polk, Armstrong was forced to abandon Owen's Ford and Glass Mill to a mere picket guard, which in turn upset Hill. Fortunately, Hill's panicky dispatch of the night before suggesting the Yankees were crossing in force at Owen's Ford proved false, but the whole contretemps forced Bragg to devote more attention than he probably cared to in straightening things out on the left.

Among the orders Bragg issued at Thedford's Ford that morning included instructions to Wheeler to close up on the army's flank and "develop the enemy;" to Armstrong to move to Red House Bridge (superseded by Forrest's request for help), and, via Polk, orders for Hill to close the gap between his own force and Hindman's division, left vacant by Armstrong's departure.[7]

Thus far in three weeks of active campaigning, D. H. Hill had shown little perspicacity or initiative. Early in the campaign, Hill seemed irrationally aggressive, but since leaving Chattanooga he seemed to be slipping deeper into continual pessimism. There is a natural tendency for any commander to view his sector as of primary importance, but an effective subordinate must also be able to discern a real threat from a feint. While still in Chattanooga back at the beginning of the month, Hill was one of those fooled into thinking Rosecrans's diversion north of the city was the real attack, and he had misadvised Bragg accordingly. In the McLemore's Cove affair, Hill failed to grasp that Negley's advance was an opportunity to destroy a piece of Rosecrans's army; instead, Hill

6   J. F. Wheless Memoir, TSLA.

7   *OR* 30, pt. 4, 671.

viewed the threat from Alpine as the real danger. Even after the Union XX Corps was in full retreat, Hill was still wrongly reporting that La Fayette was in imminent danger from the south, information that forced Bragg to move most of the army back south on September 14. The misfired affair at Davis's Crossroads left Bragg wondering about Hill's willingness to attack. All of this led to a deterioration of the relationship between Bragg and Hill, an association that could never be harmonious or end well. Neither man suffered fools gladly, nor held his tongue to assuage an aggrieved subordinate. How Hill would behave during the upcoming battle remained to be seen.

On the morning of the 19th, Hill's mood took an upswing when he determined to find out what the Yankees in his front might be up to. Benjamin H. Helm's brigade of John Breckinridge's division reached Glass Mill, on the east bank of West Chickamauga Creek four meandering miles upstream (or two direct miles south) from Lee and Gordon's Mills. Just after dark on September 18 Helm established a picket line along the east bank of the creek. John Beatty's Federals established a similar line just before dawn on the 19th, after the confusion about replacing William Hazen's brigade of John Palmer's command was cleared up.

A low hill overlooked Glass Mill from the east bank, while the western bank was essentially flat, sloping upward very gradually about 800 yards to a farmhouse on the north side of the Glass Mill Road, which crossed the Chickamauga via a wooden bridge. The plain between the house and the mill was a patchwork of field and woodlots. A ford crossed the creek about one-third of a mile downstream from the bridge.

D. H. Hill, mindful of the larger Confederate movement underway to his north, now "determined to make a diversion" at Glass Mill, and gain some useful intelligence, if possible. On Hill's orders, the newly arrived pickets slipped across the creek near Glass Mill to probe Beatty's lines. Helm's men, Kentuckians all, comprised the storied "Orphan Brigade" of Confederates who prided themselves on being an elite force within the army—volunteer patriots from a state that hadn't even left the Union. At first light they pushed across to the west bank only to encounter more Federals from Beatty's command. Hill, who was observing the reconnaissance, decided to up the ante and ordered Helm to reinforce his skirmishers. "An hour after sunrise" according to Lt. Col. Martin H. Cofer, both the 2nd and 6th Kentucky crossed the creek to "develop the position of the enemy." The Yankees responded in kind. Major Rice E. Graves, Breckinridge's artillery chief, sent forward a section of Capt. Robert Cobb's Battery to support the infantry. The guns opened fire on a house 500 yards distant and thought to be sheltering Federals. The gunfire accomplished little except to provoke a response from Capt. Lyman Bridges's Illinois battery. Cobb withdrew and a lull ensued.[8]

Hill wasn't finished. Part of his job was to draw as much Federal attention to himself as possible, and he decided a larger diversion was needed. At 9:00 a.m. he ordered the effort renewed. Word passed down the chain of command to send the rest of Helm's brigade, three more of Cobb's guns, and an additional two sections of Capt. Cuthbert H. Slocomb's 5th Battery of the Washington Artillery across the stream to engage the enemy. The infantry pushed west beyond the creek, but the focus of the fight shifted to the big guns. With the firepower of nine artillery pieces at his disposal, Graves boldly pushed them right up among Helm's infantry, where they unlimbered and opened a rapid fire.[9]

Initially, Graves focused his fire against Bridges's overmatched battery. Within a short time, however, the Federals equalized the contest when Lt. Eben P. Sturges galloped onto the scene with half of Capt. Frederick Schultz's Battery M, 1st Ohio Light Artillery. Nine Union tubes matched the Rebels shot for shot. Bridges's gunners were having a hot time of it when Sturges arrived: "[I] found [them] still under a severe fire, with a number of horses killed, some men lost, and their ammunition running a little short."[10]

Confederate Lt. Joseph E. Charlaron, serving in Slocumb's 5th Battery of the Washington Artillery spotted Sturges's Union guns coming up and rode over to inform Graves, who was standing behind the New Orleans battery directing the action. "I see it," Graves sharply replied before ordering Slocumb to close the range by rolling his cannon even farther forward, by hand; the Yankee fire was too intense to limber and advance in conventional fashion. The order surprised Charlaron, who did as instructed and managed to gain about 100 yards. The Yankees had their range, however, and pummeled the Louisianans with every yard.[11]

---

8   Ibid., pt. 2, 140, 211, 214.

9   Ibid., 140.

10   Entry for September 19, Eben Sturges Diary and Letters, AHEC.

11   Joseph E. Chalaron, "Memories of Major Rice E. Graves, C.S.A." *Daviess County Historical Quarterly*, vol. 3, no. 1 (January 1985), 11. Originally printed in the *New Orleans Messenger*, May 27, 1900.

As Union crew members dropped around Bridges's guns, members of the 104th Illinois infantry, who were lying down behind the battery, came forward to man the pieces. Lieutenant William W. Calkins of the 104th found the long-arm fight "intensely interesting." It was also dangerous, for the regiment "lost one man mortally wounded, and eight wounded, on the skirmish line and at the battery" during the engagement.[12]

The fight lasted between 60 and 90 minutes, and it was late in the morning when the Rebels finally disengaged and fell back to the east bank of the creek, having provoked what Hill regarded as a sufficient Federal response. "The enemy," Breckinridge later reported, "was in considerable strength at the fords," but it was only "a covering force to columns passing down the center of the valley to unite with the center and left of his army."[13]

In addition to the Illinois infantry losses, Bridges's gunners suffered two killed and nine wounded. Overall Rebel losses were slightly higher, with Captain Cobb's battery reporting one killed and one wounded and Slocomb losing seven dead and five injured, many of whom fell when the men manhandled the guns forward. The Orphans, who had to bear the entire affair without firing a shot in return, suffered the most. A private in the 4th Kentucky recalled they "had to lay flat down and spread out like Cuban adders, and then were far from safe. Shells cut the young trees, and limbs from the larger ones, and they fell promiscuously over and around us. These terrible missiles would also plough the ground and burst in our midst, making sad havoc. Fourteen of our brigade were killed here before we received orders to recross the river on the Chattanooga Road." Throughout the exchange Lieutenant Charlaron watched Major Graves with growing alarm. Despite repeated orders from Breckinridge to pull back, the aggressive young staff officer "seemed loath to quit the field under the enemy's fire. His persistency," admitted the lieutenant, "probably cost us some men."[14]

The Federals correctly interpreted this probe as an effort to draw them into a larger fight, but despite the severity of the barrage at Glass Mill, most Federals

---

12 William Wirt Calkins, *The History of the One Hundred and Fourth Regiment of Illinois Volunteer Infantry. War of the Great Rebellion 1862-1865* (Donohue and Hennenberry, 1895), 129-130.

13 *OR* 30, pt. 2, 198.

14 *OR* 30, pt. 1, 374; Fred Joyce, "Kentucky's Orphan Brigade at the Battle of Chickamauga." *The Kentucky Explorer* (April 1994), 28; Chalaron, "Memories of Major Rice E. Graves, C.S.A.," 11. The bulk of those 14 casualties were wounded, not killed.

refused to take Hill's proffered bait. Beatty, whose brigade was the focus of all this Rebel attention, asked for reinforcements, but that idea was quickly quashed. Lieutenant Colonel Arthur C. Ducat, an assistant inspector general on William Rosecrans's staff, was with Maj. Gen. James Negley that morning. Ducat was Scots-Irish, born in Dublin into a noted Highland family, and schooled there until railroading brought him to Chicago. His passions were organizing fire brigades and an amateur study of military science, the latter refined by two years of war. Ducat discerned Hill's push of Helm's men across the creek for what it was: a distraction. He informed the army commander in a terse noontime note "that firing on General Negley's front is a demonstration to attract your attention from another point . . . General Beatty . . . is all right while he has nothing hurt and no musketry firing yet." Ducat also reported that the head of McCook's XX Corps was now in the vicinity, should there be need of more troops.[15]

Ducat's opinion of the engagement, as well as word of McCook's arrival were both pieces of welcome news to Rosecrans. The Union army commander was attempting to orchestrate an extraordinarily dangerous and complex mission in the face of the enemy —leapfrogging multiple divisions one by one northward towards General Thomas, towards Rossville, and ultimately, Chattanooga. Most of the XIV Corps troops were already gone, with some of them now engaged in heavy action around Jay's Mill and the Winfrey Farm. Thomas wanted Negley to follow as quickly as possible, thus reuniting his divided corps.

However, Thomas's XIV Corps wasn't the only force in motion. Rosecrans also wanted to shift John Palmer's 2nd Division of Crittenden's corps from the XXI Corps right flank, at Glass Mill, to the Corps left north of Lee and Gordon's Mills. This shift would extend the Union line northward towards Thomas's movement to the Kelly Farm, narrowing (but not closing) the gap that would remain between Thomas's and Crittenden's lines when the XIV Corps reached their destination.

Accordingly, Negley was detached from the XIV Corps and ordered to replace Palmer's force at Glass Mill, so Palmer could complete his own movement. Replacing one division with another while in the face of the enemy is always a tricky movement; it was complicated in this case by the dark of night

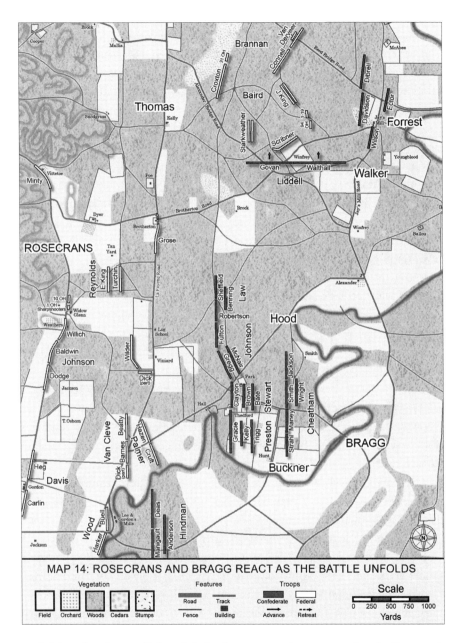

MAP 14: ROSECRANS AND BRAGG REACT AS THE BATTLE UNFOLDS

and delayed orders to Palmer's brigade commanders, as previously discussed. The resulting confusion didn't get sorted out until nearly dawn, and only after a great deal of pointless marching and countermarching.

When Palmer finally did move out, he discovered that the roads were still clogged. Not only did his columns have to use the same roads Negley's people were filling as they moved up to replace him, but Palmer also found that the tail end of Thomas's XIV Corps troops and trains were still jamming the roads northward. The limited road network in the vicinity simply wasn't extensive enough to simultaneously handle five divisions of Federal infantry and their attendant baggage, making for long delays.

All of this traffic also affected McCook's XX Corps. Rosecrans intended to use one of McCook's divisions to replace Negley—allowing him to rejoin Thomas—and the others to replace Crittenden's force, enabling the XXI Corps to continue their own shift northward until they linked up with the right of the XIV Corps. The difficulty in accomplishing these moves lay again with the limited roads, and all the troops already filling them. McCook fell short of his march objectives on the 18th because Thomas's men were blocking his path; now, despite receiving Rosecrans's orders for September 19 at 12:15 a.m. that morning, the XX Corps didn't begin moving until dawn because the roads were jammed with Negley's and Palmer's troops through most of the night.

Much of this traffic passed directly in front of Rosecrans's headquarters at the Gordon house opposite Crawfish Spring. Troops filled the roads in front of the spring most of the night and well into the morning. Major General Richard Johnson's 2nd Division, XX Corps was among them. The morning that greeted them at 5:00 a.m. was "frosty and cold," the overnight temperatures having taken an unseasonable plunge. Leading McCook's column, Johnson reached Crawfish Spring at 9:00 a.m. and halted in front of James Gordon's stately brick home. While the men broke ranks to fill canteens, Johnson reported to Rosecrans.[16]

By now, cannon fire from Thomas's engagement farther north was fully audible. Focused on that fighting, Rosecrans was still thinking aggressively. Thomas had originally conceived of a three-division attack with two of his own divisions and at least one (Palmer's) borrowed from Crittenden. Rosecrans would do him one better. Seizing the opportunity presented by Johnson's timely appearance, the army commander ordered Johnson to join Thomas, "from whom," continued Johnson, "I would receive [further] orders." Dispatching an aide forward to locate the XIV Corps commander, Johnson returned his men to the road and hustled them north.[17]

16 Cope, *The Fifteenth Ohio Volunteers*, 308-309.

17 *OR* 30, pt. 1, 535.

While Thomas could certainly use Johnson's help, the cumulative effect of Rosecrans's decisions was starting to unravel the army's command structure. Negley's division was detached from Thomas and now sandwiched between Crittenden's XXI Corps and McCook's XX Corps, while the latter two corps commanders were each giving up a division to Thomas. It was the beginning of a process that, if continued, could only lead to increased confusion and worse.

Johnson still had a considerable distance to cover (nearly six miles by road to Kelly's farmstead) before he could join Thomas. Flames still flickered along the fence rails set alight the night before, the acrid spirals of smoke filling the nostrils of the men tramping past as the rattle of musketry and heavier bass-drum thump of the fieldpieces reached their ears. A short while after resuming their march, Johnson's men were passed by Rosecrans and his entourage also heading north. Rosecrans was relocating his field headquarters to be closer to the action. Just shy of Poe Field, Johnson found General Thomas, who upon hearing Johnson's current orders directed him to "form line of battle and move forward and attack." The newly arriving troops dropped their packs and bedrolls and formed line.[18]

Other Federals were also being drawn into the growing engagement, notably Palmer's men. Most of the division commanders in the Federal armies in the Eastern Theater were graduates of West Point. In the Western Theater, however, there were fewer professionals to go around, and more civilian-soldiers rose to command large bodies of troops. Major General John McCauley Palmer was one of them. When war arrived, the prewar lawyer and influential Republican wasted little time before raising a regiment, and received his first star by December 1861. One enlisted man didn't think he looked much like a soldier: "On horseback he looked like a bag of oats; in the face, well his face would sour a lemon." Despite Palmer's unsoldierly appearance and his ongoing suspicions about the nepotism of West Pointers toward their own, by 1863 the army's senior officers held him in high regard. Professional soldier Richard W. Johnson, alongside whom Palmer was about to go into action this day, described him as "one of the ablest and best generals in the army"—rare praise from a Military Academy man for a political general. Rosecrans sustained

---

18 Ralph E. Kiene, Jr., ed. *A Civil War Diary: The Journal of Francis A. Kiene, 1861-1864* (privately published, 1974), 174-175; Henry M. Davidson, *History of Battery A, First Regiment of Ohio Vol. Light Artillery* (Daily Wisconsin Steam Printing House, 1865), 87; OR 30, pt. 1, 535; Albert Kern, ed. *History of the First Regiment Ohio Volunteer Infantry in the Civil War 1861-1865* (n.p. 1918), 19.

this opinion shortly after the battle when Palmer tried to resign by informing the War Department that Palmer was "a prudent, brave and valuable officer [whose loss] would be a serious injury to the service."[19]

As earlier noted, Col. William Grose's brigade departed on a reconnaissance before Thomas's dispatch requesting a supporting attack reached Crittenden and Palmer. Grose's movement, it will be recalled, created a great deal of uncertainty within Baird's division of the XIV Corps that morning. Not only did his brief appearance near Poe Field confuse Col. Benjamin Scribner's men, but his report back to Palmer (his own division commander) was about to induce a considerable amount of caution within Crittenden's XXI Corps. Shortly after that brief contact with Thomas's men, Grose deployed his regiments and extended his lines a short way into the timber east of Poe's Field. There, his skirmishers detected the movement of "a heavy force of the enemy, already upon their flank," elements of Walker's Confederate Reserve Corps. Shortly thereafter, Grose's men could hear "heavy volleys of musketry . . . some distance to the left," which unbeknownst to them marked the initially successful advance of Baird's division.[20]

Grose and Palmer now engaged in a series of confusing communications. Grose, at the Poe farmstead, was roughly two miles north of Palmer's current position near Lee and Gordon's Mills. In his first message back to Palmer, Grose apparently failed to report that he had established contact with Thomas, or provide any details of Baird's attack. Instead, he reported only that he "found the enemy in force" and awaited further instructions. Palmer elaborated: "About half past 10 o'clock a messenger came in from Colonel Grose in charge of one of Bragg's orderlies taken prisoner. From this prisoner . . . enough was learned to satisfy me that the enemy was near in force." Additionally, Grose inquired whether he should engage the enemy. Unsure of Rosecrans's overall intentions, Palmer ordered Grose to move back down the La Fayette Road and

---

19 Warner, *Generals in Blue*, 358; Charles B. Dennis Memoir, Rutherford B. Hayes Presidential Library, Fremont, OH. To be fair, Sergeant Dennis was not favorably disposed towards Palmer, who once turned him down for a furlough. Palmer, *A Conscientious Turncoat*, 116-119. Palmer attempted to resign due in part to turmoil within the army after Chickamauga, but also because of personal reasons: he promised his wife he would do so once the current campaign ended, and he was concerned about his son, who was very sick. Rosecrans convinced him to remain in the army.

20 Louis A. Simmons, *The History of the 84th Reg't Ill. Vols.* (Hampton Brothers, Publishers, 1866), 88; William Grose, *The Story of the Marches, Battles, and Incidents of the 36th Regiment Indiana Volunteer Infantry* (The Courier Company Press, 1891), 178.

rejoin the division, a move that unmasked Baird's right flank just as St. John Liddell's Confederates were beginning their own advance. In light of Thomas's request for support from Crittenden's XXI Corps, Palmer's recall of Grose was untimely, but Crittenden was still seeking Rosecrans's instructions at this time and so was not ready to let Palmer go forward. Communications between the various actors in the unfolding drama were not at their best that morning.[21]

By now, the whole Federal army was abuzz with speculation. Rumors that Bragg had been heavily reinforced were common within the ranks, and the captured Rebel orderly apparently said enough to confirm that belief. Private Henry F. Dillman of the 31st Indiana, one of Palmer's men, ominously noted that "Gen Bragg has been reinforced with the flower of the southern army (Gen Longstreet's Corps) besides the state militia."[22]

Before Grose's men fully retraced their steps to the vicinity of Lee and Gordon's Mills, Crittenden reached a decision. The distant roar of renewed fighting marked a larger and perhaps more desperate struggle on Thomas's front. Crittenden's own orders indicated that defending the crossing at Lee and Gordon's Mills was vital, but since his front there was quiet he decided he could spare a division for employment farther north. Complying with Thomas's request, Crittenden ordered Palmer to march north and join Thomas. Crittenden also dispatched a courier to Rosecrans (who was still at Crawfish Spring) informing the army commander of his decision. Rosecrans's response confirmed Crittenden's orders to Palmer.[23]

Palmer's troops had only just settled into their new positions north of Lee and Gordon's Mills that morning, when word to move arrived. At least while Grose's brigade was busy with the reconnaissance up the La Fayette Road, in the interim the rest of Palmer's men managed to snatch a short rest, gulp down a bit of breakfast, and even receive mail. Despite this interlude, everyone knew a fight was in the offing, and any respite was destined to be brief. "Soon we received orders," recalled Pvt. Joseph Marshall of the 90th Ohio, "to keep our harness on and be ready to move at any time." Palmer was riding the lines of his division when Col. Oliver Payne of the 124th Ohio hailed him: "'General,

---

21 OR 30, pt. 1, 713, 780. Who the orderly was, or how he came to be captured, remains unknown.

22 Entry for September 19, Henry F. Dillman Diary, Lilly Library, Indiana University, Bloomington, IN.

23 OR 30, pt. 1, 607.

there's going to be a dance down there this morning, is there not?' 'Yes,' replied [Palmer] 'and in less than an hour your regiment will get an invitation to attend.'"[24]

That "invitation" arrived at 11:00 a.m.: move at once to support Thomas. The mail from home had been abundant, the backlog just catching up after several days of marching. The poignancy of the unfolding scene struck Lt. Charles Hammer, the 124th's regimental adjutant: "[N]early every man received one or more letters from home. I sat upon my horse and read perhaps ten or twelve . . . when the movement forward was ordered, the ground was strewn by torn letters left by the men." William Hazen's brigade led Palmer's march. Fearing the La Fayette Road was by now in enemy hands, Palmer turned his troops to the left and moved up the Dry Valley Road, passing near the Widow Glenn house, which Rosecrans had just recently occupied as his headquarters. "He hailed me," recalled Hazen, "and gave me minute directions for going into action."[25]

Rosecrans had not allowed himself to become distracted by diversions to the south. At 10:00 a.m., after directing Johnson forward to reinforce Thomas, Rosecrans led his entourage north to the Widow Glenn's. "The cavalcade" noted Lt. Col. John P. Sanderson, "cantered off at a most fearful speed, raising a dust that was frightfully suffocating . . . and we soon reached the Glenn house, about 2 ½ miles nearer Rossville." It seemed a rare vantage point. "This house, a log hut, was on a high hill, surrounded on three sides by woods, [but] in front of it was a large cornfield. From this point almost the entire line of battle could be seen." The widowed occupant, 26-year-old Eliza Glenn, had lost her Confederate-soldier husband to disease the previous spring, leaving her alone with two small children—and terrified at the prospect of a battle unfolding on her doorstep. "In the house," Sanderson continued, "we found a mother, almost frightened to death, with 8 or 10 young children [evidently neighbors or other refugees] hanging on to her dress, equally scared." With the help of her

---

24 Entry for September 19, Joseph K. Marshall Diary, OHS; George W. Lewis, *The Campaigns of the 124th Regiment, Ohio Volunteer Infantry with Roster and Roll of Honor* (The Werner Co, 1894), 54.

25 Charles D. Hammer Reminiscences, 124th Ohio file, CCNMP; Hazen, *A Narrative of Military Service*, 127.

father's slave named John Camp, Eliza, the gaggle of children, and a few meager belongings all piled into an ox-cart and rolled away to the northeast.[26]

Rosecrans and his staff were not Eliza Glenn's first visitors. The 92nd Illinois Mounted Infantry, part of John Wilder's brigade, had been detached on courier duties for the past few days. The 92nd arrived at the Glenn's from Pond Spring that morning, and was now in the cornfield southeast of the cabin awaiting orders. Major John Bohn of the 92nd was observing what little he could see of the fight, which was pretty much only the dust and smoke of battle rising from the woods to the northeast. When Rosecrans rode up, his rank and uniform were obscured by an enlisted man's greatcoat. Both men focused on the noise and smoke of Thomas's distant engagement. "Rosecrans excitedly fired off a succession of queries" at Bohn: "what does it mean? Where is that fighting? How long has it been going on? What troops are engaged? How far is that from here? What does that dust mean? What does it mean?'" Bohn, more than a little overwhelmed by this sudden onslaught of questions from his commanding general, "answered promptly and as definite as I knew how."[27]

While his headquarters was being established and the field telegraph set up, Rosecrans ordered the 92nd Illinois to dismantle the fences east of the farm to ease the way for future movement. The Illinoisans made short work of the task before turning their attention to every soldier's prime need: food.

Like Bragg, Rosecrans was also seeking out local expertise. While he had no troops recruited from the area, he did have Unionist sympathizers like James Lee, who proved helpful to Wilder. Nor were the Federals above impressing local civilians at gunpoint in a pinch. At least two such Unionists joined Rosecrans here. John McDonald encountered one of Wilder's patrols that morning. When he learned the farmer intimately knew the area, Wilder sent him on to army headquarters. Dr. Robert Dyer was also scooped up and forwarded to Rosecrans. Both men that day would provide assistance and direction, willing or otherwise, to several Union generals.[28]

---

26 "Battlefield of Chickamauga," Saturday night, 10 o'clk Sep 19, 1863, John P. Sanderson Letters, OHS. Sanderson was speaking optimistically here. The Glenn house, while surrounded by more open ground than much of the battlefield of Chickamauga, still provided no direct line of sight to almost all of the fighting on September 19th. Sartain, *History of Walker County*, vol. 1, 109.

27 Baumgartner, *Blue Lightning*, 246-7.

28 Sartain, *History of Walker County*, vol. 1, 104.

Rosecrans had been closely following the unfolding action, and had a relatively firm grasp of its nature thus far. He was aware that Baird's Federal division had come to grief because it was outflanked and surprised from the south, and he took pains to warn Palmer's men of exactly that fact. The "minute directions" supplied to Hazen, and promptly passed up the chain of command to Palmer, made this clear. "At this moment," Palmer reported, "I received a note from the general commanding . . . which led to a [seemingly] slight, but what turned out to be most advantageous, change of formation. He suggested an advance *en echelon* by brigades, refusing the right."[29]

Palmer's men moved up to Poe Field, where he found Johnson's division of the XX Corps already forming for battle and about to enter the woods east of the La Fayette Road. Palmer fell in on Johnson's right, extending the Union battle line southward as Rosecrans intended, and deployed his three brigades as the army commander suggested, *en echelon*. Both Federal divisions then entered the woods, cautiously, groping for both the enemy and George Thomas's hard-fighting troops.

29 *OR* 30, pt. 1, 713.

Chapter Fourteen

The Battle for Brock Field:

Saturday, September 19: 11:00 a.m. to 1:30 p.m.

Braxton Bragg needed Ben Cheatham and his division. At 11:00 a.m., Lt. P. S. Parker of Bragg's staff handed Cheatham an order "to move to . . . the support of Major General Walker." With John K. Jackson's brigade in the lead, the division moved north to the Viniard-Alexander Road, followed it to Alexander's Bridge Road, and then turned northwest toward the sound of the fighting. A mile farther along, Cheatham halted the division and deployed his five brigades, each led by a brigadier, in two lines: Jackson on the right, Preston Smith in the center, and Marcus J. Wright on the left. George Maney's and Otho Strahl's commands filled out the second line. After informing his officers that they should not expect support on either flank, Cheatham "gave the order to advance." It was about noon.[1]

Moving on a broad front, Cheatham's brigades initially marched through open timber in the general direction of Brock Field. Each of the three leading brigades quickly lost all but the most tenuous contact with one another. Jackson's brigade, its right guiding along Alexander's Bridge Road, was the first to find Federals. Jackson expected to encounter Rebels, for he understood his men were moving to replace Walker's Reserve Corps which was furiously

1 OR 30, pt. 2, 78.

engaged somewhere up ahead, their fight audible to all. Colonel Charles P. Daniel commanded the 5th Georgia on Jackson's left flank. Earlier while forming his line of battle, Jackson cautioned Daniel to be careful because there was a friendly "line of battle in front."[2]

Captain Joseph Cumming appeared while Jackson was cautioning Daniel. Cumming served on Walker's staff, but only a month previous had been a member of Jackson's military family. The two did not part amicably. Tempers had flared over a petty grievance concerning a supply requisition, which escalated into Cumming's resignation. According to Cumming, his timely appearance saved Jackson's men from a disastrous encounter with the Yankees before they were properly formed to meet them. Jackson, he explained, was taking too long to deploy, and "would be caught in the midst of it; the enemy was near at hand and [instead] he should pivot on his right and wheel to the right into line." Jackson, he continued, did as suggested in the nick of time, since "he had hardly gotten into line [before] he was attacked." In reality, Cumming was probably mistaken, and nerves may have had something to do with it. At that instant Walker's men were crumbling in the face of Croxton's counterattack, and the moment was an urgent one. Jackson and all of his regimental commanders reported they were fully deployed and moving forward when the enemy made their unexpected appearance.[3]

This did not mean that they were not surprised. Major John B. Herring, leading the 5th Mississippi, reported "there were no skirmishers in front of the line, and I supposed from this fact that we constituted a second line. We advanced not more than 100 yards when we were attacked by the enemy directly in front, who were also advancing. We returned the fire vigorously, and after a few minutes the enemy's line gave way." "This confused my command considerably," observed Colonel Daniel of the 5th Georgia, "but in a short time we continued the advance, driving the enemy before us."[4]

Jackson's line had collided with the three right-hand regiments of Col. John T. Croxton's Federal brigade plowing through the woods near the Winfrey house. They were in considerable disarray by the time they stumbled upon Jackson's Rebels. Croxton, it will be recalled, had divided his long front into two

---

2   Ibid., 89.

3   Cumming Recollections, UNC.

4   *OR* 30, pt. 2, 89, 91.

wings. When Colonel Hays ordered his left wing to launch a bayonet charge, Croxton followed suit. "We moved through the woods like a raging storm," recalled Lieutenant West of the Union 4th Kentucky. "We drove everything before us and had come up almost to the muzzles of the guns in their battery when two bullet wounds put me out of business."[5]

Those muzzles belonged to the guns of Capt. John Scogin's Georgia battery, moving with Jackson, and consisted of a pair each of six-pounders and 12-pound howitzers. At first contact, Scogin aggressively pushed his fieldpieces into the front line alongside the 5th Mississippi, helping to check Croxton's line and then drive it back. Once fully deployed and stable, Jackson's front from right to left included the 5th Georgia, 2nd Battalion/5th Confederate, 5th Mississippi, Scogin's battery, the 8th Mississippi, and the 2nd Georgia Sharpshooters. Jackson's 1,300 infantry (plus the four fieldpieces) confronted only half of Croxton's brigade, no more than 700 effectives.[6]

Outnumbered and with both flanks exposed, Croxton ordered a retreat. Hays's wing, however, was still trying to drag away several of the recaptured Union fieldpieces from Scribner's and Starkweather's former positions. "We had determined to keep them or die," asserted Private Davidson. "Suddenly rapid musket-firing commenced on our right and our rear," recalled Captain Webster, whose company of the 10th Kentucky had been thrown forward into Winfrey Field as skirmishers to cover the artillery salvage operation. The heavy firing was Croxton's right wing conducting a stubborn fighting withdrawal.[7]

Losses were heavy on both sides. "They being in such overpowering force, and flanking us again on the right, we were compelled to fall back . . . disputing every foot of ground," reported Colonel Chapman of the 74th Indiana, who came to grief himself when his horse was shot from under him "and fell heavily upon me, breaking my arm . . . but I continued on the field." On the brigade right, Lieutenant Colonel Kingsbury of the 14th Ohio continued to flourish his musket. "[He] did not go into the fight like some officers do—swinging his sword in the air," wrote Augustus May, "but . . . on foot, with a cartridge box strapped on his shoulder and musket in his hand . . . constantly cheering on his

---

5   Granville C. West, "Personal Recollections of the Chickamauga Campaign," *MOLLUS*, vol. 45, 427.

6   *OR* 30, pt. 2, 93.

7   Ibid., pt. 1, 416; "My Dear Aunt," Chattanooga, Tenn., Feb. 19, 1864, Henry G. Davidson Letters, ALPL; Webster, "Chickamauga," *National Tribune*, July 2, 1891.

men." Captain Albert Moore of Company A, 14th Ohio, was struck in the head, a wound that gave him a ghastly appearance. Medical orderly Jonathon Wood burst into tears when he saw Moore at the field hospital with "his face all covered with blood and dirt." Luckily it was not as bad as it looked. "I found a ball had grazed the top of his head, laying the skull bone bare," explained the orderly. "I cut off the hair, washed off the blood, applied compresses and bandages, and he [was] feeling so much better that he went [back] to his command again." Plenty of others were not so fortunate. By now the 14th's makeshift aid station contained more than 100 wounded Buckeyes.[8]

Jackson's rebuff sent Croxton's line falling back several hundred yards to a small wooded rise, where, joined by Hays's regiments, the reunited Yankee brigade faced the oncoming Rebels with more equal firepower. Here, wrote Private Davidson, "The Rebels attacked us again, and again, but without success." Relief for Croxton was at hand in the form of Richard Johnson's XX Corps division, which was moving up behind Croxton's beleaguered line. Soon it would be Jackson's turn to be driven.[9]

August Willich's brigade led Johnson's command into action. Willich was arguably the best brigadier in the XX Corps and one of the best in the entire Union army. The dedicated Communist was 53 that September, a former Prussian army lieutenant who had forsaken his martial career to pursue political reform by supporting himself through the honest toil of carpentry. He had commanded troops again during the European upheavals in 1848, and fled to England in 1851. Friedrich Engels, who once served as Willich's adjutant, believed him to be the best soldier among the revolutionaries—"brave, cold-blooded, skilful, and of quick and sound perception in battle."[10]

Engels and his mentor Karl Marx were less enamored with Willich's unrelenting political style. All were dedicated Socialists, but Willich disdained Marx's more theoretical approach, as well as his university pedigrees and his liking for the swirl of English drawing room society. Willich preferred to share the adversities of the poor and espoused direct action. They formed rival political factions, and at one point the enmity between them proved so deep that Willich challenged Marx to a duel. Marx avoided the confrontation, but one

---

8   OR 30, pt. 1, 416-417; Augustus C. May, "The Fourteenth at Chickamauga," *Toledo Commercial*, October 17, 1863; Jonathan Wood Recollections, OHS.

9   "My Dear Aunt," Chattanooga, TN, Feb. 19, 1864, Henry G. Davidson Letters, ALPL.

10 Loyd D. Easton, *Hegel's First American Followers* (Ohio University Press, 1966), 169.

of his younger followers provoked a fight with the hotheaded Willich who wounded the man. That seemed to settle the matter of honor, but failed to heal the political rift. By the early 1850s Willich had settled in Cincinnati and was editing a Socialist newspaper. His military experience and anti-slavery leanings propelled him back into uniform in 1861. He joined the 9th Ohio, was elected its adjutant, and drilled its members into a crack regiment. That fall he left the 9th to raise another all-German unit, the 32nd Indiana, and instilled the same standards of drill and discipline there. After earning distinction at Shiloh, he was promoted to brigadier general in July 1862.[11]

Willich was both an egalitarian—he addressed his soldiers as "citizen" outside of formal duties—and a first-rate soldier who could handle a brigade as easily and effectively as most men commanded a regiment. Willich, noted Johnson, his division commander, "was always in the right place, and by his individual daring rendered the country great service." Willich was also a tactical innovator. He developed an infantry formation called "Advance Firing" and incorporated that into his brigade's drill during the summer of 1863. "One great advantage . . . of brigade drills under General Willich," wrote Capt. Alexis Cope of the 15th Ohio, "was that every movement was explained beforehand and directed to some definite purpose and object. We were to attack the enemy in some assumed position, or we were to be attacked . . . in front, flank, or rear, and were moved in such a manner as to meet the attack. By this method the drills were made interesting and instructive to every man in the command."[12]

At Thomas's direction, Johnson formed his division in line at the southern end of Kelly Field with Willich on the right and Col. Philemon P. Baldwin's brigade on his left, with Col. Joseph Dodge's brigade posted in reserve. The 32nd Indiana and 49th Ohio filled out Willich's first line, with the 89th Illinois and 15th Ohio forming in support. Illinois Sgt. Isaac Young of Company H, a farmer by trade, was struck by the incongruity of their pastoral surroundings: "Birds were singing . . . [and] butterflies were fluttering about," he observed. Even a "cow stood under a tree . . . and lazily chewed her cud." Not everyone thought the scene idyllic. One of Young's comrades was more focused on the

---

11 Ibid., 173-174.

12 OR 30, pt. 1, 536; Cope, *The Fifteenth Ohio Volunteers*, 280. Willich also wanted to mount his men in wagons to increase their mobility, but the idea was rejected because of a shortage of transport.

"streams of wounded and stragglers trailing out of the woods [which revealed] that the crumbling process has begun in our grand line."[13]

Croxton's men were again out of ammunition and thankful to be relieved. They disengaged, leaving Jackson's Confederates in control of the small ridge littered with casualties from both sides. Willich sent his skirmishers forward to feel out this opposition and uncovered Jackson's strong line. Major Samuel F. Gray of the 49th Ohio recalled this initial collision: "advancing about three hundred yards . . . [we] found the enemy, [and] light skirmishing at once commenced, growing hotter." Matters grew too hot too quickly, as the 49th outpaced their comrades in the 32nd Indiana: "The skirmish line of the Forty-Ninth," recorded Sgt. Maj. Andrew J. Gleason, "advancing too far . . . was outflanked on the right and had to retire a short distance. We then lay down under a murderous fire of musketry and artillery." Part of that "murderous fire" was being performed by Scogin's Georgia battery. "The rebels played on us fearfull from a battery in our front, and canister flew thick while shells burst all around us," recalled Pvt. Francis Kiene of the 49th Ohio's Company I. "[A] shell . . . struck Samuel Perill by my side and tore away all of his left hip, inflicting a fatal wound."[14]

While the fight between Willich and Jackson escalated, two more of Cheatham's Confederate brigades moved up and engaged another Union division. Preston Smith's and Marcus Wright's commands, Tennesseans all, advanced on a broad front south of Jackson moving toward the Brock farmstead. At 1,642 men Smith's was the largest brigade in Cheatham's division, while Wright's, with 1,113 rank and file was one of the smallest. Their combined frontage amounted to more than 800 yards, which only expanded with each step they took as they made their way through the open timber.[15]

The Brock homestead lay empty by 1863. Farmer John Brock was 65 at the time of the battle, and with his two oldest sons having followed the drum and Major Gordon off to war, the old man took the rest of his brood to a cabin near McFarland's Gap a half mile or more west of the McDonald place. Perhaps his farm was too much to handle with his two eldest absent, for Brock Field was

13 OR 30, pt. 1, 538; Isaac K. Young, "Chickamauga—The Battle As I Saw It," *National Tribune*, April 22, 1886; Anonymous, "Willich at Chickamauga," *Rock Island Argus*, October 19, 1863.

14 OR 30, pt. 1, 551; Cope, *The Fifteenth Ohio Volunteers*, 309-10; Kiene, *A Civil War Diary*, 175.

15 Powell, "Numbers and Losses," CCNMP.

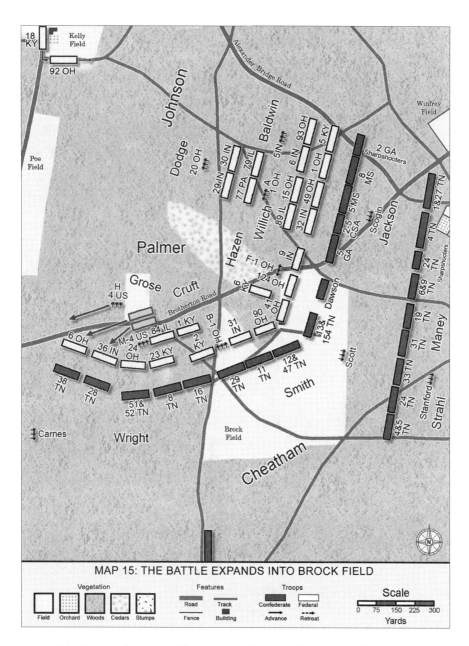

MAP 15: THE BATTLE EXPANDS INTO BROCK FIELD

Vegetation					Features		Troops		Scale				
Field	Orchard	Woods	Cedars	Stumps	Road / Fence	Track / Building	Confederate / Advance	Federal / Retreat	0	75	150	225	300

Yards

one of the larger cleared holdings on the battlefield. A west-facing, L-shaped open area ran 600 yards south from the Brotherton Road. It was 250 yards wide at the northern end, doubling to more than 500 yards at its southern terminus, with the Brock cabin sitting right at the angle of the L on the west side of the clearing. Brock had also begun clearing more land along the east side of his field

Brock Field, looking southwest towards the L-shaped corner. The line of monuments in the foreground mark Hazen's positions. Frank Cheatham's Confederates would emerge from the treeline in the distance. Note that the field was considerably larger then. The treeline to the south (the right in the picture) was another 400 yards farther back.

Harvey Scarborough

and north of the road, where dead standing trees and tangled brush piles marked his unfinished work.[16]

Smith's and Wright's Rebels were about to collide with John Palmer's division. Approaching the farm from the west, Palmer's three brigades were deployed in a staggered formation echeloned to the right, alert to Rosecrans's earlier suggestion to be wary of being flanked from the south. It was Palmer's intention to bring his command alongside Johnson's, connect with Willich's right flank, and present a united front against whatever Rebels lay ahead. Hazen led the formation. Brigadier General Charles Cruft's brigade occupied the divisional center, his front 100 yards behind and to Hazen's right. Grose's men, having fallen in at the rear of the column earlier as it passed, took position staggered in similar fashion behind and to Cruft's right.[17] Each brigadier deployed his command in the standard formation of a double line of regiments and set off. One-half mile east of the La Fayette Road, they found the enemy.[18]

16 Sartain, *History of Walker County*, vol. 1, 105.

17 *OR* 30, pt. 1, 729.

18 Hazen to Lossing, August 23, 1866, Palmer Collection, WRHS.

Moving on Jackson's left, Smith's brigade front approximated the length of Brock Field's eastern edge. Both Smith and Hazen had swarms of skirmishers in front of their respective lines, and the first contact between them provoked a short-lived conflict that deceived each side into thinking the other was retreating. Smith ordered Maj. William Green of the 11th Tennessee, commanding Dawson's Sharpshooter Battalion, to "advance and check the enemy," but before Green could deploy more than two of his five companies, the impatient brigadier ordered the rest of the brigade forward. Smith's regiments drove the Yankee skirmishers an estimated 400 to 800 yards west and north until they met Hazen's main line.[19]

Hazen's men initially formed with the 41st Ohio on the right and the 9th Indiana to their left, a frontage of only some 200 yards. Behind them trailed the 6th Kentucky and 124th Ohio, formed in "double column at half distance," a formation two companies wide by five deep, with room enough between the lines to deploy into a line in almost any direction. To Col. Aquila Wiley of the 41st Ohio, Smith's Rebels appeared to give way first. "Passing through an open wood," he reported, "our skirmishers soon became engaged with those of the enemy, and drove them. On emerging from the wood, we came to an open field about 400 yards in width, with another skirt of woods beyond."[20]

A narrow strip of timber that would become a prominent feature of the ensuing fight bisected the field parallel to the brigade's front. The 41st's lieutenant colonel, Robert L. Kimberly, watched as "[our] skirmishers passed through this belt and a few yards beyond, and were then driven back by an overpowering fire." The Buckeyes of the 41st surged forward through the tree belt to reinforce their skirmishers when, continued Kimberly, "the edge of the forest beyond, in front, on the right and on the left, was suddenly fringed with a line of flashing fire." Wiley's report disagreed slightly with his executive officer's memory. The 41st's main body, claimed Wiley, had not yet reached the strip of trees when Smith's Rebels opened fire, and Wiley thought the Confederates intended to seize the timber strip first and use it as cover. "We were too quick for them," he reported, "gaining it first, and delivering our fire

---

19 *OR* 30, pt. 2, 115.

20 Ibid., pt. 1, 708; Lewis, *Campaigns of the 124th Regiment*, 55-56; *OR* 30, pt. 1, 773. Double column at half distance was a normal formation for the two supporting regiments in a Union brigade. *OR* 30, pt. 1, 773.

by battalion at short range, sent them back into the woods from which they started."[21]

Hazen's line was clearly overmatched. Fighting on the left of the 41st, Capt. Amasa Johnson of the 9th Indiana recalled that "the contest was terrific. We advanced, driving the enemy back step by step . . . [into] the field. Our loss in this our first part of this engagement was very heavy." Here the two blue regiments halted, using the tree line and some brush piles as cover, and let the enemy come to them. In the butternut line facing Hoosier Captain Johnson, Capt. Alfred Fielder of Company B, 12th Tennessee, witnessed the same bloody struggle: "In a few minutes [we] were engaged in an awful fight, the enemy disputing every inch of the ground." Colonel Alfred Vaughan led the combined 13th and 154th Tennessee forward in a spirited charge, driving the Federals back "to their temporary breastworks [the brush piles] where they made a stubborn stand."[22]

As Hazen's men moved forward and a gap opened between the Hoosiers and the 41st Ohio, the brigadier directed the inexperienced 124th Ohio forward to fill it. Sworn into Federal service in September 1862, the 124th joined the Army of the Cumberland in early 1863, but were new to the terrors of actual combat. Their baptism of fire was proving difficult. At first contact, the fresh Buckeyes had gone to ground behind the 41st Ohio, lying prone while the musketry duel opened in front of them. On Hazen's order, Col. Oliver H. Payne directed his 124th to rise and shift left. The regiment fumbled its inaugural battle command. "Companies A, H, and part of D, not understanding the order" failed to move. They subsequently fell in with the veteran 6th Kentucky and performed credibly, which meant the 124th would fight shorthanded the rest of the day.[23]

Despite the already raging firefight, the inexperienced Payne ordered Capt. George Lewis to take Company B forward and deploy as skirmishers. "This movement was executed under fire, and not in very good style," admitted Lewis. Once deployed, Lewis found himself a mere 100 yards from a Rebel line, where he watched in growing alarm as Scott's Tennessee battery pushed its way

21 Kimberly, "At Chickamauga," 715; *OR* 30, pt. 1, 773.

22 Amasa Johnson, "Chickamauga," *National Tribune*, June 16, 1887; Entry for September 19, Alfred Fielder Diary, TSLA; *OR* 30, pt. 2, 112. Vaughan mistook the downed trees and brush piled by Brock for prepared Federal defenses.

23 Ibid., pt. 1, 775.

into the front line and unlimbered. Company B concentrated its fire on this new threat and, noted Lewis with pride, his "farmer boys had shot down every horse and not one of the gunners could approach a gun." Lewis exaggerated, but only slightly: the Rebel artillerymen manage to fire, but the gunners clearly faced some grim moments. Captain William L. Scott was out sick and the battery went into action under Lt. John H. Marsh, who was cut down almost at once leaving Lt. A. T. Watson in command. The gun crews indeed suffered heavily: "2 privates . . . killed, 3 seriously wounded, and 10 slightly," plus 14 horses. Colonel Vaughan of the 13th Tennessee watched Marsh attempt to unlimber "under a heavy and destructive fire, so much so that a number of men and horses were disabled before the battery was placed for action."[24]

When Watson's crews opened, their shells rendered Company B's situation even more precarious. With no time to rectify his mistake and recall the skirmishers, Payne ordered Lewis's men to lie flat. The "main line opened fire over us [and] . . . it was difficult to tell from which we suffered the most, the fire of the enemy or the bad marksmanship of the line in the rear," Lewis lamented. Colonel Payne fell during this fighting with a bad wound, and Maj. James B. Hampson assumed command of the regiment. Despite the lethal danger of trying to run back across the open ground—"The enemy's fire, which had by now become very heavy, [was] telling fearfully in our ranks" —Hampson ordered Lewis to return with his men and reform on the left side of the embattled regiment. This they managed to do, and the Ohioans concentrated on pouring fire into the Rebels. Hazen finally had a solid battle line with which to oppose Smith's large brigade.[25]

The Confederates had troubles of their own. On the parade ground, Smith's 1,600 men required a quarter-mile of frontage; advancing over rough timbered ground during a battle considerably attenuated that line. Gaps appeared as units lost contact with those on their flanks. When the combined 13th/154th Tennessee wheeled more to the right to confront the 41st Ohio head-on, Col. William Watkins and the 12th/47th Tennessee—the next regiment in line to the left—failed to follow suit. Instead, Watkins and the 11th Tennessee continued to march straight forward. This move split Smith's line into two parts. The 500 Rebels of Dawson's Battalion and the 13th/154th

24 Lewis, *Campaigns of the 124th Regiment*, 57; OR 30, pt. 2, 107, 117. Captain Scott was sick and unfit for duty on September 19, 1863.

25 Lewis, *Campaigns of the 124th Regiment*, 57-59; OR 30, pt. 1, 776.

Tennessee confronted Hazen's line, while Smith's remaining 1,100 Tennesseans moved west into the southern portion of Brock Field. Under other circumstances, Smith's left would have merely collided with Cruft's Federals, then moving in line on Hazen's right. Rosecrans's earlier injunction to advance *en echelon*, however, had altered Cruft's course in the battle.[26]

Charles Cruft was a lawyer from Terre Haute who witnessed the clash at Bull Run as a civilian in 1861 and thereafter helped raise the 31st Indiana. He won promotion to brigade command with a proven combat record and steadiness under fire. His bravery was something of a legend. Cruft was wounded three times at Shiloh with "a bullet in the shoulder, a second in the thigh, and a piece of shell in his skull, but 'he picked them out, without dismounting, as coolly as a man would draw a splinter from his finger' and only quit the field after the fighting ended that day." Advancing to bolster Hazen's right-rear, Cruft and his men could be counted on to secure the brigade's exposed flank.[27]

With the 90th Ohio on the left and the 2nd Kentucky on the right, Cruft's brigade picked its way through wooded and hilly terrain. As they approached Brock Field, they discovered what Cruft described as a plateau, with an abrupt drop-off. They also encountered Smith's skirmishers, and observed Hazen's men moving into action just a short distance to the northeast. The 90th Ohio moved up to try and join their line to that of their fellow Buckeyes in the 41st, and in doing so Col. Charles H. Rippey also advanced the right of the 90th so its fire angled against the flank of the 13th/154th Tennessee. Rippey was pleased with his initial position, perched on "the crest of a swell in the ground along which was some fallen timber and other cover."[28]

The 2nd Kentucky on the far right did not fare as well. When Cruft halted the brigade, complained Col. Thomas B. Sedgewick, the 2nd was "left . . . in a very undesirable position, on low ground and exposed to a terrible fire from three sides." With the rest of Smith's Rebels swinging around to face more north than west, Cruft's front was about to be outflanked. Grose's brigade had

26 Ibid., pt. 2, 111.

27 Civil War Indiana Website, Charles D. Cruft Biography, http://civilwarindiana.com/biographies/cruft_charles_d.html, accessed 11/3/2012.

28 *OR* 30, pt. 1, 730, 756.

not yet moved far enough west to connect with Cruft's right, leaving his line dangerously exposed.[29]

Seeing the danger, Cruft deftly reoriented his entire line to face southeast, extending his line back at about a 45-degree angle off Hazen's right. He also ordered the 31st Indiana up into the center of the brigade line, leaving only the 118 men of the 1st Kentucky as a reserve behind his right. Moving forward to deploy between the 90th Ohio and 2nd Kentucky, the 31st was exposed to the full fury of the enemy fire: "All at once a terrible shower of musketry was let into our ranks," wrote Pvt. John Day of Company K, and "not more than 40 or fifty yards away rose a cloud of smoke . . . marking the position of the enemy." The Federals eschewed a formal battle line and scrambled to make use of whatever cover they could. "The 31st fought in her accustomed way, lying down," wrote Henry F. Dillman, a private in Company G. Logs and stones were thrown together to form "a temporary breastwork" just as Smith's Rebels attacked.[30]

While Cruft's men were receiving the attention of both the 12th/47th and 11th Tennessee, Smith's remaining regiment, the left-flank 29th Tennessee, broke contact with the 11th and drifted even farther west, lost and by now in disarray. "Having double-quicked some distance over rough ground," admitted the 29th's Col. Horace Rice, "the line of the regiment was considerably broken and some confusion prevailed at the time we halted." The 29th's officers were struggling to reform the regiment when "a volley from the enemy . . . added still more to the confusion."[31]

That volley marked Union Col. William Grose's entry into the fight. With five regiments and two batteries, Grose had a relative abundance of troops, and formed accordingly. The 24th Ohio and 23rd Kentucky deployed in his first line, on the right and left, respectively, while the 36th Indiana and 84th Illinois fell in behind them in support. The 6th Ohio, together with Batteries H and M of the 4th U.S., trailed along in reserve. All told, Grose carried 1,631 men and 10

29 Ibid., 752.

30 Entry for September 19, John Day Diary, InHS; Entry for September 19, Henry Dillman Diary, Lilly Library, Indiana University, Bloomington, IN. Only four companies of the 1st Kentucky were present.

31 OR 30, pt. 2, 114.

fieldpieces into the spreading combat. Even in such a compact formation, they overlapped the 29th Tennessee's front by a good margin.[32]

Another Hoosier, Grose had been a lawyer, politician, and judge before the war but he had no military experience. The brigade's larger-than- normal size might have posed a challenge for him, but he had proven himself capable as early as the battle of Shiloh, and he worked hard to compensate for his lack of prewar martial credentials. Grose proved to be a by-the-book disciplinarian, much to the dismay of at least some in his command. At the beginning of September, Christopher Wetsel of the 84th Illinois described "this tyrannicle General" in a letter home. In what another veteran from another war would come to call a classic *"Catch-22,"* no man could leave camp without a pass, Wetsel complained, but then Grose "will not sign [any] passes." Fires on guard or picket were prohibited. When the mail arrived after dark one night, "we was all anxious to read our letters," but Grose ordered the camp guard to arrest any man burning a light. Colonel Louis Waters of the 84th Illinois interceded to get the men released, but Wetsel was convinced that Grose now had it in for the regiment. "If there was any necessity of it, I should not grumble, but all it is done for—is revenge!"[33]

Grose and his men were entering a tactically complicated situation. They were still moving east by southeast and so not yet fully aware of Cruft's convex and curving deployment, adopted under duress to extend and protect Hazen's right. Moreover, neither Grose nor his regimental commanders had a clear picture of their opposition. In addition to the wayward 29th Tennessee, Confederate Brig. Gen. Marcus J. Wright was moving his brigade north and west groping for a Union flank while discovering the 29th's exposed left in the process.

Like the man whose brigade he would soon fight, Marcus Wright was also a lawyer. Unlike Grose, however, he had a smattering of antebellum military experience in the prewar militia. Wright was a veteran of Shiloh and Perryville, but this was his first time leading a full brigade under fire. His appointment was not without controversy. Originally, the brigade had been led by Brig. Gen. Daniel Donelson, a West Pointer and competent commander who at age 62 suffered from poor health and was not fit for a field command. Donelson left

---

32 Ibid., pt. 1, 780.

33 Christopher Wetsel Letters, Western Illinois University, McComb, IL. Joseph Heller wrote the classic WWII novel *Catch-22*.

Marcus Wright. New to command, Wright
was not popular with his men.
W. J. McMurray

the brigade in January 1863 and died of illness that April. Most of the brigade's rank and file expected Col. John H. Savage of the 16th Tennessee to assume command, and "were surprised and mortified to see Col. Wright" get the promotion.[34]

Wright had served on Cheatham's staff and obviously won his superior's confidence. He had a strong patron in Tennessee Governor Isham G. Harris, who was also a personal friend. In the fall of 1862, Wright commanded the post and camp of instruction at McMinnville training draftees, but was eager to get back into the fight with a field command. Harris lobbied hard on Wright's behalf, writing letters of recommendation from himself and for Cheatham to sign, and "induced Bragg and Leonidas Polk to request Wright's appointment" to brigadier. Harris assured Wright that "the War Department shall have no peace" until the commission came through. True to the governor's word, Wright was promoted that December. In January, Harris's son Eugene was appointed a first lieutenant and joined Wright's staff, further cementing their relationship.[35]

The issue of what command Wright would assume remained in question. He was originally considered for the top slot of the famous Kentucky Orphan Brigade, which had lost its brigadier at Murfreesboro. The Orphans, however, demanded (and loudly) that a fellow Kentuckian lead them; the job fell to Bardstown native Ben Hardin Helm. Donelson's illness opened another door. Even better, Wright's promotion would circumvent Colonel Savage's

---

34 Warner, *Generals in Gray*, 75, 346; Lindsley, *Military Annals of Tennessee*, vol. 2, 344. Wright's most notable contribution came after the war when he served as the Confederate agent for the *Official Records*, helping to gather thousands of pieces of scattered correspondence for that momentous project.

35 Sam Davis Elliott, *Isham G. Harris of Tennessee* (Louisiana State University Press, 2010), 129, 134-135.

ambitions, which suited both Cheatham and Governor Harris. John Savage was a longtime political opponent of both men, and disliked Donelson to boot, so much so that he was sometimes disputatious to the point of insubordination. One historian recently described Savage as "egocentric if not paranoid[.] Savage often imagined everyone was aligned against him, and personalized every situation." This time his suspicions were correct: both Cheatham and Harris wanted him gone. When Wright assumed command of the brigade, the outraged Savage resigned in protest. The men in the ranks sided with their enraged colonel, however, and the brigade continued to hold a grudge against the man they considered an interloper. Wright would have to work hard to earn their trust.[36]

As he entered the fight, Wright was not fully aware about the rest of the division's deployment. He initially expected to come up behind W. H. T. Walker's line, and assumed Maney's brigade would be on his left since it was behind him during the approach march. Instead, Maney's men were being held in reserve behind Jackson's brigade on the division's right. Instead of finding and replacing Walker's Rebels, Pvt. Carroll Clark of the 16th Tennessee remembered almost blundering into a line of Federals. "Colonel [David M.] Donnell told us to be careful and not shoot our pickets as they fell back to our line. . . . Advancing in the woods, Jim Martin said 'yonder they are.' . . . Col. Donnell [cautioned] 'don't shoot they are our men.'" Martin's eyes were keener than the colonel's. "Our men hell!" exclaimed the private, "and bang went his gun, which opened the ball for us. The Yanks were swinging around and never saw us."[37]

This burst of Confederate fire delivered a nasty shock for Grose's Federals, who were focused on supporting Cruft's embattled men. The hammer blow fell on the 24th Ohio, which quickly gave way in a surprised panic. The 24th was comprised of veterans who performed well at Stones River, maneuvering under fire to repel repeated Rebel attacks under the masterful direction of Col. Frederick C. Jones. That fight killed Jones and several other officers and left the much-reduced regiment in the hands of a captain. After the battle, Capt. David

---

36 Ibid., 135; Kenneth Noe, *Perryville: This Grand Havoc of Battle* (The University Press of Kentucky, 2001), 195. At Perryville, Savage's willful recklessness led the 16th Tennessee into a slaughter. The regiment lost nearly 60% of the 370 men engaged, as opposed to the rest of the brigade, which suffered a loss rate closer to 25%. Despite this blunder, he remained a popular officer.

37 *OR* 30, pt. 2, 118; Carroll Henderson Clark Memoirs, TSLA.

J. Higgins was recalled from detached duty and promoted to colonel to take command of the 24th. Higgins was not a well man. Crippled with rheumatism, he was often absent and incapable of leading in the field. The next in rank, Maj. Thomas D. McClure, was also not up the task, and the regiment's confidence suffered. Now, with untested leadership and bullets ripping through their ranks from an unexpected direction, their confidence collapsed.[38]

Grose quickly reacted to the crisis. "On meeting the enemy" he wrote, "the troops on the right of my brigade gave way, and the Thirty-Sixth Indiana was immediately changed to the right to defend the flank." To Grose, Wright's continued movement westward appeared to be an attempt to flank him, so he threw the 6th Ohio into line on the right of the 36th, and at the same time reoriented the 23rd Kentucky to attach on the 36th's left. Shortly thereafter, the unsteady 24th Ohio rallied and moved back into line alongside the 6th Ohio. Grose's new front now faced entirely south, stretching roughly 500 yards, though not quite in contact with Cruft's right flank. Once aligned, Grose's men poured their fire into Wright's Rebels.[39]

To Wright, the circumstances suddenly confronting his new brigade were wholly unsatisfactory. At one point the 16th and 8th Tennessee emerged into a corner of Brock Field, only to be raked by Union fire. Wright hastened them back into the woods again, but in doing so he lamented, "My line of battle . . . advanced obliquely to the right, instead of being parallel to the enemy's line." The situation quickly deteriorated. Separated from the rest of the brigade by a small ravine, the 16th Tennessee experienced a "very heavy fire from a battery of the enemy, about 150 yards in front of the left wing of [the] regiment. This fire wounded a considerable number of my men," reported Colonel Donnell, and the rest of the regiment "fell back 10 or 15 paces to seek protection behind trees." At first Donnell believed "the line was giving way, but the men maintained their [new] position, firing as rapidly as they could through the thick undergrowth." Private Clark remembered receiving an intense fire from the Yankees. A bullet cut the strap of his canteen, forcing him to stuff it in his haversack. "Boys were being killed and wounded all around. A grapeshot stuck a tree . . . and a piece of bark struck my nose a glancing lick, tearing off a lot of

38 OR 20, pt. 1, 571-573; John Rutherford, 24th Ohio website, http://www.geocities.com/ CapitolHill/Senate/1861/higgins.html, accessed 8/16/2013.

39 OR 30, pt. 1, 780; Hannaford, *Story of a Regiment*, 463.

hide." The 16th, firmly rooted behind whatever cover they could find, returned that fire as best they could.[40]

Wright struggled to turn his brigade to face this threat from his right. His five regiments, formed in order from right to left, included the 16th, 8th, 51st/52nd, 28th, and 38th Tennessee; the last included the men of the 22nd Tennessee Battalion, merged with the 38th that summer. Every command was significantly understrength, however, and Wright's entire brigade amounted to just 1,100 men. Even without the 84th Illinois in the firing line, Grose's Yankees brought to bear at least 200 more muskets, and both Batteries H and M of the 4th U.S. were firing. In stark contrast, Capt. William W. Carnes's Tennessee battery fell behind in the long movement to contact and had yet to reach the front.[41]

Colonel John H. Anderson and his men in the 8th Tennessee, fighting just 200 yards from the Yankee line, watched in dismay when the 16th Tennessee on their right fell back to seek better cover. Within minutes, the 51st/52nd Tennessee on their left also retired, leaving them painfully exposed. Anderson determined to hold his regiment in place. Like most of Wright's regiments, Col. John G. Hall of the 51st/52nd found he had drifted too far to the right during the advance. So too did the 8th Tennessee, which "gained some ground on me by a movement by the right flank." The result was that Hall's regiment lost contact with Anderson's 8th. Alongside Hall's command on his left, the 28th Tennessee went prone and returned fire from that position.[42]

Colonel John C. Carter's 38th Tennessee, holding Wright's exposed left flank, was feeling especially vulnerable. Like Wright, Carter went into action expecting to find Maney's regiments on their left. With Maney nowhere to be found, Wright instructed Carter to halt and the 38th went to ground about 150 yards short of the Union line. The Tennesseans blazed away, with Carter later admitting, "I cannot definitely say what loss I inflicted upon the enemy." When Captain Carnes's four Tennessee guns finally arrived, Wright dispatched them to the left flank to support Carter. Carnes requested Carter to clear his infantry from in front of his guns and opened upon the Federals with canister.[43]

---

40 *OR* 30, pt. 2, 118, 124-125; Carroll Henderson Clark Memoir, TSLA.

41 *OR* 30, pt. 2. 118.

42 Ibid., 123, 126, 129.

43 Ibid., 128.

It was now shortly after 1:00 p.m. Cheatham's three leading brigades were fully engaged, squared off against five enemy brigades from Johnson's and Palmer's divisions (Col. Joseph Dodge's brigade was in reserve). Neither side was strong enough to drive the other. The resultant fight, mostly a medium- to long-range musketry duel, inflicted about equal losses and emptied cartridge boxes at an alarming rate, but accomplished little else.

Northeast of Brock Field, meanwhile, Confederate brigadier John Jackson was in trouble. Had Willich's brigade been alone, Jackson's men might have prevailed. The Southerners' longer frontage and artillery support gave them the edge in firepower. However, Col. Philemon Baldwin's Federal brigade arrived on Willich's left. His 1st Ohio came alongside their fellow Buckeyes in the 49th, and with the 5th Kentucky added their fire to the escalating fight. "[B]y order of the general commanding brigade the [whole] first line advanced to the work under a heavy fire of musketry," reported Major Gray of Willich's 49th Ohio. The reinforced Federal line overmatched Jackson's brigade, and leveraged the Rebels into a slow retreat.[44]

Holding Jackson's left, Colonel Daniel's 5th Georgia was running short of ammunition. The first man he sent back to bring up more was shot down before he could find the wagons. Before the second runner could return, Daniel claimed "we were ordered to retire—which we did in as good order as the thickness of the undergrowth would admit." Alongside Daniel on his right Major Gordon's 2nd/1st Confederate followed suit. "The command began a retrograde movement," wrote Gordon, "and moved back some several hundred yards." Gordon also insisted the retreat was ordered, though "by whom the order was given, I have not been able to ascertain."[45]

What we do know is that those orders did not come from Jackson. "Seeing troops on the left retiring, I sent to inquire the meaning of it," the irate brigadier reported after the battle. Gordon and Daniel blamed Preston Smith's brigade, which was falling back on their left after striking Hazen's line. In any case, the damage was done. Their retreat exposed Captain Scogin's artillery "to [a] cross-fire, killing several of my horses, and forced me to abandon one piece and one caisson." Opposite them, Francis Kiene with the 49th Ohio gloated over

---

44 Ibid., pt. 1, 551.

45 Ibid., pt. 2, 87, 89.

the turnabout: "We . . . routed the 8th Miss. Regt. and took the rebel battery which annoied us so."[46]

Holding Jackson's center, the 5th Mississippi had "maintained it's position gallantly," insisted Major Herring, "though exposed to a galling fire . . . until Lieutenant Colonel Sykes, observed that the line had retired on the left, gave the command to fall back." Still, insisted Herring, "we fell back [only] about 100 yards, faced about and renewed the fight."[47]

While the rest of the brigade line was unraveling left to right, Col. John C. Wilkinson of the 8th Mississippi added to the harassed brigadier's woes when he "informed General Jackson, through my adjutant, that the enemy was flanking us on the right." The 2nd Georgia Sharpshooters, holding Jackson's far right, were not able to stop the progress of Baldwin's recently arrived Yankees, and Jackson was faced with the prospect of a double envelopment. Fortunately, Maney's Tennessee brigade was but a few hundred yards to his rear, and Jackson called upon Maney to come to his aid. Preston Smith on Jackson's left was also having problems, and had asked Brig. Gen. Otho Strahl to move his brigade as well.[48]

Frank Cheatham and Leonidas Polk were with the reserves when requests for help arrived. "Gen. Cheatham came riding rapidly down in front of our line," recalled William J. Worsham of the 19th Tennessee, part of Strahl's brigade, "saying, 'Give them hell, boys, give them hell;' he was not out of sight and scarcely out of hearing when Gen. Polk came in full tilt on his heels, and said, 'Give them what Cheatham says, we will pay off old chores today.'" Strahl and Maney moved their brigades forward shortly before 2:00 p.m. The heavy fire they stepped into probably convinced many in the ranks that they were more likely to receive hell than dish it out.[49]

Maney's command included five regiments consolidated into three tactical formations, as well as a small battalion of sharpshooters. The 1st/27th Tennessee, numbering 703 officers and men, anchored his right. The much smaller 4th Tennessee occupied the center with a mere 179 troops, while the

---

46 Ibid., 84, 93; Kiene, *A Civil War Diary*, 175. Kiene meant the 5th Mississippi.

47 *OR* 30, pt. 2, 91.

48 Ibid., 84, 93.

49 William J. Worsham, *Old Nineteenth Tennessee Regiment, C.S.A., June 1861-April 1865* (Guild Bindery Press, 1992), 88-89.

6th/9th Tennessee aligned on the left, 368 strong. Instead of deploying as skirmishers, the 24th Tennessee Sharpshooter Battalion added their 43 men to the ranks of the 4th. This was the first action for most of the sharpshooters. Maney's line faced intense Federal shelling even before Jackson's men cleared their front. Private Sam Watkins of the 1st Tennessee recalled falling shells inflicting fearful losses during a final halt to dress their ranks: "Three soldiers are killed and twenty wounded. Billy Webster's arm was torn out by the roots . . . and a fragment of a shell buried itself in Jim McEwin's side, also killing Mr. Fain King, a conscript." One of Watkins's fellow 1st Tennessee men, Pvt. Marcus Toney of Company E, remembered the regiment charging "gallantly, amidst a terrible cannonade." Further complications arose when Maney's line reached the area of freshly felled timber and dead standing trees that marked Brock's recent field-clearing efforts. This area "presented some difficulty to easy passage in line," admitted Maney. Once through, the brigade halted and opened fire at the Federal line as soon as they crested a slight ridge.[50]

Maney expected to advance in conjunction with Strahl, whose regiments from right to left included: the 19th, 31st, 33rd, 24th (not to be confused with the 24th battalion, above) and 4th/5th Tennessee. All told they numbered 1,181 of all ranks. They waited 300 yards east of (behind) Smith's embattled line for the better part of an hour until Smith sent word he was almost out of ammunition and needed support right away. Strahl responded with alacrity and hurried forward, losing contact with Maney's left flank as he did so, much to the latter's dismay. Subsequently, neither brigade would get much support from the other.[51]

Strahl's line moved past Smith and his staff, with Smith cautioning them not to fire too soon for fear of hitting his own men who were still disengaging. The result was the intermingling of the two brigades, which caused some alarm amongst the new arrivals. "We met . . . more men coming out wounded then [there] were of us going in," Worsham of the 19th Tennessee recalled. "The sight was anything else than inspiring or encouraging." More complications followed. Due to the curving nature of the Federal line, the 19th and 31st

50 Powell, "Numbers and Losses," CCNMP; OR 30, pt. 2, 104; Sam R. Watkins and Ruth Hill Fulton McCallister, ed., Co. Aytch: Maury Grays, First Tennessee Regiment, or, A Side Show of the Big Show (Providence House Publishers, 2007), 109; Toney, The Privations of a Private, 60; OR 30, pt. 2, 94.

51 Ibid., 130.

Tennessee faced the Yankees head-on and at close range. The rest of Strahl's troops, however, were blocked by elements of Wright's brigade. The 24th and 4th/5th Tennessee didn't fire a shot during the entire action for fear of shooting people on their own side.[52]

Cheatham struggled to control this wayward fight but achieved little other than to add an additional layer of confusion, as exemplified by Strahl's report. Smith's line was disengaging when Smith informed Strahl that Wright's men were still masking his left, and that Maney was not where he was supposed to be because "my right flank was not supported by any one, and that I was in a position to be flanked," continued Strahl, "unless I immediately moved in that direction." Strahl demurred, fully grasping the "great danger of attempting a flank movement" under the current circumstances. He also believed Maney would be up momentarily. Besides, Wright's line was either retiring or would be very soon. A short while later, Smith returned bearing orders from Cheatham to "close the gap between [Strahl] and Jackson." However, by this time Jackson was gone—something Cheatham should have known. Did Cheatham mean Maney? If so, it was an unfortunate mistake because Strahl "concluded that General Maney had been ordered elsewhere" and now believed there was a brigade-sized hole in the line between his right and Jackson's brigade. There was no choice but follow orders by facing right and moving to close up that gap.[53]

Disaster struck immediately. We "had hardly commenced the movement," Strahl continued, "before the enemy met the front of my column with a murderous and destructive fire, enfilading nearly the whole of my line." Captain Frazier of the 19th Tennessee found himself caught up in this savaging: "We extended a flank movement to the right . . . under a terrible fire of canister, shot and shell, not firing a gun ourselves. A solid sheet of lead seemed [to be] coming at us." In the 4th/5th Tennessee, Private Rennolds expressed his own frustration: "[We] again advanced across the field and were fired on, and again ordered back, while all were expecting to be allowed to fire."

The permission to pull triggers never arrived. Finally, admitted Worsham of the 19th, "We had to fall back some fifty or a hundred yards." Some 200 of

---

52 Entry for September 19, E. H. Rennolds Diary, TSLA; Worsham, *Old Nineteenth*, 89; Entry for September 19, William Sylvester Dillon Diary, TSLA.

53 *OR* 30, pt. 2, 130-131.

Strahl's men added their names to the casualty lists during this brief action, while inflicting virtually no damage upon the enemy.[54]

Maney, of course, had not been ordered elsewhere. Several factors conspired to leave a sizable gap between his left line and Strahl's right. The felled timber and scrub in their sector impeded Maney's advance, making it impossible for the two brigades to simultaneously advance. In addition, Jackson's move westward guiding along the Alexander Bridge Road pulled his brigade farther right—away from Preston Smith's track toward Brock Field. This left a large gap in Cheatham's front just minutes after his assault got underway. The hole was still there when Maney moved ahead to replace Jackson's exhausted brigade and Strahl did the same for Smith. This was the "gap" Cheatham ordered Strahl to close when he came to grief. His bloody retreat further exposed Maney's left. It is also important to note that Jackson's line became engaged with Willich considerably farther west than where Hazen and Smith squared off, and when Jackson's men fell back, the Federals did not launch an aggressive pursuit. When Maney's troops reached Jackson's former position, they took up a line at least 150 yards west of where Smith (and subsequently Strahl) entered the fight in Brock Field.

Maney's men groped their way forward to where Scogin's abandoned gun rested, but they saw little sign of Jackson's brigade, which seemed to have vaporized into fragments during their retreat. Colonel Hume Field of the 1st/27th Tennessee figured out where to place his line when he stumbled across Jackson's wounded, who were still lying where they fell. Colonel George Porter, leading the combined 6th/9th Tennessee, attempted a frontal assault as he neared the Federal line, only to be met with "a most deadly concentrated fire, both of small arms and artillery . . . my regiment at the time being in full view and at short range of the enemy's guns." To Tennessee Pvt. Robert Gates of the 6th's Company H, it seemed that "to advance was madness; to stand was nearly as bad." Formation soon went by the wayside as the Rebels scattered for cover. "We entered the fight at a charge," Pvt. Van Buren Oldham of Company G, 9th Tennessee declared, but soon "halted and lay down." To Oldham, the moment must have been especially nerve-wracking. His last time under fire was at

---

54 Ibid., 131; S. J. A. Frazier, "Reminiscences of Chickamauga," *The Lookout*, May 20, 1909, Hamilton County Library, Chattanooga; Rennolds Diary, TSLA; Worsham, *Old Nineteenth*, 91.

Perryville, where he was wounded and captured. Now everything seemed to be coming apart all over again.[55]

To the Federals, Maney's effort appeared unimpressive. Willich and Johnson were more concerned with the fact that there was also a gap in the Union lines between Willich's right and Hazen's left. After he had routed Jackson, Willich—who Johnson often turned to for advice—asked Johnson if there were friendly troops off to his right. He was "assured by the divisional inspector that a division of another corps was on [the] left" but no one seemed to be on the right flank. Willich asked Colonel Rose of the 77th Pennsylvania (Dodge's brigade, then in reserve) to reconnoiter. Rose returned to inform Willich the next troops in line off to his right belonged to Hazen, and they were "more than a mile distant." Rose overestimated the gap by a wide margin, but his general point remained: Willich's flank was exposed.[56]

Rose also brought word that Hazen's troops were running low on ammunition and were "heavily pressed." Johnson decided it was time to commit his reserves and send Dodge's regiments in at once. "Off to our right," Dodge recalled, "it was evidently 'red hot.' In a moment I received an order . . . to go to the relief of Gen. [Hazen.] We marched by the right flank, perhaps a quarter of a mile, when we arrived on the ground."[57]

Other reinforcements, equally unlooked for, were headed Hazen's way. XIV Corps leader George Thomas was also aware of not just one but several gaps in his still-coalescing line, and sought more troops to fill them. Major General Joseph Reynolds's Fourth Division of the XIV Corps was available. Without Wilder, Reynolds's division was a small one, and thus far his two brigades had been held in reserve. On the night of the 18th, Reynolds followed Baird and Brannan during their overnight march, halting for the morning in the woods south of Dyer Field. And there, Joe Reynolds awaited his next orders.

Reynolds was a professional soldier. He graduated from West Point in 1843 and was a lifelong friend was fellow classmate Ulysses S. Grant. He had little

---

55 *OR* 30, pt. 2, 99, 102; Lindsley, *Military Annals of Tennessee*, vol. 2, 216; Entry for September 19, Van Buren Oldham Diaries, University of Tennessee, Martin, TN.

56 *OR* 30, pt. 1, 539. The divisional inspector was wrong. A similar gap existed beyond Baldwin's left as well. The nearest Federals to the north were Brannan's men, a half-mile distant on the Reed's Bridge Road.

57 Ibid., 535; Joseph B. Dodge, "The Story of Chickamauga, part two," *Northern Indianan*, February 11, 1875.

actual field experience under his belt, however. After a short stint in Texas he returned to West Point in 1846 as an instructor, a post he would hold for nearly a decade. In 1855, he was transferred to field duty for two years, but the settled life of a teacher appealed more to him than duty on a frontier army post, and he resigned two years later to teach mathematics at Washington University in St. Louis. He remained in that position for just three years before moving to Lafayette, Indiana, where Reynolds entered the grocery business with his brother.[58]

With war broke out Reynolds quickly returned to uniform. He commanded the 10th Indiana under General Rosecrans in western Virginia, where he proved to be "an able leader . . . demonstrating competence and energy." Despite this success, and Rosecrans's esteem, Reynolds left the army again, this time citing family business matters. He could not stay away for long, however, and re-entered the army in the fall of 1862 with an appointment to command the newly raised 75th Indiana. He never assumed that duty, however, for West Pointers were too rare to command mere regiments. Within two months Reynolds was a major general, and Rosecrans trusted him enough to hand over command of a division. Because his troops were not engaged at Stones River, Reynolds began 1863 with limited combat experience on a small scale—and none at the head of a division. This lack of experience didn't stop him from enjoying the high opinion of Rosecrans as well as George Thomas. Several times during the current campaign, Reynolds led not only his own division but exercised command over John Brannan's division as well, leading a sort of demi-corps.[59]

It was 12:30 p.m. when Thomas decided to commit Reynolds's two brigades to the fight. His first impulse was to send his men north to the McDonald house, where they could either backstop Brannan's and Baird's divisions, reforming astride the Reed's Bridge Road after their morning's exertions, or perhaps fill in between Brannan's right and Johnson's left, making good the earlier assertions of Johnson's staff to Willich. Accordingly, with Brig.

58 David M. Kapaun, Jr., "Major General Joseph J. Reynolds and his Division at Chickamauga: A Historical Analysis," Master's Thesis, U.S. Army Command and General Staff College, Fort Leveavenworth, KS. 1999, 8-10.

59 Ibid., 12; "From Chattanooga," *The Lafayette Daily Courier*, Lafayette, Indiana, September 14, 1863.

Gen. John B. Turchin's four regiments leading the way, Reynolds started his small division north along the La Fayette Road.[60]

And then Thomas changed his mind. Some time after 1:00 p.m., at Thomas's direction, Reynolds caught up with the rear of Turchin's brigade at the McDonald house and ordered it to reverse course and "take position southeast of Kelly's Crossroads." Reynolds did not ride to the head of the brigade to personally speak with Turchin. Instead, he transmitted the order to the 18th Kentucky and 92nd Ohio, the two rear regiments in Turchin's column. Their commanders responded with alacrity but failed to send word of the revised instructions up the line to Turchin. The Russian, meanwhile, continued marching north for some time with only half his brigade (the 11th and 36th Ohio) before discovering his other half had plunged into the forest somewhere behind him, apparently in support of Palmer's left. As far as Turchin was concerned, they had disappeared without a trace. Sometime later Capt. William B. Curtis of the brigade staff arrived bearing revised orders to lead the now-furious Turchin back to the scene of the fight. It would take some time for him to find his wayward troops.[61]

With Turchin now moving in the right direction, Reynolds rode back south on the La Fayette Road and rejoined his remaining brigade under Col. Edward A. King. It was about 2:00 p.m. when Thomas found Reynolds with King's men just south of the Poe farm. The corps commander seemed worried, even pessimistic. "He told me," recounted Reynolds, "that our people were very hard pressed and expressed doubt about their maintaining themselves." Thomas instructed Reynolds "not to send any of my artillery" into the woods, mindful of the fact that Baird's division had already lost 14 of his 18 guns in the morning's action. The two men discussed how best to place and support the batteries, and then Reynolds, perhaps unsettled by his boss's worried mien, "asked Thomas distinctly if our people could maintain themselves. . . . He said he was not sure." If that is the case, reasoned Reynolds, "they must have some rallying point. Thomas then said I should exercise my own judgment and give help where it was needed if I could."[62]

---

60 OR 30, pt. 1, 473; Turchin's report makes it clear the division's first destination was the McDonald house. It is possible this was the "division of another corps" mentioned above.

61 Ibid., 440, 476.

62 Reynolds Statement, September 19, CCNMP.

A bit farther south, Brotherton field ran parallel to and west of the La Fayette Road, crowned by an open ridge running the length of the field about 75 yards west of the road. It seemed an ideal location for artillery, and Reynolds posted the 21st Indiana battery there and ordered King's 75th Indiana to support it. He positioned King's three remaining regiments in the vicinity of the field and awaited developments.[63]

Meanwhile, back on the firing line, Hazen, whose troops were still in the act of savaging Strahl's Rebels as they struggled to maneuver to the right under that deadly Yankee fire, was about to get a great deal of support. He needed it. Hazen's front line was firing so rapidly that ammunition was running short, and after about 30 minutes he ordered the 6th Kentucky (with the wayward three companies of the 124th Ohio still attached) forward to replace the bullet-less 41st Ohio. In some ways, the Kentuckians found that rotating into the front line was a relief, for now at least they could shoot back. The men of the 6th had already suffered several losses while lying in reserve, including Col. George T. Shackelford, who was wounded by a Rebel ball that passed through "the right arm, just below the shoulder, shatter[ing] the bone, and [becoming] imbedded in his back." Command passed to Lt. Col. Richard Rockingham. The 6th was a veteran unit, having faced combat at Shiloh and defended the infamous Round Forest at Stones River. They were up to the task here. The Kentuckians numbered 302 in their own ranks, with perhaps another 135 Ohioans from the attached 124th, and thus provided a fresh surge of firepower just in time to further cripple Strahl's command.[64]

A few minutes later, Turchin's two detached rear-most regiments arrived and Hazen immediately commandeered them. The 92nd Ohio relieved their fellow Buckeyes in the newly-baptized 124th, while the 18th Kentucky replaced Colonel Suman's 9th Indiana. By now, some of Hazen's men had fired nearly 100 rounds per man. Their weapons were badly fouled and almost too hot to touch. The new men had an easier time, as Strahl's Rebels were now retreating and hardly shooting back, but the renewed swell of musketry as the two fresh regiments opened fire drew attention from another quarter. This was the sound

---

63 *OR* 30, pt. 1, 440.

64 Reinhart, *6th Kentucky*, 212. One of the first monuments erected on a Civil War battlefield was built at Stones River by Hazen's men in 1863, six months after their furious contest on the site. See Reinhart, *6th Kentucky*, 168.

that had attracted Johnson's attention, and triggered the decision to send in Col. Joseph Dodge's brigade.[65]

Joe Dodge's four regiments moved south through the trees to appear directly behind Hazen's line at the north end of Brock Field. Dodge deployed his men for an attack, forming his regiments "thirty or forty feet in rear of Gen. [Hazen's brigade] and hidden . . . from them [and the enemy] by the thick undergrowth." With only 1,130 men in his brigade, Dodge placed all of his regiments in a single line, with the 30th Indiana on the left, and in order to the south, the 79th Illinois, 77th Pennsylvania, and 29th Indiana. On Dodge's signal his troops rushed forward, moving through Hazen's line toward the enemy. Dodge described both Hazen and his men as "thunderstruck."[66]

Dodge's advance produced mixed consternation and awe among their fellow Yanks. Private A. C. Shafer of the 92nd Ohio (Hazen) remembered they had only been "engaged some 15 minutes [when] Johnson's Division . . . charged and drove the enemy far away into the forest—Dodge's Brigade . . . running over us." Captain Lewis of the 124th Ohio marveled at the manner in which the men went into action: "The first regiment at double-quick rushes through and past our broken and decimated ranks, not stopping until they come close to the Confederate line, then halting abruptly, deliver a well directed volley in the face of the enemy, fall and reload while the next regiment rushes over them . . . to repeat [the process]. . . . It would be almost idle to add that the confederates were compelled to fall back. . . . I had seen many noble looking men before; I have seen many since, but have never seen any such men . . . as composed that charging column that relieved us that dismal afternoon at Chickamauga."[67]

While Dodge was hurrying to Hazen's aid, Confederate George Maney was becoming increasingly concerned about his right flank. It was protected only by a thin screen of cavalry skirmishers brought forward by Forrest when W. H. T. Walker's troops fell back. These cavalrymen belonged to George Dibrell's brigade, shifted south from the Reed's Bridge Road after the fighting ended there. Dibrell's troopers, however, faced Colonel Baldwin's entire brigade of Federal infantry, and Forrest informed Maney that he was "unable to sustain

---

65 OR 30, pt. 1, 768.

66 Dodge, "The Story of Chickamauga, part two."

67 A. C. Shafer, "An Incident of Chickamauga," *National Tribune*, May 21, 1914; Lewis, *Campaigns of the 124th Regiment*, 59-60.

himself against the strong force . . . pressing him." The situation on the right deteriorated further a short while later, when Maney heard artillery open a rapid fire from his right rear. Riding to investigate, Maney found Forrest "had been forced in" and in an effort to stave off disaster, brought up both Huggins's and Huwald's Tennessee batteries as reinforcements. Forrest was personally directing their fire, but not sanguine that he could hold back "the enemy [who] was certainly approaching in force from [the north]."[68]

As if the problems on the right were not enough, this was the same time Maney became aware of Colonel Dodge's advance on his left front. "I was soon convinced," reported the harassed Maney, "that my command was greatly overmatched." Earlier, he sent most of Lt. William B. Turner's Mississippi battery 300 yards to the rear to find a position suitable for the employment of artillery, leaving him only one brass Napoleon on the brigade firing line. Maney directed that lone piece to angle south in the hope it could rake Dodge's advancing line if the Yankees turned his left, but what were really needed were more infantry—and fast. Accordingly, Maney sent couriers to both Cheatham and Strahl imploring them for help.[69]

Strahl did his best to respond. By now his men had rallied after having fallen back in the wake of their disastrous flanking move. Strahl hastily advanced back into action, and Dodge's troops slammed directly into them. Strahl dolefully reported that "my three right regiments (the Nineteenth, Thirty-First, and Thirty-third) were thrown forward . . . and took possession of a small skirt of woods which they held until the line on their right had fallen back so far that they were again exposed to a severe enfilading fire."[70]

Dodge had no way of knowing it, but his advance had penetrated the lingering gap between Maney and Strahl that had vexed Cheatham. Each Confederate brigade thought the other had given way, exposing their own flank, and each commander was feeling isolated and threatened with disaster. Certainly Colonel Porter of the 6th Tennessee felt imperiled. "About this time the enemy [Dodge] . . . made a rapid advance upon my line both in front and flank, and . . . would have killed or captured the whole command had I not deemed it proper . . . to abandon the position and fall back." On the way back he

68 Jordan and Pryor, *Forrest's Cavalry*, 322; *OR* 30, pt. 2, 94.

69 *OR* 30, pt. 2, 95.

70 Ibid., 131-132.

met Maney, who after demanding to know why the 6th/9th was retreating, acquiesced and ordered Porter to fall back on Preston Smith's brigade line and reform. To Pvt. William H. Davis of the 9th Tennessee, the fight here "was desperate beyond description." A number of Tennesseans were captured, and for the moment, all was confusion. At least one of those Rebels, Pvt. Drew Brock, managed to free himself when a Federal officer took charge of him and the pair "drifted off some hundred yards from the main line." Finding a spring, the incautious Federal knelt to drink, whereupon Brock brained him with a large rock and hid in the nearby bushes for the duration of the fight. Several other Confederates were not so lucky, including regimental Sgt. Maj. J. H. Crothers, who was captured in this same action. The combined 6th/9th Tennessee was effectively out of the fight.[71]

Already decimated by losses, Maney's 4th Tennessee was the next to go. By now, the 4th was being led by Capt. Joseph Bostick of Company A. The regiment's colonel, James A. McMurray, was mortally wounded and the other field officers cut down earlier in the action. Bostick ordered the 4th and their attached sharpshooters to fall back once Dodge's Federals closed to within thirty paces. The single Napoleon of Turner's battery went with them, escaping capture by seconds.[72]

This left only the 1st/27th Tennessee on the right of Maney's line. Thus far its losses had been significantly fewer than those suffered by their comrades down the line to the left, but the collapse of the rest of the brigade rendered their position untenable. Private Watkins recalled a furious firefight. At one point Watkins seized the regimental colors as the bearer toppled over, shot through the brain. Watkins had no intention of being the next color-bearer to die, however, and thrust the banner into the hands of another man and resumed fighting. "It was a question of who could load and shoot the fastest," he explained. Events climaxed when General Forrest rode up with grim news: "Colonel Field," he barked, "look out, you are almost surrounded, you had better fall back." What was left of Maney's front dissolved into rout. "I ran through a solid line of bluecoats as I fell back," recalled Watkins. "They were

---

71 OR 30, pt. 2, 102; Entry for September 19, William H. Davis Diary and Letters, Emory University, Atlanta, GA; Lindsley, *Military Annals of Tennessee*, vol. 2, 216. As far as is known, Pvt. Drew Brock was not related to the Brocks of Brock Field.

72 OR 30, pt. 2, 100.

upon the right of us, they were upon the left of us, they were in front of us, they were in the rear of us. It was a perfect hornet's nest."[73]

When Jackson's Rebels gave way earlier, the Yankees did not aggressively pursue them. Now, however, with Dodge attacking farter south, General Johnson decided to commit the rest of his Federals to the fight. Willich and Baldwin both advanced, driving Maney's disordered regiments before them. Willich brought forward the 89th Illinois alongside the 49th and 32nd, leaving the 15th Ohio in reserve. He ordered his men to use "Advance, Firing," his experimental new formation. "The movement was quite simple," recounted Alexis Cope of the 15th Ohio, "being a line of battle in four ranks, each rank advancing a few paces in front and firing, then stopping to load while the other ranks advanced alternately, thus keeping up a steady advance and a steady fire all the time." The result was a methodical advance combined with a wall of fire, delivering a volley every 10 or 15 seconds while still sustaining a measured forward progress. Executed properly, "Advance, Firing" offered a devastating tactical advantage. The brigade used the new technique for the first time during the Tullahoma campaign at Liberty Gap, Tennessee, on June 25, 1863, with significant success.[74]

That success was duplicated at Chickamauga. "Away we sped on double-quick with a whoop, driving the enemy," remembered Allen Wilkins of the 49th Ohio. "[W]e advanced for more than a mile, and five pieces of artillery were taken." Scogin's abandoned fieldpiece was probably still on the field, not yet recovered, but the Yankees pushed forward far enough to also stumble on the remnants of Loomis's Michigan battery, of Baird's Division, which had already exchanged hands multiple times. Croxton's earlier efforts had not secured all of the 1st Michigan's guns, and now a new wave of Bluecoats swept over this repeatedly embattled ground and laid their own claim to the Wolverines's lost fieldpieces.[75]

Maney's battered command might have had more trouble disengaging if Baldwin's advance had been more aggressive. As Pvt. Levi Wagner of the 1st Ohio indicated, however, the Federals were wary of plunging headlong into the

---

73 Watkins, *Co. Aytch*, 109. Time likely dimmed Watkins's recollections. The 1st/27th suffered 13% losses in the battle. The 4th lost more than one-third of its men, while the 6th/9th suffered a staggering 57% loss on the other flank.

74 *OR* 30, pt. 1, 538-539; Cope, *The Fifteenth Ohio Volunteers*, 279.

75 Allen Willkins, "Soldiering With a Vengeance," *National Tribune*, Februry 15, 1900.

attack: "We advanced some distance through the heavy timber, driving the Rebel skirmish line . . . until our regiment came up to a rail fence, with an open field in our front. . . . The enemy were in heavy force beyond this field, which was narrow and sloped down into a hollow, beyond which [lay more] heavy timber. If they had got the 1st to advance through that field in line, there might have been none of [us] left to blow about their deeds of valor." This open "narrow and sloped" ground was Winfrey Field, and the skirmish line Wagner recalled driving was Dibrell's dismounted Rebel cavalrymen, who had done about as well as could be expected screening Maney's exposed right flank.[76]

Matters were not as well under control to the south on Willich's front. There, the 89th Illinois was exposed to a severe fire of both musketry and artillery during their attack. Catching sight of some Rebel gunners dragging off their Napoleon by hand, Companies A, B, and E of the 89th broke ranks to give chase and suffered considerably for their rashness. For a moment, confusion reigned. Lieutenant Colonel Duncan Hall mistook the excitement for a collapse of his flank and ordered the rest of 89th's companies to fall back a short distance and rally. The chaos caught Willich's attention. "Standing in front of the regiment and amid the shower of bullets . . . [he] complimented the regiment for its impetuous advance, calmed their excitement, instructed them how to advance firing and maintain their alignment. . . . After dressing and drilling them in the manual of arms for a short time," Willich moved them back into line with the brigade at the edge of Winfrey Field.[77]

The 89th had run into a new Confederate line. Maney's decision to send three of Turner's artillery pieces rearward to establish a fallback position proved wise. While Maney engaged Willich's Federals, Jackson reformed his own command alongside Lieutenant Turner's guns and added Scogin's surviving pieces "so posted as to have a crossfire in front of Turner's Battery," where, he reported, "the enemy's advance . . . was checked at this point."[78]

Willich and Baldwin established a strong line along the western edge of Winfrey Field, with Baldwin's regiments still holding the division's left. Willich sent word of their success back to divisional commander Johnson, who now realized his division did not have support on either flank. He halted any further

---

76 Levi Wagner, "Recollections of an Enlistee, 1861-64," AHEC.

77 *OR* 30, pt. 1, 543.

78 Ibid., pt. 2, 84.

advance and ordered Willich "to hold his ground." Two Union batteries added their potential firepower to this position. Captain Peter Simonsen's 5th Indiana unlimbered on Baldwin's left to place a crossfire across the open field. Willich instructed Capt. Wilbur F. Goodspeed to deploy sections of his Battery A, 1st Ohio Light Artillery, behind the brigade's center and right while Goodspeed's caissons took their turn retrieving what they could of Baird's abandoned fieldpieces.[79]

In the meantime, Dodge drifted back to the new line. In the midst of the charge against Strahl, Dodge's horse had been killed and the dying beast threw him some distance. "I never knew how far," he later recorded, but it took some time for him to regain his feet and his wits. While he was on the ground his troops had charged into the woods, only to come up against the same Rebel artillery storm that had rained metal into Willich's men; they fell back again in considerable disorder. Once he regained control, Dodge reformed his brigade in two lines on Willich's right, angled to the southwest to refuse the flank. By now, the nearest Federals (Turchin's men, who had replaced Hazen) were even farther off to the right.[80]

Johnson's remaining battery was the 20th Battery, Ohio Light Artillery, commanded by Capt. Edward Grosskopf. Thus far it had been of little use. Grosskopf and his men were somewhat of a bad odor among the rest of the division. The captain had taken over the battery in June after Capt. L. Smithwright was invalided out of the service—or, as Grosskopf averred, allowed to resign because of incompetence. Grosskopf found the battery to be ill-disciplined and unruly. He struggled to restore order and gain the confidence of his new command, with limited success. The battery's junior officers and NCOs were apparently not up to their tasks either, and as the division entered the fight Grosskopf had "to see to every detail . . . and manage the whole battery [by] himself." Willich showed little tolerance for Grosskopf. Levi H. Sipes of the 29th Indiana recalled that while climbing Sand Mountain just a few days earlier, Grosskopf's battery had fallen far behind the line of march. "It took him so long to get his guns up," wrote Sipes, "that Gen. Willich got out of patience and told the Captain to send some of his men on ahead and plant some corn and

79 Ibid., pt. 1, 535; 5th Indiana Battery Tablet, NE corner of Winfrey Field, CCNMP; Battery A, 1st Ohio Tablet, Brotherton Road, CCNMP.

80 Dodge, "The Story of Chickamauga, part two."

potatoes, they would be fit to eat by the time he got his guns up." So far, the 20th Battery had not fired a shot. Dodge placed them in the rear of his brigade.[81]

By 3:00 p.m., the fight for Brock Field was over. Cheatham's Southern division had attacked superior numbers of Federals and been repulsed all along the line. His men were now mostly resting and reorganizing in the woods several hundred yards to the east. The battle was now shifting south once again, as both sides fed more troops into the growing fight.

81 Edward Grosskopf to Edward Ruger, June 23, 1867, Thomas Papers, RG 94, NARA; John Otto Papers, "History of the 11th Indiana Battery," InHS; Levi H. Sipes, GAR Questionnaire, Chicago Historical Society.

Chapter Fifteen

Governed by Circumstances:

Saturday, September 19: 11:00 a.m. to 2:30 p.m.

Major General Alexander P. Stewart enjoyed a quiet, if somewhat frustrating, morning. At dawn, his troops resumed crossing West Chickamauga Creek, as did the other division of Simon Buckner's Corps under Maj. Gen. William B. Preston. Once across, both divisions maneuvered to close up alongside the left flank of Bushrod Johnson's Provisional Division of John B. Hood's Corps. This took some time, as the creek made a sharp angle northward and then a hairpin bend back south at the vicinity of the Hall farmstead. This sharp twist left most of Buckner's troops in line behind this bend and unable to advance directly west if ordered to do so. Hours were consumed shifting this way and that in an effort to unmask his infantry lines, an effort that proved only partially successful. By midmorning Stewart's brigades were formed in successive lines on Johnson's left, with Preston's troops on Stewart's left. Stewart's front was unobstructed, but Preston's front still faced the creek. It was far from an ideal position, but it was the best Buckner could manage under the circumstances.

At 9:00 a.m., Buckner ordered Capt. McDonald Oliver, commanding the Eufala Light Artillery, to unlimber on a ridge overlooking the creek near the Hall house and engage some distant Federals (probably men of Wood's or Van Cleve's divisions guarding Lee and Gordon's Mills). The Alabama gunners only managed to fire two rounds from their 3-inch ordnance rifles before Federal return fire drove them back. Some of this incoming fire fell amongst Stewart's

Alexander P. Stewart, who found his orders
to be unclear.

Miller's The Photographic History of the Civil War

infantry, but caused no serious disruption. During this shifting of lines and short artillery barrage, Bucker's men listened to the growing battle developing to the north.[1]

Just before noon Maj. Pollack Lee, ignoring standard protocol, bypassed Buckner and handed Stewart an order from Braxton Bragg instructing the division commander "to move to the point where firing had commenced, which," explained Stewart, "seemed to be a considerable distance to the right and somewhat to the rear of us." That was the extent of the command, and Major Lee was unable to elaborate.[2]

Alexander Stewart was a West Pointer, an 1842 graduate with both James Longstreet, soon to be fighting alongside him at Chickamauga, and William Rosecrans. Despite his education Stewart spent only one year on active duty before returning to the academy in 1843 to teach mathematics. In 1845 he resigned to take a similar position at Cumberland University in Tennessee. Stewart remained an educator until the war broke out in 1861, when he leveraged his military schooling for an early commission in the Confederate forces. He led brigades in all the army's major battles to date, and was promoted to major general and a division command on June 2, 1863. Despite his dearth of active prewar experience he was a capable soldier. Brave under fire, always calm and collected, Stewart earned the sobriquet "Old Straight" from the men he led.[3]

---

1 OR 30, pt. 2, 361, 400; Eufala Battery Tablet, Battleline Road, CCNMP.

2 Ibid., 361.

3 Elliott, *Isham G. Harris of Tennessee*, 9-13; Warner, *Generals in Gray*, 294; Elliott, *Isham G. Harris of Tennessee*, 80.

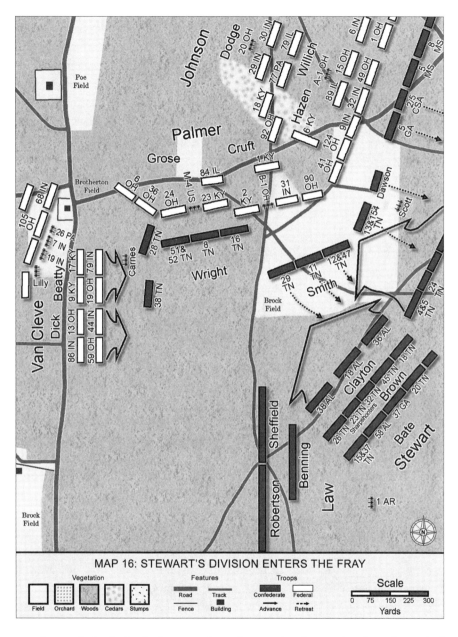

MAP 16: STEWART'S DIVISION ENTERS THE FRAY

Vegetation: Field, Orchard, Woods, Cedars, Stumps

Features: Road, Track, Fence, Building

Troops: Confederate, Federal, Advance, Retreat

Scale: 0 75 150 225 300 Yards

Stewart's logical mind, attuned to the precise demands of mathematical proofs, was unsure what to think or how to handle the perplexing order now in hand. There was little of substance in Bragg's vague directive "to move to the point where firing had commenced." After notifying Buckner, Stewart rode to Bragg's headquarters a mile or so to the rear near Thedford's Ford to seek clarification from the army commander himself. He found little satisfaction there, either. Bragg "informed me," Stewart later wrote, "that Walker was engaged on the right, was much cut up, and the enemy was threatening to turn his flank; that General Polk was in command on that wing, and that I must be governed by circumstances." Bragg and Polk had just parted company a short while before. Polk and his aide, Capt. J. F. Wheless, had conferred with the army commander while Ben Cheatham was moving up his division, and had departed to supervise the Tennessean's entry into the fight. Bragg likely assumed Stewart would take further instructions from Polk, who presumably had a better grasp of the tactical situation. Polk, however, was no George Thomas.[4]

When contrasted with Rosecrans's astute instructions to Palmer upon going into action about this same time, Bragg's directive comes off poorly. The Rebel commander didn't even mention that Cheatham's men had been similarly ordered into action a short time before, or from what direction the enemy might appear next. His reference to Polk only informed Stewart who was supposed to be in control on that part of the field, but he could not supply any detail on where Polk might be found. Dutifully, Stewart rode back to his men and ordered them to move out.

Bragg's order also further weakened the army's command structure. Earlier, Bragg divided Polk's Corps when he sent Cheatham into battle out of necessity. Cheatham's division was in reserve and not holding a place in the line, and were thus on hand when fresh troops were needed on the right side of the line. This was not true for Stewart's division. Between Stewart and the spreading fight farther north were two divisions of Hood's First Corps—six brigades numbering nearly 7,000 men. Stewart had to pull his men out of line, march behind Hood's formations, and then turn west again to come to grips with whatever Yankees he might find. This move also split Buckner's corps, with Stewart fighting north of Hood while Buckner continued to hold the line with Preston's division south of Hood. Marching around Hood's First Corps took time, and neither Stewart nor his aides could readily find Polk. Stewart found one of Polk's aides, Lt. William B. Richmond, who was unable to pinpoint the bishop's location. Stewart's leading elements were halted near the south end of the Brock cornfield, "beyond which the heaviest firing was heard," when Richmond rode upon the scene. Stewart had made the decision to insert

4   OR 30, pt. 2, 361; J. F. Wheless Memoir, TSLA.

his command when Richmond rode up and confirmed the decision. "From what he knew," reported Stewart, "a better point at which to attack . . . could not be found."[5]

By now it was now close to 2:00 p.m. Most of Cheatham's troops were either already disengaged or in retreat. Only Marcus Wright's brigade was still slugging it out with Federals in the woods between the Brock farm and the Brotherton Road, and Wright was getting the worst of it.

Alexander Stewart was not the only general officer who felt as though he was groping about in the dark. Opposing Stewart at the southern end of the Union line was Maj. Gen. Thomas L. Crittenden, who fretted away most of the morning listening to the sounds of battle growing louder as the fight worked its way down the line from the north. George Thomas's XIV Corps was heavily engaged, but beyond that Crittenden knew little. Little had been heard from General Palmer since his division had marched to support Thomas before noon. Shortly after Palmer departed, Crittenden received a plea from Thomas asking for a second division if he could spare the troops. Crittenden sent Maj. John Mendenhall, his own chief of artillery, and Col. Joseph C. McKibbin, one of Rosecrans's aides-de-camp who happened to be present, to investigate. They returned a short time later to report they had run into Rebels but had not found Palmer. This news, reported Crittenden, "led me to believe that . . . Palmer was not only fighting in his front, but was attacked in his rear and perhaps surrounded."[6]

The Crittenden name was a famous one in Kentucky. Thomas's father, John J. Crittenden, was the U.S. Senator who famously tried to forge a compromise and avoid war in 1860. When that effort failed, Thomas joined the North while his older brother George went South. Both were generals in opposing armies by the next year. Thomas L. Crittenden was a lawyer, not a soldier, though he did have experience as an aide on Gen. Zachary Taylor's staff in Mexico. His early promotion was undoubtedly due to the political importance his name carried in Kentucky, a state Lincoln determined to keep in the Union at all costs. By 1863 Crittenden had seen action at Shiloh and commanded a corps at both Perryville and Stones River. He proved competent enough during the latter battle to be awarded a brevet promotion. Thomas

---

5   *OR* 30, pt. 2, 361.

6   Ibid., 607.

Crittenden was not destined to emerge as one of the war's great leaders, but he was not about to let one of his divisions be cut off and captured, either.[7]

Aside from some long-range artillery fire, affairs were quiet on Crittenden's front, so the XXI Corps commander took a risk. With Palmer's detachment, Crittenden had only five infantry brigades left to him. Brigadier General Thomas J. Wood's division had only two brigades on hand, since Brig. Gen. George Wagner had been left to garrison Chattanooga. Brigadier General Horatio Van Cleve's division had its full complement of three brigades. Wood's men were defending the crossing site at Lee and Gordon's Mills, but some of Van Cleve's troops might be spared to help Thomas. Crittenden summoned Van Cleve to order him to march two of his brigades north where they could push on after Palmer. Before Van Cleve arrived, Crittenden sent a courier to Rosecrans at the Widow Glenn's to seek permission to meet Thomas's request. Both Van Cleve's leading elements and Rosecrans's agreement reached Crittenden about the same time. As a result, Crittenden led Van Cleve and his brigades up the La Fayette Road and into battle, trusting Wood to defend the Mills on his own.

Van Cleve later reported the timing of his order to march north as 1:00 p.m., but it was probably somewhat earlier. Horatio Van Cleve was also a West Pointer, though a decade older than most of his fellow academy alumni in the U.S. Army. Graduating in 1831, he left the military in 1836 to pursue a varied career: farming, teaching, surveying, and engineering in Michigan, Ohio, and finally Minnesota. He was the 2nd Minnesota's first commander, did well enough to garner promotion, and had led both a brigade and his division in combat. Like A. P. Stewart, Van Cleve was also unhappy with his orders. The instructions themselves were clear enough: "support General Palmer on our left, who was then hotly engaged." The division leader, however, was worried about dividing his command. Only Brig. Gen. Samuel Beatty's and Col. George F. Dick's brigades would accompany him; Col. Sidney M. Barnes's four regiments were to stay with Wood and watch the crossing.[8]

Samuel Beatty's troops led the column. Two of Dick's regiments, which had supported Wilder the night before, withdrew at dawn to cook breakfast and

---

7   Warner, *Generals in Blue*, 100.

8   Warner, *Generals in Blue*, 521; OR 30, pt. 1, 803.

hustled after Beatty. Dick's two other regiments remained in the vicinity of Viniard Field and joined the rear of the formation as it passed.

The men in the ranks were keyed up and ready for something to happen. All morning long the crescendo of combat had kept them on edge. Captain James R. Carnahan of the 86th Indiana later waxed poetic in describing the moment: "[T]he sound of the contest begins to gather and grow in strength. It comes on like the blasts of the tornado . . . until it comes in a great rush and roar . . . before which those who hear it and are not of it stand in awe." Soon enough they weren't standing, but moving quickly up the La Fayette Road toward the spreading fight. They did so in a brown fog. As Lt. Jason Hurd of Company G, 19th Ohio, later recalled, "we struck a double-quick: clouds of dust enveloped us and hid from view every surrounding object. Even the men . . . could scarcely distinguish each other."[9]

Just south of the Brotherton cabin, General Beatty's four regiments halted and faced right, fronting toward the woods farther east. The 19th Ohio and 79th Indiana formed in front, while the 9th and 17th Kentucky fell in behind. Both Crittenden and Van Cleve supervised this deployment, and immediately sent Beatty's troops into the trees. It was about 2:00 p.m. Colonel George Dick's four regiments were still hurrying up the road, and would have to catch up as best they could.[10]

No fewer than five Union generals watched Beatty's men step off into the woods or were within a few hundred yards of their lines when they deployed. In addition to Crittenden and Van Cleve, division commanders Palmer and Reynolds were both active in Brotherton Field at this time, and George Thomas was in the immediate vicinity, probably nearer Poe Field. Command confusion, however, was not just a Confederate problem this day. None of the latter three officers seemed aware of Van Cleve's arrival, or if they were, took little note of it. A coordinated forward movement by Van Cleve's new arrivals and Palmer's existing force could have rolled up much of Cheatham's division, but that did not happen.

As described earlier, after his encounter with Thomas, Reynolds positioned himself near the Brotherton farm. John Palmer found Reynolds there as Beatty's men were deploying. Palmer's men had been fighting for nearly two

9 James R. Carnahan, "Personal Recollections of Chickamauga" *MOLLUS*, vol. 9; Jason Hurd Diary, CSI.

10 *OR* 30, pt. 1, 808.

hours and ammunition was growing scarce. Turchin's arrival had allowed Hazen to rotate out of line to re-supply, but Palmer needed support for Grose and Cruft. Mindful of Thomas's earlier instructions to "give help where it was needed," Reynolds offered Edward King's brigade less the 75th Indiana, which Reynolds retained to guard his artillery line.[11]

Instead of merely replacing part of Palmer's embattled line with King's men, someone conceived the idea of sending King to strike the flank of the Rebels facing Cruft. It was a sound tactical plan, but neither Palmer nor Reynolds appeared to realize that Van Cleve, in the form of Sam Beatty's fresh brigade, was already moving to do exactly that. Behind Beatty to the south came Dick's tramping regiments, deploying along the La Fayette Road to do the same thing. Groping for an opening in the Union line where he could go into action pursuant to Palmer's intentions, King ended up moving south past Van Cleve's division to enter the woods on Dick's right. The need to work around Van Cleve's two brigades delayed King's deployment even more so than Dick's, so that all three brigades entered the ensuing fight at staggered intervals, Beatty first, then Dick, and finally, King. This disorder was apparent even to the men in the ranks. Albion Tourgee of the 105th Ohio, King's brigade, observed "the winding roads were full of lost staff officers. The commander of a regiment rarely saw both flanks of his command at once. . . . Confusion reigned even before the battle began." At one point, "seeing a group of officers in consultation" one wag of an Ohioan "guessed they were 'pitching pennies to decide which way the brigade should front.'"[12]

The Confederates upon whom this avalanche of Federal regiments was about to fall were largely unaware of their peril. Marcus Wright's command was Frank Cheatham's last brigade still in the fight. Wright was worried about his exposed left flank, but could do little about the problem. His men stepped into action westward, but their orientation drifted roughly 90 degrees so that they were now facing north and engaging elements of Cruft's and Grose's Federals. This change of direction exposed Wright's left flank, which was now perpendicular to, and only about 400 yards east of, the La Fayette Road. In an

---

11 Ibid., 440.

12 Albion W. Tourgee, *The Story of A Thousand: Being a History of the Service of the 105th Ohio Volunteer Infantry, in the War for the Union from August 21, 1862 to June 6, 1865* (S. McGerald & Son, 1896), 219. King was killed in action the next day, so no reports for the brigade or the regiments are found in the *Official Records*. Neither Palmer nor Reynolds in their postwar writings offer details of the orders given to King.

effort to protect that vulnerability, Wright placed Lt. William Carnes's Tennessee battery on the left, hoping its firepower could make up for the lack of infantry. Carnes, however, was still oriented toward Grose's line in an effort to answer the fire of Batteries H and M, 4th U.S. Artillery, whose guns were working over Wright's infantry.

Sam Beatty's men were perfectly positioned to enfilade Wright's formation; in naval parlance crossing his "T". Beatty was a competent practical soldier, a man with Mexican War experience and two terms as sheriff of Stark County, Ohio. When war broke out he helped raise the 19th Ohio infantry and was elevated to brigade command after Shiloh. Before him waited the perfect tactical opportunity. On the brigade right, Lieutenant Hurd and the rest of the 19th plunged into "a pine forest, thick with low bushes. . . . In less than five minutes, we ran full upon the left flank of a Rebel Battery heavily supported by infantry." Simultaneously, a member of the 79th Indiana also spotted Carnes's guns and alerted Col. Frederick Knefler, who ordered his Hoosiers to open fire on the Rebels to "disable the men and horses."[13]

Knefler, a Hungarian exile from the 1848 revolution, was also a rarity in nineteenth century America: he was Jewish. He served under Maj. Gen. Lew Wallace, first in the 11th Indiana and then on the general's staff at Fort Donelson and Shiloh. Knefler did well enough in those actions to earn an appointment to command the 79th in August 1862, and continued to impress both subordinates and superiors. He was not initially a popular figure in the 79th due to his European notions about military discipline, but no one doubted his competence or bravery in combat, which was enough to win over the rank and file.

The two leading Federal regiments numbered 684 men, and their fire swept through Carnes's gun crews with devastating effect. The battery had only just opened fire, having had to clear ground through the trees with axes before they could unlimber and engage Grose's Federals just 300 yards to the north. Beatty's sudden arrival forced Carnes to turn some of his guns 90 degrees to engage this new threat.

Federal rifle fire splintered limbers and trails, thudded against wheels and into men. Confederate Lt. Lucius G. Marshall watched in mingled shock and horror as the upraised lid of a limber chest drew a tremendous fire: "the white pine of the unclosed cover . . . attracted hundreds of hostile infantry shots,

13 Jason Hurd Diary, CSI; OR 30, pt. 1, 811.

which, passing through the wood and puncturing the outside tin, made the chest resemble a huge grater." A surprised Marshall noted that none of the men retrieving ammunition out of the chest were hit by this fire, but that luck proved fleeting. Before long both men and horses were rapidly falling. The Rebel crews managed to reply with a few rounds of canister, poured into the faces of their attackers, but within minutes Carnes recognized the situation was hopeless and ordered his gunners—those still on their feet—to retreat. Worried the Yankees would recognize the normal bugle call for "cease firing," Carnes ordered his bugler to instead sound "Assembly." The ruse did little to fool the oncoming enemy. Every gun, limber, and 49 mangled horses were left on the field. Manpower losses are harder to calculate. Of the 90 or so men serving with the battery on September 19, Carnes officially reported only seven killed and 16 wounded. Official reports and reality, however, are not always the same thing. Many of his men were hit multiple times. Lieutenant A. Van Vleck took a thigh wound early in the action, but stayed at his post until a second bullet inflicted more serious damage. Carnes detailed an extra man to help the ambulance corpsmen take the lieutenant to the rear (Van Vleck was a big man) when a third round pierced his heart, killing him on the spot.[14]

When he learned of Beatty's approach, Wright made his way to the left on foot. The surprised brigadier recognized he had no chance of stopping the assault and sent aides scrambling through the brush with orders for both the brigade and the battery to retreat. Wright credited Carnes's sacrifice with buying time to allow most of his brigade to disengage in good order, the regiments falling back one by one as their commanders' instructions traveled down the line. Only the 28th and 38th Tennessee, Wright's two left-most regiments, were severely disrupted by Yankee fire during this movement. Lieutenant Spenser Talley of the 28th recorded that the woods where his regiment fought, caught between Grose's men on their right and Beatty's to their new front, turned into "a hideous and blood curdling scene. The trees were shattered into splinters and dead and wounded men covered with [wood] fragments. . . . Trees as large as my body were severed in twain." Colonel Sidney Stanton, Talley's commander,

---

14 *OR* 30, pt. 2, 81. In 1893, Carnes recalled his losses were 11 killed and 27 seriously wounded, for a total of 38, plus three more men slightly wounded who remained on duty. "All included," he wrote, "we had 41 men shot in the fight on Saturday." "My Dear General," Oct. 22, 1893, James William Eldridge Papers, Huntington Library, San Marino, CA.; Lindsley, *Military Annals of Tennessee*, vol. 2, 821-822; "My Dear Hickman," W. W. Carnes to Col. Jno P. Hickman, Oct. 3d, 1905, Carnes's Battery file, CCNMP.

reported that the effort to disengage "more fully exposed [the regiment] to the fire of the enemy" resulting in heavy losses as the 28th fell back about 150 yards to reform. The 38th Tennessee on the far left had already disappeared, recalled Lieutenant Marshall, when their colonel, John C. Carter, strolled coolly into the maelstrom of fire sweeping the battery "as if for a social visit." However, Marshall admitted, the infantry "probably did right to leave, for otherwise they would have been annihilated."[15]

Delighted with their success, Beatty's Federals made the most of seizing Carnes's guns as trophies. Men from all of his four regiments helped haul some of the guns back toward the La Fayette Road. Major David Claggett of the 17th Kentucky was in the brigade's second line, supporting the 79th Indiana. "[We moved on the] double quick for about a mile with the finest prospect for a fight," he cheerfully recorded in his diary that night, "and were soon hotly engaged—we drove the enemy and captured a battery of four guns and got them off the field. I got the battle flag myself." Colonel Knefler of the 79th noted that his Hoosiers lost more than a few men charging the guns, but it could have been much worse if Carnes's crews had been allowed to fire their final rounds. Once the battery was captured, the exhausted but jubilant Hoosiers discovered the gun tubes loaded to the muzzles with double canister waiting to be discharged. The gunners had been shot, captured, or had retreated just in time to prevent what could only have been a slaughter.[16]

While Beatty's Federals were overrunning Carnes and turning Wright's brigade out of position and into retreat, another Rebel brigade halted several hundred yards to the east trying to make sense of the fight. Brigadier General Henry Delamar Clayton was an Alabama politician and another lawyer-turned-soldier. He was competent enough in that new profession to earn the command of a combat brigade. He had only three regiments,

---

15 OR 30, pt. 2, 118; "Memories of Spenser Bowen Talley," 26, AHEC; OR 30, pt. 2, 126; Lindsley, *Military Annals of Tennessee*, vol. 2, 822.

16 Entry for September 19th, 1863, David M. Claggett Diary, 17th Kentucky file, CSI; George W. Parker, *History of the Seventy-Ninth Regiment Indiana Volunteers Infantry in the Civil War of Eighteen Sixty-One in the United States* (The Hollenbeck Press, 1899), 90. Exactly how many of the guns were hauled away, and how far they were taken, is open to question. Confederate accounts credit John C. Brown's brigade with recapturing Carnes's battery and restoring the guns to Confederate ownership. In later years, the park commission's proposed text concerning the capture of Carnes's battery noted the assistance of other regiments, which incensed Colonel Knefler who remained adamant his 79th captured the battery by itself—despite language to the contrary in his own official report.

Alabamians all: the 18th, 36th and 38th regiments. Of these, only the 18th had seen combat, and that was at Shiloh nearly a year and a half before. After the battle the regiment rode the rails to Mobile, where the latter two commands joined them in garrisoning the city until the entire brigade was transferred north to join Bragg in the spring of 1863. By Army of Tennessee standards, all three regiments were large, their numbers not yet worn down by field service. The brigade numbered 1,446 officers and men when it advanced into action.

The day thus far had been a frustrating experience for the brigade and its brigadier. The Alabama command had spent the past couple of hours tramping through the woods. "We were 'right-flanked' and 'left-flanked' and 'forwarded' so often and so fast," lamented soldier-correspondent Capt. Ben Lane Posey of the 36th, "that we were bewildered, somewhat disordered and quite out of breath before we [even] reached the enemy." Worse yet, the woods were "full of stragglers . . . skulkers and wounded. Whole companies, regiments, and brigades seemed scattered to the winds. . . . The fugitives told the wildest tales of flight and massacre." Rumors telegraphed their way through the ranks. Private Richard M. Gray of the 37th Georgia (which was bringing up the rear of A. P. Stewart's division some 800 yards behind Clayton's Alabama brigade) confessed that all they understood was that our "orders were to march to the center which, being hard pressed by Gen. Thomas's Corps needed help, and a heap of it." Clayton's understanding was just as vague for Stewart could do no more than pass on Bragg's formless instructions. "[A]fter having more definitely located the enemy," Clayton reported, "I would have to act for myself and be governed by circumstances."[17]

During their withdrawal, Colonel Carter of the 38th Tennessee and General Wright stumbled into Clayton's line, which was still facing north as if to assault Grose's Yankees. Carter warned Clayton of the danger approaching from the west and urged him to change front to meet it. Wright found one of Clayton's regiments and, still horseless and with time of the essence, cast aside protocol to urge the regimental commander to "move to my left and protect the men . . . retiring." One of Wright's aides, a young officer named Harris, found division leader Stewart about this time and reported that "Wright's Brigade was

---

17 "Clayton's Brigade at Chickamauga," *Mobile Reader and Advertiser*, October 23, 1863. Captain Posey signed his articles with the pen name "Ben Lane." R. M. Gray Reminiscences, 86, UNC. Gray wrote his recollections in 1867. It is doubtful that he or his comrades knew who they were facing when they started to move on September 19. OR 30, pt. 2, 401.

much cut up by an enfilade fire: that Carnes' Battery had been lost, and that help was wanted."[18]

Stewart spurred his mount forward, only to find that Clayton had already reoriented his lines to face west and was ready to advance. Sitting his horse amidst the ranks of the 18th Alabama, Stewart paused only long enough to order the men to give "three cheers for Alabama" before sending them into the fight. The advancing Alabamians caught Beatty's Yankees still celebrating their earlier victory, enmeshed in drawing off their artillery trophies. Now, with no warning, it was their turn to be caught by surprise. When Wright fell back, Beatty halted his main line just short of Carnes's abandoned position to reorganize his brigade and wait for Dick's brigade to move up on his right. The Federals needed some untangling. During their charge, the 19th Ohio angled to the left, crossing the front of the 79th. Ohio Pvt. J. A. Reep recalled that "three or more companies" of the 79th were "directly behind us." Before things could be set right, however, Clayton's three large Alabama regiments came crashing through the woods.[19]

Clayton's nearly 1,500 men overwhelmed Beatty's front of fewer than 700, and the Rebel flank extended almost a full brigade front beyond Beatty's right. For a few short minutes this advantage seemed to be enough. Beatty's front line gave way as the 19th Ohio, fearing a flank attack, fell back behind the brigade reserve just 60 yards to the rear. The Hoosiers of the 79th Indiana followed suit in considerable disorder to a new position behind the 17th Kentucky, which then opened fire. "We was laying down to support them," Hoosier Pvt. William H. Huntzinger recalled, when orders arrived to get back into line, "as our regiment was scattered some out in front." Just then, a bullet struck William's younger brother Levi in the calf; William helped move Levi back an additional 50 yards before being ordered to return to the fighting line.[20]

Things might have been worse but for the steady presence of the 17th Kentucky. The men of the Bluegrass state were commanded by Col. Alexander

---

18 OR 30, pt. 2, 119; B. L. Ridley, "Southern Side at Chickamauga, Part II," *Confederate Veteran*, vol. VI, no. 11 (November, 1898), 515. The Harris in question was Governor Isham Harris's son.

19 OR 30, pt. 2, 404; J. A. Reep, "Guttmachrala, or Four Years at the Front as a Private," 19th Ohio file, CSI.

20 William H. Huntzinger Diary, http://www.lafavre.us/huntzinger/hunt_v.htm, accessed 8/22/2012. Levi survived his wound and was sent home to recuperate.

Stout who, according to Lt. Jefferson Jenings, "was a very brave man [who] could repeat the tactics verbatim [but] who could hardly apply the most unimportant portion to any practical movement. Hence we always looked to [Lieutenant] Colonel [Robert] Vaughan for orders in action." Fortunately both men were present today. With Stout's presence providing the inspiration and Vaughan's head for tactics, the 17th proved a bulwark behind which the Hoosiers rallied.[21]

Clayton's attacking Rebels might have finished outflanking Beatty's line and rolled up yet another Federal command if Col. George Dick and his brigade had not arrived "in rear of and to support the First Brigade." Like so many on both sides, Dick was also confused. Initially he thought his brigade was to follow Beatty's, not move up abreast on his right. Beatty's earlier oblique to the left, however, exposed Dick's two frontline regiments, the 59th Ohio and 44th Indiana, which slammed into the other half of Clayton's long Rebel line. The two Federal regiments combined numbered just 519 officers and men, and so were undersized compared to the Alabama commands. Even when added to Beatty's rifles, the combined Union line was still overmatched, but surprise made up for the numerical disparity. Opposite the 59th, one Rebel recorded the moment of contact: "The left wing of the 38th Alabama . . . ran into an ambuscade of the enemy . . . [with] a fatal volley which instantly killed Major [O. S.] Jewett and Captain [W. Ripley] Walsh, and brought down about a score" of others. The men of 38th were still in column when they met the Buckeyes and scrambled into a disordered line in an effort to return fire.[22]

Both sides halted about 100 yards apart and began exchanging a heavy, steady, and static fire. The woods here were thicker than on most of the field, and a number of men on both sides commented on the unusual density of the undergrowth. The brush, however, provided little protection from bullets and casualties mounted. Beatty's former front line rallied behind the two Union Kentucky regiments, now roughly aligned with the 44th and 59th of Dick's brigade. With his men taking a pounding, Clayton ordered them prone. While this offered greater protection, it reduced firepower and accuracy. That wouldn't do at all. "The firing seeming to be too much at random," reported the brigadier, and "I passed down and up the line, calling the attention of officers to

21 J. H. Jennings to Ezra Carman, November 28, 1893, Carman Papers, NYPL.

22 *OR* 30, pt. 1, 823; "Clayton's Brigade at Chickamauga," *Mobile Register and Advertiser,* October 23, 1863.

the fact." Many years later the Reverend (then corporal) Edgar W. Jones recalled the firefight: "Standing in line the firing began, seemingly without any command, and in three minutes the engagement was something awful. The slaughter was dreadful . . . Company G had fifteen men wounded in less than that many minutes." Down the Southern line in the ranks of the 38th, Pvt. Joseph H. Findley also experienced the horror. "They cut as all to pieces," he informed his father. "I have no idea how many men were killed, on either side, but there was a heap of them."[23]

The slugfest lasted about half an hour, with the Alabama men getting the worst of things. The Federal fire was so effective that Clayton believed his brigade was outnumbered, with both flanks overlapped, and that his men were caught in a crossfire. He had to do something, so he dispatched his staff to inform the regimental commanders to prepare for a charge, but abruptly changed plans when he learned his men were running short of ammunition. Clayton asked Stewart if he could fall back to re-supply. Stewart agreed, and ordered John C. Brown's brigade to move up to replace him.

Clayton's brigade lost nearly 400 men during the action, including several officers. One of them was the 18th Alabama's colonel, James T. Holtzclaw. According to the official report, the officer "was thrown from his horse and so badly hurt" that he had to leave the field. Another account claimed he was stunned after his horse "struck a tree." Corporal Edgar Jones, however, suggested another cause. Just before going into action, Jones remembered "a field officer turning up a bottle which I supposed contained whiskey, and I further thought he was trying to steady his nerve. I was not surprised when I learned afterward that his horse had fallen with him and disabled him to such an extent that he had to go to the rear."[24]

A brief lull ensued as Clayton's troops melted back into the woods. Colonel Dick ordered a charge, but it did not amount to much and the Yanks halted to

23 OR 30, pt. 2, 401; Edgar W. Jones, and Zane Geier, ed. "History of the 18th Alabama Infantry Regiment," 18th Alabama file, CCNMP; Joseph H. Fendley, "Fendley's Civil War Letter," *Clarke County Historical Society Quarterly*, vol. 7, no. 4 (Spring, 1983), 108.

24 OR 30, pt. 2, 401, 405. Clayton also estimated the fight lasted an hour, but this seems too long when considering the other engagements going on around them. Thomas W. Cutrer, ed. *Oh, What a Loansome Time I had: The Civil War Letters of Major William Morel Moxley, Eighteenth Alabama Infantry, and Emily Beck Moxley* (University of Alabama Press, 2002), 140; Jones, "History of the 18th Alabama," CCNMP.

await further developments. Thus far Federal losses had been much lighter, probably no more than 200 men killed and wounded.

Farther west and a bit north in Brotherton Field, Joe Reynolds was still trying to be useful. By now, his command consisted of only Col. Milton Robinson's 75th Indiana and Capt. Samuel J. Harris's 19th Indiana battery. Still, Reynolds was thinking of contingencies. While Van Cleve's infantry watched the Rebels retreat, Reynolds sketched out the ghost of a Federal line in Brotherton field. He posted Harris's six guns on the crest of the small ridge running the length of the field and instructed Robinson to support his fellow Hoosiers. In the meantime, two of Van Cleve's batteries that had been following their brigades arrived and prepared to enter the woods. First up was Capt. A. J. Stevens's 26th Pennsylvania artillery, trailing Beatty. Stevens also had six guns, all brass: four of the outdated Model 1841 six-pound smoothbores and two James rifles, which were simply six-pounders re-bored with rifling in an effort to update them. Stevens split his battery, dispatching the section of James rifles to a position alongside Harris before plunging into the woods with the four smoothbores. He unlimbered behind the 9th and 17th Kentucky and was preparing for action when the infantry advanced and disappeared into the foliage. With the woods too thick for limbered artillery, Stevens split the battery again, this time by ordering the crews of the two smoothbore sections to advance their guns by hand to support Beatty's men with canister if the Rebels broke through. The risky decision separated the guns from their limbers and caissons and would make them nearly impossible to quickly withdraw should the need arise.[25]

Captain George R. Swallow's 7th Indiana Battery, following Dick's brigade, was the second to arrive and also faced a similar quandary. Swallow's battery had been divided earlier, when he was directed to leave two of his 10-pound Parrott rifles near Lee and Gordon's Mills. Now up at the front, he ordered his remaining two Parrotts and two Napoleons into the woods behind the infantry. There, Swallow found his guns all but useless as he took several positions without finding any viable targets. Reynolds caught wind of Swallow's troubles and, mindful of Thomas's admonition about saving artillery, recalled the 7th and posted the guns on the ridge south of Harris.[26]

25 *OR* 30, pt. 1, 820.

26 O. H. Morgan and E. R. Murphy, *History of the 7th Independent Battery Indiana Light Artillery* (Bedford, IN, 1895), 23; Reynolds Statement, September 19, 1863, CCNMP.

Reynolds was slowly accumulating a sizable force in Brotherton Field. His scratch command grew again when Col. Smith Atkins arrived at the head of the 92nd Illinois. Normally part of John Wilder's brigade, Atkins and his men had not seen much of Wilder the past few days. Until September 18, the 92nd had been on duty with Thomas's XIV Corps headquarters, which in turn passed them on to Reynolds to act as couriers and a mounted telegraph line while he was in McLemore's Cove. Atkins was sent that morning to re-join Wilder, but the reunion was cut short when Wilder informed him that General Thomas wanted him to report to Reynolds, "near Brotherton's." The delighted Reynolds warmly welcomed the 92nd's arrival. "[I] was ordered . . . to hitch all my horses in the woods," wrote Atkins, "and moved up to and on the right of a battery planted . . . in reserve to King's Brigade."[27]

Back on the Confederate side of the line, meanwhile, John Calvin Brown, yet another Tennessee lawyer-turned-soldier, led his veteran brigade into the fight. Brown was a competent combat officer who had taken a wound at Perryville and would eventually rise to division command. His men were Tennesseans all, four regiments and a battalion numbering 1,340 rank and file. While his line was slightly shorter than Clayton's had been, the Federals were still formed in two lines, and most of their losses had come from the front rank, meaning the two Union brigades probably mustered only about 1,000 rifles along their entire front. Moreover, Dick's recent pursuit left his two lead regiments disordered and exposed some distance in advance of Beatty's line.[28]

Brown's Tennesseans hit the Yankees hard. Patches of fire touched off dropped shells and cartridges, and the smoke made seeing even a few yards difficult. "The dead and dying of both sides covered the ground," recalled Cpl. Thomas J. Corn of the 32nd Tennessee. As the 32nd swept through Carnes's former position, Corn took note of a horrific sight: "thirteen dead [animals] in one pile." The small arms fire rose to a dizzying crescendo. "The engagement was the most severe and constant of any that I ever witnessed," recorded George W. Dillon of the 18th Tennessee, fighting on Brown's right. All of the 18th's field officers fell, most of them early in this charge.[29]

27 Wilder Revised Report, CCNMP; OR 30, pt. 1, 456.

28 Warner, *Generals in Gray*, 36.

29 T. I. Corn, "Brown's Brigade at Chickamauga," *Confederate Veteran*, vol. XXI, no. 3 (March, 1913), 124; Entry for September 19, 1863, George W. Dillon Diary, TSLA.

Brown's men pressed home their attack with firm determination. "We had made one charge and drove the Rebs," wrote Company A's John Warbinton of the 59th Ohio, "but was not able to hold our ground. [A]s we was falling back and Just before I passed the line that was in our rear I was hit. I felt the ball when it struck but it didn't hurt so I . . . fell in and . . . helped the Capt. form the Co." Warbinton's mangled finger was later amputated. The Buckeyes were all but routed. "[After the charge]," reported Lt. Col. Granville A. Frambes, the 59th's commander, "I then observed that my line was in advance of the . . . [44th Indiana] . . . and my right flank was unprotected. . . . I then halted and had to lie down and fire at will. Shortly after I gave this order I discovered the enemy was flanking me on my right and the line on my left was falling back rapidly. . . . I then gave the order to fall back."[30]

The Hoosiers of the 44th Indiana suffered a similar fate. They were nearly isolated, well in advance of Beatty's men on their left and disconnected from the 59th on their right. Lieutenant Colonel Simeon C. Aldrich of the 44th "ordered a slow retreat, fighting our way back to a small ravine, where I rallied my men again." With his front giving way, Dick moved his men back far enough to rally them into a single line. An order from Van Cleve directed Dick to close up and align all four regiments alongside Beatty's newly-reformed second line, now consisting of the 19th Ohio and 79th Indiana.[31]

Brown's attack had also forced Beatty's front line—the 9th and 17th Kentucky—to the rear. Colonel Alexander M. Stout of the 17th witnessed the 44th Indiana's retreat and described it as considerably more chaotic than had the 44th's own Lieutenant Colonel Aldrich. "They broke to the left and rear in great disorder," claimed Colonel. Stout. "My regiment at once felt the enemy's fire . . . and to escape capture fell back to the left and rear by companies." To Lt. Samuel Cox of the 17th's Company C, the Rebel fire was so intense that as he walked backwards, trying to retreat while keeping his face to the enemy, it looked as if "a wall of rifle bullets" pursued him.[32]

Things were even more desperate in the ranks of the 9th Kentucky. Directly behind these Kentuckians were Captain Stevens's four six-pounders of the 26th Pennsylvania battery. When the troops on his right fell back, Stevens

30 "Dear Aunt," Oct. 4, 1863, John J. Warbinton Letters, AHEC; OR 30, pt. 1, 833.

31 *OR* 30, pt. 1, 827, 823.

32 Ibid., 816; John Blackburn, *A Hundred Miles, a Hundred Heartbreaks* (Reed Printing Company, 1972), 126.

made his way to the 9th's commanding officer, Col. George H. Cram, who urged "the Captain to give [the enemy] some of his 'most suitable pills.'" Stevens complied, and the ensuing canister ripped through Brown's Rebels with devastating effect.[33]

Brown's Tennesseans, in turn, hurled themselves at this last holdout. "We were ordered . . . double-quick through the smoke of powder, and charged a battery supported heavily by infantry," recalled the 18th Tennessee's Pvt. Noah J. Hampton. "Some of us lay our hands on the artillery, and the cannoneers fought at us with their sabers. . . . We were so close to the cannons that we were burned by the powder. One poor fellow standing within ten steps of the cannon got his head shot off, his brains and hair falling on my left shoulder." Despite fearful losses, momentum and numbers were in Brown's favor.[34]

Lieutenant Marcus Woodcock was one of those embattled Kentuckians. From the ranks of the 9th he watched with increasing alarm as "presently the rebel infantry fell with resistless force upon our right . . . the woods [here] were so open, that we could see to a considerable distance." The visibility in his narrow sector offered no comfort. "Soon [the 17th] begins to waver, and then fall back in great disorder, upon which the rebels set up a deafening yell and bound forward in pursuit. The rebels . . . came down upon . . . our regiment with the fury of a tornado." Matters took an even darker turn when friendly fire began bursting within the 9th's ranks, "which broke the line into disorder." The fire came from Harris's 19th Indiana battery, part of Reynolds's scratch line in Brotherton Field. Harris reported that he tried to fire only "when we could do so without endangering the lives of our own men," but admitted to Beatty after the fight that he had been ordered to open fire (presumably by Reynolds) and had little choice but to comply. Woodcock recalled "one of the shells bursted in the midst of Cos. G and K and severely stunned Lieut. Rodes and several men." This new assault was simply too much to bear, and threw the 9th into confusion.[35]

Alone, nearly surrounded, and struggling to save Stevens's 26th Pennsylvania's guns, the 9th finally broke and ran. Stevens's cannon paid the

33 Noe, *A Southern Boy in Blue*, 198.

34 Noah J. Hampton, *An Eyewitness to the Dark Days of 1861-1865, Or a private Soldier's Adventures and Hardships During the War* (Privately printed, 1898), 31.

35 Noe, *A Southern Boy in Blue*, 199; OR 30, pt. 1, 808; Ibid., 471, 808; Noe, *A Southern Boy in Blue*, 199.

price when Brown's Rebels made for their trophies. The limbers had come forward in a belated effort to withdraw the pieces, but it was too late. "It was impossible to check them," reported Keystoner Lt. Samuel McDowell, "[B]y the time the battery had limbered up the horses of three pieces were nearly all shot and one limber blown up." The three captured Pennsylvania pieces proved a partial repayment for the earlier loss of Carnes's guns.[36]

Brown had successfully routed two Union infantry brigades (Dick and Beatty, a combined eight regiments) and overrun at least three guns. The Federals were struggling to reform in the timber several hundred yards to the west, almost at the La Fayette Road. Whether they could have held that line or not in the face of the vigorous oncoming pursuit is something that will never be known. With his moment of triumph at hand, it was Brown's turn to be assailed from an unexpected direction.

Unbeknownst to the Tennesseans, just a few hundred yards to their right were Colonel Grose's Yankees. In theory, Grose's men posed the same threat to Brown's flank that they had to Clayton's, but if Grose advanced south by southwest he would break his connection with the rest of Palmer's division, which was facing generally east. Further complicating the issue was the loss of Grose's right-most regiment, the 6th Ohio. Initially held in reserve, the 6th had been sent to extend Grose's right early in the fight against Wright's Tennesseans. The Buckeyes had suffered dozens of losses and were out of ammunition. General Palmer sent them to the rear to find more, but he did so without informing Grose that the regiment securing his right flank was no longer there.[37]

The 6th Ohio marched back north to the Brotherton Road, then west until it reached the Brotherton farmstead, where the Buckeyes found General Reynolds still trying to be helpful. The Ohioans, reported the division commander, "had come to the rear in great disorder," cut up by their earlier fight. Reynolds ordered Col. Nicholas Anderson to take his 6th "back to the fence [on the west side of Brotherton Field] and get themselves into shape." In the meantime, Palmer worried about Grose and especially about Battery H of the 4th U.S. Artillery, which was left exposed by the 6th's departure. Palmer

36 *OR* 30, pt. 1, 820.

37 Ibid., 796.

dispatched a courier to Reynolds requesting the loan of yet another regiment to take the 6th's place on Grose's exposed flank.[38]

The only infantry Reynolds had left when Palmer's request arrived was the 75th Indiana. Turchin's brigade had replaced Hazen's command, and Edward King with three regiments was still groping for a place in line south of Van Cleve's pair of brigades. Reynolds had a personal connection to the 75th, having been the regiment's first colonel, however briefly, at its muster-in in 1862. He still retained a proprietary interest in the command. His real worry, however, was in further stripping his already thin defensive line. He was pondering what to do when Palmer arrived and "said that he wanted a regiment very much. I had one," replied Reynolds, "but did not like to spare it. Palmer repeated his request, stating again "that he wanted the regiment very much. . . . He had whipped them [the Rebels] and just wanted more force to give them a final clinch." Reynolds acquiesced, reasoning that he could swap the 75th for the 6th Ohio and still retain a semblance of a reserve. Colonel Robinson would take his 360 Hoosiers forward and report to Palmer.[39]

Private James G. Essington of the 75th's Company D recalled the command was "marching 'left in front' [when] Gen. Palmer halt[ed] us [and] ordered Col. Robinson to move by the right flank." The Hoosiers advanced through the timber into the gap between Grose's now denuded right and Sam Beatty's left—straight into the right front and flank of Brown's advancing Tennesseans. Corporal William B. Miller of Company K thought they arrived there in the nick of time. "Our command was 'Fix Bayonet' and the race was for the guns, one of which was fast on a sapling and nearly all the horses were dead and only a few of the men left with their lieutenant. We got to the battery first and broke files around them and met the enemy 'face-to-face.' They haulted and we opened fire, and they began to waver and finally broke, but [first] our regiment received a volley that left its impression on our ranks."[40]

38 Reynolds Statement, September 19, 1863, CCNMP.

39 Ibid.

40 Entry for September 19, 1863, James G. Essington Diary, InHS. "Left in front" refers to the way the regiment would face in battle. Normally, a regiment formed up "right in front" so the men in the front and the rear ranks always fought in the same place. "Left in front" meant the regiment was essentially backward, and if it had to go into line the rear rank would now be in the front, and vice versa. While not a problem for properly trained troops who could fight and maneuver from either orientation, "left in front" was a less familiar facing, and a complication that no regiment would choose to have when entering battle unless dictated by necessity. Entry

The stuck gun belonged to Lt. Harry C. Cushing's Battery H of the 4th U.S. Artillery, fighting in the woods just south of the Brotherton Road. Cushing had split his battery, with one section under Lt. Robert Floyd supporting Grose's center, while he personally led the other section to the brigade's right. Unaware that the 6th Ohio had withdrawn, Cushing was fighting his two guns, including a "liberal use of short-fused case shot and canister." The artilleryman felt he was holding his own, but admitted that "the arrival of General Reynolds' troops completed [the rebels'] discomfiture."[41]

The 75th's attack broke the momentum of Brown's charge. The Rebel reported that just as his success seemed complete, "a force of the enemy appeared on my right flank, and had well-nigh turned it, compelling the 18th and 45th Tennessee Regiments to retire rapidly and in some confusion . . . ." Colonel Anderson Searcy of the 45th recalled that "a perfect shower of grape and canister enfiladed our line," confirming Cushing's own opinions about the accuracy of his fire.[42]

At the head of the 18th Tennessee, the ill Col. Joseph B. Palmer suffered a grievous wound when a bullet ripped into his right shoulder and severed an artery. Someone was smart enough to immediately apply a field tourniquet that stopped the bleeding and saved his life. With the battle still raging around them, his men were afraid to move him. When the regiment abruptly retreated, however, they shifted their colonel to a less exposed location and left. Palmer had the unfortunate knack of attracting enemy metal. He suffered at least three wounds in his last battle at Murfreesboro and spent the first four months of 1863 recuperating. He survived that difficult episode and he would this one as well, though by the thinnest of margins. He remained on the field all night, sick and, according to family history, pressing his thumb into the wound to keep from bleeding out. He would not rejoin the Army of Tennessee for 10 months, and when he did it was with a permanently paralyzed arm.[43]

While Palmer lay suffering, Brown hurried to the right side of his line to help rally the 18th and 45th Tennessee. Worse was yet to come for the

---

for September 19, 1863, William Bluffton Miller Diaries, InHS. Miller misidentified this battery as F, 4th Ohio, a unit that did not exist.

41 OR 30, pt. 1, 799; Ibid., pt. 1, 371.

42 Ibid., pt. 2, 380.

43 Lindsley, *Military Annals of Tennessee*, vol. 1, 364; Robert O. Neff, *Tennessee's Battered Brigadier: The Life of General Joseph B. Palmer, CSA* (Hillsboro Press, 2000), 99.

Tennesseans. The brigade might have recovered and driven the 75th back in turn, unsupported as the Hoosiers were, if not for the timely intervention of the rest of King's brigade, which struck almost simultaneously against Brown's left. King's troops, it will be recalled, had originally been sent to help Grose's brigade of Palmer's division. Initially posted near the 19th Indiana battery, King had barely started to move when one of Palmer's aides rode up, followed by Palmer himself. "The Genl ordered us to the left to help the right of his division, which was hard pressed," recalled John M. Kane, a sergeant with Company A of the 101st Indiana. King tried to follow Palmer's orders, only to find two other Union brigades (Beatty and Dick) in the way.[44]

After a fitful and frustrating march King's men entered the woods at "a point about five hundred yards south of the Brotherton House . . . moving at a quick walk without skirmishers." King formed his truncated command in two lines, with the 68th and 101st Indiana in front (left to right) and the 105th Ohio behind them. Short the 75th Indiana, King's front line numbered 756 rank and file with a frontage of roughly 150 yards. The 105th added another 310 officers and men in the second line. Future regimental historian Edwin High recalled passing the 26th Pennsylvania battery to the 68th's left as they went in. A short while later, High recalled the rising crescendo of fire marking Brown's engagement with Van Cleve's men to the north, and that "the roar of artillery and sharp rattle of musketry indicated that the fight was drawing close."[45]

King had long held martial aspirations and had amassed a considerable résumé. When he failed to get into West Point in 1831, he raised a company of

---

44 Joseph E. Suppinger, ed. "From Chickamauga to Chattanooga: The Battlefield Account of Sergeant John M. Kane," *East Tennessee Historical Society Publications*, no. 45 (1973), 101.

45 Edwin W. High, *History of the Sixty-Eighth Regiment Indiana Volunteer Infantry, 1862-1865, with a Sketch of E. A. King's Brigade, Reynolds' Division, Thomas' Corps, in the Battle of Chickamauga* (n.p., 1902), 64-65; Dean H. Keller, ed., "A Civil War Diary of Albion W. Tourgee," *Ohio History*, vol. 74, no. 2 (Spring, 1965), 121. The park monuments tell a different story with King's regiments in a single line, the 101st Indiana on the left and the 105th Ohio on the right. However, there are no reports in the OR for King's brigade; King was killed the next day (September 20) and his regimental reports did not reach army headquarters. Only one is known to exist, that of Lt. Col. Thomas Doan, 101st Indiana, in the files of the Indiana State Adjutant General's files for that regiment. Doan lists the regiments in the same order as the monuments, but does not state that this was how they entered the fight. High's history and other sources make it clear the 68th encountered Brown's Confederates first, something possible only if they held the brigade left, and Tourgee's diary specifically states the 105th Ohio formed the rear line. Two companies of the 105th Ohio were back with the trains. The full complement of the 105th on September 19 was 382 officers and men.

volunteers and joined the Texas Revolution in 1836 before finally entering the U.S. Army as a captain in the 15th U.S. Regulars in 1847—just in time to see extensive combat in Mexico (where he was wounded). He was a civilian in 1861 and joined the rush to the colors when the cannons opened. In 1862, he was captured at Munfordville while in command of the 68th Indiana. September 19, 1863, was the first major combat for King's 68th and 101st Indiana, but the 105th Ohio had been savagely bloodied at Perryville, losing 265 men out of nearly 750 present. King's task was a challenging one, groping for a Rebel flank in murky smoke-shrouded woods, equally in the dark about both the enemy's location and that of any friendly troops.[46]

Their first intimation of contact boded ill. "We . . . moved to the left, then forward, then back to the right—and the bullets were whistling thick—and then forward into line," recalled Pvt. John Beale of the 68th Indiana. "There was one regiment to our left and in advance of us. They broke and ran through our men." The fleeing regiment was the 59th Ohio of Dick's brigade. King had stumbled across the end of the Union line. Short of all of its field officers, the 68th went into battle led by Capt. Harvey Espy; Colonel King spent much of the advance just behind the regiment to keep an eye on it. Watching the 59th Ohio retreat, King reoriented the 68th so Espy's line faced northeast, and waited. Soon, "a force of the enemy, which seemed to be a brigade, appeared on the left front of [our line] moving in a northwesterly direction, with their left flank exposed to us. The dense underbrush hid us from their view."[47]

This unsuspecting Confederate force was in fact the 26th Tennessee on Brown's left flank. From the 68th's perspective, the 26th Tennessee appeared to advance with "the precision of a parade," but in fact the Tennesseans had already been hit hard. Their regimental commander, Col. John M. Lillard, turned the regiment to the northwest aiming for what he thought was another Union battery in the woods, but was in fact those pieces of Carnes's battery not yet drawn off the field. Already under heavy shell and infantry fire, the 26th crested a low ridge in the woods when King finally ordered the 68th Indiana to fire. According to Tennessee Maj. Richard Saffell, "the enemy's reserve line opened a most destructive fire upon us. Here Colonel Lillard fell mortally

46 Kapaun, *Major General Joseph J. Reynolds*, 31-32.

47 John Beale to wife, September 24, 1863, John Beale Papers, InHS; High, *Sixty-Eighth Indiana*, 65.

wounded by a shell, and command . . . devolved upon me. The fire from the enemy's troops at very short range threw our line into some confusion."[48]

Saffell was on his own. Lillard was down and Brown was busy at the other end of the brigade, which was simultaneously dealing with the sudden repulse of the 18th and 45th Tennessee. The Federals on his flank were mauling his own line, and beyond the 68th other Federals were moving up to engage his flank. Major Saffell quickly grasped that he faced more than a single Yankee regiment. Neither charging nor staying put seemed like good options. In the absence of instruction from above, Saffell ordered a retreat which, he admitted, "was not executed in very good order." The 26th tumbled back several hundred yards through the woods after having lost 73 of their 239 officers and men, for a 30% casualty rate.[49]

With both flanks retreating, Brown's center soon followed. The 32nd Tennessee, 341 strong, and the green 23rd Tennessee Battalion, another 144 rank and file, were set to pursue Van Cleve's brigades when Col. Edmund Cook of the 32nd realized his peril. Beatty and Dick's men appeared to have rallied, he noted, and another Union battery seemed to be throwing shells into his line. Just then, "Major [John P.] McGuire approached and informed me that we had no support on either the right or the left, and were about to be flanked by the enemy." Like Saffell, Cook was alone; Brown was still busy elsewhere, and he had a decision to make. On his own hook, the colonel decided he, too, had no choice but to retreat. The regiment did so promptly, though in better order than the units on either flank. The 23rd Battalion, having lost Maj. Tazewell Newman to a wound in the first charge, was now in the hands of Capt. W. P. Simpson, who simply followed Cook's example. Brown's entire brigade fell back 200 yards and set about reorganizing.[50]

The timely intervention of King's line allowed both Dick and Sam Beatty's brigades to regain some measure of their composure. Lieutenant Woodcock, who along with his comrades in the 9th Kentucky had barely escaped their ordeal around the 26th Pennsylvania's cannon, noted that this pause allowed "a partial rally of our regiment and some others. . . . As the rebels had stopped

48 High, *Sixty-Eighth Indiana*, 65; OR 30, pt. 2, 376.

49 OR 30, pt. 2, 376.

50 Ibid., 378; It is possible that the 23rd Tennessee Battalion had been acting as a part of the 32nd Tennessee from the start of the action. Captain Simpson's report is very sketchy on the details of the 23rd's action for either day at Chickamauga.

shooting for a moment no doubt to reform their lines we got a sort of line rallied."[51]

Brown's Tennesseans soon resumed shooting, but did not attempt another charge. Both sides exchanged fire for another 30 minutes, but the respite had given Van Cleve's line a chance to reform, so Brown's lone battered brigade was now outmatched by three brigades of Yankees. With his ammunition running low, it was now Brown's turn to appeal for help. A. P. Stewart, Brown's division commander, once again responded with celerity with his decision to commit his last reserve. Brigadier General William B. Bate would take his mix of Georgia, Alabama, and Tennessee troops into the fight and replace Brown.

As Bate prepared his men, events on other parts of the field guaranteed the battle would spread even further. Just then, another engagement was touching off near the Viniard house a little less than a mile south of the Brotherton farmstead. This fast developing action would finally draw Bragg's carefully hoarded main body into the fight.

51 Noe, *A Southern Boy in Blue*, 200.

Chapter Sixteen

Viniard Field:
Davis Opens the Fight:

Saturday, September 19: 2:00 p.m. to 3:00 p.m.

Sergeant Lewis Day of Company E, the 101st Ohio, part of Brig. Gen. William Carlin's brigade, awoke to a "beautiful Indian Summer morning, perfect in every respect." Day and his comrades, who marched with Jefferson C. Davis's division of McCook's XX Corps, were camped just north of Pond Spring several miles south of Crawfish Spring. Despite the overnight cold, theirs was a restful night. They had been marching hard since General Rosecrans recalled McCook's corps from Alpine, and only lately had that pace slowed. They had another day's march ahead of them. Only two of Davis's brigades were present along with some Federal cavalry; Col. Sidney Post's four regiments had been detailed the day before to guard Stevens's Gap through Lookout Mountain.[1]

Davis received the next day's orders from McCook at 3:30 a.m.: Brig. Gen. Richard Johnson's division would be moving at "early dawn," and Davis would follow. No mention was made of combat or even of a destination; only that once on the road, Davis would receive "proper directions where to encamp."

---

1 L. W. Day, *Story of the One Hundred and First Ohio Infantry* (The W. M. Bayne Printing Co., 1894), 152; OR 30, pt. 1, 507.

The innocuous instructions notwithstanding, most of the men expected to be in a fight soon, this day or the next.[2]

Jefferson C. Davis was a veteran officer, though not a military academy graduate. He enlisted in an Indiana regiment at the start of the Mexican War only to discover he was good at soldiering. After securing a commission in the Regulars at the end of that conflict, Davis spent the 1850s in various duty stations and found himself in April 1861 defending Fort Sumter. After the fort fell, Davis left the Regulars to secure a commission as colonel of the newly forming 22nd Indiana. He did well in the chaotic early days of the war, quickly rising through the ranks to command a division at Pea Ridge.[3]

In September 1862, however, he earned instant notoriety by pulling a pistol during a heated argument and killing his superior officer, Maj. Gen. William 'Bull' Nelson. The incident that triggered the quarrel was at heart a trivial one over command and some public embarrassment. Davis was arrested but soon released. Incredibly, departmental commander Maj. Gen. Horatio G. Wright thought Davis acted in self-defense. Davis also had the support of his good friend, Indiana governor Oliver P. Morton. Civil authorities brought an indictment for murder; Davis posted bail and returned to his division. After two years of postponements the charge was dropped. Davis never went to trial. He had a reputation as a good combat soldier. Fighters, as Lincoln once said about General Grant, couldn't be spared.[4]

Three months later a disaster of a different kind (and not of his making) found Davis at Stones River. The Rebels launched a massive dawn attack against McCook's Right Wing that surprised and routed both Johnson's and Davis's divisions. Davis and his men fought hard (and surprisingly well) once over their initial shock. They held on as long as they could under difficult circumstances. The battle left the command tainted with an odor of bad publicity. Many newspapers inaccurately reported that Davis's men had acted badly, fueling whispered rumors that swept through the ranks of the rest of the army. Rosecrans, however, valued Davis, praised him in his report, and even suggested he was worthy of promotion. Like the other officers in the Right

---

2   Ibid., 123.

3   Warner, *Generals in Blue*, 115.

4   Nathaniel Cheairs Hughes, Jr., and Gordon D. Whitney, *Jefferson Davis in Blue: The Life of Sherman's Relentless Warrior* (Louisiana State University Press, 2002), 100-126. This is an excellent biography of Davis. The chapter cited here examines the shooting in great detail.

Wing, no official blame was attached to Davis's performance on December 31, 1862.[5]

Shortly after Stones River, outstanding penmanship and writing skills landed Pvt. Charles Dennis of the 101st Ohio at Davis's headquarters, where he witnessed firsthand the hard feelings flying fast and thick within the division. Dennis remained one of Davis's aides for the rest of the war. Initially, Dennis found his new boss difficult to work for. "He was a man who never gave credit for any good act, not even for an act of bravery," complained the private, "but he was not so neglectful of those who did not do well, or showed any desire to flaunt the white feather." Much to his dismay, Dennis also found that Davis enjoyed being at the forefront of any action. "There was no lack of opportunity to see war, and for that matter, to be right in it," grumbled Dennis, "for General Davis loved War. . . . It seemed to me that he was high as a church steeple, and that I was the only man in the army that was a good mark for the enemy's sharpshooters." As time passed, however, the "old man" grew on Dennis, who later admitted, "I liked him better after a year than I did when I first entered his high presence."[6]

Davis had other quirks. His politics were a source of friction. He was a Democrat, none too fond of the Emancipation Proclamation, and suspicious of abolitionism in the Army of the Cumberland—especially at the top. He thought Rosecrans's support for the proclamation was destructive to the army's morale, and made little effort to hide his opinions at a time when "copperhead-ism" was increasingly seen as disloyalty. On the field at Stones River, in the midst of that unfolding disaster, he shocked Brig. Gen. William P. Carlin when he exclaimed, "this will teach Rosecrans a lesson! This will teach the d——d abolitionists a lesson! Rosecrans was too sanguine!" The stunned Carlin wondered why Davis was even "on the Union side." Apparently Rosecrans was not aware of Davis's views, or at least overlooked them in lieu of his fighting qualities when recommending him for promotion. However, relations would soon sour between the two men.[7]

---

5 *OR* 20, pt. 1, 198.

6 Dennis Memoir, 6-7, Rutherford B. Hayes Presidential Library, Fremont, OH.

7 Girardi and Hughes, Carlin Memoirs, 90. Hughes and Whitney, *Jefferson Davis in Blue*, 147-148, details some of the friction between the two men. Rosecrans came to believe that Davis was spreading lies about him to politicians.

William P. Carlin did not get along with
divisional commander Jeff. Davis.

Spillard F. Horrall

Davis's command was not a happy
one in the fall of 1863. Tensions ran
hard between Davis and Carlin, who
was the only other Regular Army man
in the division. Carlin commanded
Davis's Second Brigade. He was an
excellent soldier, calm under fire, but
like so many prewar professionals,
jealous of rank and attention. Carlin
believed Davis's report of Stones River
was not effusive enough with praise for him and his men. His step to correct
that in the form of a supplemental report, something Davis's modern
biographers described as "a rebuttal—a rebuke, if you will," miffed Davis, who
took offense at Carlin calling his version of affairs into question. The dispute
hardened into enmity between the two men, which would never be overcome.
It "all began at Stones River," Carlin informed Maj. Gen. William T. Sherman in
April 1865. From then on, "I was under command of an enemy." Once, Carlin
and Col. Hans Heg of the 15th Wisconsin called on Rosecrans in person to ask
that Davis be relieved. Rosecrans refused.[8]

Further trouble arose in the ranks when Col. William E. Woodruff
resigned. Woodruff was not unhappy with Davis, but with the army. He'd been
removed from command of his regiment, the 2nd Kentucky, during the
confusion of the Perryville campaign to take charge of a brigade in Davis's
division. This was all well and good until Woodruff was injured at Stones River,
given medical leave—and apparently forgotten. He wanted to return to either
the 2nd Kentucky or be promoted to brigadier general. When neither option
seemed likely, he resigned on January 19, 1863. His departure elevated Col.
William Caldwell of the 81st Indiana to command of the Third Brigade.
Caldwell had been ill since Perryville and Lt. Col. John Timberlake led the

---

8   Hughes and Whitney, *Jefferson Davis in Blue*, 143-144.

Hoosiers in action at Stones River, but Caldwell was now healthy enough to return.[9]

Caldwell might have been acceptable to Davis, since their politics were similar. He was not, however, acceptable to Rosecrans. Caldwell was also highly critical of the Emancipation Proclamation and of the current of abolitionism within the ranks of the army. Like Davis he was willing to express his opinions loudly and often. Unlike his immediate boss, however, Caldwell lacked political influence. That April, Caldwell was relieved from command for uttering "disloyal sentiments," and was dismissed from the service that July. According to Carlin, Caldwell was brave enough, "full of spirit and gallantry [but] accused by some . . . of [his] officers of . . . 'Copperheadism' and . . . dismissed for it." Caldwell's departure further disrupted a regiment already in difficulty. None of Caldwell's immediate subordinates could stomach his views, either, and they refused to serve under him. Lieutenant Colonel Timberlake had already resigned. His successor, Lt. Col. Hiram Woodbury, declined the command when offered it and turned in his resignation on April 30. Next up was Maj. Leonidas Stout, who also refused the honor and transferred to a cavalry regiment. This turmoil left the brigade leaderless and the regiment in the hands of a none-too-steady Capt. Nevil B. Boone.[10]

The problem of brigade command was finally solved when Colonel Heg and his Wisconsin regiment were transferred from Carlin's command into the Third Brigade. To compensate for the loss of Heg's men, the 81st Indiana was transferred to Carlin's brigade.

Heg was senior to the other colonels, had proven himself competent under fire as a brigade commander in Carlin's absence, and perhaps as importantly, had the right amount of zeal for the Union cause. Heg was a Norwegian immigrant who had achieved political success in his adopted state of Wisconsin. He was a free-soiler and noted antislavery advocate. He enjoyed a good relationship with Carlin and had a high opinion of his former brigade commander, proudly informing the editor of the Milwaukee *Sentinel* that

9 Ibid., 146.

10 W. H. Terrill, *Report of the Adjutant General of the State of Indiana* (Indiana Adjutant General's Office, 1866), vol. 3, 37; Girardi and Hughes, *Carlin Memoirs*, 89. Caldwell fell afoul of Order Number Nine, issued by Union Brig. Gen. Milo S. Hascall that April. Hascall had been recently transferred from the Army of the Cumberland to take charge of the District of Indiana in an effort to crack down on desertion. Hascall's efforts shut down a number of Indiana newspapers for publishing disloyal material; Caldwell was caught up in the furor.

Rosecrans thought Carlin was "one of the best officers in the army." Heg added, "I wish I could say as much for our division commander, but I cannot." In fact, Heg found a great deal to dislike about Davis, and was willing to say so. On January 20, 1863, Heg had words with Davis in person. He described the incident to his wife: "I had quite a spat with . . . our Division Commander . . . and told him what I thought of proslavery Generals-I have no good feeling for him, and have made up my mind that I will not go into another Battle under his command."[11]

Davis could count on at least one friend still in the division. Col. Philip Sidney Post of the 59th Illinois still led the First Brigade. Post had served under Davis since the early days of the war in Missouri, and had been wounded at Pea Ridge. A fellow Democrat, Post had also been repeatedly recommended for promotion by Davis, but the Federal government was ever stingy with rank, and Post remained an acting brigadier. Davis's trust in the colonel was well-founded. A civilian lawyer, Post was also a first-rate soldier and a proven leader who would go on to earn a Medal of Honor at Nashville during the closing months of the war. Unfortunately Post was not with the division on September 19. Tasked with bringing up the rear and guarding Stevens's Gap, his regiments were still a dozen or so miles to the south, far from the scene of any fighting. They would see no combat at Chickamauga.[12]

Interestingly, just a week before Chickamauga, Davis's wife Marietta (Mary) tried to intercede with Heg on her husband's behalf. Recall that Mary and her friend, Clara Pope, traveled with Davis on campaign until September 12, when it looked very much like the Army of Tennessee was going to fight instead of retreat. The ladies were hustled back to Stevenson in haste, but sometime during the lull at Valley Head Mary made several social calls on Heg. The Norwegian found her to be a "fine, young, intelligent woman, but not handsome." Heg also failed to note whether or not she improved her husband's standing in his eyes.[13]

Heg and Carlin's men spent much of the morning that September 19 marking time. Despite the overnight order, Johnson's division did not clear the road in front of Davis's men until about 8:00 a.m., when Heg's regiments stood,

11 Theodore C. Blegen, ed. The Civil War Letters of Colonel Hans Christian Heg (The Norwegian-American Historical Foundation, 1936), 178, 187.

12 *OR* 8, 253.

13 Hughes and Whitney, *Jefferson Davis in Blue*, 169.

formed, and led the column. The day was fine but the march was a miserable one. One member of the 8th Kansas recalled that "our route lay along a dusty road. . . . Fragments of rails were yet smoldering amid the ashes, adding to the intolerable dust dense volumes of stifling smoke." Private William E. Patterson of the 38th Illinois's Company K, Carlin's brigade, focused on the sounds of battle that could be heard almost from the first step. The deep boom of cannon fire, "2 or 3 miles in front of us," reached them first, followed later by "skirmishing a few hundred yards to our right flank." The column passed McCook's headquarters on the left, the XX Corps flag flying while orderlies shuttled to and fro. Patterson's regiment suffered its first casualty of the day near an open field when "a rebel ball from the woods" on the right wounded an unsuspecting soldier. The shot was a stray round from the distant skirmishing. The column continued on without further incident until it reached Crawfish Spring where, Patterson noted, they halted for "about an hour."[14]

The stop allowed the troops to refill canteens, and in some cases, wash their filthy feet. Davis's men arrived only shortly after Rosecrans shifted his headquarters north to the Widow Glenn house, and the troops observed that beehive of activity with interest. McCook had already informed Davis that he was to report to either Rosecrans or Thomas (Rosecrans was still thinking of feeding Thomas's line with fresh troops as they arrived). Davis rode ahead to find Rosecrans and receive orders. His men, meanwhile, lounged, listened to the developing fight, and pondered what it all meant for them.[15]

By the time Davis caught up with the army commander, Rosecrans had already committed Palmer's division and approved Tom Crittenden's decision to send Van Cleve's division into the growing fight. When Davis reported his command "ready for action," Rosecrans seized the opportunity. "General Rosecrans ordered me to place one of my batteries in position . . . in front of his headquarters," wrote Davis, "and to move forward as speedily as possible in the direction of the heaviest firing, and to make an attack with a view, if possible, to turn the enemy's left flank."[16]

14 Adjutant General of the State of Kansas, *Military History of the Kansas Regiments* (Kansas State Printing Company, 1896), 123; William E. Patterson Memoir, Western Historical Manuscript Collection, University of Missouri, Rolla, MO.

15 James E. Love Autobiography, Missouri Historical Society, St. Louis, MO.

16 *OR* 30, pt. 1, 498.

A new urgency marked the division's movements. Via courier, Davis instructed Heg and Carlin to "march [their brigades] . . . at double quick time to the north and east along the La Fayette Road" until Davis met them. Crawfish Spring was three miles south of the Glenn house, and many troops recalled covering this distance at a breakneck pace. "[We] made a run of three miles," recalled Sgt. Ben Strong of the 101st Ohio. Carlin agreed, estimating that the "brigade went three miles at this exhausting step before . . . Gen. Davis caused me to halt, to face to the right, and to go into the woods." Ahead of them and on Carlin's left were Heg's troops already moving east.[17]

Davis ordered his artillery chief, Capt. William Hotchkiss, to lead the 8th Wisconsin battery to the forward slope in front of the newly relocated army headquarters, where the Badger gunners would enjoy a substantial field of fire. From there, they had nearly 1,000 yards of open ground to their front across the fields of Brock's farm until the wood line fringing the La Fayette Road obstructed their view. The Wisconsin men would enjoy an unparalleled view of the coming fight.[18]

About 400 yards south of that same Brock cabin, east of the La Fayette Road, stood a small structure known as the Log School. Another 250 yards to the south, on the west side of the road in a small grove of trees, stood the Viniard house. Who the Viniards were, or how many people lived there, is a question lost to history. The family had only recently arrived in the neighborhood, and did not linger long after the battle. Viniard Field was a large rectangle beginning at the La Fayette Road and running east about 450 yards to a narrow fringe of trees tracing a watercourse. From there, another smaller field ran another 250 yards to the east. The field extended south approximately 600 yards. West of the La Fayette Road was a smaller roughly rectangular field connecting with the Brock property. The western edge of this smaller field was marked by the rise where Col. John T. Wilder had established his battle line

---

17 William P. Carlin, "Military Memoirs," *National Tribune*, April 16, 1885. Carlin meant the Dry Valley Road. Benjamin T. Strong, *3 Years or During the War* (Charles R. Green, 1913). There are no page numbers in this pamphlet. Carlin, "Military Memoirs," April 16, 1885.

18 OR 30, pt. 1, 508. There were three Brock families living in the area during or close to the time of the battle, but information on them remains sketchy. We know the most about John Brock, as recounted in Chapter 9, but very little about the others. From the look of the 1860 Census, it is possible this was the residence of John Brock, but *Sartain's History of Walker County* does not agree. Tradition names this farmstead as the Benjamin Brock farm, but little else exists to confirm that information.

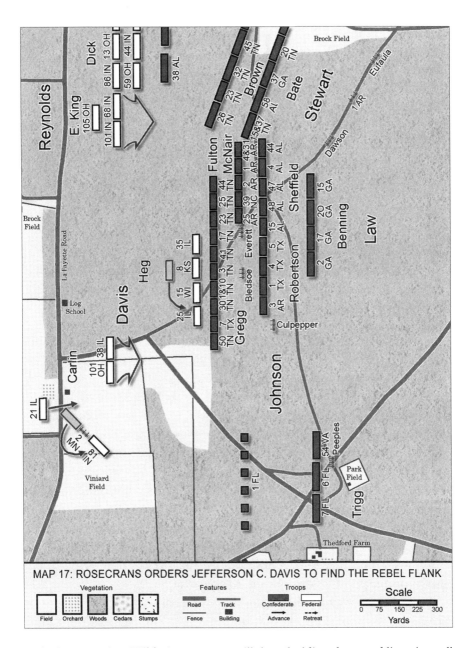

MAP 17: ROSECRANS ORDERS JEFFERSON C. DAVIS TO FIND THE REBEL FLANK

early that morning. Wilder's men were still there holding the wood line. A small dry creek with steep, sharply cut banks bisected this western field. With or without water the creek bed, which in September 1863 was more of a ditch than anything else, was roughly chest-deep in most places, but too wide to easily or

Looking east into Viniard field. The road in the foreground is the La Fayette Road. Here Carlin aligned his regiments, awaiting the order to advance. *Harvey Scarborough*

safely jump and too hard to climb into (or get out of). It would feature prominently during the later stages of the fight.[19]

Heg's regiments were marching east and nearing the La Fayette Road when Davis decided his line was too far north. According to Col. John A. Martin of the 8th Kansas, Heg's brigade first moved east through the woods dividing the Brock and Brotherton fields. It did not form into a line of battle until after marching nearly one mile, after which it sidled south "three quarters of a mile to the right."[20]

Heg's command consisted of four regiments: the 25th and 35th Illinois, 8th Kansas, and his own 15th Wisconsin. The 8th was a long way from home, one of the few trans-Mississippi regiments in the Army of the Cumberland. The 15th was also distinctive, intended as an all-Norwegian unit recruited largely by Heg's own efforts. When Norwegians alone couldn't fill up the ranks, some Swedes and Danes rounded out the complement, marking the 15th as "the Scandinavian Regiment." The brigade numbered only 1,218 officers and men. The 15th was especially understrength at just 176 rank and file. Two of its companies had been detached to garrison Island No. 10 on the Mississippi

19 Sartain, *History of Walker County*, 108.

20 *OR* 30, pt. 1, 520.

River more than a year past, and had yet to be recalled. Heg ordered three regiments into his front line, with the 35th Illinois on the left, the 8th Kansas holding the center, and the 15th Wisconsin anchoring the right. The 25th Illinois formed Heg's sole reserve. This deployment placed nearly 900 of the brigade's 1,200 men at the fore, with a frontage of about 220 yards. The brigade faced the woods east of the La Fayette Road, centered on the Log School, with its right resting at the edge of a cornfield. Davis, who had accompanied Heg to this point, ordered the Norwegian to continue into the woods while "simultaneously feeling for the Confederate left and the Federal right." With Heg's course now charted, Davis rode to find Carlin. The time was about 2:15 p.m.[21]

Carlin's men doggedly followed the march east and south. As the 38th Illinois moved forward, Private Patterson noticed Capt. William A. Hotchkiss's 2nd Minnesota battery as it "dashed off through the woods to the right, got into position and opened on the Rebels." Hotchkiss posted his guns at the southern end of the big field just east of the La Fayette Road, his pieces angled northeast to better support the intended flank attack. Carlin, meanwhile, deployed his regiments on Heg's right. From the slight rise west of the Viniard house, Cpl. William H. Records of the 72nd Indiana, Wilder's brigade, watched them come: "They . . . passed down through the farm in front of us . . . [coming] on at the double quick, cheering and swinging their hats [and] right-flanked into line." Carlin's line formed with its left on or near the dirt track of the Viniard-Alexander Road and extended south into the field, but fell short of connecting with the guns of the 2nd Minnesota.[22]

Carlin aligned his 1,215 men in a single line along the La Fayette Road, with the 38th Illinois on the left, and the 101st Ohio, 81st Indiana, and 21st Illinois forming successively to the right. Before he completed this deployment, however, Davis intervened. The division commander wanted the 21st Illinois—at 416 men the largest by far of Carlin's regiments—to withdraw and comprise a divisional reserve. A few minutes later, Davis detached the 81st Indiana to also pull back and form in support of the 2nd Minnesota battery at

21 Ibid., 529, 533; Hughes and Whitney, *Jefferson Davis in Blue*, 173.

22 Patterson Memoir, University of Missouri, Rolla, MO; Entry for September 19, Records Diary, InSL.

the southern end of Brock Field. "My command," an angry Carlin penned after the battle, "was therefore reduced to two regiments of infantry."[23]

It was at this inopportune time that Capt. Nevil Boone demonstrated his unfitness to command the 81st. Boone wasn't up to the task of maneuvering the full regiment into line. Corporal George Morris of the 81st, who later penned the regimental history, charitably noted that "owing to some misunderstanding, part of the regiment fell back and were thrown into confusion, but through the efforts of the line officers . . . [and] some of General Davis's staff . . . were halted and reformed. The remainder of the regiment was then withdrawn in good order." Once things were sorted out, Boone "asked to be relieved." Carlin, looking on in disgust, was in no mood to be kind. "The incompetency displayed by Captain Boone early in the action," Carlin reported, "induced me to supersede him by Major James E. Calloway, Twenty-First Illinois Volunteers, a vary gallant and efficient officer." The Hoosiers in the ranks of the 81st were relieved to see Calloway arrive. The major, "a brave and fearless officer . . . assured the boys that he would stay with them as long as they would stay by him," recalled Corporal Morris.[24]

With the misadventures of the 81st underway, Davis ordered Carlin's men to lie down as he rode the length of the brigade's truncated line, an instruction Cpl. Lewis Day and his comrades in the 101st Ohio "cheerfully obeyed." The sounds of combat to the north, where Van Cleve was engaging, had reached a thunderous climax. "The roar of musketry seemed to be almost constant," remarked Day, "sometimes rolling off further to the left, then surging back toward us . . . while . . . the crash of cannon by single piece, section, or entire battery hammered and pounded and shook the very earth." From behind them, the 8th Wisconsin's six fieldpieces added their bark to the din, and an unwelcomed bite as well: "The battery fired so low," Ohio Sgt. Ben Strong remembered, "that some of our own men were hit." Strong's comrade, Leonard Cole of the 101st, watched with alarm as fire plagued them from both sides. "Serg't Wise of Co. E was wounded in the head by a piece of one of our own

---

23 *OR* 30, pt. 1, 515.

24 George W. Morris, *History of the Eighty-First Regiment of Indiana Volunteer Infantry in the Great War of the Rebellion 1861 to 1865* (Franklin Printing House, 1901), 58; Letter from "Rambler," *New Albany Daily Ledger*, September 26, 1863; OR 30, pt. 1, 515.; With his efforts found so publicly wanting, Boone resigned his commission on October 8, 1863.

shells," lamented Cole, while at the same time, "two corporals of Co. C were killed by Rebel sharpshooters."[25]

While Carlin was doing his best to accommodate Davis and get his men ready for battle, Heg's men were moving into the woods, driving Rebel skirmishers before them. Wisconsin Capt. Mons Grinagar of the 15th described their first contact: "We . . . advanced in line of battle over a slight elevation . . . and on ascending the top, the enemy's skirmishers opened fire on us, but with little effect. We drove them in." Like that area of the battlefield where Van Cleve's men went into the fight, underbrush in the woods here was also quite thick, often described as jack-oak or scrub, which limited visibility to an unusual degree. This factor colored the accounts of Union and Confederate participants as lines of troops stumbled upon one another at very close range. Grinagar's report added that Heg's line continued on only "a short distance farther [until] we received a heavy volley from the enemy's line immediately in our front." Waldamar Ager, also in the 15th Wisconsin, recalled "a terrible rifle salvo just as a battery opens on [our] left wing."[26]

In the brigade center, the Kansans faced a similar fusillade. To the Federals it seemed as if the enemy line suddenly appeared, brutally close, from behind a rock ledge. "In an instant [we] were furiously engaged in desperate combat," wrote one regimental historian. With his regiment checked, Martin struggled with this "destructive fire," but his men "replied with promptness. . . . The roar of musketry at this time was deafening." Several Kansans were shot down on the rise in this first fire, including "Old Soldier," the regimental dog.[27]

Despite the exchange of fire with their pickets, many of the Confederates were equally surprised by Heg's appearance. The Rebels belonged to John Gregg's and John Fulton's brigades of Bushrod Johnson's Provisional Division, Hood's Corps. These troops had been lying in line all day listening to the fight while waiting for something to do. Though they did not know it, they formed the center of General Bragg's main body, poised to strike at what the

25 Day, *One Hundred and First Ohio*, 160; Strong, *3 Years*; "Brother Jim," Leonard Cole to James M. Cole, James M. Cole Papers, ALPL.

26 OR 30, pt. 1, 533; Waldemar Ager, *Chickamauga: Colonel Heg and his Boys* (Norwegian-American Historical Society, 2000), 58.

27 Adjutant General's Office, *Official Military History of Kansas Regiments during the War for the Suppression of the Great Rebellion* (W. S. Burke, 1870), 123; OR 30, pt. 1, 529; Bill McFarland, *Keep the Flag to the Front: The Story of the Eighth Kansas Volunteer Infantry* (Leathers Publishing, 2008), 146.

Confederate commander believed was Rosecrans's left flank. Bragg had siphoned away Ben Cheatham's division and A. P. Stewart's after that, but what was left still comprised an imposing mass of soldiers. John Hood's six brigades, along with William Preston's three more arrayed farther south, numbered nearly 13,000 bayonets. Other than some small movements in the woods as the generals rearranged their battle lines to their liking and accommodated late arrivals, the men were well rested and had yet to fire a shot.

The hours of enforced inactivity had made the troops a bit slapdash. Captain William H. Harder of the 23rd Tennessee, Fulton's brigade, remembered that a low hill covered the brigade front and "our men were lying down behind their stacks of guns in line, talking, entirely careless of all the firing." When the sounds of battle grew near, Fulton sent out "a skirmish line to our left center, which was no sooner deployed to the front, than they were attacked with great fury and . . . driven back." Lieutenant Colonel James T. Turner, commanding the 30th Tennessee recalled that Gregg's brigade had "a heavy picket line, but it was rapidly driven in." Gregg ordered Turner to take charge of the skirmishers, rally them, and "see what was in our front." It was no use. "I could not get anything out of the pickets or rally them as they rushed past me," Turner complained, and in a minute or so he could see why: "I took a peep through the thick young pines, and in fifty yards of me two lines of Federals were rapidly advancing. Just as I turned to retreat I was shot nearly through . . . but succeeded in reaching our lines before falling." The Federals closed rapidly, and when they crested the rise a storm of fire erupted. As Harder would later write, a number of men were hit before they had time to take arms. Farther down the front, opposite the 15th Wisconsin, Lt. Clarence C. Malone of Company C, 10th Tennessee, watched aghast as Federal fire swept through his ranks: "In less than ten minutes our regiment had lost one hundred men of 168." Malone can be excused for overestimating the numbers of dead and dying: the casualties were heavy enough. His regiment would be heavily engaged on this day and the morrow and lose a total of 114.[28]

The opposing soldiers fell to it with a will, loading and firing while slugging it out at close range. Heg was determined not to give an inch to the equally

---

28 Harder Reminiscences, TSLA; J. T. Turner Report, 30th Tennessee file, CCNMP; Lindsley, *Military Annals of Tennessee*, vol. 1, 451. Turner's account in the *Annals* is similar to, but not the same as the report in the CCNMP file, above; "Dear Miss Florence," September 28, 1863, Martha Harper Clayton Papers, Duke University.

stubborn Rebels. The result was a static and very bloody firefight. Dramatic scenes played out up and down the blazing front. One involved Kansan Color Cpl. Charles Rovohl, who was mortally wounded early in the action. Badly hurt, he passed the flag to another of the guard. When two of his comrades scrambled to pull him from the firing line to gain the limited shelter of the reverse slope, Rovohl protested, "Keep the flag to the front."[29]

Unbeknownst to Colonel Heg, his brigade had struck the seam between Gregg and Fulton's Rebel brigades, whose combined line overmatched his by wide margins on both flanks. In addition, Bushrod Johnson's line included Brig. Gen. Evander McNair's brigade in support behind Fulton, and divisional artillery totaling 12 guns in three batteries. It didn't take Heg long to discover something was lethally amiss, and he extended his front south by bringing the 25th Illinois out of reserve and into line on the 15th Wisconsin's right. The move, however, was no more than a stopgap. "Still the brigade held its ground," reported Colonel Martin, "cheered on by the gallant . . . Colonel Heg, who was everywhere present, careless of danger." With his brigade fully committed and facing heavy pressure, Heg sent a courier to find Davis and ask for more help.[30]

Back in Viniard Field, meanwhile, an exasperated Carlin was trying to figure out what was expected of him. Davis had ordered Carlin's remaining regiments to lie down "without giving me or them additional instructions," complained the brigadier. At least some good news arrived in the form of one of Colonel Wilder's aides, who pulled up his mount to inform Carlin that two of Wilder's regiments were in the wood line on the west side of the road behind him, securing his right flank.[31]

When he received Heg's request for support, Davis ordered Col. John W. S. Alexander's 21st Illinois, part of Carlin's command, to move up and help the embattled Norwegian. The 21st was a fighting regiment that bore the distinction of having Ulysses S. Grant as its first commander. Colonel Alexander had led the 21st since Grant's elevation to higher command. Though they saw little combat during their first year of service, the Prairie-staters more than made up for that at Stones River, where the regiment suffered a staggering 303 casualties. Alexander earned unstinting praise from Carlin for his leadership

29 John A. Martin, *Addresses: By John A. Martin delivered in Kansas* (Kansas Publishing House, 1888), 147.

30 *OR* 30, pt. 1, 529.

31 Ibid., 515.

in that bloody affair. Heg's men had been fighting for about 45 minutes when Alexander led his men diagonally across Viniard Field and entered the brush in an effort to find their right flank. Once Alexander had stepped off, Davis ordered Carlin to advance with what was left of his brigade under his direct control: the 38th Illinois and 101st Ohio.[32]

Carlin was moving out as four more Union regiments were entering Viniard Field, brought there by the earlier action of Major General Crittenden. Colonel Sidney Barnes's brigade of Van Cleve's division had been left behind at Lee and Gordon's Mills when Van Cleve was ordered north into the fight at midday. When that fight spread, however, Crittenden summoned Barnes to come up and help.

Tom Crittenden was having a busy day. By 1:00 p.m., Van Cleve's two brigades were fully committed in their fighting to support Palmer's troops. Crittenden needed additional help. Only three brigades of his corps were left to call upon: Barnes's men and Tom Wood's two brigades, both of which were still guarding the bridge at Lee and Gordon's Mills. McCook's troops were supposed to be coming up to replace them there, and were expected soon. Accordingly, Crittenden sent his chief of staff, Maj. Lyne Starling, to report to Rosecrans and ask that Wood's men be released to come forward. Within minutes Starling galloped back with a belligerent reply: "Take them all in." Crittenden immediately dispatched Maj. John Mendenhall to bring up Wood, and ordered Starling to do the same with Barnes's regiments.[33]

When Starling reached Barnes about 1:30 p.m. and told the colonel he was sorely needed, Barnes not unreasonably asked for clarification: "I asked to whom I should report, upon whom I should form, and where was the enemy." The reply was less than satisfactory. According to Barnes, the staff officer told him to "go forward at once and engage the enemy, that they were on the right of the road . . . that our army was driving them, that I could take them in flank; to go in an act on my own judgment." The frustrated Barnes could have commiserated with any number of officers over the vague orders, Union and Confederate alike. At least he wouldn't be going in alone, for Starling also told him that Wood's division had orders to come up right behind him.[34]

---

32 Ibid., 499; OR 20, pt. 1, 282.

33 OR 30, pt. 1, 982.

34 Ibid., 839.

Barnes, a Kentucky lawyer and a stout Unionist who raised the 8th Kentucky in 1861, had little combat experience and no military training before the war. He had led the 8th since the war's first November, but the regiment missed the fighting at Perryville. The Kentuckians were heavily engaged at Stones River, but Barnes was absent recovering from an illness and commanding convalescents in Nashville. Seniority of rank elevated him to brigade command in April 1863. Now, five months later, he was faced with a difficult situation and virtually no guidance about how to accomplish his mission.[35]

Still, orders were orders, however vague they might be, so Barnes formed his brigade into two lines and moved in column of companies up the La Fayette Road for about one mile until he reached the timber at the southern limit of the Viniard farmstead. From there, he bore off the road to the right, deploying his men "over rough ground and into thick timber." The move consumed about one hour. From this vantage point Barnes paused to observe the unfolding action in Viniard Field while his aides galloped off to find either his division or corps commander to seek additional instructions. Neither could be located. He spotted Carlin's men (though he didn't know what command it was at the time) and what looked like a Confederate battle line in the trees beyond, driving Federals westward. If he went in on Carlin's right, reasoned Barnes, he could strike the Rebels in the flank, just as Crittenden's aide directed. Even better, his own right flank would be protected because Brig. Gen. Thomas J. Wood's two brigades were marching up right behind him.[36]

Tom Wood did not understand the situation any better than Barnes. When Mendenhall delivered Crittenden's orders, all he could tell Wood was the corps commander wanted him to "take position . . . on the right of some part of General Van Cleve's division." The directive left Wood in something of a quandary. His two brigades represented the last force guarding the crossing at Lee and Gordon's Mills. Departing would expose the Federal rear to a quick lunge by the Rebels across the river (Thomas Hindman's division of Leonidas Polk's divided corps). Wood had little choice but to obey, and he did so with alacrity. He put his men in motion and sent an aide off to army headquarters to report the movement and urge that replacement troops be sent at once. Along

35 8th Kentucky Compiled Service Records, NARA.

36 *OR* 30, pt. 1, 839.

the way the aide met General McCook, whom Rosecrans had already charged with holding the right flank, and who promptly sent troops from Maj. Gen. Philip Sheridan's division to secure the now-exposed crossing. Sheridan's men were handy, having followed Davis's troops to Crawfish Spring.[37]

Properly relieved, Wood set off north along the La Fayette Road in Barnes's wake. Wood was possessed of a short temper, and the vague instructions set it off. "The order directed me to take position on the right of General Van Cleve's command," he complained, "but I was totally ignorant of his position . . . and met no one on my arrival . . . to enlighten me[.] I found myself much embarrassed for the want of information." At some point Starling informed Col. Charles Harker, who commanded Wood's lead brigade, that he would be going in on Barnes's right as part of a larger flank attack; presumably this was the "some part" of Van Cleve's division Mendenhall had referred to earlier.[38]

It was at this point that Major Starling became the conduit for a series of conflicting instructions. Unlike Wood, Starling found Crittenden easily enough, and reported Barnes's impending arrival. Almost immediately, Crittenden sent him back down the road with further details for Wood: "He might make a very advantageous [movement] on the enemy's flank . . . [since] Van Cleve was driving the enemy rapidly in a direction parallel to [the La Fayette Road]." However, cautioned the corps commander, Wood should "understand distinctly" that this was "only a suggestion, not an order." Once he delivered his message Starling rode back to find the corps commander but Crittenden had left to report to Rosecrans at the Widow Glenn's. Jefferson Davis rode up, however, and "expressed great anxiety" about his command, which was being "much pressed by the enemy. He said he wished very much he had a brigade, as it would save him." Impressed by the urgency of the moment, and using his authority as the corps chief of staff, Major Starling "told him [Davis] I would immediately bring him one."[39]

The ubiquitous Starling galloped back down the road and found Col. Charles G. Harker, who was expecting to move to protect Barnes's right flank. Instead, Starling diverted the Ohioan farther north to help Davis. Harker was

37 Ibid., 487, 631.

38 Ibid., 631, 691.

39 Ibid., 982-983.

moving when up rode Tom Wood, angry and annoyed by his vague and ever-changing orders. "Why is there no staff officer to show me what position to take?" snapped Wood, loudly. "I am here for that purpose," soothed the major. "General Davis's forces are already engaged. He knows their position and can best direct you." As Wood and Davis worked out the details of Wood's placement, Crittenden returned and joined the discussion, all the while under a distant Rebel fire.[40]

By re-directing Wood to go help Davis at once, Crittenden was abandoning—or at least postponing—his earlier intention to send Wood and Barnes into action against the Rebel right flank. This made sense, since Davis's line was verging on collapse and needed help immediately, plus locating the unknown enemy flank might take some time.

Talking to Wood, Davis sketched in the details of what had transpired thus far in the woods to their east. As they conversed, one of Heg's officers reported the alarming news that the Norwegian "could not maintain his position" in the woods any longer. As if to drive home the danger, "a stream of fugitives pour[ed] out of the woods." Heg's line had given way. Wood quickly moved up and formed his two brigades in the road behind Davis's line.[41]

There were now six Union brigades active in the Viniard Field sector, elements of four divisions from all three of the army's infantry corps. The command situation was understandably confused. Crittenden, who commanded Wood and Barnes, but not Davis, remained focused on the idea of a flank attack to relieve Van Cleve. Wilder's custom, practice, and forte was independent operations, but thus far his troops had played the role of spectators to the rapidly unfolding fight. Davis and Wood were at least trying to cooperate, but in everyone's haste no one thought to inform Sidney Barnes of Wood's changed orders, leaving him with the impression that a full Union division was still on his right rear to lend weight to his own attack.

Additional Confederate troops were also about to enter the fray. John Bell Hood had grown tired of waiting for orders while fighting seemed to rage all around him. The first of Lee's reinforcements from Virginia were moving up to take a hand.

---

40 Ibid., 983.

41 Ibid., 631.

Chapter Seventeen

Viniard Field:
Hood Engages:

Saturday, September 19: 2:30 p.m. to 4:30 p.m.

The 19th of September was a restless and even anxious day for Maj. Gen. John Bell Hood. He was a man of action and there was much to do, but he was not in a position or location to do much of anything. He arrived in north Georgia the day before and thus far had little chance to get to know or even to meet many of the Army of Tennessee officers he would be commanding or fighting alongside. St. John Liddell chatted with him briefly the evening of Hood's arrival and "found him affable, but his conversation was too short to enable me to form an estimate of his ability and military views." Brigadier General Henry L. "Rock" Benning's brigade arrived that night, followed later that morning by an Alabama brigade under Brig. Gen. Evander M. Law. Their arrival, together with the appearance of Simon Buckner's two-division corps on Bushrod Johnson's left flank precipitated a wholesale shuffling of troops.[1]

Everyone was expecting a battle would soon begin. Braxton Bragg might not have been aware of George Thomas's overnight march to Kelly Field, but

---

1 Hughes, *Liddell's Record,* 141; William C. Oates, *The War Between the Union and the Confederacy and its Lost Opportunities with a History of the 15th Alabama Regiment and the Forty-eight Battles in which it was Engaged* (Neale Publishing Company, 1905), 254. Oates says his command, the 15th Alabama, did not cross Chickamauga Creek until 10:00 a.m., but this is much too late. If he had crossed at that time, he would have been entangled in the fighting at the north end of the field.

the wholesale Federal activity did not go completely unnoticed. The night was cold, fires were prohibited, and many of the Rebels were still wet after crossing Chickamauga Creek on the 18th, which meant most of them did not get a good night's rest. It was so chilly Lt. James Thompson of the 3rd Tennessee gave up trying to sleep about 2:00 a.m. "to warm myself by exercise." While he was pacing in the dark, Thompson wrote, "I entertained myself until daybreak by listening to the movements of the enemy. I could distinctly hear the artillery moving and the voices of the drivers. They came nearer and nearer until I could hear the tread of infantry. I knew then that a battle must soon ensue." At dawn, Col. John Fulton, now heading up Bushrod Johnson's brigade, organized a reconnaissance to investigate that noise—a "detail of intelligent men . . . five from each regiment." The patrol returned at 10:00 a.m. to report Yankees just a mile and a quarter distant. By the time the patrol returned, Hood's and Buckner's Corps were deployed in line, with Hood's men north of the Viniard-Alexander Road and Buckner's divisions packed in tightly between the Park and Hunt farmsteads. Cheatham's men were filing into reserve behind them, until tapped by Bragg for commitment in Brock Field.[2]

By then, the fighting on the right farther north had grown into a sustained engagement. The sounds of battle filled the forest all morning, but orders to advance were not forthcoming. Officers passed along the lines encouraging the men, but had little news to offer. Some of Hood's men had seen him yesterday, saluting him on the Reed's Bridge Road. For the Alabamians of Law's Brigade, however, this was their first glimpse of their gaunt, angular general since his wounding at Gettysburg, and they now made the happy discovery that their commander was with them instead of recuperating in Richmond. Catching sight of Hood, they cheered, and he saluted in return.[3]

Troop units were not the only things being reshuffled that morning. Hood had led a division in Lt. Gen. James Longstreet's First Corps of the Army of Northern Virginia before being wounded on July 2. He wasn't Longstreet's senior division commander, however. That bragging right belonged to Maj. Gen. Lafayette McLaws, whose commission predated Hood's by five months.

---

2 Robert W. Ikard, "Lieutenant Thompson Reports on Chickamauga: A Comparison of Immediate and Historical Perspectives of the Battle," *Tennessee Historical Quarterly*, vol. 44, issue 4 (Winter, 1985), 420. Thompson was writing to his brother on October 18, 1863. *OR* 30, pt. 2, 472.

3 J. Gary Laine and Morris M. Penny, *Law's Alabama Brigade in the War Between the Union and the Confederacy* (White Mane Publishing, 1996), 144.

However, neither Longstreet, nor McLaws (nor any of McLaws's troops) had reached the battlefield on September 19. Their absence left Hood in charge of Longstreet's corps, which had been augmented to a sizable force with the attachment of Bushrod Johnson's Provisional Division. Hood's elevation created a ripple effect in the ladder of command. General Law left his brigade to step up to command Hood's division, which in turn bumped up Col. James L. Sheffield of the 48th Alabama to assume Law's former duties. Sheffield did so under a bit of a handicap: he had no staff because Law kept the brigade staff with him. Sheffield couldn't strip the 48th of the rest of the regiment's officers to assist, so he would go into battle without much of a brigade staff of his own. Controlling a brigade's formation without aides riding the line would be problematic during the upcoming battle's two heaviest days, as "the brigade would [repeatedly] become split, fight piecemeal, and lose much of its striking power."[4]

The troops from Virginia were eyed with great interest by Army of Tennessee veterans, and vice versa. Longstreet's men arrived sporting new uniforms, so the first thing most Westerners noticed was that these strangers were better dressed. The uniform coats were especially distinctive, dyed so dark they "looked more blue than gray." One of the results was ill-founded conclusions: the Easterners thought the Army of Tennessee men were nothing but ragamuffins, while the Western troops decided Gen. Robert E. Lee's men got the best of everything. "Easterner" Lawrence Daffan of the 4th Texas (Jerome Robertson's brigade) wrote that "Bragg's army had never seen a well-uniformed Confederate regiment before." An adjutant with the 4th Alabama, Robert Coles (Law's/Sheffield's brigade) remembered that "frequently, Bragg's men proposed to exchange a 'Bragg jacket for a Lee jacket'" as they stood by the road watching the newcomers march past.[5]

None of the troops from Lee's Army of Northern Virginia had yet done much fighting in the Western Theater. Bushrod Johnson's three brigades, who had led the day before (September 18) at Reed's Bridge, had come from Mississippi or were transferred from other parts of Bragg's army. They now

---

4 Ibid.

5 Col. Harold B. Simpson, *Hood's Texas Brigade: Lee's Grenadier Guard* (Landmark Publishing, 1999), 324; Kate Daffan, *My Father As I Remember Him* (Press of Gray and Dillaye, 1907), 41; Robert T. Coles, "History of the 4th Alabama" 4th Alabama Regimental file, ADAH. Despite the fact that no Virginia regiments actually came west with Longstreet, the Westerners repeatedly referred to them as such.

comprised Hood's front line. As the fighting spread on the morning of the 19th, other troops had been drawn off to shift to the right (north); first Cheatham's division and then A. P. Stewart's men. All the while, Longstreet's troops remained in their hasty bivouacs, yet to fire a gun in combat in North Georgia. That was about to change.

It was about 2:00 p.m. when Colonel Heg's Union brigade line crested the ridge sheltering Bushrod Johnson's main line, and the killing began in earnest. Fulton and Gregg's brigades fought in place and suffered significantly as a result. The 50th Tennessee of Gregg's brigade was said to have suffered 12 killed and 45 wounded *before* the regiment even moved from their morning position. Lieutenant Thompson worked as an assistant surgeon in charge of the regimental infirmary corps behind the 3rd Tennessee, another of Gregg's regiments. Soon after the fighting started, he recalled "the wounded came in rapidly."[6]

Bushrod Johnson effectively dealt with Heg's first attack, but only on a localized level since he had no orders to advance in the wake of the Norwegian's withdrawal. Except for the 17th Tennessee's leftmost companies, most of Fulton's line was not directly engaged, and Johnson was able to direct some of their fire into Heg's flank. Unlike the Federals, Johnson had ample artillery support. Lieutenant William S. Everett's Georgia battery and Lt. R. L. Wood's Missouri artillery supported Fulton and Gregg, respectively, hurling shell and canister downrange as fast as they could ram the fixed ammunition down the tubes. Johnson also ordered Capt. James F. Culpepper's South Carolina gunners forward from the reserve line to come into action on Gregg's left. Heavily overmatched and without any artillery of his own, Heg appealed for help, which prompted Davis's order to send in Carlin's 21st Illinois.[7]

It was now about 3:00 p.m. John Bell Hood was at the front, and he decided he had had enough of waiting for orders. His corps was under attack. He was a man of action, there was much to do, and now he was in a position and a

---

6 *OR* 30, pt. 2, 453. There is some inconsistency in the casualties for Johnson's regiments. The Memphis *Daily Appeal* for October 1, 1863, reported the 50th only lost nine killed and 46 wounded for the entire battle. The 50th, it should be recalled, had already had its share of suffering in this campaign. It was one of the units involved in the locomotive collision on September 14 that killed 13 and injured another 75. Unknown Memoir, 50th Tennessee Infantry, TSLA; Ikard, "Lieutenant Thompson Reports," 422.

7 *OR* 30, pt. 2, 453.

location to do something about it. Hood ordered Johnson to lead a general advance.

Hood never wrote a report of his Chickamauga experience, and he covered the fighting of September 19 in a single paragraph of his autobiography. As a result, divining his intentions at this moment remains difficult. When Hood initiated this movement, Hood's own division, now under Law, was on the right, two brigades forward and one in reserve. Bushrod Johnson's command was left, south of Law, also with two brigades forward and one in the second line. Hood's orders, as passed on in the reports of several subordinates, raise a number of questions about what he intended Johnson to achieve. Hood ordered the division commander to wheel to the right and guide to the right as he moved. Thus, instead of advancing due west toward the Viniard farm, Hood's orders reoriented Johnson's line northwest toward Brotherton Field. When Evander Law's line began moving, however, it drifted to the left. This drift may have been intentional, with Hood trying to form an assault column by stacking one division behind the other, or it might have been purely accidental.[8]

Unfortunately, Law—who was in a position to cast additional light on the reason for this peculiar movement—also never wrote a formal report or even a memoir of his time at Chickamauga. Intentional or not, the net effect was to set the two divisions off at divergent angles, and split them both in two. As a result, about two-thirds of Johnson's command moved out of the Viniard Field sector and became involved in events elsewhere, leaving only Gregg's brigade to face Heg. Law's former brigade, now under Sheffield, followed suit, but not so the rest of his division. Robertson and Benning both came into action with their brigades on what used to be Johnson's front. Each division was disrupted. In turn, their brigades also fragmented and disconnected.[9]

John Fulton's four small Tennessee regiments set the pace. Holding the right of Johnson's front line, Fulton's 874 men moved past the 35th Illinois on Heg's left and advanced unopposed for 600 to 700 yards through the timber before they found more Federals, who turned out to be Edward King's three regiments of Reynolds's division (Thomas's IV Corps). King's men, it should be remembered, were looking to outflank A. P. Stewart's Rebels facing Van

8　Ibid.

9　William Glenn Robertson, "The Chickamauga Campaign: Chickamauga, Day 1" *Blue & Gray Magazine*, vol. XXIV, no. 6 (Spring, 2008), 44-46. Dr. Robertson has termed this odd movement "The X Maneuver."

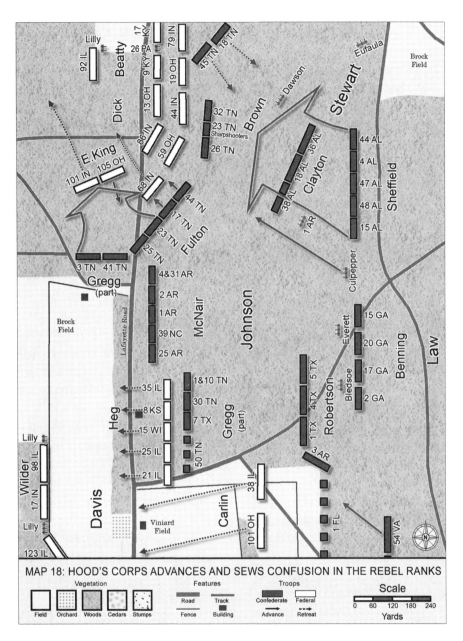

MAP 18: HOOD'S CORPS ADVANCES AND SEWS CONFUSION IN THE REBEL RANKS

Cleve's line, and the sudden appearance of Fulton's Confederates coming up from the southeast was quite a shock. The collision was unplanned by either side, but Fulton got the better of it. His line entered the fight in a perfect position to turn King's right flank. Fulton's thrust also, however, effectively removed his brigade from the struggle with Jefferson Davis's Yankees, an affair we shall return to soon.

Farther south off Fulton's left flank, John Gregg's brigade faced Heg's line in an experience much different than the one Fulton was going through. John Gregg was 34 years old, a transplanted Texan born and educated in Alabama. He studied law in Tuscumbia, but took a judgeship in Texas in the 1850s. When war came he recruited and led the 7th Texas, rising to brigade command in August 1862. Gregg was a proven fighter. In May of 1863, his 2,500 Rebels stood off more than 10,000 Federals for several hours at Raymond, Mississippi, during the complex Vicksburg operations. This time, his Rebels held a numerical advantage, though admittedly a slight one. Gregg counted 1,419 troops, while Heg numbered 1,218 in his ranks. Casualties had by now reduced both formations, but with many of Gregg's men surprised by Heg's sudden appearance, the Confederates suffered more than the Yanks in that first collision. Gregg's return fire, augmented by Rebel cannon, began to take a grim toll on Heg's men.

Heg stepped off with the 35th Illinois, 8th Kansas, and 15th Wisconsin in his first line, arrayed north to south. After the first contact, Heg moved the 25th Illinois out of the reserve to extend his brigade line to the south, on the right of the 15th Wisconsin. Heg's Unionists and Gregg's Confederates traded volleys for a few minutes. At some point during this fight the Federals fell back "10 or 15 paces" toward the low crest behind them. Mainly, however, this initial phase of the action was largely static. Lieutenant Colonel Ole C. Johnson, commanding the 15th Wisconsin, thought his line was holding firm until he noticed "the 8th Kansas on our left begin to slacken and waver." Fellow Badger Capt. Mons Grinager reported the Wisconsin men were ordered to "fix bayonets and charge the line immediately in our front." The 15th pressed on until about 30 yards ahead of the Kansans, where Johnson realized his line was unsupported and Captain Grinager reported there was no support on the right flank. Heg's order to charge either never reached the 25th Illinois, or the 25th could not make any headway. When the Kansans on their left began retreating, Johnson ordered his Scandinavians back as well. According to Colonel Martin of the 8th Kansas, "The enemy was constantly reinforced, and at last they flanked us on the left, pouring a destructive fire down our line."[10]

---

10 *OR* 30, pt. 1, 533; Ole C. Johnson to his Brother, November 3rd, 1863, Albert O. Barton papers, WHS; *OR* 30, pt. 1, 533, 529.

This fire came from the 3rd and 41st Tennessee on Gregg's right, which outflanked the 35th Illinois and sent it reeling back toward the La Fayette Road. Thereafter, the 3rd and 41st veered to the right in an effort to maintain contact with Fulton's brigade, as previously ordered. Within minutes these regiments were out of this part of the fight and Gregg would not see them again that day. This tactical error robbed Gregg of his two largest regiments—nearly one-half of his strength at a critical time. Their unexpected departure, however, did little to ease the pressure on the 35th Illinois because Bushrod Johnson, aware that Gregg's line was becoming attenuated, ordered Evander McNair to move two of his regiments into the growing gap.

McNair tasked this mission to the 25th Arkansas and 39th North Carolina, a pair of small commands that numbered together no more than 380 officers and men. Although all told they fielded only the strength of a single average regiment, timing and position made up for their paucity in numbers. The two regiments charged forward under the overall command of the 39th's colonel, David Coleman. Johnson would later report the units entered the fight on the left of Gregg's 7th Texas, but Coleman's own report suggested they went in farther north. Coming up, Coleman observed Gregg's men "under a terrific fire" and ordered his troops forward. "Passing over the left of Gregg's brigade [we] drove the enemy in rapid flight through the thick woods, across the Chattanooga [La Fayette] Road, past the small [Brock] house 100 yards on, and into the cornfields beyond." Hammered in the flank by two Rebel regiments, and then pursued so vigorously by two more, the 35th had little choice but to run for their lives.[11]

The 35th's collapse exposed Martin's Jayhawkers to a similar thrust by the 10th and 30th Tennessee. The 8th Kansas fell back under better discipline, but dragged the rest of Heg's line with it. Bowing to the inevitable, Heg ordered a general retreat, conducted "slowly and in good order" until his men stumbled onto Colonel Alexander and the 21st Illinois, who were just going into line on Heg's right. Heg halted his line again and reformed the men for another try at the Rebels.[12]

The engagement thus far had been less than satisfactory for Alexander's men. It was their first battle, and they had but the vaguest of notions where the

11 OR 30, pt. 2, 454, 500.

12 Ibid., pt. 1, 533.

enemy was. According to Sgt. William W. Hensley, the 21st "advanced ... firing into the timber but [we saw] no rebels. Pretty soon we were ordered back . . . and formed our lines again and made another advance still firing. . . . but seeing no rebs. Then the shots came on us thick and fast and we were ordered back again."[13]

Fortunately for the Federals, instead of turning south to capitalize on the exposed nature of the Kansas regiment's flank, Coleman's men moved straight west following the discomfited 35th Illinois. Even more fortunately, the remaining 800 Rebels of McNair's brigade did not join in, halting instead in the woods east of the road. These fragmented Confederate movements, coupled with the earlier separation of the 3rd and 41st Tennessee, allowed Heg time to reform. Gregg's other units stretched wide in an effort to cover Heg's front. The 50th Tennessee, on Gregg's left, stretched so much it became little more than a skirmish line. When Heg's Federals fell back out of contact, Gregg's troops did not pursue.[14]

Anchored around and behind the 21st Illinois, Heg's men scrambled back into order. Losses had been heavy, with many stragglers. On the brigade's northern (left) flank, few if any from the battered 35th Illinois managed to stop until well past the Brock farm. Instead, they fell back into and through Brock Field, bursting out of the trees just north of where Brig. Gen. Tom Wood's brigades (Harker and Buell) were forming in the La Fayette Road. Wood spotted both the danger and with it, a potential opportunity. The division leader dispatched Major Mendenhall to "rally the fugitives rushing across the road," and ordered his left-most brigade under Harker to pivot. Colonel Charles Harker's regiments were initially deployed in the standard two-line formation facing due west, parallel to the road. Wood's new orders wheeled Harker so that his line faced northeast in an effort aimed at striking the pursuing Confederates in the flank. Before Harker could reorient his front, however, another staff officer arrived with news the Rebels "had gained the road and was advancing up it, i.e. in the direction of Gordon's Mills." This report was somewhat misleading, but the confusion was understandable in the heat of the moment. It is also unclear if the report was mistakenly describing Fulton's Rebels moving

---

13 William Wallace Hensley Autobiography, Virginia Polytechnic Institute and State University, Blacksburg, VA. Hereafter VPI.

14 Powell, "Numbers and Losses," CCNMP. The 3rd Tennessee numbered 274; the 41st had 325 in action. *OR* 30, pt. 2, 454.

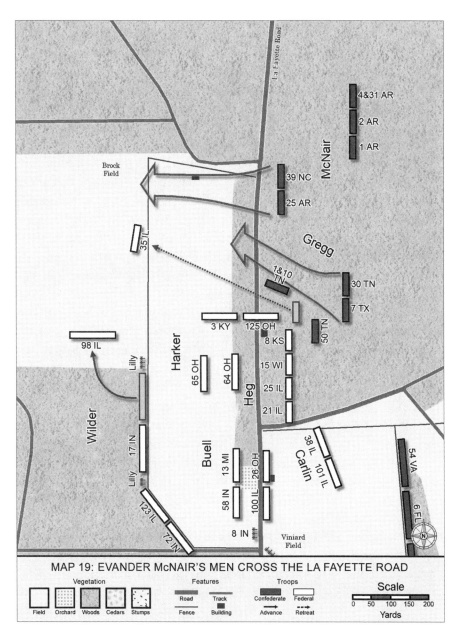

MAP 19: EVANDER McNAIR'S MEN CROSS THE LA FAYETTE ROAD

north to threaten Van Cleve, or the more immediate threat posed by Coleman's two-regiment thrust west, which Wood could easily see for himself. In any case, Wood recognized the danger to his own exposed flank and ordered Harker to further refuse his left. Once completed, the brigade front formed a shallow inverted "V" with the apex pointed north along the road. The 3rd Kentucky and

125th Ohio formed the first line with the 64th and 65th Ohio comprising the second. While Wood was reorienting Harker, Coleman halted his Rebels to figure out what to do next. His Arkansans and North Carolinians had outstripped any possible support and were essentially alone in the open fields around the Brock cabin. Menacing Federal formations were visible off to their left-rear.[15]

Farther south by southwest in the woods lining the fields, John T. Wilder's Federals watched Coleman's unsupported pursuit near the Brock cabin with interest. Years later, Wilder would recall "the enemy halted in column of division just opposite my left flank and within 50 yards of it. I immediately brought a regiment and two guns with canister to bear on them." Wilder's memory was mistaken about the range, since the cabin was 400 yards north of his left flank, but he soon closed the distance. The regiment and guns he brought "to bear on them" were the 98th Illinois and Lieutenant Scott's section of the 18th Indiana battery. With a starting strength of 485 men and equipped mostly with Spencer repeaters, the Illinoisans were superior in both numbers and firepower, and once in position they opened fire. "Finding [our] tired and weakened line exposed to a fatal flanking fire . . . with an enemy's battery near on the left," reported Coleman, "a strong enemy reinforcement [Harker] approaching, and our ammunition nearly exhausted, the impracticability of longer holding this . . . exposed position was immediately manifest." Coleman's men swarmed east back across the La Fayette Road and into the sheltering woods beyond. It was still before 3:30 p.m.[16]

All of this happened before Harker could finish redeploying. Wood was still concerned about threats from that direction, however, so about 3:45 p.m. he ordered Harker's 1,346 men to proceed up the road. They moved cautiously northward—the 3rd Kentucky and 65th Ohio to the left of the La Fayette Road, the 125th and 64th Ohio in the timber to the right of the roadway—to restore the Union line and drive whatever Rebels they found back east of the La Fayette Road. Wood accompanied Harker "nearly half a mile" before breaking off. "Having perfect confidence in his ability to handle his brigade," Wood

---

15 Ibid., pt. 1, 632.

16 Wilder Revised Report, CCNMP; Baumgartner, *Blue Lightning*, 223; *OR* 30, pt. 2, 500. While Wilder exaggerates Coleman's proximity, which was closer to 150 yards or more, and the formation—Coleman was in line, not in column—the bulk of the description is accurate.

reported, I remarked to [Harker] that I would leave him and go to look after my other brigade." Harker's own confidence was perhaps less certain. "About this time," he reported, "there was very great confusion . . . and no one seemed to have any definite idea of our own lines or the position of the enemy."[17]

Harker's men took fire even before they started to move. They were, after all, directly in the rear of a terrific contest off to the east between Heg and Gregg, and there were reported to be considerable numbers of Confederates ahead to their left and front. During their initial deployment, the 65th Ohio was hit by a "murderous volley" which dropped several officers and men. As Harker's men worked their way north, stray Rebels came in from their left. The unsettling discovery suggested Harker's command was moving into the rear of the advancing Rebel army. The woods on their right to the east also swarmed with stragglers, a legacy of the rift in Gregg's brigade front. One of these stray Rebels turned out to be General Gregg himself.[18]

Just before 4:00 p.m., Gregg was in the woods near the La Fayette Road trying to locate elements of his scattered command and determine the extent of the Federal lines. According to his friend Dr. Dudley Saunders of Marietta, Georgia, the brigadier cut an imposing figure: "Large, tall, handsome, and well-proportioned," his most prominent feature was his "massive head." Somehow, he and his staff stumbled into skirmishers of the 64th Ohio. The 64th's adjutant, Charles Woodruff, recalled that Gregg came "quite near" before realizing he was among Yankees. "Expressing his surprise with a word or two," continued Woodruff, the transplanted Texan made to ride away. "When . . . told to surrender," wrote an amused Woodruff, "he declined with a touch of profanity." Shots rang out and Gregg toppled from the saddle with a neck wound presumed fatal. Souvenir-minded Federals scrounged his spurs and sword, but when the general asked for a surgeon, he was told there was no time. "Oh my God, this is awful," moaned the stricken Gregg. It was also war. Harker's men moved on. Like Fulton's Confederates before them, Harker's brigade moved out of the purview of the Viniard Field struggle to become

17 OR 30, pt. 1, 632, 691.

18 Wilbur F. Hinman, *The Story of the Sherman Brigade. The Camp, the March, the Bivouac, the Battle, and How "The Boys" Lived and Died During Four Years of Active Service* (Press of the Daily Review, 1897), 120.

involved in the swirling action around Brotherton Field. Both commands will be examined more fully in a later chapter.[19]

Gregg's loss, meanwhile, came at a critical time for the Rebels. It would be at least another hour before Col. Cyrus Sugg of the hard-hit 50th Tennessee received word that Gregg was down and that Sugg was in charge of the fragmented brigade. Until then, Gregg's command was divided and leaderless, which meant his veteran brigade would contribute little more to the rest of the afternoon's fight.

With Heg's men reformed, Jefferson Davis's Union division was advancing anew. This time Heg held the numerical edge. Colonel Alexander's 21st Illinois added 416 Yankees to the firing line, while the loss of the 3rd and 41st Tennessee subtracted 599 muskets from Gregg's command. Without reckoning the casualties, and assuming that none of the 35th Illinois rallied in time to join in this drive, Heg could now deploy some 1,350 men against Gregg's remaining 800 or so—proportions that likely held true even with casualties factored into the mix. This explains how and why the Federals drove Gregg's Tennesseans and Texans back through shattered timber already clotted with gore by earlier combat. To Colonel Martin of the 8th Kansas, the fire seemed "more severe than before," but Heg's reformed line steadily pushed the enemy eastward, albeit slowly.[20]

The advance ground to a halt when another Rebel battle line appeared: Jerome Robertson's brigade was moving into contact. Robertson commanded one of the best combat units in the entire Confederate army, the famed Texas Brigade of the Army of Northern Virginia. Hood was its first commander, and its members had conducted more than their share of brutal, hard-hitting assaults. They broke the Yankee center at Gaines's Mill in June 1862 and cut a swath through the Federal ranks in Miller's Cornfield at Sharpsburg that September. That fame, however, was earned with staggering casualties. In Robertson, the brigade had a competent commander of significant experience. Once a Kentuckian, Robertson joined the Texas republic in the 1830s, fought Indians on the frontier, and started his Confederate career in the 5th Texas. He had led the brigade since the summer of 1862 and been wounded twice, first at

---

19 James Edmunds Saunders, Early Settlers of Alabama (L. Graham and son, Printers, 1899), 202; C. Woodruff, "Wide of the Mark, a New Version of the Death of the Rebel Gen. Gregg." *National Tribune*, January 28, 1892.

20 "Letter from Colonel Martin," *Freedom's Champion*, October 8, 1863.

Second Manassas and again at Gettysburg. His attention to the care of his men had earned him the nickname of "Aunt Polly."

As part of Law's division, Robertson's men originally angled southwest, cutting behind Bushrod Johnson's front, and were now moving up behind Gregg's attenuated line. Despite their heavy losses at Gettysburg that July, Robertson's four regiments (the 1st, 4th, and 5th Texas, and 3rd Arkansas) had largely recovered from that ordeal and numbered 1,300 officers and men. All day long they had listened to the battle rage to their north and front, expecting to be called into action at any moment. Private John C. West in Company E of the 4th Texas likened the rise and fall of volleys of gunfire to "rain on a tin roof, where at intervals the storm rages with tremendous fury, then lulls, but still continues as sound grow faint or distinct according to the direction of the varying wind." As Gregg retreated in the face of Heg's renewed advance, Robertson reoriented his line to pass through what was left of Gregg's ranks and counterattack.[21]

Robertson stepped off with orders to keep his right in contact with Colonel Sheffield's Alabamians. A series of factors soon made that impossible. First, Sheffield's brigade did not follow the divisional drift to the left but instead tracked right—perhaps additional evidence that the entire maneuver was more accidental than planned. Next came a report from Col. Van Manning of the 3rd Arkansas holding Robertson's left flank: "I advanced about 300 yards when the enemy made an appearance so far to my left as to necessitate a change of my front." Robertson initially thought Manning's report described only a "small force meant to make a diversion" against his left and authorized Manning to detach two companies to watch the brigade's flank. Within a few short minutes, however, Manning realized it would take more than a handful of men to deal with this threat, and wheeled his entire regiment toward the southwest. This posed Robertson with a dilemma: he could not maintain a connection with Sheffield's line and keep contact with Manning. It was a difficult choice. The veteran commander informed General Law that he "had necessarily to detach my brigade" from the rest of the division.[22]

The Texas brigade made a number of minor changes of direction during its approach, rendering it difficult to pinpoint where or how Robertson entered the

21 John C. West, "Fourth Texas Infantry at Chattanooga," *Houston Tri-Weekly Telegraph*, November 12, 1863.

22 *OR* 30, pt. 2, 511-512.

fight. The War Department tablets for both Law's (Hood's) division and this brigade are oriented southwest inside the tree line bordering the north end of East Viniard Field, which suggests the entire brigade (aligned 5th, 4th, and 1st Texas, and 3rd Arkansas, right to left) came into action from this angle. It is more likely the brigade formed an irregular 'L' with the longer shank facing west while the Arkansans oriented southward. Robertson reported the 5th and 4th Texas moved through heavy timber, while the 1st Texas and the Razorbacks bordered an open field. The woods also prevented the brigadier from knowing what was on his right. This helped open "a considerable gap" in the middle of the brigade front, and the 4th and 5th fought largely on their own for the next hour or so. As they moved up, the 4th and 5th also met some of Gregg's men falling back, their formation lost. Corporal Joseph Polley of Company F, 4th Texas, recalled "they [Gregg's men] came toward us in squads, and, though not running, they were not idling by the wayside. 'You fellers'll catch h-ll in thar' one of them shouted as he came near us."[23]

That warning could have applied equally to the Federals. Heg's second advance was more confused and more disorganized than his first effort, and when his line slammed into the Texans, it immediately ground to a halt. To a dismayed Colonel Martin of the 8th Kansas, Robertson seemed to bring "overwhelming numbers" into action against him. In fact, the numbers were probably about even, but Martin's men were tired and surprised by the appearance of a fresh line of the enemy troops. After a short firefight, the Federal line was again retreating. The Texans pursued. The Union regiments fell back in stages, giving way over and through each other with much confusion. At one point the 15th Wisconsin retired behind the 25th Illinois, ordered back into a supporting position, where Heg personally complimented his old command for their "gallant fight." The breather was short-lived. When the 25th suddenly fell back, its commander promised Wisconsin Lt. Col. Ole Johnson that his men would reform in turn. The retreating 25th, however, found the 21st Illinois already deployed behind the Scandinavians, and so kept moving back to reform behind Colonel Alexander's line. In the swirling confusion, Alexander thought the 25th's passage cleared his front of friendly troops. When he ordered his men

---

23 Robertson Brigade Tablet, Viniard Field, CCNMP. In fact, the tablet suggests the entire brigade, not just the 3rd Arkansas, wheeled to the left to meet Carlin and Barnes, but other accounts suggest only the 3rd and perhaps the 1st Texas actually did so. *OR* 30, pt. 2, 511; Ibid., 514; Polley, *Hood's Texas Brigade*, 209.

to open fire, their volleys ripped into the rear of the 15th Wisconsin. That proved too much to bear. "Being attacked from the rear by our own troops was more than we had bargained for," wrote Johnson, "and I told everyone to take care of himself." The Wisconsin men scattered, their cohesion shattered for the day.[24]

Sergeant Hensley of the 21st Illinois found this fight no less confusing than the earlier action. "As I started back I met Adjutant [Charles B.] Steel[e]. The Adjutant had a palsied left arm and could not handle his bridle very well. Just as I came near him his nice black mare . . . received a shot and was jumping about [so] I asked the Adjutant if I could help him and he said 'no, I can handle her' and I went on back where the Colonel was forming the regiment in line." Hensley hunted up Capt. William H. Jamison, commanding Company C, to voice his concern. "This won't do, fighting here in the brush where we can't see the enemy," Hensley protested. "The boys are getting discouraged and we can't hold them much longer." Hensley was right, and a short time later the 21st Illinois broke in turn, routed by a "deadly fire upon our left." Colonel Alexander led the survivors southwest toward Carlin's position.[25]

Limited visibility also initially hampered the Texans. Corporal Polley remembered the first contact and the stubborn retreat through the woods: "For almost a minute we failed to locate their line. Then we discovered they were lying down . . . and shooting from behind cover, and we commenced firing as we advanced rapidly toward them. Their main body gave way before our impetuous rush, but with a reluctance that was not encouraging, and [they] formed another line a hundred yards in rear of the first." Another Texan noted the slaughter already apparent "at every step, passing over the dead and wounded" from earlier combat.[26]

Texas Pvt. John West "advanced to within one hundred yards of the yanks before I saw them lying and squatting . . . in the scant undergrowth. Just as . . . I was about to shoot," West continued, "a cry passed down the line that they were our own men, but very few seemed to regard it, and a pretty heavy though irregular fire was opened on them." The Federals facing the 4th Texas were

---

24 *OR* 30, pt. 1, 529; Ole C. Johnson, "From Libby Prison," *Wisconsin State Journal*, December 23, 1863.

25 Hensley Autobiography, VPI; *OR* 30, pt. 1, 519.

26 A. V. Winkler, *The Confederate Capital and Hood's Texas Brigade* (Eugene Von Boeckmann, 1894), 144.

confused and disorganized, and so returned a halting fire. "I believe myself that this line of yanks would have surrendered, had an opportunity been afforded them, they seemed so passive. I fired two shots . . . when the entire line in front of us suddenly seemed to be panic-stricken and fled, except [for] two or three companies behind a house and two our left."[27]

James T. Hunter, a captain with the 4th Texas, would later write the report for his regiment's Chickamauga service. According to Hunter, his men drove the Yankees all the way back to the road and into Viniard Field beyond, though some Federals took shelter among the Viniard farm buildings while others holed up in the Log School just to the north. The 5th Texas on Robertson's right picked up support from some of Gregg's scattered command and had a slightly easier time of it. Captain Tacitus Clay noted the timber concealed the 5th's strength from the Yankees. "The impression prevailed among them . . . that they were flanked, and after delivering a feeble fire," Clay continued, "they fled across the field to the woods beyond." "With a Texas yell we went at them and drove them," boasted Pvt. Robert Campbell of Company A, "run them like dogs—until our regiment, the 5th, got so far ahead of the brigade."[28]

During the advance, the Texans stumbled upon the seriously wounded John Gregg. Someone organized a detail to carry him back to the brigade hospital. Gregg recovered and within six months would be leading the very men who saved him.[29]

Unfortunately for the Confederates, the pursuit of Heg's men disrupted the Texans' formation. Reckless with the excitement of the moment, Private West of the 4th Texas found himself in trouble. As he later admitted to his wife, "I got mixed up with the Yanks by being too fast," though he hastened to add, "I have the credit of doing some good work at close quarters." West had just removed his bayonet ("it hurt my hand in loading rapidly," he explained) when a Federal turned and fired from less than 30 feet away. "The bullet hit the handle of my bayonet, which had not been in the scabbard two seconds, and . . . it was

27 West, "Fourth Texas at Chattanooga," *Houston Tri-Weekly Telegraph.*

28 OR 30, pt. 2, 514, 516; Robert Campbell, *Lone Star Confederate: A Gallant and Good Soldier of the Fifth Texas Infantry* (Texas A&M University Press, 2003), 97-98.

29 Goodrich, "Gregg's Brigade," 264. When he was fit for duty, Gregg was assigned to command the Texas Brigade in the spring of 1864 after Robertson secured a transfer back to Texas. Gregg's respite from death was short lived. He was killed leading a charge in October 1864 outside Richmond.

driven against me with great force, blinding and sickening me so that I fell and was supposed to be fatally wounded. It seemed to me a thousand bullets and grapeshot tore up the ground around me." In a letter to his brother, West added a little more detail. When he was struck, he wrote, "[I] fell almost upon the body of a severely wounded Yank, who asked me to unbuckle his belt, which I did with great difficulty, for I was very sick and spitting blood myself. He died before he had time to thank me." West deemed his survival "a miracle," though he managed to make his way to the rear. Once there, West discovered he was only badly bruised, and after a night's rest returned to his regiment for the next day's long bloody combat.[30]

Heg's collapse cleared the way of Federals almost to the La Fayette Road. Small knots of Federals attempted to stand, most notably in the Log School. The defenders were by now disorganized and, in some cases, demoralized and did not hold out for long. Polley described one Texan, Juluis Glazer, who single-handedly charged the Log School and, despite taking several wounds, captured a number of Norwegians from the 15th inside.[31]

Beyond the school farther south, meanwhile, Col. George P. Buell's men of Wood's division were deployed in line and still awaiting orders. When Harker's troops moved off to the north, Buell's line, deployed just east of the Viniard buildings, remained behind. For a short while they were spectators to the fight swirling around them. They were about to find themselves in the thick of the action.

With Harker gone, Buell's left flank was more vulnerable than even Heg's had been, and the Texans were not slow to exploit their advantage. The 4th and 5th Texas regiments angled southwest, their lines disordered but in a perfect position to savage Buell. In the meantime, Robertson's other two regiments (1st Texas and 3rd Arkansas) renewed their attack from the west across Viniard Field. Both wings of the Texas Brigade were converging on Buell's four exposed regiments.

Things could have been worse for Buell. Of Bushrod Johnson's three brigades, Fulton's was already out of the picture, having moved off to the northwest about 3:00 p.m. John Gregg's command was savaged and badly disrupted, and with its brigadier down likely out of the fight for the rest of the

---

30 John C. West, *A Texan in Search of a Fight, Being the Diary and Letters of a Private Soldier in Hood's Texas Brigade* (Press of J.S. Hill & Co, 1901), 107, 114.

31 Polley, *Hood's Texas Brigade*, 212.

day. By the time Robertson's men came into the fight, Gregg's line was chopped into at least three segments: the 3rd and 41st Tennessee were off with Fulton, the 10th (along with the 1st Battalion) and 30th Tennessee were operating against the northern half of Heg's line, and the 7th Texas and 50th Tennessee were operating more or less as a skirmish line.

In theory, this still left Brig. Gen. Evander McNair's 1,207 men, who thus far had seen virtually no action except for Colonel Coleman's limited foray across the road, handily repulsed by the 98th Illinois. McNair was still being held as the divisional reserve in the woods about 300 yards east of the La Fayette Road, facing the gap between the 41st and 10th Tennessee. In part due to the uncertainty created by Harker's move, the bulk of McNair's men would not become heavily engaged on September 19. In his report, Coleman noted that after the 25th Arkansas and 39th North Carolina reformed in the woods, they were "marched back to nearly their original position to await ammunition, where they were joined by the rest of the brigade." There, McNair and his men waited out the rest of the afternoon's fight. Bushrod Johnson seems to have forgotten about McNair's troops after Johnson's earlier orders to send Coleman forward. McNair, for his part, undertook no initiative of his own. He would be badly wounded on the morrow, and thus never write a report of his brigade's actions on the 19th, nor has any postwar account been located. His inactivity remains one of the battle's unanswered questions. If he had decided on his own to support Robertson, or if Johnson had ordered him into action here, the Federals would have been in dire straits.[32]

No official blame or approbation was directed McNair's way for whatever happened that afternoon, but he would not serve again with the Army of Tennessee. After he recovered, he was transferred to the Trans-Mississippi, where he finished the war. Gregg's wounding and McNair's decision to fall back removed the bulk of Johnson's division from the Confederate battle line at a critical time, and in a place where the Federals could no longer mount much of an effective defense.

32 OR 30, pt. 2, 500.

Chapter Eighteen

Viniard Field:
Carlin Comes to Grief
Saturday, September 19: 2:30 p.m. to 4:30 p.m.

Heg's bitter fight did not take place in a vacuum. While his troops were pushing and being shoved in the timber, Brig. Gen. William P. Carlin was trying to advance as well, moving to engage the other half of Robertson's Texas Brigade when it appeared on the far side of Viniard Field. Carlin moved slowly, however, reluctant to expose his men by pushing deeper into the open field with the Rebels holding the timber on the far edge. "We had the great disadvantage of being distinctly seen by the enemy, while they were seldom visible to us," explained Carlin. "Our line was in very open woods, or in the cleared land. . . . Their scouts and skirmishers in butternut clothes could be seen clinging to the trees on the far side." And, of course, Carlin had already lost the 21st Illinois to Heg, while division commander Davis had dispatched the 2nd Minnesota artillery and 81st Indiana to the southwest corner of the field early in the fight. Pushing into the open with only half of his brigade would be the height of foolishness.[1]

Carlin's attention was fixed on the two regiments comprising Robertson's right wing. The 1st Texas and 3rd Arkansas appeared in force in the scattered timber just beyond the northeast corner of the field. Manning's Arkansans

---

1 Carlin, "Military Memoirs," *National Tribune*, April 16, 1885.

Viniard Field, midfield, from the Union position, looking northeast. The tablet
to the left of the Viniard-Alexander Road marks the spot where the
1st Texas and 3rd Arkansas entered the field. *Harvey Scarborough*

stepped into view first, changing front (as noted in the previous chapter) to refuse their flank and protect it from what looked to be an open expanse filled with Federals. They were soon joined by Capt. R. J. Harding's 1st Texas, which also turned to face south in response to the Federal activity threatening Robertson's left. Together the two regiments numbered 789 officers and men. Rebel accounts from these regiments are considerably sparser than those penned by men in the 4th and 5th Texas, and those few that do survive tend to be brief and with few details. For example, Harding's regimental report summed up several hours of fighting in a couple of sentences: "the regiment was immediately marched by the left flank to meet [Carlin's] advance. We found them posted in large numbers in a ravine covered by thick undergrowth. We immediately charged them, killing a colonel and driving them across a field." In reality, it was not so easy as all that.[2]

The Rebels on Robertson's left flank initially did not meet with the same rush of success as did the 4th and 5th Texas. In addition to Carlin's musketry, Manning's Arkansans and Harding's Texans were also drawing artillery fire from several Union guns, first the 2nd Minnesota battery and then some of Eli Lilly's 18th Indiana pieces, ranged back on the rise with Wilder. This fire was

2   OR 30, pt. 2, 513.

enough to give the Rebels pause. For a while, the fight ground on in a static exchange of fire.

Captain William E. Hotchkiss of the 2nd Minnesota, who was serving as Davis's divisional artillery chief, had ample reason to be satisfied with his gunners. "The service the [battery] did at this point was of great importance," he later reported. "[I]t prevented the enemy from forming and extending his left with the evident purpose of flanking General Davis' right." Private D. H. Hamilton of Company M, 1st Texas, recalled the intensity of the shelling even before they were ordered into the attack: "By this time the Yankee batteries had about topped all the timber around us. The shells kept every man as busy as a Cranberry Merchant dodging their flying fragments."[3]

For a while, the Minnesota artillery received support from Wilder, who could also see the potential flanking threat. Early in the developing fight, Tom Crittenden ordered Wilder to move his entire brigade forward across the La Fayette Road. When the 2nd Minnesota seemed in danger, Wilder sent the 72nd Indiana and 123rd Illinois into Viniard Field as an additional counterweight to any Confederate flanking effort. This move certainly gave Robertson pause and sent additional firepower into his ranks. Just how significant this portion of the fight became is open to debate. In his diary, Capt. Ambrose Remley of the 72nd wrote that "about noon our brigade was ordered across the field and formed along the edge of the woods. At this time, the Rebels made a determined charge and drove the infantry [Davis] back to where we were. After part of our lines had been engaged a while . . . we fell back to our old position." Hoosier Sgt. Benjamin Magee recalled the movement by his regiment as a dramatic charge that saved Davis's men from what he called "annihilation." Wilder, however, was more restrained and merely noted that the enemy were repelled "in handsome style" while Colonel Miller, writing the 72nd's official report, recorded only that they "entered the woods and checked the enemy." Shortly afterward, Wilder maneuvered his entire line back to his original position west of the road in order to respond to a new threat: the 25th Arkansas and 39th North Carolina under Colonel Coleman had slipped past Heg's flank into the West Brock Field (as described earlier). Wilder dispatched the 98th Illinois to

---

3 Ibid., pt. 1, 502; D. H. Hamilton, *History of Company M, First Texas Volunteer Infantry* (W. M. Morrison, 1962), 31. "Busy as a Cranberry Merchant" is an outdated colloquialism similar to "busy as a beaver." I confess that I don't know why cranberry merchants would be busier than other folks.

deal with that problem. By this time East Viniard Field was getting crowded. A number of additional Federals were arriving from the south.[4]

These new arrivals belonged to Sidney Barnes, who halted his regiments in the open timber bordering the southern edge of Viniard Field roughly 800 yards south of the current fight. Barnes, it will be recalled, had been ordered up from Lee and Gordon's Mills along with General Wood's division. In fact, Barnes was still expecting Wood's men to cover his own right flank because he was never informed that Colonel Starling subsequently summoned Wood to another part of the field entirely. In keeping with his original orders, Barnes was looking for a way to assail the left flank of the Rebels engaged with Heg. Accompanying Barnes was Lt. Courtland Livingston's 3rd Wisconsin battery of four 10-pound Parrott rifles and two 12-pound howitzers, as well as one section of Capt. George R. Swallow's 7th Indiana battery. While Barnes assessed the situation, Wood's staff officer Maj. John Mendenhall rode over and took charge of the artillery. Mendenhall ordered Livingston to deploy his six guns on high ground in a peach orchard to the south and east of the 2nd Minnesota's pieces, where they also engaged Robertson's Rebels. From there, recalled one Wisconsinite, "the ten guns rendered the enemy's situation . . . quite an uncomfortable one, for they made tremendous efforts to dislodge us." Barnes's four regiments closed up behind the artillery, coming to a halt inside the trees south of Viniard Field.[5]

While Mendenhall was deploying Livingston's guns, Colonel Starling led Tom Wood's two brigades (Harker and Buell) north up the La Fayette Road. Wood's men passed to the rear of Barnes's line, now some distance off the road to the east, behind the 3rd Wisconsin and 2nd Minnesota positions out in Viniard Field, and halted between and behind Carlin's and Heg's brigades. It was at this point Wood became involved in sending Harker's men farther north on their uncertain mission into the woods toward Brotherton Field, leaving Col. George P. Buell's brigade idling in the road near the Viniard house. Buell's battery, the 8th Indiana, unlimbered, with "the left half of [the] battery deployed in woods and the right in an open field." Both the infantry and the artillery were on lower ground near the road and house. Their view of the battle—and any

---

4 OR 30, pt. 1, 447; Linville, *Battles, Skirmishes, Events and Scenes,* 83; Magee, *History of the 72nd Indiana,* 174-176; OR 30, pt. 1, 447, 452.

5 OR 30, pt. 1, 622; Anonymous, *History of the Services of the Third Battery, Wisconsin Light Artillery in the Civil War of the United States, 1861-65* (Courant Press, n.d), 27.

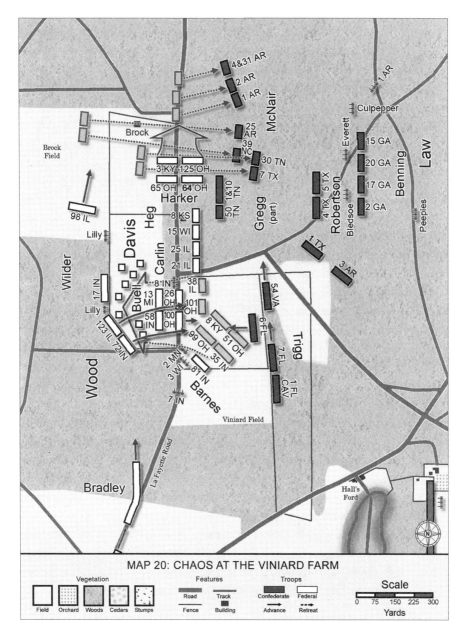

MAP 20: CHAOS AT THE VINIARD FARM

Vegetation				Features		Troops		Scale
Field	Orchard	Woods	Cedars	Stumps	Road	Track	Confederate	Federal

reasonable field of fire—were mostly blocked by the rising terrain in midfield to the east.[6]

The commander of the Hoosier battery, Capt. George Estep, found the circumstances disturbing. There was fighting to his front, though he could see little of it, and word reached him that Rebels were driving in the blue infantry. Afraid that if he opened fire he would send metal flying into friendly troops, Estep rode over to Lieutenant Livingston's 3rd Wisconsin battery for clarification. The news was alarming: "[Livingston] told me that he had been firing at a range of 800 yards, but that the distance was growing less very fast." Estep galloped back to his own guns and ordered the right half of the battery to cut the fuses on their shells for 700 yards in the hope it would prevent any of his rounds from dropping among fellow Federals.[7]

Mendenhall, meanwhile, began riding over to Wood's newly arrived formation and noticed the wayward section of the 7th Indiana battery seemingly bereft of responsibilities. "I posted it in the field in the rear of where General Wood's head of column was entering the woods," explained Mendenhall. The two Hoosier gun crews moved as ordered into a situation that would soon prove perilous.[8]

While all this activity was unfolding, Barnes spent a considerable period of time halted at the southern end of the field. Carlin and other senior officers seemed oblivious to his presence. Carlin would have been heartened to know another Union brigade was so close at hand, but he was busy with his own problems. The departure of his 21st Illinois left Carlin with just 544 officers and men composed of the 38th Illinois on his left, and the 101st Ohio on the right. This was less than one-half of Carlin's original combat power, with which he was expected to push across the field and take on an unknown number of Confederates waiting for him in the tree line. Thus far these men had been more spectators than participants. The 38th watched as Heg's line came tumbling back the first time and the 21st Illinois rushed to bolster it and open fire on Gregg's pursuing Confederates. "Then," noted the 38th's Pvt. William Patterson, "Colonel Heg again drove the rebels before them . . . and disappeared into the woods under a heavy fire." Despite Davis's instruction to Carlin to join in this second advance, Patterson recalled that the 38th Illinois remained in the road, and the regiment was still there when Heg's men came tumbling back again, this time pursued by the Texans of the 4th and 5th regiments.[9]

---

7   Ibid., 677.

8   Ibid., 622.

9   Patterson Memoir, University of Missouri, Rolla, MO.

The men of the 101st Ohio, however, recalled the opposite. Captain Leonard D. Smith, upon whom it would fall to write the 101st's report, claimed Carlin ordered the regiment "forward to the fence dividing the corn-field from the woods" bordering Viniard Field to the east. "We were ordered to our feet and into the woods directly in front of us," agreed Sgt. Lewis Day, further noting that "the order was obeyed with alacrity. We had but little difficulty in clearing our front of skirmishers and sharpshooters. Advancing cautiously, but steadily . . . we soon struck a strong rebel force advancing obliquely across our front toward our left." These troops were probably the 1st Texas trying to turn Heg's southern flank. (Manning's Arkansas still seemed to be facing south into the field.) Carlin's line halted and opened fire. While his men exchanged shots with the enemy, a surprised Carlin observed an unknown brigade of Yankees cut across his own right-front.[10]

Sidney Barnes's intentions may have been sound, but his execution was surely flawed. While Livingston's artillery of his 3rd Wisconsin was going into action, Barnes decided to advance. He first encountered not Rebels but some of Wilder's men retreating, probably members of the 123rd Illinois who "caused some little confusion" as they passed through his ranks. After taking a moment to sort things out Barnes resumed his advance. Unfortunately, his battle line was on a course to mask Carlin's regiments by moving across their right-front, and he was also exposing (unwittingly) his own brigade to a flank fire from Rebels in the distant trees on the east side of the field. As these new and as yet unidentified Federals halted and opened a sustained fire on Robertson's Rebels, Carlin tried to compensate by ordering the 101st Ohio to execute a left-half wheel and angle its fire more to the northeast. With bullets zipping around him, Carlin spurred his horse to the newcomers to see who they were and what they were doing. Before he could do little more learn the brigade belonged to Barnes, however, disaster struck.[11]

Carlin had been right to be wary of the woods. Within them lurked the 1,536 officers and men of Col. Robert C. Trigg's brigade, part of William Preston's division. Originally, Maj. Gen. A. P. Stewart's division was in this area until plucked out of the line at midday and sent north to support Ben

10 OR 30, pt. 1, 527; Day, *One Hundred and First Ohio*, 160. Day also recalled the regiment advancing "through a dense woods," but all the other accounts have the 101st out in the field at this time.

11 OR 30, pt. 1, 516, 839.

Cheatham's embattled division. When Stewart departed, corps commander Simon Buckner ordered Preston to shift Trigg's brigade north and cover the gap. Trigg did as ordered and also advanced the 1st Florida Cavalry (dismounted) forward another 300 yards as skirmishers.[12]

Robert Craig Trigg was an 1849 graduate of the Virginia Military Institute and a veteran officer. He began the war as a captain in the 4th Virginia and fought under Stonewall Jackson at First Manassas. Soon after that battle he won permission to raise his own regiment, recruiting the 54th Virginia from his native southwestern Virginia. He and the 54th served in that region and were part of Buckner's command when Knoxville, Tennessee, was evacuated during late summer 1863. His brigade consisted of his Virginians, the 1st Florida Cavalry, and the 6th and 7th Florida. Both Preston and Buckner thought highly of Trigg and urged his promotion. "His personal gallantry," wrote Buckner 10 days after the battle, "his qualifications as a commander and his conduct on the field . . . entitle him . . . to permanently command the brigade."[13]

The 1st Florida watched Davis's Federals deploy along the La Fayette Road and skirmished with Carlin's men at long range, but Trigg did not bring up the rest of the brigade until close to 3:00 p.m. It was about that time when Gen. John B. Hood decided to advance. He notified General Bragg of his decision, and Bragg in turn instructed Buckner to "reinforce [Hood] as far as I could." That reinforcement proved to be Trigg's command. Like so many other commanders that day, Trigg received little in the way of guidance from above. His instructions consisted of little more than a vague injunction to "move in the direction of the firing." He initially moved by the right flank, sidling northward. Within minutes he met one of Hood's staff officers who directed him to face his line west and move forward. Trigg had only the sketchiest notion of where Hood's line was located. He thought the staffer's order was intended to put his brigade into line supporting Hood's rear, alongside Henry Benning's brigade. In fact, Trigg was still several hundred yards south of Robertson's left flank.[14]

A second staffer appeared and, as Trigg reported, "claimed my support for General Robertson's Brigade." Trigg continuing moving west until he reached a

---

12 Ibid., pt. 2, 414.

13 Anonymous, "Col. Robert C. Trigg, of Virginia" *Confederate Veteran*, vol. XVII, no. 2 (February, 1909), 65; Endorsement, Sept 30, 1863, Wyckliffe-Preston Papers, University of Kentucky, Lexington, KY.

14 OR 30, pt. 2, 357, 430.

point where he could at last get some sense of the battle swirling in his area. Things did not appear to be going well. "I came near a cornfield, in which the enemy had a battery . . . supported by a long line of infantry," Trigg then continued. "The enemy was advancing when I first discovered him, and had passed about one-third of the length of the field. [Our] troops that had won the wooded ridge . . . to my right were falling back in some confusion." The view also seems to have triggered uncertainty in Trigg's guide, who asked him to "halt until he could learn precisely what position I could take." By now the brigade was under heavy fire, but Trigg agreed to stop. Robertson himself soon appeared to inform Trigg his own men were under pressure and in danger of "being beaten back unless quickly reinforced." Robertson hurried Trigg into a right oblique that finally brought the Virginian's line of battle up to the fence bordering the east side of Viniard Field—a position from which he could provide effective support.

Once there, the 1st Florida Cavalry (which up to this time had remained deployed as skirmishers across Trigg's front) fell in on the brigade left. Once his front was clear, Trigg's men unleashed a stunning volley into Carlin's line and savaged the flank of Barnes's brigade. "The enemy broke in confusion to the left and rear," Trigg noted with satisfaction.[15]

Despite Trigg's belief that the whole Federal force in Viniard Field was concentrating their fire on him, neither Carlin nor Barnes realized there was more than a Confederate skirmish line present that might pose a threat to their own flanks. Barnes's attention was almost wholly focused on Robertson's right wing and especially the 3rd Arkansas, which Barnes thought he could take in the flank. Carlin's men had Barnes's regiments between them and the east side of the field, so they paid little attention to what lay beyond and couldn't see much in that direction in any event.

Captain Thomas Wright of the 8th Kentucky, holding the left front of Barnes's advancing brigade, certainly had no intimation of disaster. He recalled the 8th delivering "a steady fire on the enemy's line to our front. Our men appeared in the best of spirits," he continued, "notwithstanding the heavy fire they were pouring on us." Wright recalled the brigade halted to deliver a more accurate fire into Robertson's line. Some of the 8th had already fallen when the Arkansans appeared to fall back. "We were expecting momentarily to be ordered forward," continued Wright, "when, to our surprise, we were

15 Ibid.

completely flanked on our right." Sergeant Samuel Kessler, fighting on the right of the Kentuckians with Company C, 51st Ohio, was one of those who bore the brunt of this new attack. "We were moved to another part of the field," he wrote, "without any support but two other regiments and the rebels made a most desperate charge to gain this position." Barnes watched with horror as "the right of the first line . . . Fifty-First Ohio, gave way, then the entire regiment, and then the 8th Kentucky. . . . They both retired fighting, passing the second line, which was then lying down."[16]

Colonel Peter Swaine of the 99th Ohio had charge of the support line. He manfully tried to hold his ground and buy enough time for the first line to reform. Swaine was a Regular, a West Point graduate of the class of 1852 who had been appointed to lead the 99th in December 1862. He replaced Col. Albert Langworthy, dismissed after a controversial decision to retreat during the Kentucky campaign. Swaine had his work cut out for him, for Langworthy was thrown out despite the objections of his disgusted men. Swaine found a regiment in ramshackle condition, but his excellent leadership and drillmaster skills changed that. Under his supervision, the 99th "became unrivaled among volunteers and unabashed in everything that pertained to the soldier, even in the presence of regulars, not at all omitting the actual shock of battle." Now, as the brigade's front line collapsed, Swaine ordered his men to their feet and shoved them forward to meet Trigg's sudden challenge. "The advance . . . was gallantly made in the face of a deadly fire," Swaine reported, "the Irishmen [of the 35th Indiana] and Buckeyes keeping up a perfect flame of fire. "Our line staggered for a moment," he continued, "[but] were dealing terrific punishment to the foe, when another line opened upon our right flank."[17]

Swaine was being charitable. The Rebel fire was heavy and accurate, scything through his men from both front and right flank. Swaine's executive officer, Lt. Col. John E. Cummins, "who knows not what fear is," ordered Companies B and D to change front to the right, but they could not hold their ground. Farther up the regimental line, "a minnie ball struck my left thigh about halfway between my knee and hip," wrote Capt. Thomas Honnell of Company

16 Thomas J. Wright, *History of the Eighth Regiment Kentucky Volunteer Infantry* (St. Joseph Steam Printing Co. 1880), 189; Samuel Kessler to "Dear Uncle," Letter of October 1, 1863, Thomas J. Kessler Papers, Navarro College, Corsciana, TX; *OR* 30, pt. 1, 839.

17 Kevin B. McCray, *A Shouting of Orders: A History of the 99th Ohio Volunteer Infantry Regiment* (Xlibris, 2003), 33; Woods, *Steedman and His Men at Chickamauga*, 112-113; *OR* 30, pt. 1, 849.

C, and while it struck "the bone, [it] did not break it." Barnes's entire brigade—flanked, surprised and torn apart by Trigg's fire—was soon in full retreat. Some of the men fell back into and through Carlin's rightmost regiment, the 101st Ohio, which disgusted a Buckeye private named Leonard Cole: "The rebels flanked them in turn, and instead of their acting like men they run like cowards."[18]

When Barnes's men broke and ran, Carlin's line largely followed suit. The 38th Illinois essentially dissolved. Lieutenant Colonel John Messer kept at least part of the 101st Ohio in order while conducting a fighting retreat, but everyone was now heading for the La Fayette Road. Carlin later confessed his men were "panic-stricken. . . . Riding into the midst of them," he wrote, "I pleaded with them and begged them to return. I then tried to shame them, but they heeded not my pleading nor my ridicule. Then anger overcame me, and I used words more forcible than polite." As the general later wrote in his memoirs, his aide, Lt. Joseph W. Vance, "exclaimed 'General, they are shooting at us,' meaning these panic-stricken men of ours. 'Oh! That surely cannot be true,' [Carlin] replied." Some of the men had "discharged [their muskets] in the air at an elevation and to their rear." Whether these shots were aimed at them or were the unthinking reactions of panicked men scrambling for safety, the rout was complete. There would be no rally and renewed advance on this side of the road.[19]

To Colonel Trigg, the moment seemed one of splendid opportunity. "I ordered my brigade to charge before he could rally," Trigg reported, and at once the 6th Florida obeyed. Lieutenant Colonel John J. Wade, who led the 54th Virginia on the brigade's right, attempted to follow suit. "In my regiment an irregular fire was kept up for several minutes," explained Wade, "which prevented my order to advance from being heard [immediately.]" As a result, the Floridians were already well out in front of the brigade line when Wade got his excited Virginians to cease fire, cross the fence, and move out in the 6th's wake. Farther down the line to the left, the 7th Florida and 1st Florida Cavalry were still behind the fence line.[20]

18 Ibid., 850; "October 26, 1863," Thomas C. Honnell to Henry Honnell, Honnell Papers, OHS; "Brother Jim," September 17-22, 1863, James M. Cole Papers, ALPL.

19 *OR* 30, pt. 1, 516; Girardi and Hughes, *Carlin Memoirs*, 99-100.

20 *OR* 30, pt. 2, 430, 439.

Viniard field, from the southwest corner, looking northeast. The large monument to the far right marks the position of the 81st Indiana. The cannon in the center belong to the 2nd Minnesota Battery. Carlin's line is to the left. While the line of low rectangular monuments just beyond the cannon commemorate Bradley's Brigade (see chapter 19) they also mark the approximate line of advance for Barnes's regiments. The treeline to the right-center of the image concealed Trigg's Confederates. *Harvey Scarborough*

What should have been a grand moment for Trigg turned out to be something altogether different. He impetuously led the 6th forward about 200 yards and crested a small rise where, for the first time, he could see the entire Union position in Viniard Field. Six Union regiments were in full retreat. Only the 81st Indiana remained formed in support of the guns of the 2nd Minnesota on Trigg's left. Alongside Trigg, the 6th's colonel, J. J. Finley, noted also the presence of two more batteries, one plying his Floridians with "a raking fire" about 300 yards to the left, and the third "diagonally to our right." These guns were those of the 3rd Wisconsin, planted earlier in support of the Minnesotans, and the newly arrived 8th Indiana battery of Wood's division, which had halted with Buell's brigade at the northwest corner of the field. Finley paid little attention to Buell's infantry. Both he and Trigg focused on what looked to be the exposed and thus vulnerable Union guns. At least two cannon directly in front of the 6th Florida—the orphaned pieces of the 7th Indiana battery, bridging the gap between Buell's line and the 2nd Minnesota—appeared especially ripe for the taking.[21]

21 Ibid., 439.

While the Floridians of the 6th regiment continued forward, however, Trigg realized he was alone: none of his other three regiments had advanced. The 6th, now unsupported out in midfield, was at least 200 yards ahead of the rest of the brigade. The colonel spurred his horse back toward the fence line to bring up the laggards when he saw them beginning to cross the fence to move forward. Satisfied they were coming on in "good order," Trigg turned to rejoin the 6th. Within minutes, however, a second look back again filled him with dismay. Instead of moving west across the field toward the Yankees, his three regiments were moving north away from the fight. The stunned colonel rode hard in their direction to discover what was amiss.[22]

The abrupt course change came at the behest of Brigadier General Robertson. Determined to see what was delaying his own support, Robertson found Colonel Wade of the 54th Virginia and ordered a change of direction. Robertson, wrote the Virginian, informed Wade that "we were going wrong, and that our formation should be made on his (Texas) brigade in the woods to the right." Because he knew of the previous instruction to support Hood's men, Wade obeyed and "moved my regiment by the right flank . . . to the woods." The 1st and 7th Florida regiments followed suit.[23]

The Floridians of the 6th regiment, meanwhile, plunged on without help into a hellish maelstrom. "Our regiment acted nobly," Capt. Hugh Black of Company A informed his wife, but "every company suffered right severely. . . . I was never in such a place before. It is strange to me how anyone escaped for I assure you the bullets seemed to search every nook and corner of the field. The 6th's advance exposed its flank to the 81st Indiana. The Hoosiers, still in Major Calloway's capable hands, had been personally repositioned by General Davis to help a regiment Davis mistook for the 38th Illinois. In fact, the formation was Barnes's support line under Colonel Swaine's direction, still getting in some licks as it fell back. Calloway's men leveled their rifled muskets and enfiladed Colonel Finley's Rebels from about 200 yards: "We immediately opened a well directed fire, first by volley and then by file."[24]

Perhaps a more veteran regiment would have broken off the attack earlier or not pressed forward quite so rashly. Despite having been in service since the

22 Ibid., 430.

23 Ibid., 439.

24 Elizabeth Coldwell Frano, *Letters of Captain Hugh Black to his Family and Friends during The War Between the States 1862-1864* (Evansville Bindery, 1998), 58; OR 30, pt. 1, 523.

spring of 1862, the men of the 6th were new to combat. Except for extensive marching and little shooting during Bragg's unsuccessful Kentucky invasion that fall, they had spent nearly all of their time in East Tennessee. Chickamauga was their first experience in full-fledged battle. Finley recorded that his men closed to within "150 yards" of a Federal battery (the two-gun section of the 7th Indiana) but once on the crest of the ridge midfield, Union fire from three directions ripped through his ranks. The worst of it came from the left, where the 81st Indiana, 2nd Minnesota, and 3rd Wisconsin "kept up without intermission an enfilading fire upon my whole line, which told with terrible effect." Somehow Finley's men managed what he described as a "well directed fire" that drove away the Union gun crews of the 7th Indiana, "leaving the guns unmanned and the battery flag cut down." Fighting unsupported in the open, however, left him with little chance of prevailing, and Trigg ordered Finley to withdraw his regiment. The brave foray cost the Floridians 35 killed and 135 wounded out of 402 engaged.[25]

The fate of the two guns of the 7th Indiana battery was nearly lost to history. Captain Swallow and the bulk of the battery were engaged farther north with Dick's brigade, and would have their own dramatic tales to tell of fighting on the 19th. As a result, the actions experienced by this detached section, engaged in Viniard Field were never described in an official report. Major Mendenhall's passing reference about placing the pair of Hoosier guns in the field that day confirmed their presence there. Captain Hotchkiss of the 2nd Minnesota provided additional clues. Concerned about the advancing Floridians, Hotchkiss decided to "retire the 2nd Minnesota and a section of an Indiana battery, then on the left of the Minnesota battery slowly . . . about 250 yards across the only open ground in our rear . . . [but] . . . the drivers and men of the . . . Indiana battery . . . became panic-stricken, and stampeded with their caissons and gun limbers . . . through the [left section of] the Second Minnesota." By implication, the two guns remained on the field, which matches Colonel Finley's description of driving away Union gun crews from their pieces. Once the Floridians were driven back, however, the men of the 7th reclaimed their guns and the section rumbled northward to find the rest of the battery, having had enough of being orphaned in the middle of a battle.[26]

---

25 *OR* 30, pt. 2, 435-436.

26 Ibid., pt. 1, 504. Even today there is no position marker anywhere in Viniard Field to denote the presence of the Indiana section.

With the 6th Florida's abrupt withdrawal, Trigg's men were now out of the fight. The colonel led Finley's 6th back across the body-strewn field in search of the rest of his regiments, which were now halted a couple of hundred yards to the north in the timber behind the field's eastern fence line. None of his other three regiments had suffered like the 6th, though all had taken some loss. The next heaviest loss was in the 54th Virginia, which suffered three killed and 35 wounded for an eight percent casualty rate. Despite Robertson's urgent summons at perhaps the worst possible moment for the Confederates, Trigg's brigade was not called upon for further duty that day even though Robertson needed additional assistance.

The action on the southern end of Viniard Field may have been falling into fitful gunfire, but the fighting at the northern end was intensifying. The collapse of Carlin's and Barnes's commands encouraged the men of the 1st Texas and 3rd Arkansas to complete their own attack. Both regiments charged, cresting the rise north of where the Floridians had run into trouble, in an effort to strike the Union line around the Viniard farm. They started forward about the time the lone assault of the 6th Florida reached its apogee and came apart, but neither formation reported seeing the other. Viniard Field wasn't that large, but it was large enough that three regiments could pass within a couple of hundred yards of one another—one falling back east and two charging west—and not realize other regiments were close at hand in the same open patch of ground. This fact is a clear testament to how confusing the fight had become to all its participants.

Trigg's absence did not mean that Robertson's right wing had to fight on wholly unsupported, however. The advance of the 1st Texas and 3rd Arkansas transpired about the same time Robertson's left wing (the 4th and 5th Texas) was breaking Heg's line as it swept in from the northeast. More by chance than by design, all four of Robertson's regiments were converging on the Viniard cabin and Col. George P. Buell's four regiments of Yankees.

Colonel Buell, a first cousin to former army commander Don Carlos Buell, reached brigade command by dint of hard service. He was a civil engineer and not a professional soldier, though he did graduate from Norwich Military Institute. At the war's outbreak, Buell returned home from the Colorado Territory to enlist in the Union cause as lieutenant colonel of the 58th Indiana. He commanded the 58th at Stones River until thrust into brigade command in the middle of that bitter fight, where he "performed every duty gallantly and well."[27]

Buell halted his men in the road south of Harker's brigade, where he formed the brigade in two lines facing east in a reserve position straddling the La Fayette Road. The six pieces of the 8th Indiana Battery had already unlimbered east of the road, so Buell formed his front alongside the artillery. The 339 men of the 100th Illinois fell in on the battery's right, while the 26th Ohio, 377 strong, moved up on the left. The 58th Indiana deployed behind the 100th just south and west of the farmstead. The 13th Michigan did the same behind the 26th. Buell's second line numbered 617 officers and men. His whole frontage, including the battery, occupied about 270 yards. Their field of fire, however, was poor. The right half of the brigade was in the field, but behind the crest of the rise to their front, while on the brigade left, Capt. Walden Kelly of the 26th Ohio observed "the underbrush of and under the timber prevented us from seeing more than a short distance."[28]

One more Federal battery was loitering in the vicinity of the Viniard farm at this time. Captain Cullen Bradley's 6th Ohio was halted in the road south of Buell. Bradley's guns were nominally attached to Colonel Harker's brigade, but when Tom Wood dispatched Harker on his mission northward, Bradley's guns did not follow his infantry. Instead, they waited in column, limbered, while Bradley followed Harker's line on horseback to see where his pieces might be needed. Losing track of the infantry as they moved off through the timber, Bradley trotted back to his guns and awaited instructions. In the interim, he ordered his men to unlimber their pieces in the road to the right and rear of Buell's new position.[29]

Colonel Harker's departure north along the La Fayette Road about 4:00 p.m. not only left Heg with no reserves, but also exposed Buell's left flank. When the 4th and 5th Texas subsequently broke Heg's line and swept toward the La Fayette Road, the Texans found that open flank an irresistible target.

---

27 Hight and Stormont, *Fifty-Eighth Regiment*, 569; OR 20, pt. 1, 472. Norwich sent 750 graduates to the Civil War, second only to West Point, and including 60 who served in the Confederate ranks.

28 Welden Kelly, *A Historic Sketch, Lest We Forget - Company "E" 26th Ohio Infantry in the War for the Union 1861-65* (n.p., 1909), 12. Note that the title page of this publication spells Captain Kelly's first name as Weldon, but the roster has him listed as Walden.

29 OR 30, pt. 1, 649.

Their attack from the north, in conjunction with that of the 1st Texas and 3rd Arkansas from the east, bore down upon Buell's unsuspecting men.

Buell's situation was rendered considerably worse by the sudden torrent of Heg's panicked Federals sweeping through his ranks. Lieutenant Colonel William H. Young of the 26th Ohio reported that "in a moment more dozens, then scores, and finally hundreds of straggling soldiers came rushing . . . over my line in the wildest disorder and most shameful confusion." Buell's brigade did not join in the rout, but the mob entirely obscured their field of fire. Captain Estep, commander of guns of the 8th Indiana, watched as his "battery was filled with men falling back through it in great confusion." Once they cleared his front, thought Estep, "I thought I would then be able to deal a destructive fire on . . . the enemy, but he was pressing so close . . . his shots taking effect on my horses, that I was compelled to retire." The fire from his left was especially destructive, and Estep admitted he was forced to abandon one gun and limber in the left section when five of the piece's horses were cut down.[30]

Sergeant Hensley of the 21st Illinois was one of those men pouring through Estep's gun line. Emerging from the timber, Hensley noted that someone "had run one of our cannons in just behind us and as we passed it in the brush some of the horses to the [caisson] were shot and were lunging about." Swept up in the rout, Hensley watched the caisson "run over Captain Jamieson . . . I went to him and asked if he needed help." When the stunned but apparently uninjured officer refused Hensley's aid, "I went on after the regiment. We passed out of that brush into a field[,] climbing over a rail fence."[31]

Buell was struggling to hold his brigade in position when General Wood, who was observing the rout from a position near the brigade's right, intervened. Heg's collapse and Estep's hasty retreat endangered Bradley's 6th Ohio battery still in the road just to the south. In an effort to save his division's cannon, Wood dispatched an aide to Col. Fred Bartleson, heading up the 100th Illinois on Buell's right-front. "General Wood wants the 100th to make a bayonet charge," overheard Capt. Harlow B. Godard, commanding Company H.[32]

The order suited Bartleson, who was aggressive to a fault. The prewar prosecutor and Illinois State's Attorney in Joliet was said to be the first man to

30 Ibid., 669, 677.

31 Hensley Autobiography, VPI.

32 "Dear Adela," September 19, 1863, 100th Illinois File, CCNMP.

Thomas J. Wood. Despite a crippling fall from his horse, Wood was seemingly everywhere in Viniard Field on September 19.

Library of Congress

enlist in Will County. He lost an arm at Shiloh with the 20th Illinois. Undaunted, he secured a promotion to colonel of the newly raised 100th Illinois in August 1862 and led the command into its first battle at Stones River the previous winter, where the regiment lost 45 men. Now alone, Bartleson ordered the 100th to charge into Viniard Field to oppose the 3rd Arkansas and 1st Texas. Captain Godard recalled the "boys responded with a cheer" and advanced. The Rebels faltered for a minute or two before finding their footing, leveling their rifled muskets, and firing. The men of the 100th "endured a short but murderous fire" and, "Not being properly supported," explained Pvt. J. C. Lang of Company D, "we were compelled to give way."[33]

On the brigade left, the 26th Ohio was also in great distress. Already informed by General Wood that his position "must be held," Lieutenant Colonel Young had to wait some time before friendly stragglers and routed men cleared his front. Then, just as he was ready to open fire and deliver a charge of his own, an unknown officer galloped through the 26th's ranks shouting "for God's sake don't fire; two lines of our own troops are still in the woods!" As if in answer, a raking fire from those same woods enfiladed the Buckeyes, "cruelly cutting" into the left half of the regiment. Sergeant Elias Cole of Company C was one of those hit in this first fire, struck in the right shoulder. "We had just got into position, and a poor one it was . . . [when] they fired a volley into our

33 "Letter from a Soldier," *Joliet Signal*, October 6, 1863.

ranks, cutting us up desperately." Colonel Young's horse went down. "The rebel line appeared in front, within 20 yards, advancing firing. I ordered . . . a charge, but the command could be only partially heard; and the charge was not made." Instead, Young noted "the [8th Indiana] battery . . . had already . . . withdrawn [and] a heavy line of rebels were . . . rapidly gaining my rear." Staying put, thought Young, meant "the certainty of capture." He ordered the regiment to retreat.[34]

With his two front line regiments falling back and the entire brigade in considerable disorder, Buell attempted to restore the situation by ordering his second line to charge. Colonel Joshua B. Culver took the 13th Michigan forward about 100 yards while the disorganized 26th Ohio broke for the rear. The Wolverines fared no better than the Buckeyes. "We held [this position] about ten minutes," Culver noted, "delivering a destructive fire into the enemy's massed columns, but as our left flank had been turned, and being raked by an enfilading fire, we were compelled to retire." Buell's own 58th Indiana had an even worse time. When the 8th Indiana battery fell back, it rolled over the prone ranks of the 58th: "Two guns came running," wrote the regiment's historian, "and turned, pell-mell, through our Regimental lines. Several of our men were injured [and] our line was sadly broken." Ordered to charge, the men of the 58th scrambled to their feet and "pressed forward as best they could, but the line could not be maintained, on account of the house, the fence, the stable, and the endless confusion of the hour."[35]

More a mob than a battle line, the 58th managed to move forward into a moment of comparative silence, somehow unnoticed by the Rebels. Their peaceful sojourn ended quickly when a sudden fire ripped though their left flank. The 1st Texas and 3rd Arkansas might have been momentarily checked by the individual, if uncoordinated, charges of Buell's regiments, but the 4th and 5th Texas were not. Having cleared their own front of any Federals with Heg's collapse, these two regiments simply turned south and savaged the left flank of each of Buell's regiments in turn. Now it was the 58th's turn. Like the rest of the regiments before them, the 58th had little choice but to break and run. When he spotted the 6th Ohio battery still in the road about 150 yards to

34 Elias Cole, *Journal of Three Years' Service with the Twenty-Sixth Ohio Volunteer Infantry in the Great Rebellion . . . 1861-1864* (n.p. 1897), 44; OR 30, pt. 1, 669.

35 Ibid., 667; Hight, *Fifty-Eighth Regiment*, 131.

the south, Lt. Col. James T. Embree ordered the 58th to fall back and support the guns, hoping to at least get them to safety.[36]

Captain Bradley and his 6th Ohio had much the same experience as Estep's Hoosiers: a cacophony of confusion, fighting all around, but unable to shoot because of the mass of fleeing Federals swarming through and around them. The 6th might have been overrun if not for Bradley's professionalism. A Southerner by birth, Bradley spent 15 years in the Regular Army and rose to 1st Sergeant in the 2nd U.S. Artillery, before resigning to accept a commission as captain of the 6th. He had been in tight spots before, having nearly been overrun at Stones River (where he performed gallantly); he was up to the challenge now. Bradley ordered his imperiled battery to retire by section, with the final two guns retreating by prolonge and firing as they fell back. The 6th withdrew in a superb display of tactical competence about 200 yards all the way to Wilder's brigade line, where Bradley took up a position on the left of the 72nd Indiana and continued firing at the Rebels around the Viniard house.[37]

Colonel Heg, whose regiments had been battling all afternoon, was desperately trying to reform his survivors behind whatever protection Buell's brigade could offer. Heg's command was almost hopelessly disorganized, but small clumps of men were still in the fight. According to Lt. Col. Ole Johnson, the 15th Wisconsin "was now so much scattered that I found it impossible to get together more than a small squad," which Johnson rallied and deployed alongside some of Wilder's men. Heg was struggling from horseback to bring his own collection of oddments into line directly behind Buell when the Texans swept down from the northeast. A nameless Rebel squeezed a trigger and the lead round struck Heg in the abdomen. Most accounts agree Heg rode about a quarter of a mile before falling to the ground in front of members of his old regiment. A small squad of men carried him to Davis's divisional field hospital at Crawfish Spring, where Heg died the next day. Colonel Martin took command of what was left of the brigade, most of which was scattered in the woods west of Wilder's entrenchment.[38]

---

36 *OR* 30, pt. 1, 663.

37 Hinman, *The Sherman Brigade*, 44; 6th Ohio Tablet, Viniard Field, CCNMP. "Retire by prolonge" meant dragging the guns with 50-foot ropes attached to the trails, pausing to fire canister as they did so.

38 Ole C. Johnson, "From Libby Prison," *Wisconsin State Journal*, December 23, 1863. Accounts vary about the timing and nature of Heg's death. One suggests Heg was struck closer to 3:00

Buell's infantry also fell back on Wilder's position, though with considerably less panache than the gunners of the 6th Ohio. A small stream had carved a deep ditch through the field west of the Viniard farm that meandered across the front of Wilder's position from north to south. The drought-dry streambed was anywhere from two to four feet deep, and made an ideal impromptu trench into which wounded and stragglers from both Buell's and Heg's commands poured by the score. Most of the men in those two brigades crossed the ditch and kept going, but Lieutenant Colonel Young of the 26th Ohio was not one of them.

When the 26th first broke, Young fell back only as far as the fence line bordering the west side of the Viniard farmstead, where he again rallied the regiment. He attempted to hold for a few minutes while the rest of Buell's line fell, domino-like, to the enfilading fire from the 4th and 5th Texas. It didn't take Young long to discover an additional vulnerability in his new position: he taking fire from the Texans and from Union troops in the ditch just behind him. With the ditch looking more attractive by the second, Young ordered his surviving men to fall back once more.[39]

Young aligned his Buckeyes in the ditch jammed with both stragglers and wounded and engaged the Rebels milling about the Viniard farm. "From [here] another defense was now opened," wrote the colonel, "and for a few moments vigorously . . . maintained." The natural trench, however, proved to be no safe haven. Once again, Confederates worked their way around the vulnerable Union northern flank and delivered an enfilading fire down its length while lead rounds passed overhead in both directions as Wilder engaged the Texans. Company C's Sgt. Elias Cole, who had been struck a few minutes earlier in the shoulder, had taken shelter in the streambed only to watch in horror as his supposed haven became a battleground. "Here the balls . . . fell like hail," he wrote, "and many were wounded [a] second and third times, and some killed." The 26th Ohio had to go. "A hasty retreat was made to the fence on the . . . west

---

p.m. as the brigade advanced against Robertson, while another claims he was hit by a spent ball after dark. One observer even claimed Heg was hit, fell from his horse, and then jumped up, remounted, and rode the quarter of a mile to find his own command. The placing of the monument on the field, however, suggests he was hit just before or as Buell was being outflanked. See Ager, *Colonel Heg and His Boys*, 59, 202-204.

39 *OR* 30, pt. 1, 670.

Viniard Field, northwest corner, looking south. This is the view presented to the
4th and 5th Texas after routing Heg's Federals, and turning south to outflank Buell's men.
The monuments closest to us (directly behind the park road gate) mark Buell's line.
The Viniard house and barn sat in the trees on the right side of the image.

Harvey Scarborough

side of the field," recalled Captain Kelly, "where, with a promptness under fire
never excelled, the regiment rallied and again opened fire on the enemy."[40]

In Young's wake, Robertson's Rebels crossed the road and reached the
farm. With some exaggeration, a later historian of the Texas Brigade described
the Viniard house as "a veritable fortress of hewed logs." While this description
overstated the case, the farm and outbuildings offered a substantial obstacle
occupied by Yankees from a number of different regiments. The 4th and 5th
halted, almost as disordered in victory as the Federals were in defeat and retreat.
What followed was a vicious hand-to-hand struggle as the Texans began rooting
out the Federals.[41]

Those Texans not bogged down with bayonets and musket stocks in the
fighting around the Viniard house crested another rise in the timber just east of
the La Fayette Road and moved into relatively cleared land around the road,
where other Union troops could now fire upon them. Wilder's men, in
particular, enjoyed an excellent field of fire, and artillery support to boot.

40 Ibid; Cole, *Journal of Three Years' Service*, 44; Kelly, *A Historic Sketch*, 13.

41 Simpson, *Hood's Texas Brigade: Lee's Grenadier Guard*, 318.

Captain Hunter led part of the 4th Texas forward in a charge after Lt. Col. John P. Bane was wounded in the arm. Hunter later recalled that "the left wing of the regiment had forced the gunners away from a section of artillery [the 8th Indiana] that stood one hundred and fifty or two hundred yards obliquely to our left. I at once conceived the idea of making a rush, capturing and bringing out those guns." Hunter's decision to make "a rush" proved to be a bad one. The attack passed diagonally along the front of part of Wilder's position. "Just across [the] road," Hunter continued, "there was a staked and ridered rail fence and behind it a strong line of battle. . . . When we had covered half the distance or more, this line opened upon us . . . and gave us an enfilade as well as direct fire. We got to about fifty yards of the fence, but the fire was so heavy . . . that we were forced to fall back." The 4th Texas nearly lost its colors here, the flag bearers shot down by Wilder's men and other Yankees firing from the dry streambed, but Hunter personally dashed back to retrieve them. The bloodied men of the 4th had to content themselves with helping to clear out the last resistance in the Viniard farm buildings.[42]

This last fighting proved especially deadly. The 4th Texas would later find and bury 22 of its dead in and around the Viniard farm. One Confederate remembered as many as 200 unburied Federals also littered the area. A number of senior officers fell here, including both the 4th and 5th Texas's regimental commanders. Even after pulling back, Robertson indicated in his battle report that the Federals still had some fight in them. He described a brief Yankee counterattack to retake the crest of that second rise once the Texans retired to shelter behind it. Yet another Rebel charge was required to drive them off.[43]

Similarly, the 1st Texas and 3rd Arkansas closed on the farm from the east. Private Hamilton of the former regiment remembered "the Yankees . . . occupied an old farm; they had torn down the rail fences and made breastworks of them for about a mile in length and were lying behind this barricade when we charged them. When we got within about one hundred yards," he continued, "they arose, fired one volley, and ran like turkeys. That one volley, however, was very destructive." Advancing on the far right, the Arkansans suffered the worst for they were still exposed to a galling fire from the south. Their heaviest loss also came when they crested the rise just east of the Viniard farm, at which time

42 J. T. Hunter, "Hard Fighting of Fourth Texas," *Confederate Veteran*, vol. XIV, no. 1 (January, 1906), 22.

43 Simpson, *Hood's Texas Brigade: Lee's Grenadier Guard*, 318; OR 30, pt. 2, 511.

they became fully exposed to fire from multiple directions. A Razorback private named Sam Emerson, fighting in the ranks of Company F, recalled the moment: "As soon as we reached the top of the hill . . . they opened upon us with grape and canister from two batteries . . . .We forced them to desert a battery that occupied a position in front of [us]." The 3rd's commander, Col. Van Manning, was knocked from his horse although not severely wounded. Major John W. Reedy was killed instantly, musket in hand, while urging the men forward. A score of others fell with him.[44]

Despite this last knot of resistance around the farmstead, Buell's Federals were already hopelessly compromised and retreating. Most of the fire Robertson's men endured during that final effort came instead from the Union cannon to the south, mainly the 2nd Minnesota and 3rd Wisconsin batteries, and rifle fire from Wilder's line west of the road. In addition to Wilder's infantry and their deadly rapid-firing Spencers, Eli Lilly's 18th Indiana battery and the guns of Bradley's 6th Ohio studded along Wilder's line added their shells against Robertson's Rebels.

By this time, however, Major Calloway and his 81st Indiana, together with the guns of the 2nd Minnesota, were alone on the east side of the La Fayette Road. Calloway had watched the fighting rage to his north for some time, lending support where he could. So far, "owing to the admirable position occupied . . . [the 81st] was not suffering very greatly, but the position was [now] so flanked as to endanger my entire command." Calloway led his Hoosiers back to a fringe of timber along the west side of the La Fayette Road and halted. After a few minutes of firing from this position, Calloway was informed that if he fell back another 50 yards, he could take up a position behind part of the breastworks Wilder's men had thrown up that morning. No fool, he did exactly that. The guns of the 2nd Minnesota also retired, taking up a new position somewhere near the southwest corner of West Viniard Field behind the 81st Indiana. From there, both the infantry and artillery resumed firing at the now-distant Texans and Arkansans.[45]

---

44 Hamilton, *History of Company M*, 32; Samuel Henry Emerson, *History of the War of the Confederacy*, 61 to 65 (n. p. 1913), 47; Calvin L. Collier, *"They'll Do To Tie To!" The Story of the Third Regiment, Arkansas Infantry, C.S.A.* (Pioneer Press, 1959), 158. The "battery" was probably the gun from the 8th Indiana battery, abandoned here.

45 *OR* 30, pt. 1, 523.

With their support evaporating to the north, the 3rd Wisconsin battery also fell back and reoccupied its initial position on a knoll just east of the La Fayette Road, the same area where Barnes's brigade had halted earlier. Once there the Wisconsin gunners felt a little more secure, for behind them a bit farther south were elements of Philip Sheridan's advancing division (XX Corps). Sheridan had spent most of the day defending Lee and Gordon's Mills, but about 4:00 p.m. received orders to march north and support Crittenden. Leaving one-third of his command behind to guard the crossing, he moved with the brigades of Cols. Luther P. Bradley and Bernard Laiboldt north along the La Fayette Road, with Bradley's four Illinois regiments leading the way. Sheridan knew almost nothing of the chaotic situation in Viniard Field, so he halted well short of the fight and sought orders from someone who did.[46]

Despite their tactical success east of the La Fayette Road, the Confederates were unable to make additional progress. Wilder's line proved an effective backstop, bolstered by all or parts of four Union batteries and the quickly rallying infantry of Wood's and Davis's disordered divisions. According to Captain Harding, when the 1st Texas reached the road, "we lay for some time under a heavy fire . . . from a battery about 200 yards in advance." All this enemy attention convinced Robertson to pull his injured and disorganized brigade back beyond the crest of the rise to avoid the incoming rounds.[47]

The Texas Brigade had turned in an outstanding day's work. Aggressive regimental leadership, coupled with some luck, allowed Robertson's four regiments to engage and defeat more than twice their number. Heg's brigade of Yankees had already been bled substantially in the earlier contest with Bushrod Johnson's men, but Buell's four regiments and Carlin's rump of a brigade were essentially fresh when they encountered the Texans. Unfortunately for the Union men, Barnes's sudden rout from Trigg's fire disrupted Carlin at the worst possible moment, while Harker's departure northward left Buell's left flank hopelessly compromised.

The Texans might have had a much worse time of it had Charles Harker's brigade still been in place along the road, or if Harker had attacked in support of Heg as originally planned. Its absence at the Viniard Farm was sorely missed. Harker's 1,346 officers and men would have been a nasty surprise for the 570

---

46 3rd Wisconsin Tablet, CCNMP; *OR* 30, pt. 1, 579.

47 *OR* 30, pt. 2, 513.

Rebels in the 4th and 5th Texas. Instead, as indicated earlier, these troops pivoted and moved north to render what would be invaluable assistance elsewhere later that day.

The Texans paid a heavy butcher's bill for their success. Each regiment lost at least 100 men, or about 450 out of the 1,300 engaged in just a bit more than one hour of fighting. Little more could be expected of them that day. Robertson knew his command had been severely damaged and appealed for help. "Immediately upon reaching the hill," he reported, "I sent a courier for reinforcements, and a staff officer for a battery." Brigadier General Henry L. "Rock" Benning's Georgia brigade promptly moved up to assist him. Artillery proved much harder to come by.[48]

48 Ibid., 511.

Chapter Nineteen

Viniard Field:
Benning Attacks:

Saturday, September 19: 4:30 p.m. to 5:30 p.m.

The retreat of Robertson's brigade granted the disorganized Federals a short reprieve. In the middle of a carpet of dead and wounded, General Wood chivvied Buell's men back into ranks "for the purpose of advancing to recover the lost ground." Wood was almost certainly in a great deal of pain. Shortly after ordering the 100th Illinois to make its charge, Wood's horse had been shot and killed, hurling the general forward onto his saddle. The sudden collision ruptured his right groin, but he refused to quit the field. Instead, reported Colonel Young of the 26th Ohio, Wood led a scratch force comprised of the "bulk" of the 26th, "a few men of the 13th Michigan . . . and another fragmentary regiment of, I think, Davis's division," back to reoccupy their old ground around the Viniard house. Along the way, Young added, they were joined "by many brave fellows who had staid in the ditch, and a few others . . . by the fence." The Texans weren't completely ready to surrender their gains, however, so the movement was conducted under what Young called "a galling fire." The Federals reclaimed the 8th Indiana's abandoned gun, and the rest of the battery soon came up to support the advance.[1]

---

1 OR 30, pt. 1, 633; "My Dear Friend," April 6, 1878, Wood to William B. Blair, William Blair Papers, InHS. This hernia, "a severe inguinal rupture" of the groin, would trouble Wood for the

One of those men in the ditch was Sergeant Hensley of the 21st Illinois, who had taken refuge there with several comrades. Crossing the La Fayette Road, Hensley was hurrying back toward Wilder's line when he noticed more Union artillery arrayed to his front trying to fire on the Rebels. "We lay down in the ditch," recalled Hensley, so "that our battery might fire a little sooner. Then the battery opened on them and drove them back." With that, the sergeant and several others from the 21st gamely joined in the advance.[2]

Estep's 8th Indiana guns occupied a new position close to their first one, but one from which they could effectively fire over the rise. Once there, however, the gunners discovered they might have made a mistake. The Rebel infantry hadn't fallen back more than 100 yards; both sides opened fire. "I am positive . . . I did the enemy serious injury," wrote Estep, who admitted the Texans gave as good as they got. "His musketry fire became so terrible . . . that to remain . . . only insure[d] that I would not have a horse left."[3]

General Carlin was also active during this Federal resurgence even though he was approaching complete exhaustion. His horse had also been shot, the round going through the body behind the saddle, but had borne the wound so well that Carlin failed to notice the animal was wounded until an aide mentioned it. "He carried me often at a gallop, from right to left of my line," recalled the general. There was no time to seek a replacement. "I determined not to dismount so long as he could move." Just a few minutes earlier, Carlin had met with Heg and both agreed to reform their lines by rallying on Wilder's position. Heg, of course, fell shortly thereafter. Carlin's own formations were so thinned and disordered as to be little more than a skirmish line, but when Wood led Buell's troops forward, Carlin followed suit. So, too, did Major Calloway with his 81st Indiana, leading what was perhaps Carlin's only intact regiment. Seeing the surge of other Federals moving after the Rebels, "we immediately followed his retreating forces and re-took our former position," Calloway tersely reported. A little to the north of the 81st, Sergeant Hensley remembered passing the Viniard farmstead, "some old cabins out in the field where some

---

rest of his life, forcing him to wear a medical truss to prevent a "protrusion of the bowels." Despite what must have been a very painful wound, Wood refuse to quit the field for the remainder of the battle. OR 30, pt. 1, 671.

2 Hensley Autobiography, VPI.

3 *OR* 30, pt. 1, 677.

rebels took shelter to fire on us. We . . . drove them away and went a little further and laid down . . . in a cornfield."[4]

Lewis Day of the 101st Ohio observed that the Rebels "had not ventured over the brow of the ridge," but were instead "lying flat on their faces, they hoped to command . . . the road. Their lines were hammered most unmercifully" by Federal cannon. "Seeing they were wavering," Day continued, "instantly our line was in motion." Finally, it seemed as if fortune's tide was running in favor of the Federals. Day thought the Rebels were unable to stand the concentrated fire of the Union guns and were in full retreat, until he and his comrades crested that same ridge: "to our horror we beheld a splendid line of fresh Confederates issuing out of the woods facing our left."[5]

Robertson's appeal for support had borne fruit in the form of Brig. Gen. Henry Benning's brigade. The command was drawn up in a single line, from north to south as follows: the 2nd, 17th, 20th, and 15th Georgia regiments. Clad in newly issued uniforms, Benning's men must have indeed looked "splendid," though they were lacking in numbers. Not only had the Georgians suffered heavily at Gettysburg, but this was their first trip home in two years. A number of men seized the opportunity for a bit of informal leave. Benning's command numbered 1,200 when it detrained in Atlanta, but Benning himself estimated he led only about 850 men into action on September 19. The fitful nature of the Western and Atlantic's traffic added to the problem by delivering the brigade to Ringgold in dribs and drabs over several days leading up to the battle.[6]

Benning was a big and hearty man. At 49, he was also older than most of the officers in the Confederate army. He'd grown up among plantation society outside Augusta, Georgia, but after earning a law degree, in 1835 moved across the state to Columbus, which at that time was little more than a frontier town. He prospered there, and by the time of the secession crisis was a Georgia Supreme Court justice and an established figure in society and politics. He was also an ardent fire-eater who not only helped lead Georgia out of the Union, but was sent to Richmond as a Confederate emissary to urge the all-important state of Virginia to join the new nation as well. When rhetoric gave way to war,

---

4 Girardi and Hughes, *Carlin Memoirs*, 100; OR 30, pt. 1, 524; Hensley Autobiography, VPI.

5 Day, *One Hundred and First Ohio*, 165. Day mistakenly identified this line as Trigg's brigade.

6 OR 30, pt. 4, 652 and OR *Supplement*, 30, 697. The brigade numbered 1,500 on June 30, 1863, and took 1,400 men into the fight at Gettysburg on July 2.

Benning took command of the newly formed 17th Georgia, soon to be part of General Lee's army in Virginia. A forceful man with few subtleties and solid leadership skills, he rose to brigade command in January 1863. Despite his wealth and position Benning retained the common touch. When his command detrained at Ringgold, he and his staff were without their horses, still en route and several days away. Undeterred, Benning led his men from the platform on foot and shouldered an axe instead of a sword. By the 19th, however, he had located enough animals to mount himself and his staff.[7]

Initially part of Evander Law's reserve line back in the timber several hundred yards east of the La Fayette Road, Benning's troops had also spent most of the day listening to others do the fighting. Benning's line initially trailed behind Sheffield's and Robertson's regiments, a movement that was further slowed when two forward brigades began to drift apart. Then, when Robertson called for help, Law ordered Benning to move out. Unsure of the nature of the Union positions, Benning led his Georgians towards the Viniard farmstead, about 600 yards distant. "I found him [Robertson] with his brigade hotly engaged with a superior force of the enemy's infantry aided by a battery," reported Benning. One of his Georgians recalled that "the enemy were charged and driven across a plain and into their trenches on a hill, where they had erected temporary fortifications and planted several batteries."[8]

Once again, the Rebels had the advantage of position. In response to Robertson's summons, Benning had shifted his line to the left, and the Georgians entered the fight from the northeast, the line angling through the woods just north of the Viniard-Alexander Road. With the Confederate right overlapping the Federal left, Wood's line was outflanked a second time. Confederate Sgt. William Houghton recalled that the 2nd Georgia "was opposite the part of their [Federal] line which was in the woods. For some reason that gave way first, and we pushed ahead and swung around against the fence just as the Yankee line in the field began to give way. As they ran back through the open field we stood there behind the fence and trees shooting them down. . . . We would shout at them to surrender and they would tell us to go to

<hr />

7 J. David Dameron, *General Henry Lewis Benning: "This was a Man"* (Iberian Printing Co., 2000). 14, 99-100.

8 *OR* 30, pt. 2, 518; "Benning's Brigade in the Fight" *Columbus Sun*, September 24, 1863.

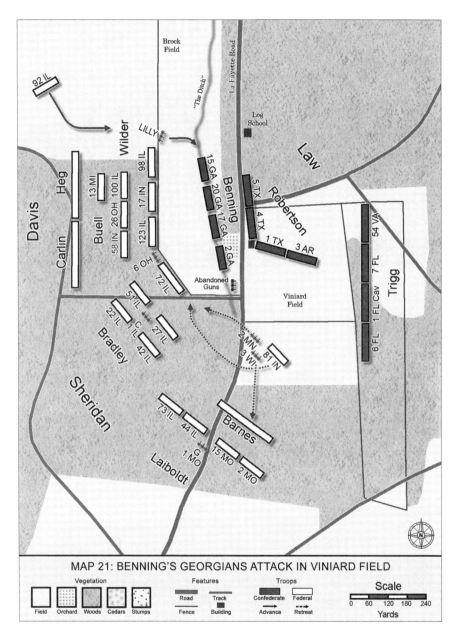

MAP 21: BENNING'S GEORGIANS ATTACK IN VINIARD FIELD

hell, and then down they would go. It was," concluded Houghton, "a horrible slaughter."[9]

The collision between Wood's Federals and Benning's men produced yet another horrific fight in and around the Viniard house. The 8th Indiana battery

9   W. G. Houghton Memoir, 2nd Georgia File, CCNMP.

As Benning's Georgians emerged from the trees just north of Viniard Field, this was their view. The pyramid monument to the right marks Colonel Heg's mortal wounding. The fringe of trees and small brush just beyond denote the creek-bed, subsequently named the Ditch of Death. Just in front of the trees in the far distance, the line of monuments there marks Wilder's position. *Harvey Scarborough*

was once again a target, and Captain Estep ordered the guns to leave. "[T]he execution of the order had scarcely begun when the infantry began to fall back," reported the officer, "being charged by the enemy *en masse*, who came yelling like devils." Corporal James Treahorn of Company K, 26th Ohio, remembered how the Georgians's gunfire scythed through the battery horses. "A severe hand to hand combat occurred: bayonets and clubbed guns were freely used," wrote Treahorn. "One large fierce rebel thrust his bayonet through the breast of a little wounded boy. Lt. [Benjamin W.] Shotwell drew his revolver and shot the rebel dead, and was himself shot." A Hoosier artillery sergeant named Samuel Day remembered how the Confederates "made an overwhelming charge and Drove our infantrie from our support before we could Limber up and at the same moment shot down the most of our horses." Gunner P. L. Hubbard and his fellow crewmen tried to save their piece by hand, "the cannoneers running to the rear with the gun down a long slope into a ditch," but they could not manhandle the gun across that obstacle, and abandoned it there. This time, noted Captain Estep, "three of my pieces were left on the field" in the hands of the enemy. His battery had been all but wrecked twice within 90 minutes.[10]

10 OR 30, pt. 1, 677; James Treahorn, "From the 26th Regiment," *Madison County Union*, October 8, 1863. Treahorn mistakenly reported Shotwell as having died. The lieutenant

William Hensley of the 21st Illinois also found himself in peril once again. Hensley was busy fighting a private war, sniping at a Confederate in a tree several hundred yards distant on the far side of Viniard Field. Hensley was loading his rifle with a double charge of powder to make sure the round would carry when Benning's Georgians struck. "[T]he rebels came up on our left and gave us a raking fire and we retreated," was how Hensley recalled the event. "They captured 14 of our men that were near the fence and among them was color bearer Sgt. [George W.] Beam. They did not get our flag as it was laying between to corn rows and [they] . . . did not see it."[11]

Major Calloway and the 81st Indiana once again had a ringside seat to this latest round of slaughter. The Hoosiers had taken up their former position on the knoll at the southern end of Viniard Field, a good vantage point from which to watch Benning's impressive attack sweep the farmyard clear and turn Carlin's flank. "The general and his command made a most gallant and heroic resistance," Calloway reported, "but being overpowered were shattered and driven back with fearful loss, leaving the colors of the Twenty-First Illinois Volunteers in the hands of the color-sergeant, who was shot dead on the field." Calloway may have been skippering the 81st, but he could not leave the colors of his own regiment (the 21st Illinois) abandoned to the enemy. The fire delivered by the Hoosiers obliquely to the left on Calloway's command helped check the Rebels long enough to recover the colors and cover the 101st Ohio as it helped some of Estep's 8th Indiana guns back across the field. The 81st's effective fire was observed by Sergeant Hensley, who wrote that the Confederates "were in a hurry to get away from there themselves."[12]

Benning's momentum cleared the farm of organized Federals a second time and drove the opposition from the La Fayette Road. John Wilder's brigade

---

survived, but resigned in September 1864 when he was unable to take the field. Jeffrey A. Hill, *The 26th Ohio Veteran Volunteer Infantry: The Groundhog Regiment*, 2nd ed. (Authorhouse, 2010), 720; Entry for September 19, 1863, Samuel Day Diary, Lilly Library, Indiana University, Bloomington, IN; P. L. Hubbard, "The Capture of the 8th Indiana Battery," *National Tribune*, June 6, 1907; *OR* 30, pt. 1, 677.

11 Hensley Autobiography, VPI.

12 *OR* 30, pt. 1, 524; Hensley Autobiography, VPI. Calloway reported that the 81st's fire "repulsed" the Confederates with "immense slaughter." He was probably actually firing on some of Robertson's men who had joined Benning's advance, but did not again cross the road. Benning's own accounts do not mention having their southern flank turned or repulsed. By now, the field was so covered with casualties from previous actions that it was hard to discern how much damage any particular fire was doing.

remained intact in the woods on the western edge of the field, once again a bulwark and a rallying point for Davis's and Wood's troops. Studded with all those Federal guns, Wilder's position looked considerably more formidable than the Federals a few minutes earlier holding a cleared position around the farm. Benning paused to reorganize his line.

The seemingly endless charges and counter-charges impressed and dismayed Lt. Joseph A. Scott, the commander of the First Section of Eli Lilly's 18th Indiana battery. Stationed on the left of Wilder's brigade near the 98th Illinois and 17th Indiana, Scott and his gunners enjoyed a perfect view of the unfolding spectacle. They watched as Benning, supported by at least some of Robertson's Texans, reformed his men using the road for alignment. The grand display was so impressive that Scott wrongly believed it was composed of "Three divisions, those of Generals Longstreet, Hood, and Johnson . . . massing . . . in plain view of our position. I turned to Col. Wilder . . . and said, 'That means another charge on our line.' He said, 'Yes, be ready.' I called the Sergeants and instructed them to carry the canister up to the muzzles of the guns and break off two charges of powder out of three."[13]

Benning may have wished he had three divisions. He certainly wished he had some artillery, the lack of which he would complain about in his official report. His four under-strength regiments were almost certainly not enough to carry Wilder's position, but he had thus far been successful. Perhaps one more hearty effort would finish the fight and win the day. And so with their lines reformed the Georgians went forward under the admiring gaze of their Federal opponents.[14]

Not a one of the Federals who admired the enemy advance let the grandeur of the moment interfere with the grim business at hand. Federal artillery opened first on Benning's line, followed by the infantry. Together with Lieutenant Scott's triple-shotted canister, Wilder's repeating rifles pumped a huge volume of lead into the enemy ranks. "We began to shoot at the oncoming rebels as fast as our . . . rifles would permit," noted Theodore Petzoldt of the 17th Indiana. "It was too fierce for human beings to face long, but the rebels came on until they reached a deep ditch . . . in front of where we lay." Like so many Yankees before them, the Georgians found the cover offered by the dry streamed too

13 Joseph A. Scott Reminiscences, InHS.

14 *OR* 30, pt. 2, 518.

compelling to leave behind. All four of Benning's regiments went to ground there.[15]

Once again, Wilder's unshakable line had saved the Federal position in Viniard Field. West of the ditch, the ground gradually rose for about 100 yards to Wilder's breastworks, the entire distance blanketed with a deadly fire of infantry rounds and canister balls. Worse still for the Confederates, these Yankees were not demoralized or disorganized. As the field below them cleared of friendly troops, Wilder's brigade, supported by hundreds of rallied men from the other Union brigades that had earlier fought here, engaged Benning's line with a stunning display of firepower.

On Wilder's right, Sergeant Magee of the 72nd Indiana was fighting lying down behind the barricade, wholly absorbed in adding his bullets to the storm of fire, when he received a nasty shock. Unbeknownst to him, one of the 6th Ohio's guns had unlimbered directly behind him. "The first intimation I had that the gun was there was when I heard the most deafening clap of thunder and it seemed to me I bounced 2 feet high," wrote the stunned infantryman. "The gun was so close to me the concussion entirely disabled my right ear." Firing directly above prone men was a dangerous use of artillery, but normal safety concerns no longer applied.[16]

Captain John J. McCook also witnessed this fight. At just 18, John was the youngest of the combative McCook clan and served on General Crittenden's staff. Despite his youth, the captain was already a veteran of Perryville and Stones River, but the intensity of the fighting in Viniard Field left a deep impression upon him. "The musketry and cannonading was perfectly terrible," he informed his sister, "the guns were fired so often and so many at a time that you could not distinguish the sound of any particular cannon . . . the enemy . . . debouched from the woods and came forward with a shout. [A]s soon as they were in the bare corn field we opened on them with six batteries, thirty guns, on their exposed lines. [T]his," he assured her, "kept them back until we had reformed our infantry." Although it may have seemed like 30 guns were firing,

---

15 Theodore Petzoldt, "Recollections," 17th Indiana file, CCNMP.

16 Benjamin Magee Recollections, InHS; see also Baumgartner, *Blue Lightning*, 237.

there were probably no more than 20 pieces of all calibers playing on the Rebel advance.[17]

The sheet of lead and iron filling the air above their heads effectively trapped the Georgians in the ditch. When his requisitioned horse was shot out from under him, and with his "uniform torn by several bullets," Benning decided to join his men in the defile. The question foremost in his mind was what to do next. Going forward was impossible, but scrambling back out the other side would expose them to the same overwhelming fire. He had managed to drive his men close to the enemy line, and concluded additional help would arrive to join him in defeating the Federals. "The place we held was much exposed," he admitted, but "I thought I could hold it till the reinforcements (every minute expected) should arrive, when a general advance might be made." Accordingly, the Georgians clung to both the ditch and the farmstead, firing as best they could at the heavy line of Yankees across the way.[18]

This stage of the fighting lasted for some time, and the seeming stalemate frustrated the combative Wilder. Ensconced in their natural trench, the Rebels were proving as hard to move as his own men. The solution arrived in the form of a creative use of artillery. If a few guns could be advanced far enough forward to fire down the length of the ditch from the northwest, the strong natural defensive position would be converted into a deathtrap. Without any support on his right flank, Benning could do little to counter such a maneuver. Wilder conferred with Captain Lilly, and Lieutenant Scott's two guns, supported by a battalion of four companies drawn from the 17th Indiana, were selected for the dangerous duty.[19]

"I ran the guns forward by hand," remembered Scott, "and changed front to the right . . . which brought the right flank of the enemy in direct line with the fire of the two guns, and for several minutes we raked the ditch with double-shotted guns." The battery's bugler, Henry Campbell, was overwhelmed by the noise: "[T]he roar was perfectly awfull—nothing can be compared with it—if ten million pieces of sheet iron were shaken at once it

---

17 "Dear Sister," September 22, 1863, John J. McCook Letters, Gilder-Lehrman Collection, New York Historical Society, NYC. John was the youngest brother of both Daniel McCook, brigade commander in the Reserve Corps, and Alexander McCook, commander of the XX Corps. He was also the nephew of Edward M. McCook, who led a brigade in the Cavalry Corps.

18 *OR* 30, pt. 2, 518; Baumgartner, *Blue Lightning*, 238.

19 Wilder Revised Report, CCNMP.

wouldn't be a drop in the bucket." As he watched, remembered Campbell, "Capt. Lilly moved forward two guns . . . to a position where he could rake the ditch from end to end [and] opened out with thrible charges of canister." Gunner W. D. Crouse thought the guns did terrible execution, as they were "loaded to the muzzles with canister." With his men manning his right being ripped to pieces without being able to defend themselves, Benning had little choice now but to order a retreat. The Georgians tumbled out of the streambed and ran back east as best they could. Some, however, refused to leave, preferring the shelter in the bottom of the ditch and likely captivity to the deadly risk of negotiating the storm of Federal fire in the open.[20]

Benning was engaged for a little short of an hour and his losses had been heavy. The 2nd Georgia lost eight officers and 88 men. The 20th Georgia lost 17 of its 23 officers, though the regiment's total casualties went unrecorded. Benning's men would also be heavily engaged on the 20th, and most regiments did not break their losses out by day, but at least two-thirds of the brigade's reported 492 casualties fell during the Viniard Farm fighting on the 19th, or about 325 of the 850 or so men who entered the fight that afternoon.[21]

Many of Wilder's men marveled at the execution they had wreaked upon the Georgians. Shortly after the battle, Wilder returned home on sick leave and described the battle to an eager public. "It actually seemed a pity to kill men so," he informed a reporter, "they fell in heaps, and I had it in my head to order the firing to cease to end the awful sight." Corporal Frank Evans of the 18th Indiana battery described the carnage in the ditch. He "saw men that was shot all over[,] some with their legs shot off and some shot in the face[,] some shot in the head . . . the rebs lost a grate many more men than we lost for we mowed them down like . . . grass." Martin Hamilton of the 17th Indiana, observing the carnage from Wilder's main line described the bloody day to his parents. "Our brigade . . . was posted at the edge of the woods. . . . Here we remained the day in sight of the whole doings," he explained. "In a little while two [Confederate] divisions ran in out front . . . Some came through our lines [Davis's and Wood's divisions] but the rebs could not walk over the brigade. [The Federal infantry in

---

20 Joseph A. Scott Reminiscences, InHS; "Three Years in the Saddle," Henry Campbell Journal Transcript, Wabash College, 106; W. O. Crouse Papers, Tippecanoe County Historical Association, Lafayette, IN.

21 "Dear Father and Mother," September 20, 1863, Theodore Fogle Letters, Emory University, Atlanta, GA; OR 30, pt. 2, 518.

front of us] made three different attempts to rally and go up on the rebs in our front but failed. Loss I suppose heavy.”[22]

Lilly's decision to rake the ditch with artillery was one of the cruel necessities that war so often produces. Most of the casualties incurred at the ditch were probably already wounded from previous actions, men who had used their last strength to seek shelter from the fighting. Benning's casualties did not occur on a pristine part of the battlefield. Dead and wounded men from half a dozen brigades, blue and gray, littered the Viniard family property. Early in the fight, the ditch looked like a haven to many of the Federal wounded, and later, took form as a defensive fighting position. It was already filled with bodies both living and dead well before Benning's Georgians sought cover there. Lieutenant Scott's deadly crossfire, while tactically necessary, killed or inflicted additional injury on many of the wounded Yankees hiding there. In the aftermath of the battle, the ditch was choked with corpses—many more than just Benning's Georgians. It was an especially horrific few minutes during an afternoon of endless horrors.

Despite the chaotic nature of his retreat, Benning reported only a handful of missing—presumed captured—men in this fight. By now most of the Federals were also completely disorganized, and the chaos of the battlefield helped a number of Rebels get away. One of these was Capt. John H. Martin, commanding Company B of the 17th Georgia. Lightly wounded in the foot, Captain Martin and a comrade were taken prisoner by men from the 8th Kansas. Years later, recalled Martin, “orders were given to take us off to General Crittenden's headquarters but we delayed all we could and before they could get us off of the battlefield and while the fighting was terrific some Confederate cavalry dashed out on our left and rather in the rear of the Yankee line . . . the Yankees became panic stricken and broke. . . . We rejoined our regiment without ever having been gotten off the battlefield at all.” Who the Rebel cavalry were remains a mystery, since no Confederate mounted regiments were operating anywhere near the Viniard farm.[23]

22 Baumgartner, Blue Lightning, 241; Indianapolis Daily Journal, September 28, 1863; Gerald S. Henig, ed., “‘Soldiering is One Hard Way of Serving the Lord.’ The Civil War Letters of Martin D. Hamilton,” Indiana Military History Journal, vol. 2, no. 3 (October, 1977), 10.

23 J. H. Martin Reminiscences, UDC Collection, vol. XI, GDAH; Two companies of the 1st Louisiana Cavalry were serving as General Hood's escort on September 19, and may have been the mounted men mentioned in Martin's account. However, even a mounted brigade staff

Benning's troops fell back in disorganized throngs east of the La Fayette Road to join Robertson's brigade. Both commands took shelter behind the rise of ground just east of the Viniard farmstead which Robertson had used previously. Benning was not alone in his frustration about the lack of artillery to contest the Federal long arm. "I sent three different messengers for a battery, all of whom returned without any," Robertson complained. "I then went myself, but could not get the officer in command of the only one I could find to bring his battery up. I have no hesitation in believing that if I could have gotten a battery in position we could have inflicted heavy loss on the enemy, as his infantry was massed in heavy columns."[24]

The Texas Brigade commander's complaint points once more to a decided lack of tactical coordination above brigade level. After acquiescing to Robertson's need to shift southward during the initial advance, division commander Evander Law seems to have played only a minor role in the subsequent engagement. Nor was Hood mentioned in any of the brigade or regimental reports. The difficulties the First Corps experienced during the early stages of its advance required Hood and Law to understandably focus much of their energies elsewhere, and Robertson and Benning paid the price for that inattention. Although Law had no artillery to send to Robertson (even if he was aware of the brigadier's need), the same cannot be said for Hood and Simon Buckner.

Most of the Army of Tennessee's artillery was nominally organized in battalions at the divisional level for administrative purposes, but they did not fight that way. For combat purposes, the army still followed the practice of assigning a battery to each brigade. In the Eastern Theater, both the Union and Confederate armies were moving to consolidate cannon in tactical battalions (or "brigades," in the nomenclature of the Army of the Potomac) for use by higher echelon commanders. Division and corps commanders often had artillery that each officer could commit at critical moments and locations, instead of devolving that control to individual brigadiers. By way of contrast, in Bragg's Army of Tennessee, 33 of the army's 42 batteries were usually assigned to brigades. The remaining nine batteries, however, were organized into two

---

might have triggered the Federal panic. By the close of this part of the fighting, confusion was the norm.

24 *OR* 30, pt. 2, 511. Robertson probably encountered one of Bushrod Johnson's batteries, occupying its original line in the woods several hundred yards to the east.

reserve battalions, one of five batteries normally attached directly to army headquarters, and one of four batteries serving with Buckner's Corps.[25]

Because the First Corps's own artillery had not yet arrived from Virginia, Hood moved to the front without any artillery support. On September 18, one of the reserve artillery battalions was assigned to Bushrod Johnson's Provisional Division. Since each of Johnson's brigades had a battery assigned to it, the battalion was removed from Johnson's command structure on the morning of the 19th and reassigned to Hood's control, meaning it was now available to support his own division under Evander Law. This battalion of five batteries (18 guns) was commanded by General Roberston's own son, Maj. Felix H. Robertson. Unfortunately, despite their theoretical availability, when Robertson called for artillery support, the guns under his son's command were nowhere to be found.[26]

The battalion's location and actions on September 19 remain something of a mystery. Neither Major Robertson nor most of his battery commanders filed a battle report. Even the park commission, usually so reliable in documenting the actions of individual batteries, did not place tablets for these units on September 19. It appears the battalion did not serve as a single unit, but was instead parceled out as per normal Army of Tennessee practice. Johnson noted in passing that Robertson commanded only "eight pieces" (two batteries) on the morning of the 19th. Sometime early that afternoon, Capt. Overton Barret's Missouri battery of two six-pounders and two 12-pound howitzers was detached and sent to support Marcus Wright's brigade of Ben Cheatham's division. Wright's men were lying in reserve in the woods east of Brock Field after their trying ordeal at midday, and since Carnes's battery had been completely wrecked in that same fighting, either Wright or General Cheatham appealed for a replacement. Given that Cheatham's division still had four other batteries in a more or less effective state, Barret's reassignment was probably an overreaction.[27]

Still, some of Major Robertson's guns should have been available to go help his father's brigade. Unlike Bushrod Johnson's batteries, which unlimbered

---

25 In theory, each division's artillery was organized into a battalion in the Army of Tennessee as well, but this was mainly for administrative purposes. When the shooting started, those batteries were parceled out to their brigades.

26 *OR* 30, pt. 2, 453.

27 *OR* 52, pt. 1, 85.

alongside their respective brigades that morning before the fighting became general, the Reserve Battalion's pieces never made it into the front line even though they had all morning to come up. None of the three aides General Robertson sent back to request artillery support knew where to find these batteries that, apparently, were specifically tasked with supporting Law's division. The dangers and problems of throwing commands together on the fly were becoming evident.

Felix Robertson did not receive any official criticism for his role—or lack thereof—in the fighting of September 19. He would go on to serve as Gen. Joe Wheeler's chief of artillery and eventually receive a brigadier general's wreath and command of a cavalry brigade. However, his rise in rank might have had more to do with well-cultivated relationships with his superiors than any innate tactical talents. Historian Peter Cozzens dismissed Major Robertson as "a miserable sycophant" of Braxton Bragg's, because at Bragg's request, the then-captain Robertson rewrote his report of the battle of Stones River in order to cast additional blame on John C. Breckinridge for making what proved to be a disastrous attack on January 2, 1863. Promotion to major followed soon thereafter.[28]

In addition to Major Robertson's guns, the four batteries of Maj. Samuel C. Williams's battalion, totaling 14 cannon, were also reasonably close at hand. Attached to Buckner's Corps, this battalion crossed Chickamauga Creek early that morning and fell in behind Buckner's massed infantry. Williams's guns were not engaged or even deployed until midday. "I was held as the reserve," Williams reported, "and posted accordingly in [the] rear . . . where I remained for several hours." Williams's artillery was in addition to the batteries already assigned to each brigade of both Preston's and Stewart's divisions. Detaching Williams's pieces to help Robertson or Benning (or both) would not have deprived Buckner's troops of artillery support.[29]

At 11:00 a.m., Buckner was called upon to give up Maj. Gen. A. P. Stewart's division to reinforce Cheatham's embattled division fighting farther north. Stewart's departure left a gap in Buckner's line between Hood's left to the north and the right flank of Preston's division. As explained in detail earlier, Buckner deployed Colonel Trigg's brigade to plug that gap. At the same time, Maj.

---

28 Cozzens, *This Terrible Sound*, 203; Cozzens, *No Better Place to Die*, 215.

29 *OR* 30, pt. 2, 449.

Thomas Porter, Buckner's chief of artillery, reported that "Brigadier General Mackall, General Bragg's chief of staff, ordered that all the artillery that could be spared from the corps should be placed in the position just vacated by General Stewart." Accordingly, Williams brought up Capt. Putnam Darden's Mississippi and Capt. R. F. Kolb's Alabama batteries. In addition, Capt. Robert P. McCants's Florida battery was sent to support Trigg's infantry, which was in line just to the west. Williams deployed all these guns at a position where they could "check the enemy in case our infantry, then hotly engaged . . . should be driven in." Williams's remaining battery, consisting of only two 3-inch rifles under the command of Capt. Edmund Baxter, was sent to reinforce Preston's front line. All of these guns were operating within just a few hundred yards of where Robertson and Benning wanted and needed them to engage.[30]

Instead, they did very little. The men serving in Williams's battalion had an especially trying afternoon. Positioned 800 or 900 yards southeast of Viniard Field, Kolb's, Darden's, and McCants's gunners could see much of the fighting that raged across that farmstead. In between infantry clashes, Union artillery (most likely the 3rd Wisconsin and 2nd Minnesota) frequently shifted their aim to drop rounds among the three Rebel batteries, inflicting some losses to Darden's and Kolb's commands. The Confederates could not fire back because, as Porter explained, "our fuses are so uncertain that [we] would have run the risk of killing our own men by firing over their heads." Near sundown, Porter ordered Williams to collect all three batteries and fall back to his original reserve position behind Buckner's Corps. They had observed, endured, and suffered during that terrible fighting without contributing more than one or two pulls on the lanyard.[31]

Buckner's own role on September 19 can perhaps best be described as passive. He exercised very little command and undertook nothing on his own initiative. In fairness, A. P. Stewart's division was taken from him before the fighting began, and he never received a direct order to attack. Bragg's directive to Buckner to support Hood, however, generated almost a non-response. Only Trigg's brigade entered the fight. There was much more that could have been done on that front, and an aggressive commander would have done it. One of the quirks of Buckner's chosen position massed Preston's division behind a

---

30 Ibid., 360, 450. Williams gave the time of this order as 2:00 p.m., but it was probably closer to noon. A. P. Stewart would have been gone almost three hours by 2:00 p.m.

31 Ibid., 360.

north-looping bend in the Chickamauga, where his infantry held a high ridge overlooking Hall's Ford. If ordered to engage the enemy, Preston's men could not have simply marched west. This same idiosyncrasy in the creek's course also meant that Buckner's southern flank was almost invulnerable to any Union attack—expected or otherwise; Preston's division wasted precious hours holding a part of the line where it was essentially unneeded.

If Buckner had instead committed Preston's 4,600 infantry and the seven batteries of artillery still available to him, he would have struck a powerful blow against Davis, Wood, and Wilder. For reasons that remain unexplained, he did not do so. Despite his high rank and the respect of many of his peers, Buckner had only limited combat experience as a senior officer, and that service had been a mixed bag. His abilities as a commander, therefore, were essentially still a question mark. He did well enough at Perryville when given a direct order, but his halting and unsteady performance at Fort Donelson earlier that year, where he was working in tandem with a man he despised and without clear-cut direction from above, suggested he was a cautious, risk-averse sort of commander. His poisoned relationship with General Bragg all but guaranteed he would continue his established pattern of refusing to make independent decisions or show any initiative on the field.[32]

With the support of either infantry or artillery, Robertson and Benning fell back into the trees that sheltered two of Bushrod Johnson's brigades (McNair's, and at least part of Gregg's now under Colonel Sugg), and Trigg's combined command of Floridians and Virginians. There the two brigadiers from the Virginia army would pause, reorganize, take note of their losses, and await new orders. Or so they believed.

The Federals were not quite finished, however. The survivors of Wood's and Davis' shattered ranks were willing to try and reoccupy the contested ground one more time, especially since they were now bolstered by yet another Federal division. Two brigades of Maj. Gen. Philip Sheridan's division (XX Corps) were now present. Sheridan, as usual, was ready and even anxious to advance.

Earlier, as he moved up the road from Lee and Gordon's Mills, Sheridan placed his brigades in line on an angle similar to where Sidney Barnes formed his four regiments just before they entered the fight about mid-afternoon. Colonel Luther P. Bradley's four Illinois regiments formed a double line west of the road, extending behind the breastworks held by Wilder's right and the 81st Indiana. Colonel Bernard Laiboldt placed the 44th and 73rd Illinois, and the 2nd and 15th Missouri, in a single line on the east side of the road in and around the guns of the 3rd Wisconsin artillery. Captain Mark Prescott's Battery C, 1st Illinois Light Artillery followed Bradley, while Laiboldt moved the guns of Lt. Gustavus Schueler's Battery G, 1st Missouri, to the center of his line.

Sheridan arrived on the scene just as the Federals were retreating in the face of Benning's advance, and in time to witness Estep's battery being overrun for the second time that day. He also observed the hectic retreat of the fragments assembled by Wood and Carlin. Sheridan intended to commit his troops as soon as they came up in order to retrieve Union fortunes. Since Bradley's Illinois regiments led the march, they moved into battle first.

Colonel Bradley was another amateur soldier. He was born in Connecticut in 1822 but had been living in Chicago since 1855. He had prewar militia experience in both places, which help elevate him to second in command of the 51st Illinois in September 1861. Bradley did well at regimental command, and at Stones River jumped to brigade command when the senior colonel was killed on December 31, 1862. As his men moved forward through and past Wilder's line, Bradley recalled that "the rebels had turned our right and captured Estep's battery. So it was an old fight and a pretty hot one. Sheridan ordered me to drive back two brigades—Tegg's [Trigg's] and Robinson's [Robertson's] of Longstreet's Corps, which had made the trouble on our right."[33]

Like so many of their comrades that day, the men in the brigade had alternated between interminable waiting and haste. Sergeant George Pratt, Company A of the 51st Illinois, went in on the left of the brigade's front line. "We took up and abandoned several positions until about 4:00 p.m. when we double-quicked over a mile by the road . . . then by the right flank through the woods-over a marsh-up a ridge-past 'Vineyard's' log house crossing the La Fayette Road into an open field which had been several times fought over already." To Pratt's right, Pvt. Henry C. Dixon of Company E, 27th Illinois, recalled that same field "covered by the dead and wounded from the heavy fighting done by the division whose place [we] took."[34]

---

33 Luther P. Bradley Papers, AHEC.

34 George Pratt Recollections, ALPL; Henry C. Dixon, "Sheridan's Division at Chickamauga," *National Tribune*, December 18, 1918.

Just as he was going forward, Colonel Bradley observed corps commander General Crittenden, who by now seemed distraught. "I noticed Crittenden riding down the rear of the line in an excited manner, and it impressed me that his manner was unfortunate under the circumstances." The strain of the difficult battle was wearing on the XXI Corps leader, but Bradley would soon have other reasons to take a jaundiced view of the general.[35]

The sight of Bradley's four regiments sweeping into Viniard Field impressed those who witnessed it. "I heard a cheer, loud and ringing," wrote a correspondent for the *Cincinnati Commercial* following the brigade's advance, "and riding up behind the line. . . I saw four noble regiments far across the field, pouring swift volleys into the flying foe." James Riley soldiered in the ranks of Company E, 42nd Illinois, and recorded his impression of the fight: "We started on with a yell, charged over the 13th Mich. Reg't . . . drove the Rebels back, and recaptured a battery which the Rebs had taken from our men."[36]

Private Dixon of the 27th Illinois observed General Sheridan as that officer watched Bradley's brigade go into battle. Sheridan, thought the private, "seemed in his glory, as he always did in a fight." Manning the rails of the barricade with the rest of the 72nd Indiana was Sgt. Ben Magee, who was perhaps unsure what to think of "Little Phil." "We hear a commotion to our right rear," recorded the Hoosier, "and looking around we see Gen. Sheridan on his black horse . . . and in front of him a staff officer . . . carrying the General's flag, and as he approaches the rear of our regiment he calls out: 'Make way for Sheridan! Make way for Sheridan!' Of course we gladly open ranks and let the general and his staff pass through."[37]

Sheridan followed Bradley's brigade about as far as the La Fayette Road some 200 yards in front of the 72nd Indiana's line. Bradley's own line continued to the small rise that bisected Viniard Field another 100 yards east of the road near the point where the 8th Indiana battery's guns had been lost the second time. Colonel Nathan Walworth of the 42nd Illinois, commanding Bradley's second line, reported that "the brigade moved steadily forward across a piece of

---

35 Bradley Papers, AHEC.

36 Orderly Sergeant B. B. Atwater, "From the 27th Regiment," Chattanooga, Tenn., November 15, 1863, as quoted in Gene Kelly, *Collection of Civil War Letters Written by Mercer County Soldiers*, (n.p. n.d.); C. W. Denslinger, ed., *Civil War Diary of James Wesley Riley who served with the Union Army in the War Between The States, April 22, 1861-June 18, 1865.* (n.p., 1960), 54.

37 Magee, *History of the 72nd Indiana*, 177.

open, level ground and ascended a gentle slope." Colonel Jonathon Miles of the 27th Illinois, on the right of the first line, recalled that he advanced "about 60 rods [300 yards] up that same "gentle slope," halting near the four abandoned guns and two caissons of the 8th Indiana. Some of the battery's gunners, he believed, were still trying to work the guns as Bradley's men arrived.[38]

Bradley's Federals crested the rise only to meet "a most withering fire . . . which cut down Colonel Bradley." The four Illinois regiments discovered the hard way that, while the Rebels might be falling back, they were not routed. By now, these Confederates had an afternoon of back-and-forth fighting under their belt, so few Southern accounts distinguished between these various Union counter-blows. Bradley's men, however, were fresh to the fight and recalled the moment with precision. "The 3rd Brigade charges across the open field," wrote Lt. Henry Weiss of the 27th to his wife back home in Shipman, Illinois, "driving the foe 'helter-skelter' into the woods beyond. Here their fire was hot and heavy on us exposed in the field. . . . We were flanked, but unwilling to give way."[39]

Bradley's line had entered the same sort of trap Barnes's men had run afoul of earlier. Focused on the woods at the northern end of the field, Bradley's men pursued Benning's and Robertson's remnants at an angle, ignoring the tree line to their right. Trigg's Confederates, however, were still in those woods, willing and able to savage Bradley's exposed right flank. "We had a monkey and parrot time of it for a while," admitted Bradley, who was hit twice by this fire. "When we reached the battery every horse of the twelve teams of the limbers and caissons was on the ground, dead or wounded."[40]

The 27th and 51st Illinois were hit hard. The severely wounded Bradley passed command to Colonel Walworth but refused to immediately leave the field. Walworth ordered the first line back behind the crest of the rise and brought up the 22nd and 42nd Illinois to take its place, directing their fire at both Hood's men and Trigg's line.[41]

The Confederates, however, were about fought out. This firefight lasted about half an hour before the Southerners fell back deeper into the covering

---

38 *OR* 30, pt. 1, 594, 597.

39 Ibid., 595; Transcript of Letter, October 16th, 1863, Henry M. Weiss to his wife, 27th Illinois file, CSI.

40 Bradley Papers, AHEC.

41 *OR* 30, pt. 1, 595.

woods. The lessening of the firing allowed Captain Estep's guns to be dragged to the rear, saved by Company G of the 27th Illinois, much to the thanks of Estep and General Wood. Still, the Illinois ranks had been badly thinned. A captain in Company F of the 27th Illinois named John Glen admitted, "in less time than it takes to write it they killed and wounded near 300 of us. This was doing bully yet we held our own, drove them, took a few prisoners, and sent a large number over the 'River Jordan.' They fought well and understood their business," continued the captain, "[but] they found they were not fighting the Army of the Potomac and their wounded both officers and privates acknowledge we fight better than the eastern army, so they told me." Of the 1,391 officers and men that entered the fight, Bradley's brigade lost roughly 250, or nearly 20% casualties in just a few minutes.[42]

After he witnessed the initial part of this fight from his vantage near the La Fayette Road, Sheridan rode back to try and bring up Laiboldt's men. His mission offered the boys in the 72nd Indiana a moment of levity. Bradley's first line came "pouring back over the ridge in confusion," noted Sergeant Magee with a touch of derision. "When Sheridan sees his men retreating he turns and comes back—having exposed his person in a fool-hardy manner. As he approaches our line we begin to shout, with a spike of irony, 'make way for Sheridan!—make way for Sheridan!'" In fact, Laiboldt's regiments were not needed, and by the time Sheridan reached the rest of his division the fighting here was over.[43]

Colonel Bradley, meanwhile, was making off the field to seek aid for his wounds. "I was faint, and a little shaky," recalled the brigade commander, who had an aide helping him. "'What are you doing here, Sir! What are you doing, a Colonel helping off wounded men!' I looked up, and there was Crittenden," who had mistaken Bradley for a skulker. "He recognized me, and apologizing hastily, he rode off." The apology did no good. The incident soured Bradley on Crittenden, who the colonel felt lost control of himself. Perhaps he had. The Kentuckian spent the difficult afternoon watching brigade after brigade come apart amid fearful slaughter. However, he clearly did not see that Bradley was

---

42 "Dear James," September 29, 1863, John A. Glenn Letters, ALPL.

43 Magee, *History of the 72nd Indiana*, 177-178. Magee goes on to describe Bradley's brigade as being completely routed, even worse than Davis's had been. His account, published in 1882, is at odds with contemporary reports, letters, and diaries, all of which have Bradley's line holding in Viniard Field.

being helped by an aide, not doing the helping. Crittenden's initial conclusion was not unreasonable, but it was a little hasty.[44]

The horrific fighting in Viniard Field ended around 6:00 p.m. The Confederates fell back into the woods north and east of the field and came to rest haphazardly once they were out of sight and range of Yankee muskets and artillery. Robertson's and Benning's brigades were intermingled with Colonel Sugg's regiments, while Trigg's remained largely intact in the woods farther south.

The Rebel withdrawal left the Federals in control of the field, where they reclaimed the 8th Indiana's guns and worked to bring in at least some of the 3,000 or so casualties, blue and gray, littering the area. Jefferson C. Davis, meanwhile, began the hard work of reforming Carlin's and Heg's shattered brigades in the trees behind Wilder's stout line. Colonel John Martin of the 8th Kansas took Heg's place in the command hierarchy. Tom Wood drew a skirmish line from Buell's intermingled ranks and advanced the men into the woods just east of the Log School, where so many of Heg's men had fallen. With this advance warning line in place Wood next set about reforming his regiments alongside Wilder's position. Sheridan's division formed up south of Wilder, anchored on Laiboldt's line. Sidney Barnes, with little hope of locating the rest of his division, rallied his men alongside Laiboldt. Colonel Walworth held his men in Viniard Field itself until well after dark before pulling back, leaving the field a ghastly no-man's land.

It took some time for the Union survivors to drift back to their units. All of them were tired, hungry, and thirsty, and many were wounded. At the start of the fighting, Sgt. William Hensley of the 21st Illinois shed his blanket roll, haversack, and other personal accoutrements, retaining only his weapon and ammunition. "If I get killed," he reasoned, "I won't need them, and if I don't there will be lots of such things left on the battlefield." Hensley emerged unscathed, but his intended pragmatism failed him. When it dawned on him that it was likely to be a "cool night," Hensley "came to where a Major and his horse had been killed. . . . One of the Major's legs was under the horse and a fine roll of blankets tied behind the saddle." When he moved to appropriate the bedding, however, "something seemed to say, 'No, don't rob the dead.'" The major's trappings remained untouched and Hensley moved on. He spent the

---

night shivering, his only meal a hastily issued piece of beef cooked by the expedient of wrapping it around his ramrod and roasting it over a campfire.[45]

The battle's aftermath affected more than sergeants. "The shadows of the ridges had been cast by the setting sun across the La Fayette Road," wrote General Carlin. "The enemy withdrew out of sight and gave up the contest for the night. My poor horse waited for me to dismount; then he lay quietly down in the dusty La Fayette Road and died without a struggle. Removing the saddle with the help of one of my men, I seated myself on it, and then gave way to a long, hysterical crying spell, which I could no more have checked than I could have checked the setting sun . . . . I was overcome," he admitted, "because I was not as successful that day as I deserved to be, though my troops . . . did as well as any troops could have done. . . . I felt a disappointment I had never experienced before, because I had never been called on before to put forth such incessant exertions."[46]

45 Hensley Autobiography, VPI.

46 Girardi and Hughes, *Carlin Memoirs*, 101.

Chapter Twenty

Johnson Flanks Van Cleve:

Saturday, September 19: 3:00 p.m. to 4:00 p.m.

The fighting that opened with a limited clash near Reed's Bridge that morning spread like a wildfire, gathering strength and intensity as it shifted south along the seam of the two armies to culminate with the bloodiest action of the day in Viniard Field. The fighting farther north, however, did not die out when the storm passed. Instead, it ignited as a backfire when Rebels from Bushrod Johnson's lead brigade carried the action back northward as it moved toward Brotherton Field. While the struggle raged in Tabler Viniard's front yard, combat flared anew all along the front.

Johnson faithfully attempted to execute John Bell Hood's order to wheel his entire division slowly to the right. For Col. John S. Fulton of the 44th Tennessee, now in charge of Johnson's former brigade, the order translated into an instruction for "the left regiment to touch to the right until we reached the [La Fayette] road, when the right would move slowly . . . thus to change direction slightly to the right; but," Fulton reported, "this order was not fully carried out." Even this partial wheel, however, was enough to discomfit the entire division. As described earlier, John Gregg's brigade line stretched until it eventually broke, and Evander McNair's supporting regiments lost sight of Fulton's men and halted in confusion.[1]

---

1   OR 30, pt. 2, 473.

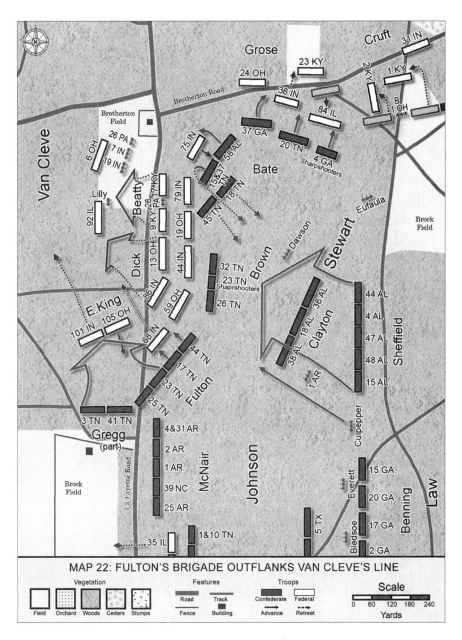

MAP 22: FULTON'S BRIGADE OUTFLANKS VAN CLEVE'S LINE

Fulton's brigade, meanwhile, continued advancing in good order. John Fulton was one of five brothers from Fayetteville, Tennessee. He and three of his siblings donned the gray, while brother James remained a civilian paymaster for the Union Navy despite his state's (and his family's) secessionist inclinations. A prewar lawyer, John enlisted as a private in the 44th Tennessee.

Bushrod Johnson. He struggled to coordinate his provisional division on the afternoon of September 19.
Library of Congress

Even at that low rank while fighting at Shiloh, his leadership abilities were obvious and he was elected captain, and then colonel, of the 44th. He was an excellent choice, successfully leading the regiment at both Perryville and Murfreesboro. Now, in September 1863, he had an opportunity to prove his worth at brigade command. Despite difficult terrain, the brigade maintained its integrity and combat effectiveness. Fulton guided his new command northwest through 700 yards of woods where, well before it reached the La Fayette Road, the four Tennessee regiments ran into more Yankees.[2]

The Federals comprised the three regiments of Col. Edward A. King's brigade of General Thomas's XIV Corps. As described in detail in an earlier chapter, King's line had played a critical role in checking Confederate Brig. Gen. John C. Brown's command just as Brown's Rebels were driving the disorganized Union brigades of Sam Beatty and George Dick (Van Cleve's division, XXI Corps) through the woods east of the La Fayette Road. King had fortuitously appeared on the Confederate left at the apogee of Brown's success and, along with a similar intervention by the 75th Indiana on Brown's other flank, forced the Tennesseans back, buying time for Beatty and Dick to restore some semblance of order within their own ranks.

Confusion prevailed here just as it did everywhere else on the Chickamauga field. Initially, King thought he was moving to support Col. William Grose's brigade of John Palmer's division, Tom Crittenden's XXI Corps; he had little notion of who Van Cleve's routing men were or where they came from. King did understand that there was no support on his right flank for a considerable distance, and he worried about a threat from that direction. For their part,

2   Lindsley, *Military Annals of Tennessee*, vol. I, 536.

neither Brown nor his immediate commander, A. P. Stewart, had any idea Bushrod Johnson's Rebel line was coming up from the southeast and was in a perfect position to either turn King's flank or support Brown. Brown's Tennesseans were hanging on—checked but not overwhelmed, trading fire with Beatty, Dick, and King's men. They were also running short of ammunition. Stewart had already decided to replace Brown with his last fresh brigade under Brig. Gen. William B. Bate, but Bate was 600 yards to the rear and would be some time coming forward.

Bushrod Johnson's arrival on King's right changed the equation completely, but the confusion that prevailed in Johnson's command from the left wheel reduced his force. Instead of three full brigades, he now had only six regiments. Fulton's brigade (the 17th, 23rd, 25th, and 44th Tennessee, from left to right) was deployed in a single line of battle while the 3rd and 41st Tennessee, the fragment of Gregg's command that had retained contact with Fulton's flank, moved on the left of the 17th. These 1,400 Rebels were about to fall on King's formation.[3]

King's front line consisted of only two regiments, the 68th Indiana and 101st Indiana, with the 105th Ohio trailing in support. Thus far King had taken few losses because he had caught Brown's Tennesseans by surprise, but his entire brigade numbered under 1,100 officers and men, and fewer than 800 were in the first line. King sorely missed the 360 men of his 75th Indiana, off helping Palmer. King was alert to trouble, however, and expected Rebels to appear at any moment. As a result, Fulton's line stumbled into a bit of an ambush.[4]

"After a short lull . . . the enemy appeared in heavy columns," explained the historian of the 68th Indiana. King ordered the Hoosiers to hold their fire "until he gave the order. As the enemy approached, his admonitions about firing were frequent. A look of eager expectancy was seen on the faces of the men, many of them having cartridges between their teeth, awaiting the order, 'Fire.'" The Tennesseans stepped to within 50 yards when the 68th unleashed "a thunderous volley." Fulton's Rebels halted and replied in kind, "and the

---

3   Fulton's regiments numbered 874 men, while the 3rd and 41st Tennessee added another 599. However, Fulton's command had already experienced some losses on the 18th. See Powell, "Numbers and Losses," CCNMP.

4   Powell, "Numbers and Losses," CCNMP. The three regiments took 1,138 into action, but suffered some loss in the fight with Brown.

fighting was heavy for about twenty minutes." Fulton remembered much the same thing when he wrote, "The enemy opened fire on us . . . and we became hotly engaged." A Union battery added its fire to King's musketry, "throwing in rapid succession grape and canister," but the real damage came from the Yankee infantrymen, "whose fire," admitted Fulton, "was heavy, well directed, and disastrous."[5]

Fulton's regiments squared off against King's line in a straight-up, head-to-head fight, and if they had been advancing alone might not have prevailed. Both sides recorded a sustained firefight of some duration in the tangled smoky woods. The battle began well for John M. Kane, the first sergeant of Company A, 101st Indiana. Earlier, when he and his comrades went into action against Brown, Kane recalled, "we raised the Hoosier yell, and went in on a run. We drove the enemy nearly a quarter [mile] before firing a shot. We could see them running like wild turkis." The tide turned with Fulton's arrival. "But just as we were going down a hill only slightly wooded, the enemy, who had rallied on the edge of a thicket only sixty yards from us, open . . . a fierce, searching fire." Fighting on King's right front, Kane and the rest of the 101st slugged it out with the Rebels at a range between just 50 and 100 yards.[6]

Unbeknownst to any of King's men, Fulton was not alone. Within the ranks of the 105th Ohio, Lt. Albion Tourgee observed what could only be an ominous development. While the two front line Hoosier regiments engaged the Confederates, recalled Tourgee, "[we] saw the enemy's columns pass the right of our brigade. The One Hundred and First Indiana began to bend backwards like a willow wand: presently it broke." The detailing of Companies C and D to guard the divisional wagon trains had left the Buckeyes short-handed, and they were about to face nearly double their numbers as the 101st Indiana crumbled.[7]

The Rebels flanking King's right were the 3rd and 41st Tennessee regiments of Gregg's brigade. Their numbers extended Fulton's line well beyond King's flank, and all or part of both the 3rd and 41st managed to work around the Yankees. Once flanked, King's otherwise stout defensive effort began to melt way.

5   High, *Sixty-Eighth Indiana*, 66; OR 30, pt. 2, 473.

6   Suppinger, "From Chickamauga to Chattanooga," 101.

7   Tourgee, *Story of a Thousand*, 219; Switzer, *Ohio Volunteer*, 124.

Lieutenant Colonel Thomas Doan, commanding the 101st Indiana, recalled the Rebels making two distinct efforts to drive his line before "finally, our right flank being turned, our position became obviously untenable and our brigade commander drew us off to a strong position in the rear." Sergeant Kane of the same regiment experienced a calm sense of detachment despite the fact that "balls were flying thick and fast [and] men were falling every second[.] This was my first fight. I felt cool, fearless and reckles as if there were no enemy in miles. Shots commenced coming in from the right flank and the order came to retreat," he concluded, "which was done in tolerable good order, the men turning to shoot as we retired."[8]

Confederate John Fulton agreed with Kane, at least at first. "The enemy opened fire upon us and . . . the entire brigade became hotly engaged," reported the colonel, "which lasted nearly an hour, the enemy making a stubborn resistance, gradually retiring, he having the advantage of both undergrowth and ground." However stubbornly they fought while falling back, the retreat exposed the flank of the 105th Ohio, which was trying to maneuver into the breach. The Buckeyes did not fare as well. In his diary, Lieutenant Tourgee freely admitted, "We were again outflanked and after a volley or two we turned and left. Of course [the] retreat, after turning with a charging enemy in front, became a perfect rout." Tourgee ran too, "crying and shouting to the men to stand. I became completely tired out," he added, and "was only aroused to further exertion by fear of being gobbled."[9]

The 68th Indiana followed suit. If any theme emerges from the desperate fighting in the woods of Chickamauga on September 19, it is that men of both sides who were willing to stand firm in the face of a deadly fire to their front became rattled and routed by even the suggestion of a surprise flank threat. The 68th's regimental historian Edwin High covered the retreat in a few terse words: "Colonel King gave the order to withdraw, and the brigade was soon in motion [as far as] the slope south of the Dyer House, to what is now known as Lytle Hill," nearly 1,000 yards to the rear.[10]

---

8   Thomas Doan Report, 101st Indiana Infantry file, Adjutant General's Records, Indiana State Archives, Indianapolis, IN; Suppinger, "From Chickamauga to Chattanooga," 102.

9   OR 30, pt. 2, 473; Keller, "A Civil War Diary of Albion W. Tourgee," 121.

10   High, *Sixty-Eighth Indiana*, 66.

In his history of the 68th regiment, High did his best to justify King's withdrawal. Dick's brigade was the next in line on King's north, he explained, and it was already gone by the time King ordered his retreat. A retirement, therefore, was inevitable. This might have been so. Dick's four regiments were still fighting off Brown's Tennesseans (and doing a credible job of it) when they also caught wind of Fulton's Rebels moving around their flank to the south. Dick's men were still on edge after their earlier collapse, and their line was considerably jumbled. "Confusion seems to have taken possession of our lines," recorded James Carnahan of the 86th Indiana, "and to add to it, the lines to the right have been broken and the enemy is sweeping past our flank." Whoever broke first mattered as little then as it does today. What mattered was that once the Rebels gained their flank, neither King nor Dick could main his position and the Union line crumbled.[11]

On the 68th's left flank was the regimental rear guard commanded by Company E's Lt. Robert J. Price. The rear guard comprised some of the last troops to leave, explained Frank Wilkinson in a letter to Price's parents. The "Co[mpany] [was] made up by detail from all the other Co's . . . whose duty it is to prevent all straggling and marauding." Price's small command started behind the main body of the 68th, but, Wilkinson recalled, "So heavy was [the enemy's] fire that in less than 15 min[utes] we had lost about 150 men" and Captain Espy ordered Price to fill in on the regiment's left. There, just before the 68th fell back, Price was struck three times. The first ball merely tore his blouse, but the second ripped open his shoulder. With that, Price turned "his head partly round and pointing to the wound said to one of his sergeants, 'look at that will you.' Just as he said this . . . a ball struck the right side of his head and he immediately dropt forward onto his face." There was no time to recover Price's body, Wilkinson added sadly, and he was left on the field.[12]

Behind King's line, in a small ravine just east of the La Fayette Road, Dr. William B. Graham of the 101st Indiana established an aid station where he could triage the wounded before hurrying them back to the divisional hospital at Crawfish Spring. Without prior warning, recalled the doctor, King sent him an urgent order "to immediately ship all the wounded back . . . at once, as our

11   James A. Barnes, James R. Carnahan, and Thomas H. B. McCain, *The Eighty-Sixth Regiment Indiana Volunteer Infantry: A Narrative of its Services in the Civil War of 1861-1865* (The Journal Company, Printers, 1895), 181.

12   Frank M Wilkinson to Mr. D. Price, Robert J. Price Letters, InHS.

line was broken and the enemy was coming." Somehow Graham managed to shift his charges out of harm's way just in time.[13]

The sudden retreat of these two Union brigades sparked a similar response among Sam Beatty's regiments. In the 19th Ohio, Lt. Jason Hurd was by now thoroughly confused. "The Confederates advanced until they came into range of our guns before it was discovered that they were not fronting our line, but enfilading us." Beatty's efforts to change front to the southeast to meet this threat "caused some confusion in our ranks. In the din of the battle's roar, no voice could be heard, and the commands were only a waste of breath." The underbrush also proved to be an obstacle, and if that weren't bad enough, Union artillery posted in Brotherton Field again began to drop shells into the brigade's ranks. An Ohio private named James Nash, also a member of the 19th, thought the Buckeyes were doing well and falling back in good order until "our artillery—some twelve guns planted upon an eminence in our rear—opened up a terrific fire . . . which scattered our men pell mell." Finally, admitted Hurd, the whole command gave way, heading for the "comparative safety" of the Union guns. "When we came [out of the woods] and up the slope where Swallow's [7th Indiana] battery was planted, we saw chaos and confusion as our men went plunging across that open field."[14]

Dick's line might already be crumbling, but with King's retreat, Dick's and Beatty's withdrawal was now a foregone conclusion. The rapidity of that retreat (or more accurately, collapse) was the byproduct of earlier fighting. Dick's and Beatty's combined eight regiments, already rattled by their earlier retreat in the face of Brown's successful attack, succumbed to the soldier's universal dread of being surrounded and captured. Fulton's Rebels only needed to turn and drive north a short distance to roll up the Union flank; fear and surprise completed the job. The result was that the tactical situation in the woods east of the Brotherton farmstead had been completely reversed.

General Van Cleve found himself in the midst of this untimely collapse where, with three of his aides, Capts. E. A. Otis, Carter Harrison, and Thomas Murdock, he attempted to stop the retreat. When a round struck Otis, the staffer dismounted and was pleased to discover the lead slug had not penetrated his uniform. Another volley of Rebel metal blasted Murdock from his horse

13   Robert E. Walker, *Old Sorrel: The Life of Gilbert Moore* (n.p., 1994), 99.

14   Entry for September 19, James M. Nash Diary, WRHS; Jason Hurd Diary, CSI.

with the mortal round lodged in his neck, and just a few seconds later fire felled Murdock's mount. With the situation collapsing around them, Van Cleve and his aides joined the retreat. Murdock's loss and abandonment was especially hard on Van Cleve, who was deeply fond of his young aide. "Your brother was to me as a son," confessed the division leader in a letter to James Murdock dated September 25, "deeply beloved by his associates on my staff and by all who knew him."[15]

Things might have gone much worse for the Union brigades if William Bate's Confederate brigade had already replaced Brown and been in a position to attack at that time. Instead, Brown was still trying to withdraw his mostly bullet-less command. Affecting a prompt and organized passage of lines between brigades was a complicated exercise even on a parade ground; in woods while under fire it was time-consuming chaos to sort things out. The result was the lack of immediate pursuit by any of A. P. Stewart's troops, which in turn gave the Federals a short reprieve.

To Maj. Gen. Joseph Reynolds, who was still trying to manage the battle from Brotherton Field, the collapse also came as a shock. Reynolds had been building something of a reserve line along the ridge running down the center of the field, mostly by acquiring stray units that stumbled his way. As noted, the 6th Ohio was one of the first, but a number of other troops followed. The core of Reynolds's strength centered around four Union batteries. First Lieutenant Harris's 19th Indiana battery had been in place since midday, his four Napoleons and two three-inch rifles deployed about 250 yards south of the Brotherton cabin. A short time later, a pair of bronze James rifles from Capt. A. J. Stevens's Battery B, 26th Pennsylvania, unlimbered near the cabin on Harris's left. The rest of the battery followed Beatty's brigade into the woods, where three of the guns were overrun by Tennessee Rebels. Lieutenant Sam McDowell managed to salvage one of his six-pounders and, when he emerged from the woods, Beatty ordered him to plant the surviving piece alongside the James rifles. Next in line were the two Parrotts and two Napoleons from Captain Swallow's 7th Indiana Battery, recalled to the ridge after a similarly fruitless effort to take position in the woods behind Dick. When Dick's brigade retreated the first time (in the face of Brown's attack) Swallow crossed the road and took position between Stevens and Harris. There, his two remaining

---

15   Horatio Van Cleve to Captain James Murdock, Sept. 25, 1863, Horatio Van Cleve Letters, MinnHS.

Parrott rifles joined him after their near-disaster in Viniard Field. This gave Reynolds a budding grand battery of 15 guns.[16]

Four more fieldpieces joined the line some time after 3:00 p.m. Lieutenant Harry Cushing's Battery H, 4th U.S. Artillery, consisting of four model 1841 12-pound howitzers, galloped up and reported to Reynolds just as Fulton's Tennesseans first engaged King's regiments. After being rescued by the 75th Indiana, Cushing emulated the 6th Ohio and fell back to reload his limber chests. The renewed intensity of the firing drew him southward. Reynolds remembered Cushing as "a little fellow . . . [asking] 'Can you tell me where I can find a general officer?'" Once Reynolds identified himself, Cushing "told me he would like to find something to do. That he had his battery and was looking for a place to go in." Reynolds placed his pieces between Harris and Swallow.[17]

Nineteen cannon were a fearful force—if they had targets. As they rolled into line, however, there was little at which to shoot. That was about to change. Unfortunately for the gunners, they also lacked infantry support. Reynolds had given away nearly all of his own men to help Palmer, and had on hand only the 6th Ohio (part of Palmer's division) and Col. Smith Atkins's 92nd Illinois Mounted Infantry, sent to him by Thomas's order of earlier that morning.

Smith D. Atkins was an unusually outspoken and even cantankerous colonel. A prewar lawyer and newspaper editor in Freeport, Illinois, he possessed strong opinions about the way things ought to be done. One member of the 92nd considered him to be "a peculiar man, a talented lawyer by profession . . . [who] used his talents to save wrong-doers from getting justice done to them. . . . He had a slick tongue . . . was fond of speech-making, and had a high appreciation of what he said and did." Atkins would later claim he had wrangled a transfer for himself and the 92nd to Wilder's brigade in June 1863 after quarrelling with his then-commanding officer, the Reserve Corps's commander Maj. Gen. Gordon Granger. That officer, Atkins asserted, wanted to turn him over to the civil authorities in Kentucky to stand trial for the crime of "nigger-stealing"—a charge stemming from Atkins's employment of a black servant. Atkins thought the charge ridiculous and dismissed it out of hand as nothing more than a manifestation of Granger's animosity toward him. The charge may have been technically true, for Atkins and his regiment were strong

16   *OR* 30, pt. 1, 820, 836.

17   Reynolds Statement, September 19, CCNMP; *OR* 30, pt. 1, 799.

abolitionists who often recruited blacks or otherwise liberated them from bondage, even in loyal states where this activity was still strictly proscribed.[18]

Fearing eternal rear guard duties, Atkins petitioned army headquarters in July 1863 to transfer his regiment to "some active command at the front," preferably John T. Wilder's brigade of mounted infantry. Wilder's men were enjoying newfound fame because of their exploits at Hoover's Gap during the Tullahoma campaign. Riding with Wilder sounded good to the outspoken (and ambitious) Atkins. The 92nd's commander pulled whatever strings he could, including one leading to Col. John W. Taylor, the Army of the Cumberland's chief quartermaster who also happened to be Atkins's law partner's brother-in-law back in Freeport. The application was successful and that August the men of the 92nd were mounted, issued enough Spencers to arm five companies, and joined Wilder's command near Wartrace. This move was wildly popular with the men, who were delighted at the prospect of riding rather than walking, being armed with repeating weapons, and most especially, out from under Granger's command thumb. The 92nd, in the words of James A. Colahour, found "Gen. Gordon Granger [to be] a West Point Dahm Phool." When the new order arrived Atkins was commanding a brigade in the Reserve Corps, and Granger ordered him not to take his regiment and join Wilder. In a final act of defiance, Atkins ignored Granger's directive and, reasoning that only the departmental commander could issue an instruction like that, joined his men. This remarkable feat of insubordination, if it actually happened as Atkins related, passed unmarked.[19]

Once with Wilder, the 92nd Illinois Mounted Infantry was often sent on detached missions. Atkins and his Illinois troops led Thomas J. Wood's infantry into Chattanooga on September 9 while the rest of Wilder's brigade was still operating north of the Tennessee River, and were repeatedly used by Rosecrans to establish lines of mounted couriers between various high-level headquarters. Because of these missions, they were not operating with the brigade at the opening of the battle on September 18.

---

18 Swedberg, *Three Years with the 92nd Illinois*, 7-8; Smith D. Atkins, *Remarks by Smith D. Atkins, Late Colonel of the 92nd Illinois Volunteer Infantry (Mounted.)* Wilder's Brigade Reunion, (Effingham Illinois, September 17, 1909), 4.

19 *Ninety-Second Illinois Volunteers*, 88-89; James A. Colehour Reminiscences, ALPL. This story is recounted in the 92nd's regimental history, and elsewhere in Atkins's writings, but there is no evidence in the *OR* or from Granger to support it.

Now, with the battle raging heavy in the woods farther east, Reynolds ordered Atkins to dismount his men, tie the horses in the trees on the west side of Brotherton Field, and deploy in support of his burgeoning gun line. The regiment, he informed Atkins, was his "only reserve."[20] The dismounted infantry took up a position somewhere south and east of Harris's artillery. With two companies detached and guarding trains, the Illinois regiment numbered only about 380 men, and of those only about 150 carried Spencers. The rest were still armed with Enfield rifle-muskets.[21]

While Reynolds accumulated bits of infantry and batteries and sections of artillery between roughly 2:00 p.m. and 3:30 p.m. (with most of his men and guns arriving after 3:00 p.m.), King, Beatty, and Dick waged a bitter life-and-death struggle in the woods to the east. The sounds of their fighting, rising and falling as the Rebel attacks surged and ebbed, engulfed the waiting line. When Johnson's Tennesseans menaced King's flank, the brigadier sent back word of his problems to Reynolds, who in turn ordered Atkins to take the 92nd forward and help out. One of Reynolds's staff officers led the 92nd east to the La Fayette Road with the vague and generally unhelpful order to "keep down the road" until he found King's line. The 92nd was still moving south in column when the Rebels found them.[22]

A very heavy body of the rebs came upon us very suddenly," was how 22-year-old Cpl. Charles Edwin Cort of Company H described it, "and the 6th [9th] Kentucky run through us and broke our ranks." Marching along in Company A, Pvt. William Boddy spotted "a brigade of our men . . . falling back. Then . . . the rebels rushed out on our regiment pouring into us a heavy volley of musketry . . . not having time to form a line of a battle [We were] thrown somewhat into confusion. The other regiments kept breaking through our ranks. It was impossible to get the [92nd] into line.[23]

Company B Pvt. John M. King remembered that the head of the 92nd had just turned east and the regiment was in an L-shaped column when disaster struck. "Thirty men in the 92nd were shot in less than three minutes," he wrote,

20 *Ninety-Second Illinois Volunteers*, 109.

21 Baumgartner, *Blue Lightning*, 157.

22 *OR* 30, pt. 1, 456.

23 Helyn W. Tomlinson, ed., *"Dear Friends:" The Civil War Letters and Diary of Charles Edwin Cort* (n.p., 1962), 105; Berkenes, *Private William Boddy's Civil War Journal*, 77.

and unable to form ranks in the road, "we were ordered to fall back in haste." Many of the regiment had to scramble over the fence and back into Brotherton Field. King was doing so when he was struck with what he later regarded a foolish notion: "I . . . saw a rebel carrying a rebel flag coming towards us walking in a crouched position to keep the balls from hitting him. I conceived the idea to stop . . . just long enough to shoot that rebel." King leveled his rifled musket and fired (without noting for posterity whether he hit the man) and added, "to cap the climax to my foolishness, feeling elated I commenced to reload my gun." King carried an Enfield instead of a Spencer, so this took some time. When the Union private looked up, he discovered the 92nd formed behind him ready to fire, and a heavy Rebel line to his front preparing to do likewise. Stranded in no-man's land, King now thought better of his decision and made for his regiment. He was running west when, to his horror, he realized he was in front of one of the Spencer-armed companies and the men were beginning to fire. King dove to the ground as hundreds of lead rounds whistled overhead, trapped but still alive and unhurt.[24]

Joe Reynolds was absorbing the calamity unfolding at the southern end of the field when he saw virtually all of Van Cleve's survivors pouring out of the woods east of the La Fayette Road. "They were being driven," explained Reynolds, "but I could not see who was driving them. They were not firing at the time I saw them and were going northward in the rear of my line." Reynolds also spotted Van Cleve, "but could not speak to him." His fellow division commander was some distance off, explained Reynolds, "and I had my hands full." He did, however, hear the old general yell out to "the boys to go slow, or something of the kind; trying to stop his men," but the words were of no use.[25]

As noted earlier, the Union collapse could have been an even greater calamity had Brown or Bate been ready to strike at this time. They would come with their brigades soon enough, and create crisis enough, but their lack of immediate pursuit gave the Federals in Brotherton Field a few precious minutes of respite. Not all of Van Cleve's retreating men refused to stop. Indeed, fragments from most of the regiments rallied in or around Reynolds's artillery position, though they did so haphazardly and without regard to preserving brigade formations or chains of command.

---

24 Swedberg, *Three Years with the 92nd Illinois,* 118-9.

25 Reynolds Statement, September 19, CCNMP.

Out of these same woods at the same time emerged a furious Brig. Gen. Samuel Beatty, determined to find out which Union battery had wreaked such havoc on his command. The brigadier guided his lathered mount up to Capt. Samuel Harris, whose 19th Indiana battery "was firing on our own men," reported Beatty. By this time several batteries were active, and in truth any (or several) could have been the culprit. Harris's guns, however, had been more active than most. In his own defense, Harris protested "that he was ordered to do so," a disclaimer that did little to lessen the damage or the general's justifiable anger. Once he spoke his piece, Beatty began the arduous work of trying to set his command back to rights before the Confederates could overrun the new line.[26]

Few members of Beatty's 9th Kentucky rallied on this line. After running through and disrupting the 92nd Illinois, "we soon passed through several batteries that were parked along a low ridge in an open field," noted Lieutenant Woodcock of the 9th. Straggling was heavy. "I don't think one half of the Brigade was present when we halted some distance to the rear," Woodcock admitted. Few of the Kentuckians rallied, leaving the regiment combat ineffective. Fellow Kentuckian Pvt. DeWitt Downing recounted that "our men were so badly scattered [that] we did not fight any more that day." The 9th Kentucky's commander, Col. George Cram, managed to halt a handful of his men behind Cushing's Battery H artillery Regulars, but this small pool amounted to little more than a corporal's guard. Even Cram was honest enough to admit they did not linger long there and soon retreated as far west as the Dry Valley Road.[27]

The 19th Ohio, also of Beatty's brigade, fared little better. Lieutenant Hurd would later estimate that Union artillery rounds killed or wounded up to a quarter of the unfortunate Buckeye regiment and completely scattered the survivors. Hurd reached the strip of timber lining the west side of Brotherton Field with only about a dozen men of his regiment. There, they met Lt. William Erb, formerly of Company A and now serving on Beatty's staff, who led the survivors to a point "a few rods west" of their current location. When they

---

26 *OR* 30, pt. 1, 808.

27 Noe, *A Southern Boy in Blue*, 200; "Dear Parents," September 25th, '63, DeWitt Clinton Downing Letters, Western Kentucky University, Bowling Green, KY; *OR*, 30, pt. 1, 813.

arrived at this point, somewhere near the Dyer house, Hurd found another "50 to 75 of the 19th Ohio collected and awaiting orders."[28]

The rest of Beatty's men managed to form closer to the line of guns. Colonel Stout and Lieutenant Colonel Vaughan managed to hold together some portion of the 17th Kentucky and reform the survivors in the rear of Harris's 19th Indiana battery (likely behind the 92nd Illinois). Colonel Knefler did best of all, managing to hold much of the 79th Indiana together and post the regiment at the northern end of Brotherton Field along with a number of men from other regiments until "a force was rallied to support the batteries."[29]

Dick's regiments were similarly scattered. The 44th Indiana and 13th Ohio were severely disrupted. Lieutenant Colonel Aldrich of the 44th reported only that his regiment was "obliged to leave the field." Despite his claim that his men fell back in "tolerable good order," the 44th did not regroup until that evening near the Dry Valley Road. The Ohioans of the 13th fell back through Brotherton Field. Some of them halted in the woods farther west, stopped by the efforts of Lt. Col. Elhannon Mast, but their stability was tenuous at best. Colonel Granville Frambes of the 59th Ohio, another of Dick's regiments, "succeeded in rallying a part of the regiment behind a line of artillery . . . in an open field. Here we succeeded in checking [the enemy] by the aid of artillery and the stubborn fighting of fragments of several different regiments for some time."[30]

None of these units fielded anything close to the numbers with which they had entered the fight. Beatty and Dick went into action with just more than 2,400 men in the ranks, and when the time came to take stock of the day's fighting on September 19, each regiment had lost an average of 20%. While on paper this suggested that nearly 2,000 men were still with their colors, reality was something altogether different. The chaos and disruption of heavy combat, coupled with heavy straggling, left most regiments with fewer than 100 men organized and present at this time. A precise count is of course impossible, but a good estimate suggests each brigade rallied about 300-400 men in and around

---

28   Jason Hurd Diary, CSI. The number of men Hurd thought felled by Union guns was much too high, but demonstrates just how destructive the firing was perceived to be by the men who suffered under it.

29   *OR* 30, pt. 1, 811.

30   Ibid., 827-828; Joseph C. McElroy, *Chickamauga: Record of the Ohio Chickamauga and Chattanooga National Park Commission* (Earhart & Richardson, 1896), 35; *OR* 30, pt. 1, 833.

Brotherton Field. Combined with the 6th Ohio and 92nd Illinois, Reynolds probably cobbled and held together only about 1,200 to 1,500 infantry to support his 19 fieldpieces. The majority of those bayonets were now of very uncertain morale, having been routed twice within the past 90 minutes.

Horatio Van Cleve's own morale had also suffered. Having failed to arrest the retreat of his men short of Brotherton Field, Van Cleve sought help elsewhere. He dispatched two officers to find General Crittenden, who was at that time down in Viniard Field. The first courier to reach Crittenden found out the corps commander had no troops to offer. He also discovered he could not return the same way because the La Fayette Road had been overrun behind him and was swarming with Rebels. The second aide never found the corps commander at all. The result left Van Cleve feeling more isolated than ever. When neither aide returned in a timely fashion, Van Cleve and Capt. E. A. Otis, his assistant adjutant general, rode north toward Poe Field hoping to find men there. On the way they met Brig. Gen. William B. Hazen, who like Captain Cushing heard the swell of firing to the south and had been drawn to it.[31]

Hazen described Van Cleve as "riding wildly up the road, with tears running down his cheeks." Van Cleve demanded if Hazen had "any troops, as they were needed 'just down there,'" adding that "he had not a man he could control. . . . His distress was not feigned." Fortunately, Hazen did have troops to lend him. Around 2:45 p.m., Brig. Gen. John Turchin's brigade (Reynolds's division) had replaced Hazen's men on the firing line at Brock Field, leaving Hazen to march his brigade back to Poe Field for more ammunition. Even though his command had lost nearly 400 men in the midday fight, it had not been driven or routed during its earlier action and, except for the green 124th Ohio, was still in good order. Hazen left the 124th to reform and guard the ammunition wagons in Poe Field while he moved with the rest of his brigade south to support Van Cleve.[32]

While Reynolds organized and Van Cleve agonized, the Confederates gathered to advance. William Bate's passage of John Brown's line slowed A. P. Stewart's renewed assault and created something of a pause, but the respite was a short one. John Fulton's Tennesseans continued their own advance, albeit cautiously, and still retained the advantage of position over the milling and

31   Ibid., 803.

32   Hazen, *Narrative*, 128.

largely disrupted Federals. As a result, the entire scenario that had routed Van Cleve's line in the woods east of the road played out once again in Brotherton Field about 4:00 p.m. Confederates appeared first on the right, rolling up Joe Reynolds's line from south to north, and then appeared from the east when A. P. Stewart's troops joined in.

Chapter Twenty-One

Breakthrough in Brotherton Field:

Saturday, September 19: 4:00 p.m. to 5:30 p.m.

In the wake of their rapid retreat to Brotherton Field, some of Van Cleve's disorganized men found a few moments to catch their breath. For most, however, there was no pause. Rebel infantry was already pushing forward aggressively in the wake of their fleeing opponents. At the southern end of the field, Bushrod Johnson's Confederates continued advancing to engage yet another vulnerable Union flank.

The 92nd Illinois Mounted Infantry, part of Wilder's brigade, certainly experienced no respite. The bursting through of their ranks by King's panicked men disrupted the Illinoisans, and Colonel Atkins and Lt. Col. Benjamin Sheets struggled mightily to reform the regiment's ranks. "King's brig[ade]" observed an assistant surgeon named Thomas Winston, "had broken through the 92nd while [we] were forming on the field. This, together with the fact that our men were ordered not to fire by the officers . . . fearing to shoot our men as they were emerging from the woods, caused the greatest confusion in the Reg't."[1]

Confederate infantry appeared soon thereafter, and the 92nd Illinois had no choice but to engage regardless of how many Federals might still be in their front. Colonel John Fulton was not plunging headlong toward the next Union

---

1 Thomas Winston to "my Dear Wife," September 25, 1863, Thomas Winston Papers, ALPL.

line. His 17th and 44th Tennessee halted in the open woods before crossing the road, and when they spotted the 92nd, "opened fire on the enemy, distant about 200 yards." Fulton had no intention of charging straight ahead into a frontal assault and risk a mauling from Union artillery (visible in large numbers) crowning the open ridge ahead. And before long, he discovered he didn't have to. Instead, "the Twenty-fifth and a portion of the Twenty-third Tennessee Regiments crossed the road [to the south] . . . gained the cover of the woods and moved to flank . . . the enemy's battery."[2]

Lieutenant Colonel Robert Snowden of the 25th Tennessee initiated the flanking movement. Snowden had initially halted east the road, awaiting orders from Fulton. From his vantage point he could see Harris's 19th Indiana Battery just to the north "pouring a deadly fire" into the 44th Tennessee. "I hesitated for a moment whether to cross the road with a single regiment," explained the Rebel officer, but when a Federal gun began lobbing shells his way, Snowden made up his mind and went forward into the sheltering cover of the trees at the southern end of the field. King's men, in full retreat ahead of the Tennesseans, didn't resist the advance. It is possible the Yankees assumed Snowden's Tennesseans were more of King's men, for Snowden was able to position his entire command at a right angle to the chaotic Federal line, either unnoticed or unfeared. The textbook opportunity occurred but rarely on a real battlefield. Once in position, the patient Snowden ordered his men to fire, reload, and charge.[3]

Captain Harris of the 19th Indiana was game. Instead of immediately retreating, he struggled to reorient his guns. "Receiving a close and destructive fire on my right, I ordered the piece on the right to retire, with the purpose of changing the front of the right half-battery, so as to enable me to meet the fire of the enemy." A gutsy decision, it went awry in the chaos of combat when the crew of the rightmost piece misunderstood the command. Harris tried to set things right, but was struck by a spent ball that did not break the skin but temporarily disabled him. The now-leaderless battery limbered under fire, losing horses and men as it did so. Snowden's Tennesseans shot down enough horses to capture one gun, as well as a number of gunners. And what of the

2   OR 30, pt. 2, 473. Fulton explained that in the open woodland bordering the southern end of Brotherton Field, the enemy were in "full view."

3   Ibid., 489.

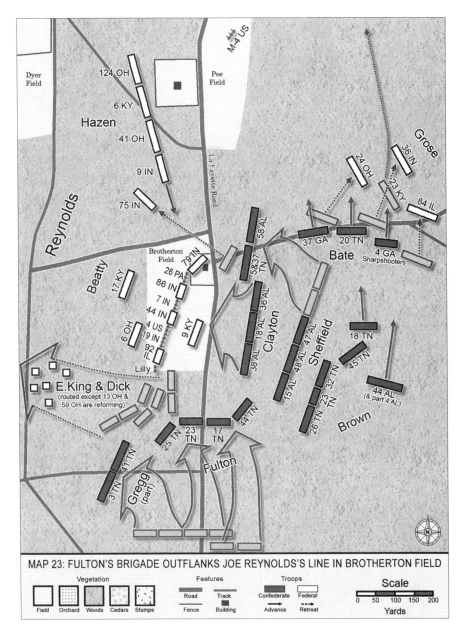

MAP 23: FULTON'S BRIGADE OUTFLANKS JOE REYNOLDS'S LINE IN BROTHERTON FIELD

92nd Illinois and 6th Ohio? Harris would only report that, "receiving no support from the infantry detailed for that purpose, the battery fell back."[4]

4   Ibid., pt. 1, 471.

The south end of Brotherton Field, looking north. From here the rise of the ridge in the middle of Brotherton field is easily discernible. The fence across the middle of the image marks the historical southern boundary of Brotherton field, with the ground on this side of the fence covered in open timber. *Harvey Scarborough*

Corporal James Colehour of the 92nd Illinois recalled that earlier, when they arrived on scene, "we tied our horses to trees and sailed in, taking the place of a brigade which had been routed and don't you think for a minute that the bullets, shot, shell, bark and dirt did not fly. I had fired three or four shots," he continued, "when I thought someone struck my shoulder with a club." Colehour fell out of ranks, unable to continue. "Just then," he added, "Gen. Reynolds rode up and says 'For God's sake men fall back you are being surrounded.' He had to strike two or three men to make them fall back as they did not know we were nipped." Most of the men in the 92nd Illinois needed no such encouragement; the threat of being outflanked was enough. Atkins later noted his men had already repulsed three Confederate charges with rapid Spencer fire, "but they swarmed on my right flank in great force, and I was compelled to withdraw." Atkins also had his horses to worry about, still tied off in the trees behind his line. "I perceived that the other regiment supporting the battery had given way and men falling back . . . were taking our horses." That "other regiment" was likely one of Van Cleve's fragmented units, but in any case, the flank was quickly crumbling and, from the Federal perspective, soon became a matter of *sauve qui peut* (every man for himself).[5]

5   James A. Colehour Reminiscences, ALPL; Atkins, *Useless, Disastrous Battle*, 10; *OR* 30, pt. 1, 456.

The 6th Ohio, part of Grose's brigade, also became caught up in this latest collapse. Its colonel, Nicholas Anderson, was anxious to return to his own brigade and division. Anderson was apparently unaware of the impromptu bargain struck between Generals Reynolds and Palmer that traded his regiment for the 75th Indiana of King's brigade. Once resupplied, Anderson began leading the Ohioans back to his own division until Reynolds appeared. "Reynolds said he feared he would lose the battery," recalled a lieutenant who witnessed the exchange. With that, the division leader spurred his horse away, thinking he had prevailed. Anderson, however, had no intention of becoming orphaned if he could help it. He still believed his duty was to return his regiment to the brigade, and a short while later he started the 6th Ohio off once again to find Grose's command. The Buckeyes had just entered the woods east of the La Fayette Road (somewhere south of the Brotherton Cabin) when Van Cleve's line gave way, refugees streaming back through the trees into the field in that same rush of disorder that disrupted the 92nd Illinois. At that moment one of Reynolds's aides galloped up, "begging [Anderson] to come save the battery," and the 6th Ohio "double-quicked back."[6]

The 6th Ohio had barely reached its previous position in the tree line bordering the west side of Brotherton Field behind Harris's battery when the battle reached them. Buckeye William Webber, a private in the 6th Ohio, remembered that "we were not allowed to stay there more than probably twenty minutes when we were outflanked from our right." The Ohio troops witnessed the retreat of Atkins's 92nd Illinois and the desperate struggle over Harris's guns. Once the five surviving pieces of the 19th Indiana departed, the Ohioans began shooting. Faced with threats from multiple directions, Anderson alternated his fire. After delivering a volley to the east against that part of Fulton's brigade line still in the trees on the far side of the La Fayette Road, they "changed front to the rear on the tenth company" and fired a volley to the south against Snowden's surging 25th Tennessee. They did this repeatedly in the hope of checking the onrushing Rebels.[7]

Fulton's men had dislocated the southern end of the Federal line, but without support their attack would eventually falter. Fortunately for the Tennesseans, support was on the way. Unlike during the earlier fight against

---

6 Hannaford, *Story of a Regiment*, 463.

7 Webber to Henry Boynton, December 3, 1900, 6th Ohio file, CCNMP; Hannaford, *Story of a Regiment*, 464.

Van Cleve, this time A. P. Stewart's men were fully re-supplied and advancing—two Confederate brigades poised to come into action at precisely the right time and place.

Brigadier General William Brimage Bate's brigade led Stewart's command. For two hours, his troops had endured shelling and the occasional casualty while being held in reserve behind Henry Clayton's and John Brown's brigades. Now it was Bate's turn to move to the front. His brigade included a mix of troops from three states: 413 Tennesseans in two regiments, the 20th and combined 15th/37th; 517 Georgians in the 37th regiment and 4th Battalion Sharpshooters, and 287 Alabamians of the 58th regiment. Bate placed the 4th Battalion on the right, extending his line left with the 20th Tennessee, 37th Georgia and 58th Alabama. For the time being, the 15th/37th followed in support.[8]

Bate's orders were to replace Brown's brigade. In Brown's mind, the greatest threat to his command had come from the right, where he had witnessed the arrival of the 75th Indiana and the damage the Hoosiers had dealt from that quarter. Brown passed the information along to Bate as his line retired, which in turn induced Bate to reorient his formations. Instead of advancing due west as had both Clayton and Brown, Bate angled northwest toward the intersection of the La Fayette and Brotherton roads. And thus it was by chance that he struck the seam between Palmer's Federals west of the road and Reynolds's mixed line cobbled together at the Brotherton farm. The space between the two Union divisions was wide, more of a fissure than a seam. Roughly 600 yards separated Palmer's right from Reynolds's left. Between these two divided wings stood only some 300 men of the 75th Indiana—directly in Bate's path. Lieutenant William J. McMurray of Company B, 20th Tennessee, was standing near Col. Thomas B. Smith when Bate appeared. The general was "riding his old single footing sorrel. . . . Bate rode hurriedly to him and said 'Now Smith, now Smith, I want you to sail on those fellows like you were a wildcat.'"[9]

With nearly 1,000 men in his first line, Bate outmatched the 75th Indiana three times over. This time, the Hoosiers could count on neither surprise nor an advantageous tactical position to aid them. If Bate hoped to simply envelop the

---

8 *OR* 30, pt. 2, 383-384.

9 Dr. W. J. McMurray, "The Gap of Death at Chickamauga," *Confederate Veteran*, vol. 2, no. 11 (November, 1894), 329.

smaller 75th, however, he was sorely disappointed. Before his Rebel line could close with the Indiana troops, the 4th Battalion and 20th Tennessee received a punishing fire from Col. William Grose's brigade. All but forgotten during the struggle with Van Cleve's Yankees, Bate's angle of advance allowed Grose to get back into the fight with a vengeance. The Georgia 4th Battalion Sharpshooters and the 20th Tennessee pivoted eastward in response, a move that also pulled the 37th Georgia in that direction. Colonel Bushrod Jones and the 58th Alabama could not follow suit, for to have done so would have exposed Jones's own left flank to fire from the 75th Indiana.

That act of stopping to pivot east, however, irrevocably split the brigade in two, with the right "wing" engaged with Grose while the left portion of the brigade (58th Alabama and 15th/37th Tennessee) headed off on a divergent angle.

The upshot of the sudden appearance of Grose's brigade was that, initially at least, Jones and his Alabamians confronted the 75th alone. Jones moved forward into what he described as an "open, woody country" and "within 200 or 300 yards" found the Hoosiers, though trees and smoke obscured much of the enemy line. Uncertain of what he faced or whether he had support, Jones held his regiment in check. Instead of charging, his 287 Alabamians engaged the like-sized 75th Indiana in a static firefight for (according to Jones) about 30 minutes. Fortunately for the Alabamians, the 15th/37th Tennessee had followed Jones's regiment and not the rest of the brigade. At some point during this exchange, Tennessee Col. Robert C. Tyler brought his combined command up alongside the 58th's left. Both regiments drifted a little to the south as they moved, and before long were oriented back more to the west than to the northwest.[10]

A. P. Stewart probably did not know Bate's line had split. His worry was for Bate's left flank, which he understood was unsupported. He knew Federals were rallying in Brotherton Field, and was at least vaguely aware Bushrod Johnson's Tennesseans were engaging those Federals at the southern end of the field. To fill the gap between Jones and Johnson, Stewart ordered Henry Clayton back into the fight.[11]

10 *OR* 30, pt. 2, 389.

11 Ibid., 362.

Joseph J. Reynolds. He was still trying to give
help where it was needed.
Albion W. Tourgee

Clayton's three Alabama regiments had also been re-supplied and though significantly depleted in manpower, had recovered sufficiently from their earlier ordeal to fight again. Between casualties and stragglers, the brigade now numbered no more than perhaps 1,000 men, down nearly one-third from its original fighting strength. They were still willing to go forward, however. The 38th Alabama held the brigade right, the 18th the center, and the 36th was again on the left. Much of Clayton's line moved up initially behind Bate's 58th Alabama and 15th/37th Tennessee. Each of Clayton's regimental commanders would remark that they passed through Bate's lines during their advance.

Clayton's formation struck Joe Reynolds's line in Brotherton Field head on, and might have been bloodily repulsed if Fulton's Tennesseans had not already started to leverage the Federals out of position from the south. The men of the 92nd Illinois were already gone, having fallen back to save their horses. Captain Harris was disabled from the spent ball and his battery in the act of withdrawing, sans the gun seized by the 25th Tennessee. These departures left Lieutenant Cushing's 4th U.S. Regular Battery next in line, still firing as fast as its gunners could load, the 6th Ohio facing south trying to fend off Johnson's Tennesseans, and fragments of Beatty's, Dick's, and King's men who refused to quit the field.

Among those fragments was Sgt. John Kane of the 101st Indiana (King's brigade), who had become separated from the rest of his command. "The Regulars worked in splendid stile," wrote Kane admiringly. "A gun would recoil about ten feet by the time three or four men had the gun in position: It was swabed, loaded, primed, ready to fire. And they did not wait long to fire. At first they fired case shot. I supposed they used canister towards the last," he continued, "But the [incoming] fire was too hot. Some of their men were killed and many of their horses, so they had to retire."[12]

The 38th Alabama on Clayton's right faced the brunt of this barrage. Before these Alabamians awaited not only Cushing's thumping fieldpieces, but the tempting target of the 6th Ohio's exposed left flank. The 38th Alabama moved smartly forward, seemingly unchecked by the big guns blowing hot metal into its ranks. Later, a dismayed Ohio lieutenant would explain why the cannon of both Cushing's and Harris's batteries were unable to stop this charge: "the men at the guns worked well," he concluded, "but fired somewhat too high." The result, from the Union perspective, was that too few Alabamians went down. The 6th's Ohio position was untenable. "We were now flanked on both sides, while the rebels were bearing down upon us in front. Things looked desperate, and I began to think of Libby." Reynolds made an appearance, and just as he had done with Atkins's men, ordered the Buckeyes to retreat. They did so in considerable confusion, falling back into the trees to the west. Reynolds lost a mount at this time when it was shot out from under him, but he escaped to the north.[13]

The exact composition of the Union line here is impossible to state with certainty. The 7th Indiana and 26th Pennsylvania batteries stood to Cushing's left toward the cabin, while parts of the 9th Kentucky and 44th and 86th Indiana regiments provided some infantry support. Where exactly those infantry commands were placed, however, remains conjecture. Lieutenant Woodcock of the 9th described what he could see of Clayton's advance in vivid detail. "We got a sort of a line rallied," Woodcock wrote. "Just then Corporal Clarke . . . pointed through an opening in the timber, and not more than 300 yards off, I espied the rebel line advancing and their flag was distinctly visible. Clarke said 'Do you see that G-d d——nd yaller rag? Oh how I would love to shoot its bearer.'" The Alabamians proved quicker to the trigger, unleashing "a terrible volley . . . which was too much for our thin and straggling line to withstand." The Kentuckians of the 9th managed to return fire once before breaking again for the rear. The 9th was likely positioned forward of the Federal artillery, perhaps at the edge of the La Fayette Road, for Woodcock

---

12 Suppinger, "From Chickamauga to Chattanooga," 102.

13 Hannaford, *Story of a Regiment*, 464. The "Libby" to which he referred was Libby prison, a notorious facility in Richmond, Virginia.

remembered that during this last retreat, "we soon passed through several batteries that were parked along a low ridge."[14]

James Carnahan recollected that the 86th Indiana was sandwiched between the 7th Indiana battery and Cushing's Regulars, and recalled a heroic stand against at least two attacks on the ridge. Carnahan put the best face he could on the fighting, but in fact the Union line quickly fell apart. Captain Swallow, commanding the guns of the 7th Indiana, did not think much of the infantry support. When "our line fell back . . . across the road," he wrote, "I then opened upon the enemy a rapid fire of canister, and kept it up until two regiments fell back through the battery in confusion and disorder; Part of the 13th Ohio then rallied on my right and rear, but their lieutenant colonel being killed, they too, fled in disorder." Feeling deserted and having expended his canister, Swallow also limbered "with some difficulty," narrowly escaping capture.[15]

Colonel Dick concurred with Swallow's assessment when he admitted his command was unsteady and scattered. His line held on here for only "a short time." Dick was slightly farther north along the open ridge with that portion of his command supporting the 26th Pennsylvania battery. Captain Stevens and the 26th, it will be recalled, had already had a difficult time of it earlier in the afternoon having lost three guns to Brown's Rebels back in the woods. Now the remaining half-battery tried to stand off this new assault. It was no use. "Having the enemy still on my right," reported Dick, "I was compelled to fall still farther back to another and higher ridge," on the west side of Dyer Field, about a half-mile to the rear. Without infantry, the guns simply could not remain in place.[16]

While recent history was repeating itself in Brotherton Field, the 75th Indiana (King's brigade) was locked in its static slugging match with the left half of Bate's brigade. Clayton's impetuous advance ended that fight as well. Coming up behind Colonel Jones and the 58th Alabama, Clayton's 36th Alabama surged through Jones's static line and together the Alabamians charged. The enthusiasm spread to both of Bate's regiments, which joined in the assault. Jones admitted that "the noise of battle was so great I could not hear

---

14 Noe, *A Southern Boy in Blue*, 200.

15 Carnahan, "Personal Recollections of Chickamauga," *MOLLUS*, vol. 1, 13-14; *OR* 30, pt. 1, 836. One of the two regiments retreating through Swallow's position must have been the 9th Kentucky.

16 *OR* 30, pt. 1, 823.

any command," but in this case it mattered not a bit. "The movement began at the moment when the Thirty-Sixth Alabama . . . was in the act of passing over my command . . . and the two regiments, comingled, charged in a run . . . The enemy gave way and fled in confusion."[17]

This final onslaught was simply too much for Colonel Robinson's Hoosiers to withstand. Already weakened from its earlier fight with Brown, the 75th suffered additional heavy losses during the long range exchange of volleys with Jones's and Tyler's Rebels. Writing home on October 2, Sgt. William Hilligos of Company G informed his aunt that "it was here we suffered the most." The new hammer-blow was Clayton's advance, both in front and working around to the south of the Hoosiers, ended the affair. "We are trying to hold the ground," chronicled James Essington of Company D, "with many in our front . . . [when] Capt. Steel says they are flanking us." When the Rebels halted and leveled their rifled muskets to fire, Essington continued, "From our officers [we hear] 'Retreat! Retreat!'"[18]

The Hoosier line buckled and a few moments later gave way altogether. Many of the Rebels were shooting high, but not too high. According to the regimental historian, no less than seven men in Company A, holding the regimental right flank, were shot in the head during this retreat. The 75th nearly lost their state colors when Cpl. James Stewart went down with a wound, but the color sergeant named Jacob Lair gallantly rescued them. Lair, who was already carrying the national flag, demonstrated his physical strength and emotional courage when he slung Stewart across his back, picked up the state banner, and carried all three out of the fight. The unfortunate Stewart, however, took another bullet "from right to left immediately under his armpits" that instantly killed the corporal. It was only when Lair stopped that he discovered he had been carrying his friend's corpse.[19]

The 75th's retreat deteriorated into a rout as the fractured command stumbled back into the northern end of Brotherton Field. Sergeant William B.

17 Ibid., pt. 2, 389.

18 William Hilligos Letter, John Q. Thomas Papers, InHS; James G. Essington Diary, InHS. Captain Steel was Capt. Samuel Steele of Company A. Essington attempted to record a detailed timeline of his fight on the 19th, breaking the action down into a number of discrete charges and counter-charges.

19 David Bittle Floyd, *History of the Seventy-Fifth Regiment of Indiana Infantry Volunteers, its Organization, Campaigns, and Battles* (1862-65) (Lutheran Publication Society, 1893), 142-143.

The North end of Brotherton Field, looking south. The monument on the far left marks the position of the 9th Indiana. The line of monuments running south in the distance denotes Reynolds's original line, now being outflanked by Fulton. The rest of Hazen's brigade deploys across the ground to the center and right.

Harvey Scarborough

Miller of Company K had been wounded earlier in the fight and left the line to seek aid. He was still in Brotherton Field being treated when his comrades fell back around him. "Our men kept falling back as the Rebels pressed them and finally came out into the open field and from where I was I could see the battle. The Rebels seem to be desperate. Some say they are drunk and they made one charge after another and our men made terrible havoc in their ranks." Havoc or no, the Rebels were not to be denied.[20]

It was here a rumor began that would haunt Colonel Robinson of the 75th Indiana for many years after the war. Separated from his own 101st Indiana of the same brigade, Sergeant Kane stumbled into the midst of the 75th during this retreat. According to Kane, "neither Colonel [Robinson] or Lieut[enant] Colonel [William O'Brien] was in sight. Presently I saw them behind a straw stack. When we retired again, Lt. Col. O'Brien disappeared. I did not see or hear from him again until after the men were rallied and the brigade reformed. The Reg't all say he showed the white feather." Worse yet, alleged Kane, the next day

20 Entry for September 19, William Bluffton Miller Diaries, InHS.

O'Brien "left the field with a scratch on the arm and had two men help him to Chattanooga."[21]

If true, Kane's charges should have been enough to discredit and ruin both men. Robinson, however, commanded the regiment in action at Missionary Ridge two months later and again in a fight near Dalton, Georgia, in February 1864 before resigning his commission that March. O'Brien fought with the regiment until the end of the war, and after Robinson resigned earned several plaudits while commanding the 75th through the Atlanta campaign. None of the surviving accounts from members of the 75th Indiana confirm Kane's assertions or disparage either man.[22]

The remnant of the 75th stumbled out of the woods, which now "seemed filled with missiles of death," when the Hoosiers spotted another line of battle halted at the northern end of Brotherton Field. "Noticing strange troops, we inquired: 'what regiment?' Their reply was: *The Bloody Ninth!*' It was the Ninth Indiana." The arrival of yet another regiment of Hoosiers could not have been more timely.[23]

The appearance of Col. Isaac C. B. Suman's 9th Indiana was due entirely to the quick-wittedness of his brigade commander, William B. Hazen. After meeting Van Cleve on the La Fayette Road, Hazen retrieved his brigade and led it south into the unfolding crisis. When he reached the Brotherton farm, he

---

21 Suppinger, "From Chickamauga to Chattanooga," 108.

22 Kane's entire account raises a number of questions. While it contains a great deal of detail and seems to be relatively contemporary to the events described, he also seems to shift scenes from the 101st to the 75th and back again several times. He never explains why, if he did indeed fight with the 75th Indiana, he was not in the ranks of Company A, 101st Indiana—where as 1st Sergeant he clearly belonged. I cannot satisfactorily resolve all the discrepancies raised, and so settled on the narrative above, i.e., that somehow Kane became separated from his own unit after its first retreat on September 19 and fell in with members of the 75th (which was at least from his brigade). It is also possible that, being from a different regiment, he might have mistaken other officers for Robinson and O'Brien. Much to Robinson's annoyance, the rumor resurfaced during a political campaign in 1872. Robinson was standing for local office as a "Grant Man" when John M. Palmer, who had led a division in the Army of the Cumberland, came to town. Palmer, a good Democrat, was stumping for the Horace Greeley ticket. Robinson explained to Palmer that a local Greeley candidate had raised charges of cowardice at Chickamauga against him, and asked Palmer to refute them. Despite a few minutes of teasing designed to make his former comrade-turned-rival squirm, Palmer backed Robinson completely and cleared the colonel's name. Robinson won the election. The camaraderie of combat, at least in this instance, outweighed political rivalry. Palmer, *Personal Recollections*, 180-181.

23 Floyd, *History of the Seventy-Fifth Regiment*, 141.

placed the 9th Indiana near the cabin, facing southeast, with the 6th Kentucky alongside it on the right. Both regiments formed at a roughly 45 degree angle to the road. After their fight in Brock Field, these two regiments numbered no more than about 250 muskets each.[24]

Hazen's next immediate objective was to extend that line with the 300 additional men of Col. Aquila Wiley's 41st Ohio, but before he could place Wiley's regiment, the brigadier's attention was drawn to the 75th Indiana's scrambling retreat and the swell of musket fire due east of his position at the intersection of the Brotherton and La Fayette roads (where the rest of William Bate's Rebel brigade was sweeping past Grose's flank). A Rebel force of unknown size was heading northward past the 9th Indiana's left flank directly toward Poe Field and Palmer's divisional ammunition wagons, which were defended only by the shaky 124th Ohio. With a word, Hazen spurred his horse north to see what sort of defense he could muster to stem this new enemy thrust.[25]

Cast adrift without additional orders, Colonel Wiley was moving his 41st Ohio down the western side of Brotherton Field when Van Cleve's line broke for the last time. The Buckeyes came into line at least 100 yards beyond the 6th Kentucky's right flank, creating a gap in the brigade line. Wiley, however, had more immediate problems, for his own regimental line was being buffeted by waves of stragglers pouring through his ranks. "Seeing the coming avalanche of fugitives," penned Lieutenant Colonel Kimberly, "[Wiley] broke his line to the rear by companies and allowed the flying mass to pass through the intervals."[26]

Hot on their heels came the Rebels. Clayton's 18th and 38th Alabama were flushed with apparent "victory" after overrunning two of the now-deserted brass smoothbores of the 26th Pennsylvania in the woods east of the road. Like a number of other batteries that lost guns on September 19, these pieces would be "captured" multiple times as the battle ebbed and flowed around them. Both Alabama regiments mistook them for the Federal guns pounding them from Brotherton Field. Some members of the 38th Alabama asked Lt. Col. Agustus R. Lankford for permission to fall out and take the guns to the rear as trophies. "Being engaged in a successful charge upon the enemy retreating in confusion,"

---

24 *OR* 30, pt. 1, 762.

25 Hazen, *Narrative*, 128; and *OR* 30, pt. 1, 762.

26 Kimberly, "At Chickamauga," 715.

Lankford reported, "I thought it best to continue the pursuit." He would come to regret his decision. Later, when there was time to secure the guns, the dismayed Alabamians discovered that Bate's men had already hauled them off and claimed their capture.[27]

Despite losing credit for the cannon, Lankford's instincts were correct. During a fluid battle there is never a good time to thin your ranks to seize a trophy. The Union line was cracking and pressure had to be maintained to drive it back. Once out in the open with most of the Yankees in full retreat, Lankford's men, with some help from Snowden's 25th Tennessee working its way northward through the field, slammed into Colonel Wiley's 41st Ohio.

The 41st "delivered a volley by battalion on the advancing foe," explained Lieutenant Colonel Kimberly. The Alabamians, "ranks loose, as usual in a headlong pursuit," staggered and stopped—at least for the moment. Not so for the 25th Tennessee working around the Ohioans's right and rear. Facing near-encirclement, Colonel Wiley resorted to a series of risky and rather daring maneuvers, unwittingly duplicating the 6th Ohio's evolutions of just a few minutes earlier. "At a double quick," explained Kimberly, "Wiley changed front to the rear on his left company and sent another volley among the swarming enemy on his right." The well-drilled 41st repeated the smart tactic twice more, falling back each time and alternating volleys to the east and south until they could break clear and reach the rest of the brigade. The technique was fraught with risk, for each time he changed front Wiley presented a flank to one Rebel regiment or another. Even a hint of panic within the 41st may well have collapsed the entire regiment. The Buckeyes paid a heavy price for their discipline with 115 Ohioans killed, wounded or reported missing during the course of the battle (32% of their engaged strength). The bulk of these men fell here.[28]

While Wiley was expertly extricating his regiment from the middle of the field, the 6th Kentucky and 9th Indiana had their hands full battling four Rebel regiments. Clayton's 18th Alabama entered the gap Wiley had left between his 41st Ohio and Lt. Col. Richard Rockingham's 6th Kentucky. At the same time, the 36th Alabama, together with the 15th/37th Tennessee and the right-most portion of the 58th Alabama—all intermingled—struck the 6th and 9th

27 *OR* 30, pt. 2, 409.

28 Kimberly, "At Chickamauga," 716.

regiments head-on. The bulk of the 58th Alabama overlapped the 9th Indiana's line and threatened to flank the Hoosiers on their left. The blue line bowed, giving ground on both ends; within minutes a brutal crossfire was scything through each regiment.

The already bloodied 6th Kentucky was wrecked within a few minutes and with nearly 40% killed, wounded, and missing suffered the highest percentage loss of the brigade. Colonel Shackelford fell earlier that afternoon in Brock Field, and now Lt. Col. Richard Rockingham—who had just returned from sick leave and had been in command barely two hours—went down. Four captains and five lieutenants were also lost, devastating the company command structure. "It was here the Sixth Kentucky lost so fearfully . . . from the mortality among its officers," reported Hazen, "was very much broken and its fragments were attached to other regiments of the brigade."[29]

The 9th Indiana suffered almost as much. Captain Amasa Johnson in Company D recalled that while the 9th was "heavily engaged" with the enemy in front, "the rebels had broken and penetrated our lines to our right . . . their fire was enfilading our regiment." Just when the Confederates were "on the eve of striking our flank and rear . . . and giving us the full benefit of their 'Rebel Yell,'" Gen. Reynolds approached and gave us orders to fall back."[30]

Major General Joseph Reynolds was seemingly everywhere in Brotherton Field that afternoon. No man could have done more to try and salvage the crumbling tactical situation. Men from one regiment after another recalled his presence, usually when ordering command back just in time to avoid being surrounded. This time, Reynolds instructed Col. Isaac Suman to take his 9th Indiana back to the fence line bordering the northern corner of the field. The shattered remnants of the 6th Kentucky fell in alongside them to the west. Having retreated first into the timber on the west side of the field, Wiley's 41st Ohio worked its way up through those same trees and joined up with the 6th's right flank.

Hazen's three regiments might not have been sufficient to turn back Clayton's and Bate's men even without the presence of Fulton's Tennesseans, whose flanking maneuver precipitated the entire crisis, but their bloodletting

---

29 *OR* 30, pt. 1, 771; Hazen, *Narrative*, 128.

30 Amasa Johnson, *The Ninth Indiana Regiment at Chickamauga: An Address Given August 25th, 1887, during the Fifth Annual Reunion of the Ninth Indiana Veteran's Association* (Watseka Republican Book Print, 1888), 2.

bought time to save three Union batteries. Both Cushing's Battery H, 4th Regulars, and Swallow's 7th Indiana escaped (though just barely) without the loss of a gun. The 26th Pennsylvania was not quite so lucky and lost another fieldpiece, but only because it was damaged and rendered immobile. Unable to limber it, the Pennsylvanians abandoned the piece, their fourth loss of the day. That total would have been higher if not for the arrival of Hazen's troops, who drew every Confederate eye to them as they entered the action. Even Colonel Wiley's inadvertent error in overshooting the brigade line and advancing too far south into the field played out to Union advantage, for the 41st Ohio's location interposed a Union line of battle between Clayton's Alabamians and the escaping gun crews.[31]

Despite those heroics, however, nothing could now disguise the fact that Fulton and Clayton, along with two of Gregg's regiments and two of Bate's, had ripped a significant hole in the Yankee line. It was just this sort of gap that General Rosecrans feared the most, and he was desperately scrambling to plug it. What he did not know was that another pair of Confederate brigades were positioned to potentially exploit that success. John Brown's Tennesseans, battered but re-supplied and rested, stood behind Clayton's line and were ready to go back into action. Moving up behind Brown and off to his left were the five regiments of Brig. Gen. Evander Law's Alabama brigade (Hood's division) under Col. James L. Sheffield of the 48th Alabama. With 1,500 veterans in its fresh and unbloodied ranks, Sheffield's brigade was in theory ideally suited to seize whatever opportunity beckoned in Brotherton Field. Ideally situated, that is, if there were a firm hand at the helm.

As was typical of the fighting on September 19, many senior commanders went into battle uninformed about what to expect in front and who was on their flanks or behind them in support. At this time and in this location, all or part of six Rebel brigades (Clayton, Brown, Bate, Fulton, Sheffield, and half of Gregg) from three different divisions (Stewart, Johnson, and Law) of two different corps (Hood and Polk) were present. The most senior officer in the vicinity was division commander A. P. Stewart, who had thus far done an admirable job of controlling his own command. He was only dimly aware, however, of the presence or intentions of the other formations around him. The whereabouts of Bushrod Johnson and Evander Law remained a mystery. Each division commander had to divide his attention between two fronts: Brotherton Field

---

31 *OR* 30, pt. 1, 820.

and the fighting farther south. Both lost control of their commands and by about 3:00 p.m. neither was functioning as an intact formation. Johnson's brigades moved off on divergent angles. In all probability, Johnson was riding back and forth struggling to bring his brigades back together and back under control.

Law's division began the fighting behind Johnson's division and suffered a similar fate. Sheffield's brigade was in Law's front rank on the right, with Jerome Robertson's brigade on the left and Henry Benning's brigade in reserve. Sheffield's brigade line extended about 300 yards, with Col. William Perry's 44th Alabama on the brigade's far right, the 4th Alabama formed on Perry's left, and the 47th and 48th Alabama regiments extending the line. Holding the brigade's left was Col. William C. Oates and his 15th Alabama. Colonel Sheffield placed himself in front of his right-center at the head of the 4th and shouted, in a "tremulous and quavering voice peculiar to him . . . 'Forward, 4th Alabamians, forward! You have a name that will never, never die.'"[32]

Things went wrong almost immediately. Law's influence on the September 19 battle seems almost nonexistent. Shortly after 3:00 p.m., just after Law's division stepped off, Robertson's courier arrived asking Law for authority to shift to the left. Law agreed and sent word of the move to Sheffield. Sheffield's line, however, did not follow suit and instead headed straight west. Robertson and Benning, as we have seen, spent their afternoon fighting in Viniard Field. Law's decision irrevocably split his division.

One problem facing the officers commanding the newly arrived troops from Virginia was the lack of horseflesh. In order to speed the movement of the infantry to North Georgia, all of the corps' horses, artillery, ambulances, and other transportation had been held back, to be sent forward when space permitted. The result, a serious one which no one seemed to have foreseen, left most of Hood's officers scrambling to find mounts locally or face the prospect of going into the fight dismounted. Not so with Colonel Sheffield, however, who against orders somehow managed to bring his "magnificent iron gray" along with him. He and the horse, however, saw almost no action. Within minutes of beginning the advance, a shell burst startled the animal and threw Sheffield to the ground, injuring his back. Command should have then passed

---

32 Laine and Penny, *Law's Alabama Brigade*, 145. The 15th Alabama was made famous by its struggle for the extreme left flank of Little Round Top at Gettysburg on July 2, where Oates and his men fought Col. Joshua Lawrence Chamberlain and his 20th Maine.

to Colonel Perry of the 44th, who was holding the brigade's right flank. Unfortunately, Perry, the 44th regiment, and a good chunk of the 4th Alabama were not in contact with the rest of the brigade.[33]

As it moved through the smoke-shrouded woods already filled with the detritus (human and otherwise) of previous actions, the Alabama brigade line fractured. Perry recalled moving about 600 yards forward and passing two lines of Confederates. The first line must have been Brown's men, who informed him that they were out of ammunition. The next line was composed of either some of Clayton's fellow Alabamians or members of Bate's brigade. In either case, shortly after this the 44th Alabama stumbled into a line of Yankees. The collision sparked a confused firefight during which the 44th Alabama and the right wing of the 4th Alabama peeled off to the north, eventually intermingling with Bate's men in their battle with Grose's Union brigade.[34]

The result of this schism left one-half of the 4th Alabama, together with the 47th, 48th, and 15th regiments, tramping west and as of yet unengaged. The left wing of the 4th drifted north, perhaps trying to reconnect with the other half of the regiment, but in doing so lost contact with the rest of the brigade. These Alabamians found Colonel Tyler and his combined 15th/37th Tennessee just in time to join in the charge against the 9th Indiana. The 4th's adjutant, Robert Coles, remembered this attack: "Advancing blindly and rapidly through a dense undergrowth, we ran unexpectedly right into a column of infantry which poured a deadly fire into our ranks." More confusion arrived when another field officer went down. The round struck Lt. Col. Laurence H. Scruggs "close to his sword belt buckle and had come out through his sword belt on the opposite side. We pronounced him mortally wounded," added Coles, "and so informed him, but on closer examination found that the ball had struck the edge of the buckle and passed halfway around his body . . . very much bruising him but scarcely breaking the skin." Scruggs had been leading the regiment in the absence of Col. Pickney D. Bowles, who was sick and in the hospital at LaGrange, Georgia. Scruggs's incapacitation effectively left the 4th Alabama leaderless.[35] While the regimental staff was misdiagnosing Scruggs, Coles

---

33 Robert T. Coles, "History of the 4th Alabama," ADAH; Laine and Penny, *Law's Alabama Brigade*, 148.

34 William F. Perry and Curt Johnson, eds., "A Forgotten Account of Chickamauga," *Civil War Times Illustrated*, (September/October, 1983), 54.

35 Pinckney D. Bowles Compiled Service Record for September and October 1863, NARA.

admitted that "for a moment the regiment was stunned and dazed from the suddenness of the fire."[36]

Something had to be done, and quickly. Colonel Tyler of the 15th/37th Tennessee (Bate's brigade) incorporated "about 40 or 50 men" of the 4th as an ad hoc company and attached them to his own left flank. Immediately after the volley described by Coles, Tyler "charged them [the 9th Indiana] from the hill in utter confusion and fired several volleys . . . as they retired to a skirt of woods some 200 yards" distant. The rest of the 4th followed suit, halting somewhere out in Brotherton Field. By now the 4th was completely disorganized. Elements of the regiment were operating with Perry's 44th Alabama, Tyler's 15th/37th Tennessee, and a third fragment of unknown size was trying to retain a connection to Sheffield's brigade.[37]

The remainder of Sheffield's command, moving and fighting without a brigadier, halted in the woods east of the La Fayette Road. In a rare mention of Law's influence on September 19, one of his aides reached the 15th Alabama's Colonel Oates to inform him that Sheffield's injury and Perry's disappearance left him in charge of the brigade. Oates assumed command and somehow got the brigade moving forward again—but not far. "[S]oon after crossing the La Fayette Road," he wrote, "[I] halted for the reason that I could not see any enemy to our front." Like so many commanders this day, Oates had no idea what to do or where to do it, and he decided to wait for someone to give him orders. He could see friendly troops, including elements of Fulton's Tennesseans farther south in the field, but the real fighting seemed to have moved on. During the lull, several of his men busied themselves by securing the spoils of war. Adjutant Henry Figures of the 48th Alabama was one of them. He found his counterpart, an adjutant named John H. Shepherd of the Union 9th Kentucky, wounded on the field. After appropriating Shepherd's sword, Figures sent the Federal to the rear as a prisoner.[38]

---

36 Coles, "History of the 4th Alabama," ADAH.

37 OR 30, pt. 2, 395; Coles, History of the 4th Alabama," ADAH. It is interesting to note that Coles makes no mention of the virtual dismemberment of his regiment at this time, though he did observe that his 4th Alabama lost contact with the 44th Alabama early on during the movement.

38 Laine and Penny, *Law's Alabama Brigade*, 148; Oates, *The War Between the Union and the Confederacy*, 254; Laine and Penny, *Law's Alabama Brigade*, 148; Henry Figures to "Dear Mother," September 26, 1863, http://www.mqamericana.com/4th_AL_Hds_Brig_Chick_btieh.html, accessed 9/19/2011.

Not every Confederate halted in the field. Clayton's Alabamians pursued the retreating Yankees through the narrow belt of timber to the west and out into Dyer Field beyond. They certainly could have used some help. The Dyer farmstead was one of the larger cleared areas on the battlefield. It was roughly bounded by the Glenn-Kelly Road on the eastern edge and the Vittetoe-Chickamauga Road to the west. A farm lane called the Dyer Road bisected the property. The field was slightly more than a mile long from south to north, and varied in places between a quarter of a mile and one-half mile in width. For troops who had thus far stumbled into bloody encounters in smoke-shrouded woods with half-seen opponents, the contrast proved startling. The sudden view was also disturbing: large bodies of Union troops seemed to be converging on Clayton's men from multiple directions.

Chapter Twenty-Two

We Bury Our Dead:

Saturday, September 19: 4:00 p.m. to 5:30 p.m.

William Bate was an ambitious and determined man. Much like Colonel Atkins of the 92nd Illinois Mounted Infantry, Bate had been both a newspaper editor and lawyer before turning to politics in 1854 and winning the office of prosecuting attorney for Nashville, Tennessee. Bate was a decade older than the Illinoisan, however, and accumulated both a Mexican War record and successful stint in the state legislature in 1849. A Breckinridge elector in 1860, when war came Bate was among the first to join up.

In May 1861 Bate was elected colonel of the 2nd Tennessee and shipped east to Virginia. Although present at First Manassas that summer, he and his regiment were not engaged. They would not experience Civil War combat until April 6, 1862, at Shiloh, Tennessee, where one-third of the regiment fell killed or wounded in a single attack. Bate's younger brother Humphrey was among the dead, and Bate himself nearly lost his left leg when a musket ball mangled the limb. A surgeon wanted to amputate, but Bate held off the saw-wielding doctor at gunpoint. He kept the leg in exchange for a pronounced limp and a permanent need for a crutch.[1]

---

1 Daniel, *Shiloh*, 163.

By the spring of 1863, Bate had been recently promoted to brigadier general and was rumored to be available to replace Isham G. Harris as governor of Tennessee. Bate, however, who did not lack for political ambition and always had one eye on his reputation, made it clear he would not leave the army with the war still on. His brigade opposed Wilder's Federals at Hoover's Gap that June during the Tullahoma campaign, where Bate pressed a vigorously unsuccessful attack, suffered significant losses, and suffered a second wound. Thus far, few chances to shine had come his way. All of that was about to change.[2]

Trailing the division, "I had thrown out no skirmishers," Bate reported, and before advancing "200 yards . . . a battery on my extreme right played constantly and with terrible effect upon that wing." The enemy guns belonged to Lt. Francis Russell's Battery M of the 4th U.S. Grose's brigade was unique in the Army of the Cumberland in that it had two batteries assigned to it, both from the 4th U.S. Lieutenant Harry Cushing's Battery H had been rescued by the 75th Indiana and had subsequently taken up a new position in Brotherton Field, but Lieutenant Russell's four Napoleons and two 24-pound howitzers were still supporting Grose's infantry.[3]

As already described, when Bate's right elements (Georgia 4th Battalion Sharpshooters and the 20th Tennessee) turned east to meet the Union fire head-on, his brigade bifurcated because the 58th Alabama and 15th/37th Tennessee could not reorient themselves without exposing their left flank to an enfilading fire from the 75th Indiana. As a result, the latter elements ended up fighting in Brotherton Field with some success, but Bate lost about half of his strength for the rest of the afternoon.

Grose's Federals were not without problems of their own. The brigade had endured several hours of enemy fire and suffered accordingly, and ammunition was running low. In addition to losing Cushing's battery, the 6th Ohio was gone (removed to Brotherton Field) which left the 24th Ohio once again holding Grose's right flank. Beset with leadership problems, the Buckeye regiment was still shaken from its earlier discomfiture on meeting Wright's Rebels about 2:00 p.m. Once the regiment reformed and returned to the firing line, however, it did well enough in the hours thereafter, but all that fighting had been at long range

---

2 Dennis Kelly, "Back in the Saddle: The War Record of William Bate," *Civil War Times Illustrated*, vol. XXVII, no. 8 (December, 1988), 29.

3 *OR* 30, pt. 2, 384.

and without threat of a flank attack. Lieutenant Colonel Foy of the 23rd Kentucky, whose flank would be exposed if the 24th Ohio broke again, was not convinced the regiment was fully reliable and kept a cautious eye on Colonel Higgins's Buckeyes. At one point in the earlier fight against Brown's Tennesseans, Foy "noticed the Twenty-Fourth Ohio giving slowly back. I immediately sent an officer to see what was the matter. He brought the word back 'all right' and that they intended to hold their ground." Only partially reassured, Foy resolved to spare extra attention to the Ohioans in case of trouble. Just before 4:00 p.m., and just before Bate advanced, Foy's 23rd Kentucky fell back into reserve, with the 84th Illinois taking its place. Colonel Grose also shifted the 36th Indiana into the front line on the 84th's right, between it and the 24th Ohio.[4]

All three of these Federal regiments were facing Bate's "wildcats" and, together with Russell's Battery M of the 4th U.S., opened a heavy fire against them. It was this hail of enemy lead and iron that oriented Bate's three rightmost regiments northeast. Grose's roughly 900-musket front line had a numerical edge, as Bate's 4th Battalion Sharpshooters, 20th Tennessee, and 37th Georgia counted no more than perhaps 700 men at this stage. The Rebels, however, had full cartridge boxes and were eager to charge.

The 24th Ohio and 36th Indiana proved unable to hold them off. Colonel David Higgins of the 24th Ohio was battling both the enemy and a flare-up of his rheumatism that all but crippled him this day. In all probability he didn't see much of the fight. The regiment, his report tersely noted, "receiv[ed] and return[ed] a heavy fire throughout the day, never shrinking from the deadly contest except when outnumbered and crushed by mere weight of numbers." In fact, his men were "shrinking" quickly against numbers not overwhelmingly disadvantageous. At the head of the 23rd Kentucky, Foy prepared for the worst. As this new threat developed, he faced the 23rd from south to southwest so his men were behind and north of the 24th. Foy later praised the 24th's effort, noting "they stood as if every man was a hero for a half an hour." Still, Foy could not completely overlook the fact that when pressed, the Ohioans fell back behind Foy's own line of ready muskets.[5]

4   Ibid., pt.1, 792-793.

5   Ibid., 798, 793.

The Confederates were less charitable about the Union stand. According to Tennessean Lieutenant McMurray, "In five minutes all the horrors of war that a soldier ever witnessed were there, [but] in fifteen minutes we were in possession of every piece of artillery, had broken Palmer's line . . . and cut our way so far into the Federal rear that they began to close in behind us. A newly promoted sergeant named James Cooper of Company C, 20th Tennessee, remembered that "we pressed forward unchecked by the murderous discharges of their small howitzers . . . and drove the first line from their position."[6]

With the 24th retreating, the 36th Indiana did likewise. In a letter home, Hoosier Capt. Pyrrus Woodward of Company C explained that the regiment had already exhausted 120 cartridges per man, "and were compelled to fall back, which [we] did in tolerable good order, leaving our hospital under fire of the enemy." Major Gilbert Trusler reported the 36th moved about 200 yards to the rear and rallied on some artillery, where they fixed bayonets for a last stand.[7]

The retreat of the 24th Ohio and 36th Indiana left only the 23rd Kentucky and 84th Illinois holding the line, alone and exposed. The 23rd still faced southwest, and the 84th more south than west. The departure of the 36th Indiana left a gap of some considerable size between the two remaining regiments, a problem that would bedevil the Illinoisans more than Foy's Bluegrass men. Kentucky Sgt. Arnold Brandley recalled the moment, though less charitably than did Foy. "The 24th [Ohio] passed over our regiment" to take position in front, explained Brandley, "but the pressure was too great, and the [24th] began to falter. . . . We obstructed their retreat, ordering them to fall in on our left. 'Allow no one to pass through H Company!' yelled Captain Claudius Tifft." The Kentuckians opened fire, but couldn't hold on much better than had the Buckeyes. "The company ranks had been considerably thinned out," Brandley continued," so we did no longer touch elbows." A Rebel appeared and demanded Brandley's surrender. The surprised soldier glanced around only to discover he was alone; the rest of the 23rd had given way. Brandley dashed for the rear in a frantic zigzag pattern right into the middle of Russell's battery, which was packing up in a rush to flee. When a desperate

6 McMurray, "The Gap of Death at Chickamauga," 329; James L. Cooper Reminiscences, TSLA. Both McMurray and Cooper have mistaken earlier captured guns—perhaps some of Carnes' pieces—for Russell's M, 4th U.S., which lost no cannon in this fight.

7 "Interesting Letter From Chattanooga," *New Castle Courier*, October 29, 1863; *OR* 30, pt. 1, 788.

artillery officer implored him to help shift one of the cannon, Brandley lent a shoulder. It would be some time before he stumbled on his regiment again.[8]

Unbeknownst to Brandley, Colonel Foy had ordered the 23rd to retreat when he noticed some of Bate's charging Rebels had worked around his right and were responsible for the deadly crossfire cutting through his ranks. Foy guided the regiment north, despite the Rebel threat to his right, but in doing so threw the command into considerable disorder, as Sergeant Brantley had discovered. Foy was forced to retreat much farther than the rest of the brigade before he and his regiment found friendly troops. They eventually "took a new position about 300 to 400 yards" to the east, coming into line near Lt. Giles Cockerill's Battery F, 1st Ohio Light Artillery, which had been assigned to Hazen's brigade. Grose's other regiments, meanwhile, fell back northeast toward Cruft's command, which likely saved many the fate of having to visit a Rebel prison. The withdrawal, however, also opened a door for Bate's men directly into the Federal rear. First, however, Grose's last regiment had to be disposed of.[9]

Private Wetsel might have thought Grose bore the 84th Illinois a grudge, but Grose himself described the 84th's solitary struggle here with fulsome praise: "Now came the time for the 84th Illinois to [step] into the breach. The Colonel [Waters] changed front to the right, and with his brave and hitherto-tried regiment contested every inch of the ground until compelled to give way before overwhelming numbers, the enemy having reached his . . . right flank (our former rear.) All was retired in tolerably good order, which ended my fighting for the day." The enemy had indeed outflanked the 84th, which was holding the worst of all positions. The small but steep hill (formerly defended by the 36th Indiana) dominating their front and right flank was now crowned with surging Rebels. According to Sergeant Cooper of the 20th Tennessee, "here occurred the prettiest fighting of the whole war. We rushed up on a little hill, and the enemy were just below us, all crowded together in a deep hollow. Our rifles were in prime condition and our ammunition so good that I really enjoyed the fight."[10]

---

8 A. Brandley, "A Kentucky Regiment at Chickamauga." *National Tribune*, February 15, 1894.

9 *OR* 30, pt. 1, 793.

10 *OR* 30, pt. 1, 780-781; James L. Cooper Reminiscences, TSLA. For Private Wetsel's comment, see Chapter 14.

Not a single member of the embattled 84th "enjoyed the fight." Somehow most of the men managed to hold their ground for a few minutes, but they suffered severely for it. Worse was to come when another Rebel regiment appeared on the other flank. The 84th Illinois was caught up in a double envelopment. Here, recorded an Illinois private named James B. Suiter of Company B, "they came in overwhelming numbers on our left flank . . . and we were compelled to fall back." The 84th's heaviest losses were incurred during their break for the rear. "All the men we lost were shot [while] falling back," fumed Company's G commander, Capt. Frederick Garternich. Broken and battered, the 84th followed most of the rest of the brigade northeast.[11]

The new threat had come in the form of the 276 officers and men of the 44th Alabama of Sheffield's brigade, who had purely by chance advanced into an exposed enemy flank. As noted earlier, the 44th started the battle holding Sheffield's right, and should have been moving west. Initial contact with the Yankees confused nearly everyone. The 44th's Col. William Perry thought a concealed line of Federals lying prone in the woods had ambushed him from no more than "sixty yards away." When the aggressive Perry ordered his men to charge, however, nothing happened. "My men . . . fail[ed] to respond promptly, and [were] showing symptoms of unsteadiness," reported the regimental leader. "I shouted the order to lie down [instead.]" For a few minutes the 44th blazed away at what was essentially an invisible enemy while Perry, now dismounted and using a tree for cover, watched the action. In fact, he and has men had stumbled upon the left flank of the 84th Illinois, which was simultaneously fighting Bate's Rebels on its right flank. It was during this engagement that the 4th Alabama Sharpshooters split apart from Bate's brigade line and made its way to Perry's position. This confusion added an unknown number of men to Perry's ranks, though Perry wasn't even aware he had been reinforced until later.[12]

Thus far, Perry's involvement with Grose's 84th Illinois had been peripheral. In the heat of combat Grose's Yankees could not distinguish between different regiments or brigades of Rebels. No one, for example, mentioned the new uniforms sported by Perry's Army of Northern Virginia troops. However, as each of Grose's regiments fell back in turn, effectively

11 Entry for September 19, James P. Suiter Diary, ALPL; *Keithsburg Observer*, October 15, 1863.

12 Perry and Johnson, "A Forgotten Account of Chickamauga," 54.

abandoning the 84th, "the fire of the enemy perceptibly slackened." Perry now saw his chance—if he could get his men to move. "I ordered a charge and started toward the enemy at a run." This time the men of the 44th "responded with a yell and a bound."[13]

Alabamian Joab Goodson, a captain commanding Company B, was exultant. "The Yankees," Goodson recalled, "fought us manfully as long as we lay and fought them, but when . . . we raised a yell and went at them at the double-quick . . . they went at a double-quicker. I tell you they skedaddled in fine style." With the 84th broken and retreating, the 44th took off in hot pursuit. A short while earlier Perry could not get his men to charge; now, he couldn't get them to stop. "My men soon passed me. . . . [When] prudence dictated a halt . . . I was unable . . . to get them under control. On they went, a broken mass of howling demons. I followed . . . shouting *halt! halt!*"[14]

Except in the most general sense, it is unclear where Perry's men appeared or how they struck Grose's line. They blundered onto an already confused battlefield, and their chaotic charge only served to further muddy the waters of understanding. General Bate was focused on driving his brigade northward, not back to the east, where the bulk of Grose's Yankees were heading. Even as Bate struggled to get his own three regiments under control, Perry's mob dashed through his ranks. The 37th Georgia, which entered the fight anchoring the center of Bate's line and became its left-flank regiment when the 58th Alabama and 15th/37th broke away, became badly intermingled with Perry's troops. "On charging the enemy . . . [we] became mixed up with a regiment of Law's Brigade," explained the 37th's Lt. Col. Joseph Smith, "and in the confusion incident to such a state of things about 50 men, including several line officers, and myself . . . became separated . . . and pursued the fleeing enemy in a right oblique direction."[15]

Just as Perry did not know members of the 4th Alabama Sharpshooters had filtered into his line, neither did Bate realize Perry's intruders had struck his, moving at cross-purposes to Bate's intended direction of advance. When exactly Bate learned of Perry's disruption is unknown since Bate failed to note the collision in his report. Instead Bate's focus was drawn northward. Despite

---

13 Ibid.

14 Hoole, "Letters of Joab Goodson," 150; Perry and Johnson, "A Forgotten Account of Chickamauga," 54.

15 *OR* 30, pt. 2, 392.

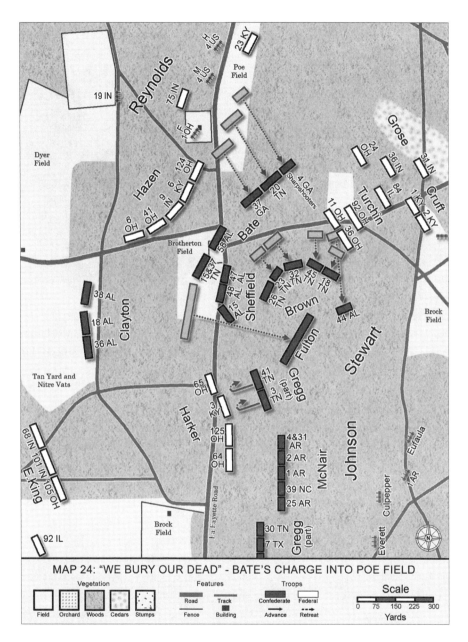

MAP 24: "WE BURY OUR DEAD" - BATE'S CHARGE INTO POE FIELD

having broken the first Federal line and nearly captured a battery, "Another [line] revealed its hydra-head immediately in rear," wrote Bate in colorful prose, "hurling its death-dealing missiles more destructively, if possible, upon our still-advancing but already thinned ranks."[16]

16 Ibid., 384.

William Babcock Hazen. His quick thinking in
Poe Field demolished Bate's Confederates.

Miller, The Photographic History of the Civil War

The distance between the
Brotherton Road and Poe Field was
about 300 yards. The Poe farm was
similar to the Brotherton homestead, a
narrow strip of cleared land alongside
the La Fayette Road about three times
as long as it was wide. The Poe cabin
and barn sat west of the road, while the
bulk of the cleared land lay east of it.
The farm was deserted, abandoned by
the family that morning. Larkin H. Poe
was serving as a teamster in the 4th Georgia Cavalry. His wife Sarah was the
oldest daughter of George and Mary Brotherton just down the road. With battle
looming, Sarah packed up her two young children, Hilliard and Gussie, and fled
into the hills west of the Snodgrass farm.[17]

Today, the monuments marking Grose's final position stand about 450
yards east of the intersection of the Brotherton and La Fayette roads, and just
south of the former. Bate's advance angled through the woods in a
northwesterly direction. His left (the 37th Georgia, minus Smith and his
detachment) may have been visible through the woods (and if so, just barely),
despite the smoke created by both gunpowder and the numerous accidentally
kindled small brush fires. Somehow William Hazen saw Bate's movement,
realized its import, and acted decisively to head it off.

To Hazen, at least, everything seemed in flux. "The enemy . . . came down
with wonderful force driving completely from the field Van Cleve's division,"
penned the brigadier. "Reynolds on our right shared nearly a like fate, and our
two other brigades—Gros[e] and Cruft—came pouring back like herds of
cattle." Having already committed his own brigade to stem the Rebel tide at
Brotherton's, Hazen rode back to Poe Field where, to his great relief, he found
not only his own 124th Ohio and Battery F of the 1st Ohio Artillery, but three

17 Sartain, *History of Walker County*, 99.

other Union batteries as well. The ever-eager Harry Cushing had rolled his four guns here after escaping Brotherton Field, and Russell's Battery M had retreated to the northern end of Poe's clearing when Grose's line gave way. Also present were the surviving guns from Harris's 19th Indiana (now without Harris)—five pieces commanded by Lt. Robert S. Lackey.[18]

"To get these in position to take the enemy's line in flank," Hazen recalled, "was scarcely the work of a minute." Twenty-one Union fieldpieces formed a curved line along the west side of Poe Field that arced across the La Fayette Road at the northern end. For artillery, the range was almost point-blank: no more than 200 to 400 yards from the gun line to where Bate's regiments would burst into the southeast corner of the field. The curving line of pieces was perfectly situated to catch the onrushing Rebels in a deadly crossfire.

Bate led the way into the field astride his second horse of the day. His first mount, "an old sorrel," had gone down during the attack against Grose's line. "General Bate had his black mare brought up and . . . was soon again in the hottest of the fight with crutch in hand," recalled one eyewitness. Despite the sharp contest with Grose, Bate had thus far suffered only moderate losses. Disruption more than casualties had shed men from the ranks of all three regiments. As a result, Bate probably led no more than 500 men out of the woods and into Hazen's well-placed artillery field of fire.[19]

First Sergeant Richard M. Gray of Company K, 37th Georgia, was one of those hundreds who followed Bate into the clearing. The 37th, recalled Gray, had just charged home against the last of Grose's Yankees, "and completely overwhelmed them . . . so they turned and fled." Without pause, the Rebels pursued. Hazen's artillery line opened fire when they reached the edge of Poe Field.[20]

Bate was among the first to fall. Both the general and his mare went down in a heap just 300 yards from where his first mount had collapsed. The mare was dead, but the fortunate Bate struggled to his feet with the aid of his crutch

18 Hazen to Benjamin Lossing, August 23rd, 1866, Palmer Collection, WRHS; 19th Indiana Battery Monument, CCNMP. Today, there is a position marker for the 19th Indiana in the woods at the south end of Poe Field, south of the Poe house site, and west of the La Fayette Road. However, the text for that marker states that the battery was engaged at the "north end of Poe Field."

19 W. J. McMurray, *History of the Twentieth Tennessee Regiment Volunteer Infantry, C.S.A.* (The Publication Committee, 1904), 291.

20 R. M. Gray Reminiscences, UNC.

Poe Field, looking north, from where Bate's Brigade entered the clearing. The large marker in the foreground is the Georgia State Monument, commemorating all Georgians who fought at Chickamauga. This image clearly shows the long, narrow nature of the field, with Union artillery in the trees to the left and the far distance. The La Fayette Road can be noted by the presence of the vehicle in the image's left-center. *Lee White*

without a mark on him. Others were not so lucky. The Yankee iron was slaughtering men all around him. The 20th Tennessee's magnificent regimental flag led the men into the clearing. The banner had been hand-sewn by Maj. Gen. John Breckinridge's wife and presented to the regiment in March 1863, an award for being the best drilled and disciplined unit in Breckinridge's division. Company B of the 20th reported losing 19 of its 26 officers and men in the battle, most of them in Poe Field, which regimental historian William J. McMurray attributed to being "raked by an enfilading fire." The 37th Georgia would lose 194 of its 425 taken into action; 140 fell on the 19th of September. Major T. D. Caswell, Capt. Benjamin Turner, and 33 others of the diminutive

4th Georgia Sharpshooters were struck, leaving the 50-odd survivors under the command of a lieutenant.[21]

A Federal lieutenant named Ambrose Bierce witnessed the carnage while serving on Hazen's staff. Although he was a topographical engineer, Bierce's real talent was as a wordsmith. Bierce reached the field at Hazen's side just in time to help alert the Union artillery. "A moment later," he wrote, "the field was gray with Confederates. . . . Then the guns opened fire with grape and canister for perhaps five minutes—it seemed an hour—nothing could be heard but the infernal din of their discharge and nothing seen through the smoke but a great ascension of dust from the smitten soil. When all was over, and the dust cloud had lifted, the spectacle was too dreadful to describe. The Confederates were still there . . . but not a man was on his feet . . . and so thickly were all covered with dust that they looked as if they had been reclothed in yellow. 'We bury our dead,' said a gunner, grimly."[22]

Hazen's description was much more matter-of-fact, but just as clear as to the outcome: "Opening at short range on their flank with canister, we sent them back." The sharp and bloody repulse began and ended so quickly that the various infantry units and fragments Hazen was attempting to rally at that time had little or nothing to do but watch Bate's Rebels be torn apart. Lieutenant George Lewis of the 124th Ohio was one such spectator.[23]

Lewis's first day of battle was proving to be quite eventful. When Hazen's brigade departed from Brock Field, Lewis lingered to try and help some of his men wounded on the skirmish line. When he lost track of the rest of his regiment he nearly panicked, but soon found his fellow Buckeyes a few minutes before Bate's attack lying prone in line behind a six-gun battery. Everything was quiet, but Lewis took note that the gun crews had prolonge ropes ready, prepared to quickly fall back, if needed. It was then, he later wrote, "I saw coming . . . a solid mass of Confederate Infantry; their stars and bars flaunting

21 McMurray, *Twentieth Tennessee*, 291-292; Entry for September 19, 1863, Diary of Isaac V. Moore, 37th Georgia Infantry, http://www.knoxscv.org/csa.htm, accessed 2/15/2010. The 20th Tennessee was part of Breckinridge's division when awarded their flag, but served in A. P. Stewart's division at Chickamauga.

22 Ambrose Bierce, *Ambrose Bierce's Civil War* (Wing Books, 1996), 33. Bierce would become a famous, if troubled, man after the war, a journalist and the author of rather sardonic short stories, the most famous of which is entitled "An Occurrence at Owl Creek Bridge." Bierce vanished in Mexico in the early 1900s.

23 Hazen to Benjamin Lossing, August 23rd, 1866, Palmer Collection, WRHS.

gaily." Lewis was certain the battery would be overrun. Federals were still falling back all around him, and off to the right in Brotherton Field, Yankees appeared to be in full retreat as well. "I turned to see . . . what would become of the battery when their six guns opened one after the other in rapid succession, and I saw lanes and alleys open in the solid ranks of Confederate gray. This was repeated as rapidly as the guns could be worked . . . [as] that grand old United States Battery poured its double-shotted canisters at half distance into the now panic-stricken and flying rebel horde." Both the 75th Indiana and Lieutenant Colonel Foy's 23rd Kentucky had rallied behind Hazen's grand battery and, like Lewis, had little to do but watch the gory spectacle unfold before them.[24]

Bate's men were too disorganized and far too few to take four batteries of artillery in a frontal attack. The Confederates should have halted well short of Poe Field to at least determine what they were up against. Instead, flushed as they were with the relatively easy victory over Grose's Unionists, Bate and his men launched a rash charge that cost the brigade dearly and gained nothing. Perhaps it would have been impossible for Bate to stop his surging regiments—even if he had wished to do so. In the end, his Rebels (or at least some of them) tumbled back into the woods nearly as quickly as they ran into Poe Field.

Colonel Perry's 44th Alabama and assorted oddments, meanwhile, were making a similarly reckless headlong charge to the northeast in pursuit of the 84th Illinois. This move might have visited further disaster upon Palmer's Federals, if not for steady nerves and quick reactions among the Yankees.

Flank attacks, even by relatively small forces, had been breaking determined defensive lines on both sides all day. Perry's disorganized advance threatened Charles Cruft's brigade on what was once Grose's left. Had Cruft maintained his original position facing south, Perry's advance may well have struck his right flank. Fortunately for the Federals, however, both Cruft and Palmer were alert to the threat.

Charles Cruft was as unflappable at Chickamauga as he had been at Shiloh. He and his men could clearly hear the sounds of Bate's burgeoning engagement with Grose, and they realized the swelling cacophony of combat was coming

---

24 Lewis, *Campaigns of the 124th Regiment*, 61-62. Lewis's account suggests that he thought he was observing a Regular battery, which could only have been Lt. Francis Russell's Battery M of the 4th U.S., but it is more likely he was watching Lieutenant Cockerill's Battery F, 1st Ohio Artillery.

their way. Private Henry Eby of the 7th Illinois Cavalry, who served as one of General Palmer's couriers, liked Cruft the best out of the three brigade commanders in the division. He regarded him as "very kindly, and pleasant to his companions," and not nearly the disciplinarian Hazen was; but that did not mean he wasn't a capable soldier. As far as Eby was concerned, Cruft "knew his duty and he did it."[25]

Palmer provided the first real warning that Grose's line was giving way. The general had been riding back and forth along the Brotherton Road from somewhere near where Robinson's 75th Indiana was engaged to a point in Cruft's rear, trying to monitor the fight. He had just completed one such circuit and had come from the Hoosiers when, "as I rode forward in a gallop I looked down a hollow to my right front and saw a Rebel line advancing up a hill in the direction of Cruft's brigade . . . [who] had not noticed the approach of the enemy."[26]

Palmer rode into the ranks of Cruft's men at a full gallop shouting the alarm, and he did so just ahead of the approaching Confederates. He missed being swept up in Bate's attack by mere minutes. Cruft's laconic report noted only that "orders were now received from General Palmer to move such portion of my command as was possible to Colonel Grose's aid." Fortunately for these Federals, the pressure on Cruft's original front had long since eased with the withdrawal of Ben Cheatham's Tennesseans, leaving Cruft in a position to quickly react.[27]

Cruft's 1st Kentucky had already turned to face the threat. Because most of the regiment was away guarding the trains, the 1st was a mere rump of a command numbering only 118 men in four companies. The regiment was also still in a bad odor with Cruft over the affair at Peavine Creek on September 10, where almost an entire company was captured by Rebel cavalry. Cruft worried there might be "some want of confidence between officers and men hitherto unsuspected," and so chose not to hazard the 1st in his front line. The 1st initially supported Cushing's battery, and after Cushing left, some of Russell's guns. Cruft need not have worried. When Grose's line started to unravel on his

25 Henry H. Eby, *Observations of an Illinois Boy in Battle, Camp, and Prisons—1861-1865* (n.p. 1910), 95.

26 Palmer, *Personal Recollections*, 177.

27 *OR* 30, pt. 1, 730.

right, Lt. Col. A. R. Hadlock quickly faced his small line to the right and began to rally Grose's regiments.[28]

Cruft quickly reinforced Hadlock with the 2nd Kentucky and 31st Indiana, both plucked from his now-quiet front line, leaving just the 90th Ohio to watch for any renewed threat from that quarter. All three regiments experienced difficulties when Grose's men ran through their ranks. Colonel Thomas Sedgwick of the 2nd Kentucky reported that "finding the enemy was . . . gaining ground on the right, I changed front perpendicularly to the rear, to be ready as a support, but had scarcely got my line reformed before we were thrown into disorder by retiring troops."[29]

Cruft ordered the 2nd Kentucky and 31st Indiana to advance and retake Grose's original position, but that idea was soon abandoned. Instead, most of Cruft's men fell back a short distance—Colonel Sedgwick estimated 200 yards—and reformed. Grose's men rallied behind and around them. Private Suiter of the 84th Illinois (Grose's brigade) thought Cruft's support a godsend, for it stemmed any pursuit and saved the 84th and the rest of their brigade any further losses. Even better, additional help was on the way. John Turchin was also aware of the trouble on the right.

As a trained and experienced European officer, Turchin considered himself the equal or better of just about any commander on the field. He was still seething over Joe Reynolds's interference in splitting his command earlier in the afternoon. By "separating his own small division into two parts," contemptuously wrote Turchin, "and placing those parts on the opposite flanks of another division . . . and leaving them without anyone to direct their movements . . . while [Reynolds] remained in the rear to organize something out of nothing . . . does not look like generalship." The furious racket and rapid progression of the fight on Grose's front was nearly half a mile from where Turchin occupied Hazen's former position in Brock Field, but it was clearly audible. There was no time to wait for orders.[30]

Like the son of any good Cossack officer, Turchin believed in the spirit of the offensive. He regarded the bayonet as the decisive weapon and that men trained in its use were more confident on the battlefield. His first regiment, the

28 Ibid., 726, 745.

29 Ibid., 753.

30 Turchin, *Chickamauga*, 75.

19th Illinois (now serving in James S. Negley's Second Division, XIV Corps) adopted Zouave dress along with drill and training in bayonet technique. At the helm of an infantry brigade, Turchin continued that trend. He aggressively drilled his men in the weapon's use, and put that training to practical effect whenever possible. Now, reasoned the Russian, was a fine time to implement the doctrine. He peeled off two regiments, the 11th and 36th Ohio, ordered them make an abrupt right face, and charge. "We could tell from the swiftly approaching roar of battle," recalled Robert Adney of Company B, the 36th, "that they were driving our men in almost a rout. We changed our course to a direct right angle . . . and started not at a double-quick, but at a keen run through the brush and timber." Close behind came the 18th Kentucky and 92nd Ohio. The Russian was leaving no one behind.[31]

Turchin's lines passed through Cruft's men and Grose's rallying troops. Palmer was mesmerized by the maneuver. The general had just fired his pistol at a Confederate officer when he saw Turchin leading the charge. "In an instant, all was changed. The Rebels [principally the 44th Alabama] had by this time become disordered and they were unable to withstand our assault. They broke and we pursued them." Lieutenant Colonel Hiram Devol of the 36th Ohio was at this time handed command of the regiment. Devol recalled that "the retreating line passed through ours, which brought us face to face with an exultant enemy. We opened fire and they took cover behind trees and logs." The Buckeyes of the 36th suffered considerable loss in this affair, including Col. William G. Jones, who fell mortally wounded. Thrust abruptly into command and unable to locate Turchin, Devol "assumed the responsibility and ordered the line up and forward. They responded with bayonets fixed and the old time yell. The enemy was terror-stricken, and retreated in great haste."[32]

Cruft and Grose likely would have stopped the Rebels on their own, since both brigades rallied quickly and outnumbered the 44th Alabama by a considerable margin, but Turchin's counterattack did more than just stop the

---

31 Rob Adney, "Account of the Battle of Chickamauga," 36th Ohio file, CCNMP. Zouaves were French Regiments of native infantry, recruited from North Africa. In 1859, Elmer Ellsworth toured the country at the head of the "Chicago Zouave Cadets," an exhibition troupe that became a national sensation. Naturally, when war came, a number of "Zouave" regiments were formed. The 19th Illinois was notable for containing a number of the original Chicago Cadets who had toured with Ellsworth.

32 Palmer, *Personal Recollections*, 177; Hiram F. Devol, *Biographical Sketch* (Hudson Kimberly Publishing Co., 1903), 37.

attack. Turchin's arrival shoved the Confederates all the way back to and through Grose's original position. Moreover, the 44th's original path of advance carried it northeast, so that Turchin's two regiments took the Alabamians at least partly in flank. Colonel William Perry of the 44th continued the struggle to control his own command. Perry, it will be recalled, had lost control of his men when they charged off like a "broken mass of howling demons" and outdistanced him by some 400 yards through the timber. They also stumbled onto another Union battery at close range, which was probably Capt. William W. Andrews's 21st Indiana Light Artillery (attached to Turchin's brigade). Andrews admitted to a hasty change of front to the right at this time, and to "throwing a few rounds of canister" in that direction before Turchin's men counterattacked.[33]

To Perry, Andrews's artillery unleashed a terrible fire. "The ground shook, and a storm of grape and shrapnel swept the woods." Not realizing the Federal guns were well supported, Perry thought that "an organized line of battle could easily have silenced the battery with a single volley," but it was of no matter for his men were anything but organized. "A retreat as rapid as had been the advance" now swept the 44th past their own commander, the Alabamians scattering to the rear like a covey of frightened quail. One of A. P. Stewart's artillery batteries was also nearly caught up in this rout after attempting to follow the brigades through the woods as they advanced. Swamped with Confederate infantry in sudden retreat, the battery (which remains unidentified) abruptly turned around and headed for safety. Thinking he would get ahead of his men and rally them, Perry jumped on one of the limbers and raced off with the gunners. His plan worked in that he managed to get ahead of his retreating men. It was then Perry had the unfortunate luck of running across General Law, who watched as a single regiment from his former brigade ran for its life while the commander raced to the rear atop a limber chest. The furious Law ignored Perry and ordered Maj. George Cary to rally the 44th. Later that evening, a mortified Perry confided to Colonel Oates of the 15th Alabama that he was sure Law thought him a coward.[34]

33 21st Indiana Tablet, Brock Field, CCNMP.

34 Perry and Johnson, "A Forgotten Account of Chickamauga," 54; Laine and Penny, *Law's Alabama Brigade*, 154; William C. Oates, "General W. F. Perry and Something of his Career in War and Peace," *Montgomery Advertiser*, March 2, 1902. Laine and Penny have a discussion of which Confederate battery might have been involved.

Both Turchin and his troops were exultant. "We routed, as we learned from the prisoners afterward, Law's brigade . . . a crack brigade from the rebel army in Richmond." George Turner of the 92nd Ohio similarly crowed, "we engaged a part of Longstreet's boasted force . . . and drove back in confusion Law's brigade." Even better, Turner continued, "in the charge we lost no men." Among the trophies claimed were the oft-captured brass guns of the 26th Pennsylvania. Like most of the other troops who laid hands on them, however, Turchin's men had no time to drag them off and so the guns remained on the field for the Confederates to squabble over. Ultimately, Capt. Thomas H. Dawson's Georgia battery (now under the command of Lt. Ruel Anderson) tried to haul them off by hand, but made it only 150 yards before giving up the effort. And there the Union guns remained until finally policed up by Confederate salvage parties after the battle was over.[35]

While Perry's men furnished the bulk of the captures (and thus identified Law's brigade for Turchin's report), in fact, beyond the 44th and that fragment of the 4th Alabama Sharpshooters attached, no other Alabamians were involved. A smattering of Bate's men had been caught up in the affair, but additional resistance came from yet another Southern brigade, lost and adrift, that blundered into the scene of action.

John Brown's Tennessee regiments, resupplied and reorganized, wanted to reenter the fight. The problem was, where? Brown knew nothing of Law, Sheffield, or Perry. He understood that Bate's brigade, also of A. P. Stewart's division, was off to his north, and apparently thought fellow brigade commander Henry Clayton was still behind Bate in support. By this time Brown was also aware that Bushrod Johnson's men (the brigades of Fulton, Gregg, and McNair) were in action somewhere to the southwest. One of Stewart's staff officers found Brown and informed him that "the enemy had penetrated between Bate's left and Johnson's right, and that his skirmishers were moving upon my flank." That was all Brown needed.[36]

The Tennessean ordered his brigade to counter the threat "at the double-quick," but found no Yankees. In fact, while the staffer's information probably summarized Stewart's understanding of the current situation, it bore only limited resemblance to reality. Brown didn't mention Clayton's men, who

---

35 OR 30, pt. 1, 474; George Turner to "Dear Mother," September 23, 1863, George Turner Letters, OHS.

36 OR 30, pt. 2, 371.

had already moved between Bate and Johnson to rather handily clear Brotherton Field with their own impetuous charge. Federals were indeed moving in to threaten Johnson's left, a threat that would ultimately send all the Confederates in this area scrambling back eastward across the La Fayette Road, but that was happening several hundred yards farther south. No one was threatening Brown's or Bate's flanks from that quarter. Brown discovered as much in short order, halted his men, and sent word back to Stewart that "the enemy had either retreated, or the alarm was a false one."[37]

Brown and his brigade were in the woods somewhere southeast of the intersection of the Brotherton and La Fayette roads. They had no additional orders, and Brown had no idea where the battle was developing. Wherever his line formed in this much fought-over patch of timber, it must have been oriented to the northwest. His right flank regiment, the 18th Tennessee, was far enough east to run afoul of the now-retreating 44th Alabama. Private Jasper Hampton of the 18th's Company B recalled that by this time in the fight, "there was such a volume of smoke that we could not distinguish the enemy from our own men ten steps away." Hampton was aware that a portion of "Longstreet's Corps made a right flank movement . . . and our regiment, thinking they were our enemies, fired a volley into them, killing or wounding thirty or forty of our own men." The volley had found Alabama flesh belonging to Perry's 44th regiment. Hampton overestimated the damage inflicted, for the 44th reported only five killed and 43 wounded on the 19th (most of which fell fighting against Grose, Turchin, and Cruft), but this additional blow served to further damage the Alabamians's morale.[38]

With Perry's 44th out of the way, it was Turchin's turn to feel exposed and vulnerable. "After consulting General Cruft," wrote the Russian, "we decided to fall back [and] reform our line on the original position." This retreat almost certainly allowed Bate's shattered ranks to slip back southward unmolested after their ordeal in Poe Field, though how many of Bate's men had already fallen back before Turchin's counterattack remains an open question. What is clear is that after a brief volley and a limited advance by Brown's 18th Tennessee (in which yet another regiment laid claim to the 26th Pennsylvania's guns),

---

37 Ibid.

38 Hampton, *An Eyewitness*, 31; In his 1888 history of the battle, Turchin attempted to correct his wartime report to show that his brigade routed Brown instead of Law, but in fact Brown's troops held their ground. See Turchin, *Chickamauga*, 187.

Brown's men formed a bulwark behind which Bate and Perry could reform their commands.[39]

These vicious Rebel assaults, as haphazard as they were, still tore a tremendous hole in the Union army's center. Bate had been repulsed from Poe Field, but large numbers of Confederates swarmed Brotherton Field, firmly astride the La Fayette Road. Restoring the integrity of the Union line in this sector of the field now became William Rosecrans's urgent priority.

39 OR 30, pt. 1, 474.

Chapter Twenty-Three

Shoring up the Center:

Saturday, September 19: 5:30 p.m. to 7:00 p.m.

Once William Rosecrans established his new headquarters at the Widow Glenn's, the place became a focal point of activity. From there, "little could be seen of the fighting lines," admitted Charles Kirk of the 15th Pennsylvania Cavalry, but it was ideally situated to most of the action. "The smoke and dust of the conflict and bursting of shells could be plainly seen above the trees. Here the General, with a common blue overcoat about his shoulders and a light colored felt hat on his head, paced up and down, glass in hand, directing his troops and receiving reports." A constant flow of "officers and orderlies" brought news of the fight, and carried orders back to the lines. More "messages flashed over the field telegraph," remembered Kirk. "It was a scene of great interest and intensity."[1]

Excitable at the best of times, Rosecrans was on edge, as an incident with that field telegraph demonstrated. The operator, 18-year-old Jesse Bunnell, saw a lot of the Army of the Cumberland's commander, "who, appreciating . . . the importance of the field wire and its uninterrupted efficiency, gave much attention to it." Bunnell set up his apparatus "on a little table at one end of the porch in front of that memorable Widow Glenn's house . . . Rosecrans

---

stationed himself at the other end of the porch." Because of the "lack of moisture," Bunnell had trouble finding a suitable ground for the wire until he hit upon the idea of "running it down into [the Widow Glenn's] well." This did the trick, and Bunnell kept the wires humming with traffic until without warning his connection went down. The fault lay with some of those cavalrymen from the 15th Pennsylvania, who flocked to the well to "cool their parched throats." One of the buckets hauled up Bunnell's ground wire. When Rosecrans demanded to know why the telegraph had stopped working, Bunnell pointed out the offending troopers. "General Rosecrans became greatly excited. He savagely ordered the cavalrymen to replace 'that wire' and to leave 'that well.'" Within a short time communications were restored.[2]

Rosecrans had spent much of the day feeding troops into the battle as they arrived, intent on filling the gap between George Thomas's and Thomas Crittenden's corps lines. The Union army leader had thus far committed no fewer than five of his 10 divisions to that task, and for most of the fight the gap had gone unexploited by the enemy. In the waning afternoon Confederate infantry, more through luck than by design, finally established a foothold squarely between the two halves of the Union army. For Rosecrans, sealing the breach was now his most urgent mission. But where were the troops to do so?

Rosecrans had only one fresh force at hand. Major General James S. Negley's division of the XIV Corps was still watching the crossing farther south at Glass Mill. The only excitement in that sector had come earlier that morning when John C. Breckinridge's Rebels launched a foray across the creek and provoked a sharp artillery duel. The diversion was easily repulsed. By mid-afternoon quiet had once again returned to Glass Mill. The bulk of the Union army's trains, meanwhile, had passed to the north and were out of any immediate danger. Rosecrans ordered Negley to leave a brigade behind as a rear guard and join the rest of the army. Now, at what was perhaps the most critical point of the day's fight, Negley and his other two brigades were approaching the Widow Glenn's.

James Scott Negley, one of Pittsburgh's leading sons, had strong military credentials for a citizen soldier of that era. After graduating from the Western University of Pennsylvania, he joined the local militia and served throughout

<hr>

2   Jesse H. Bunnell, "General Thomas and the Telegraph Operator," in Tim Goff, ed., *Under Both Flags: Personal Stories of Sacrifice and Struggle During the Civil War* (The Lyons Press, 2003), 451-452.

the Mexican War. He remained in the militia after returning home and by the time the Civil War erupted was a brigadier general in the state forces. In October 1861, he was commissioned brigadier general of U.S. Volunteers and served in Kentucky and Tennessee for the next two years. When Confederate Gen. Braxton Bragg invaded Kentucky in the fall of 1862, Negley successfully defended Nashville from various Rebel probes. He and his division won acclaim for their gallant stand at Stones River at the end of the year. The battle also earned Negley his promotion to major general after Rosecrans made a personal recommendation on his behalf.[3]

Negley was the senior division commander in Thomas's XIV Corps, and was trusted by both Rosecrans and Thomas. It was Negley's division that led the corps's advance on La Fayette during the second week of September and very nearly came to grief in McLemore's Cove on September 10-11. Negley escaped disaster, but the strain of the moment told on him. On the night of the 12th he sought out Surgeon R. G. Bogue, the division's medical director, who diagnosed the general with diarrhea and gave him medicine. His condition failed to improve, and by September 15 Negley was too sick to move. He spent that day and the next in bed. Fortunately, his division remained stationary on both days waiting for other Federal units to catch up. September 17, however, required a march and Negley attempted to return to duty. He rode a horse, but as a precaution an ambulance trailed him wherever he went. Even simple horseback riding at a leisurely pace exhausted him. Nevertheless, when his division marched once more on the 18th, Negley was back in the saddle. He was also up most of that night seeing to various details of his command and trying to sort out the confusion of replacing Palmer's men at Glass Mill.

At 3:30 p.m. on September 19, when he received an order from Rosecrans "to withdraw my command [from Glass Mill] and push forward as rapidly as possible to the support of Major General Thomas," Negley promptly responded. Two of his brigades under Cols. Timothy R. Stanley and William Sirwell were in reserve and could move at once. Brigadier General John Beatty's men, however, were picketing West Chickamauga Creek and in contact with Rebel skirmishers; they would need more time to disengage.[4]

---

3 Heidler and Heidler, *Encyclopedia of the American Civil War*, vol. 3, 1403-1404. Today, Western University is the University of Pittsburgh.

4 *OR* 30, pt. 1, 329.

Rumors coursed through Negley's ranks. His troops knew the climactic battle for control of Chattanooga was underway and that Rebel reinforcements were being rushed in from other parts of the Confederacy. Lieutenant Robert Dilworth in Company I, 21st Ohio, part of Sirwell's brigade, noted that morning that "some of our forces captured a rebel courier with a dispatch to [General Joseph E.] Johns[t]on to report to Chattanooga as soon as possible. Jeff Davis has ordered Bragg to retake Chattanooga at all hazards." Still, mused Dilworth, "If we have the amount of troops here which has been reported I think we have enough to whip old Bragg's forces out of Georgia." Dilworth was a rare optimist; most Federals believed they were facing more than 100,000 Rebels, including most of Robert E. Lee's men, and so were badly outnumbered.[5]

Moving up the Dry Valley Road, Negley estimated he had about three miles to march. His men moved quickly, though most of his units paused at Crawfish Spring to drink and fill their canteens. Given the general scarcity of water, Negley allowed the break, though to members of the 37th Indiana, Sirwell's brigade, he did seem "vexed at the deliberation of some of the men when . . . filling their canteens." The 37th had been heavily engaged at Stones River and its men were no strangers to combat. Still, it was disconcerting to many to view the wake of a major battle. "We moved forward rapidly and soon began to meet wounded men and stragglers—many were badly wounded and many were only scared—stampeded," recalled the regiment's historian. So many stragglers amid the wounded suggested to these veterans that things were not going well at the front.[6]

Negley's column reached Rosecrans's headquarters at the Widow Glenn's about 4:30 p.m. Just as the head reached the house it crested a ridge overlooking the battlefield. Members of the 78th Pennsylvania, also in Sirwell's brigade, recorded the scene as "a panorama of war on a grand scale. The battle was raging fiercely in the forest along the Chickamauga; batteries of artillery and brigades of infantry were moving on double quick to the support of our forces on the battle lines. [W]e could see the smoke of battle rising above the trees, almost shutting out our view of the forest, while the roar of artillery and the

---

5 Entry for September 19, Robert S. Dilworth Journal, OHS.

6 George H. Puntenney, *History of the Thirty-Seventh Regiment of Indiana Infantry Volunteers: Its Organization, Campaigns, and Battles-Sept., '61-Oct., '64.* (Jacksonian Book and Job Department, 1896), 54.

rattle of musketry was deafening." The Pennsylvanians were watching Jefferson Davis's and Tom Wood's divisions wage their desperate struggle around the Viniard farm. Out of the woods "pour[ed] thousands of wounded soldiers and stragglers. It was a sight never to be forgotten."[7]

As far as Rosecrans was concerned, Negley arrived in the nick of time. The army commander ordered him to take his two brigades, locate General Thomas, and attack into the teeth of the Confederate advance at Brotherton Field and restore the Union line. Stanley's brigade led the column with the 11th Michigan in the van. A short distance beyond, the Wolverines spotted General Rosecrans a few rods north of the Glenn cabin observing the fight. As each company of the 11th passed the commanding general, its members raised their rifles in salute, a gesture smartly returned by a thankful Rosecrans. "Make it warm for them, Michigan boys," Rosecrans called, provoking cheers in response. James Martin of Company H recalled that Rosecrans "told us if we had a fight with the Rebels to give them fits." Once past the memorable meeting point Stanley's men moved out into South Dyer Field and formed a line of battle facing east. Sirwell's brigade was right behind them. The Hoosiers of the 37th Indiana did not get cheering words from Rosecrans, but some of them exchanged words with a wounded Federal heading for the rear. When asked how the fight was going, he replied, "well, it is about nip and tuck and d——d if I ain't afraid that tuck has the best of it." With this unsettling observation ringing in their ears, the Indiana men advanced into the field and deployed with the rest of Sirwell's troops on Stanley's right.[8]

George Thomas was also fretting about the threat to the army's center and bedeviled by the same question: where could he find more men? Rosecrans looked south and found Negley, but Thomas turned his eyes in the opposite direction. By mid-afternoon, both John Brannan's and Absalom Baird's divisions of his XIV Corps had been out of action for several hours, recovering from their bloody morning ordeal. These six brigades were in line astride the Reed's Bridge Road on a ridge about a half mile east of the La Fayette Road.

7　J. T. Gibson, *History of the Seventy-Eighth Pennsylvania Volunteer Infantry* (Pittsburg Printing Company, 1905), 97.

8　Charles E. Belknap, *History of the Michigan Organizations at Chickamauga, Chattanooga, and Missionary Ridge, 1863* (Robert Smith Printing Company, 1897), 113; "Dear Parents" October 24, 1863, James A. Martin Letters, Bentley Historical Library; Puntenney, *Thirty-Seventh Regiment of Indiana Infantry Volunteers*, 54.

After their heavy combat the battle progressed southward and things quieted down on their front.

At 3:00 p.m., Thomas ordered Brannan to leave John Croxton's brigade in line on Baird's right and march his other two brigades south. Croxton's large brigade had suffered heavily in the morning fight, the others less so, making them the obvious choice for renewed action. With 2,400 of his men in tow, Brannan moved quickly to comply.[9]

Initially, Thomas seemed uncertain about where to commit these reinforcements. Colonel John Connell, who led one of Brannan's brigades, reported he was directed only to move to the rear some distance, "about 1 mile from the hospital." The divisional hospital was at Cloud Church on the La Fayette Road, which placed the location of Connell's stopping place somewhere in Kelly Field, where his and Col. Ferdinand Van Derveer's troops waited for further instructions. Orders passed down the line for the men to pile their blankets and knapsacks "so as to give the men freer action." Connell had a brief and unsatisfying discussion with Brannan, who in turn had just spoken to Thomas. "It was all sixes and sevens," said Brannan, "adding, 'General Thomas knows no more of any plan . . . than we do.'" The divisional commander added a note of reassurance: "I think all we will do this evening will be to move for position for the opening in the morning."[10]

By about 4:00 p.m. the picture was becoming clearer. Thomas knew he had to help both Reynolds and Palmer. He also knew that drawing off Brannan would leave a significant gap in his front between Baird and General Johnson's division of Alexander McCook's XX Corps, which was in line just west of the Winfrey farmstead. Accordingly, Thomas ordered Brannan to retrieve Croxton's brigade and move with his entire division (three brigades) to join Reynolds. Thomas also directed Baird to leave Colonel King's battered brigade of Regulars behind to watch the Reed's Bridge Road while the rest of his First Division moved southeast through the woods to find and connect with Johnson's right. By 4:30 p.m., Thomas had virtually his entire left flank in motion.[11]

9   OR 30, pt. 1, 401.

10 Ibid., 409; Charles T. DeVelling, *History of the Seventeenth Regiment, First Brigade, Third Division, Fourteenth Corps, Army of the Cumberland, War of the Rebellion* (E. R. Sullivan, Printer and Binder, 1880), 102.

11 OR 30, pt. 1, 250.

Brannan's division marched toward what seemed to be the point of greater danger. Croxton's five regiments arrived and, passing the other two brigades, took the lead south along the Glenn-Kelly Road. As they did so, the swell of cannon fire thundering to repulse Bate's Rebels in Poe Field must have been audible, even above the general racket of the battlefield. Neither Croxton nor Brannan had much of an idea of where they were needed, but it seemed obvious they weren't simply repositioning for tomorrow's fight. Today's battle was still very much alive.

Though neither Rosecrans nor Thomas knew it, one more Federal force was moving to help contain the breach. Colonel Charles Harker's four regiments were still moving cautiously north along the corridor of the La Fayette Road below Brotherton Field. As noted earlier, after witnessing large numbers of Confederates moving across the road and, apparently, directly into the unprotected Federal rear, division commander Tom Wood had reoriented Harker's men and ordered them northward a few minutes before 4:00 p.m.

Harker's lone brigade set off on what looked to be a dangerous mission, attacking unsupported into an unknown number of Rebels. Harker was only 28, but had confidence in both himself and his men. Born in New Jersey and orphaned young, he managed to secure an appointment to West Point and graduate 16th in a class of 27 in 1858. In late 1861, he accepted an appointment as colonel of the forming 65th Ohio and by 1862 was in command of a brigade. Harker earned a solid reputation for his performance at Stones River, where General Rosecrans personally ordered him and his men to rush to the defense of the Nashville Pike on the morning of December 31, 1862. His command suffered a staggering 539 casualties but earned Rosecrans's thanks and approval. Harker was recommended for a star soon after, though by September 1863 Congress had yet to act on that promotion.[12]

Three of Harker's regiments were veterans of that earlier action. His fourth, Col. Emerson Opdyke's 125th Ohio, had yet to face a stand-up fight despite a year's service. Fortunately for these Buckeyes, their colonel had learned his trade as a junior officer in the 41st Ohio under William B. Hazen; they would not disappoint now.

As will be recalled, Harker first deployed facing west and just north of the Viniard Farm. He did so alongside Buell's brigade and behind Hans Heg's

---

12 Warner, *Generals in Blue*, 207; James B. Fry, *Official Register of the Officers and Cadets of the U.S. Military Academy, West Point, New York* (John F. Baldwin, Printer, 1858), 7.

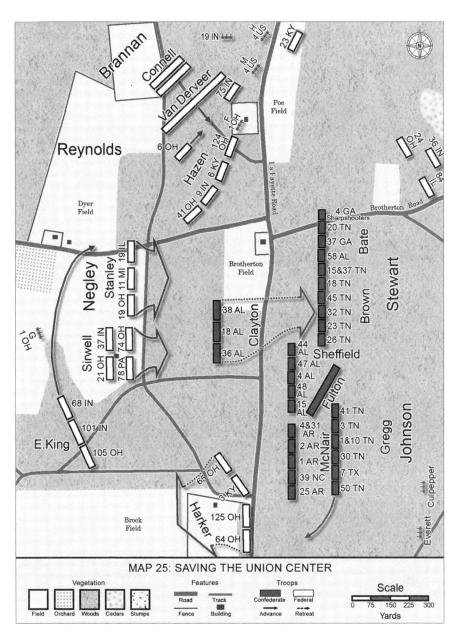

MAP 25: SAVING THE UNION CENTER

troops who were engaged in the woods to the east. The 125th Ohio was on the
right and the 64th Ohio just to their south on their left, with the 3rd Kentucky
and 65th Ohio in the same order behind them. "About this time" Harker noted,
"there was very great confusion among the troops which had been engaged, and
no one seemed to have any definite idea of our own lines or the position of the

enemy." When Confederates swarmed across the La Fayette Road to the north, Harker's plans were changed. Wood ordered him to move northward in response.[13]

Initially, Harker's line formed something of a semicircle as the 125th Ohio and 64th Ohio kept pushing east while Harker threw the 3rd Kentucky and 65th Ohio out at an angle to the northeast. This proved an impossible formation to control, especially after the Kentuckians made several changes of front in response to what seemed to be enemy threats from both the right and left. Then they found Rebels. The 65th Ohio got the worst of things in the initial encounter. Lieutenant Wilbur F. Hinman of Company E recalled a confusing advance. Shorter evergreens fringed the edge of the woods here, a dense thicket hard to push through and which limited visibility. Hinman and his fellow Buckeyes had picked their way about 100 yards when "we received from the enemy a murderous volley" that dropped four officers and "many excellent soldiers." The men were trying to adjust to the frontal fire when a flanking threat developed. The 3rd Kentucky and 65th changed front to the rear to face north, a move that pulled them west back across the La Fayette Road. The 65th Ohio's commander, Lt. Col. Horatio Whitbeck, fell wounded here, leaving Maj. Samuel Brown in command.[14]

This reorientation left the brigade spread out over a considerable distance, straddling the La Fayette Road with at least part of the command still in the woods. In order to facilitate command control, Harker sent word to Opdyke, the next ranking Colonel, to act as a wing commander by taking charge of both his own regiment and the 64th east of the road. Harker recalled the fighting here as severe, but the Rebels had by now lost most of their cohesion and aside from the 65th's unfortunate casualties, the action produced more noise than damage. The 125th Ohio, for example, reported only one sergeant and 11 privates as wounded for the entire day.[15]

It is impossible to determine with precision which Confederate troops Harker engaged. It is nearly certain most of the Rebels hailed from John Gregg's brigade (by now badly scattered), but Lieutenant Hinman of the 65th

---

13 OR 30, pt. 1, 691; See Chapter 17 for a description of Harker's arrival on the field.

14 Hinman, *The Sherman Brigade*, 420.

15 OR 30, pt. 1, 692; Entry for September 19, E. G. Whitesides Diary, AHEC. Despite the newness of his regiment, Opdyke was in command of Harker's left wing because he was the senior regimental commander in the brigade and a veteran of earlier service under Hazen.

Ohio also reported taking prisoners from James Longstreet's Corps. The new arrivals were distinctive in their new uniforms, observed Hinman, as opposed to the "go-as-you-please-manner" found in the Army of Tennessee, where "every imaginable variety of garments and head-covering" was the rule. The Army of Northern Virginia troops must have been Texans from Jerome Robertson's command. Soldiers from Evander McNair's brigade were also in the vicinity, and part of Colonel Coleman's regiment had made a foray into East Viniard Field a short time earlier. Any of these troops could have resisted Harker's movement.[16]

If Harker had been able to discern the opposition he potentially faced, he likely would have halted or even fallen back. The distance between the Log School (where Harker first deployed) and the southern edge of Brotherton Field was less than 1,000 yards. By 4:30 p.m., the Rebels swarming in and around Brotherton Field numbered several thousand, and had just routed Joe Reynolds's scratched-together line of blue. These Southern troops included Fulton's four Tennessee regiments, plus two of Gregg's, Clayton's and Sheffield's (now Oates's) seven Alabama regiments, Brown's Tennesseans, and two regiments under Bate. Even after suffering sizable casualties and large numbers of stragglers, this was a daunting enemy force.

Harker, of course, had no way of knowing what he faced, but he did possess a significant advantage that had trumped all others that September 19: position. He and his brigade were advancing into the flank and rear of all these Confederate commands. Uncertainty was not confined to the Union troops this day, and if anything was an even greater factor among the Confederates.

Harker's advance, coupled with Negley's and Brannan's approach, conspired to create a three-pronged Union counterstroke aimed directly at the expanding crisis in the Union center. It wasn't planned. None of the three prongs knew the others were there. Independent decisions by several Union commanders on different parts of the field, however, had aligned to create a spontaneous harmony of concerted action right where it was needed most. It was not long before the Confederates became aware of all three of these developing threats, with the Federals seemingly materializing out of nowhere

---

16 Hinman, *The Sherman Brigade*, 423. It was about this time that the 64th Ohio had its encounter with Confederate brigadier John Gregg that left him badly wounded and rendered his brigade leaderless at a most inopportune time for the Rebels engaged in and around Viniard Field. See Chapter 17 for details on Gregg's wounding.

from several directions at once. Precipitate retreat became the only viable Rebel option—especially since the various brigades in question lacked concerted command of their own.

Harker's appearance initiated this sequence of retreat. The Federals first appeared on the "left and rear" of the 3rd and 41st Tennessee, the two regiments of Gregg's brigade that had tagged along with Fulton's men. Colonel Calvin Walker of the 3rd Tennessee was now commanding both units in the absence of more senior leadership. The Union advance prompted Walker to order the regiments back east across the La Fayette Road. He also instructed Lt. Col. James Tillman of the 41st Tennessee to find Fulton and alert him to the new threat.[17]

When Colonel Tillman of the 41st rode up and reported that "the enemy would soon be in my rear," recalled Fulton, he received the report with outright skepticism. The senior colonel was still under the impression that Johnson's divisional line was intact. "Our lines were connected on our left and . . . a flank or rear movement could not, therefore, be made by the enemy," he insisted. To Fulton's horror, however, Tillman informed his brigade commander that only two regiments of Gregg's brigade had kept up and now, on Col. Calvin Walker's order, they were gone as well. The disbelieving Fulton trotted over to see for himself, and got an eyeful when he did. He watched in stunned disbelief as the Federal 3rd Kentucky appeared behind the 17th Tennessee, and he "heard distinctly the commands 'halt,' 'front,' and immediately their fire was pouring on our flank and rear. Here," admitted Fulton, "a general stampede ensued."[18]

The warning simply arrived too late, and the enemy was moving too quickly. "The movement of the enemy . . . was so prompt," reported division commander Bushrod Johnson, "that they penetrated our line on the left of [Fulton's] line . . . and fired a volley into its rear" before the Rebels could react. Years later, Capt. William Harder of the 23rd Tennessee recalled speculating with his commanding officer, Col. Robert H. Keeble, about how vulnerable the brigade's left had become. "I asked [the] Colonel if he had seen our left was not supported . . . remarking that if any federal officer had the daring . . . he with a few men might put our whole brigade in disorder." Charles Harker was instilled with just such daring, and his move triggered a scramble to the rear. Johnson

17 James Van Eldik, *From the Flame of Battle to the Fiery Cross: The 3rd Tennessee Infantry* (Yucca Tree Press, 2001), 170.

18 *OR* 30, pt. 2, 474.

noted that Fulton's "brigade now moved by one impulse to the right and fell back to the east of the road . . . leaving 11 officers . . . 60 men, and the captured battery in the hands of the enemy."[19]

With Fulton's men "stampeding," other troops in the vicinity could not help but take notice. Colonel Oates of the 15th Alabama witnessed the rout. Also bereft of orders and unable to find anyone to tell him what to do, Oates had faced his four Alabama regiments west and parked them in Brotherton Field. His experience mimicked Fulton's. Drawn by the activity to his south, Oates ordered the 15th to change front, but the Federals advanced too quickly. A Union volley ripped into the Alabama flank, killing two men and wounding several others. Oates ordered a retreat. "As soon as the movement fairly began," recalled the infuriated officer, "I saw that a panic had seized the command. I gave the order to halt at the road and for the officers . . . to shoot any man who crossed it without orders." Fortunately for Oates and his men, there were far more Rebels to pursue than Harker had Yankees, and Oates's Alabamians managed to regroup short of fratricidal gunplay. From there, the brigade fell back farther east in a more organized fashion, with Oates ordering out two companies of skirmishers from each unit to try and distract Harker from inflicting any further damage.[20]

In news that would have certainly surprised Oates, Harker also had retreating on his mind. Once in Brotherton Field, the Union brigadier realized he stumbled into a viper's nest of Rebels, routing two brigades with just the 3rd Kentucky and 65th Ohio. His men claimed the capture of 204 Confederates, but both Union regiments had taken punishment and were a bit disorganized. Every mounted officer save one was dismounted, a half-dozen officers of the 3rd Kentucky had been killed or wounded along with "a great many of the enlisted men." Thus far Harker's luck could be attributed to surprise, but the Confederates were now regrouping and outnumbered him several times over. Even without Oates's skirmishers harrying him along, Harker decided to fall back to the southern edge of the field, pull in Colonel Opdyke and his other two regiments, and from there fall back to rejoin the division.[21]

---

19 OR 30, pt. 2, 455; Harder Reminiscences, TSLA. Harder had a knack for inserting himself into the middle of every incident, and making himself the hero, but in general his recollections ring true. OR 30, pt. 2, 455. The "captured battery" refers to the gun from the 19th Indiana.

20 Oates, *The War Between the Union and the Confederacy*, 254-255.

21 OR 30, pt. 1, 692.

Despite his departure, Harker's movement had undermined the entire Confederate position around Brotherton Field. Not only were Bushrod Johnson and Oates retreating, but now Henry Clayton and that portion of William Bate's command that had not followed its brigadier into Poe Field were left feeling quite unsettled.

Clayton's three regiments had pushed the farthest west after unraveling the Union line in Brotherton Field. Images of running Yanks had whipped up excitement among Clayton's men to a fever pitch, and they couldn't be recalled. "We . . . pursued the flying enemy in a mad, wild, reckless charge," recounted Capt. Ben Posey of the 36th Alabama. "Only once were we momentarily checked" when officers tried to regain control of the command, explained Posey, but "a few stepped to the front and urged on the charge, which was again renewed."[22]

By Clayton's estimate, the brigade moved about half a mile in advance of any other Confederates, passing over Brotherton Field and through the belt of timber separating the Brotherton farm from South Dyer Field before finally halting there just beyond the tree line. Winded and disorganized, the Alabamians realized their deep thrust had outstripped any support, and as Posey noted, "to go further placed us in imminent danger of being ourselves captured." In fact, the charge had significantly disrupted Clayton's regiments. Captain Posey ordered Companies A and K to halt "in a turnpike" (the Glenn-Kelly Road) bordering the west side of the woods, but could not find the rest of his regiment. Lieutenant Colonel Augustus R. Lankford, commanding the 38th Alabama, had a similar problem. Finding Posey in the road, he ordered the captain to wait while he rode to locate his own regiment, intending to bring the 38th into line alongside Companies A and K. Lankford returned a few minutes later to announce he could not locate his men, either. In fact, the entire brigade was in disarray. Major Peter Hunley of the 18th Alabama reported that "after the route of the enemy, the regiment being a good deal scattered, the pursuit was somewhat in confusion." Hunley also noted that, by the time everyone halted, parts of both the 36th and 38th regiments were mixed in with his command.[23]

---

22 Ben Lane, "Clayton's Brigade at Chickamauga," *Mobile Register Reader and Advertiser*, October 23, 1863. Again, 'Ben Lane' was Posey's pen name.

23 Ibid.; *OR* 30, pt. 2, 405.

Henry Clayton, no stranger to hard-fought battlefields, had a problem. His regiments were disorganized and too far advanced for their own good, and he knew it. The sun was dipping quickly on the western horizon, and Federals were visible from several points on the compass. Worse yet, no other Rebel commands were within sight or known to be operating nearby. He was in no shape to deliver a strong assault, withstand a counterattack, or stand firm and wait for help to arrive since none was forthcoming. Clayton was contemplating what to do when a report reached him that "the enemy was advancing in strong force from the right." Just moments later, Clayton's assistant-adjutant general, Capt. J. M. Macon, reined in his mount. Macon's message, transmitted from yet another staff officer Macon did not recognize, informed Clayton that Union cavalry was menacing his left. The force on the right, part of Brannan's division, was moving into the northern end of Dyer Field. The Union "cavalry" on the left was either a reference to Harker's men or part of John Wilder's mounted infantry command. Back by the Widow Glenn cabin, some of Negley's Federals had also seen mounted skirmishers riding into the woods east of them, men who almost certainly belonged to Wilder's command. The threat of having both flanks turned at once was enough to convince Clayton to retreat, and he ordered his three regiments to fall back. The Alabamians withdrew nearly a mile before coming to rest in the woods east of the La Fayette Road, the same spot they first engaged in combat earlier that day.[24]

Harker's success in disrupting the Confederate thrust into the gap between the Union corps wings cost his command significant losses during his engagement with Fulton and Oates. The appearance of John Brannan's Federals, however, was in and of itself enough to convince the remaining Confederates to fall back without further bloodshed. John Croxton's five regiments at the head of Brannan's column met General Reynolds, who was still trying to organize a defense in the area of Poe Field. Bate's Rebels had already been repulsed by the Union artillery, but Reynolds was acutely aware that Clayton's Confederates were "pushing still further to our right and rear." Accordingly, Reynolds commandeered Croxton and, with his brigade as the nucleus, "formed a double line of some ten or twelve regiments" facing generally south. Then, with Croxton leading, he ordered the whole force, not unlike a giant gate studded with bayonets, "to swing round on the left flank as a

24 *OR* 30, pt. 2, 402.

South Dyer Field, from Negley's position, looking east. The trees in the distance are the belt of timber separating Brotherton and South Dyer Fields. Clayton's Alabama troops emerged from that tree line, only to find themselves unsupported and threatened from the front and flanks. When Negley's men advanced down the slope, they found that the Rebels were gone.

Author Photograph

pivot. Our rear," concluded Reynolds with evident satisfaction, was "thus entirely cleared of the enemy."[25]

Unbeknownst to Reynolds, Clayton had already ordered a retreat, so the only Rebels encountered by Croxton's sweep were stragglers and wounded men. None of Brannan's troops recalled any serious fighting here. Once the sweep ended, the men set up camp (such as it was) in north Dyer Field. With darkness falling, Brannan pulled his entire division back into this field, facing generally south. The regimental history of the 82nd Indiana, part of Connell's brigade, lamented the fact that they no longer had their blankets with them: "We arrived there about dark and camped in an open field, in which there was a straw stack. It was a very chilly evening; the men were without blankets, having left them where they prepared to enter the battle in the morning, the ground of which was now occupied by the enemy."[26]

Meanwhile, James Negley deployed his command according to Rosecrans's instructions. He remained unaware of either Brannan's or Harker's offensive

25 Ibid., pt. 1, 441.

26 Hunter, *Eighty-Second Indiana*, 63.

actions. Negley's troops formed in line in south Dyer Field facing east, while atop the ridge behind the infantry two of Negley's artillery batteries prepared to go into action. The high ground here was a perfect artillery platform, and in fact would become the site of Rosecrans's headquarters the next day because of the excellent panorama it offered. Now, in the late afternoon of September 19, a dozen Union guns unlimbered here to support the expected attack. With his line ready, Negley sent word to Rosecrans that he could not find General Thomas, but that he had located the Rebels. Should he hold or advance? His courier returned just a few minutes later with Rosecrans's instructions: "That is right, fight there, right there, push them hard."[27]

Everyone expected to a hard engagement. The sense of urgency was palpable, and the crisis seemed at hand. With only six regiments totaling 2,450 bayonets, Negley must have wondered if he and his men were being sacrificed to buy time for additional reinforcements. If he could have waited, the other four regiments of Beatty's brigade and the 74th Ohio, then detailed as a train guard, might have joined his attack. However, there was no reason to expect the Rebels to resist the opportunity to press their advantage immediately, and so no time to wait for the rest of the division.[28]

When Negley finally charged, however, it proved anticlimactic. In the ranks of the 78th Pennsylvania, J. T. Gibson recorded what happened next. "We seemed to be entering the center of the fiercest conflict," he recorded, "and we fully expected to bear the brunt of the battle that evening. Instead of attacking our front . . . as expected," he added, "the enemy seemed to fall back." Lieutenant Colonel Ward, his 37th Indiana following the 78th Pennsylvania in support, wrote that "it appeared that we would be very heavily engaged but, as we rapidly advanced, the roar of musketry in our front suddenly ceased. We gained and occupied the position to which we were ordered without firing a gun and with only one man wounded."[29]

Resistance abruptly collapsed in front of Stanley's brigade as well. Lieutenant John Young of the 19th Illinois dismissed the fight as no more than "severe skirmishing," although many did not think the fighting rose to even that level. In the front rank, the 11th Michigan charged, "driving the Rebels before

---

27 Entry for September 19, 1863, Eben Sturges Diary and Letters, AHEC; OR 30, pt. 1, 347.

28 Powell, "Numbers and Losses" CCNMP.

29 Gibson, *History of the Seventy-Eighth Pennsylvania*, 97-98; Ward Journal, DePauw University, 138.

them like chaff before the wind." Despite the ominous gloom of the smoky woods, strewn with the dead and wounded from earlier fighting, the danger proved largely illusory. It is doubtful that General Clayton was even aware of Negley's presence because the Confederate brigadier only mentioned in his report the threat to his flanks and not to his front, and that the Rebels were already falling back (before Negley had been ordered into action).[30]

Negley, however, was uneasy about his new position. He had been thrust into a situation without any real understanding of the larger picture and felt isolated. Once his men halted, he sent word back to Rosecrans that he could not locate friendly troops to his left or to his right. As far as he could tell, his six regiments were holding a forward position alone. Thousands of troops under Brannan and Reynolds were close by, but they were no more aware of Negley's presence than he was of theirs. These other two Union columns were busy reforming troops in Poe and Dyer fields a few hundred yards farther north, while Davis, Wood, and Wilder were regrouping west of the Viniard farm an equal distance to the south.[31]

Negley halted both his brigades inside the west edge of the woods separating Dyer and Brotherton fields, where his men also settled in for a very uncomfortable night. Inside the tree line, the men "threw up a slight breastworks of logs, rails and trash," scribbled one man in his diary. Due to the proximity of the enemy, fires were prohibited. The night was cold, and some of these men were also short of blankets after having been forced to leave their packs behind at Davis's Crossroads a week earlier. Wounded men on both sides littered the ground all around them, their cries producing a low chorus of pain and misery throughout the night.[32]

John Beatty's brigade never caught up to the rest of the division. Negley had dispatched Maj. James A. Lowrie to bring up Beatty's command. Once with Beatty, however, Lowrie could not relocate Negley after that general advanced into the gap. Instead, he sought Rosecrans and was asking the commanding general about what to do when Negley himself rode up. Beatty's men were still a mile or more short of the field and had left their picket lines in place at the ford

30 J. Henry Haynie, *The Nineteenth Illinois: A Memoir of a Regiment of Volunteer Infantry Famous in the Civil War of Fifty Years Ago for its Drill, Bravery, and Distinguished Services* (M.A. Donahue, 1912), 238-239; Belknap, *History of the Michigan Organizations*, 113.

31 *OR* 30, pt. 1, 329.

32 Entry for September 19, 1863, James Fenton Diary, ALPL.

near Glass Mill until well after dark. Negley elected to put the brigade in reserve near the Osborn house about a quarter of a mile south of the Widow Glenn's. Having done all he could do, Negley returned to the ridge where his cannon rested overlooking his infantry line and waited for further orders and dawn.[33]

The evening would not pass quietly. Just as Negley's men were settling in, fighting erupted in the woods about a mile off their left-front. Stabs of flickering musket discharges and the deep booms of artillery split the early evening darkness. The fighting lasted by some accounts an hour or more, but seemed to come no closer. Once again uncertainty spiked within the Federal ranks. Night attacks were rare and this was more than a skirmish-line squabble. Indeed, it was a sustained combat. What Negley and the other Federals did not realize was that Confederate Maj. Gen. Patrick R. Cleburne's division had reached the field.

33 *OR* 30, pt. 1, 367.

Chapter Twenty-Four

Return to Winfrey Field:

Saturday, September 19: 3:30 p.m. to 9:00 p.m.

W**hile** the action raged that afternoon across the Brock and Viniard farmsteads, the northern end of the battlefield remained quiet. The main Winfrey Field action ended about noon, leaving in its wake only skirmishing between Federals of Richard Johnson's division and George Dibrell's Southern cavalrymen at the north end of the battlefield. That lull would not last.

Shortly after 3:00 p.m., Lt. Gen. Leonidas Polk ordered Brig. Gen. St. John Liddell's division back into the fight. Polk's call came in response to the collapse of Frank Cheatham's divisional line at 2:30 p.m., assailed by Brig. Gen. Richard Johnson's and Maj. Gen. John Palmer's Yankees. When George Maney's brigade was outflanked and routed by Brig. Gen. August Willich's and Col. Philemon Baldwin's Federal brigades, Polk had no recourse but to call upon the men of Maj. Gen. W. H. T. Walker's Reserve Corps a second time. He also notified General Bragg that more support was needed in his sector.[1]

Fortunately for the Confederate Right Wing, the Federals broke off after only a limited pursuit of Cheatham, giving Liddell ample time to get his men up and deployed. Liddell's two brigades had been resting in the vicinity of the Youngblood farm near the Jay's Mill Road. Liddell's formations had each lost

---

1   See Chapter 14.

about one-quarter of their combat strength in the morning's fight, and now numbered between 2,500 and 3,000 officers and men. Polk instructed Liddell to move his brigades north and align them on Cheatham's right, thinking that perhaps the Federals could be flanked in turn. That had, after all, been the pattern of the day's fighting. Deploying as ordered, however, proved more difficult than anticipated because Cheatham's men had come to rest in a rather haphazard manner facing generally northwest. As a result, Liddell had some trouble locating Cheatham's flank. According to Liddell, his new line "formed an obtuse angle" with Cheatham's front.[2]

Colonel Daniel Govan's brigade occupied Liddell's right, with Brig. Gen. Edward Walthall's Mississippians on Govan's left providing the connection to Cheatham. Once the men were in position about 3:30 p.m., Liddell ordered his division to advance.

Govan and Walthall were crossing familiar ground, albeit from a different direction. Four and a half hours earlier, this same battle line swept across Winfrey Field from south to north to plunge into the woods beyond. That earlier attack mauled Absalom Baird's Union division, nearly routed the three brigades of Scribner, Starkweather, and King, and captured most of the division's guns and many prisoners. Liddell's Rebels also left Winfrey Field and the surrounding timber carpeted with their own dead and wounded, intertwined with stricken Yankees. Subsequent fighting saw this same terrain change hands several times. Most recently it had been held by Johnson's Federals. Now it was a no-man's land, abandoned when Johnson's line fell back to the field's western edge. Walthall's five Mississippi regiments faced the field itself, while Govan's Arkansans moved through the trees to the north, where they had overrun King and Starkweather. This time, however, the tactical situation was much different. That morning Liddell's attack had fallen upon the flank of an unsuspecting Union line; now, his men faced a frontal assault against a prepared foe in Winfrey Field.

After the rout of Cheatham's Confederates, General Johnson pulled his three Union brigades back into a compact line along the west side of the Winfrey farm, reverting to the standard deployment of two regiments up and two back. Colonel Joseph Dodge's brigade held the farmyard and extended perhaps 100 yards to the south. August Willich's four regiments aligned along

---

2 OR 30, pt. 2, 252.

the fence on the west side of the field, the 49th Ohio and 89th Illinois in front, and the 15th Ohio and 32nd Indiana in support. Colonel Philemon P. Baldwin's men held the left. Baldwin's 1st Ohio anchored the northwest corner of the field, connecting to their fellow Buckeyes in the 49th, while the 5th Kentucky extended the front up into the remnants of Van Pelt's ruined Battery A, 1st Michigan Light Artillery, which had been repeatedly overrun in the morning's action. The 93rd Ohio and 6th Indiana were in support. The six cannon of Capt. Peter Simonson's 5th Indiana battery extended Baldwin's left so its fire could rake any Rebel line entering the field. Goodspeed's Battery A, 1st Ohio, was on Willich's right behind the support line, while the 20th Ohio battery stood to arms behind Dodge's center. Most of the Yankee infantry made some effort to augment their defenses. When Capt. Henry Richards of the 93rd Ohio returned to the regiment with a re-supply of ammunition, he discovered that "during my absence our regiment made temporary breastworks of logs." If attacked frontally, Johnson's line was likely to withstand virtually any assault. With only 800 yards of frontage, however, the position was in danger of being turned from the north. Even worse, no other Federals were close enough to help in case that threat materialized.[3]

Johnson and his brigade commanders understood their vulnerability, but could do little to correct it. About 3:30 p.m., Colonel Dodge sent Lieutenant Colonel Pyfer and a detachment of the 77th Pennsylvania out to the southwest to reconnoiter. Pyfer returned to report "a heavy picket force of the enemy [about] five hundred yards to [the] front and right," and more distressingly, that the closest Federals in that direction belonged to Turchin's brigade, about three-quarters of a mile distant. An alarmed Dodge strengthened his pickets, but had no spare troops to send into the yawning gap. He didn't know it, but within another hour this problem would only get worse, as Turchin's command would strike off farther to the west to help repulse William Bate's attack. Things to the north were no better. Willich's earlier inquiry had produced only the vague assurance that Baird's division lay off in that direction, but how far? In fact, at this hour Baird's line was at least a mile distant astride the Reed's Bridge Road, but even that would change when George Thomas plucked Brannan's men out of that line to help deal with the crises in Brotherton and Poe fields.

---

3 "Dear Father," September 22, 1863, Henry Richards Letters, Richards-Gilbert Papers, Havighurst Special Collections, Miami University, Oxford, OH.

The result was that Johnson's division was marooned a mile or so in advance of the rest of the army and ignorant of the progress of the larger battle.[4]

Many of Johnson's men took note of the grim nature of their surroundings. Captain Charles Briant of the 6th Indiana recalled that the setting "was not a very pleasant place to rest, for while the wounded had been carried to the rear, the dead of both sides were all around us. . . . I stood in one spot and counted thirty-five dead, some dressed in gray and some wearing the blue." Ignoring the carnage, a number of men wolfed down crackers and bacon—their first chance to eat in many hours. It wasn't long before they were called back to arms.[5]

Aimed squarely at Willich's and Baldwin's line, Walthall's Rebels advanced "some 300 or 400 yards," driving Federal skirmishers before them until the Mississippians reached the eastern edge of the field. There, Walthall explained, they found the enemy "strongly posted, [who] delivered a very heavy fire of artillery and small arms." Few of the Mississippians ventured out into the field, which was by now an obvious killing ground. Major James M. Johnson of the 30th Mississippi halted his men at the eastern fence line, where they went prone and tried to return the Union fire. Colonel Brantly, commanding the 29th Mississippi, noted only that they "met the enemy in a field, where we fought him until the commands on my right (Twenty-fourth and Twenty-seventh Regiments) commenced falling back to protect themselves." The entire fight probably lasted just 15 or 20 minutes, with Walthall's brigade finally falling back about 200 yards and reforming in a ravine. The caution exhibited by the Mississippians kept their losses low.[6]

St. John Liddell's other brigade under Daniel Govan experienced more confusion and bloodshed than their Mississippi comrades. Initially things went well for the Arkansans, for their line overlapped the Union flank by a wide margin. Only Govan's leftmost regiment, the combined 6th/7th Arkansas, directly faced any Yankees at all. Govan was moving his long brigade line through woods, however, and so had trouble discerning either the extent of the Union position or Walthall's difficulties. The noise of Walthall's engagement

---

4   *OR* 30, pt. 1, 555. Dodge gives the time as 4:00 p.m., but the text of his report suggests Pyfer's trip occurred before St. John Liddell's attack struck home.

5   Charles C. Briant, *History of the Sixth Regiment Indiana Volunteer Infantry, of both Three Months' and Three Years' Services* (Wm. E. Burford, 1891), 230.

6   *OR* 30, pt. 2, 273-274, 281.

was clearly audible to Govan's left, but when the 6th/7th Arkansas joined in, a baffled Govan sought out Lt. Col. John Murray of the 5th/13th Arkansas (alongside the 6th/7th to the north). With all of his staff officers away on other missions, Govan asked Murray to step in, find Col. David A. Gillespie of the 6th, and order him to cease fire.[7]

Thus far, Colonel Gillespie had experienced a thoroughly miserable afternoon. His command initially lagged behind the rest of Govan's line because a section of one of Liddell's two artillery batteries unlimbered in their midst, throwing both the regiment and the gun section into disarray. These guns were commanded by Lt. John Phalen of Capt. William H. Fowler's Alabama battery. Phalen was trying to find a position from which to support his Mississippi comrades in their unequal match against Johnson's Yankees. Phalen mistook the 6th/7th for the 24th Mississippi, and decided to follow the Arkansans into action. Instead of following along behind, Phalen blundered into the midst of the Arkansans and then halted to deploy his guns.[8]

It took a few confused minutes to untangle the mess. Gillespie barely had his regiment moving again when, 100 yards farther, his left flank was savaged by infantry and artillery fire. The left wing of Col. Philemon Baldwin's Union brigade had caught sight of the Rebels. The whizzing lead sent the Arkansans to ground and started firing back. Govan's temporary staffer, Lt. Col. John Murray of the 5th/13th Arkansas, rode up at this time. "Though I was immediately in [their] rear," he noted, "I could not see at what they were firing.". Murray delivered Govan's orders to stop wasting ammunition (doubtless to Gillespie's exasperation) and promptly rode back to his own command, convinced Gillespie's men were shooting at phantoms. The heavy Federal fire, however, showed no sign of slackening.[9]

In fact, both sides were experiencing difficulties. Captain Richards of the 93rd Ohio, part of Baldwin's brigade, thought the situation was becoming a bit dicey for his side: "They came on with a rush," he noted, "and we poured a galling fire which checked them for a moment, but another line came immediately behind, pressing us so hard that we were forced back a short distance." One of the privates in Captain Richards's Company F named Alfred

---

7   Ibid., 264.

8   Ibid., 267.

9   Ibid., 264.

Demoret vividly recalled the moment: "The fight now raged in deadly earnest. The firing of musketry and artillery was one unceasing roll, while the canopy of smoke that hung like a pall overhead almost shut out the sunlight. About this time," Demoret continued, "the rebels sought to plant a section of artillery within seventy-five yards of our lines." The private was describing Phalen's pair of artillery pieces. About this time, the 93rd's Col. Hiram Strong was badly wounded, and his fall sent ripples of some panic through his regiment.[10]

Colonel Baldwin was fully alert to the danger poised to fall against his left flank. Govan and Murray might not be able to see many Yankees, but Baldwin had a good view of Govan's men. All the Rebels had to do was turn their line 90 degrees to face south, advance, and roll up Baldwin's exposed flank. While the 93rd Ohio battled the 6th/7th Arkansas, Baldwin sent word to General Willich describing the threat to the Federal left and asking for help. Willich promptly responded, shifting the 49th Ohio northward to keep a firm connection with Baldwin's 1st Ohio. Willich suggested Baldwin "take his two rear regiments and charge to the rear and left."[11]

Willich's suggestion struck Baldwin as an excellent idea. He brought up Lt. Col. Hagerman Tripp and the 6th Indiana—the only regiment of the brigade not fully engaged. "Intimations being received . . . of an attempt [by] the enemy to flank us," reported the 6th's major, Calvin Campbell. "[W]e then changed direction to the left and deployed upon the line." The 6th arrived in the nick of time, just as Colonel Strong was wounded and the 93rd had begun to give ground. Seizing the colors of the 93rd, Baldwin personally led the Ohioans into the countercharge. "The regiment rushed forward with a cheer, and driving the enemy, captured two pieces of artillery," boasted Campbell. Alongside them, the 6th joined in the attack.[12]

Fielding fewer than 300 muskets, the 6th/7th Arkansas was in real danger of being overwhelmed by 800 advancing Yankees. Things went from bad to worse when Lieutenant Phalen's Rebel guns, which were enthusiastically banging away, began dropping shells into Govan's ranks. Unable to advance, and unwilling to remain still under a friendly iron rain, Colonel Gillespie had

10 "Dear Father," Richards Letters, Miami University; Alfred Demoret, *A Brief History of the Ninety-Third Regiment Ohio Volunteer Infantry: Recollections of a Private* (Graphic Printing, 1898), 22; OR 30, pt. 1, 575.

11 Ibid., 539.

12 OR 30, pt. 1., 567; McElroy, *Chickamauga and Chattanooga National Park Commission*, 88.

little choice but to order a retreat. Following Walthall's earlier example, Gillespie's move soon degenerated into a wholesale scramble for safety. The retreat astounded the still-oblivious Lieutenant Colonel Murray, whose 5th/13th Arkansas was next in line on the right. "I was wholly unable to see any reason for this extraordinary movement," he reported, "and therefore ordered my men to stand fast."[13]

Unlike Murray, Lieutenant Phalen had no trouble seeing the Yankees. "My guns were left without support," lamented battery commander William Fowler in describing his subordinate's ordeal. "All the horses of one piece were killed and all but one of the horses of the other piece. . . . Many of the cannoneers or drivers of the section were killed or wounded at their posts, fighting the guns to the last extremity." Both guns were briefly captured by the Ohioans, but could not be hauled off; Fowler would get a chance to recover them later that evening. The two dozen men and 27 horses lost there, however, could not be so easily replaced.[14]

With Gillespie's line routing and Phalen's guns overrun, Lieutenant Colonel Murray's own command proved equally unsteady. Despite his orders to stand fast, only Murray's two right-flank companies of the 5th/13th Arkansas did so. The rest of the regiment fell back about 100 yards. Murray remained perplexed, still insisting he "could not see any enemy." The collapse did not stop with Murray's regiment. Next in line to the north lay Maj. Anderson Watkins's 8th Arkansas, whose members also bolted when they spotted the men on the left flee. Watkins was equally baffled. "I could see no reason for this sudden panic. It is true we were considerably annoyed by the artillery of the enemy," he continued, but the 8th suffered no more than "a scattering fire of small arms."[15]

With the situation on his right unraveling, Govan ordered his entire brigade to fall back. He eventually reformed his line some 200 to 300 yards northeast of Winfrey Field in the same low ground that sheltered Walthall's Mississippians.

13 See Powell, "Numbers and Losses," CCNMP; *OR* 30, pt. 2, 264. The 6th Indiana numbered 467 going into action, while the 93rd Ohio numbered 459. So far, their losses had been light, certainly less than 100 men combined. The Arkansans initially numbered 388, but suffered heavily during the earlier fights. They lost at least 165 men during the battle, most of whom fell on September 19.

14 *OR* 30, pt. 2, 286-287.

15 Ibid., 264, 268.

The attack had accomplished little, and the men in the ranks were becoming increasingly frustrated by the day's outcome. That night, Pvt. Jacob Grammer of Swett's Mississippi battery complained, "we were repulsed several times today as our corps commander allowed us to be flanked every time we became engaged with the Yanks." Despite the afternoon's setback, St. John Liddell was certain that an opportunity for greater success was still present—if only enough troops could be found to exploit it.[16]

On the opposite side of the field, Brig. Gen. August Willich shared Liddell's sentiment. Willich had watched with enthusiasm both Walthall's repulse and Baldwin's counterattack that dispersed Govan's Confederates. "[A] spontaneous advance of the division to our left [coupled] with our own advance," argued Willich, "[meant] we could have attacked the enemy's broken flank by changing front to the right." Willich was mistaken; there was no division on Johnson's left. By this time, General Thomas had ordered Brannan's division back into action, but not to move to support Johnson. Brannan, as noted earlier, was dispatched to Poe Field to shore up the army's shattered center, leaving Baird's men alone on the Reed's Bridge Road. At the moment, Thomas had more needs than he had troops.[17]

Reinforcements were coming to Liddell's aid, though they would be some time in arriving. At midday, Lt. Gen. D. H. Hill reported to General Bragg's headquarters at Thedford Ford for additional instructions. Major General Patrick R. Cleburne's division was close behind Hill marching north, and Bragg intended to use these troops to reinforce his embattled right wing.

Patrick Ronayne Cleburne was a rising star in the Confederate army, though his reputation had yet to reach its zenith. Irish-born in 1828, he grew up a member of the Protestant gentry, though his family was far from rich. His father was a doctor, and the younger Cleburne studied to be an apothecary but failed to enter the profession. In 1846, the Potato Famine pushed him into the ranks of the British army. He was just two weeks shy of his 18th birthday.[18]

Cleburne served three years, all of it on occupation duty in his native Ireland, before purchasing his discharge and emigrating to America to seek a better life. Fetching up in the river town of Helena, Arkansas, Cleburne went to

---

16 Entry for September 19, Jacob Grammer Diary, Warren Light Artillery file, CCNMP.

17 *OR* 30, pt. 1, 536.

18 Symonds, *Stonewall of the West*, 21.

work as a druggist. He eventually owned his own store and studied law. It was in Helena that he met fellow lawyer Thomas C. Hindman, and the two became friends. Shy and reticent, Cleburne seemed an odd match for the diminutive firebrand Hindman, but they soon became political allies as well as friends. In the turbulent politics of the 1850s, Cleburne—repelled by the anti-immigrant rhetoric of the Know-Nothings, which infused much of the newly formed Republican party—became a staunch Democrat.[19]

Before the war Cleburne joined a local militia company named the Yell Rifles as a private soldier, but was quickly elected to a captaincy. As he learned quickly, his three years of professional service proved a ready steppingstone for higher command. He led his company during the seizure of a Federal arsenal in Little Rock in early 1861 and when his adopted state of Arkansas left the Union, the Yell Rifles formed as part of the 1st Arkansas, which was soon thereafter re-designated the 15th Arkansas. Cleburne jumped from captain of a company to the colonel of the new regiment. He was again promoted, this time to brigadier general, in March 1862 and given a brigade just in time for his first real combat at Shiloh, where he performed as well as anyone could have in that confused bloody fight. Just four months later in August he led a provisional division of two brigades in Kentucky at the battle of Richmond, a stunning Confederate victory that owed much to Cleburne's skill in handling men in battle. Just before Stones River, he was given permanent division command and once again demonstrated notable acumen and leadership in that fight.

Cleburne's division had once belonged to Simon Buckner before that general was promoted away to departmental command. The command underwent considerable change during the months leading up to Chickamauga. It was originally comprised of four brigades commanded by Brig. Gens. St. John Liddell, Bushrod Johnson, S.A.M. Wood, and Lucius Polk. In June 1863, however, Johnson's brigade was transferred to a new division under A. P. Stewart, replaced by a brigade of Texans under Thomas Churchill. Churchill's brigade was none-too-welcome in the Army of Tennessee. Its men had surrendered the fort at Arkansas Post the previous January, and questions persisted about their failure to vigorously defend the bastion. Rumors of their poor fighting ability or even disloyalty were patently unfair, but linger they did. Cleburne welcomed the Texans, however, and in doing so earned their loyalty. With Cleburne setting the example, the new men were accepted by the rest of

---

19 Ibid., 26-41. Symonds's biography has an excellent summation of Cleburne's prewar career.

the division. as staff officer Irving Buck would later put it, "[we] gained as fine a body of soldiers, officers and men, as ever existed."[20]

Churchill was sent back to Arkansas while his men remained with Bragg's army under the command of a young newly promoted brigadier general and graduate of West Point named James A. Deshler. In early September, Liddell's brigade was also detached for service with the newly formed Reserve Corps, and both Johnson and Liddell were elevated to command divisions of their own. The result was that Cleburne was left with just Wood's, Polk's, and Deshler's brigades, a total of 5,380 officers and men, and a dozen guns.

Cleburne was very close to Lt. Gen. William J. Hardee, and might have had some misgivings when that officer transferred to Alabama and was replaced by Daniel Harvey Hill. The acerbic Hill and Cleburne, however, quickly developed a solid rapport. Bragg respected Cleburne and encouraged that relationship. In early September, when Bragg and Hill were contemplating ways to strike the Federals, the army leader urged Hill to "consult Cleburne. He is cool, full of resources, and ever alive to a success."[21]

Hill had other good reasons to respect and rely upon his new subordinate: Pat Cleburne was a thoughtful and careful soldier, a man who paid attention to detail and worked hard to instill professionalism within his command. He took a special interest in marksmanship. With the advent of rifled muskets, it was theoretically possible to substantially increase the effective range of infantry fire. Smoothbores were dangerous out to about 100 yards, but the new rifles were sighted to as much as 800 or even 900 yards. For a variety of reasons, however, actually hitting something at such a long range took a great deal of specialized training and practice. Although the British army did not adopt a rifled musket as a standard weapon until 1852 (three years after Cleburne left the red-coated ranks), Cleburne's interest in marksmanship continued. In 1853, the British established a School of Musketry at Hythe. There, selected men from each British infantry regiment learned the arts of long range shooting, including range estimation—a vital skill given the relatively low muzzle velocity of rifled muskets. Once trained, these men returned to their commands and, in turn, taught their comrades how to use the new weapons.[22]

20 Ibid., 128; Buck, *Cleburne and His Command*, 127.

21 *OR* 30, pt. 4, 594.

22 Joseph Bilby, *Civil War Firearms* (Combined Books, 1996), 48.

In the spring of 1863, Cleburne applied these same techniques to the regiments in his division using a copy of the British Regulations for Conducting Musketry Instruction in the Army. Cleburne's efforts impressed Bragg, who ordered Maj. Calhoun Benham of Cleburne's staff to travel to Richmond and oversee the printing of a Confederate edition of this booklet for widespread army use. Benham's publication came too late for the army to benefit much in 1863, but it would serve as the basis of such training the following year.[23]

In addition to training entire regiments, Cleburne also took the lead in establishing a corps of sharpshooters within his division. A shipment of highly accurate Whitworth and Kerr rifles reached the Army of Tennessee in the summer of 1863. These exceedingly rare weapons were not suited for standard combat use, but they were deadly accurate at the previously unheard-of ranges of 1,000 or even 1,500 yards. Each weapon cost $1,000, and each division only received five, issued only to the best marksmen as determined by shooting competitions that proved to be the excitement of the army that summer. Once selected, these specialists were excused from regular duties, and on the battlefield their role was to pick off officers, couriers, and gun crews. While Cleburne did not originate the idea of the Whitworth sharpshooters, his enthusiastic embrace of the concept has forever linked his name with the idea.[24]

In short, Cleburne can be classified as a "scientific" soldier, a man dedicated to mastering his new profession through reading and practical training. He studied all aspects of soldiering, and had excelled at regimental, brigade, and now divisional command. He was also, as his deft touch with the disgraced Texans proved, a leader who understood how to inspire men as well as train and discipline them. And now, these men were about to go into action at Chickamauga.

While Cleburne's men were moving up, D. H. Hill and Cleburne consulted with Bragg at Thedford Ford. Mindful of General Polk's earlier appeal for reinforcements, Bragg directed them to report to that officer, who was still in charge of the arm's right wing. Bragg expected Cleburne to "take position on the extreme right and begin an attack" as soon as he could. No one was under

23 Calhoun Benham, *A System for Conducting Musketry Instruction* (J. W. Henry Publishing, Inc. 1998), ii-iii.

24 John Anderson Morrow, *The Confederate Whitworth Sharpshooters* (self-published, 1989), 26-28. Unlike most sharpshooters of the Civil War era, who were really trained skirmishers, these troops truly were snipers in the modern sense.

any illusions about when Cleburne would be able to get into action. It would him take several hours to reach the position directed and form for an assault, and it was already mid-afternoon. Bragg's instructions set the stage for a night engagement, the most difficult of all Civil War actions. And as Cleburne would soon discover, the path of advance led through mostly wooded ground. The combined confusion of the darkness and difficult terrain would make an effective assault problematic at best. Despite these complications, Bragg expected nothing less than a large-scale attack. After the miscarried fiasco of McLemore's Cove, D. H. Hill was not inclined to dispute these instructions.[25]

Cleburne's men had varied recollections about the urgency of this march. Sergeant William E. Bevens of the 1st Arkansas was in Lucius Polk's brigade leading the division. Bevens recalled that the pace advanced to the double-quick. When they reached the ford, he explained "we began to pull off our shoes to wade when General Cleburne came along saying 'Boys, go through that river, we can't wait.'" Jim Turner, a private in Company E of the 6th Texas also recalled the event, noting "away we went dashing through the Chickamauga river, almost waist deep, and double-quicked to the front." The dunking would prove to be a later misery, as most of Cleburne's men would have to fight through the closing hours of the 19th soaked to the waist, and thereafter spend a cold fireless night.[26]

Not everyone received such a thorough soaking. In Wood's brigade, John H. Smith of the 33rd Alabama recalled that he and his comrades "marched . . . in quick and double-quick time," but according to another man in the same regiment, removed their clothes before crossing. William E. Preston of the 33rd wrote that the regiment halted at the ford, "and after taking off our shoes, socks, pants, and drawers walked through it and put on our clothes." Because Wood's troops were following Polk's, they had more time to dress and undress while waiting for Polk's regiments to cross. Behind them, however, Deshler's Texans also splashed through the ford without a pause and emerged soaked to the bone.[27]

---

25 *OR* 30, pt. 2, 140.

26 William E. Bevens, *Reminiscences of a Private: Company "G" First Arkansas Regiment Infantry* (n.p. 1913), 30; Jim Turner, and Deanne Labenski, eds., "Jim Turner Co. G, 6th Texas Infantry, C.S.A from 1861 to 1865," *Texana*, vol. 12, no. 1 (1974), 163.

27 Entry for September 19, John Henry Smith Diary, 33rd Alabama file, CCNMP; William E. Preston Memoir, Auburn University, Auburn, AL.

While his men were crossing, Cleburne located Polk and received orders to "form a second line in rear of the right of the line already in position." Despite the day's battering, Polk was still looking to attack. Polk's aide-de-camp and son-in-law, William D. Gale, recounted the bishop-general's attitude to his wife, Polk's daughter, the following Monday: "Walker fought them for three hours & was whipped," wrote Gale, "then Cheatham went in and got whipped . . . .Walker went in again and was whipped again . . . by this time it was 4:00 p.m. and both sides seemed willing to stop. Not so your father."[28]

The column moved northwest past the smoldering remains of the deserted Alexander cabin, set afire the day before by shells from Liddell's artillery. From there, Lucius Polk's infantry left the Alexander Bridge Road to turn north on the Jay's Mill Road. They went into line of battle when they reached the mill. "My right," Cleburne reported, "rested in front of . . . Jay's Mill . . . [and] extended from the saw-mill almost due south for nearly a mile, fronting to the west." Directly in front of Cleburne's right stood St. John Liddell's two brigades (Govan and Walthall), both significantly weakened after their bloody repulse. A sizable portion of Frank Cheatham's command masked Cleburne's left. Beyond lay the heavily visited Winfrey Field, thickly carpeted with the dead and the maimed of both sides.[29]

Liddell was delighted to see his former commander. "I pressed Cleburne to move to the attack at once, with his fresh troops, and drive the enemy back, as they must be greatly exhausted from our constant fighting." If you wait, Liddell warned, "the enemy would be found entrenched and fully prepared. . . . No time was to be lost." Much to his former subordinate's frustration, Cleburne demurred. D. H. Hill was not yet present, and Cleburne's men were still deploying. The Irishman was not going to launch an attack without Hill's authorization, which arrived a few minutes later in the form of Hill himself. Liddell made his pitch once more to Hill, who proved considerably more enthusiastic then Cleburne. Besides, Bragg and Polk were both expecting just such an attack. Cleburne would go in.[30]

Despite winning his point, Liddell seemed unhappy. By this time he may well have been too agitated and exhausted for sound thinking, but one thing

28 "My Dear Wife," William D. Gale to Katherine Polk Gale, Sept. 21, 1863, Gale-Polk Family Papers, UNC.

29 *OR* 30, pt. 2, 154.

30 Hughes, *Liddell's Record*, 143.

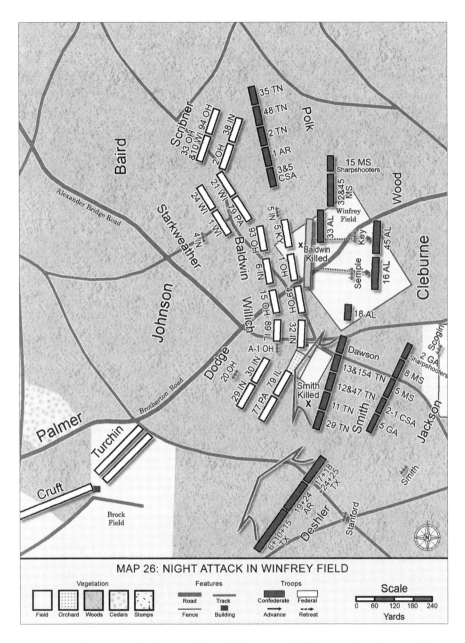

MAP 26: NIGHT ATTACK IN WINFREY FIELD

was certain: he was still obsessed that Cleburne and Hill act with all haste. Once Hill authorized the attack, Liddell turned once more to Cleburne and urged, "General, I hope you will be quick, for a minute now will be worth an hour tomorrow." To the Louisianan's dismay, "He took his time, nevertheless, losing a half an hour of daylight, at least."[31]

Liddell expectations were wholly unrealistic. Moving and deploying 5,000 men took time, something Liddell should have known from his own combat experience. Cleburne's division was moving onto an unfamiliar battlefield to face an unknown enemy. While the troops were shifting from column into line, Hill and Cleburne used that time profitably to scout the Federals in front of them. "It was [a] rule of General Hill's never to put his men into a fight until he had seen the ground himself," wrote Capt. J. W. Ratchford, one of Hill's aides. "Here he went with the skirmish line until driven into the main line" by the advent of the advance. In addition, General Polk ordered Frank Cheatham to support Cleburne with his battered division, some of which lay astride Cleburne's intended path forward. Details on that support would have to be arranged. Liddell's evident annoyance was misplaced. Things were progressing about as fast as could be reasonably expected.[32]

Darkness was gathering when the attack began. Once again the Rebel line lapped the Union flanks by a considerable margin. Lucius Polk's front replicated Govan's former line and was again positioned to turn Johnson's exposed left. S.A.M. Wood's Mississippians faced Johnson's line directly, and would have to cross Winfrey Field, but Deshler's Texans were perfectly positioned to turn the Federal right.

Even though Cleburne was deploying just behind them, Cheatham's men had little expectation of renewing the fight that night. Word had not yet filtered down to Preston Smith's and John K. Jackson's brigades that a new attack was forthcoming. About 5:00 p.m., Capt. Thomas E. King, who was serving as a volunteer aide to General Smith, took a moment to jot in his diary, "All is quiet along the lines. The result I do not yet know. Sharp shooters are pegging away, but no brigade is engaged."[33]

King was a recent addition to Smith's staff—as recent as that very day. He last saw action in command of Company H of the 7th Georgia at First Manassas in July 1861. There, a Federal musket ball shattered his ankle and it never fully

31 Ibid., 144.

32 Statement of J. W. Ratchford, D.H. Hill Papers, North Carolina Department of Archives and History; OR 30, pt. 2, 79.

33 Rev. Joseph C. Stiles, *Captain Thomas E. King; or, a Word to the Army and the Country* (The South Carolina Tract Society, 1864), 7.

recovered. Invalided out of the army, King returned home to Roswell, Georgia. It was a year before he could walk without crutches, and even then he could do so only with a cane while in constant pain. King was a son of one of Georgia's most prominent families. The town of Roswell was founded and named for his grandfather, Roswell King. His clan owned the woolen and cotton mills that made them rich and Roswell an important contributor to the Confederacy's war effort. Each of the King sons went to war. When Rosecrans's Army of the Cumberland crossed the Tennessee River and invaded Georgia, only Thomas and his younger brother Joseph, who was also crippled at Manassas, were home. Despite his physical limitations, Captain King left Roswell on September 14 to join the Army of the Tennessee. He hoped to find a place as a volunteer aide, "this being the only service in the field where my help will avail anything." On the morning of the 19th, King stumbled into Smith's command and was granted a place on his staff.[34]

King was not the only new man. Captain Henry Hunter Smith had just rejoined his uncle Preston after having served with Nathan Bedford Forrest since last March, when he had been temporarily loaned out to the noted cavalryman. Sometime that same day, Forrest and Captain Smith were riding past Cheatham's line of battle when General Smith spotted his nephew and informed Forrest he needed him back. After the general introduced King to the rest of the officers, Captain Smith recalled, "I remarked to him if he wanted to keep himself whole, he had made a mistake joining General Smith for, if he followed him, he would surely get a bullet buried in him." Still, things seemed quiet at the moment. "About seven o'clock General Smith started with his staff down the line of his division, telling his men, who were reclining on the ground, to sleep with 'one eye open,' for they were liable to be called into ranks at any moment," remembered Henry, who also thought he could hear the Federals felling trees for breastworks.[35]

The Yankees were not preparing further defensive works, though they had piled brush and logs along their main line. Across the way, both Richard Johnson and George Thomas understood the precarious nature of Johnson's position. In fact, since mid-afternoon Thomas had been trying to rectify those

---

34 Stiles, *Captain King*, 24.

35 "Reminiscences of the Late War," Henry Hunter Smith Memoir, Hargrett Library, University of Georgia, Athens, GA. From Notes Taken by Dr. Keith S. Bohannon, June 4, 2011.

faults, but more urgent matters kept diverting his efforts. Thomas intended to withdraw both Johnson's and Palmer's divisions (still defending Brock Field) to a more compact and defensible line 800 or 900 yards farther west, but only when it was safe to do so. In the meantime, Thomas's last orders to Absalom Baird were to shift two brigades of his division southward as a support to find and connect with Johnson's right. Thomas issued that order about 4:00 p.m., with Baird getting underway about 30 minutes later.

Like Cleburne's preparation on the opposite side of the line, the move took a while to execute. Baird was uncertain of Johnson's exact location and groped his way slowly through the woods with two very battered brigades. He did so alone as far as he could tell. It was likely between 6:00 and 6:30 p.m. before his troops came to a halt several hundred yards behind and just north of Johnson's left flank. Baird soon found Johnson and the two generals worked out the intended deployment of Scribner's and Starkweather's brigades, with Baird requesting help from Johnson's aides to show his brigadiers exactly where to deploy.

By this time the fighting around the Poe and Brotherton fields had subsided, allowing George Thomas to turn his attention elsewhere. Johnson and Baird were in the process of posting Baird's men when the corps commander arrived and outlined his plan to fall back to a more compact line. The men were to begin the move after dark once the danger of an attack was gone. Echoing Captain King's diary entry, Baird noted that, "with the exception of an occasional shot from rebel sharpshooters, entire quiet prevailed along the line [as] Johnson and myself rode back with . . . General [Thomas] to ascertain the position we would occupy." It was a reasonable decision, especially given that the actual movement would be conducted in the dark. The timing, however, could not have been worse.[36]

At 7:00 p.m., even as Preston Smith was cautioning his men to "sleep with one eye open," Cleburne's brigades stepped off to attack. By now, of course, Cheatham's officers had received word of the impending attack and that Cleburne's line would pass through their ranks. Once that happened, all five of Cheatham's brigades were to move out in support. Polk and Wood's regiments moved steadily westward, transiting Liddell's line with few problems. For reasons that remain unclear, however, Deshler's Texans drifted south almost from the first step. Once they moved through Cheatham's line (part of which

---

36 *OR* 30, pt. 1, 270.

was masking Cleburne's left), they drifted even farther south and by doing so, opened a brigade-sized gap in Cleburne's wide front.

Preston Smith's brigade lay directly in front of Deshler, with John K. Jackson's line behind and in support of Smith. Deshler's Texans passed through both lines, and once through Smith ordered his own troops to follow. Because he expected that Deshler's entire brigade would cover his front, Smith did not deploy skirmishers. It was dark by the time the movement was fully underway.

S. A. M. Wood's combined Mississippi and Alabama brigade made first contact with the Federals, with the fighting once again taking place in Winfrey Field. Sterling Alexander Martin Wood was an Alabama lawyer and politician elected to command the 7th Alabama in 1861. He led a brigade at Shiloh and Perryville before being wounded in the head by a shell fragment during the latter engagement. He recovered in time to lead his brigade into action again at Stones River, where his command suffered nearly 50 percent losses. At first glance he seemed a capable brigadier, but after Shiloh, rumors suggested he failed to obey orders and his brigade retreated "in a run in line of battle" under fire. These accusations were widespread and stung enough for Wood to demand a court of inquiry. The investigative body that convened in June 1862 exonerated him of any misconduct. At Perryville and Stones River he handled his men capably enough, and the rumors subsided.[37]

Like Edward Walthall before him, Wood ran into difficulties as soon as he entered Winfrey Field. Many of the Rebels making this advance were unclear of its object. Captain Daniel Coleman commanded a company in the 15th Mississippi Sharpshooters on the right of Wood's line. Even after the brigade deployed and started forward through the woods, Coleman "had no idea of meeting the enemy that evening." He and the rest of the brigade were in for a rude surprise. First, however, they passed through Liddell's line where, recalled William Preston of the 33rd Alabama, they "recognized our blue and white flag, and cheered us as we passed." Within 15 minutes, however, Wood's skirmishers fell back into the ranks and a short time later the entire line was facing the Federal defenses. One soldier-correspondent of the 16th Alabama described the affair as a "terrible night charge . . . made on an almost impregnable position of the enemy."[38]

37 OR 20, pt. 1, 898; OR 10, pt. 2, 606-607.

38 Entry for September 19, D. Coleman Diary, UNC; William Preston Memoir, ADAH; Letter from "Dixie Rebel," *Huntsville Confederate*, October 3, 1863.

With 1,982 officers and men in six regiments and two battalions, Wood's brigade frontage extended about 500 yards. The length of the formation would have been unwieldy even in daylight; in the looming darkness, Wood soon lost control of his men. In the brigade center, Col. E. B. Breedlove led his 45th Alabama straight on for the Yankees, driving enemy skirmishers back through the field until he could glimpse "their line . . . just across the [far] fence, protected by temporary defenses." The Rebels were about halfway across the field when Federal infantry and artillery opened fire. Breedlove pushed his command ahead in an effort to cross the fence. The brigade guided on the 45th Alabama, so when Colonel Breedlove thrust his regiment ahead, so did Maj. John McGaughy in command of the 16th Alabama next in line to the south.[39]

Most of the rest of the brigade, however, did not follow suit. Colonel Mark P. Lowrey, commanding the combined 32nd/45th Mississippi, was immediately to Breedlove's right holding the brigade's right flank with only the two companies of the 15th Mississippi Sharpshooters on his right. Instead of guiding on Breedlove's Alabamians, however, Lowrey understood that "the sharpshooters would dress on Polk's Brigade, and I would dress on them"—in other words, Lowrey's job was to try and keep the brigade aligned with Polk's men on his right farther north. Lowrey, at least, understood that he was making an attack. "If I encountered a battery of the enemy," he explained, he was to "charge and take it." In trying to guide on Polk's line, however, the 32nd/45th Mississippi lagged behind the 45th Alabama and began indiscriminately firing into the darkness. Some of that fire peppered Breedlove's men as they surged forward into the field.[40]

Lieutenant Colonel Harris Lampley, second in command of Breedlove's 45th Alabama, was in charge of the regiment's right wing. The Mississippians's fire revealed to Lampley that his men were about 75 yards ahead of Lowrey's blazing line. Lampley ordered the 45th Alabama to halt. The right half of the regiment immediately complied. Breedlove and the left side, however, pressed on toward the Union line. A vicious little fight erupted at close range, an action Breedlove cut short when he discovered Lampley's half of the regiment had fallen behind. The colonel ordered his part of the 45th Alabama to fall back and

---

39 Powell, "Numbers and Losses," CCNMP; *OR* 30, pt. 2, 167. Two regiments, the 32nd and 45th Mississippi, were combined.

40 *OR* 30, pt. 2, 169.

reform. This abrupt retreat under fire and conducted in darkness threw the 16th Alabama on Breedlove's left into confusion.

A week after the fight, another member of the 16th Alabama described his frustration to his father in a letter home: "In 15 minutes from the time we started forward we were upon them and over their line of fortifications. Our right was literally mixed up with theirs and many [of them] were so surprised that they forgot to run." A confused hand-to-hand combat was being waged over the rudimentary breastworks when disaster struck. According to a letter written home after the battle, "The 45th Alabama on our right gave way and Maj. McGaughy, intending to keep on a line with them . . . [ordered a] retreat & instead of marching away in an orderly manner two companies . . . of our right wing ran disgracefully from the field." The rest of the regiment was thrown into "great confusion." Captain Frederick Ashford, charged with writing the 16th's report, singled out "companies E and G [who] acted badly." Captain [George W.] Archer of Company G "made no effort to rally his men when ordered to halt, but led them in retreat." The bulk of the two companies fled the field, with a few of them not rejoining the regiment unit Monday the 21st.[41]

With Wood's center falling back or milling about in disorder, Col. Samuel Adams of the 33rd Alabama halted as well. Adams commanded both his own regiment and the three companies of the 18th Alabama Battalion occupying Wood's left. He, too, was lagging behind. William Preston remembered dismantling a "worn rail fence [by] push[ing] off alternate or . . . opposite corners, as we had been instructed to do." Once they had done so, they too found the Union line which Preston noted, "checked us." Adams reported that he halted the regiment because the 16th Alabama on his right was also stopped, and he was afraid that if he got in front of them they might fire into his own flank, which is what had already happened to Breedlove's 45th Alabama.[42]

Within just a few minutes, Wood's entire brigade was thoroughly disrupted. The center was in full retreat while both flank regiments were halted and looking for orders. A strong hand was needed to sort out the confusion, but Wood was not to be found. Apparently, he too had lagged behind. In the days after the fight, talk swept through the brigade that "he acted very badly" and the

---

41 "Dear Father," from Wilson. Steiner Family Papers, Auburn University, Auburn, AL; *OR* 30, pt. 2, 163. There were 11 men named Wilson in the 16th, and the exact author of this letter remains unknown.

42 William Preston Memoir, ADAH.

specter of cowardice raised its ugly head. The old aspersions of Shiloh resurfaced; this time, there would be repercussions.[43]

The Yankees were not having things all their own way, however. When the fighting flared, Baird and Johnson hurried back to their respective divisions only to find an unraveling situation: Colonel Baldwin was dead. Baldwin was dismounted and standing behind his old regiment, the 6th Indiana, when the attack began. When he realized this new Rebel assault would break on his front, Baldwin reasoned that a charge had worked before, so why not again? The Hoosiers watched in shock as the colonel climbed back into the saddle. "He immediately rode through our ranks and called on the 6th Indiana to follow him," recalled the 6th's Captain Briant. "This, of course, placed him between the two fires, which were only a few yards apart, and both him and his horse were killed instantly. . . . Very sensibly," Briant continued, the regiment "did not obey an order which should never have been given, but did just as they should have done: 'Stand fast and give 'em 'ell!' . . . it was a practical demonstration of the American idea—majority rule—and, as usual, it proved to be right." William H. Doll, also of the 6th Indiana, remembered that Baldwin "fell to the ground, pierced by nineteen bullets."[44]

Baldwin might have lived had he not mounted his horse. Despite the intensity of the fight, neither side was inflicting much punishment. According to Colonel Lowrey of the 32nd/45th Mississippi, "the enemy had fired rapidly, but as it was getting dark they overshot us." Much the same was true for the Confederate return fire. By elevating himself on horseback, however, Baldwin offered himself up as a perfect target. His body was never recovered, and was eventually buried on the field by the Rebels.[45]

About 400 yards to the south, another brigade was coming to grief, only this one was led by a Confederate. Brigadier General Preston Smith led his brigade forward after Cleburne's men passed. According to Col. Alfred J. Vaughan of the 13th Tennessee, Smith's line was supposed to follow 500 yards behind Deshler. Someone blundered, however, and "instead of marching to the front [Deshler] obliqued to the left." Deshler drifted far enough south to completely bypass Dodge's Federals, who anchored Johnson's right. Smith's

---

43 "Dear Arthur," October 9, 1863, Robert Lewis Bliss Letters, ADAH.

44 Briant, *History of the Sixth Regiment*, 233-234; William H. Doll Memoir, 249, InSL.

45 *OR* 30, pt. 2, 170. Colonel Baldwin's remains were probably reinterred under an anonymous headstone in Chattanooga National Cemetery.

Tennesseans still numbered some 1,300 men after their afternoon fight, but they expected to move into the night assault in support, not as part of the front line. Within a couple of hundred yards of stepping off, however, a battle erupted to their right as Wood's brigade engaged the Federal line. Shortly thereafter, a Rebel battle line (assumed to be part of Deshler's brigade), fell back through Smith's ranks. In fact, these troops composed Wood's left front, some of the 33rd Alabama or perhaps even some panicked souls from the widely scattered 16th Alabama. In any case, Smith grew cautious and halted his own line while he and a small knot of staff officers rode forward to ascertain what to do next.[46]

Captain Henry Smith recalled that the headquarters party rode forward and found "General Deshler's brigade . . . very much out of line." After remonstrating with some of Deshler's men, the party rode on—and blundered into trouble. "While in a thick cluster of woods we ran into the ranks of the enemy before we knew it, and General Smith called out to them to keep in line, thinking they were his troops." When the unidentified unit demanded to know Smith's identity, the Southern general announced himself and demanded, in turn, that they do likewise.[47]

The party of Rebel officers had ridden directly into the formed ranks of the 77th Pennsylvania, part of Dodge's brigade. When the Pennsylvanians identified themselves, the surprised Smith tried to bluff his way out by calling upon them to immediately surrender. Instead, about 30 of the Pennsylvanians leveled their rifled muskets and fired. The rounds mortally wounded General Smith and Capt. Thomas King; both died within a few minutes. Henry Smith was hit as well, his leg shattered by a musket ball. The captain would spend a long, cold, and painful night lying on the field waiting for help to arrive. Another aide, Capt. John Harris, narrowly escaped. Colonel Vaughan, who had followed Smith, was luckier than the general. The man Vaughan had questioned missed him but struck another of Smith's aides, Capt. John S. Donelson. Vaughan quickly backpedaled, calling on the 13th Tennessee to return fire.[48]

---

46 Alfred J. Vaughan, *Personal Record of the Thirteenth Regiment Tennessee Infantry by its Old Commander* (McClain Printing Co., 1975), 29-30.

47 Smith Memoir, UGA. Captain Smith incorrectly recalled the Federals as the 69th Indiana.

48 "Dearest Ma," September 25, 1863, John Harris letter, Tennessee Civil War Sourcebook, http://tennessee.civilwarsourcebook.com/collection.pdf/1863-09/1863-09-Article-323-Page 412.pdf, accessed 5/28/2011.

Donelson's demise marked yet another of the Civil War's tragic ironies. John Donelson was one of only a handful of children to be born in the White House (May 18, 1832). His parents were serving President Andrew Jackson, his father as the President's confidential secretary and his mother as a hostess since the President was a widower. John's father, Andrew Jackson Donelson, was also Jackson's foster son, and the president became A. J. Donelson's guardian when his parents died when he was five. Jackson and the Donelsons were so close that Jackson willed Captain Donelson's father his most prized possession—the magnificent sword presented to "Old Hickory" for his military triumphs in the War of 1812. In bequeathing the blade, Jackson charged Donelson to "defend [his] country against all foes, foreign and domestic." It was a charge he took seriously, for he remained a Union man despite the fact that his brother Daniel S. Donelson became a Confederate general and his sons strong secessionists who flocked to the stars and bars. The resulting rift in family relations was deep and painful.[49]

The nascent firefight died out almost as soon as it ignited. Before Smith fell and was still trying to make sense of what was transpiring, Deshler's troops reappeared—behind Dodge's Federals. When the Yankees realized they were being cut off, several hundred began to surrender and the rest were thrown into complete confusion.

Deshler can be forgiven for his wayward course. The brigade's drift left was through terrain almost entirely forested, and by now filled with the smoke of several fires. Private Jim Turner of the 6th Texas went in that evening on Deshler's left. The 6th, which was consolidated with the 10th Texas and 15th Texas Dismounted Cavalry, moved across some of the most heavily contested ground of the day. The left flank of Deshler's advance brushed the eastern edge of Brock Field, picking its way through the dead standing timber where Otto Strahl's Rebels had fought hours earlier. To Private Turner, the entire experience was surreal: "the blaze of the guns had set fire to the high sedge grass in the field. The fence was on fire and the tall dead trees in the field were blazing high in the air. Dead and wounded men were lying there in great danger of being burnt up." The place seemed the very "vortex of Hell."[50]

---

49 See http://www.hickorytales.com/andrew.html; and http://bullyforbragg.blogspot.com/2008/12/old-hickorys-ties-to-chickamauga.html, for details on the Donelson family and their relationship to Jackson. Both sites accessed May 28, 2011.

50 Turner, "Jim Turner Co. G, 6th Texas Infantry," 163-164.

Turner also recalled a fair amount of incoming Federal fire, but these rounds almost certainly were random shots. Few if any Yankees were in place opposite them. Dodge's earlier fears about the gap between his own and Turchin's lines were now exacerbated by the fact that Turchin's attentions had already been fully occupied in repulsing General Bate's breakthrough to the southwest. Even as Preston Smith was running afoul of the 77th Pennsylvania, Dodge discovered "that a heavy column was moving against my flank. . . . I immediately withdrew my battery to the rear, just in time to save it, as this column swept round on my right and rear, delivering at the same time a very heavy fire."[51]

Deshler's line fully enveloped the 77th Pennsylvania and penetrated into the rear of the right of the 79th Illinois. It did not, however, envelop Dodge's support line comprised of the 29th and 30th Indiana regiments. The flanking effort captured 73 Pennsylvanians, or 28% of the regiment's engaged strength. While that was bad enough, the losses included "all the field officers, four captains . . . two lieutenants [and] the regimental colors." For all intents and purposes the regiment ceased to function as a unit for the rest of the battle, and no battle report was ever filed. The survivors of the 77th were attached to the 79th Illinois. The 79th actually fared worse in terms of raw numbers, losing 97 men including four captains and eight lieutenants, but Col. Allen Buckner led the main portion of his command out of the trap and personally seized one of the flags to lead his men to safety. The bewildered soldiers fell back to the support line of Hoosiers, who were by this time delivering a confused fire into Deshler's ranks, having finally grasped that Rebels had somehow penetrated the brigade front. The night attack struck Lt. Montraville Reeves of the 79th Illinois as patently unfair. "It would be a rebel trick to attack us [in the dark]," he grumbled in a letter home.[52]

The brigade leader himself, Colonel Dodge, was one of those initially trapped by the Rebel "trick." Neither side's fire was very effective, and officers along both lines were trying to halt the firing for fear of shooting their own men. Dodge later recalled that the two lines were no more than 20 feet apart, and he

---

51 *OR* 30, pt. 1, 555.

52 John Obreiter, *The Seventy-Seventh Pennsylvania at Shiloh. History of the Regiment* (Harrisburg Publishing Company, 1905), 129-130; Allen Buckner, *The Memoirs of Allen Buckner* (The Michigan Alcohol And Drug Information Foundation, 1982), 19; "Dear Brother," October 5, 1863, Montraville Reeves Letters, Illinois Historical Survey, University of Illinois, Champaign, IL.

was in the midst of them. "I went to work as quietly as I could to withdraw my men," he recollected. "I run across Col. Buckner, who thought he had his regiment all right, and said he had just spoke to Col. Rose [of the 77th Pennsylvania] not ten feet from where we then were. I went in the direction he gave me but could find nothing of Rose." The decision was nearly disastrous for Dodge, who spent the next hour trying to find his way back to friendly lines.[53]

Dodge first realized he was lost when he stumbled across two unidentified men. He was about to ask their identities when they began speaking. According to Dodge, they sounded like senior Confederate officers; Dodge thought one was a division commander and the other a brigadier—Cleburne and Deshler, perhaps? The Union colonel wisely kept quiet and continued on until, thoroughly lost, the frustrated officer sat down by a tree. When two Confederate ambulance-corpsmen stumbled upon him in the dark, Dodge uttered "a pardonable untruth" and told them he was wounded. When they tried to help him, Dodge pulled his revolver and "told them in a low but firm voice who I was, explained how I had come where I was . . . and told them they must take me into our lines, assuring them I would kill one of them at any rate, or both if possible, if they made any noise or done anything to betray me. . . . They concluded to obey my orders." After more stumbling and fumbling around in the dark, all three made it back to Union lines, where Dodge found "the remnant" of his brigade "under command of Colonel Buckner about ready to fall back."[54]

Things were just as confusing on the other Union flank. There, Colonel Baldwin's death left his brigade leaderless because no one on his staff could initially locate and notify the outfit's executive officer, Col. William H. Berry of the 5th Kentucky. As a result, Baldwin's brigade fragmented. The front line, now composed of the 1st Ohio and 6th Indiana, helped Willich repulse S. A. M. Wood's assault, and even ceased firing for a few moments. To their left, however, Confederate Brig. Gen. Lucius Polk's brigade was moving past them to the west. Berry spotted the movement and took the reserve line (consisting of his own 5th Kentucky and the still-shaken 93rd Ohio) back in the hopes of connecting with Baird's Federals, who were just coming up, and preventing Polk's Rebels from striking into the rear of the division.

53 Dodge, "The Story of Chickamauga."

54 Ibid.

Polk's experience initially duplicated Govan's. Colonel James A. Smith commanded the combined 3rd/5th Confederate Regiment, 290 men strong, moving on Polk's left. Smith's men moved through Colonel Gillespie's ill-fated 6th/7th Arkansas and encountered the same fierce fire that brought the Arkansans to an abrupt halt. Smith, a 32-year-old West Point graduate of the class of 1853, admitted the fire "stopped us for a short time." Polk's reaction to this firefight, however, was quite different than Govan's. Instead of trying to get the 3rd/5th to cease firing, Polk started to turn the rest of his brigade south, angling to get at the Union flank.[55]

Had the 5th Kentucky's Colonel Berry simply faced his two regiments north and formed a line behind and north of the 6th Indiana, duplicating the deployment used to defeat Govan, Polk would have had a much more difficult time. Berry, however, first moved west trying to find and connect with Baird's arriving brigades. That movement, in turn, allowed some of Polk's Rebels free access to the 6th Indiana's exposed left flank.

Holding what had been the center of Johnson's line, Brig. Gen. August Willich received Johnson's hastily penned orders to withdraw about 6:30 p.m., before Johnson returned from his reconnaissance with Baird and Thomas. Before that instruction could be implemented, Wood's Confederates attacked and were repulsed. From there, however, things started to go very wrong.[56]

With S. A. M. Wood's brigade halted or in retreat, Cleburne's attack might have been in trouble. Major Benham would later write that "fiends and malignant demons seemed at work," what with all the sound, sight, and fury of a night battle. With some poetic license, Benham insisted that Cleburne's "line, with that commander, was superior to terror. . . . [Cleburne] rode like a fury from brigade to brigade—horse and rider seemed frenzied alike." With the attack faltering, Cleburne intervened as Benham had never before witnessed. "I never saw Cleburne before or after so demonstrative," marveled the major. "I suppose, knowing it was indispensible that the charge should be successful . . . he deemed it necessary to encourage [the men] as much as possible."[57]

Major Thomas R. Hotchkiss, however, proved equal to the moment. Hotchkiss commanded Cleburne's artillery, three batteries encompassing 12

---

55 OR 30, pt. 2, 180.

56 Ibid., pt. 1, 539.

57 Calhoun Benham, "Maj.-Gen. P.R. Cleburne," *Kennasaw Gazette*, April 1, 1889.

guns. Each battery began the advance by following behind the lines with little prospect for action. Deshler told Capt. James Douglas, commanding the Texas battery, that Douglas would likely not even be needed. Given the late hour and the "roughness of the country, he did not think my battery could be made effective with safety." Within a few minutes of moving out, however, Major Hotchkiss called all three batteries up to support Wood's faltering men.[58]

Hotchkiss was capable and aggressive. He began the war as a private on a gun crew, but soon rose through the ranks, first to lead a battery and then a battalion command. Hotchkiss was not a scientific gunner, but he was "a firm disciplinarian [who] expected strict obedience to his orders," which did not always sit well with his battery commanders. Lieutenant Thomas Key, commanding Calvert's Arkansas battery, grumbled that "a captain under this battalion management is a perfect automaton." Hotchkiss was fearless, even "reckless at times when it is unnecessary."[59]

On this night, Hotchkiss displayed his aggressive nature. Lieutenant Key and Capt. Henry C. Semple were originally ordered to bring their batteries along behind Wood, with Hotchkiss in direct command. When the 45th Alabama collapsed, Hotchkiss ordered both batteries forward into action. By this time night engulfed the field, the eight Rebel guns closed to within 60 yards of the Union line and opened fire. In full daylight a maneuver like this would have been foolhardy and almost certainly fatal for the gun crews. Cloaked in the darkness, however, the engagement was "more noisy than destructive." Lieutenant Goldthwaite, in Semple's battery, reported there was nothing to aim at but the "flash of [the enemy's] guns," and, the Southern cannoneers were so worried about firing on their own men that "we were obliged to train our guns farther and farther to the left after each round." One of the few casualties among the Rebels was Hotchkiss himself, wounded in the foot and obliged to yield command to Semple. Within 20 rounds, the Federals began retreating. The action was over quickly, and by the time Captain Douglas's Texas battery arrived there were no targets left to engage. The success of the guns motivated Wood's disordered infantry to renew their own advance.[60]

58 Ibid., pt. 2, 197.

59 Buck, *Cleburne and His Command*, 29.

60 Semple Battery Tablet, Winfrey Field, CCNMP; *OR* 30, pt. 2, 174.

If this sudden storm of shell and canister didn't kill many Yanks, it certainly had a substantial moral effect. To Willich it suddenly seemed as if Rebels were everywhere. "A shower of canister and columns of infantry streamed at once into our front and both flanks. My two front regiments were swept back to the second line." In danger of being surrounded, Willich shifted his entire brigade (now formed in a long single line) back another 250 yards, where he deployed it in a giant semicircle around the 1st and 20th Ohio batteries.[61]

Willich thought his men were the last to leave the original line, but he was mistaken. Baldwin's first line was still clinging to the fence bordering Winfrey Field, and Willich's retreat left the 1st Ohio exposed—a fact a Buckeye private named Levi Wagner realized with considerable alarm. "A terrible onrush of the enemy caused our weakened line to fall back to the main line, but not until after a terrific fight ensued. . . . We had to fall back through heavy timber, and the gloom of the forest and impenetrable pall of smoke from the firing caused such a darkness that nothing could be seen but the flash of the Rebel guns." The retreat of the Buckeyes, in turn, exposed the 5th Kentucky and Captain Simonson's 5th Indiana battery to envelopment and triggered another disordered rush to the rear. Simonson's gunners limbered and battered their way through the woods in such haste that one limber became "lodged on a tree." The men were struggling to free the piece when one of the horses was shot and fell still in the traces. With Rebels almost upon them, the gunners abandoned the cannon and limber, escaping only "because the enemy could not see who they were."[62]

Colonel Berry of the 5th Kentucky discovered the 1st Ohio's retreat only when one of his officers "called my attention to the right . . . and there stood a rebel line of battle pouring its fire into the second line of the brigade." Berry already knew he was being flanked from the north by Polk's Confederates. With the 1st Ohio gone, "I was completely cut off," realized the colonel. His solution was simple: pretend they were Rebels. Berry cautioned his men to hold their fire and passed the word that the regiment would fall back. His Kentuckians complied so well that a number of Yankees missed the movement. Private Christian Ehrisman of Company E was one of them. "I, and another comrade,

---

61 Ibid., 539.

62 Levi Wagner, "Recollections of an Enlistee," AHEC; *OR* 30, pt. 1, 577; Daniel H. Chandler manuscript, 5th Indiana Battery file, Stones River National Battlefield Park.

did not notice until the rebels were almost upon us and called on us to surrender, but of course we remembered that we had business at some other place, and regardless of flying bullets, we started on a run." Ehrisman was hit in the right shoulder but kept going. Eventually he reached a Union field hospital.[63]

Berry's deception worked too well. The Confederates seemed to think the 5th was one of their own regiments, but so too did other Yankees. Federals from either Col. Benjamin Scribner's or Brig. Gen. John Starkweather's brigade fired into the Kentuckians as they approached, a tragic event that Berry lamented, "killed many of my men."[64]

Under normal circumstances, Baird's two brigades would have been ideally positioned to turn the tables on the Confederates. Both Federal brigades were in line facing east, and as Lucius Polk's line turned to the south to turn Johnson's left, they exposed their own right to these new Union arrivals. Similar turns of fate had been occurring in these woods all day, but this time the confusion in the dark of night precluded it from happening again.

Neither Scribner nor Starkweather had a clear understanding of the tactical situation, and neither brigade was aligned correctly. Somehow the commands deployed angled inward facing one another, a shallow "V" with Scribner's men facing southeast and Starkweather's line facing northeast. If they opened fire, there was a good chance they would hit friendly troops.

The 38th Indiana was on the division's left, and Polk's men bumped into these Hoosiers first. Lieutenant Colonel Daniel F. Griffin reported that "the enemy came in at this point, advancing in the darkness and pouring a volley of musketry on our flank that caused the line to retire a few hundred yards." W. H. Springer remembered a confused fight in the gloom. At one point, he noted, the 2nd Ohio, "just next to us . . . foolishly . . . fired right on us." Things only got worse. General Starkweather thought the fire was coming from several directions, much or all of it friendly: Scribner's men, he wrote, "having . . . obliqued to the right instead of moving parallel . . . opened . . . fire upon the left regiments of my brigade and the left of Johnson's division, thus destroying my men." In response "Johnson's troops . . . faced about and fired into my right."

63 *OR* 30, pt. 1, 569; Christ Ehrisman, "An Incident of the Battle of Chickamauga," *National Tribune*, January 1, 1891.

64 *OR* 30, pt. 1, 569.

Not surprisingly, both of Baird's brigades fell back precipitously a couple of hundred yards before they could stop and regroup.[65]

The Union retreat did not become general because the Confederates quickly broke off any pursuit. Colonel Lowrey of the 32nd/45th Mississippi explained the myriad of problems that shut down any Rebel advance: "Major Hawkins of the [15th Mississippi] Sharpshooters, reported to me that the left of Polk's brigade was pressing into his battalion . . . and that we would do more harm to our friends than to our enemies. I immediately commanded to cease firing." Lowrey made it to the Union fence line, but halted there. "I discovered that our whole line, as far as I could see, was so deranged that it ought to have been regulated before we advanced farther." Daniel Harvey Hill apparently agreed. According to Lowrey, at this juncture "he rode up and directed me to await further orders from General Cleburne." Polk and Deshler, the latter intermingled with Cheatham's men, reported similar disruptions.[66]

Cleburne's night attack accomplished nothing of significance. Approximately 300 Yankees were captured, but beyond that, actual losses on both sides were light. Each side lost a brigade commander and a couple of cannon. Moreover, many of the battle casualties on both sides were self-inflicted, as friendly units in both blue and gray repeatedly fired into each other by mistake. Although on the brink of a potentially larger success, Cleburne's division became so entangled that additional organized movement and pursuit proved impossible. The Rebel attack failed to hurt Johnson's division, as his men would prove with hard fighting the next day. The ground captured proved equally unimportant. Had Cleburne's men waited an hour, Johnson and Baird would have been gone, pulled back toward Kelly Field in accordance with George Thomas's instructions. Cleburne's attack was launched not because an important tactical opportunity beckoned (St. John Liddell's agitation notwithstanding), but because General Bragg expected it, Polk wanted it, and D. H. Hill likely felt he couldn't disobey another attack order from Bragg. Hill would wax enthusiastically about the fight in both his report and in various postwar writings, describing the charge as "magnificent."

---

65 Ibid., 291; William H. Springer Recollections, InSL; *OR* 30, pt. 1, 300-301.

66 *OR* 30, pt. 2, 170.

In truth, the encounter was a footnote to the main battle, should never have been launched, and accomplished nothing except additional bloodshed.[67]

---

67 Wood reported more than 100, Polk added 50 prisoners and three cannon, while Deshler's captures totaled 175. See *OR* 30, pt. 2, 160, 176, 188; Hill, "Chickamauga," 652.

Chapter Twenty-Five

Securing the Flanks:

Saturday, September 19: All Day

While the infantry fight raged between the Reed's Bridge Road in the north and nearly all the way south to Lee & Gordon's Mills, both Generals Rosecrans and Bragg remained mindful of their operational flanks. Crossing points along Chickamauga Creek above and below the fighting posed mutual threats and opportunities. Throughout the day, the opposing commanders took steps to cover these crossings, which in turned provoked a variety of fighting. While none of these actions raged with the fury of the main contest, they periodically drew the attention of both army leaders.

As it had been for days, Red House Bridge remained one of the most critical crossing points. It was several miles north of Reed's Bridge, and thus of limited tactical use in the current battle. However, Rosecrans could not ignore the threat the Federal Road posed to Rossville, and Bragg understood the potential of a renewed Union thrust against Ringgold via Red House Bridge.

On September 18, Confederate Col. John Scott's cavalry brigade spent the day guarding the Federal Road and skirmishing with Yankees dispatched there for the same purpose. Scott blundered that night when he took his entire brigade south to camp with the rest of Brig. Gen. John Pegram's division. His withdrawal left the critical crossing unprotected. Near dawn, while Nathan Bedford Forrest was mounting Davidson's troopers to scout toward Jay's Mill, he also ordered Scott back to the crossing he had so carelessly abandoned the night before. Forrest never expressed official displeasure with Scott's inexplicable decision, but it is not difficult to picture the words and demeanor of the short-tempered Tennessean in his demand for Scott to lose no time in getting back there. Some members of his brigade recalled the speedy return to the bridge. Second Lieutenant William G. Allen of the 5th Tennessee Cavalry, who was acting as the regimental adjutant, recalled the brigade received no rest at all that night. After Scott's command reached Forrest's camp late on the night of the 18th, wrote Allen, "we sat on our horses some two hours and [then] were ordered back to [Red House] Bridge. Travel was slow going and coming." Private William Sloan of Company D recalled being sent back with haste. "Later in the day [night of the 18th] we were ordered back again in double quick time." Scott's return, however, was too late. "It was near sunrise," continued Allen, "when we reached the bridge and found [the enemy] in possession."[1]

In fact, neither side held the crossing that morning, though the Federals at least maintained control of the road. The Yankees Scott encountered belonged to Brig. Gen. Walter C. Whitaker's brigade of Brig. Gen. James Steedman's division, part of the Union Reserve Corps. These were the same troops Scott had skirmished with the day before on September 18. Major General Gordon Granger sent Brig. Gen. Walter Whitaker's brigade, 2,600 infantry and six cannon, to watch the bridge on the afternoon of the 18th. During the night, Whitaker took note of Scott's departure and thought it a ruse. "Having good reason to believe . . . that the rebels were changing their position to the rear of my command," explained Whitaker, he pulled his brigade back to higher ground at McAfee Church about two miles west of the bridge. At 8:00 a.m. on September 19, Whitaker ordered Col. Nelson Trusler of the 84th Indiana to send three companies of skirmishers back east to secure the crossing, which set the stage for another collision with Scott's Louisiana and Tennessee troopers.[2]

Major A. J. Neff led the Union infantry patrol. About half a mile from camp, Neff halted the column and selected Capt. William Boyd to take his Company A forward while the other two companies remained in reserve. Boyd was none too happy about being tapped for the mission. "The major came forward and ordered me to take my company and skirmish forward to a bridge a mile or two towards the enemy somewhere—he could not tell where. I asked

---

1   William Gibbs Allen Memoirs, TSLA; William E. Sloan Diary, TSLA.

2   *OR* 30, pt. 1, 861; Nelson Trusler Report, 84th Indiana Infantry file, September 28th, 1863, Adjutant General's Records, Indiana State Archives.

how we were to be supported and what we were to do if we got to the bridge or met the enemy in force at any place," Boyd continued, "to all of which he said he did not know. I did not know too."[3]

Despite the uncertainty, orders were orders and Boyd and his men set out. He and Company A met Rebels well short of the bridge on the Federal side of the creek. The gray troopers comprised the leading elements of Scott's column, but proved to be of little hindrance. "We pushed forward rapidly exchanging shots with them for a mile and a half until we came in sight of the bridge. . . . The enemy," admitted Boyd, "were there in force." Resistance stiffened, with Colonel Trusler reporting, "the skirmishing was very sharp until the enemy was driven into his camps beyond the Chickamauga . . . [then] the enemy opened with two pieces of artillery."[4]

These guns belonged to Lt. Winslow Robinson, who commanded a section of Louisiana artillery attached to Scott. Robinson's section was an anomaly. A normal artillery section was comprised of two guns, but Robinson had four pieces—two 3-inch rifles and two mountain howitzers. The mountain howitzers did not qualify as normal field artillery in either army by 1863. These small short-ranged light guns were more suitable for mule transportation in wilderness operations than for use in a major battle, but some units still trundled them along nonetheless. Like Captain Lilly's ad hoc attachment of four such guns to his 18th Indiana battery in support of Wilder's brigade, Robinson's augmentation of his section was probably an informal arrangement. With the appearance of infantry from the 84th Indiana, all four guns set to banging away with a will. Charles Leverich, a member of the battery, tersely noted his busy day: "Reported to General Forrest at 11 A.M. Crossed Chickamaugy but returned, opened fire, drove them back, fired all the ammunition."[5]

On the receiving end of Leverich's fire, Boyd was none too happy about the current state of affairs. By now it was late morning. He would later grump, "we were all surprised to learn that while we were fighting . . . the whole brigade was 8 miles to the rear taking breakfast." Forced to face Rebel cannon with nothing but rifled muskets, Captain Boyd ordered several men to concentrate their fire

---

3 Trusler Report, Indiana AG records; William A. Boyd Journal, University of California at Berkeley.

4 Boyd Journal, University of California, Berkeley, CA; Trusler Report, Indiana AG records.

5 Entry for September 19th, Charles E. Leverich Diary, Louisiana State University, Baton Rouge, LA.

on the gunners, which may have disconcerted the artillerists, who "[fired] over our heads at our suppose[d] support." All the while Boyd hoped someone would send Union artillery forward to equalize the fight. When that failed to happen, the frustrated captain ordered his company to fall back to a safe distance and establish a picket line.[6]

A factor beyond enemy artillery that likely contributed to Boyd's decision to retreat was the appearance of Rebels off to his left front. With only three companies, Major Neff leading the Union patrol could do little more than screen the main crossing. When he realized any move directly across the bridge would be vigorously opposed, Colonel Scott settled on a flanking move. Lieutenant Allen remembered his 5th Tennessee Cavalry waded the Chickamauga at "an old ford some distance downstream." The Yankees were less numerous there, and "[we] drove the enemy back about a mile and a half, when we [once again] found ourselves close to the Red House Bridge . . . on the west side of the river."[7]

So far, the men of the 5th Tennessee thought they were fighting dismounted cavalry instead of Boyd's Hoosier infantry. As the morning drew on the sounds of the fight, especially the noise made by Robinson's sweating gunners burning through their ammunition stocks, drew General Whitaker's attention. He ordered Colonel Trusler to take the rest of the 84th Indiana and a section of the 18th Ohio battery forward to support Major Neff and the irascible Captain Boyd. "On arriving at Kingston's house," noted the colonel, "I posted some companies behind the fence on the right of the road." The posting would provide a nasty shock to the Rebels.[8]

With Boyd's Yankees pulling back, Colonel Scott ordered the 2nd Tennessee to move directly across the bridge while the 5th Tennessee was still working its way down from the north. Lieutenant Colonel Henry C. "Hal" Gillespie had been heading up the 2nd since its colonel, a cunning and careful fighter named Henry M. Ashby, fell with a disabling wound back in June. The 2nd would need Ashby's tactical skills this day. Gillespie plunged recklessly forward, charging Company D directly up the road in column. "The road was narrow and passed through an old field covered with scrub pine," recollected

---

6   Boyd Journal, UC Berkeley.

7   Allen Memoirs, TSLA.

8   Trusler Report, Indiana AG records.

Lieutenant Allen, and "they ran into an ambush. Some ten or twelve men were killed, and many horses, blocking the road." With this bloody check fresh in hand, Scott ordered the 2nd and 5th Tennessee to dismount and more cautiously engage the enemy.[9]

This deployment took time. Scott placed the 5th south of the road, while the bloodied 2nd deployed to the north. The Kentuckians of John Hunt Morgan's former command and the 1st Louisiana extended this line north and south, respectively. On the other side of the field, General Whitaker reinforced the Hoosiers of the 84th with the 40th Ohio, putting both combatants on a more equal footing. Scott's brigade numbered roughly 1,100 men (approximately 800 after deducting for horse-holders) and four cannon, while the Union force now counted roughly 900 bayonets and two guns. It was midday or early afternoon before the action flared up again.[10]

Both Allen and Pvt. William Sloan remembered the afternoon's fight as a desperate one. The private thought the 5th Tennessee was assigned a particularly bad spot in the line. "The space between us and the enemy was entirely clear of obstructions, it being a small farm. . . . The ground descended with a gradual slope for two thirds of the distance . . . and then rose again . . . to the enemy's line." It was a perfect killing ground, dotted with "head high" scrub pine that provided only sporadic concealment. Gillespie's impetuous decision to send Company D thundering up the road had already left the center of battlefield dotted with corpses.[11]

Lieutenant Allen had little love for Colonel Scott, an officer he believed a drunkard. On September 17, for example, Scott ordered Allen to take two men and "charge the Yankee videttes off of Reed's Bridge, proceed up the Bird's Mill Road, and ascertain how many troops was on this road. I protested," recalled a still-angry Allen many years later, "but he was drunk. I took two of his regiment, as I did not expect to return and did not want to sacrifice my boys." Allen also asked for the order in writing. All three men survived the forlorn

---

9 Allen Memoirs, TSLA.

10 William G. Allen, *Reminiscences of William G. Allen: McKenzie's 5th Tennessee Regiment* (Rhea County Historical and Genealogical Society, 2000), 35. Allen recorded multiple accounts of this action, some published and others unpublished, all of which agree on the outline of events, but each of which provide additional details of the affair. Allen also remembered the 6th Georgia as being present instead of the Morgan detachment, but based on other accounts from the 6th Georgia, this is clearly in error.

11 Sloan Diary, TSLA.

hope mission, more through luck than skill, but the incident left Allen with a thinly disguised disgust for Scott. This was not the only instance of drunken leadership plaguing the brigade. Allen, a teetotaler, also had little good to say about the officers of the 2nd Tennessee. Allen was acting as rear guard during the retreat from Knoxville the previous month when he came upon "Major [Pharoah H.] Cobb and Captain [John H.] Kuhn tussling over a dipper" in the streets of Loudoun. "I saw a bucket of whiskey sitting near them and each wanted the first drink." Disgusted, Allen kicked over the bucket, denying both men their swig. All the while, Union artillery shells had been dropping into the village.[12]

Now, at Chickamauga, Lieutenant Allen observed more of the same reckless behavior. "[D]uring the hottest of our fight on the hill [Captain] Coon [Kuhn] left his regiment and rode across to our part of the line and commenced telling us how to shoot." A Federal bullet clipped Kuhn's ear and produced substantial bleeding, but "he did not seem to know it." Private Sloan, who also witnessed this remarkable display, recalled "the last time I saw him, he was a bloody sight. The truth is he had been imbibing a little too much before the battle."[13]

Something was surely affecting the judgment of Scott and his commanders on September 19. After a sustained static fire, with neither side gaining nor giving ground, Colonel McKenzie of the 5th Tennessee decided his troopers had picked off enough horses in Lt. Charles Aleshire's 18th Ohio battery to demoralize the Federal gun crews. "Adjutant!" barked the colonel to Lieutenant Allen, "take [companies] A and D and capture that battery!" The directive horrified Allen, but his orders were clear. The two companies combined numbered about 60 men who, together with Allen and six commissioned officers, would have to cross 200 yards of open ground into the face of a well-supported enemy battery.[14]

As a member of Company D, Private Sloan participated in this attack. More optimistic than Allen, Sloan vividly described the event as a near-triumph: "The charge was made with as much promptness, courage and enthusiasm as could

---

12 Williams Gibbs Allen, "Questionnaire" *McKenzie's Fighting Fifth: Questionnaires of Veterans of the 5th Tennessee Cavalry Regiment, Confederate States of America* (Rhea County Historical and Genealogical Society, 2001), 10-11.

13 Allen, *McKenzie's Fighting Fifth*, 11; Entry for September 19, Sloan Diary, TSLA.

14 Allen, *McKenzie's Fighting Fifth*, 12.

be imagined, and notwithstanding the battery was supported by a line of infantry which outnumbered us two to one, we would have taken it easily had there been no enemy there but those in sight." Unfortunately for the Tennesseans, Sloan and his comrades failed to notice the 40th Ohio, present on their flank. One of the Buckeyes, Pvt. William H. Yeo of Company B, helped beat back the assault. As noted earlier, the Ohio infantry had deployed behind an "old fence," a good position with a clear field of fire. As the inviting targets approached, recalled Yeo, "we . . . commenced pouring it into their line, as they were in this old field about midway."[15]

The Union fire was devastating. "We had made it nearly two thirds of the distance to the battery," lamented Sloan, "when we found ourselves in a veritable trap. A line of infantry which looked to be a regiment rose up from a wash . . . and gave us a fearful flank fire." Every one of the six Rebel officers accompanying Allen fell, and then it was his turn to be struck—multiple times. "I had a minnie ball through my left arm, a minnie ball through my left lung, and two through my right leg below the knee." The fortunate survivors dashed back to their own line, where the fight once again became a static affair.[16]

The fighting on this part of the field cost the two Union regiments about 50 casualties, mostly wounded. Scott's brigade recorded 20 killed and 80 wounded for the battle, most of them falling during this phase of the fighting. Scott later claimed that he had been heavily outnumbered, facing "seven regiments and a battery," and yet drove this superior force back two miles with only "500 men." Realty was something altogether different. In fact, the odds were about even. Most of Whitaker's Union force was not needed and was never engaged. The 96th Illinois recorded that the regiment's only loss of the day came when one of the regimental officers, acting as a courier between Whitaker and the 84th Indiana at the front, blundered into a Confederate patrol and was taken prisoner. General Steedman joined Whitaker at McAfee Church that morning, and both officers monitored the action. Neither felt the need to reinforce Colonel Trusler beyond sending forward the 40th Ohio.[17]

---

15 Sloan Diary, TSLA; W. H. Yeo, "Chickamauga" *National Tribune*, November 21, 1889. Yeo's name in the National Tribune is misspelled.

16 Sloan Diary, TSLA; Allen, *McKenzie's Fighting Fifth*, 12.

17 John N. Beach, *History of the Fortieth Ohio Volunteer Infantry* (Shepherd & Craig, Publishers, 1884), 42; Powell, "Numbers and Losses," CCNMP; *OR* 30, pt. 2, 531; Partridge, *Ninety-Sixth Regiment Illinois*, 172.

The affair at Red House Bridge seems not to have unduly alarmed General Rosecrans, but it did suggest the Rebels were still probing the northern crossings and the threat from that direction could not be ignored. Accordingly, while the 84th Indiana was fending off Scott about noon, Rosecrans decided to reinforce Granger by sending Col. Robert Minty's cavalry to Rossville. After their exertions on September 18, Minty's troopers spent the morning of the 19th resting and refitting near Crawfish Spring. The brigade's casualties had thus far been surprisingly light given the size of the enemy force Minty's men had faced and the duration of the previous day's action. The constant patrolling meant both men and animals had been on the go for the past two days and were in desperate need of rest and forage. Their respite proved short-lived.[18]

"While I was taking my cup of coffee and eating a piece of hardtack," explained Minty, "an officer of the 15th Pa. Cav. informed me that Gen. Rosecrans requested me to report to him in person." Minty found Rosecrans at the Widow Glenn's, where he received new instructions: "It is reported that Forrest is between us and Chattanooga playing havoc with [our] transportation and I want you to go back there and take care of him." Minty set off almost immediately. His men escorted trains headed into Chattanooga as far as Rossville, only to find the road "entirely unobstructed." He reported this happy fact to Rosecrans, who passed him on to George Thomas. By now it was mid-afternoon, and Thomas was fully involved in managing the main infantry battle. The burly Virginian sent Minty on to report to Granger at Rossville, where he arrived late in the afternoon with his men trailing behind him. It would be well after dark before Minty's troopers could replace Whitaker's infantry on the Federal Road, so Granger told the cavalryman to make camp and be ready to move out early the next morning.[19]

*   *   *

Each army's southern flank also merited attention. Rosecrans's main concern was pulling in the last of his army's trains and troops from Alpine. By the morning of September 19, most of the Union infantry was present on the field or close by. Most of the Union Cavalry Corps and at least one brigade of

---

18 See Chapter 8 for the fight on September 18.

19 Minty, "Minty's Saber Brigade;" *OR* 30, pt. 1, 923.

infantry escorting McCook's supply train, however, were still well south of Glass Mill and trying to close up with the main body.

Most of Bragg's Army of Tennessee was also up or near the field, but D. H. Hill's entire infantry corps and Maj. Gen. Thomas C. Hindman's division was still deployed west of the creek that morning between Lee & Gordon's and Glass mills. These Confederates numbered more than 15,000 men and nine batteries of artillery—a powerful force Bragg desperately wanted and needed in the main fight then heavily underway. Except for Hill's spoiling effort at Glass Mill that morning, none of these troops had contributed anything to the larger effort.

The reason for this enforced inactivity was simple: Maj. Gen. Joseph Wheeler was once again neglecting his duties. As earlier described, Bragg had been issuing a steady stream of orders to Wheeler since September 17 to ride north and guard the army's left flank. He was to have replaced Frank Armstrong's cavalry division on September 18 so that Armstrong could re-join Forrest. Wheeler failed to execute the order. He was ordered again on the night of September 18 to come up and cover Hill's front to at least free up Armstrong early on the morning of the 19th. Wheeler once again failed to execute the order. Hill's alarmed dispatch reporting a phantom Union drive across Owen's Ford a couple miles south of Glass Mill prompted yet another urgent order from Bragg demanding Wheeler to come forward at once. Even that unambiguous directive triggered only the most languid reaction from the Rebel cavalry commander.[20]

Daniel Harvey Hill had little to do after the attempted diversion at Glass Mill wound down. Hill was not a patient man, and one can only assume he chafed at being kept on the sidelines while the main event roared farther north. Some of the impetus behind sending Ben Helm's Kentucky infantry brigade across the creek that morning stemmed from this restlessness, though the move was well within the scope of Bragg's intentions to do so. That affair, however, ended late in the forenoon when Hill instructed General Breckinridge to disengage and march his division to a point about "three miles south of Lee and Gordon's Mills," where he could cover both the Glass Mill crossing and the road to La Fayette. Breckinridge dutifully complied.[21]

20 OR 30, pt. 2, 665, 667.

21 Ibid., 198.

Hill fully expected his corps to be called northward at any moment. He understood Bragg's larger intentions and was also aware that much of the army had already moved to the right. If Hill anticipated a similar marching order, he was smart to have done so. Around noon, instructions arrived from the commanding general to do exactly that.[22]

Bragg's orders revealed an army in motion. Hill was to report in person to Bragg's headquarters at Thedford's Ford, accompanied by Maj. Gen. Patrick R. Cleburne's division. Breckinridge's division was ordered to replace Hindman's command (still led by Brig. Gen. J. Patton Anderson since Hindman was ill) of Leonidas Polk's corps opposite Lee and Gordon's Mills. Anderson, in turn, was to cross Chickamauga Creek and move up behind Generals Buckner and Hood, effectively replacing Ben Cheatham's division, which by this time had been called away to help W. H. T. Walker in his fight with Thomas's Federal XIV Corps. This shuffling continued the process of disrupting the command structure of the Army of Tennessee. It was still relatively early in the day, but divisions were already fighting on their own hooks while separated from their corps, and doing so alongside units often wholly unfamiliar to them. Corps commanders had little or no idea where their subordinates were being sent, or why. Hill's new orders exacerbated the unraveling of the command fabric of Bragg's army.[23]

While all this was underway, Joe Wheeler finally made his appearance, though it took yet another flurry of orders to accomplish it. At 10:00 a.m., Bragg sent Wheeler a directive "to immediately remove your command to near this place [Glass Mill.]" Bragg followed up that peremptory command with a second directive providing more specific instructions to "closely observe" the crossing at Lee and Gordon's Mills. As late as midday, however, D. H. Hill was still looking for cavalrymen so he could call in the last of his pickets. At 12:10 p.m., Hill sent yet another urgent dispatch to Wheeler noting that Glass Mill was uncovered save for "a regiment and a section of a battery" which Hill "begs you will relieve . . . as soon as possible."[24]

Why it took Wheeler almost 48 hours to comply with Bragg's clear intentions remains a mystery. Suffice to say, Wheeler's failure to respond

22 Ibid., 140.

23 Ibid., 32, 140, 198.

24 Ibid., pt. 4, 672.

promptly to these new orders greatly hampered Confederate efforts on both the 18th and 19th. As Frank Armstrong noted in frustration on September 18, Brig. Gen. John Wharton's cavalry division spent the day camped near Dr. Anderson's house just a few miles away. Dr. Peter Anderson was a leading citizen, wealthy by local standards, and his substantial dwelling along the La Fayette Road near Rock Springs was well-known to the Confederates. His home, less than three miles southeast of Glass Mill and perhaps four miles east of Owen's Ford, served as headquarters for Generals Polk, Hindman, and Hill at various times the past 10 days, and most of the rest of the army had tramped past or camped nearby during that same period.[25]

W. B. Corbitt was one of Wharton's men serving in the 3rd Confederate Cavalry of Col. Thomas Harrison's brigade. Early on the morning of September 19, Corbitt recorded clearly hearing the sounds of battle: "Cannonading resumed at 8 o'clock . . . the great battle just begun. Cannonading very heavy." At 10:00 a.m., he noted, "Adam's Brigade of Breckinridge's Division is engaging the enemy about two miles from our command." As late as 2:00 p.m., Corbitt added, "all quiet at this hour. No firing to be heard." Robert F. Bunting was chaplain of the 8th Texas Cavalry, also in Harrison's brigade, and a regular correspondent of the *Houston Tri-Weekly Telegraph*. In a letter to the paper dated September 29, Chaplain Bunting similarly described the cavalry's uneventful morning: "On Saturday, the cannonading increased quite early and we are ordered to 'saddle up' and proceed 'to the front.' After <u>standing in line for several hours</u> [emphasis added] for a respectable distance in the woods we move briskly to a point lower down on the Chickamauga." Clearly Wheeler was in no hurry to get Wharton's troopers to the front.[26]

It was well into mid-afternoon before Wharton's troopers filed into position to replace Hill's men. In doing so, they initiated another round of skirmishing that occupied most of the rest of the day because Wheeler had spotted a Union cavalry column coming north out of McLemore's Cove.

The Union cavalry was widely scattered on the morning of September 19. Minty, of course, who belonged to Brig. Gen. George Crook's division, had been detached from Crook's command since August, and was taking his orders

25 See Powell, *Failure in the Saddle*, for a comprehensive discussion of Wheeler's movements during this period of the battle.

26 Entry for September 19, 1863, William E. Corbitt Diary, Emory University, Atlanta, GA; Letter from Robert F. Bunting to Editor, Telegraph, September 29, 1863, TSLA.

directly from General Rosecrans. Colonel Louis Watkins's brigade of Edward McCook's division was still at Valley Head, some 40 miles distant, the last major Federal force still that far south. Watkins had charge of the last of the trains, some of the Federal sick, and a few prisoners. The other three brigades of the Cavalry Corps were closing in on Crawfish Spring.

At dawn, Brig. Gen. Robert Mitchell, who commanded the corps, was camped with McCook's division (minus Colonel Watkins's men) in McLemore's Cove within two miles of Blue Bird Gap. McCook's force consisted of two brigades under Cols. Archibald P. Campbell and Daniel M. Ray. General Crook and Col. Eli Long's brigade were at Dougherty's Gap, at the very southern tip of the cove. One other regiment, Col. Thomas Harrison's 39th Indiana Mounted Infantry of Willich's brigade, was also in the vicinity. Harrison and his 539 Hoosiers spent the night of September 18 at Pond Spring.[27]

Stanley's dislike and low opinion of Mitchell explained why Stanley remained with the corps as long as he did, despite his illness and incapacitation. His decision to finally relinquish command and get back to Stevenson and find a hospital plunged Mitchell into a dangerous and confusing situation. Without Minty and Watkins, the cavalry was understrength: McCook's two brigades numbered only 2,726 officers and men, and Crook's command added about 1,800 more. Wheeler's Confederate cavalry, some 7,000 strong, occupied the gaps in Pigeon Mountain and lurked north of La Fayette. Wheeler, should he decide to act agressively, was in good position to interpose his troopers between Mitchell and the rest of the army which, in turn, would force the Federal cavalry back up Lookout Mountain via Stevens's Gap to try and come at Chattanooga via Lookout Valley. A withdrawal like that would be doubly difficult because the Union cavalry was burdened with substantial baggage trains. By the evening of September 18, however, Mitchell was in contact with Alexander McCook's XX Corps via the 39th Indiana's courier line to Pond Spring. This allowed Mitchell to inform General Rosecrans that the direct path to rejoin the army was still open. At dawn on the 19th, Mitchell and the First Division began riding

---

27 OR 30, pt. 1, 393, 548. Blue Bird Gap was the southernmost of the four gaps in Pigeon Mountain. Union Col. Thomas Harrison of the 39th Indiana Mounted Infantry should not be confused with a Confederate colonel of the same name leading a brigade of cavalry in John Wharton's cavalry division, Joe Wheeler's Cavalry Corps.

for Crawfish Spring, while Crook and Long's brigade descended Dougherty's Gap for Pond Spring.[28]

Most of the ride passed in uneventful fashion for the Union horsemen, though the distant mutterings of the larger battle were clearly audible to many as they rode. In his diary, Robert S. Merrill of the 1st Wisconsin Cavalry noted as they neared "La Fayette we could hear the cannon & knew a battle was being fought. Our whole command halted in the roads & waited for the train to pass: Cannonading pretty heavy while we halted." Most of the men were plagued with more mundane discomforts. "Last night we slept in fear of snakes, which seemed abundant," admitted Henry Hempstead of the 2nd Michigan Cavalry. "No one was bitten, however. This morning it is still cold, with a high wind and dust flying in blinding clouds." "It is suffocating to travel on the roads," agreed Wisconsinite James W. Skeels, for "the dirt is six inches deep." It was this dust rising in billowing clouds that drew Rebel attention.[29]

"At 2:00 p.m.," reported Joe Wheeler, "I learned the enemy's cavalry were moving up McLemore's Cove. I moved across the river and warmly assailed their flank, dividing the column and driving the enemy in confusion in both directions." This short boastful paragraph is the only report Wheeler offered for his actions on all of September 19. A later biographer expanded on its grandiosity, if not its thin details: "With most of his command dismounted, [Wheeler] fought the enemy's infantry with great success. Towards evening he forced the passage of Chickamauga Creek, warmly attacking the enemy, driving him from two positions, and securing a number of prisoners." Unfortunately, none of these claims are borne by either Union observations or those of Wheeler's own troops.[30]

What we do know is that, in response to the approaching Union column, Wheeler instructed Wharton to take Harrison's brigade across the creek at Owen's Ford and attack the Yanks. "We move briskly to a point lower down on

28 Ibid., pt. 3, 743; Powell, "Numbers and Losses," CCNMP; Itinerary of Second Division, Cavalry Corps, CCNMP.

29 Entry for September 19, Robert S. Merrill Diary transcript, Carroll College, Waukesha, WI; Entry for September 19, Henry Hempstead Diary, Bentley Historical Library; "Dear Sister," September 25, 1863, James W. Skeels Letters, Wisconsin Veterans Museum, Madison, WI.

30 OR 30, pt. 2, 520; W. C. Dodson, Wheeler and His Cavalry 1862-1865 (E. F Williams and J. J. Fox, 1997), 106. Dodson, whose book was first published in 1899, offered no additional citations concerning Wheeler's actions on the 19th, but he was clearly paraphrasing Wheeler's own report.

the Chickamauga to intercept a Federal train," recalled Chaplain Bunting. "After some time . . . Gen. Wharton and Col. Harrison go to the front" along with the 8th and 11th Texas Cavalry. "Coming into an open space . . . the dust which rises from the valley indicates the position of the advancing enemy. The Rangers [8th Texas] were ordered to form on the left in the open field, whilst the 11th was dismounted on the right."[31]

The Rebels had indeed divided the Union column, though not by much. In fact, they almost let the Yankees pass entirely unmolested. None of the men in Colonel Campbell's brigade recorded any action on the 19th, and Campbell reported that his brigade arrived at Crawfish Spring without incident that afternoon, beyond a "slight skirmish" that incurred no losses. Major Leonidas Scranton, commanding the 2nd Michigan Cavalry in Campbell's brigade, recorded quite clearly that the "enemy [Wheeler's troopers] were more or less in sight all day, and fired some shots at long range; but we wasted no powder." When Campbell's men reached Crawfish Spring, Mitchell ordered Campbell to establish pickets along Chickamauga Creek between Glass and Lee & Gordon's mills, replacing Maj. Gen. James S. Negley's recently withdrawn Federal infantry that was either already engaged elsewhere or hurrying northward onto the main field.[32]

Most of Colonel Ray's brigade also managed to pass without incident, with the 2nd Indiana Cavalry and the brigade trains bringing up the rear. A gap had indeed opened between the 2nd Indiana and the rest of the brigade, however, just as Colonel Harrison's Rebels appeared on the scene. "Some stragglers behind the 4th Ind[iana Cavalry]," noted John A. Mendenhall, a hospital steward with the 2nd, "caused our regiment to get cut off from the balance of the column." Fellow Hoosier James M. Jones explained in more detail: "In front of our Reg. was a lot of pack mules and refugees that other Regs. had gathered up . . . ." Lagging behind, this detachment of oddments caused a gap to open up within the column, and "the first thing we knew the Rebs. had got between our Reg. and the one in frount [sic] and cut us off from our command."[33]

31 "Dear parents and Home Folks" October 3, 1863, Thomas Coleman Letters, Western Historical Manuscript Collection, University of Missouri, Rolla, MO; Bunting Letters, TSLA.

32 *OR* 30, pt. 1, 899, 902.

33 Entry for September 19, John A. Mendenhall Diary, InHS; "Sketch of Army Life of James Madison Jones," 2nd Indiana Cavalry file, CSI.

With Rebels seeming to appear out of thin air blocking the way forward, Hoosier Maj. David Briggs, commanding the 2nd Indiana, dismounted a skirmish line to confront them and dispatched two men to alert Colonel Ray of the threat. Although unlooked for, Briggs also found support from fellow Hoosiers in the form of Col. Thomas J. Harrison's 39th Indiana, who had been waiting for Ray's column to pass before moving up to Crawfish Spring themselves. Harrison dismounted his own men and sent them forward alongside the troopers, adding the considerable firepower of their Spencers to the Union battle line.[34]

Colonel Ray reacted equally quickly when Briggs's messengers arrived, sending both the 4th Indiana and 1st Wisconsin Cavalry regiments back down the trail. The sudden reappearance of these two units from the north rendered Confederate Col. Thomas Harrison's position untenable. Badger Col. Oscar La Grange saw a chance to work half of his regiment around Harrison's flank, threatening to cut the Confederates off from the ford. With the tables neatly turned, the Rebels had no choice but to flee and did so, narrowly escaping disaster. The entire affair disgusted Chaplain Bunting. "Seeing our men exposed," he grumbled, "they dismounted, and crossing the creek they crept up through the bushes and opened a heavy fire upon us. It was badly planned and we were the sufferers." He also knew where the blame lay: "Gen. Wheeler . . . is responsible for the failure," Bunting continued, "for instead of sending us alone to that position, his whole force should have been thrown across the creek and hurled upon the enemy. . . . It is evident that we have too many commanders and not enough of system."[35]

Losses on each side amounted to a couple of dozen men, with a good many Texans narrowly missing a free trip to a Northern prison. If Wheeler captured any Yankees, they were mostly from the detachment of refugees trailing the 4th Indiana Cavalry. Ray's brigade reported only 11 men missing for the entire battle of Chickamauga. By that evening (September 19), the entire Yankee column was safely at Crawfish Spring without further incident.[36]

---

34 *OR* 30, pt. 1, 909.

35 *OR* 30, pt. 1, 912; Bunting Letters, TSLA. Again, there are two men named Thomas Harrison in this fight; a Federal, commanding the 39th Indiana and the other a Confederate, commanding a brigade in Wharton's Division.

36 Powell, "Numbers and Losses," CCNMP.

This short engagement was Wheeler's sole contribution to the struggle on the 19th. Safely extricated, John Wharton pulled his cavalry division back to its camp near Anderson's house that evening, detailing in its wake only a few companies to guard the various crossings once held by D. H. Hill's infantry. Wheeler finally ordered William Martin's division, still holding the gaps in Pigeon Mountain, to ride forward at this time, though these troopers would be late arriving. In the meantime, Company D of the 8th Texas was sent to picket Glass Mill, and there had one brief encounter with Yankee horsemen before everything quieted down for the night.

As noted, Colonel Campbell sent similar details out that evening, detachments from the 9th Pennsylvania and 2nd Michigan. A Wolverine Sergeant named Henry Hempstead of Company M was part of the force sent to guard Glass Mill. "After going a couple of miles our advance was fired upon by the pickets of what appeared to be a small cavalry force," wrote Hempstead. "We dismounted and reconnoitered their position . . . at a mill on the opposite side [of Chickamauga Creek] where the bank had quite an elevation. We fell back a short distance after sustaining a skirmish with them long enough to develop their strength, which seemed to be greater than ours." Neither side suffered any loss in this light exchange of fire. Once out of range, both the Texans and the Michiganders settled in for the night, prepared to renew the fight in the morning.[37]

That evening, far to the south, Col. Sidney Post's infantry brigade of Jefferson C. Davis's division, XX Corps, halted atop Lookout Mountain at Stevens's Gap. Post's four foot regiments and their attached battery were escorting the last of McCook's XX Corps trains up from Valley Head. They were still a hard day's march behind the rest of the army. From their camps, however, Post's men enjoyed a vast panorama of war. "Within a mile of camp," wrote a quartermaster sergeant named Orlando French of the 75th Illinois, "we could overlook the whole Confederacy. . . .The two lines of battle could be discerned although not very distinct, as the whole valley was one cloud of smoke and dust. The distance was too great to hear musketry but the roar of artillery was incessant and the clouds of smoke ascending showed us plainly this position. [N]ight," he continued, "put a stop to the conflict [and] the campfires of the two armies sparkled brightly in the night air, presenting a beautiful

37 Hempstead Diary, Bentley Historical Library.

picture but the scene lost much of its beauty when we thought of the suffering wounded soldiers that must lie on the cold ground."[38]

*   *   *

Thus ended the second day of the battle of Chickamauga. The fighting on September 19 was confused and chaotic, with each commander largely reduced to reacting to events, rather than seizing the initiative. Here also ends volume one of *The Chickamauga Campaign: A Mad Irregular Battle*. Overnight, both sides would pause, take stock, and devise new plans. While the next day's battle would have its own share of missteps and strategy gone awry, the fighting on September 20 would be more organized, more focused. That day's story will be told in the second volume of *The Chickamauga Campaign* trilogy, *Glory or the Grave*.

---

38 "Dearest Lydia," Sept 27th 1863, Orlando L. French Letters, University of Tennessee, Knoxville, TN.

Order of Battle
with Strengths and Losses

Unit strengths are taken from official reports, returns, and a variety of other sources, chiefly regimental histories and newspapers. Some strengths are estimated. Losses are taken from official reports, augmented by copious newspaper information. Volume 3 of The Chickamauga Campaign will contain a detailed, fully sourced expansion of this information.

Army of the Cumberland

Maj. Gen. William S. Rosecrans

General Headquarters
1st Battalion Ohio Sharpshooters (154 engaged): No losses
10th Ohio Infantry (396 engaged): 1 missing = 1
15th Pennsylvania Cavalry (438 engaged): 2 wounded, 3 missing = 5
Detached, serving as mounted infantry
Wilder's Brigade (First Brigade, Fourth Division, XIV Corps)
92nd Illinois (383 engaged) 2 killed, 22 wounded, 2 missing = 26
98th Illinois (485 engaged): 2 killed, 31 wounded, 2 missing = 35
123rd Illinois (422 engaged): 1 killed, 13 wounded, 10 missing = 24
17th Indiana (513 engaged): 4 killed, 10 wounded, 2 missing = 16

72nd Indiana (480 engaged): 3 killed, 16 wounded, 2 missing = 21
18th Indiana Battery (10 guns) Capt. Eli Lilly: 1 killed, 2 wounded = 3
Brigade total (2,283 engaged): 13 killed, 94 wounded, 18 missing = 125

XIV Corps

Maj. Gen. George H. Thomas

Provost
9th Michigan (384 engaged): no losses
Co. L, 1st Ohio Cavalry (57 engaged): no losses

First Division: Brig. Gen. Absalom Baird
First Brigade: Col. Benjamin F. Scribner
38th Indiana (354 engaged): 13 killed, 57 wounded, 39 missing = 109
2nd Ohio (412 engaged): 9 killed, 50 wounded, 122 missing = 181
33rd Ohio (415 engaged): 14 killed, 63 wounded, 83 missing = 160
94th Ohio (309 engaged): 2 killed, 22 wounded, 22 missing = 46
10th Wisconsin (240 engaged): 11 killed, 55 wounded, 145 missing = 211
Brigade total (1,730 engaged): 49 killed, 247 wounded, 411 missing = 707

Second Brigade: Brig. Gen. John C. Starkweather
24th Illinois (362 engaged): 19 killed, 68 wounded, 56 missing = 143
79th Pennsylvania (390 engaged): 16 killed, 67 wounded, 42 missing = 125
1st Wisconsin (391 engaged): 27 killed, 84 wounded, 77 missing = 188
21st Wisconsin (369 engaged): 2 killed, 43 wounded, 76 missing = 121
Brigade total (1,512 engaged): 64 killed, 262 wounded, 251 missing = 577

Third (Regular) Brigade: Brig. Gen. John H. King
1st Battalion, 15th U.S. (276 engaged): 9 killed, 49 wounded,
102 missing = 160
1st Battalion, 16th U.S. (308 engaged): 3 killed, 19 wounded,
174 missing = 196
1st Battalion, 18th U.S. (300 engaged): 19 killed, 71 wounded,
68 missing = 158
2nd Battalion, 18th U.S. (287 engaged): 14 killed, 81 wounded,
50 missing = 145
1st Battalion, 19th U.S. (204 engaged): 3 killed, 17 wounded,
116 missing = 136
Brigade total: (1,375 engaged): 48 killed, 237 wounded, 510 missing = 795

Artillery

4th Indiana Battery (6 guns) Lt. David Flansburg: 1 killed, 14 wounded, 5 missing = 20

A, 1st Michigan Battery (6 guns) Lt. George W. Van Pelt: 6 killed, 7 wounded, 12 missing = 25

H, 5th US Battery (6 guns) Lt. Howard M. Burnham: 13 killed, 18 wounded, 13 missing = 44

Second Division: Maj. Gen.James S. Negley
First Brigade: Brig.Gen.John Beatty

104th Illinois (299 engaged): 2 killed, 46 wounded, 16 missing = 64

42nd Indiana (328 engaged): 1 killed, 52 wounded, 53 missing = 106

88th Indiana (259 engaged): 3 killed, 33 wounded, 16 missing = 52

15th Kentucky (305 engaged): 5 killed, 42 wounded, 15 missing = 62

Brigade total (1,191 engaged): 11 killed, 173 wounded, 100 missing = 284

Second Brigade: Col. Timothy R. Stanley

19th Illinois (333 engaged): 10 killed, 45 wounded, 16 missing = 71

11th Michigan (341 engaged): 5 killed, 42 wounded, 19 missing = 66

18th Ohio (344 engaged): 5 killed, 55 wounded, 14 missing = 74

Brigade Total (1,018 engaged): 20 killed, 142 wounded, 49 missing = 211

Third Brigade: Col. William Sirwell

37th Indiana (361 engaged): 1 killed, 8 wounded, 2 missing = 11

21st Ohio (561 engaged): 28 killed, 84 wounded, 131 missing = 243

74th Ohio (300 engaged): 1 killed, 2 wounded, 6 missing = 9

78th Pennsylvania (507 engaged): 2 wounded, 3 missing = 5

Brigade total (1,729 engaged): 30 killed, 96 wounded, 142 missing = 268

Artillery

Bridges' Battery (6 guns) Capt. Lyman Bridges: 6 killed, 16 wounded, 4 missing = 26

G, 1st Ohio Battery (6 guns) Capt. Alexander Marshall: no losses

M, 1st Ohio Battery (6 guns) Capt. Frederick Schultz: 4 wounded = 4

Third Division: Brig. Gen. John M. Brannan
First Brigade: Col. John M. Connell

82nd Indiana (285 engaged): 20 killed, 68 wounded, 23 missing = 111

17th Ohio (454 engaged): 16 killed, 114 wounded, 21 missing = 151

31st Ohio (465 engaged): 13 killed, 134 wounded, 22 missing = 169

38th Ohio (16 engaged): no losses (rest of regiment guarding trans)

Brigade total (1,220 engaged): 49 killed, 316 wounded, 66 missing = 431

Second Brigade: Col. John T. Croxton

10th Indiana (366 engaged): 24 killed, 136 wounded, 6 missing = 166
74th Indiana (400 engaged): 22 killed, 125 wounded, 10 missing = 157
4th Kentucky (351 engaged): 25 killed, 157 wounded, 9 missing = 191
10th Kentucky (421 engaged): 21 killed, 134 wounded, 11 missing = 166
14th Ohio (460 engaged): 35 killed, 167 wounded, 43 missing = 245
Brigade total (1,998 engaged): 127 killed, 719 wounded, 79 missing = 925

Third Brigade: Col. Ferdinand Van Derveer

87th Indiana (366 engaged): 40 killed, 142 wounded, 8 missing = 190
2nd Minnesota (384 engaged): 35 killed, 113 wounded, 14 missing = 162
9th Ohio (502 engaged): 48 killed, 185 wounded, 16 missing = 249
35th Ohio (391 engaged): 21 killed, 139 wounded, 27 missing = 187
Brigade total (1,643 engaged): 144 killed, 579 wounded, 65 missing = 788

Artillery

D, 1st Michigan Battery (6 guns) Capt. Josiah W. Church:
7 wounded, 4 missing = 11
C, 1st Ohio Battery (6 guns) Lt. Marco B. Gary: 4 killed, 9 wounded = 13
I, 4th U.S. Battery (4 guns) Lt. Frank G. Smith: 1 killed, 21 wounded = 22

Fourth Division: Maj. Gen. Joseph J. Reynolds
First Brigade (Wilder)

detached and serving as mounted infantry

Second Brigade: Col. Edward A. King

68th Indiana (356 engaged): 17 killed, 108 wounded, 12 missing = 137
75th Indiana (360 engaged): 17 killed, 108 wounded, 13 missing = 138
101st Indiana (400 engaged): 11 killed, 90 wounded, 18 missing = 119
105th Ohio (382 engaged): 3 killed, 41 wounded, 26 missing = 70
Brigade total (1,476 engaged): 48 killed, 347 wounded, 69 missing = 464

Third Brigade: Brig. Gen. John B. Turchin

Provost Guard: A, 18th Kentucky: 29 engaged): no losses
18th Kentucky (266 engaged): 7 killed, 46 wounded, 33 missing = 86
11th Ohio (433 engaged): 5 killed, 36 wounded, 22 missing = 63
36th Ohio (484 engaged): 12 killed, 65 wounded, 14 missing = 91
92nd Ohio (400 engaged): 6 killed, 68 wounded, 17 missing = 91
Brigade total (1,612 engaged): 30 killed, 215 wounded, 86 missing = 331

Artillery

19th Indiana Battery (6 guns) Capt. Samuel J. Harris: 2 killed, 16 wounded,
2 missing = 20
21st Indiana Battery (6 guns) Capt. William W. Andrew: 12 wounded = 12

XX Corps

Maj. Gen. Alexander McDowell McCook

Provost
I, 2nd Kentucky Cavalry (39 engaged): no losses
D, 1st Ohio Infantry (41 engaged): no losses
Detached, serving as mounted infantry
39th Indiana (First Brigade, Second Division, XX Corps) (581 engaged):
5 killed, 35 wounded = 40

First Division: Brig. Gen. Jefferson C. Davis
First Brigade: Col. P. Sidney Post
(guarding trains, only lightly engaged)
59th Illinois (285 engaged): 1 wounded, 1 missing = 2
74th Illinois (354 engaged): 1 wounded, 4 missing = 5
75th Illinois (200 engaged): 10 missing = 10
22nd Indiana (400 engaged): 1 killed, 2 wounded, 4 missing = 7
Brigade total (1,239 engaged): 1 killed, 4 wounded, 19 missing = 24
Second Brigade: Brig. Gen. William P. Carlin
21st Illinois (416 engaged): 22 killed, 70 wounded, 146 missing = 238
38th Illinois (301 engaged): 15 killed, 87 wounded, 78 missing = 180
81st Indiana (255 engaged): 4 killed, 60 wounded, 23 missing = 87
101st Ohio (243 engaged): 13 killed, 82 wounded, 51 missing = 146
Brigade total (1,215 engaged): 54 killed, 299 wounded, 298 missing = 651
Third Brigade: Brig. Gen. Hans C. Heg
25th Illinois (337 engaged): 10 killed, 171 wounded, 24 missing = 205
35th Illinois (299 engaged): 17 killed, 130 wounded, 13 missing = 160
8th Kansas (406 engaged): 30 killed, 165 wounded, 25 missing = 220
15th Wisconsin (176 engaged): 13 killed, 53 wounded, 45 missing = 111
Brigade total (1,218 engaged): 70 killed, 519 wounded, 107 missing = 696
Artillery
2nd Minnesota Battery (6 guns) Lt. Albert Woodbury: 2 wounded = 2
5th Wisconsin Battery (6 guns) Capt. George Q. Gardner: no losses
8th Wisconsin Battery (6 guns) Lt. John D. McLean: no losses

Second Division: Brig. Gen. Richard W. Johnson
First Brigade: Brig. Gen. August Willich
89th Illinois (391 engaged): 14 killed, 88 wounded, 30 missing = 132
32nd Indiana (378 engaged): 21 killed, 81 wounded, 20 missing = 122

39th Indiana (detached)
15th Ohio (325 engaged): 10 killed, 77 wounded, 33 missing = 120
49th Ohio (405 engaged): 10 killed, 59 wounded, 30 missing = 99
Brigade total (1,499 engaged): 55 killed, 306 wounded, 114 missing = 475

Second Brigade: Col. Joseph B. Dodge
79th Illinois (263 engaged): 3 killed, 21 wounded, 97 missing = 121
29th Indiana (315 engaged): 11 killed, 92 wounded, 69 missing = 172
30th Indiana (299 engaged): 10 killed, 55 wounded, 61 missing = 126
77th Pennsylvania (253 engaged): 3 killed, 28 wounded, 73 missing = 104
Brigade total (1,130 engaged): 27 killed, 198 wounded, 307 missing = 532

Third Brigade: Col. Philemon P. Baldwin
6th Indiana (467 engaged): 13 killed, 116 wounded, 31 missing = 160
5th Kentucky (334 engaged): 14 killed, 79 wounded, 32 missing = 125
1st Ohio (367 engaged): 13 killed, 96 wounded, 33 missing = 142
93rd Ohio (459 engaged): 15 killed, 86 wounded, 29 missing = 130
Brigade total (1,627 engaged): 56 killed, 378 wounded, 125 missing = 559

Artillery
5th Indiana Battery (6 guns) Capt. Peter Simonson: 1 killed, 7 wounded,
1 missing = 9
A 1st Ohio Battery (6 guns) Capt. Wilbur F. Goodspeed: 2 killed,
14 wounded, 4 missing = 20
20th Ohio Battery (6 guns) Capt. Edward Grosskopf: 2 wounded, 2 missing = 4

Third Division: Maj. Gen. Philip H. Sheridan
First Brigade: Brig. Gen. William H. Lytle
36th Illinois (358 engaged): 20 killed, 101 wounded, 20 missing = 141
88th Illinois (449 engaged): 12 killed, 62 wounded, 14 missing = 88
21st Michigan (299 engaged): 16 killed, 73 wounded, 17 missing = 106
24th Wisconsin (487 engaged): 3 killed, 73 wounded, 29 missing = 105
Brigade total (1,593 engaged): 52 killed, 309 wounded, 80 missing = 441

Second Brigade: Col. Bernard Laiboldt
44th Illinois (269 engaged): 6 killed, 64 wounded, 34 missing = 100
73rd Illinois (300 engaged): 13 killed, 57 wounded, 22 missing = 92
2nd Missouri (281 engaged): 7 killed, 56 wounded, 29 missing = 92
15th Missouri (250 engaged): 11 killed, 67 wounded, 22 missing = 100
Brigade total (1,100 engaged): 37 killed, 240 wounded, 107 missing = 384

Third Brigade: Col. Luther P. Bradley
22nd Illinois (314 engaged): 23 killed, 76 wounded, 31 missing = 130
27th Illinois (463 engaged): 2 killed, 79 wounded, 10 missing = 91
42nd Illinois (305 engaged): 15 killed, 123 wounded, 5 missing = 143
51st Illinois (309 engaged): 18 killed, 93 wounded, 38 missing = 149
Brigade total (1,391 engaged): 58 killed, 372 wounded, 84 missing = 514

Artillery

C 1st Illinois Battery (6 guns) Capt. Mark H. Prescott: 4 wounded = 4

11th Indiana Battery (6 guns) Capt. Arnold Sutermeister: 3 killed,
12 wounded, 4 missing = 19

G 1st Missouri Battery (6 guns) Lt. Gustavus Schueler:1 killed,
3 wounded, 1 missing= 5

XXI Corps

Maj. Gen. Thomas L. Crittenden
Provost

K, 15th Illinois Cavalry (83 engaged): 3 wounded = 3

First Division: Brig. Gen. Thomas J. Wood
First Brigade: Col. George P. Buell

100th Illinois (339 engaged): 23 killed, 117 wounded, 24 missing = 164

58th Indiana (397 engaged): 16 killed, 119 wounded, 34 missing = 169

13th Michigan (220 engaged): 13 killed, 67 wounded, 26 missing = 106

26th Ohio (377 engaged): 27 killed, 140 wounded, 45 missing = 212

Brigade total (1,333 engaged): 79 killed, 443 wounded, 129 missing = 651

Second Brigade

(not engaged): stationed at Chattanooga

Third Brigade: Col. Charles G. Harker

3rd Kentucky (401 engaged): 13 killed, 78 wounded, 22 missing = 113

64th Ohio (325 engaged): 8 killed, 50 wounded, 13 missing = 71

65th Ohio (306 engaged): 14 killed, 71 wounded, 18 missing = 103

125th Ohio (314 engaged): 16 killed, 84 wounded, 5 missing = 105

Brigade total (1,346 engaged): 51 killed, 283 wounded, 58 missing = 392

Artillery

8th Indiana Battery (6 guns) Capt. George Estep: 1 killed, 9 wounded,
7 missing = 17

6th Ohio Battery (6 guns) Capt. Cullen Bradley: 1 killed, 8 wounded = 9

Second Division: Maj. Gen. John M. Palmer
First Brigade: Brig. Gen. Charles Cruft

31st Indiana (380 engaged): 5 killed, 61 wounded, 17 missing = 83

1st Kentucky (118 engaged): 2 killed, 26 wounded, 3 missing = 31

2nd Kentucky (367 engaged): 10 killed, 64 wounded, 18 missing = 92

90th Ohio (415 engaged): 7 killed, 62 wounded, 15 missing = 84

Brigade total (1,280 engaged): 24 killed, 213 wounded, 53 missing = 290

Second Brigade: Brig. Gen. William B. Hazen
9th Indiana (328 engaged): 13 killed, 91 wounded, 22 missing = 126
6th Kentucky (302 engaged): 12 killed, 95 wounded, 11 missing = 118
41st Ohio (360 engaged): 6 killed, 100 wounded, 9 missing = 115
124th Ohio (453 engaged): 15 killed, 92 wounded, 34 missing = 141
Brigade total (1,443 engaged): 46 killed, 378 wounded, 76 missing = 500

Third Brigade: Col. William Grose
84th Illinois (382 engaged): 13 killed, 83 wounded, 9 missing = 105
36th Indiana (347 engaged): 13 killed, 99 wounded, 17 missing = 129
23rd Kentucky (263 engaged): 11 killed, 52 wounded, 17 missing = 80
6th Ohio (362 engaged): 13 killed, 102 wounded, 17 missing = 132
24th Ohio (277 engaged): 3 killed, 60 wounded, 16 missing = 79
Brigade total (1,631 engaged): 53 killed, 399 wounded, 65 missing = 517

Artillery
B 1st Ohio Battery (6 guns) Lt. Norman Baldwin: 1 killed, 8 wounded,
4 missing = 13
F 1st Ohio Battery (6 guns) Lt. Giles J. Cockerill: 2 killed, 8 wounded,
2 missing = 12
H 4th U.S. Battery (4 guns) Lt. Harry C. Cushing: 5 killed, 17 wounded = 22
M 4th U.S. Battery (6 guns) Lt. Francis D. Russell: 2 killed, 6 wounded = 8

Third Division: Brig. Gen. Horatio P. Van Cleve
Provost
A, 9th Kentucky (30 engaged): no losses

First Brigade: Brig. Gen. Samuel Beatty
79th Indiana (300 engaged): 1 killed, 44 wounded, 10 missing = 55
9th Kentucky (213 engaged): 2 killed, 45 wounded, 13 missing = 60
17th Kentucky (487 engaged): 6 killed, 105 wounded, 15 missing = 126
19th Ohio (384 engaged): 7 killed, 60 wounded, 23 missing = 90
Brigade total (1,384 engaged): 16 killed, 254 wounded, 61 missing = 331

Second Brigade: Col. George F. Dick
44th Indiana (229 engaged): 3 killed, 61 wounded, 10 missing = 74
86th Indiana (261 engaged): 1 killed, 31 wounded, 21 missing = 53
13th Ohio (304 engaged): 5 killed, 47 wounded, 22 missing = 74
59th Ohio (290 engaged): 7 killed, 41 wounded, 30 missing = 78
Brigade total (1,084 engaged): 16 killed, 180 wounded, 83 missing = 279

Third Brigade: Col. Sidney M. Barnes

35th Indiana (229 engaged): 5 killed, 23 wounded, 37 missing = 65
8th Kentucky (297 engaged): 4 killed, 47 wounded, 28 missing = 79
51st Ohio (319 engaged): 8 killed, 35 wounded, 55 missing = 98
99th Ohio (357 engaged): 3 killed, 30 wounded, 24 missing = 57
Brigade total (1,202 engaged): 20 killed, 135 wounded, 144 missing = 299

Artillery

7th Indiana Battery (6 guns) Capt. George R. Swallow: 8 wounded, 1 missing = 9
26th Pennsylvania Battery (6 guns) Capt. A. J. Stevens: 2 killed,
14 wounded, 1 missing = 17
3rd Wisconsin Battery (6 guns) Lt. Courtland Livingston: 2 killed,
13 wounded, 11 missing = 26

Reserve Corps

Maj. Gen. Gordon Granger

First Division: Brig. Gen. James B. Steedman
First Brigade: Brig. Gen. Walter C. Whitaker

96th Illinois (419 engaged): 39 killed, 134 wounded, 52 missing = 223
115th Illinois (426 engaged): 22 killed, 151 wounded, 10 missing = 183
84th Indiana (374 engaged): 23 killed, 97 wounded, 13 missing = 133
22nd Michigan (455 engaged): 32 killed, 96 wounded, 261 missing = 389
40th Ohio (537 engaged): 19 killed, 102 wounded, 11 missing = 132
89th Ohio (389 engaged): 19 killed, 63 wounded, 171 missing = 253
18th Ohio Battery (6 guns) Capt. Charles C. Aleshire: 10 wounded = 10
Brigade total (2,695 engaged): 154 killed, 654 wounded, 518 missing = 1,326

Second Brigade: Col. John G. Mitchell

78th Illinois (353 engaged): 17 Killed, 77 wounded, 62 missing = 156
98th Ohio (181 engaged): 9 killed, 41 wounded, 13 missing = 63
113th Ohio (355 engaged): 21 killed, 98 wounded, 12 missing = 131
121st Ohio (235 engaged): 9 killed, 83 wounded, 7 missing = 99
M 1st Illinois Battery (6 guns) Lt. Thomas Burton: 2 killed, 9 wounded
1 missing = 12
Brigade total (1,124 engaged): 58 killed, 308 wounded, 95 missing = 461

Second Division: commander not present
Second Brigade: Col. Daniel McCook

85th Illinois (371 engaged): 2 wounded = 2
86th Illinois (420 engaged): 1 killed, 1 wounded, 5 missing = 7

125th Illinois (439 engaged): 1 killed, 2 wounded, 4 missing = 7
52nd Ohio (517 engaged): 5 wounded = 5
69th Ohio (350 engaged): 13 missing = 13
I 2nd Illinois Battery (6 guns) Capt. Charles M. Barnett: no losses
Brigade Total (1,997 engaged): 2 killed, 10 wounded, 22 missing = 34

Cavalry Corps

Maj. Gen. David S. Stanley, Brig. Gen. Robert B. Mitchell

First Division: Brig. Gen. Robert B. Mitchell,
Col. Edward M. McCook
Escort
I, 4th Indiana (32 engaged): losses unknown
First Brigade: Col. Archibald P. Campbell
2nd Michigan (273 engaged): 2 killed, 7 wounded, 2 missing = 11
9th Pennsylvania (397 engaged): 3 missing = 3
1st Tennessee (678 engaged): 1 missing = 1
Brigade total (1,384 engaged): 2 killed, 7 wounded, 6 missing = 15
Second Brigade: Col. Daniel M. Ray
2nd Indiana (388 engaged): 1 killed, 4 wounded = 5
4th Indiana (316 engaged): 2 wounded, 7 missing = 9
2nd Tennessee (476 engaged): 1 killed, 2 wounded = 3
1st Wisconsin (384 engaged): 2 wounded, 4 missing = 6
D 1st Ohio Battery (2 guns) Lt. Nathaniel M. Newell: no losses
Brigade total (1,564 engaged): 2 killed, 10 wounded, 11 missing = 23
Third Brigade: Col. Louis D. Watkins
4th Kentucky (288 engaged): 1 wounded, 94 missing = 95
5th Kentucky (363 engaged): 20 missing = 20
6th Kentucky (524 engaged): 2 killed, 7 wounded, 122 missing = 131
Brigade total (1,175 engaged): 2 killed, 8 wounded, 236 missing = 246

Second Division: Brig. Gen. George Crook
First Brigade: Col. Robert H. G. Minty
3rd Indiana Bn (detached, in Chattanooga)
4th Michigan (489 engaged): 1 killed, 12 wounded, 6 missing = 19
7th Pennsylvania (496 engaged): 5 killed, 13 wounded, 1 missing = 19
4th U.S. (711 engaged): 1 killed, 5 wounded, 1 missing = 7
Brigade total: (1,696 engaged): 7 killed, 32 wounded, 8 missing = 47

Second Brigade: Col. Eli Long

2nd Kentucky (347 engaged): 11 killed, 50 wounded, 2 missing = 63
1st Ohio (404 engaged): 2 killed, 13 wounded, 7 missing = 22
3rd Ohio (550 engaged): 2 killed, 7 wounded, 8 missing = 17
4th Ohio (545 engaged): 4 killed, 9 wounded, 21 missing = 34
Brigade total (1,846 engaged): 19 killed, 79 wounded, 38 missing = 136

Artillery

Chicago Board of Trade Battery (7 guns) Capt. James H. Stokes: no losses

Army of Tennessee

Gen. Braxton Bragg

General Headquarters

Druex Co. Louisiana Cavalry (68 engaged): no losses
K, 3rd Alabama Cavalry (68 engaged): no losses
Miners and Sappers (160 engaged): no losses
C, 1st Louisiana Regulars Infantry (48 engaged): no losses

Polk's Corps

Lt. Gen. Leonidas Polk

Escort

Greenleaf's Co. Louisiana Cavalry (33 engaged): losses unknown

Cheatham's Division: Maj. Gen. Benjamin F. Cheatham

Escort

G, 2nd Georgia Cavalry (32 engaged): losses unknown

Jackson's Brigade: Brig. Gen. John K. Jackson

2nd Bn, 1st Confederate (194 engaged): 10 killed, 73 wounded = 83
2nd Georgia Sharpshooters (108 engaged): 3 killed, 27 wounded = 30
5th Georgia (353 engaged): 27 killed, 165 wounded, 2 missing = 194
8th Mississippi (404 engaged): 10 killed, 84 wounded = 94
Brigade total (1,311 engaged): 54 killed, 419 wounded, 4 missing = 477

Maney's Brigade: Brig. Gen. George Maney
1+27 Tennessee (703 engaged): 14 killed, 75 wounded = 89
4th Tennessee (PA) (179 engaged): 10 killed, 43 wounded, 12 missing = 65
6+9 Tennessee (368 engaged): 26 killed, 168 wounded, 17 missing = 211
24th Tennessee Sharpshooters (43 engaged): 19 wounded, 3 missing = 22
Brigade total (1,293 engaged): 50 killed, 305 wounded, 32 missing = 387

Smith's Brigade: Brig. Gen. Preston Smith
11th Tennessee (383 engaged): 8 killed, 44 wounded = 52
12+47 Tennessee (351 engaged): 11 killed, 76 wounded = 87
13+154 Tennessee (222 engaged): 8 killed, 67 wounded = 75
29th Tennessee (413 engaged): 4 killed, 66 wounded, 1 missing = 71
Dawson's Sharpshooter Bn (273 engaged): 7 killed, 49 wounded, 6 missing = 62
Brigade total (1,642 engaged): 38 killed, 302 wounded, 7 missing = 347

Strahl's Brigade: Brig. Gen. Otho F. Strahl
4+5 Tennessee (380 engaged): 3 killed, 30 wounded = 33
19th Tennessee (266 engaged): 8 killed, 66 wounded, 20 missing = 94
24th Tennessee (245 engaged) = 43 total losses
31st Tennessee (168 engaged): 1 killed, 26 wounded = 27
33rd Tennessee (122 engaged) = 53 total losses
Brigade total (1,181 engaged): 250 total losses

Wright's Brigade: Brig. Gen. Marcus J. Wright
8th Tennessee (285 engaged): 3 killed, 78 wounded, 1 missing = 82
16th Tennessee (266 engaged): 1 killed, 67 wounded = 68
28th Tennessee (279 engaged): 9 killed, 76 wounded = 85
38th Tennessee (278 engaged): 4 killed, 56 wounded, 5 missing = 65
51+52 Tennessee (255 engaged): 13 killed, 102 wounded = 115
Brigade total (1,113 engaged): 30 killed, 379 wounded, 6 missing = 415

Artillery
Capt. William W. Carnes's Tennessee Battery (4 guns): 7 killed, 16 wounded = 23
Capt. John Scogin's Georgia Battery (4 guns): 1 killed, 11 wounded, 1 missing = 13
Scott's Tennessee Battery (4 guns) Lt. John H. Marsh: 2 killed, 14 wounded = 16
Smith's Mississippi Battery (4 guns) Lt. William B. Turner: 2 wounded, 5 missing = 7
Capt. Thomas J. Sanford's Mississippi Battery (4 guns): 4 wounded = 4

Hindman's Division: Maj. Gen. Thomas C. Hindman

Escort
I, 3rd Alabama Cavalry (65 engaged): losses unknown

Anderson's Brigade: Brig. Gen. J. Patton Anderson
7th Mississippi (291 engaged): 10 killed, 64 wounded, 1 missing = 75
9th Mississippi (355 engaged): 9 killed, 75 wounded, 9 missing = 93
10th Mississippi (311 engaged): 17 killed, 59 wounded = 76
41st Mississippi (502 engaged): 24 killed, 164 wounded, 9 missing = 197
44th Mississippi (272 engaged): 81 total losses
9th Mississippi Sharpshooters (134 engaged): 36 total losses
Brigade total (1,865 engaged): 80 killed, 454 wounded, 24 missing = 558

Deas's Brigade: Brig. Gen. Zachariah C. Deas
19th Alabama (515 engaged): 34 killed, 158 wounded, 12 missing = 204
22nd Alabama (371 engaged): 44 killed, 161 wounded = 205
25th Alabama (330 engaged): 15 killed, 95 wounded, 2 missing = 112
39th Alabama (340 engaged): 14 killed, 82 wounded = 96
50th Alabama (500 engaged): 17 killed, 81 wounded, 8 missing = 106
17th Alabama Sharpshooters (76 engaged): 1 killed, 9 wounded, 2 missing = 12
Brigade total (2,132 engaged): 125 killed, 586 wounded, 24 missing = 735

Manigault's Brigade: Brig. Gen. Arthur M. Manigault
24th Alabama (381 engaged): 22 killed, 91 wounded, 3 missing = 116
28th Alabama (629 engaged): 266 total losses
34th Alabama (329 engaged): 38 total losses
10+19 South Carolina (686 engaged): 26 killed, 210 wounded = 236
Brigade total (2,025 engaged): 656 total losses

Artillery
Capt. S. H. Dent's Alabama Battery (6 guns): 3 killed, 13 wounded = 16
Capt. James Garrity's Alabama Battery (4 guns): 5 wounded = 5
Water's Alabama Battery (4 guns): Lt. Charles H. Watkins = no losses

Hill's Corps

Lt. Gen. Daniel H. Hill

Escort
Raum's Co. Georgia Cavalry (51 engaged): losses unkown

Breckinridge's Division: Maj. Gen. John C. Breckinridge
Adams's Brigade: Brig. Gen. Daniel W. Adams
32nd Alabama (145 engaged): 4 wounded = 4
13+20 Louisiana (309 engaged): 16 killed, 54 wounded, 44 missing = 114
16+25 Louisiana (319 engaged): 21 killed, 49 wounded, 36 missing = 106
19th Louisiana (349 engaged): 28 killed, 114 wounded, 11 missing = 153

14th Louisiana Sharpshooters (99 engaged): 7 wounded = 7
Brigade total (1,221 engaged): 65 killed, 238 wounded, 91 missing = 394

Helm's (Orphan) Brigade: Brig. Gen. Benjamin H. Helm

41st Alabama (357 engaged): 27 killed, 120 wounded, 11 missing = 158
2nd Kentucky (302 engaged): 13 killed, 107 wounded, 25 missing = 145
4th Kentucky (275 engaged): 7 killed, 51 wounded = 58
6th Kentucky (220 engaged): 2 killed, 32 wounded = 34
9th Kentucky (230 engaged): 11 killed, 89 wounded, 2 missing = 102
Brigade total (1,384 engaged): 60 killed, 399 wounded, 39 missing = 498

Stovall's Brigade: Brig. Gen. Marcellus A. Stovall

1+3rd Florida (298 engaged): 9 killed, 70 wounded, 13 missing = 92
4th Florida (238 engaged): 9 killed, 67 wounded, 11 missing = 87
47th Georgia (193 engaged): 11 killed, 59 wounded, 6 missing = 76
60th North Carolina (168 engaged): 8 killed, 36 wounded, 16 missing = 60
Brigade total (897 engaged): 37 killed, 232 wounded, 46 missing = 315

Artillery

Capt. Robert Cobb's Kentucky Battery (5 guns): 3 killed, 7 wounded = 10
Capt. John W. Mebane's Tennessee Battery (4 guns): 1 wounded
5th Company, Washington (Louisiana) Artillery (6 guns) Capt. C. H. Slocumb:
11 killed, 22 wounded = 33

Cleburne's Division: Maj. Gen. Patrick R. Cleburne

Escort

Sander's Co. Tennessee Cavalry (51 engaged): 1 wounded = 1

Deshler's Brigade: Brig. Gen. James Deshler

19+24 Arkansas (226 engaged): 8 killed, 97 wounded, 1 missing = 106
6+10+15 Texas (700 engaged): 20 killed, 95 wounded, 28 missing = 143
17+18+24+25 Texas (767 engaged): 24 killed, 174 wounded = 198
Brigade total (1,693 engaged): 52 killed, 366 wounded, 29 missing = 447

Polk's Brigade: Brig. Gen. Lucius E. Polk

1st Arkansas (430 engaged): 13 killed, 180 wounded, 1 missing = 194
3+5 Confederate (290 engaged): 13 killed, 104 wounded, 1 missing = 118
2nd Tennessee (264 engaged): 13 killed, 145 wounded, 1 missing = 159
35th Tennessee (236 engaged): 7 killed, 54 wounded = 61
48th Tennessee (170 engaged): 10 killed, 65 wounded, 3 missing = 78
Brigade total (1,390 engaged): 56 killed, 548 wounded, 6 missing = 610

Wood's Brigade: Brig. Gen. S.A.M. Wood
16th Alabama (414 engaged): 25 killed, 218 wounded = 243
33rd Alabama (459 engaged): 19 killed, 166 wounded = 185
45th Alabama (423 engaged): 22 killed, 95 wounded = 117
18th Alabama Bn (87 engaged): 5 killed, 34 wounded = 39
32+45 Mississippi (541 engaged): 25 killed, 141 wounded =165
15th Mississippi sharpshooters (58 engaged): 3 killed, 23 wounded = 26
Brigade total (1,982 engaged): 96 killed, 680 wounded = 776

Artillery
Carlvert's Arkansas Battery (4 guns) Lt. Thomas J. Key: 6 wounded = 6
Capt. James P. Douglas's Texas Battery (4 guns): no losses
Capt. Henry P. Semple's Alabama Battery (4 guns): 10 wounded = 10

Reserve Corps

Maj. Gen. William H. T. Walker

Gist's Division: Brig. Gen. States Rights Gist
Colquitt's Brigade: Col. Peyton H. Colquitt
(not engaged on September 19)
46th Georgia (591 engaged): 5 killed, 48 wounded, 19 missing = 72
8th Georgia Bn (399 engaged): 14 killed, 59 wounded = 73
24th South Carolina (410 engaged): 30 killed, 144 wounded, 17 missing = 191
Brigade total (1,400 engaged): 49 killed, 251 wounded, 36 missing = 336

Ector's Brigade: Brig. Gen. Matthew D. Ector
Stone's Alabama Bn (111 engaged): 5 killed, 17 wounded, 1 missing = 23
Pound's Mississippi Bn (42 engaged): 1 killed, 8 wounded, 1 missing = 10
29th North Carolina (215 engaged): 14 killed, 72 wounded, 25 missing = 111
9th Texas (145 engaged): 6 killed, 36 wounded, 18 missing = 60
10th Texas DC (272 engaged): 11 killed, 84 wounded, 24 missing = 119
14th Texas DC (197 engaged): 10 killed, 47 wounded, 29 missing = 86
32nd Texas DC (217 engaged): 13 killed, 65 wounded, 40 missing = 118
Brigade total (1,119 engaged): 60 killed, 329 wounded, 138 missing = 527

Wilson's Brigade: Col. Claudius C. Wilson
25th Georgia (383 engaged): 29 killed, 123 wounded = 152
29th Georgia (220 engaged 24 killed, 97 wounded, 8 missing = 129
30th Georgia (334 engaged): 20 killed, 106 wounded = 126
1st Georgia Sharpshooters (152 engaged): 5 killed, 52 wounded, 4 missing = 61
4th Louisiana Bn (228 engaged): 21 killed, 48 wounded, 68 missing = 137
Brigade total (1,317 engaged): 99 killed, 426 wounded, 80 missing = 605

Artillery

Capt. Evan P. Howell's Georgia Battery (6 guns) 7 wounded = 7

Liddell's Division: Brig. Gen. St. John R. Liddell
Govan's Brigade: Col. Daniel C. Govan

2+15th Arkansas (349 engaged) = 150 total losses

5+13th Arkansas (450 engaged): 38 killed, 131 wounded, 32 missing = 201

6+7th Arkansas (388 engaged) = 165 total losses

8th Arkansas (387 engaged): 14 killed, 92 wounded, 65 missing = 171

1st Louisiana Regulars (401 engaged) = 170 total losses

Brigade total (1,975 engaged): 73 killed, 502 wounded, 283 missing = 858

Walthall's Brigade: Brig. Gen. Edward C. Walthall

24th Mississippi (428 engaged): 10 killed, 103 wounded, 19 missing = 132

27th Mississippi (362 engaged): 10 killed, 88 wounded, 19 missing = 117

29th Mississippi (368 engaged): 17 killed, 139 wounded, 38 missing = 194

30th Mississippi (362 engaged): 5 killed, 76 wounded, 38 missing = 119

34th Mississippi (307 engaged): 15 killed, 91 wounded, 19 missing = 125

Brigade total (1,827 engaged): 57 killed, 497 wounded, 133 missing = 687

Artillery

Capt. Charles Swett

Capt. William H. Fowler's Alabama Battery (4 guns): 6 killed,
17 wounded, 1 missing = 24

Warren (Mississippi) Light Artillery (4 guns) Lt. H. Shannon:
2 killed, 6 wounded = 8

Buckner's Corps

Maj. Gen. Simon B. Buckner

Escort

Clark's Co. Tennessee Cavalry (20 engaged): losses unknown

Train guard

Companies from 63rd Virginia and 65th Georgia (80 engaged): no losses

Preston's Division: Brig. Gen. William Preston

Gracie's Brigade: Brig. Gen Archibald Gracie, Jr.

43rd Alabama (400 engaged): 16 killed, 83 wounded = 99

1st Alabama/ Hilliard (260 engaged): 24 killed, 144 wounded = 168

2nd Alabama/Hilliard (230 engaged): 16 killed, 75 wounded = 91

3rd Alabama/Hilliard (285 engaged): 5 killed, 45 wounded = 50

4th Alabama/Hilliard (205 engaged): 15 killed, 87 wounded = 102

63rd Tennessee (402 engaged): 16 killed, 184 wounded = 200
Brigade total (1,782 engaged): 92 killed, 618 wounded = 710

Kelly's Brigade: Col. John H. Kelly

65th Georgia (251 engaged): 4 wounded = 4
5th Kentucky (377 engaged): 14 killed, 75 wounded, 2 missing = 91
58th North Carolina (322 engaged): 46 killed, 114 wounded, 1 missing = 161
63rd Virginia (196 engaged): 6 killed, 48 wounded = 54
Brigade total (1,145 engaged): 66 killed, 241 wounded, 3 missing = 310

Trigg's Brigade: Col. Robert C. Trigg

1st Florida DC (300 engaged): 3 killed, 24 wounded = 27
6th Florida (470 engaged): 35 killed, 130 wounded = 165
7th Florida (431 engaged): 4 killed, 34 wounded, 5 missing = 43
54th Virginia (477 engaged): 4 killed, 43 wounded = 47
Brigade total (1536 engaged): 46 killed, 231 wounded, 5 missing = 282

Artillery

Capt. William C. Jeffries's Virginia Battery (5 guns): no losses
Capt. Tyler M Peeples's Georgia Battery (4 guns) 1 killed, 2 wounded = 3
Capt. Andrew M. Wolihin's Georgia Battery (4 guns): no losses

Stewart's Division: Maj. Gen. Alexander P. Stewart

Escort

Foules's Co. Mississippi Cavalry (35 engaged): 1 killed, 1 missing = 2

Bate's Brigade: Brig. Gen. William B. Bate

58th Alabama (287 engaged): 21 killed, 128 wounded = 149
37th Georgia (425 engaged): 19 killed, 168 wounded, 7 missing = 194
4th Georgia Sharpshooters (92 engaged): 2 killed, 36 wounded = 38
15+37th Tennessee (230 engaged): 15 killed, 102 wounded, 4 missing = 121
20th Tennessee (183 engaged): 8 killed, 80 wounded = 88
Brigade total (1,211 engaged): 65 killed, 515 wounded, 11 missing = 591

Brown's Brigade: Brig. Gen. John C. Brown

18th Tennessee (362 engaged): 20 killed, 114 wounded, 1 missing = 135
26th Tennessee (239 engaged): 12 killed, 79 wounded, 1 missing = 92
32nd Tennessee (341 engaged): 9 killed, 112 wounded, 2 missing = 123
45th Tennessee (254 engaged): 13 killed, 85 wounded = 98
23rd Tennessee Sharpshooters (144 engaged): 3 killed, 29 wounded = 32
Brigade total (1,340 engaged): 57 killed, 419 wounded, 4 missing = 480

Clayton's Brigade: Brig. Gen. Henry D. Clayton

18th Alabama (527 engaged): 37 killed, 250 wounded, 8 missing = 295
36th Alabama (429 engaged): 16 killed, 133 wounded, 3 missing = 152
38th Alabama (490 engaged): 37 killed, 143 wounded, 5 missing = 185
Brigade total (1,446 engaged): 90 killed, 526 wounded, 16 missing = 634

Artillery

Capt. John T. Humphreys's 1st Arkansas Battery (4 guns): 1 killed, 3 wounded = 4
Dawson's Georgia Battery (4 guns) Lt. R. W. Anderson: 1 killed, 6 wounded = 7
Eufala (Alabama) Artillery (4 guns) Capt. McDonald Oliver:
1 killed, 13 wounded = 14

Reserve Artillery

Maj. Samuel C. Williams
Capt. Edmund D. Baxter's Tennessee Battery: (2 guns) no losses
Capt. Putnam Darden's Mississippi Battery (4 guns): 1 killed, 2 wounded = 3
Capt. R. F. Kolb's Alabama Battery (4 guns): 2 killed, 1 wounded = 3
Capt. Robert P. Mecants's Florida Battery (4 guns): 1 wounded = 1

First Corps, Army of Northern Virginia

Maj. Gen. John B. Hood

(Lt. Gen. James Longstreet not yet present)

Escort

Co's C & E, 1st Louisiana Cavalry (30 engaged): losses unknown

Johnson's Provisional Division: Brig. Gen. Bushrod R. Johnson
Fulton's Brigade: Col. John S. Fulton

17th Tennessee (249 engaged): 61 wounded, 69 missing = 130
23rd Tennessee (186 engaged): 8 killed, 77 wounded, 13 missing = 98
25th Tennessee (145 engaged): 10 killed, 45 wounded, 1 missing = 56
44th Tennessee (294 engaged): 10 killed, 88 wounded, 15 missing = 113
Brigade total (874 engaged): 28 killed, 271 wounded, 98 missing = 397

Gregg's Brigade: Brig. Gen. John Gregg

3rd Tennessee (274 engaged): 22 killed, 87 wounded, 6 missing = 115
10th Tennessee (190 engaged): 24 killed, 86 wounded, 4 missing = 114
30th Tennessee (185 engaged): 21 killed, 73 wounded, 3 missing = 97
41st Tennessee (325 engaged): 11 killed, 67 wounded, 1 missing = 79
50th Tennessee (186 engaged): 9 killed, 46 wounded = 55
1st Tennessee Bn (82 engaged): 13 killed, 24 wounded, 1 missing = 38
7th Texas (177 engaged): 10 killed, 82 wounded = 92
Brigade total (1,419 engaged): 110 killed, 465 wounded, 15 missing = 590

McNair's Brigade: Brig. Gen. Evander McNair

1st Arkansas MR (273 engaged): 14 killed, 76 wounded, 16 missing = 106
2nd Arkansas MR (139 engaged): 6 killed, 43 wounded, 3 missing = 52
25th Arkansas (133 engaged): 7 killed, 51 wounded, 3 missing = 61
4+31+4th Bn Arkansas (415 engaged): 14 killed, 60 wounded, 29 missing = 103

39th North Carolina (247 engaged): 10 killed, 90 wounded, 3 missing = 103
Brigade total (1,207 engaged): 51 killed, 320 wounded, 54 missing = 425
Artillery
E 9th Georgia Battery (4 guns) Lt. William S. Everett: 3 wounded = 3
Bledsoe's Missouri Battery (4 guns) Lt. R. L. Wood: 1 killed, 1 wounded = 2
Capt. James F. Culpepper's South Carolina Battery (4 guns): 14 wounded = 14

Hood's Division: Brig. Gen. Evander M. Law
Benning's Brigade: Brig. Gen. Henry L. Benning
2nd Georgia (427 engaged): 16 killed, 101 wounded = 117
15th Georgia (285 engaged): 7 killed, 75 wounded = 82
17th Georgia (250 engaged): 9 killed, 132 wounded, 8 missing = 149
20th Georgia (238 engaged): 28 killed, 114 wounded = 142
Brigade total (1,200 engaged): 60 killed, 422 wounded, 8 missing = 490
Law's Brigade: Col. James L. Sheffield, Col. William F. Perry
4th Alabama (249 engaged): 12 killed, 45 wounded, 1 missing = 58
15th Alabama (373 engaged): 11 killed, 121 wounded = 132
44th Alabama (276 engaged): 10 killed 71 wounded, 8 missing = 89
47th Alabama (283 engaged): 7 killed, 56 wounded, 7 missing = 70
48th Alabama (276 engaged): 19 killed, 67 wounded, 1 missing = 87
Brigade total (1,457 engaged): 59 killed, 360 wounded, 17 missing = 436
Robertson's (Texas) Brigade: Brig. Gen. Jerome B. Robertson
3rd Arkansas (322 engaged): 25 killed, 120 wounded, 12 missing = 157
1st Texas (409 engaged): 19 killed, 124 wounded, 12 missing = 155
4th Texas (322 engaged): 26 killed, 102 wounded, 5 missing = 133
5th Texas (247 engaged): 13 killed, 87 wounded, 12 missing = 112
Brigade total (1,300 engaged): 83 killed, 433 wounded, 41 missing = 557

McLaws's Divison: Brig. Gen. Joseph B. Kershaw
(not engaged on September 19)
Humphreys's Brigade: Brig. Gen. Benjamin G. Humphreys
13 Mississippi (300 engaged): 1 killed, 7 wounded = 8
17th Mississippi (338 engaged): 12 killed, 76 wounded = 88
18th Mississippi (260 engaged): 1 killed, 8 wounded = 9
21st Mississippi (328 engaged): 7 killed, 43 wounded = 50
Brigade total (1,226 engaged): 21 killed, 134 wounded = 155
Kershaw's Brigade: Brig. Gen. Joseph B. Kershaw
2nd South Carolina (225 engaged): 26 killed, 75 wounded = 101
3rd South Carolina (343 engaged): 51 killed, 151 wounded = 202
3rd South Carolina Bn (182 engaged): 7 killed, 44 wounded = 51
7th South Carolina (283 engaged): 10 killed, 76 wounded, 1 missing = 87

8th South Carolina (215 engaged): 5 killed, 23 wounded = 28
15th South Carolina (343 engaged): 14 killed, 57 wounded = 71
Brigade total (1,591 engaged): 113 killed, 390 wounded, 1 missing = 504

(Note: George T. Anderson's and Micah Jenkins's Brigades, of Hood's Division; Major General Lafayette McLaws, William T. Wofford's and Goode Bryan's Brigades, as well as the First Corps Artillery under Col. E. Porter Alexander all arrived too late to fight in the battle of Chickamauga.)

Reserve Artillery

Maj. Felix H. Robertson

Capt. Overton W. Barret's Missouri Battery (4 guns): no losses
Capt. G. Le Gardeur's Louisiana Battery (4 guns): no losses
Capt. M. W. Havis's Georgia Battery (3 guns): 1 killed, 1 wounded = 2
Capt. Charles L. Lumsden's Alabama Battery (5 guns): 1 killed, 1 wounded = 2
Capt. T. L. Massenberg's Georgia Battery (4 guns): 4 wounded = 4

Forrest's Cavalry Corps

Brig. Gen. Nathan Bedford Forrest

Escort

Jackson's Co. Tennessee Cavalry (67 engaged): losses unknown

Armstrong's Division: Brig. Gen. Frank C. Armstrong

Escort

Bradley's Co. CSA Regular Cavalry (47 engaged): losses unknown

Dibrell's Brigade: Col. George G. Dibrell

4th Tennessee (200 engaged): 2 killed, 16 wounded = 18
8th Tennessee (300 engaged): 3 killed, 11 wounded = 14
9th Tennessee (350 engaged): 8 wounded = 8
10th Tennessee (est. 474 engaged): 3 killed, 3 wounded = 6
11th Tennessee (est 474 engaged): 2 killed, 2 wounded = 4
Shaw's Tennessee Bn (est. 284 engaged): losses unknown
Capt. A. L. Huggins's Tennessee Battery (4 guns): losses unknown
Capt. John W. Morton's Tennessee Battery (4 guns): losses unknown
Brigade total: (est. 2,218 engaged): 10 killed, 40 wounded = 50 known losses

Wheeler's Brigade: Col. James T. Wheeler
Escort
E 6th Tennessee Cavalry (est. 30 engaged): losses unknown

3rd Arkansas (300 engaged): 2 killed, 2 wounded = 4
2nd Kentucky (est. 427 engaged): losses unknown
6th Tennessee (300 engaged): losses unknown
18th Tennessee Bn (164 engaged): losses unknown
Brigade total (est. 1,221 engaged): losses unknown

Pegram's Division: Brig. Gen. John Pegram
Davidson's (formerly Pegram's) Brigade
Brig. Gen. Henry B. Davidson
1st Georgia (est. 295 engaged): losses unknown
6th Georgia (est. 400 engaged): 12 killed, 72 wounded = 84
6th North Carolina (520 engaged): 5 killed, 6 wounded, 18 missing = 29
10th Confederate (250 engaged): 2 killed, 11 wounded = 13
Rucker's Tennessee Legion (385 engaged): 37 total losses
Capt. Gustave A. Huwald's Tennessee Battery (4 guns): losses unknown
Brigade total (est. 1,900 engaged): 163 known losses
Scott's Brigade: Col. John S. Scott
Morgan's Detachment (240 engaged): 3 killed, 7 wounded = 10
1st Louisiana (est. 210 engaged): 10 killed, 42 wounded = 52
2nd Tennessee (est. 300 engaged): 5 killed, 14 wounded = 19
5th Tennessee (est. 300 engaged): 2 killed, 14 wounded = 16
Lt. Winslow Robinson's Louisiana Battery (2 guns): 3 wounded = 3
Brigade total (est. 1,100 engaged): 20 killed, 80 wounded = 100

Wheeler's Cavalry Corps

Maj. Gen. Joseph C. Wheeler

Martin's Division: Brig. Gen. William T. Martin
Escort
A 3rd Alabama (est. 34 engaged): losses unknown
Morgan's Brigade: Col. John T. Morgan
1st Alabama (est. 418 engaged): losses unknown
3rd Alabama (279 engaged): losses unknown
51st Alabama Partisan Rangers (est. 418 engaged): losses unknown
8th Confederate (est. 418 engaged): losses unknown
Brigade total (est. 1,533 engaged): losses unknown

Russell's Brigade: Col. A. A. Russell
4th Alabama (est. 418 engaged): losses unknown
1st Confederate (est. 418 engaged): losses unknown
Wiggins's Arkansas Battery (2 guns) Lt. J. P. Bryant: losses unknown
2 regiments absent, on detached duty
Brigade total (est. 836 engaged): losses unknown

Wharton's Division: Brig. John A. Wharton
Escort
B 8th Texas (est. 41 engaged): losses unknown

Crews's Brigade: Col. C. C. Crews
Malone's Alabama Regiment (est. 502 engaged): losses unknown
2nd Georgia (600 engaged): losses unknown
3rd Georgia (est. 418 engaged): losses unknown
4th Georgia (605 engaged): losses unknown
Brigade total (est. 2,125 engaged): losses unknown

Harrison's Brigade: Col. Thomas Harrison
3rd Confederate (550 engaged): losses unknown
3rd Kentucky (est. 418 engaged): losses unknown
4th Tennessee (est. 418 engaged): losses about 40
8th Texas (412 engaged): losses unknown
11th Texas (est. 398 engaged): losses unknown
Capt. B. F. White's Tennessee Battery (4 guns): losses unknown
Brigade total (est. 2,273 engaged): losses unknown

Index